D1571454

A FINANCIAL
HISTORY OF
THE NEW
JAPAN

A FINANCIAL HISTORY OF THE NEW JAPAN

T. F. M. ADAMS
IWAO HOSHII

KODANSHA INTERNATIONAL LTD.,
TOKYO, JAPAN AND PALO ALTO, CALIFORNIA, U.S.A.

HG
188
.J3
A634

Distributed in the British Commonwealth (except Canada and the Far East) by George Allen & Unwin; in Continental Europe by Boxerbooks, Inc., Zurich; in Canada by Fitzhenry & Whiteside Limited, Ontario; and in the Far East by Japan Publications Trading Co., P.O. Box 5030 Tokyo International, Tokyo. Published by Kodansha International Ltd., 2-12-21, Otowa, Bunkyo-ku, Tokyo 112, Japan and Kodansha International/USA, Ltd., 599 College Avenue, Palo Alto, California 94306. Copyright © 1972, by Kodansha International Ltd. All rights reserved. Printed in Japan.

ISBN 0-87011-157-4
LCC No. 75-185642
JBC No. 0033-783091-2361

First edition, 1972

CONTENTS

III THE PERIOD OF RAPID GROWTH

PREFACE

In May 1964, my *Financial History of Modern Japan* was published. For a work on such a theme, with a limited and specialized readership, it proved surprisingly successful—so much so that a second printing was called for within a few months. That also was soon sold out, and the continuing flow of inquiries indicates that demand for such a work continues.

Much has happened, however, since the 1964 book was written. In fact, developments in Japan have been so staggering in the past seven years that the original book is now both outdated and incomplete. Hence the need for a deeper and more comprehensive work.

From the ashes of a country devastated in a lost war, with millions starving, industrial plants gutted, and transport and communications reduced to the primitive, this resilient nation has arisen like the phoenix. The Germans have called it a *wirtschaftswunder*.

Inevitably, this *wirtschaftswunder* is founded on finance. If an army marches on its stomach, so an economy is fed by finance. Nothing can be done without loans, yen, dollars, marks, or other currency, and the banking and other institutions needed to provide such necessities. To describe the sources and means of financing this complex and somewhat unique economy makes a fascinating story, unusual in its developments and unsusceptible to comparison with that of Western economies.

It is still, I believe, a fact that an up-to-date analysis of Japanese finance has nowhere else been adequately provided, at least in English. Such an analysis must give an account of the financing of trade and industry, the credit system, and the many financial institutions. With the rapid acceleration of the "internationalization" of Japan's banking, trade, and commerce and the international financial turmoil created by President Nixon's new economic policy, it is more important than ever to provide information on Japan's financial system.

This book could not have been written without its coauthor, Dr. Iwao Hoshii. I thank him and all who encouraged and helped.

I must acknowledge my debt to Messrs. Yusuke Kashiwagi, special advisor to the minister of finance, and Aritoshi Soejima, formerly of the Ministry of Finance and now director of the Tokyo office of the International Bank for Reconstruction and Development (the World Bank); and to the president and officers of the Tokyo Stock Exchange who gave me access to the records of the exchange. The president and officers of Fuji Bank kindly permitted the use of the work *Banking in Modern Japan* published by the bank; Miss Masako Hotta translated many of the original sources, and typed and retyped the manuscript. She was, always, the uncomplaining victim of such onerous work.

T. F. M. ADAMS

INTRODUCTION

Japan's emergence as a modern nation has generally been identified with her development since the Meiji Restoration (1868). The program of modernization envisaged by the early Meiji leaders comprised not only the creation of a new political order but also of a new economy, particularly the establishment of industries using Western equipment and techniques. The initiative in the economic transformation lay with the state, and national objectives, above all military preparedness, dominated the economic planning. At first, many of the new industrial enterprises were founded and managed by the state, the lack of private capital being one of the reasons for the direct involvement of the state in business.

The precarious fiscal situation in the eighties prompted a basic change in policy. An ordinance promulgated in 1880 directed the sale of state enterprises with the exception of arsenals, railroads, and telephone and telegraph lines. In this way, enterprises equipped with modern machinery and run by skilled personnel were sold to private entrepreneurs at extremely low prices and on very favorable terms. The fact that many of the entrepreneurs who bought the enterprises were neither manufacturers nor artisans was of great significance for the development of Japan's economy. The old style artisans lacked capital as well as experience to venture into factory production. The organization and management of Western-style enterprises lay beyond their tradition, and they had no connections with the bureaucracy in whose hands was the actual disposition of state properties. Hence, a large part of the enterprises was acquired by financiers who later built the *zaibatsu* and formed the leading class of Japan's economic society.

The first financial institutions patterned after Western models (as understood in Japan) were the "exchange firms," which were soon replaced by "national banks." Pension bonds issued by the government in commutation of the stipends payable to the former warrior class (*bushi*) provided much of the capital invested in banks, and for many years public funds constituted a large part of bank deposits. In Japan, modern capitalism started as financial capitalism and capital creation by the state laid its foundation. The state, or more precisely Japan's political leaders, used financial measures for directing economic development along lines conducive to the attainment of national goals. The foundation of the Bank of Japan (1882) and the "special banks" (Yokohama Specie Bank, Industrial Bank, Kangyo Bank, banks for agriculture and industry, Hokkaido Colonial Bank, and Bank of Taiwan) institutionalized the tradition of diverting public means to private purposes. Public financing of private undertakings was considered normal, and no special connection with the public interest or the common welfare was required since industrialization as such was considered a national project.

Thus, the basic traits of Japan, Inc. go back to the Meiji era. The state did not pursue economic objectives for economic (and still less for social) reasons, but the government expected private business to contribute to national goals while Japanese entrepreneurs looked to the state for help when mismanagement or business depressions threatened ruin to the economy. This system was partially responsible for the tendency of Japanese entrepreneurs to lose sight of the realities of the market and make their decisions without regard to the balance of supply and demand.

Although the effects of the governmental policies and, in particular, of the state's fiscal measures proved favorable to the entrepreneurial class, these policies were adopted in the interest of the state and not of capital. From a long-range point of view, the suppression of demand (implicit in the policies of the Meiji era, deliberate in the quasi-wartime economy of the thirties, and absolute during the Second World War) may have been detrimental to the economy, but the priority given to production greatly accelerated the country's economic growth while the relative retardation of consumption constituted one of the inherent weaknesses of Japan's economic structure and partially explains its proneness to crises and recessions.

As in the West, the Great Depression brought a period of profound social and political unrest and violent protests against the existing order. The revolutionary left and the ultra-nationalist right were equally opposed to the corrupt party system, the asocial administration of the bureaucracy, and the exploitation of the state by the capitalist oligarchy. The bizarre outcome of a number of abortive military coups was the ascendancy of the army over the government. After the Manchurian incident of September 1931, the army had pursued its own policy in China and Manchuria in open defiance of the decisions of the cabinet; from 1936 on, the army also dictated domestic policies. The country's entire administration, its economic apparatus, and its financial resources were made subservient to the military. In February 1936, the assassination occurred of Admiral Makoto Saito (lord keeper of the privy seal), Viscount Korekiyo Takahashi (minister of finance), and General Jotaro Watanabe (inspector general of military education); Grand Chamberlain Admiral Kantaro Suzuki, who headed the Japanese government at the time of the surrender, was severely wounded. In the few years between the February 1936 incident and the outbreak of the Pacific war in December 1941, a period referred to in Japan as quasi-wartime, no less than nine finance ministers tried to perform the impossible task of fulfilling the demands of the military without bankrupting the nation.

When, on December 8, 1941, Japan opened hostilities against the United States and Britain, the authorities were not too sure in just what way they could bring the war to an end. There was not the slightest chance of winning a military victory over the United States. The most that could be hoped for was to occupy the most important areas of Southeast Asia, consolidate the self-sufficiency of Japan's economic bloc, and wait for the victory of the Axis in Europe, while inflicting as much damage on the enemy as possible.

The successes at the beginning of the war, which enabled the Japanese forces to gain control, with relatively light losses, of the Philippines, the Malay Peninsula, Burma, Indonesia, and the islands in the Southwest Pacific, seemed to give support to the optimistic expectation of the authorities that the war would be relatively short. There was no serious effort to prepare for a drawn-out war of attrition. The people's standard of living, which had already been forced down appreciably before the war, gradually sank below the subsistence level. The curbs imposed after the outbreak of hostilities on the freedom of the press and of speech, assembly, and association, created an atmosphere of oppressive gloom and anxiety for the future which was only occasionally punctured by artificially stimulated outbursts of nationalism.

In June of 1943, the Japanese Combined Fleet suffered a heavy blow in the battle off Midway Island; and when the savage struggle for Guadalcanal, from August 1942 to February 1943, ended in retreat, it became clear that the war had turned into what had been considered the most appalling possibility, a long-term war of attrition. June 1944 saw the landing of American forces on Saipan which brought the industrial belts in central and eastern Japan within the range of American long-distance bombers (air raids on western Japan had already been staged by American planes operating from bases in China). The full-scale air offensive which began with the capture of Iwo Jima by U.S. Marines in February 1945 threw Japan's economy into complete confusion.

In the war theater, the Philippines and Okinawa were lost; the offensive launched against India ended in disaster with the defeat in the battle of Kohima-Imphal and the following collapse in Burma. In May 1945, Germany's surrender terminated the war in Europe and made Japan's situation completely hopeless. General Hideki Tojo had resigned in July 1944 after the fall of Saipan. General Kuniaki Koiso and Admiral Mitsumasa Yonai were ordered to form a new cabinet which, although continuing the war effort, was looking for an opportunity to end the conflict and even made an attempt at opening peace negotiations. In April 1945, Admiral Kantaro Suzuki, then president of the Privy Council, formed a new cabinet. Unfortunately, the complete change in policy indicated by Suzuki's appointment was not understood by the Allies, and Japan's explicit request to the Soviet Union in July 1945 to use its good offices for ending the war was not acted on by Stalin.

On August 6, 1945, the first atomic bomb was dropped on Hiroshima; three days later, Nagasaki met with the same fate. When, on August 8, the Soviet Union declared war on Japan despite the still valid neutrality pact of 1941, immediate surrender became inevitable. On the fourteenth, the Supreme War Council and the cabinet, meeting in the presence of the emperor, agreed to accept the Potsdam Declaration, and the governments of the United States, Great Britain, the Soviet Union, and China were notified of Japan's capitulation. At noon on August 15, the emperor's voice, heard for the first time over the radio, read to a stunned nation the text of the imperial rescript terminating the war.

Over eight years had elapsed since July 1937, when the China incident started—years of unprecedented suffering and enormous losses, and the tragic surrender wrote the end to a restless and confused epoch.

I

THE
POSTWAR
ECONOMY

1 THE ECONOMY UNDER THE OCCUPATION

1 GENERAL CONDITIONS

 TERMINATION OF THE WAR AND THE OCCUPATION

Japan's losses of military personnel and civilians attached to the armed forces numbered 2,376,000 in dead, seriously wounded, and missing, including losses in the China incident. Losses at home came to 668,000, while 8,754,000 persons lost their homes and all their belongings.

Direct and indirect losses in national wealth (deterioration, dispersal, insufficient repair, etc.) were estimated at ¥65,302 million at war-end prices, or about five times the damage caused by the Great Earthquake of 1923. The damage came to 34 percent of the national wealth as of 1935 (excluding the value of roads and historical monuments). The national wealth left at the end of the war represented a mere 1.1 percent increase over 1935—the results of ten years of economic effort had been virtually wiped out. In addition, losses in warships and aircraft amounted to ¥40,382 million, and losses in other military material to ¥29,600 million. Assets located in the territories lost through the war, or held abroad, were estimated at over $20 billion and they, too, had to be almost entirely written off.

In the peace treaty, Japan renounced all territorial acquisitions made after the Meiji Restoration, together with her claimed sphere of influence. The Japanese Empire of 1940 covered 678,000 sq. km. while the territory remaining under her administrative jurisdiction on the basis of the Potsdam Declaration shrank to 370,000 sq. km. and comprised only the four main islands of Hokkaido, Honshu, Shikoku, and Kyushu, and the adjacent islands.

The population in the remaining territory numbered 72 million, more than double the 35 million who had lived in about the same area in 1872. The repatriation of the demobilized soldiers and of Japanese living overseas was to add a couple of million to this number (the net balance of people repatriated to Japan and those leaving Japan between 1945 and 1950 added 5 million to Japan's population).

Equally great were the losses in industrial equipment, resulting directly from air attacks and bombardments, or indirectly through deterioration, relocation, or dismantling. If the maximum industrial capacity in 1944 is compared with the capacity remaining on August 15, 1945, the following ratios appear. Hydroelectric power with 102.6 percent and ordinary steel materials with 100.5 percent showed a slight increase. Industries producing calcium cyanamide, pig iron, pulp, sulphuric acid, or electrolytic copper retained 80 percent or more of their capacity. Thermal electric power with 53.3 percent had somewhat over half of its capacity left, but the average for the textile industry was 33.4 percent, and petroleum refining, automobiles, bicycles, ammonium sulphate, soap, and paper were all below 50 percent. The heavy and chemical industries were most severely hit by direct war damage while the light and consumer goods industries suffered enormous losses due to the redirection of their personnel and equipment to the munitions industry.

While a relatively large portion of the productive capacity of the heavy and chemical industries was left, the capacity of industries serving civilian demand, which were essential for stabilizing economic conditions and checking the inflation, was woefully inadequate, a situation which threatened to become a great obstacle to economic rehabilitation.

However, even the equipment that was left at the end of the war was obsolete, worn out, and badly in need of repair. In addition, transportation equipment and housing were badly damaged or in a dilapidated condition. Moreover, river regulation and conservation had been neglected, which contributed greatly to the enormous typhoon damage in postwar years.

For the ordinary people life was less nightmarish than under the constant threat of air raids during the closing months of the war, but living conditions became even more desperate with the demobilization of servicemen and the dismissal of workers in the munitions industries, with a lack of housing in the cities, with the virtual impossibility of buying even the most essential daily necessities, and, above all, with a growing food shortage.

At the end of the war, the armed forces comprised 5 million men stationed in Japan proper and 4 million overseas, a total of 9 million. The labor draft had sent another 9 million into the munitions industries, including college and high school students, plus workers from the consumer goods industries, commerce, and agriculture. Toward the end of the war, however, production of military material had fallen off and military equipment was insufficient; also, in the munitions industries, the shortage of raw materials and skilled workers could not be covered by a senseless increase in manpower. Although some efforts were made to disperse vital industries, the main industrial strength remained centered in the cities, and production suffered sharply when the workers lost their homes through air raids.

Among daily necessities, textiles were the first in which a serious shortage developed, since Japan had to rely almost exclusively on imported raw materials. Already by 1937 the use of staple fiber in woolens had been made compulsory.

The production of rice, Japan's staple food, and other agricultural products declined sharply due to the drafting of the agricultural labor force and the shortage in chemical fertilizers and other materials. The rice crop had yielded 63 million *koku* (1 *koku*=4.9629 English bushels) in 1943 and 59 million *koku* in 1944, but in 1945 it dropped drastically to 39 million *koku*, while imports from Korea and Taiwan became extremely difficult. A rationing system, based on a passbook, was enforced in Tokyo in February 1941 and soon extended to the whole country; but in July 1945 the basic rice ration had to be reduced by 10 percent and the actual delivery of the rations became most irregular.

The per capita calorie intake of the population had already declined to 97.9 percent of the minimum in 1941 and had fallen to 83.4 percent by 1945.

The extraordinary military expenditures special account was closed at the end of February 1946. The total paid into this account since 1937 came to ¥173,306 million. Funds raised by government bonds and borrowings constituted the bulk of the revenues, viz., ¥149,789 million, or 86.4 percent. (Revenues on the general account from 1937 to 1945 amounted to ¥94,255 million; of this sum, ¥22,970 million was raised through bonds and borrowings.)

Total expenditures came to ¥155,397 million; during the last months of the war the government had not paid cash but, in order to prevent inflation, had converted its accounts payable into borrowings. Expenses settled in this way came to ¥10,016 million. Besides the extraordinary military expenditures, ¥40,837 million in national defense contributions (*kokubō kenkin*) and expenses paid by appropriations from the general account after closing the special account must be added to the war costs. Appropriations in the general accounts for the army, the navy, and the Munitions Ministry, which must be regarded as direct war expenses, came to ¥24,957 million. These were the principal items of war expenditures and came to a total of ¥231,207 million. Additional expenditures are represented by a loss of ¥524,681 million on the accounts of the Overseas Funds Bank. This sum involved an enormous nominal expansion due to the inflation in the occupied territories and it is difficult to assess the actual amount of the losses.

As against the tremendous physical losses sustained by Japan's economy through the war, the nominal value of monetary assets represented by government bonds and war indemnity claims showed an enormous expansion—one aspect of the mounting inflationary flood which was to engulf the old order. Immediately after the termination of the war, the balance sheet of Japan's economy, as given in a table inserted in the Economic Planning Agency's *Postwar Economic History* (*Sengo Keizai-shi*), shows physical assets with a current value of ¥188,852 million. On the side of monetary assets, however, are privately held securities and other investments, ¥80,345 million; deposits, ¥195,404 million; adjustment items in the accounts of the Bank of Japan, ¥29,154 million; and war indemnity claims against the government, ¥105,700 million, making a total of ¥410,603 million. The balance, or rather imbalance, between the two sides therefore came to ¥221,751 million.

In view of this situation, one part of public opinion urged a thoroughgoing adjustment through the repudiation of government bonds and the cancellation of war indemnity claims, but the authorities, under the pretext of preventing confusion, dragged their feet and wasted a lot of precious time before deciding on a policy, so that it became impossible to check the inflation effectively.

The Potsdam Declaration, which constituted the basis of Japan's status under the occupation, had listed among the terms for Japan's surrender: (1) the elimination of "the authority and influence of those who have deceived and misled the people of Japan into embarking on world conquest"; (2) the destruction of Japan's war-making power; (3) the limitation of Japanese sovereignty to the islands of Honshu, Hokkaido, Shikoku, Kyushu, and minor islands to be determined; (4) complete disarmament of the Japanese military forces; (5) punishment of all war criminals; (6) removal of all obstacles to the revival and strengthening of democratic tendencies among the Japanese people. The final condition concerned Japan's economy. It read: "Japan shall be permitted to maintain such industries as will sustain the economy and permit the exaction of just reparations in kind, but not those which would enable her to rearm for war. To this end, access to, as distinguished from control of, raw materials shall be permitted. Eventual Japanese participation in world trade relations shall be permitted."

Until these objectives were accomplished, Japan was to remain under Allied occupation. On December 27, 1945, the Moscow conference of the foreign ministers of Great Britain, the United States, and the Soviet Union agreed on the establishment of a Far Eastern Commission (FEC) composed of the representatives of eleven nations. Part of its functions was: "To formulate the policies, principles, and standards in conformity with which the fulfillment by Japan of its obligations under the Terms of Surrender may be accomplished." It could review orders issued to or action taken by the supreme commander for the Allied powers (SCAP), General Douglas MacArthur, who exercised actual administrative authority. The "Terms of Reference" for the Far Eastern Commission confirmed the dominating position of the United States in the occupation of Japan by stipulating that "the Commission in its activities will respect existing control machinery in Japan, including the chain of command from the United States Government to the Supreme Commander" and by the provision that "the United States Government may issue interim directives to the Supreme Commander pending action by the Commission whenever urgent matters arise not covered by policies already formulated by the Commission."

Under SCAP, GHQ functioned as an executive organ for the implementation of occupation policies, while the Allied Council for Japan, on which the United States, the USSR, China, and the British Commonwealth were represented, was established "for the purpose of consulting with and advising the Supreme Commander," who was to be the sole executive authority for the Allied powers in Japan.

The supreme commander Allied powers was an American and the commander in chief of the armed forces Pacific, which constituted the bulk of the occupation troops. Hence the administration of occupied Japan was largely based on American policies. The "Initial Post-Surrender Policy," prepared jointly by the U.S. Department of State and the War and Navy Departments, and approved by President Truman on September 6, 1945, made it very clear: "Although every effort will be made by consultation and by constitution of appropriate advisory bodies to establish policies for the conduct of the occupation and the control of Japan which will satisfy the principal Allied powers, in the event of any differences of opinion among them, the policies of the United States will govern." This document, whose major clauses were incorporated into an FEC Policy Decision dated June 19, 1947, listed the following "ultimate objectives" of the United States:

(a) To insure that Japan will not again become a menace to the peace and security of the world.

(b) To bring about the eventual establishment of a peaceful and responsible government which will respect the rights of other states and will support the objectives of the United States as reflected in the ideas and principles of the Charter of the United Nations. The United States desires that this government should conform as closely as may be possible to principles of democratic self-government but it is not the responsibility of the Allied Powers to impose upon Japan any form of government not supported by the freely expressed will of the people.

The document then set forth the principal means to achieve these objectives:

(a) Limitation of Japan's sovereignty to the main islands.

(b) Complete disarmament and demilitarization.

(c) Encouragement of individual liberties and respect for fundamental human rights; formation of democratic and representative organizations.

(d) The Japanese people shall be afforded opportunity to develop for themselves an economy which will permit the peace-time requirements of the population to be met.

Part IV of the document dealt with the economic objectives of the occupation and explained the basic principles under the headings "Economic Demilitarization" and "Promotion of Democratic Forces." For the last-mentioned purpose, two specific policies were advocated:

(a) To prohibit the retention in or selection for places of importance in the economic field of individuals who do not direct future Japanese economic effort solely towards peaceful ends.

(b) To favor a program for the dissolution of the large industrial and banking combinations which have exercised control of a great part of Japan's trade and industry.

In the third paragraph entitled "Resumption of Peaceful Economic Activity," the document stated: "The plight of Japan is the direct outcome of its own behavior, and the Allies will not undertake the burden of repairing the damage." After laying down the basic policies for "Reparations and Restitutions," the document briefly touched on "Fiscal, Monetary, and Banking Policies" and said:

The Japanese authorities will remain responsible for the management and direction of the domestic fiscal, monetary, and credit policies subject to the approval and review of the Supreme Commander.

For the execution of the policies laid down in the document "the Supreme Commander will exercise his authority through Japanese governmental machinery and agencies," but "the policy is to use the existing form of government in Japan, not to support it."

SCAP transmitted his orders or instructions to the Japanese government in the form of directives, memoranda, or letters, while the measures taken by the Japanese authorities pursuant to these orders were embodied in laws or ordinances.

The reforms carried out under the watchful eyes of the occupation authorities over a period of years touched almost every phase of the life of the nation and may be broadly divided into demilitarization and democratization.

2 DEMILITARIZATION

(1) Japan's military establishment was completely dissolved and her entire armed forces disarmed.

(2) In the cultural field, all laws and ordinances restricting the freedom of religion, speech, press, assembly, and organization were rescinded. The wartime distortions were removed from the educational system.

(3) The right of women to participate in politics was recognized. People who had occupied important posts in the wartime political and administrative structure or in the numerous control organizations were removed from public office.

(4) In the economic sphere, the basic wartime control laws were the Law Relating to Temporary Measures Concerning Export and Import Commodities, the National General Mobilization Law, and the Wartime Emergency Measures Law—*Senji Kinkyū Sochi-hō*. While the latter was enacted in 1945, it had actually not been enforced seriously, though it gave the government still greater power than the previous laws. These laws were not immediately abrogated, because a SCAP directive (No. 3 of September 22, 1945) held the Japanese government responsible for "initiating and maintaining a firm control over wages and prices of essential commodities" and "initiating and maintaining a strict rationing

program for essential commodities in short supply, to insure that such commodities are equitably distributed." But the ordinances based on the first-named law lost their effect in July 1947, and those implementing the last two laws became, with a few exceptions, invalid in September. The Iron Works Law and a series of laws for the protection and promotion of industries, together with the Munitions Companies Law, had been abrogated by the end of 1945. But the Emergency Fund Adjustment Law regulating money supply and currency remained in force longer and was only abrogated in April 1948. The Financial Control Organization Ordinance, however, was rescinded in 1945 and the National Financial Control Association dissolved in the same year. The Important Industries Organization Ordinance was also abrogated and all control associations were disbanded in 1946.

The defeat had seriously impaired the authority of the government, which was one reason why the transition from the wartime controls over the economy to the restrictions necessary for reconversion to civilian production was far from smooth. The resulting confusion aggravated the situation in the already badly disorganized economy.

Controls over staple food like rice and other grains, as well as over coal, were kept in force, but supply was entirely inadequate. The prohibition against the use of equipment for civilian production was rescinded, and rationing for vegetables, meat, and fish was temporarily lifted in order to stimulate deliveries, but all these measures created confusion, and the relaxation of the control system, without improving the supply situation, made conditions worse.

The wartime price controls remained in effect, but, faced with the inflation, the government itself resorted to price increases, and the partial lifting of controls over commodities, without securing sufficient supplies, seriously weakened the price controls.

The dismantling of the wartime control system without positive measures for economic reorganization, the purge of the old leaders without competent replacements, the uncertain future, and the unchecked inflation brought the economy into a state of complete paralysis.

(5) The "Closing of Colonial and Foreign Banks and Special Wartime Institutions," ordered by a memorandum of September 30, 1945, formed part of the demilitarization program and had a great impact on the financial world. The measure affected the Wartime Finance Bank, the United Funds Bank, the Bank of Chosen, the Colonial Bank of Chosen, the Bank of Taiwan, the Central Bank of Manchuria, the Industrial Bank of Manchuria, the Central Reserve Bank of China, the Federated Reserve Bank of China, the Bank of Mongolia, the Southern Development Bank, the Overseas Funds Bank, and "all other banks, development companies, and institutions whose foremost purpose had been the financing of colonization and development activities in areas outside Japan or the financing of war production by the mobilization or control of financial resources in colonial or Japanese occupied territory." Specifically mentioned among the financial control organizations were the National Financial Control Association and the Far East Colonial Co.; the South Manchurian Railway Co. and the Manchurian Heavy Industries Development Co. were listed among the colonization and development companies to be dissolved. In August 1946, all control associations were ordered closed. If these associations are included, the number of institutions closed came to 1,070. The Bank of Chosen and a few other financial institutions were liquidated by the Bank of Japan, whereas the majority of these associations were liquidated by the Closed Institutions Liquidation Commission (*Heisa Kikan Seiri Iinkai*), set up in May 1947 and dissolved in March 1952.

 DEMOCRATIZATION

The chief measures for the second great objective, democratization, were the dissolution of the combines (*zaibatsu*) and the democratization of agriculture and labor.

1) Zaibatsu Dissolution—On October 31, 1945, SCAP directed that "no sale, trade or other transfer or adjustment of the capital stocks, bonds, debentures, voting trust or other forms of capital securities" of fifteen representative Japanese firms or their subsidiaries or affiliates be made without SCAP's prior approval. The four "big" *zaibatsu*, Mitsui, Mitsubishi, Sumitomo, and Yasuda realized that dissolution was inevitable and each concern worked out a plan for its dissolution. Negotiations with the minister of finance, Keizo Shibusawa, then produced a common plan, which was formally submitted to SCAP on November 4, 1945, and approved two days later. Under this plan, the four combines, referred to as the "Holding Companies," were to transfer to a "Holding Company Liquidation Commission" (HCLC) "all securities owned by them and all other evidences of ownership or control of any interest in any firm, corporation, or other enterprise." The commission was to liquidate all property as rapidly as possible, and neither the holding companies nor the members of the Mitsui, Yasuda, Sumitomo, or Iwasaki families were to purchase any of the transferred property. The directors and auditors of the holding companies were to resign all offices held by them in the companies.

SCAP's memorandum which approved the plan for the dissolution of the four holding companies demanded that the Japanese government present:

(a) Plans for the dissolution of industrial, commercial, financial and agricultural combines in addition to the four holding companies.
(b) Its program to abrogate all legislative or administrative measures which create, foster or tend to strengthen private monopoly.
(c) Its program for the enactment of such laws as will eliminate and prevent private monopoly and restraint of trade, undesirable interlocking directorates, undesirable inter-corporate security ownership and assure the segregation of banking from commerce, industry, and agriculture and as will provide equal opportunity to firms and individuals to compete in industry, commerce, finance, and agriculture on a democratic basis.

For the transition period until the establishment of HCLC, the government, on November 24, promulgated the "Ordinance Concerning Restrictions on the Dissolution of Companies," which prohibited any changes in the status of the concerns designated by the minister of finance and the disposal of shares of stock by their current holders. Gradually, several hundred firms were added to the list of "restricted concerns."

In August 1946, the Holding Company Liquidation Commission (*Mochikabu Kaisha Seiri Iinkai*) was organized and started its work with Mitsui Honsha, Mitsubishi Honsha, Sumitomo Honsha, Yasuda Hozensha, and Fuji Kogyo K.K. (i.e., Fuji Industrial Co., the holding company of Nakajima Aircraft, which had expanded rapidly during the war). Until September 1947, five designations were made, bringing the number of designated holding companies to eighty-three (with approximately forty-five hundred subsidiaries), while fifty-three members of *zaibatsu* families were designated by SCAP and required to turn over their personal security holdings (the previous measures had only affected corporations). The designated holding companies also included Mitsui Bussan and Mitsubishi Shoji, whose dissolution had been specifically ordered by GHQ, which maintained that, far from being just trading companies engaged in general merchandising, they formed the core of their respective *zaibatsu* and possessed all the characteristics of holding companies.

In November 1946, the restricted concerns and their affiliates were prohibited from acquiring stocks or debentures of other firms and were ordered to dispose, with the approval of HCLC, of the securities in their possession.

HCLC was dissolved in July 1951. During the almost five years of its existence, it disposed of 165,673,000 shares of stock (paid-up value ¥7,572 million) transferred to it by the designated holding companies and *zaibatsu* families; under its supervision the "restricted concerns" disposed of 34,366,000 shares of stock (paid-up value ¥1,545 million). This made a total of 200,039,000 shares of stock with a paid-up value of ¥9,117 million.

Of the eighty-three designated holding companies, thirty (including the four big *zaibatsu*) were dissolved; the others were permitted to remain in existence after reorganization had divested them of their character as holding companies.

Control of companies by personal ties was also broken up. Key officials in some two hundred fifty firms were purged (some twenty-two hundred business leaders were affected), members of the *zaibatsu* families designated by HCLC had to resign their posts; officers and employees of restricted concerns were forbidden to hold concurrent offices in other firms. The Law for the Elimination of *Zaibatsu* Family Control (*Zaibatsu Dōzoku Shihai-ryoku Haijo-hō*) enacted in 1948 excluded members of such families from holding any official positions in *zaibatsu* companies.

A report of HCLC contained the following information concerning the influence of the four *zaibatsu*. (In the terminology of HCLC, a firm was considered to be *zaibatsu* dominated if the parent company held more than 10 percent of the stock of the daughter firm; if in their turn these firms were holding companies, the companies under their control were included.)

The paid-up capital of the firms dominated by the Mitsui *zaibatsu* came to ¥3,061 million, or 9.4 percent of the national total at the time of the designation. In the following industries, the share of the Mitsui interests in the national total was very high: finance (banking, trust, insurance), 13.9 percent; heavy industries, 12.7 percent (including mining, 15.7 percent; machinery, 13.9 percent; chemicals, 19.1 percent); and marine transportation, 18.1 percent.

The paid-up capital of the firms under Mitsubishi control amounted to ¥2,704 million, which constituted 8.3 percent of the national total. Mitsubishi's most important holdings were finance with 13.1 percent of the national total, heavy industries with 10.7 percent (machinery and shipbuilding, 16.0 percent), and marine transportation with 40.3 percent.

The firms belonging to the Sumitomo concern had a paid-up capital of ¥1,667 million, or 5.2 percent of the national total. Its share in banking was small (5.4 percent), but it had 8.4 percent of heavy industries (metal industries, 14.4 percent; machinery, 10.6 percent).

The Yasuda combine's paid-up capital was ¥510 million, which was only 1.6 percent of the national total. It occupied a very strong position in finance, where its share came to 17.2 percent of the capital of all financial institutions, but its interests in heavy industries were an insignificant 0.7 percent.

The four big *zaibatsu* together controlled 24.5 percent of the paid-up capital of all firms, 49.7 percent of finance, and 32.4 percent of heavy industries. The corresponding figures for 1937 were 10.4 percent of the total, 22.5 percent of finance, and 14.6 percent of heavy industries. The empires of the big *zaibatsu* as well as the lesser combines were completely broken up.

In order to prevent the reappearance of a similar monopolistic domination of the economy, the Law Relating to Prohibition of Private Monopoly and Maintenance of Fair Trade (*Shiteki Dokusen Kinshi, Kōsei Torihiki Kakuho ni Kan-suru Hōritsu*, usually called the Antimonopoly or Antitrust Law) was enacted in 1947. It prohibited firms, with the exception of financial institutions, from acquiring stock of other firms; financial institutions were prohibited from acquiring stock of competing financial institutions; financial institutions with more than ¥5 million in assets were forbidden from acquiring more than 5 percent of the stock of any other firm. Interlocking directorates, mergers, and cessions were restricted; unreasonable restraints on trade and unfair methods of competition, excessive concentration of power over enterprises, and undue restrictions on production, sale, price, or technology through combinations and agreements were prohibited. Since these restrictions proved too severe, they were later modified so that the formation of holding companies for the chief purpose of dominating the management of other enterprises remained forbidden, but up to a certain extent firms could possess and acquire the shares of other firms.

2) Deconcentration—All these measures prohibited the domination of one firm over other firms, but they did not touch the problem of the size of one firm. This aspect of monopolistic domination was taken up by the Law for the Elimination of Excessive Concentration of Economic Power (*Kado Keizai-ryoku Shūchū Haijo-hō*, usually referred to as the Deconcentration Law), which intended the breakup of gigantic monopolistic enterprises and the severance of activities unrelated to the main line of business of a given enterprise. Its purpose was to dissolve, in connection with the Antimonopoly Law, those enterprises which could actually be considered as monopolistic. Pursuant to this law, HCLC designated 325 firms as representing excessive concentrations. These firms, however, comprised the bulk of Japan's representative enterprises, and the enforcement of their dismemberment would have been a serious blow to the economy.

With the change in the world situation in the latter half of 1947, occupation policies also underwent considerable modifications, and, in September 1948, a "Deconcentration Review Board" made up of five Americans, published a set of "Basic Principles" which considerably relaxed the application of the law. The result of this relaxation was that eventually only eighteen firms were found to fall under the purview of the Deconcentration Law. Among them, Mitsubishi Heavy Industries (broken up into three firms) and Japan Iron Works (broken up into four firms) were dismembered, while the coal departments of Mitsui Mining and Mitsubishi Mining were left as the original companies, and the metal mining departments were set up as new firms. Hitachi Co. Ltd. and Toshiba (Tokyo Shibaura Electric Co. Ltd.) had to divest themselves of certain parts of their factories. In addition, Nihon Hatsuden, the electric power monopoly, was reorganized by setting up nine regional power companies engaged in power generation as well as distribution. These reorganizations were completed by 1951.

The securities transferred to HCLC, those held by the Bank of Japan as liquidator of financial institutions, and by the Closed Institutions Liquidation Commission and the Ministry of Finance (securities turned over in lieu of cash tax payments under the Capital Levy Law) constituted over 40 percent of all Japanese securites. In order to prevent a collapse of the securities market, a Securities Coordinating Liquidation Committee (SCLC; *Yūka Shōken Shori Chōsei Kyōgi-kai*, the Japanese designation, would better be rendered by Securities Liquidation Coordinating Council) was established in June 1947. SCLC laid down the following policies for the disposal of the securities:

1) No sale should be permitted which would lead to the reappearance of the *zaibatsu*; the ownership of stock shall be spread as widely as possible among the masses.
2) Employees of the firms which issued the stocks should be given the right of preemption.
3) After them, the inhabitants of the localities where the factories of the firms are located should be given the right to buy such stocks.
4) The remainder should be placed on the securities market.

At that time, however, the people at large lacked both sophistication and purchasing power to invest in stocks, and the fact that the stock exchanges were closed (they did not reopen until May 1949) was another serious factor in the slow progress made in the disposal of the securities. However, when SCLC was dissolved in July 1951, it had sold 233,133,000 shares of stock with a value of ￥14,115 million in addition to ￥208 million of government obligations and corporate debentures.

These measures brought about a large-scale redistribution of stock ownership and, in particular, increased the number of individual shareholders. Ownership of stocks traded on the stock exchanges showed the following changes. Corporate ownership (except financial institutions and security dealers) fell from 24.7 percent in March 1946 to 5.6 percent in March 1950, while individual ownership increased from 53.1 percent to 69.1 percent. The character of the stock exchanges, too, underwent a transformation and changed from centers of speculation by professionals to actual trading centers. The protection given to ordinary investors and the decrease in the real value of one share due to the inflation greatly facilitated stock investment by the general public and prepared the way for the later stock boom.

3) Other Measures—Together with the dissolution of the *zaibatsu*, agricultural reform and labor legislation constituted the most important measures for economic democratization.

The gist of the land reform was to force absentee landlords to sell their tenant cultivated land to the government, while farmers who cultivated their own land could only retain 3 *chō* (1 *chō*=2.451 acres) in Japan proper and 12 *chō* in Hokkaido.

The land bought up by the government was then sold to the tenant farmers. The result of this process was that, compared with prewar conditions, about 80 percent of the tenant cultivated land was released, while the share of tenant cultivated land fell from somewhat less than 50 percent of all farmland to less than 10 percent. The proportion of landless tenant farmers was reduced from about one-fourth of the farming population to less than 5 percent. Payment of rent in kind (rice) was forbidden and rents payable in cash were not to exceed 25 percent of the crop value of paddy fields and, in the case of upland fields, 15 percent. The protection given to agriculture by the land reform, as well as the food control policies of the government, greatly contributed to the rise in the income level of the rural population.

A series of legislative measures, starting with the Labor Union Law of December 1945, also vastly improved the status of labor.

These democratization measures were an important factor in raising the real income level of the masses and helped to make the rapid postwar economic expansion possible. The basic principles underlying the demilitarization and democratization carried out not only in the economic sector but in all fields of national life were summarized in the new constitution, which came into effect on May 3, 1947.

4 ▲ DEVELOPMENT OF THE POSTWAR ECONOMY

No unanimity exists on a proper division of the postwar period. There are, however, a few outstanding events which marked the developments in Japan's economy. The first was the adoption of the "Dodge line" which put an end to the postwar inflation, and the second was the Korean War, which sparked the real recovery of Japan's industry and set the stage for the ensuing growth period.

The years immediately after the war brought the country nearer to chaos than had the war itself. The uncontrolled inflation, for which the inept economic policies of the government were largely responsible, undermined confidence, not only in the currency, but in all fixed-value obligations and wiped out whatever had been left of public savings. The inflation may be divided into three periods: the first extended from the end of the war to the enforcement of the Monetary Emergency Measures of February 1946; the second lasted until the foundation of the Reconversion Finance Bank in January 1947; and the third ended with the adoption of a balanced budget and the uniform exchange rate of $1 = ¥360 in April 1949.

After the end of the Korean War, Japan went through four business cycles, 1951–56, 1956–58, 1959–61, and 1962–70. After a slow start, economic expansion was swift so that for the whole period from 1946 to 1951 the real growth rate of GNP came to a yearly average of 11.1 percent. At about the middle of 1951, the reaction following the Korean War started the economy on a downward course, and business had to be propped up by monetary means. But the same year experienced a new upswing, which continued into 1952. In order to cope with the problem of overproduction, the government increased fiscal investments and the supply of government funds. Interest rates were lowered in order to stimulate domestic demand and other measures were taken toward easing the monetary stringency. Business derived its main support from consumer demand which had expanded greatly in the wake of the Korean War boom. In 1953 the expansionary movement shifted over to the investment sector. After the autumn of 1952, however, the international payments balance had shown a deficit, caused by the stagnation of exports, the decrease in procurement orders placed by the U.S. forces, and an increase in imports. The holdings of gold and foreign exchange (government and Bank of Japan), which had temporarily exceeded $1.1 billion, dropped to $725 million in May 1954.

The Bank of Japan had switched to a tight-money policy in September 1953, and the government changed to a policy of contraction in fiscal financing. In 1954 the economy went through a deflation; industrial production sagged and prices came down (Japanese commodity prices, which had risen appreciably above the international level through the Korean War, thus underwent an adjustment). Despite the American recession exports took a favorable turn, helped by Europe's strong postwar boom, and the international payments balance improved. The recovery in the United States, which set in soon after, gave exports an additional uplift. Each year, exports registered a substantial gain and, until 1956 when the so-called Jimmu boom (i.e., the biggest boom since Jimmu, Japan's legendary first emperor in 660 B.C., according to the old, but fictitious, chronicles) brought unprecedented prosperity to Japan, the economy achieved a remarkable expansion without being plagued by inflation.

In April 1956, the advances given by the Bank of Japan fell to their lowest postwar level (¥18,442 million), because the influx of foreign exchange (through the increase in exports) and the greatly expanded government payments had eased the monetary stringency. But since no suitable measures were taken to soak up the liquid funds, banks diverted a large part of their funds to industry, where just about this time a greatly accelerated demand for funds for equipment investment burst forth. Japan's economy thus plunged into a period of feverish overexpansion marked by rising prices, bulky imports, and an exceedingly active money market. The Suez crisis further accentuated this development. The foreign exchange balance had shown a continuous increase from the end of 1954 until the end of 1956, when it reached $941 million (according to a revised method of calculation, which omitted balances on open accounts and deposits with Japanese foreign exchange banks; based on the old method, which included these items, foreign exchange holdings came to $1,507 million). In the beginning of 1957, however, a sharp decline set in. The real growth rate of GNP for the period from fiscal 1951 to 1956 showed a yearly average of 7.9 percent.

The large deficits in the balance of payments made Japan's financial managers panicky and, in May 1957, a complete reversal in policy ushered in a period of deflation. In retrospect, the recession of 1957–58 was ascribed to inventory adjustment. Actually this was the chief result of the excessively tight money policy adopted by the government, but it was not the cause of the recession. The 1955–56 boom had encouraged inventory investment, and inventories continued to grow during the first half of 1957; from then on raw materials decreased very slowly, but manufacturers' inventories of finished goods continued to rise well into 1958. Despite sagging demand, production maintained a fairly high level. Two factors were responsible for the unexpected strength of the economy: equipment investment and consumer demand; and it was their timing, their coincidence at this particular juncture, which made the economy click despite the inept political interference. Equipment investment was stimulated by the growing impact of the scientific revolution on Japan and the realization on the part of Japan's industrial leaders that to catch up with the technical innovation already well on its way in the West was a question of life or death for Japan's industry. Characteristic of these efforts was the induction of foreign technologies in almost all fields, the growth of the petrochemical and electronics industries, and the modernization of the iron and steel industry.

Developments in consumer demand were characterized by a boom in consumer durables, particularly electric household appliances such as washing machines, television sets, refrigerators, and transistor radios. Although the increase in income was partly responsible for the boom, changed consumer attitudes and the adoption of a modified type of installment purchase plan played a great role.

The year 1959 brought a period of explosive growth. The "Economic Outlook for Fiscal 1959" published by the Economic Planning Agency had forecast a 5.5 percent increase in real national income. As a matter of fact, GNP increased 18.9 percent over fiscal 1958, for which the chief stimulant was private investment, which increased by 68.7 percent over the preceding fiscal year. A less spectacular, but still impressive gain, was achieved by individual consumption spending which rose by 8.3 percent, while the government tried not to be outdone and increased its spending by 14.9 percent. After an early peak in March 1960, economic activities dropped off slightly but picked up again in early summer and continued strong all through the rest of the year. Equipment investment supported the advance of the economy and contributed chiefly to the expansion of production in such sectors as machinery and iron and steel. In the fall of the year, the government announced its ten-year plan for doubling the national income. The plan was worked out by the Economic Council which submitted its report to Prime Minister Ikeda on November 1, 1960. The emphasis in this document was on a description of Japan's economy in the target year, fiscal 1970, and it was a statement of goals rather than an indication of steps by which the goals could be reached. The plan foresaw an average yearly increase of 7.8 percent in GNP, which was expected to rise from an average of ¥9,743.7 billion in the base period 1956–58 to ¥26,000 billion in 1970. Per capita national income was estimated to rise from ¥87,736 in the base period to ¥208,601 in the target year, and an average yearly expansion of 11.9 percent was forecast for mining and manufacturing production.

The announcement of the plan added fuel to the blaze of economic expansion. It was as if every firm wanted to reach the goals of the plan in the shortest possible time. Given Japan's scarcity of natural resources, economic expansion necessarily involves rising imports and pressure on the balance of payments. In the beginning of 1961, the balance on current account turned unfavorable and in May the overall balance showed a deficit. At the same time, a rise in consumer prices began which continued through the following year. Prime Minister Ikeda defended his "high-rate" growth policy as "basically correct," but a dramatic reversal came in September 1961, when the cabinet adopted a "Policy for the Amelioration of International Payments." Just as in 1957, the enormous increase in imports (the increase over the preceding year came to 24 percent in 1960, and to almost 30 percent in 1961) was blamed for the worsening of the payments balance, and monetary measures were again the chief means on which the government relied for implementing its new policy. But while the increase in imports in 1957 had largely been caused by speculative buying, the basic reason for the larger imports in 1961 was the overall increase in the economy, supported chiefly by the furious pace of equipment investment. Contrary to the deflations in 1953–54 and 1957–58, the policy shift did not produce an immediate change in the behavior of the economy.

GNP grew by 18.9 percent from fiscal 1960 to fiscal 1961. Between 1951 and 1961 the average annual rate of increase came to 13.3 percent. Equipment investment in fiscal 1961 rose 34 percent over the preceding year, and the increase in inventories came to 54 percent. The large inventories in finished goods led to a worsening of the economic situation after March 1962. Particularly hard hit were iron and steel. The heavy outflow of foreign exchange came to an end with the New Year 1962, and in July the current account again showed a surplus. In October the government declared that the ordeal was over. A reduction in the official discount rate and easier credit was to reanimate the flagging economy, but economic incentives were lacking and there was no immediate prospect for a new advance. The real growth rate of GNP in fiscal 1962 was down to 5.7 percent, and equipment investment remained stationary.

1 THE ECONOMY UNDER THE OCCUPATION

2 THE PERIOD OF POSTWAR CONFUSION

1 INITIAL OCCUPATION POLICIES AND THE INFLATION

On August 15, 1945, the government declared that absolutely no moratorium on bank deposits or similar measures would be taken. On September 11, the minister of finance asserted in a speech that a deflationary tendency would probably develop, since the end of the war would reduce government spending due to military expenditures and retard the currency inflation caused by the enormous increase in munitions production funds. However, for a short time after the termination of the war, war spending continued. Severance pay was given to demobilized soldiers, and munitions firms were paid outstanding bills as well as indemnities for cancelled contracts. Some of these payments were made, not in cash, but in the form of special blocked deposits; even so, cash payments came to ¥9,734 million in August and ¥8,671 million from September to November (when SCAP found out what was going on). The excess of government payments over receipts from August to November came to ¥18,393 million; government bonds issued during this period amounted to ¥16,084 million, of which the Bank of Japan took over ¥12,084 million.

On November 24, 1945, SCAP sent two memoranda to the Japanese government. One prohibited the payment of pensions and other benefits to exservicemen (with the exception of pensions for disabled soldiers); the other, entitled "Elimination of War Profits and Reorganization of National Finance," stopped payments "upon any claim arising from the production or supply of war materials, from war damage or from the construction or conversion of war plants" except into blocked accounts supervised by SCAP. The memorandum further prohibited the government from issuing bonds, obtaining or extending credit, and other transactions. This stopped the large excess of government disbursements over receipts but, on the other hand, brought about a rapid increase in bank loans. Ostensibly, these loans were for the conversion of munitions factories to civilian industries, or for wage payments, but actually the funds contributed nothing to an increase in civilian production and only helped closed enterprises from becoming bankrupt. Deposits, however, with the exception of blocked accounts decreased every month, except in September. One reason was the acute food shortage, which forced people to withdraw their deposits in order to buy food; another was the rumor that a special tax would be levied against war profits, which induced people to hide their assets. The growing imbalance between deposits and loans in turn led to a large increase in the borrowings from the Bank of Japan. Its advances had stood at ¥23,544 million at the end of August; they then showed a slight decrease but again climbed rapidly toward the end of the year and reached ¥40,956 million at the end of January 1946. The bank note circulation increased even more abruptly. It had stood at ¥30,282 million on

August 15, but went up to ¥42,300 million at the end of the month, a 40 percent increase in two weeks (due, no doubt, to the *après nous le déluge* attitude of government officials and the finance officers of the armed forces); around the beginning of February 1946, it exceeded ¥60,000 million, having doubled since the end of the war.

In order to stop the inflation, the government decided to apply a comprehensive anti-inflationary policy to finances as well as to all sectors of the economy. The most important measures taken to that effect were the Monetary Emergency Measures Ordinance (*Kinyū Kinkyū Sochi-rei*) and the Bank of Japan Notes Deposit Ordinance (*Nihon Ginkō-Ken Yo-nyū-rei*) of February 16, 1946.

As of February 17, all bank deposits were frozen and cash withdrawals were limited to monthly living expenses (¥300 for the household head, ¥100 for each member of a house-hold; but in April, the amount for the household head was reduced to ¥100), and to funds necessary to carry on the customary business of enterprises. For tax payments and trans-actions in controlled commodities, checks drawn against blocked accounts were permitted. Salaries, wages, and other regular payments could be made in cash up to ¥500 per person. On principle, bank loans were to be in the form of blocked loans paid into the blocked accounts of the borrower; according to the purposes of the payments, withdrawals were permitted either in cash or in blocked checks.

As of March 2, all Bank of Japan notes in circulation of denominations upward of ¥5, not deposited with monetary institutions, ceased to be legal tender. On the same day, ¥100 per person could be exchanged against new bank notes, but since not enough new notes were ready, stickers to be affixed to the old notes were used. As a result of this measure, the note issue was reduced from the peak of ¥61,824 million on February 18 to ¥15,200 million on March 12.

On the same date, a number of other ordinances were promulgated. They included the Extraordinary Assets Investigation Ordinance (*Rinji Zaisan Chōsa-rei*), which laid the foundation for a tax on war profits; the Hoarded Commodities Emergency Measures Ordinance (*Intoku Busshi-tō Kinkyū Sochi-rei*), which prohibited the hoarding of raw materials and finished goods beyond a certain volume; and the Emergency Foodstuff Meas-ures Ordinance (*Shokuryō Kinkyū Sochi-rei*), which sanctioned the seizure of foodstuffs in case delivery schedules were not complied with.

On March 2, the Commodity Price Control Ordinance (*Bukka Tōsei-rei*), which replaced the wartime Price Control Ordinance, fixed the government's purchase price of rice at ¥300 per *koku*, while the government sold it at ¥250. The consumer's price for one ton of coal was fixed at ¥150. In short, the government set up a price structure which would keep the living expenses of a normal household down to the ¥500 level. But since the fiscal inflation continued, this price structure could be maintained for only a few months.

The settlement of accounts for fiscal 1945, which fell partly in the war and partly in the postwar period, showed general account revenues of ¥23,487 million (including ¥9,029 million from government bonds) and expenditures of ¥21,496 million. In the special ac-counts, a deficit of ¥38,108 million (including ¥35,426 million in extraordinary military expenditures) had to be covered by bond issues and borrowings. In his administrative speech on July 25, 1946, Tanzan Ishibashi, minister of finance in the first Yoshida cabinet, formed after the first postwar general elections, made a policy statement in connection with the revised budget for fiscal 1946. In substance, his line of thought ran as follows: at that time,

Japan suffered from severe unemployment and idle equipment; under such circumstances, an increase in the currency volume and a rise in prices were not inflation in the ordinary sense of the word. The inflation at that time resulted from the destruction of the economic order and economic prostration, from famine, and from panic caused by this destruction. In order to overcome this type of inflation, the revival of economic activities was more important than a deflationary policy. To this end, fiscal deficits as well as an increase in currency circulation might be allowed to develop.

The concrete steps taken by the government comprised: (1) a rise in the price of coal paid to producers without raising the consumer price, the difference being made up by government subsidies (a similar system was adopted for foodstuffs and fertilizers); (2) promotion of financing by providing funds for the revival of production—the government and the Bank of Japan were to help by supplying funds for productive purposes through financial institutions.

The original budget for fiscal 1946 came to ¥56,088 million in the general accounts, but, with the rapid worsening of the inflation, the budget was revised seven times and the settlement of accounts showed revenues of ¥118,899 million and expenditures of ¥115,207 million. If the special accounts are included, the amount raised by government bonds came to ¥32,355 million (of which the Bank of Japan took over ¥25,730 million).

The proportionally largest items in the general accounts were the "expenditures necessitated by the termination of the war," i.e., expenses for labor and materials requisitioned by the occupation forces, which came to about one-third of the whole budget. This proportion sank to one-fourth in fiscal 1948, but government subsidies, which had not exceeded 10 percent of the total in 1946, increased to about 25 percent, so that occupation costs and subsidies constituted about one-half of all budgetary expenditures.

The deficit financing of the government and an increase in cash withdrawals from blocked accounts (the initial restrictions on withdrawals were frequently relaxed) gave a fresh impetus to the inflation, which had been temporarily checked by the emergency measures under which, unless in urgent cases the minister of finance made an exception, financial institutions were not to give credit in excess of their loan balances as of March 20, 1946. But in the beginning of June it was decided that, in principle, industrial funds should be provided in the form of advances from financial institutions.

The note issue, which had come down to ¥15,200 million through the emergency measures, eclipsed the previous high in September, when it reached ¥64,435 million, and went up to ¥100,040 million in January 1947. Advances by the Bank of Japan had fallen to ¥28,650 million by the end of March, but they climbed to ¥50,431 million at the year-end.

The discontinuation of the war indemnity payments had been a bone of contention ever since the end of the war. These payments were not suspended because it was feared that the effect of such a measure on the economy would be too drastic; for example, of the loan balance of all banks, which stood at ¥110 billion at the end of March 1946, ¥82 billion represented financing of munitions companies or wartime insurance payments. Special blocked deposits made up of payments for the wartime liquidation of enterprises, wartime insurance payments, and payments for military supplies constituted 25 percent of all deposits (an estimate by the Ministry of Finance for April 1946 put claims at ¥54 billion for munitions companies and ¥21 billion for ordinary civilian claims; indemnities for overseas assets were not included). If the indemnity payments were discontinued, the enterprises deprived of these claims would suffer great losses, banks would be unable to collect advances made to those enterprises, and the special blocked deposits, representing indemnities already paid, would have to be confiscated. It was thought necessary to find an arrangement that would not affect present and future business operations. In August 1946, however, the government decided on a complete discontinuation of indemnity payments.

Effective midnight, August 11, 1946, all blocked deposits in all financial institutions were divided into two categories. In the case of individuals, blocked accounts class A were all deposit accounts under ¥3,000; of deposit accounts exceeding ¥3,000, a sum of ¥15,000 for one household with each financial institution or a sum of ¥4,000 for each household member up to a total of ¥32,000, whichever was higher, was allowed as a class A blocked deposit. For corporations and other bodies, one account of ¥15,000 was allowed as a class A blocked deposit. The rest became class B blocked deposits. As a rule, class B blocked deposits could not be touched until the liquidation process was completed. At the end of September, the deposit total of all banks showed the following composition:

class A blocked deposits	42.3%
class B blocked deposits	13.7
special deposits	26.0
free deposits	18.0

All firms capitalized at ¥200,000 and over that could claim war indemnities were designated as Special Accounting Companies (*Tokubetsu Keiri Kaisha*), and, effective August 11, their assets and liabilities were divided into those necessary for the continuation of their business and those unnecessary for this purpose (they were labelled "new" and "old" accounts).

Financial institutions, also, carried out the same classification of new and old accounts. The assets of the new accounts consisted of cash, national and local government bonds, and claims on other financial institutions; the liabilities, of free accounts, class A blocked deposits, taxes and imposts, and liabilities to other financial institutions; the balance between assets and liabilities was set off by crediting or debiting the old accounts which consisted chiefly of loans to special accounting companies, class B blocked deposits, special deposits, capital, and reserves.

After these measures had been taken, another series of laws was enacted in October. They comprised, first, the War Indemnity Special Measures Law (*Senji Hoshō Tokubetsu Sochi-hō*), which decreed that war indemnities would be paid but that, as a rule, a tax of 100 percent would be levied against them (small amounts could be set off; affected were claims not settled as of August 15, 1945, and claims settled in the form of special deposits or in other blocked accounts). The amount of the tax was ¥72,156 million; exemptions came to ¥18,047 million, taxes payable to ¥54,109 million. Other measures were the Financial Institutions Rehabilitation and Reorganization Law (*Kinyū Kikan Saiken Seibi-hō*) and the Enterprise Rehabilitation and Reorganization Law (*Kigyō Saiken Seibi-hō*), which regulated the procedure for the liquidation of old accounts of financial institutions and other enterprises, and finally the Law for the Special Disposal of Losses of the Deposits Bureau of the Ministry of Finance (*Ōkura-shō Yokinbu no Sonshitsu Tokubetsu Shori-hō*) enacted in November. The losses resulting from the discontinuation of the war indemnities did not only fall on the shareholders but had to be borne partly by the creditors. Financial institutions, whose old accounts were not sufficient to cover the whole final loss (so that accounts would have been impaired without this measure), and the Deposits Bureau were to be indemnified; the indemnity total was first fixed at ¥10 billion but later raised to ¥16,500 million.

In connection with the discontinuation of the war indemnity payments, the levy of a capital tax must be mentioned. At first, this was conceived as a large-scale measure designed to tax wartime profits and affecting individuals and corporations alike; but when the war indemnities were cancelled, it was assessed on individual assets only and yielded ¥41 billion. Since, however, it could be paid in securities or real estate and the revenue was not used for retiring public bonds but for making up budgetary deficiencies, its effect as a counter-inflationary measure was negligible.

The repudiation of the obligations arising from government bonds was often discussed but, finally, the idea was discarded. With the progress of the inflation, the burden resulting from outstanding bonds became much lighter, and a few years later, when the principle of a balanced budget was adopted, no new bonds were issued. Outstanding bonds, which had come to about 1.9 times the national income in 1944, had decreased to about 10 percent of the national income by 1951, and the rate has continued to decline.

Together with the liquidation of the war economy, the economic reconstruction policies of the government gradually became more unified and took on definite shape.

The central organ for economic reconstruction was the Economic Stabilization Board (*Keizai Antei Honbu*) established in August 1946. After the National General Mobilization Law had been abrogated, the control of commodities was regulated by the Emergency Commodity Supply Control Law (*Rinji Busshi Jukyū Tōsei-hō*) put in effect in October; allocation and distribution of commodities were carried out according to the policies and plans drawn up by the Economic Stabilization Board. For key commodities, such as coal, petroleum, fertilizer, and foodstuffs, public corporations (*kōdan*) were set up in the following year. Their entire capital was advanced by the government and they were put in charge of the nationwide, unified distribution of these commodities.

Based on the Price Control Ordinance of March 1946, a Price Board was established in August, at the same time as the Economic Stabilization Board, in order to control prices; its chairman was the director general of the Economic Stabilization Board. In April of the following year, a Price Adjustment Corporation (*Kakaku Chōsei Kōdan*) was set up, which engaged in the purchase and sale of commodities and received or paid out price adjustment funds.

When, at the end of 1946 and the beginning of 1947, the inflation resumed its course at an accelerated pace and production tapered off, the government was finally forced to change its policies. It started a national savings campaign, limited bank advances, and resolved to reduce the size of the budget. But it was not easy to bring the inflation under control. The reason was that the chief instrument of industrial financing at that time, the Reconversion Finance Bank, used an inflationary method of supplying funds.

Since an increase in the production of iron, steel, and coal was considered vital for overcoming the economic crisis, the cabinet, in December 1946, had approved the "inclined" production formula. Under this scheme all imports of heavy oil (whose importation had been sanctioned) were to be allocated to the iron and steel industry, which was also to receive top priority in the allocation of coal. Steel materials thus produced were to be channeled into the coal industry which would then be able to increase coal production through improvements in equipment. The iron and steel industry was again to reap the chief benefit from the increased coal output. This circle would alternately increase coal and iron production, and a goal of 30 million metric tons of coal was set for fiscal 1947.

The financial institution which was to support this formula on the monetary side was the Reconversion Finance Bank (*Fukkō Kinyū Kinko*, "Reconstruction Finance Bank" would be closer to the Japanese appellation) set up in January 1947. Prior to this foundation, the Financial System Research Council (*Kinyū Seido Chōsakai*), established in 1945, recommended a special method for providing the funds required for economic reconstruction and the stablization of the livelihood of the people, if such funds could not be raised through ordinary financial institutions. For this purpose, and in order to soften the impact of the cancellation of war indemnities, the government submitted a bill for the foundation of the Reconversion Finance Bank to the Diet, and, until this institution could start its operations, charged the Industrial Bank with special financing projects. Based on the financing plans of the Reconstruction Finance Committee (*Fukkō Kinyū Iinkai*), an advisory organ to the minister of finance, the Reconstruction Finance Department of the Industrial Bank, began its activities in August 1946. Reconstruction finance loans given by the Industrial Bank until January 1947, when the Reconversion Finance Bank was founded, came to ¥4,118 million, and more than 40 percent of this sum was funneled into the coal industry (not for reconstruction, but mainly as stopgap financing until the government could pay its subsidies); the next chief recipient was the fertilizer industry. Loans advanced by the Bank of Japan helped out when sufficient funds were not available.

The Reconversion Finance Bank Law was passed in October 1946 and the bank was established on January 25 of the following year. Its authorized capital was ¥10 billion, to be furnished entirely by the government; at first, ¥4 billion was paid in. The gigantic scale of the bank's activities may be illustrated by a few figures. Its outstanding loan balance came to ¥28,845 million at the end of September 1947 and to more than double, ¥59,463 million, six months later at the end of March 1948, when it made up 25 percent of all outstanding bank loans (including those given by the Reconversion Finance Bank itself). The balance rose to ¥91,951 million in September (25 percent of the total) and ¥131,965 million in March 1949 (24 percent of the total). As of that date, its outstanding loans for equipment investment amounted to ¥94,342 million, 77 percent of the equipment loans of all banks.

One of the characteristic features of the loan policy of the bank was its concentration on coal (36 percent of the outstanding loan balance at the end of March 1949), iron, steel, and fertilizers. It played the most important role in equipment investment during that period. In addition, its funds served to make up the deficits caused by the government's policy of pegging official prices in such industries as coal, electric power, fertilizers, iron and steel, etc. It also supplied the working capital of the eleven public corporations (*kōdan*) existing up to March 1948, which, besides the four foreign trade corporations, were the governmental instruments for economic control. At the end of March 1948, the loans to these corporations made up 30.6 percent of the loan total of the bank; they decreased, however, thereafter.

Originally, the funds required for these loans were to be supplied by the government, but the necessity of balancing the budget, talked about since 1947 (only the adoption of the Dodge line in 1949 produced a balanced budget), reduced the amount of funds actually advanced by the government to only ¥25 billion by September 1948. The rest was raised by Reconversion Finance Bank bonds, and the outstanding bond issues on March 31, 1949, amounted to ¥109,100 million. Although the rate at which these bonds were absorbed by the Bank of Japan is said to have been lower in the later period, the Bank of Japan actually took over ¥115,592 million, or 69 percent, of the ¥168,000 million issued. To that extent, therefore, the note issue was enlarged, resulting in the so-called Reconversion Finance Bank inflation, which is credited by Japanese economists with having been an extremely important factor in promoting economic reconstruction on the financial side.

The rampaging inflation completely undermined the public's confidence in the currency. Withdrawals from blocked deposits were allowed liberally; "new yen," the currency for blackmarket dealings, leaked out through other channels than ordinary financial institutions, while they did not flow back into normal circulation. Due to the great demand for funds, the increase in bank deposits could not keep pace with the increase in bank loans, and, at the end of 1946, outstanding deposit balances of the eight city banks (¥72 billion) fell below the loan balances (¥86 billion), and this resulted in the so-called overloan situation.

Under these circumstances the Currency Stabilization Board (*Tsūka Antei Taisaku Honbu*; literally, "currency stability measures headquarters"; November 1946–November 1949) was established, in which the Bank of Japan played a leading role. Since November 1946 a savings campaign had been conducted. A number of devices were tried to entice people to save: time deposits with gifts or premiums and enjoyment of special tax favors, and time deposits that could be made partly with blocked deposits and that were paid out in new yen. In order to induce people, afraid of taxes, to deposit their funds, a system of "bearer" (uninscribed) time deposits was introduced in June 1947.

In the beginning of 1947, the Bank of Japan took a sterner attitude on borrowing in order to curb loans, and, in February of the same year, the cabinet decided to fix a loan ceiling which, while satisfying the fund demand of key industries like coal, fertilizers, and iron and steel, would check inflation. Financial institutions were to refrain from borrowing from the Bank of Japan, and syndicates would provide the funds for joint financing by financial institutions. At the same time, rules for supplying funds by financial institutions, together with a priority table of industrial loans, were put into effect in March 1947. This table divided industries into four new categories, A1, A2, B, and C. For equipment funds, coal, lignite, iron and steel, and fertilizers were put into A1 class and given priority for investment in new or enlarged equipment, while nonessential industries relegated to C class were not given equipment funds. For working capital, also, industries classified as A1 were to be given preferential treatment, similar to that given by the Bank of Japan to prime-grade commercial paper.

The loan ceiling was left to the "autonomous" decision of the financial institutions, and it was decided that the increase in loans was to remain within 50 percent of the prospective increase in free deposits (minus deposits of public funds and financial institutions), while 20 percent was to be invested in government bonds, another 20 percent was to be used for cash payments from blocked deposits, and 10 percent for buying bonds of the Reconversion Finance Bank.

The enforcement of these rules brought an increase in disbursements from blocked deposits, because loans to nonessential industries were kept down or funds required for the payment of the capital levy had to be provided. The scheme did not work out as planned, and it was revised in July. A committee, made up of the minister of finance, the director general of the Economic Stabilization Board, and the governor of the Bank of Japan, from then on fixed the ceiling on the loan increase for each month.

In July 1948, the system underwent another modification and a certain proportion of the increase in deposits was to be used preferentially for fiscal investments. The priority table, also, was amended many times. The importance of these regulations diminished in the course of time, but they have never been rescinded and remain on the books.

In January 1947, the minister of finance had announced a policy of discontinuing the practice of relying on deficit financing through bond issues as soon as possible. At least the general accounts were to be balanced without recourse to bonds or borrowings (relatively large amounts of bonds, however, were issued in fiscal 1947 and 1948 in order to pay indemnities for losses). Tax revenues were to be increased by increasing tax rates as well as by improving tax collection. New bond issues, therefore, experienced a sharp contraction, and the issues taken over by the Bank of Japan, in particular, were greatly reduced. But on account of the time lag between fiscal disbursements and the collection of revenue, government borrowings from the Bank of Japan increased drastically, rising from ¥15 billion to ¥58 billion in fiscal 1947, so that public finance remained an important factor in propelling the inflation. Moreover, the activities of the Reconversion Finance Bank, financed as described above largely by bonds, must be regarded as a part of the fiscal deficit financing. Of the factors responsible for the increase in the note issue during fiscal 1947 (from ¥116 billion to ¥218 billion) the fiscal sector accounted for 71 percent and the debentures of the Reconversion Finance Bank for 39 percent, while the civilian sector, which had been responsible for 54 percent of the increase in the preceding fiscal year, showed a decrease of 10 percent due to an increase in the compulsory absorption of government bonds through restrictions placed on loans and the increase in deposits. Since the pressure of fund demand concentrated on the Reconversion Finance Bank, the imbalance between deposits and loans of other financial institutions saw a slight improvement, and advances by the Bank of Japan to the public remained on the same level.

 POSTWAR SECURITIES MARKETS

1) Prohibition against Reopening the Stock Exchanges—The naming of Toshikazu Tsushima as minister of finance in the Higashikuni cabinet formed on August 17, 1945, raised hopes that the stock exchanges would soon be able to resume their functions, since he had played a prominent part in the efforts to support stock prices in the last months of the war. On the Tokyo Stock Exchange, uncompleted transactions as of August 9, 1945, involved 688,000 shares in long-term transactions and 1,132,000 shares in spot sales. Upon consultation with the association of stock exchange members, the exchange fixed August 28 as deadline for the completion of these transactions. At the same time, the reopening of the exchanges and the future form of their organization were discussed among the members of the exchanges and in the Ministry of Finance. The board of directors of the Tokyo Stock Exchange proposed October 1 as a date for the resumption of business. A total of 700 issues (excluding foreign and defense issues) were to be confined to spot transactions with delivery in five days. Talks between the Ministry of Finance and the securities dealers concerning these and other conditions were held on September 26, and on the following day the newspapers announced that all Japanese exchanges would reopen on October 1. But a SCAP memorandum dated

September 26 informed the government that stock and commodity exchanges and similar institutions were to remain closed until a plan for their operation had been approved by SCAP.

Actually, Japan's economy was not yet in a position to profit from the activities of the exchange; and since SCAP's prohibition seemed to imply that a reorganization of the exchange was unavoidable, the Tokyo Exchange Association (*Tokyo Torihikiin Kyōkai*, the successor to the wartime control association) formed a research group including the chiefs of the research departments of Yamaichi, Nomura, Nikko, and Daiwa companies in order to study the structure of the American securities market. Representatives of the Ministry of Finance joined the group and the reorganization of the exchanges on the basis of the membership principle became the main topic of the discussions.

2) Development of Collective Transactions—Although prospects for an early reopening of the stock exchanges looked dim, trading in stocks in the form of over-the-counter transactions resumed almost immediately after the war, and the number of customers grew steadily. Most of them wanted to sell their stock holdings in order to get cash for living expenses, the shares of civilian industries such as textiles, electric power, and foods being the main issues traded. With the expansion of these transactions, traders began to exchange information and, gradually, collective transactions, the so-called group trading, emerged. The traders' justification of this form of business was that they did not engage in it in their capacity as members of the exchange, but as securities dealers to which the Securities Exchange Law did not apply. Naturally, since group trading constituted an organized market, it was actually a violation of the law, but the Ministry of Finance and SCAP authorities chose to look the other way.

Group trading started in Tokyo on December 17, 1945, in an office of the Japan Securities Building. The group of about thirty people was composed mostly of market representatives of the securities companies. In the following year, the gathering started to use a room in the Tokyo Stock Exchange, but the Ministry of Finance, under instructions from SCAP, objected to it as an institution similar to an organized exchange, and the group moved back to the Japan Securities Building. A set of rules was drawn up, and the trading was supervised by the Securities Business Association. The meeting were usually attended by about three hundred (the total of accredited dealers and telephone operators was 360; floor personnel, 40; and newspaper reporters, 24; the floor space was 36 *tsubo*, 216 sq. ft.). In Osaka, group transactions started in October 1945 when seven or eight dealers met in a room of the Securities Association; in November, they moved to a vacant lot in the neighborhood. Organized trading began on December 19. In January 1946, group trading started in Nagoya; in August, in Kobe, Niigata, and Kyoto; and in October, in Fukuoka, while volume in Tokyo increased from an average 20,000 shares a day in January 1946 to 150,000 in May.

3) Influence of Currency Measures—Toward the end of the war, interest in the stock market had already shifted from defense issues to textile and amusement industry shares, and this trend continued in the group trading. The favorites were Shochiku and Toho (two movie companies), and Fuji Spinning. Initially prices stood at about 35 percent of the level of August 10, 1945, but in the fall of 1946 and the spring of 1947 prices experienced a definite upswing. Up to the reopening of the stock exchanges, the price pattern rose and fell again four times. Trading had been stimulated by rumors of the impending currency reform, which started to circulate as early as October 1945. When the reform was announced on February 16, 1946, the note issue of the Bank of Japan had already doubled compared with the end of the war, and wholesale prices had gone up 2.3 times. Barter was in full swing, and stocks were bought for protection against the inflation.

Immediately after the currency reform, the government allowed the payment of capital increases out of blocked accounts. This made stocks less attractive and trading subsided. But a week after the reform, on February 23, the government also sanctioned the use of blocked accounts for the acquisition of stocks, which could then be sold for new yen. This measure was only one of the numerous steps taken by the government that made the currency reform a complete failure, but it proved a big stimulant to stock trading. The group transactions, which had been suspended for one week after March 4 in Tokyo, Osaka, and Nagoya, were resumed and trading volume increased rapidly. The chief support grew from the distrust in the currency and the desire to turn blocked accounts into cash. On June 21, 1946, the Ministry of Finance stopped the withdrawal of blocked funds for stock pur-

Tokyo Stock Transactions

		Group Trading		Over-the-Counter
		Number of shares 1,000	Value ¥ mill.	Number of shares 1,000
1945	December	209		
1946	January	575		
	February	960		
	March	1,179		
	April	1,504		
	May	4,319		
	June	5,048		
	July	2,550		
	August	3,705	174	
	September	7,158	403	10,555
	October	5,240	300	7,523
	November	4,297	249	7,044
	December	4,564	293	8,600
1947	January	5,403	327	10,803
	February	6,888	415	17,608
	March	10,839	717	27,981
	April	16,742	1,321	34,041
	May	16,501	1,244	32,074
	June	13,530	1,026	24,711
	July	9,304	670	17,452
	August	6,323	460	12,947
	September	8,418	698	16,844
	October	6,768	494	13,180
	November	6,426	440	13,801

Source: History of the Tokyo Securities Association.

chases if the transaction was aimed at the procurement of new yen. This measure halted group trading from June 21 until July 9; from the tenth on, trading resumed on the basis of two sets of quotations, one for transactions in new yen and another for blocked account yen. The spread between the two sets of prices was about 20 percent. But, after July 29, group transactions were limited to those on a new-yen basis; over-the-counter trading, however, continued on a blocked-account basis.

Besides the stocks of the amusement industry and textiles, stocks of firms not connected with the reparations problem or the Law Concerning Emergency Measures for Company Accounting became popular, e.g., stocks of fishery companies, flour mills, and breweries. Furthermore, stocks of firms which showed themselves cooperative in getting approval for the withdrawal of the purchase price from blocked accounts were actively traded. When, in August, rumors about the resumption of foreign trade began to circulate, stocks of trading companies joined the ranks of the favorites. In June, the monthly volume of transactions reached 5 million shares, and in September the volume was so large that trading had to be suspended. The increase in taxes, the labor troubles in the beginning of 1947, and the scarcity of raw materials then dampened the mood of the market, but amusement issues experienced a second boom.

The bond market reappeared in almost the same way as the stock market. Government bonds had been sold during the war to almost everybody, and many people wanted to divest themselves of their holdings as quickly as possible. This brought prices down. About forty Tokyo securities dealers formed an organization called *Shōyūkai* ("Securities Association") on February 27, 1946, which held regular meetings twice a week. Quotations were on both a new-yen and a blocked-account basis, with a spread of about 10 percent. The redemption of war bonds gradually depleted the available issues but, in the beginning, trading was fairly substantial in 4 percent and 3½ percent government bonds, Greater East Asia discount government bonds, debentures of the Hypothec (*Kangyō*) Bank, "patriotic savings bonds," land certificates, Telegraph and Telephone debentures, and lottery tickets.

4) Resumption of Public Stock Offerings—Offerings of new stock issues resumed relatively early. On April 17, 1946, the four firms, Yamaichi, Nomura, Nikko, and Daiwa, offered 67,000 shares of the newly founded Shin Nippon Kogyo to the public, and a total of twenty-five offerings, including new foundations and capital increases, followed in the next six months. Since most of these issues could be bought with blocked accounts, they were readily absorbed.

Under the impact of the occupation policies and their emphasis on equality of opportunity, the Tokyo Dealers Association drew up regulations and organized a committee for stock offerings. Except for the stocks released by government organs, all offerings had to be reported to the committee and 50 percent of all offerings over 30,000 shares had to be turned over to the association in order to give all members a share in the business.

In July 1946, the Closed Institutions Custodian Commission (*Heisa Kikan Hokan-nin Iinkai*), set up on February 6, 1946, began to accept bids for the vast amounts of securities formerly held by the closed institutions. The first bids were submitted on September 16, 1946; the last, the thirty-fifth allotment, was made public on June 25, 1947. The commission offered a total of 5,885,320 shares; allotted were 3,599,851 shares for which ¥178,185,000 was paid.

5) Stagnation in the Issue Market—Despite these activities, the basic tone of the capital market was rather depressed. The old economy was being dismantled, and there was little incentive for new enterprises. Moreover, the issue of government bonds became dependent on approval by SCAP (November 25, 1945), as also was the use of the funds of the Deposits Bureau, Postal Life Insurance, and Postal Annuities for taking over financial debentures (January 29, 1946).

Debenture issues were few. For the last quarter of 1945, the Industrial Bank listed thirty bond issues totaling ¥12,818 million, and for the entire year of 1946 there were only eighty-five issues amounting to ¥23,948 million. Bank debentures were most numerous, but government bonds constituted the bulk of the amounts. According to the Bank of Japan, payments for newly issued stock amounted to ¥120 million in the last quarter of 1945 and to ¥2,386 million in 1946. Firms in the entertainment, food, and railroad industries formed the main enterprises in search of new capital. Although the new debenture issues were not numerous, the abolition of the wartime control machinery completely changed the issuing method. At the same time, the prohibition enjoining governmental financial institutions not to take over special bond issues did away with the differences between the various issues of local government bonds. In 1946, therefore, over 80 percent of all industrial debentures and 60 percent of local government bonds were offered to the public.

1 THE ECONOMY UNDER THE OCCUPATION

CHANGE IN OCCUPATION POLICIES

 POLICY OF ECONOMIC REHABILITATION

In March 1947, the so-called Truman doctrine was formulated, and the emphasis in the occupation policy gradually shifted from the more negative aspect of demilitarization to the reconstruction of the war-ravaged countries. The shift in policy was particularly noticeable in the approach to the reparations problem.

Soon after the end of the war, the first reparations mission, headed by Ambassador Edwin W. Pauley, had come to Japan. In a statement on the Japanese Interim Reparations Program of December 7, 1945, Mr. Pauley had outlined the basic reparations policy: "Despite all the destruction, Japan still retains, in workable condition, more plant and equipment than its rulers ever allowed to be used for civilian supply and consumption even in peaceful years. That surplus must be taken out." This implied extremely severe limitations deduced from very doubtful premises. Based on the Pauley report, the Far Eastern Commission, in May 1946, began to issue a series of "Interim Reparations Removal" directives. These directives, issued separately for different categories of surplus equipment, were partly implemented by SCAP's "Advance Transfer Program" initiated under U.S. authority, because the Far Eastern Commission was unable to reach a final decision. In January 1947, the commission had ruled that "the peaceful needs of the Japanese people should be defined as being substantially the standard of living prevailing in Japan during the period of 1930–1934." This was in effect the industry level set by the State-War-Navy Coordinating Committee in a drastic formulation of the initial punishment policy.

A reversal of this policy was clearly expressed in a speech which Secretary of the Army Kenneth C. Royall delivered in San Francisco on January 6, 1948. He stated:

> There has arisen an inevitable area of conflict between the original concept of broad demilitarization and the new purpose of building a self-supporting nation. . . . Since last summer we have had a competent group of industrial engineers in the Pacific selecting the specific plants which . . . can be dismantled with the minimum of detriment to Japanese economic recovery.

The report to which Secretary Royall referred, submitted by Overseas Consultants, Inc., bluntly opposed the removal of industrial equipment, stating that "the removal of productive facilities (except primary war facilities) which can be effectively used in Japan would hurt world production; would reduce the likelihood of her becoming self-supporting . . . would be expensive to the American taxpayer; and . . . would not be in the best interest of the claimant nations."

A few weeks later, a mission led by Major General Draper, undersecretary of the army, and including Percy H. Johnston, chairman of the Chemical Bank and Trust Co., visited Japan. In its report ("Report on the Economic Position and Prospects of Japan and Korea and the Measures Required to Improve Them," Secretary of the Army's Committee to Inquire into Economic Problems of Japan and Korea; chairman–P. H. Johnston; April 26, 1948), the committee expressed the view that "further delay in the settlement of the reparations problem . . . will hurt Japan greatly." It proposed a substantial lowering of the reparations levels, particularly of primary war facilities, below the already reduced levels recommended by Overseas Consultants, Inc.

Following these investigations, Major General Frank R. McCoy, the U.S. delegate to the Far Eastern Commission, issued a statement announcing the suspension of the Advance Transfer Program (May 12, 1949). He based this decision on the following conclusions reached by the United States:

A. The deficit Japanese economy shows little prospect of being balanced in the near future and, to achieve eventual balance, it will require all the resources at its disposal.
B. The burden of removing further reparations from Japan could detract seriously from the occupation objective of stabilizing the Japanese economy and permitting it to move towards self-support.
C. There is little or no prospect of Far Eastern Commission agreement on a reparations shares schedule . . .
D. Japan has already paid substantial reparations through expropriation of its former overseas assets and, in a smaller degree, under the Advance Transfer Program.

Facilities transferred to the Allied powers under the Advance Transfer Program came to somewhat over 60,000 tons by September 1949, but, consequent to the signing of the Peace Treaty of San Francisco, the reparations issue became a problem to be settled by negotiations between Japan and the individual claimant nations.

American help to Japan gradually assumed larger proportions. After fiscal 1947, relief chiefly in the form of food, financed by GARIOA (government and relief in occupied areas) funds and, after fiscal 1949, industrial raw materials financed by EROA (economic rehabilitation of occupied areas) funds were sent to Japan. The mining and manufacturing production index recovered to better than half of the prewar average when it rose from 37.4 in 1947 to 54.6 in 1948. Due to the revision of the price structure, wholesale prices (January 1948= 100; this index was based on a new method of calculation) advanced from 98.01 in December 1947 to 221.1 at the end of 1948, while retail prices (July 1914=100) went up from 14,552.8 to 33,512.3 during the same period. The rise in black-market prices of consumer goods, however, was less steep: from 558 to 769, and their ratio to official prices declined to 2.9 times.

2 DEMOCRATIZATION OF SECURITIES OWNERSHIP

1) Establishment of the Securities Coordinating Liquidation Commission—The various measures taken for the dissolution of the *zaibatsu* and the deconcentration of monopolistic enterprises involved a large-scale redistribution of securities. The securities came from the following sources.

(1) Securities taken over by the Holding Company Liquidation Commission. Their total value (prices as of December 1946) amounted to ¥7.8 billion (first designation, ¥1.9 billion; second designation, ¥4.1 billion; third designation, ¥1.8 billion).

(2) Securities of restricted concerns, which were prohibited from owning stock in other enterprises and had to dispose of their holdings under a plan to be approved by HCLC. Their value came to ¥0.6 billion.

(3) Securities owned by the *zaibatsu* families; value ¥0.9 billion.

(4) Securities owned by closed institutions. In May 1947, the Closed Institutions Custodian Commission was reorganized as the Closed Institutions Liquidation Commission and charged with the disposal of the assets of the closed institutions. The securities held by the commission were valued at ¥6 billion.

(5) Securities held by the Treasury. These were turned over as payments in kind under the Capital Tax Law, which became effective November 20, 1946. Their value amounted to ¥7.2 billion.

(6) Securities of which firms under the Law Concerning Emergency Measures for Company Accounting had to divest themselves. This law affected firms which had received war indemnity or insurance payments or owned assets abroad. The securities to be sold by these firms totaled about ¥2 billion.

(7) Securities given up under the War Indemnities Special Measures Law, ¥0.7 billion.

On January 17, 1947, the Law Concerning the Adjustment of the Disposal of Securities was promulgated and the disposal of the securities listed above was made subject to approval by the Securities Coordinating Liquidation Committee, which was set up later in the year. It was composed of five representatives, one each from HCLC, the Closed Institutions Liquidations Commission, the Bank of Japan, the Ministry of Finance, and the Ministry of Commerce and Industry. The commission was supposed to regulate the disposal of the shares without disturbing the market, so all five members had to agree on time, price, and volume of the sales. The organizations represented on the commission had to draw up plans, which were to be approved by the commission. In actual practice, however, the commission took over the work, with the exception of the shares sold by the firms coming under the purvue of the Special Accounting Law. The authorities were represented by two observers, who saw to it that the decisions of the commission conformed to occupation policies.

2) Democratization Movement—In September 1946, the House of Representatives adopted a resolution calling for the stabilization of the currency, and the Currency Stabilization Board, created soon afterwards, became the chief organ for carrying out a savings campaign. In connection with these endeavors, the securities companies launched a "securities democratization movement" in order to channel the securities released by SCLC into the hands of the public. An ordinance promulgated in November 1946 barred restricted concerns and their officers from acquiring and holding the securities of other firms, and these prohibitions, although with modifications, were extended to all firms through the Antimonopoly Law enforced in July 1947. These measures excluded from the acquisition of stocks some of the sectors which had accounted for a large part of stock ownership in prewar times.

The Financial System Research Council was established as an organ of the Finance Ministry in December 1945 in order to study the problems of Japan's monetary system. This council was dissolved, but another organ with the same name was formed in December 1946. A subcommittee, at first headed by Keitaro Sekiguchi, was formed to discuss questions concerned with securities; the fifteen members of this subcommittee were drawn from securities companies, banks, emission houses, and the press. This subcommittee was again dissolved, in July 1947, but some of its members became the nucleus of a committee set up by the Tokyo Securities Dealers Association to investigate the problems of the securities market. This committee studied ways and means of promoting savings through investment in stocks.

In the meantime, the government had prepared legislation regulating the disposal of securities, and the securities dealers used this occasion to set up a nationwide organization. On March 20, 1947, the National Federation of Securities Dealers Associations (*Shōken-gyō Kyōkai Zenkoku Rengōkai*)—its name was changed to National Federation of Securities Associations (*Zenkoku Shōken Kyūkai Rengō-kai*), on December 1, 1947—was formed and united seven associations in Tokyo, Osaka, Aichi (Nagoya), Kobe, Fukuoka, Kyoto, and Hokkaido. A regional organization was set up on June 14 by amalgamating prefectural chapters into nine district associations: Hokkaido, Ou, Kanto, Kita-Chubu, Chubu, Kinki, Chugoku, Shikoku, and Kyushu. Each of these districts elected one committee member to the national committee, while the Tokyo chapter was entrusted with handling current business. Rules were laid down for the sale of securities released by government organs and a committee set up to supervise these transactions. Prices, commission fees, allocation of stocks, and adjustment of demand and supply were to be discussed by the committee. Another committee was formed by the Tokyo Exchange Association, on which the old big four securities companies and other securities dealers were represented. The thirteen-member committee was to advise the chairman of the Tokyo Securities Dealers Association on all practical questions connected with the released securities.

SCAP actively supported these efforts, and, on November 4, a Securities Democratization Commission was formed on which the Ministries of Finance, Commerce and Industry, Communications, and Education, SCLC, the Currency Stabilization Board, the National Federation of Bankers Associations, and the Trust Association were represented. On December 1, 1947, a meeting was held sponsored by seven of the most important economic organizations in the country and attended by Prime Minister Katayama. Finance Minister Kurusu and Naoto Ichimada, governor of the Bank of Japan, spoke on the role of widespread stock ownership as a means of economic democratization and rehabilitation and of curbing the inflation.

3) Activation of the Stock Market and Increase in Stock Issues—By the end of 1947 the economic outlook showed some improvement, and, spurred by the democratization movement, stock buying became more active and the third stock boom was on its way. In February 1948, prices of such favorites as Mitsubishi Chemical, Toyo Spinning, and Teikoku Rayon went up rapidly, posting gains of up to ¥50 on a single day. On the unofficial market, large-scale transactions increased and some dealers were unable to make delivery. On January 23, the Osaka group suspended trading, and the same happened in Tokyo and Nagoya. Over-the-counter trading, too, came to a halt. About ten firms were expelled from the group for failure to deliver. Group trading resumed in February, except in the shares of Toyo Spinning and Teikoku Rayon. Things calmed down in March. In the summer, monetary stringency caused by the delays in government payments and the admonitions of SCAP brought the market back to normal. The general average rose from ¥66.26 in September 1947 to ¥161.96 in April 1948, and the price index (August 1946 = 100) from 113.1 in November 1947 to 281.2 in April 1948.

In October 1948, the second Yoshida cabinet was formed, and stock prices started to rise again toward the end of the year. In the spring of 1949, the fourth boom developed, centered on petroleum, chemicals, and mining issues. The rise spread to almost all sectors, except transportation and finance, and lasted until the reopening of the stock exchanges.

Average Stock Prices

	Metals	Machinery & ship-building	Textiles	General average
1947 Sept.	20.78	42.70	130.03	66.26
1948 Feb.	52.80	99.29	328.26	140.29
Mar.	70.10	123.01	397.28	159.82
Apr.	80.16	133.23	402.83	161.96

Source: Yamaichi Securities Co., Ltd.

In conformity with SCAP's instructions, the shares of stock released through SCLC were channeled into two directions: first, the employees of the companies whose shares were sold and the inhabitants of the places where their factories were located and, second, the general public. Three methods were used for the sales destined to bring the shares to the public: sales based on bids, general sales, and off-market sales. When the volume of shares released by SCLC was small, sales were held through bids; when large amounts were involved, general sales were held; they were either ordinary sales, sales through securities dealers, or commission sales. In some cases, sales were held for local markets. Off-market sales were exceptional; shares were sold immediately to securities dealers after the close of the session at the last posted price.

Group Trading

	Price index	Monthly trading volume 1,000 shares
1946 Jan.	109.6	575*
July	132.8	2,550*
Dec.	105.6	13,165
1947 May	150.4	48,575
Nov.	113.1	20,228
1948 Apr.	281.2	41,240
June	231.2	30,860
1949 May	700.3	151,489

* Group trading only; others include over-the-counter transactions.
Price index based on Fisher's formula; August 1946 = 100.
Source: Tokyo Securities Exchange.

The releases by SCLC started on July 7, 1947, with 199,174 shares representing twenty-four different issues. By the end of 1948, about 80 million had been sold; they brought over ¥5,153 million. The largest part of these shares, 58 percent, came from the Special Institutions Liquidation Commission; the shares released by the Closed Institutions Liquidation Commission accounted for the next largest group.

In the meantime, financial institutions, as well as manufacturing companies, had readied their reorganization plans in accordance with the legal provisions mentioned above. About eight thousand firms had been designated as "special accounting firms"; some were later taken off the list and others allowed to merge their old and new accounts, but even so, up to the end of January 1949, 4,769 firms filed reorganization plans. At the end of October 1947, 2,323 firms had had their reorganization plans approved; of these, 1,829 (almost 80 percent) were allowed to continue; 1,127 firms among these could make up the losses caused through the discontinuation of the wartime indemnification payments through capital reductions or by calling the unpaid portions of their capital; they could then again increase their capital. The original program had placed the reorganization of financial institutions after that of other enterprises (since the outcome of the enterprises reorganization would greatly affect the assets of financial institutions), but the Deconcentration Law delayed the reorganization of enterprises, so that the reorganization plans of financial institutions were not drawn up until the end of March 1948 and it was not until May 15 that the reorganization plans of seventy-two financial institutions (they did not include the Industrial Bank or the Bank of

Public Stock Offerings

	1946		1947		1948	
	Number of shares 1,000	Amount ¥1,000	Number of shares 1,000	Amount ¥1,000	Number of shares 1,000	Amount ¥1,000
Banks, trust companies, securities companies	400	20,000	550	27,500	14,325	806,250
Electric light & power	—	—	2,150	107,500	1,680	84,300
Paper	—	—	—	—	200	13,000
Ceramics	—	—	440	43,095	537	36,700
Real estate	—	—	710	37,350	842	50,645
Railroads & other transportation	732	42,129	458	30,642	807	52,000
Mining	—	—	—	—	—	—
Shipbuilding	70	3,500	1,187	92,233	12,328	1,469,881
Textiles	36	900	789	29,575	15,677	1,539,769
Food	1,943	84,300	785	47,404	1,385	95,250
Chemicals	—	—	605	47,105	3,436	336,420
Investment & colonization	—	—	—	—	215	12,250
Entertainments, department stores	552	26,400	850	34,595	1,906	118,420
Metals	—	—	—	—	625	39,600
Others	100	5,000	—	—	—	—
Total	3,833	182,229	9,202	532,451	54,681	4,757,033

Source: Yamaichi Securities Co., Ltd.

Tokyo) received their final touches. The reorganization programs of the local banks were approved on July 20, those of the city banks on August 24.

In addition to the capital increases of the reorganized firms, new foundations and new issues of other enterprises became more frequent in the years 1947 and 1948. On July 12, 1948, a revision of the Commercial Code made it obligatory to have all issued shares fully paid up, so that the demand for capital became even stronger. Almost 50 percent of the shares issued in the last half of 1948 (total amount, ¥28,868 million) were bank shares. Enterprises in other sectors used over 60 percent of the funds raised through new issues for debt amortization.

Public stock offerings increased rapidly after the successful flotation of the shares of the electric power companies between August 1947 and January 1948, despite the fact that the shares of the old Nippatsu, now Nihon Dengen Kaihatsu K.K. (Japan Electric Resources Development Co.), were quoted five to six yen below their face value. The total number of shares of electric power companies absorbed came to over 4.9 million, and the Kyushu, Kanto, and Tohoku power companies issued additional shares in order to meet the demand.

Stock Ownership During and After the War

	1945				1949			
	Number of owners		Number of shares		Number of owners		Number of shares	
	1,000	%	1,000	%	1,000	%	1,000	%
Government & public bodies	2	0.1	36,796	8.2	6	0.1	56,064	2.8
Financial institutions	7	0.4	49,571	11.1	14	0.3	198,262	9.9
Securities dealers	8	0.5	12,496	2.8	48	1.1	251,141	12.5
Other corporations	20	1.2	109,343	24.6	28	0.6	111,806	5.5
Individuals	1,656	96.7	230,592	51.9	4,183	97.5	1,369,554	68.4
Others	16	0.9	4,835	1.0	7	0.1	12,919	0.6
Total	1,712	100.0	443,636	100.0	4,288	100.0	1,999,748	100.0

Source: Tokyo Stock Exchange. Based on 691 issues traded on the Tokyo Stock Exchange.

Stock Ownership by Size of Holding

Size Number of shares	1945				1949			
	Number of owners		Number of shares		Number of owners		Number of shares	
	1,000	%	1,000	%	1,000	%	1,000	%
0– 100	1,150	67.1	39,615	8.9	1,428	33.3	52,225	2.6
100– 500	471	27.5	77,239	17.4	2,162	50.4	424,684	21.2
500– 1,000	46	2.7	27,999	6.3	368	8.6	232,480	11.6
1,000– 5,000	36	2.1	59,937	13.5	294	6.8	484,255	24.2
5,000–10,000	3	0.2	22,616	5.1	17	0.4	109,787	5.4
over 10,000	3	0.2	216,228	48.7	16	0.4	696,315	34.8
Total	1,712	100.0	443,636	100.0	4,288	100.0	1,999,748	100.0

Source: Tokyo Stock Exchange.

3 STAGNATION ON THE BOND MARKET AND COUNTERMEASURES

1) Stagnation on the Bond Market—Contrary to the active stock market, bonds remained dull during the greater part of the three years immediately following the war. True, there was a large increase in the amount of bond issues, but this was largely due to the vast amount of bonds of the Reconversion Finance Bank. The issues made available to the public constituted only a fraction of the total issues. The Central Bank for Agriculture and Forestry played a leading role in the absorption of bonds; other institutions which took over large amounts of bonds were agricultural cooperatives, credit associations, and local and savings banks.

The financial measures adopted for the reconstruction of the economy (increase in fiscal investments, issuance of reconversion finance bonds taken over by the Bank of Japan, investment funds channeled by the Reconversion Finance Bank into the industries selected for the "inclined" production program) led to a continuous expansion of the note issue of the Bank of Japan, a rapid rise of interest rates, and a growing inability of the city banks to take over bonds.

Bond Issues

	1946			1947			1948		
	Number of issues	Amount		Number of issues	Amount		Number of issues	Amount	
		Total	Offered to public		Total	Offered to public		Total	Offered to public
		¥ mill.	¥ mill.		¥ mill.	¥ mill.		¥ mill.	¥ mill.
Government bonds	12	21,254	—	16	55,202	45	12	37,874	12
Local bonds	15	147	85	109	745	30	67	929	120
Financial debentures (incl. Reconversion Finance Bonds)	30	1,820	534	62	42,776	400	66	88,262	52
	—	—	—	23	40,900	—	43	87,100	—
Industrial debentures	28	725	577	13	340	102	16	514	495
Total	85	23,948	1,197	200	99,063	578	161	127,581	679

Source: Industrial Bank of Japan.

2) Establishment of the Bond Issuance Adjustment Council—The Bond Issuance Adjustment Council was set up on June 2, 1947, by the institutions chiefly concerned with the flotation of bonds: the Ministry of Finance, the Economic Stabilization Board, the Bank of Japan, the Reconversion Finance Bank, the Central Bank for Agriculture and Forestry, the Industrial Bank of Japan, Kangyo, Teikoku, and Sanwa banks, and representatives of local banks. The reason for setting up the council was that the conditions prevailing on the bond market made it impossible to issue bonds in an orderly manner. The wartime planning had been discontinued, but the flotation of industrial bonds was still controlled by the Emergency Fund Adjustment Law, and local bond issues were supervised—without any legal basis—by the Ministry of Finance and the Bank of Japan, and linked to the issuance conditions of government bonds. When the monetary stringency forced the suspension of govern-

Bond Absorption

	1947								1948							
	Local bonds		Financial debentures		Industrial debentures		Total		Local bonds		Financial debentures		Industrial debentures		Total	
	¥1,000	%	¥1,000	%	¥1,000	%	¥1,000	%	¥1,000	%	¥1,000	%	¥1,000	%	¥1,000	%
City banks, special banks	—	—	25,470	6.4	1,200	0.4	26,670	30.7	15,810	13.1	5,000	9.6	35,465	7.0	56,275	8.3
Local & savings banks	22,050	73.5	46,460	11.8	214,762	75.3	283,272	40.0	33,920	28.2	14,960	28.7	200,310	39.6	249,190	36.8
Trust banks	—	—	—	—	—	—	—	—	4,000	3.3	—	—	9,785	1.9	13,785	2.0
Insurance companies	1,200	4.0	22,100	5.6	17,591	6.1	40,891	5.7	6,780	5.6	100	0.1	38,445	7.6	45,325	6.6
Central Bank of Agriculture & Forestry	1,450	4.8	237,640	60.4	36,230	12.7	275,320	38.8	24,335	20.2	26,970	51.8	83,570	16.5	134,875	19.9
Agricultural cooperatives, credit cooperatives	4,200	14.0	49,420	12.5	9,090	3.1	62,710	8.8	18,116	15.0	4,060	7.8	61,298	12.1	83,474	12.3
Mutual loan assocs.	—	—	3,810	0.9	600	0.2	4,410	0.6	2,420	2.0	20	0.0	6,700	1.3	9,140	1.3
Individuals	—	—	—	—	—	—	—	—	12,254	10.2	230	0.4	46,622	9.2	59,106	8.7
Others	1,100	3.6	8,200	2.0	5,527	1.9	14,827	2.0	2,365	1.9	660	1.2	22,805	4.5	25,830	3.8
Total	30,000	100.0	393,100	100.0	285,000	100.0	708,100	100.0	120,000	100.0	52,000	100.0	505,000	100.0	677,000	100.0

Source: Industrial Bank of Japan.

ment bond issues, conditions for local bond issues were left unchanged. Generally speaking, the rigidity of the conditions for bond flotations divorced their interest rates from those prevailing on the money market, and only the interest rates on the part of local bonds taken over through special arrangements retained some connection with market rates. Under these circumstances the stagnation in the bond market was not surprising.

The council then was formed to find a solution to these problems. Although it could not impose controls or draw up a unified program, it discussed the proper conditions for each of the various bond issues in view of market conditions, and fixed the amounts to be issued and the sequence of the bond flotations. The work was particularly difficult because conditions for government bonds remained unsettled.

The council first took up the flotation of industrial debentures. The interest rate was fixed at 6.5 percent, the issue price at ¥97.50, maturity at seven years, and the commission fee at ¥2.50. This was close enough to prevailing interest rates to make the issues attractive, and in July a ¥30 million issue of debentures of the Western Japan RR (*Nishitetsu*) was floated, the first offering in six months. In August conditions were agreed upon for government and local bonds and financial debentures. On December 15, 1947, the Temporary Money Rates Adjustment Law went into effect. When the Interest Adjustment Committee created under this law sanctioned a two-*rin* raise in the interest rate of bank loans and also higher interests on long-term deposits, a revision of interest rates for bonds became necessary. On January 21, 1948, issue conditions for industrial debentures were changed and, in February, those for local bonds and financial debentures were revised. But the inflation necessitated further changes and, after the interest rate on bank loans had gone up by three *rin* to 2.8 *sen* (July 1) and the official discount rate of the Bank of Japan had been raised by two *rin* on July 5, the interest rate on government bonds was increased to 5 percent and that on reconversion finance bonds from 1.6 *sen* to 1.8 *sen*. On August 16, the Bond Issuance Adjustment Council announced another revision of its conditions. But the inflation made these efforts for promoting bond flotations illusory, and it was only two years later that the Bank of Japan could revive the bond market.

4 REFORM OF THE SECURITIES TRANSACTION SYSTEM

1) Enactment of the Securities Transaction Law—In March 1947 the Diet passed the long-awaited Securities Transaction Law (*Shōken Torihiki-hō*). It was aimed at providing the legal framework for the democratization movement, replacing the strict control system set up during the war. On the other hand, the occupation authorities did not want a return to the old system of stock exchanges, organized as joint-stock companies and operating chiefly for their own profit, and insisted on a reorganization based on the membership principle. Under SCAP's direction, the Securities Division of the Ministry of Finance prepared the draft of the new law, which consequently showed strong American influence. Together with the enactment of the new law, the Securities Exchange Law was abolished and the stock exchanges themselves dissolved in the following month. But the only measure taken under the new law was the establishment of the Securities Transaction Committee on July 23.

2) Amendments to the Securities Transaction Law—The 1947 law left most of the details to be determined by ordinance. When the Ministry of Finance prepared such an ordinance, the official in SCAP in charge of the matter (who had different ideas from his predecessor under whom the law had been framed) revised the draft so much and put in so many new provisions that it was thought more advisable to rewrite the law itself. One of the important changes thus incorporated was the separation of banking from the securities business. The revised law regulated not only the stock exchanges but the whole field of the securities business and and thus replaced four former laws: the Japan Securities Exchange Law, the Securities Business Control Law, the Securities Underwriting Law, and the Securities Installment Sales Law. The registration system was introduced for the securities business and securities exchanges, but this liberal regulation was tightened again in 1950, when official approval again was made necessary for the opening of stock exchanges. The underwriting business was dissociated from banking and, in principle, made the exclusive province of securities firms. Thus, the basic distinction between long- and short-term financing was institutionalized. Public offerings had to be reported to the Securities Commission, created under the law for the supervision of the securities business. The revised law was approved by the Diet on April 5, 1948, and put into effect on May 7. It gave the Securities Commission more authority and entrusted it with the actual administration of the law, but the commission fell a victim to the reactionary wave that swept Japan after the Peace Treaty. The administrative reform of July 1952 abolished the commission and transferred its functions to the Ministry of Finance, which meant its end as an independent regulatory force.

The revised law of 1948 put an end to the wartime controls on the foundation of new enterprises, capital increases, and the flotation of debentures, but, in order to protect investors, all issues had to be reported. These reports, which were supposed to conform to the full disclosure principle, had to give complete information, not only on the actual situation of the firms but also on their future earning potential. Together with the report to the commission, the firms had to prepare a prospectus giving substantially the same information to the public.

Article 65 of the revised Securities Transaction Law prohibited banks, trust banks, and other financial institutions designated by the Securities Commission from offering or underwriting securities. An exception was made for issues involving no risk, such as government and local bonds or government-guaranteed debentures. The shift (instituted by the SCAP official responsible) of the bond emission business to the securities firms brought about far-reaching changes in the pattern of finance. Although securities firms had taken part in underwriting before and during the war, banks and trust companies had dominated the field, and securities companies had usually had to be satisfied with the role of subcontractors.

1 THE ECONOMY UNDER THE OCCUPATION

4 THE END OF THE INFLATION

 ADOPTION OF THE DODGE LINE

Despite numerous measures taken to stop the inflation, the rise in prices and the expansion of the note issue continued.

On December 19, 1948, General MacArthur, in a "Letter to the Japanese Prime Minister Concerning the Economic Stabilization Program," spelled out nine principles laid down in an interim directive of the United States government. The program read:

1. To achieve a true balance in the consolidated budget at the earliest possible date by stringent curtailing of expenditures and maximum expansion in total governmental revenues, including such new revenue as may be necessary and appropriate.
2. To accelerate and strengthen the program of tax collection and insure prompt, widespread and vigorous criminal prosecution of tax evaders.
3. To assure that credit extension is vigorously limited to those projects contributing to the economic recovery of Japan.
4. To establish an effective program to achieve wage stability.
5. To strengthen and, if necessary, expand the coverage of existing price control programs.
6. To improve the operation of foreign trade controls and tighten existing foreign exchange controls, to the extent that such measures can appropriately be delegated to Japanese agencies.
7. To improve the effectiveness of the present allocation and rationing system, particularly to the end of maximizing exports.
8. To increase production of all essential indigenous raw material and manufactured products.
9. To improve efficiency of the food collection program.
10. To develop the above plans to pave the way for the early establishment of a single general exchange rate.

In order to direct the necessary fiscal and monetary reforms required for the implementation of this program, Mr. Joseph M. Dodge, a Detroit banker who had previously been associated with the postwar currency reform in Germany, came to Japan in February 1949 as financial advisor to General MacArthur concerning Japan's economic stabilization. The measures which he initiated became known as the "Dodge line."

For fiscal 1949, the principle of balancing revenues and expenditures was strictly applied to all parts of the budget: general accounts, special accounts, and agencies connected with the government (government corporations, etc.). As a rule, financing by government bonds or loans was not permitted for the special accounts, nor could deficiencies be covered by transfers from the general accounts (which meant that expenditures had to be balanced by increases in railroad fares and postal rates). The emission of debentures of the Reconversion Finance Bank, one of the important causes of inflation, was stopped and all new activities of the bank were suspended.

In order to make the help given by the United States to Japan more effective, a counterpart fund special account was set up into which the proceeds from the sale of relief goods were to be paid. The accumulated funds were to be used chiefly for the redemption of government bonds and debentures of the Reconversion Finance Bank, and the surplus as construction funds for special accounts (telephone, telegraph, and national railways) or as investment funds for key industries (electric power and shipping). This made it impossible to continue the practice of using the proceeds from the sale of relief goods as subsidies for exports and resulted in a complete abolition of export subsidies, while import subsidies were to be paid from the general accounts.

Following the principle of not disturbing the price level, the government had made price adjustment payments compensating manufacturers for increases in costs. Compared with the preceding year, these disbursements showed an enormous increase in the initial budget, but they were to be abolished quickly by a revision of the list of commodities for which they were to be paid, by a lowering of costs through the rationalization of enterprises, and by an increase in the production volume. In order to cover the increase in expenditures made necessary through the increase in price adjustment payments and other factors, new taxes had to be levied, which greatly increased the tax burden.

Two of the great objectives in eliminating the fiscal causes of the inflation and achieving economic stability were the reintegration of Japan's economy as a part of the world economy and the establishment of economic autonomy.

Besides the policy of fiscal stability, measures like the adjustment of the foreign trade system and the adoption of a uniform exchange rate served the same purpose. In March 1949, a Foreign Exchange Control Board was set up, and, in May, the Ministry of Commerce and Industry was consolidated with the Board of Trade into the Ministry of International Trade and Industry (MITI). In the course of the following year, the four public corporations for foreign trade were abolished.

Concerning the exchange rate, a SCAP memorandum of April 23, 1949, urged the Japanese government "to take the steps necessary to put into effect at 0001 hours, 25 April 1949, an official foreign exchange rate of 360 Japanese yen to one U.S. dollar. Rates for other currencies will be based on this rate translated into the U.S. dollar values of such currencies as registered with the International Monetary Fund." This rate indicated the level at which Japan's economy was to be stabilized. It was somewhat lower than the rate of ¥330–350 which had been anticipated on the basis of the Bank of Japan's wholesale price index. The wholesale price index, however, did not take into account black-market prices; and although transactions based on black-market prices had already lost much of their earlier importance, a realistic price level reflecting both official and black-market prices would necessarily indicate a lower rate. Up to then, the yen–dollar exchange rate had been fixed separately for each particular branch of industry so as to make exports possible. These industries now had to achieve a high degree of rationalization in order to become competitive under the new rate.

The suspension of the activities of the Reconversion Finance Bank obliged enterprises to rely for long-term financing on capital increases or the flotation of bonds. The capital market, however, underwent a significant contraction.

The Dodge line implied first a balanced budget, in which revenues would even show a surplus; it further meant the repayment of national bonds and the funds the government had borrowed from the Bank of Japan. But if the government bonds and the debentures of the Reconversion Finance Bank held by the Bank of Japan (at the end of March 1949, 41 percent of the government's indebtedness in the form of bonds, short-term obligations, and loans from the Bank of Japan, which also held 56 percent of the debentures of the Reconversion Finance Bank) were to be redeemed by funds syphoned off from the public through the sale of the commodities received under economic aid programs, the opposite of inflation —a deflation—looked like more than a theoretical possibility. The end of the inflation and the adoption of a single exchange rate demanded a strict rationalization of the economy. This had so far been propped up by price subsidies, by an indiscriminate scattering of public funds, and by liberal advances from financial institutions to cover the operating deficits of enterprises.

For fiscal 1949, the principal feature of the bond redemption program was the amortization of the debentures of the Reconversion Finance Bank. The entire outstanding amount, ¥109,100 million, was taken up in the course of the fiscal year. The largest part of the funds required for this operation, ¥62,476 million, came from the counterpart fund, while ¥30,000 million was appropriated for this purpose in the general accounts. The redemption of government bonds and loans by which expenditures in the general and special accounts had been financed amounted to ¥35,662 million. Repayments to the Bank of Japan, coming to ¥46,900 million, made a compression of the note issue possible. It was further laid down that the funds required by the foreign exchange special account for the purchase of foreign currency and the sums needed by the food control special account for the storage of food were not to be raised through borrowings but to be appropriated in the general accounts.

In fiscal 1948, cash payments of the government to the private sector had shown an excess of ¥49 billion over receipts, but the position was reversed in fiscal 1949 when the receipts surplus came to ¥22 billion. On the financial side, the impact of the fiscal deflationary policy was cushioned by the disinflationary policy of the Bank of Japan, which aimed at preventing the outbreak of a panic and at the maintenance of stability.

When the Dodge line began to be enforced, the Bank of Japan, in conformity with the nine principles, tightened money supply; it made the penalty interest rate system stricter and extended its application to foreign trade bills and commercial bills, which had been exempt before. But later on, in July and in February 1950, the application of the penalty rate system was eased, and foreign trade bills as well as commercial bills were again exempted. After the Reconversion Finance Bank suspended its operations, the Bank of Japan granted preferential treatment to loans secured by corporate debentures in order to provide important industries with funds. It also expanded the activities of its accommodation service (a section established in 1947 to bring two or more banks together so that they could combine their resources for large loans to big enterprises). The financing regulations setting up priorities were greatly relaxed and practically abolished. Advances by the central bank, therefore, increased from ¥68 billion at the end of March 1949 to ¥109 billion on March 31, 1950. The most spectacular increase was in discounted bills, which rose from ¥3 billion to ¥42 billion.

In fiscal 1949, the bank bought up ¥46 billion in government bonds and debentures of the Reconversion Finance Bank through market operations, which began in June 1949. The government transferred funds of the Deposits Bureau to private financial institutions in order to ease the monetary stringency. Despite the government's deflationary policies, therefore, the note issue level of the Bank of Japan remained almost unchanged during the whole of fiscal 1949, amounting to ¥313 billion in the beginning and ¥312 billion at the end of the fiscal year.

Fiscal finances, which had been the chief cause of the inflation, showed a receipt surplus, resulting in the absorption of funds from the public. In the latter part of 1949, funds from the counterpart fund began to be made available for private enterprises in order to replace the financing by the Reconversion Finance Bank, which had been the chief source of equipment funds but which had now suspended its activities. These funds, however, were much smaller than expected. On the other hand fund demand for equipment investment increased, since with the adoption of a single exchange rate and the normalization of economic relations abroad, enterprises faced with international competition were pressed by the need to rationalize their investments. Furthermore, the relaxation of economic controls shifted to private enterprises the burden, so far shouldered by the government, of providing the funds for the flow of commodities. Another factor responsible for the strong fund demand by enterprises was the increase in inventories caused by the deflation.

2. REOPENING OF THE STOCK EXCHANGES

During this period, with the approval of some officials of GHQ, many petitions had been submitted by the Ministry of Finance to SCAP to reorganize and reopen the exchanges. The evidence of widespread unregulated transactions in the illegal market was repeatedly brought forward as justifying the need for the exchanges, but despite the appeals of the Japanese authorities and the support of certain SCAP officials, the supreme commander was adamant and refused even to consider the matter. The situation therefore remained unchanged until the arrival of Mr. Dodge.

On January 31, 1949, just one day prior to the arrival of Mr. Dodge, SCAP had sent a communication to the Japanese government intimating that the stock exchanges would be allowed to reopen. This was interpreted (on the following day in a communication from the chief of SCAP's Economic and Scientific Section to the finance minister, Shinzo Oya) to mean that the exchanges could reopen if and when the necessary legislative and administrative preparations were completed. General MacArthur who, until then, had been very strongly opposed to this move, recognized that the situation had changed, since Mr. Dodge had emphasized the necessity of establishing regular channels for the accumulation of capital and the free marketing of securities.

Certain Japanese securities dealers wanted to retain the old customary term transactions, including the settlement on balances, and, although they were ready to swallow the membership system, they tried to persuade SCAP to agree to the retention of some of the old customs. In the end they realized that a greater accommodation to modern usage was unavoidable and they finally endorsed a draft of the new statutes and business rules based on those of the San Francisco Stock Exchange. The SCAP official responsible realized that such regulations had to be tailored to Japanese practices and conditions, so that on a few points they gained concessions; the system of floor representatives and specialists (*saitorinin*) could be carried over into the new era, and SCAP did not stick to the original demand that the number of members be limited to 50–80 (the Japanese wanted all 135 dealers who had taken part in the group trading to become members of the exchange). The chief differences of opinion were ironed out by September 1948, the recalcitrant having decided to conform.

The Securities Commission published its first rules concerning the stock exchanges on June 30, 1948, and some changes in the commercial code, made necessary by the new Securities Transaction Law, were prepared in August. The Tokyo Stock Exchange building had long been requisitioned by the occupation forces and served as a billet, but the main floor, which had been used as a gymnasium, was, after arguments and negotiation, finally released in January 1948. The story of the trials and tribulations in getting approval to obtain facilities for and to open the exchanges has been told elsewhere. The building itself became the property of the Heiwa Real Estate K.K., founded in July 1947 by the Japan Securities Exchange in order to take over the government's interest in the property and to preserve it for the members who subscribed to the shares of the new real estate company. On February 12, 1949, a general meeting of the exchange members was called, which elected Motoichi Toyama as chairman of the board of directors and Mitsuji Kobayashi as president. Registration was completed by March 18. At the same time, preparations were rushed in various other localities for the reopening of their stock exchanges.

On April 1, 1949, Messrs. Toyama and Kobayashi met with the SCAP official in charge, who advised them of three conditions under which the exchanges would be allowed to reopen. They were: (1) all transactions on the exchange must be recorded in time sequence in the order of their occurrence; (2) members of the exchange must, with certain exceptions, transact all business on listed stocks through the exchange; (3) trading in futures would not be permitted.

The first rule, aiming at the protection of the public, met with no opposition. But there was considerable dissatisfaction among some diehards of the old school with the second rule, which was directed at off-board trading. The third rule stressed what the SCAP officials had made abundantly clear on earlier occasions, but many Japanese securities dealers were unwilling to acquiesce. However, the officials made the reopening of the exchange dependent on the acceptance of the three rules, and, although there was some disappointment among the old guard who preferred the anarchy of the old days, the wish to reopen the exchanges became the overriding consideration. A written promise to observe the three rules, signed by the president, the chairman of the board of directors, all directors, and the auditors, was handed to the chairman of the Securities Commission, and, on May 12, 1949, SCAP gave permission to reopen the exchanges in Tokyo, Osaka, and Nagoya. On May 14, a formal ceremony was held to commemorate the reopening of the Tokyo exchange and, on May 16, the first trading session was held. Trading volume that day was 1,500,660 shares. The exchanges in Osaka and Nagoya opened about one month later and those in Niigata, Kyoto, Kobe, Hiroshima, and Fukuoka resumed business in July. In April 1950, the exchange in Sapporo reopened, bringing the total number of stock exchanges to nine.

3 RECONSTRUCTION OF THE BOND MARKET

1) Promotion of Bond Issues—The suspension of inflationary financing increased the monetary stringency. Available funds were simply not sufficient and the measures taken, up to that time, in order to foster the bond market had been made ineffective by the inflation. In May 1949, the limit of the debenture issue authority of the Industrial Bank was raised from ten to twenty times its paid-in capital.

In response to the demands of industrial and financial circles, the Bank of Japan took several steps to provide funds for the emission market. Starting on June 2, 1949, the bank bought debentures held by financial institutions and accorded preferential treatment to loans secured by corporate debentures. In September, the Bank of Japan also began to buy government bonds held by city banks. Until the end of the year, the amount of reconversion finance bonds taken up by the Bank of Japan through its buying operations came to ¥4,998 million, and the amount of government bonds to ¥6,211 million. In addition, a total of ¥22,038 million in reconversion finance bonds held by city banks was redeemed by the government. These funds, therefore, gave the banks some liquidity and helped the absorption of corporate debentures. Under the preferential treatment, the Bank of Japan accepted certain specified issues of secured corporate debentures (local bonds and convertible bonds were excluded) as loan collateral under the same conditions as government bonds. The interest rate was reduced from 1.6 *sen* to 1.5 *sen*, and coverage was fixed at 95 percent of the market value (90 percent for discount debentures of the Industrial Bank). These measures enabled the banks to use their debenture portfolios for obtaining liquid funds from the central bank.

A revision of the Antimonopoly Law in June 1949 abolished the restriction that had limited the possession of corporate debentures by another firm to 25 percent of its capital. This removed a big obstacle to the absorption of debentures.

In June 1949, an amendment to the Bank of Japan Law established a policy board for the formulation of monetary policies. This policy board, which ranks as the highest organ of the bank, is entrusted with the following functions: to formulate the basic policies for the management of the business of the bank; to determine and change the official discount rate; to determine the types of paper eligible for discount and the conditions attached; to determine and change the types, conditions, and valuation of loan collateral; to fix matters pertaining to market operations; to determine and change the interest rates of financial institutions; to regulate the required ratios of payment reserves; and to regulate advances to securities dealers by financial institutions.

The Bond Issuance Adjustment Council split into two groups, one to discuss the general conditions for the flotation of bonds and underwriters' fees, the other to fix the conditions of specific issues, usually only of those acceptable as collateral by the Bank of Japan. The first group comprised representatives of the Ministry of Finance, the Bank of Japan, the Securities Commission, the Industrial Bank, the Kangyo Bank, city, local, and trust banks, the Reconversion Finance Bank, the Central Bank for Agriculture & Forestry, and securities dealers; the second group was made up of the banks involved in the particular issue and the four big securities companies, Yamaichi, Nikko, Nomura, and Daiwa. In practice, the chief task of this latter group was to consult with the Bank of Japan on the conditions under which the issue would qualify as loan collateral. Since the banks policy board controlled the whole interest system, the issue market was completely dependent on the Bank of Japan.

2) Favorable Developments in the Bond Issue Market—While new bond issues offered on the market remained rather low in the first half of 1949, they picked up in the latter half of the year and further in the beginning of 1950. The totals were as follows:

	1st half 1949		2nd half 1949		1st half 1950	
	Number of issues	Amount ¥ mill.	Number of issues	Amount ¥ mill.	Number of issues	Amount ¥ mill.
Government bonds	3	7,000	3	8,450	2	3,550
incl. public offerings		16		—		—
Local bonds	64	1,672	15	659	3	62
incl. public offerings		626		381		—
Financial debentures	38	45,022	20	11,935	29	15,917
incl. public offerings		603		1,410		1,995
Industrial debentures	40	1,910	109	14,645	130	21,465
incl. public offerings		1,905		14,645		21,415
Total	145	55,604	147	35,689	164	40,994
incl. refunding issues	20	18,140	15	651	30	4,902
incl. public offering		3,150		16,436		23,410

Source: Industrial Bank of Japan.

Convertible corporate debentures had been made possible by a revision of the Commercial Code (Articles 364–369) in 1938, but no such debentures had actually been floated before the war. The first convertible bonds issued were those of Daiwa Securities Co. in August 1948 (although several issues had been planned earlier), but these bonds were not offered to the public. The first public issues were those of Tosa Electric RR on April 5, 1949, and Takashimaya (department store chain) on April 15.

In March 1950, a law abrogating the organic laws of the special banks was passed, so that the Industrial Bank, the Kangyo Bank, and the Hokkaido Takushoku Bank lost their character of special banks and were treated as ordinary banks. At the same time, the Law Concerning the Issuance of Debentures by Banks was passed. This law provided that banks could issue debentures up to an amount equal to the difference of twenty times their own capital minus the aggregate of total deposits and the total of outstanding debentures. On the face of it, the law did not put any restriction on the type of banks which could issue debentures, and its intention was to make the emission of debentures possible for the former special banks and similar institutions: the Industrial, Kangyo, and Hokkaido Takushoku banks, the Central Cooperative Bank for Agriculture and Forestry, and the Central Bank for Commercial and Industrial Cooperatives. At that time, however, the capital of these institutions was rather small, so that the margin left for debenture issues was hardly worthwhile, and, in view of the depressed situation of the securities market, an increase in their capital seemed difficult. The government, therefore, diverted a total of ¥5,200 million from the counterpart fund for investment in preferred stocks of the above-mentioned five institutions. (These preferred stocks were to be redeemed through an accumulated special reserve set aside from the profits.)

On May 8, 1950, the Bank of Japan suspended its unconditional buying operations as part of its tight-money program, so that the bond market was again in difficulties.

Bond Absorption

	Industrial Debentures						Financial Debentures					
	1st half 1949		2nd half 1949		1st half 1950		1st half 1949		2nd half 1949		1st half 1950	
	Amount ¥ mill.	%	Amount ¥ mill.	%	Amount ¥ mill.	%	Amount ¥ mill.	%	Amount ¥ mill.	%	Amount ¥ mill.	%
City banks, special banks	471	24.8	6,602	45.1	9,459	44.1	967	27.5	4,041	35.4	5,052	34.6
Local banks	999	52.5	7,088	48.4	9,168	42.7	1,463	41.5	5,482	47.9	6,333	32.3
Trust banks	16	0.9	269	1.8	241	1.1	9	0.3	60	0.5	72	0.5
Insurance companies	40	2.1	53	0.4	799	3.7	81	2.2	28	0.3	66	0.5
Central Cooperative Bank of Agric. & For., agricultural cooperatives	73	3.9	427	2.9	1,603	7.5	158	4.5	177	1.5	524	3.6
Credit associations	46	2.4	25	0.2	45	0.2	114	3.2	124	1.1	399	2.7
Mutual loan associations	12	0.6	3	0.0	28	0.1	53	1.5	110	1.0	356	2.4
Individuals	192	10.1	107	0.7	81	0.4	590	16.7	1,206	10.5	1,790	12.2
Others	51	2.7	66	0.5	43	0.2	92	2.6	203	1.8	26	0.2
Total	1,905	100.0	14,645	100.0	21,465	100.0	3,532	100.0	11,435	100.0	14,617	100.0

Source: Industrial Bank of Japan

The city banks played a greater role in the absorption of debentures than in the preceding years, while the Central Cooperative Bank of Agriculture and Forestry was less active in the bond market. The lack of suitable material on the stock market led to increased investment in bonds on the part of the insurance companies.

Proceeds of debentures accepted by the Bank of Japan had to be used for equipment investment, and this portion of corporate debentures showed a sharp increase after June 1949. The share of debentures floated for the repayment of loans dropped from 65 percent in the first half of 1949 to something around 50 percent in the latter half.

4. CHANGES IN STOCK TRADING

1) **Stagnation in the Stock Market**—In the spring of 1949, the unofficial group trading experienced its fourth boom, and despite some oscillations and adverse factors, notably the adoption of the Dodge line and the new rules for the stock exchanges, the rise in stock prices continued on the reopened exchanges and reached a high on September 1. But the avalanche of stocks, hitting the market at a time of monetary stringency, because of the numerous capital increases by firms that had completed their reorganization, upset the supply–demand balance and sent stock prices skidding. At the same time, the stagnation in exports, the increase in inventories, and the difficulties experienced by many enterprises, involving a number of bankruptcies, made the future look rather uncertain.

In November, SCLC put off the release of shares, while special financial arrangements for the payment of shares and more buying by insurance companies were to support the market. In the following month, the Securities Commission prohibited fictitious transactions, and buying by the city banks and joint support purchases by the big securities companies tried to reinforce the props of the market. Finance Minister Ikeda, Governor Ichimada, and Iwajiro Noda, chairman of SCLC, visited SCAP and requested him, first, to permit the Bank of Japan to make loans against securities (this system, abnormal for a central bank, had been in use since the 1890 panic, although the practice was not legally authorized) and, second, to allow it to control the securities investments of the city banks. The first request was refused as being premature, while more securities investment by city banks was allowed. A securities finance company, called the Japan Securities Finance Co., was set up in Tokyo in December and in Osaka in January 1950, but various other measures for strengthening the stock market such as the foundation of a stock investment company did not materialize. Prices slipped further, and the Dow-Jones index for the Tokyo Stock Exchange (an adaptation of the U.S. Dow-Jones average), which stood at 176.21 when the exchange reopened on May 16, 1949, had slumped to 86.17 by the end of June 1950.

2) **Over-the-Counter Trading**—Before the war, when trading on the stock exchange was almost exclusively in futures, over-the-counter trading was more or less equivalent to spot transactions. Since the rules under which the exchanges were reopened prohibited futures, over-the-counter transactions took on a different meaning. It referred to trading of issues not listed on the exchanges. Some of these stocks were those of small firms which eventually expanded and were listed, and most of the issues traded over the counter were finally listed when, on October 1, 1961, a second section was added to each of the exchanges in Tokyo, Osaka, and Nagoya.

The over-the-counter trading was regulated by the Securities Dealers Association, which recognized the issues to be traded and the method of performance. Besides the shares of small firms, stock vouchers of firms about to be organized, stocks of subsidiary companies, or rights (certificates for stocks to be issued for capital increases) formed the object of over-the-counter trading. The many foundations connected with the enforcement of the Deconcentration Law stimulated these transactions. Since there was no necessity of actual delivery prior to the issuance of the shares, over-the-counter trading of rights permitted some kind of trading on balance so dear to the hearts of the old Japanese operators—which was the chief reason for its immense popularity. Excessive trading in completely fictitious transactions, where delivery was never contemplated, took place in certain "rights" or "when issued" shares. But, when the balloon collapsed and settlements of balances had to be contemplated, several securities dealers were in grave trouble and, particularly in Osaka, faced bankruptcy.

Most of the speculative trading at the time involved the rights of the three firms into which the old Mitsubishi Chemical had been split: Asahi Glass, Shinko Rayon, and Nippon Chemical (the last two firms have since readopted the name Mitsubishi). Prices had been run up by irrational speculation, but on April 11, 1950, Asahi Glass lost over ¥60; on the following day, over ¥80; and, on the thirteenth, the SCAP officials intervened and imposed a limit on the price movements of the issue. This raised apprehensions among Osaka traders, where most of the abuses had been committed, and the Tokyo and Osaka exchanges agreed to suspend trading in the three issues from the fourteenth to the seventeenth. On the eighteenth, trading resumed at a compromise price fixed by the Securities Commission after consultations between the authorities, including SCAP. The directors of the Tokyo Securities Dealers Association assumed responsibility for the incident and resigned. Actually, the over-the-counter transactions had again assumed the character of organized group trading (which was a violation of a basic principle of the exchange), although there was a certain number of legitimate transactions.

Transactions on the Tokyo Stock Exchange and Over the Counter

	Exchange 1,000 shares	Over-the-counter 1,000 shares
1949 June	36,982	33,778
July	22,833	26,268
August	48,797	49,866
September	44,870	56,175
October	27,091	39,949
November	23,679	48,826
December	28,161	46,853
1950 January	22,021	33,055
February	27,644	72,365
March	23,988	54,494
April	22,795	63,673
May	29,861	29,842

Source: Tokyo Securities Exchange; Securities Dealers Association.

5 COMMOTION ON THE EMISSION MARKET

Stock issues showed a rapid increase in 1949, partly because bank loans were severely restricted and partly because the reorganization of enterprises entered its final stage. The number of issues in 1949 reached 5,911 involving ¥81,744 million, exceeding the preceding year by ¥53 billion. Over ¥71 billion was for capital increases, which were particularly great in the field of manufacturing, centering on chemicals, machinery, and spinning. Other sectors showing a large expansion were commerce, mining, transportation, and communications. Of the funds so raised, 46 percent was for the repayment of loans, and 29 percent for investment. The absorption of the new shares was helped by the relaxation of the Anti-monopoly Law. The portion of stocks offered to the public was relatively small, 6.9 percent, as against 8.3 percent in the preceding year.

The increased emission of new shares coincided with a stepped-up release of shares by SCLC which, in 1949, disposed of 102,170,000 shares valued at ¥7,230 million. Of these, 39,927,000 shares, with a value of ¥2,043 million, were rights. The number of shares offered to the public through securities dealers almost trebled in that year.

In order to alleviate the pressure on the capital market, SCLC decreased its releases of stocks, and the government relaxed the requirements for the reorganization of firms. Originally, the reorganized companies had to increase their capital immediately after approval of their reorganization plans. On January 27, 1950, an amendment went into effect under which capital increases for improving the capital structure of the reorganized enterprises were no longer required as a condition of approval and could be put off for six months or a year.

In December 1949, a special organization for the adjustment of capital increases was created, which included representatives of the Bank of Japan, the city banks, the securities companies, SCLC, and the Fair Trade Commission. This committee regulated the capital increases to be carried out each month. As a rule, local firms and family enterprises were not made subject to the placing program of the commission. This reduced the amount of capital increases in the first half of 1950 to ¥28,644 million, of which ¥12,504 million (103 issues) was programmed by the committee. Public offerings were practically discontinued, and the number of shares released by SCLC also dropped considerably. Enterprises had to rely on bank loans or debentures for raising capital, so that their capital structures deteriorated again.

Stock Offerings by Securities Companies

	Number of issues	Number of shares 1,000	Amount ¥ mill.
1946	26	3,833	180
1947	123	12,076	660
1948	248	52,496	4,185
1949	376	147,497	14,265

2 ECONOMIC REHABILITATION

1 THE KOREAN WAR AND THE POSITIVE ECONOMIC POLICY

1 ECONOMIC RECONSTRUCTION

The outbreak of the Korean War on June 25, 1950, had a strong repercussion on the world economy but, due to her geographical proximity to the war theater, Japan's economy was particularly influenced. Special procurement orders and exports gave the economy, which had been suffering from the accumulation of inventories and unemployment, a sudden but welcome stimulus. Special procurement orders comprised military material, as well as services for the American armed forces fighting in Korea. In the beginning, these orders were placed through the headquarters of the U.S. Eighth Army, but, after the end of 1951, they were channeled through the Japan Procurement Agency. As a rule, the goods and services were paid for in dollars. Contracts from July to December 1950 amounted to $183,548,000; they came to $154,547,000 during the first half and reached $210,854,000 during the latter half of 1951. The strength of this unexpected demand proved to be powerful enough to reanimate Japan's economy, which, due to the disinflationary policy, had been in a coma.

At almost the same time, exports started on a sharp upward trend. If the first half of 1950 is assumed equal to 100, the value of exports rose to 154 in the second half of the year and climbed to 205 in the first half of 1951; but with the beginning of the armistice negotiations, in July of that year, they leveled off. Since, however, prices of export goods went up by 45 percent during this period, the increase in value does not necessarily indicate a corresponding increase in volume. In the composition of exports, textiles, just as before the Korean War, made up over 40 percent, but the rate of increase of metals, foodstuffs, chemicals, and machinery was remarkable. With one sweep, therefore, inventories estimated at ¥100 billion, accumulated through the deflation, were cleared out. Imports, on the other hand, hardly increased, due to rising prices, higher maritime freight and insurance charges, and a reduction in the U.S. aid given to Japan. The trade balance, which had been deep in the red all through the postwar years, turned favorable in the latter half of 1950. But this had the less desirable effect of provoking an export inflation. With mounting dollar receipts, the foreign exchange special account paid out larger and larger yen funds. The note issue rose, and the rise in the world market prices of export goods pushed domestic prices upward. Moreover, the liquidation of price subsidies, which had been going on since the preceding year, contributed to the price rise. The increase was so steep that domestic prices soared high above international price levels. Internationally speaking, Japan's export prices were driven up by America's stockpiling of strategic materials, but the hike in freight and insurance charges of goods imported into Japan also contributed to the increase. If June 1950 is taken as basis (100), wholesale commodity prices in June 1951 were 150 in Japan (the level around which the postwar wholesale price had become stabilized), 116 in the United States, and 125 in Great Britain. In order to stop the price rise and to prevent a shrinkage of production because of a shortage of raw materials, a number of measures were taken in the autumn of 1951 to promote imports. Consequently, imports showed a rapid expansion in 1951.

In this connection, the foreign exchange loan system adopted by the Bank of Japan in September 1950 should be mentioned. Due to the swollen exports, payments of the foreign exchange special account to the public had experienced such an enormous increase that it ran out of funds and the ceiling on its borrowings had to be raised. In order to eliminate the necessity of high loan limits, the new system aimed at promoting imports by having the Bank of Japan buy foreign exchange from the foreign exchange special account and lend these sums through the foreign exchange banks to civilian importers at the low interest rate (4 percent) prevailing on the international money markets. Another purpose of this system was to prevent advances for imports from aggravating the overloan tendency of the banks, since the economic recovery had already resulted in an expansion of general loans.

This system certainly contributed to the growth of imports for, with the opening of a letter of credit (at that time, the margin money was 50 percent, and import bills were usually sight drafts), the Bank of Japan also granted a loan. But it cannot be denied that it had some less desirable results. The contraction of the currency to be effected by imports was postponed for the usance period during which the credit given by the Bank of Japan ran, and, when the international payments balance turned unfavorable again, the expansionist trend of the economy could not be stopped. This intensified the setback suffered by the economy after the Korean War boom.

Industrial production began to pick up in the autumn of 1950 and, at year-end, lay slightly above the prewar 1934–36 average. The average for the whole year of 1950, however, came to only 93.8 percent of the prewar figure, due to the low level in the first half of the year. Production rose to 127.7 in 1951, increasing by 36 percent over the preceding year. Among the principal industries, iron and steel doubled its 1949 output and exceeded its prewar level (ingot steel: 1937, 5,801,000 tons; 1949, 2,111,000 tons; 1951, 6,502,000 tons). When the war broke out, SCAP abolished the ceiling (4 million spindles) set for cotton spinning equipment, and the industry expanded rapidly. Although production in 1951 was only a little over half of the prewar level, Japan took first place in the export of cotton fabrics. But electric power, coal, and transportation could not catch up with the fast pace of the economic growth and, temporarily at least, these sectors constituted as many bottlenecks holding up the entire economy. Together with the shortages in raw materials and the price rise, these bottlenecks showed clearly that Japan's economic recovery was far from complete.

When, in the spring of 1951, the United States suspended its purchases of strategic materials, the boom levelled off; the increased imports turned into accumulated inventories, and in summer a growing number of cancellations of export contracts, particularly of textiles, extended the glut to export commodities. Some trading firms became insolvent, and banks began to advance relief funds. Thanks, however, to the increase in equipment investment prompted by the war prosperity and the increase in personal consumption expenditure, the economy as a whole could maintain the high level. In 1951, international payments showed an unfavorable balance of $291 million in the visible trade accounts, but the supply of goods and services to the United Nations forces and the individual spending of their personnel brought in $623 million in foreign exchange, while U.S. aid to Japan added another $155 million. The overall balance on current transactions, including freight and insurance charges, gave Japan a receipt surplus of $337 million. Government holdings of gold and foreign exchange, which had been a bare $225 million at the end of 1949, reached $924 million at the end of 1951.

When the Korean War began, the Bank of Japan switched to a stronger tight-money policy in order to prevent a reappearance of the inflation, which the Dodge line had brought under control. Its measures comprised limitation of its accommodation service, restrictions on bills eligible for rediscounting, reduction of its buying operations, and a stricter enforcement of its penalty rates.

The fast acceleration of industrial activities caused a tremendous increase in the fund demand of enterprises, and fund demand became pressing again in 1951 with the large increases in imported merchandise and in inventories of goods produced for export. The overloan situation of private banks, which had been pretty bad before the outbreak of the Korean War, became even worse, starting with August 1951, and the eleven city banks in particular showed an excess of loans over deposits in almost all their monthly balances for about a year.

These conditions stirred up a discussion on the insufficiency of private capital accumulation, and, together with tax measures intended to increase the internal reserves of enterprises, interest rates on deposits were raised several times and a special tax reduction was granted for interest income from deposits. In July 1951, a voluntary credit restraint program was adopted by the Federation of Bankers Associations in order to curb bank loans.

About that time, the so-called revival of monetary policies occurred in America and Europe, where the low-interest policy enforced during the war was abandoned, and discount policies resumed their place as a powerful weapon of monetary policies. Japan, however, pursued a completely different discount policy. Because interest rates lay above the international level, efforts were made to lower them as much as possible. Private banks, which had repeatedly lowered their high loan rates since August 1949, did the same in November 1950, during the course of the Korean war. The Bank of Japan did not increase its official discount rate until October 1951 and resorted exclusively to penalty rates in order to curb reliance on central bank credit. Even after the raise in the discount rate, a wide differential remained between the discount rate of private financial institutions for eligible commercial paper, which stood at 2.2 *sen* (8.03 percent), and the rediscount rate of the Bank of Japan of 1.6 *sen* (5.84 percent).

The changes in the international situation resulting from the Korean War favored the policy of reestablishing Japan's full sovereignty by the conclusion of a peace treaty. On September 8, 1951, the majority of the countries with which Japan had been at war signed the Peace Treaty of San Francisco, which became effective on April 28, 1952. Thus, after six years and eight months, the occupation came to an end.

Compared with the prewar level (1934–36 = 100), the position of the economy was characterized by the following indices: total population, 137.2; industrial activity, 119.4; real national income, 108.3; agricultural production, 100.1; export volume, 36; import volume, 49; real personal consumption expenditure, 105.5; real total investment, 178.1. Although the overall international payments balance was favorable, the recovery of foreign trade was lagging far behind. A large part of the foreign exchange receipts consisted of payments for special procurements and foreign aid, and Japan was far from standing on her own feet.

No exact figures are available for U.S. aid to Japan prior to the establishment of the counterpart fund in April 1949. Japanese estimates (MITI) made public in June 1961, when negotiations between Japan and the United States concerning the repayment of these sums were wound up, put the value of goods received under GARIOA, EROA, and the civilian supply program at $1,717 million, while sales from army stocks came to $78 million, for a total of $1,795 million. The principal items were: foodstuffs, $1,050 million; and raw materials and fuel, $511 million. If goods for which Japan denied liability are subtracted, total aid amounted to $1,746 million. Japan agreed to repay $490 million over a period of fifteen years. This aid and the special procurement orders played a very important role in Japan's economic recovery.

The government regarded the stagnation following the suspension of U.S. purchases of strategic materials as a temporary phenomenon, and Finance Minister Hayato Ikeda urged Japanese industry to embark on a vast modernization program. The government's foreign exchange holdings were to be used to buy foreign machinery and large domestic funds were to be raised for equipment investment. This positive policy was carried over into 1953, when the Korean truce talks were resumed and the international climate did not look too favorable for foreign trade. After the autumn of 1952, the balance of payments had shown a deficit caused by the stagnation of exports, the decrease in procurement orders placed by the U.S. forces, and an increase in imports. The holdings of gold and foreign exchange, which had temporarily exceeded $1.1 billion, dropped to $725 million in May 1954.

The positive policy of the government brought a fairly large expansion in public expenditure. The general accounts of the budget rose from ¥932.5 billion in fiscal 1952 to ¥1,027.2 billion in the following year, in which expenditures (on both general and special accounts) exceeded receipts by ¥66.2 billion. This deficit was financed by foreign exchange fund bills and advances by the Trust Fund Bureau. Total government expenditures (national and local governments) came to 26.9 percent of distributed national income in 1952, 28.2 percent in 1953, and 29.0 percent in 1954. In order to finance the economic expansion, the government attempted to implement a low-interest policy by reducing the interest rates of governmental financial institutions, the Japan Development Bank, and the Export-Import Bank (import financing had been added to the functions of the original Export Bank in April 1952, when it was given its present name), depositing government funds with city banks, and lowering the interest rates of banks and other agencies. Long-term industrial financing was put on a new basis by the enactment of the Long-Term Credit Bank Law in June 1952. This law authorized long-term credit banks to raise funds by issuing debentures up to twenty times (in the case of newly founded banks, thirty times) their capital and reserves. The Industrial Bank of Japan was reorganized on the basis of this law, and a new institution, the Long-Term Credit Bank, founded, chiefly through the efforts of the Kangyo, Hokkaido Takushoku, and local banks. (Another bank organized under this law, the Japan Hypothec Bank, was founded in 1957.)

In 1952, GNP expanded by 12.1 percent over the preceding year and again by 17.4 percent in 1953. The index of mining and industrial production (1934–36=100) rose from 127.8 in 1951 to 136.4 in 1952. The gain in the first half of 1953 was particularly fast; the index climbed from 131.2 in January to 171.1 in August.

2 RISE IN THE STOCK MARKET

1) The Korean War Boom—When the Korean War broke out, the outlook was very uncertain and the Dow-Jones average fell to ¥85.25. But soon a large-scale military effort was under way, and the average topped the ¥100 level on July 15. The regular market, however, became stagnant, and interest concentrated on over-the-counter trading of rights. The Exchange Commission showed considerable concern over the speculative excesses, and the system of transactions, with settlement on the day of issue, was put into practice on November 13, 1950. The Dow average advanced 60 percent in 1951. An important factor was the distribution of gratis shares which became frequent in the middle of the year. At the same time, the resumption of investment trusts contributed to the absorption of the floating shares and to the improvement in prices.

The increased activity in the economy boosted corporate earnings, as shown in the following table:

	Number of firms	Sales ¥ mill.	Net profits ¥ mill.
1950 1st half	545	780,757	18,444
2nd half	556	1,142,496	57,549
1951 1st half	560	1,562,212	70,665
2nd half	560	1,671,001	52,216
1952 1st half	560	1,734,934	44,832
2nd half	560	1,781,143	42,639
1953 1st half	560	1,964,032	50,468

Source: Mitsubishi Economic Research Institute.

In 1952, the stock market showed all the signs of a boom, reflecting a conspicuous increase in consumption spending brought about by the first real improvement in living conditions since the war. Savings started to flow into the stock market, which experienced a sharp increase in both prices and trading. Stock prices went up three to four times, and the daily trading average jumped from 1,229,000 shares valued at ¥94.69 million in June 1950 to 10.84 million shares with a value of ¥2,362 million in February 1953, when the boom reached its peak. During the same period, the number of shares listed on the Tokyo Stock Exchange increased from 2 billion to 4.7 billion, and their market value rose from ¥121.7 billion to ¥810.4 billion. After a high on February 4, 1953, the market collapsed on the sixth, and the Tokyo exchange remained closed on the ninth in order to restore some kind of order. Bad news continued to depress the market. A rally, which started in the summer, was sparked by the inflationary policies of the government and the expectation of reconstruction demand in Korea. But, in September 1953, the Bank of Japan switched to a tight-money policy, and fiscal financing, too, changed to a policy of contraction. The number of firms reducing their dividends increased in the course of the year, but stock prices retained much of their speculative attraction.

2) Beginning of Credit Transactions—The postwar reform had tried to exclude speculative trading, but many of the old dealers hankered after the old ways and now proposed the creation of some kind of fictitious demand as a means of reviving the market. From these suggestions came the proposal to introduce a system somewhat similar to that of margin trading on American exchanges. On December 5, 1949, the Osaka Stock Exchange adopted a system of borrowing shares, by which the seller established his credit. But the Tokyo Stock Exchange feared that this system might even worsen the stagnation of the stock market and did not adopt the system, and the Osaka exchange soon discontinued it. On the other hand, preparations were made to make credit trading possible. The Tokyo Securities Co. was reorganized into the Japan Securities Financing Co. Until then, the Tokyo Securities Co. had been engaged in the delivery of shares traded over the counter and in the registration of stock transfers. In May 1950, the company started to handle loans for five issues, for buying as well as for selling. But securities dealers were not allowed to extend credit to their customers. Actually, the system was not too successful, and, in November 1950, Ryutaro Nemoto, chairman of the Liberal Party's policy board, informed Prime Minister Yoshida of the wish of the dealers to reintroduce term trading. In December, the director of the Economic Stabilization Board, Hideo Sudo, discussed the changes in the Securities Transaction Law that would be required to permit term transactions. Six of the leading members of the securities business visited the United States in order to study the problems involved in margin trading. After their return, the method of making credit available for regular way transactions was fixed, and, on June 1, 1951, credit transactions became possible. The development became very fast in 1952, when the credits extended jumped from ¥5,419 million to ¥35,354 million. The system was first applied to selected issues and contributed greatly to the brisk trading in these issues.

3) Revival of Investment Trusts—Investment trusts had been used extensively during the war, and foreign assets as well as shares of munitions firms constituted a large portion of their assets. In 1946, their market prices had dropped to about one-half of the nominal principal, and the issuing firms, whose number had been reduced from seven to four (Yamaichi, Nikko, Nomura, and Daiwa), had to cover a loss of about ¥52 million, equivalent to 80 percent of their capital. But the firms postponed repayment of the trust funds for two years (a clause in the contract made this possible), and by then the market price of the certificates had gone up to their full face value.

Efforts to revive the investment trust business started even before the redemption of the wartime issues was completed. In June 1948, the Ministry of Finance investigated the possibility of organizing investment companies modeled after American patterns, one form similar to mutual funds, the other based on trust agreements with investment companies. The first type was also to engage in the underwriting business, but this feature aroused the opposition of the existing securities companies to the scheme. Also, the occupation authorities thought the plan premature, and it was shelved.

The collapse of stock prices in 1949 and the difficulty in absorbing the new issues of reorganized companies made the mobilization of investment capital an urgent task. The four securities companies, which had formerly handled investment trusts, formulated a new plan (leaving out the mutual fund type), but again it met with objections on the part of SCAP. In January 1951, Finance Minister Hayato Ikeda agreed to have a bill introduced in the Diet. The draft of the Securities Commission was a simple restatement of the prewar rules. SCAP wanted to have two provisions added: the possibility of cancelling the contract before expiration and the guarantee of the principal. The securities companies were ready to agree to the first condition but balked at the second. A bill drafted along these lines was introduced in the Diet from the floor (in order to avoid SCAP supervision), and the Securities Investment Trust Law was enacted on May 26, 1951. The trust period was fixed at two years (later changed to three and then to five years) and the trust units fixed at ¥5,000 (later ¥1,000 units were added); the investor's interest was evidenced in the form of a bearer certificate, and partial cancellation of the contract and repurchase by the issuing company were provided for.

The four securities companies began to offer investment trusts in July 1951, and Osaka Shoji, Osakaya, and Oi also took up this business. Originally, registration with the Securities Commission, a capital of over ¥10 million, and organization as a joint-stock company were the chief requirements, but, in August 1953, registration was superseded by a licensing system. Although the beginning was slow, the investment trusts soon absorbed a large portion of the shares floating on the market. In 1952, the holdings of the investment trusts were already higher than those of the insurance companies, and, by the end of December 1953, they had grown to ¥71.1 billion, whereas all other financial institutions held a total of ¥87.9 billion in their portfolios.

Open-end trusts were started by Daiwa in June 1952. There was some doubt whether this form of investment trust could be set up without amending the law, but finally the view prevailed that no amendment was needed. This type permitted a more elastic management and gave the investor an instrument of much greater marketability. The investment companies added other refinements, chiefly to attract different classes of investors, distinguishing between income funds (emphasis on high yields) and capital gain funds (emphasis on appreciation), but basically all these forms are the same.

4) Foreign Stock Investment—Foreign funds played a very important role in Japan's postwar rehabilitation. The earliest help came through government programs, such as GARIOA and EROA; then followed loans extended by the World Bank (International Bank for Reconstruction and Development), which Japan joined in 1952. Private investment by foreigners was regulated by the Law Concerning Foreign Capital enacted in 1950. In its original form, the law imposed so many bureaucratic restrictions on foreign investment that its practical effect was to keep foreign capital out of Japan. (The fear of domination by foreign capital remains an obsession, not so much of Japanese businessmen as of the bureaucracy.) An amendment, passed in April 1951, removed some of the obstacles.

In the immediate postwar period, the Japanese government had hoped for foreign aid as a means of overcoming its economic difficulties and stabilizing the country's economic situation. America, on the contrary, insisted on economic stability as a necessary prerequisite to foreign investment. Only the reforms achieved through the Dodge line, the end of the inflation, and the adoption of a uniform exchange rate qualified Japan for foreign investment. The first case of capital induction occurred in March 1949, when, based on an ordinance concerning the acquisition of property by foreigners, Standard Vacuum Oil Co. acquired a 50 percent interest in Toa Nenryo. In August of the same year, another ordinance restored the property rights of Allied nationals in shares of stock confiscated during the war. A seven-man foreign investment board had already been set up in January 1949; in January 1950, a mixed Japan-U.S. council was organized and, in May, a law providing for the establishment of a foreign investment council was passed together with the Foreign

Investment Law. The amendment of the latter law in April 1951 enabled foreigners to acquire stock of Japanese firms on the stock market, and the first acquisition through this medium was sanctioned in May (5,000 shares of Shinko Rayon). The first foreign buying order placed with a securities firm came in June (10,000 shares of Teikoku Rayon). The Foreign Investment Law was again amended in July 1952, facilitating the repatriation of the capital (after a two-year waiting period).

INCREASE IN STOCK ISSUES

Capital increases became more frequent soon after the outbreak of the Korean War, and large firms accounted for the greater part of the increases. In 1949, 46 percent of the funds thus raised was used for repaying loans, but, in 1950 and 1951, this percentage dropped to 25 percent, and a large part was used for equipment investment. Total stock issues raised ¥81,744 million in 1949, ¥50,236 million in 1950, and ¥80,253 million in 1951. The manufacturing industry accounted for the largest share, more than 60 percent of the total. The industry was slow in rebuilding its plant, but the heavy increase in procurement orders and exports triggered by the Korean War necessitated a fast expansion.

On June 2, 1951, a law put an end to SCLC and its activities. During the four years of its existence, the commission had disposed of 230 million shares, valued at ¥41.1 billion, and ¥270 million worth of bonds. Restrictive legislation passed for the enforcement of occupation policies was gradually dismantled, and measures designed to protect domestic industry took their place. A revision of the Commercial Code, chiefly concerning the management of joint-stock companies, was passed in 1950 and went into effect in July 1951. It made it possible to issue new shares within the limits of the capital authorized by the stockholders' meeting without special approval for each issue, recognized the issue of bearer shares, and abolished limitations on the transfer of shares imposed by the statutes of a corporation (the only restrictions admissible by law are on the shares of newspaper companies). A few other amendments likewise improved the marketability and transferability of shares.

The Assets Revaluation Law passed in April 1950 was a condensation of various proposals, discussed since the end of 1947, and aimed at realigning the nominal value of corporate assets (in inflated yen) with their true worth. The situation was complicated by the problems of taxation and depreciation and the concern over the induction of foreign capital. An American tax mission, headed by Dr. Carl Shoup, finally put an end to the arguments, and its recommendations formed the basis of the 1950 law, which fixed October 1950 as the deadline for filing a revaluation application, limited the revaluation to 8.85 times the book value,

Acquisition of Stock by Foreigners Validated under the Foreign Investment Law

Period	Number of cases	Number of shares 1,000 shares	Amount of investment ¥ mill.
June 1950—Mar. 1951	125	21,029	1,144
Apr.—Dec. 1951	348 (155)	45,671 (2,536)	4,296 (279)
Jan.—Dec. 1952	1,853 (870)	42,686 (7,282)	3,537 (877)
Jan.—Dec. 1953	2,638 (940)	36,128 (3,505)	2,645 (476)

Note: Figures in parentheses refer to acquisitions through the stock market.
Source: Ministry of Finance.

and levied a 6 percent tax, payable in three years, on the excess of the reappraised over the original book value. This excess, set aside as a special reserve fund, could not be incorporated into the capital for a period of three years. The law contained a large number of obscurities and, by the end of October, only 77 percent of all corporations had filed revaluation applications, the reappraisal value coming to only 5.95 times the book value. The poor earnings position of many enterprises, following the implementation of the Dodge line, formed the chief obstacle. When the Korean War boom improved corporate earnings, an amendment made a second revaluation possible and another law permitted the incorporation of the revaluation reserve into the capital as early as July 1951. This amalgamation was to be approved by the stockholders' meeting, and, although this was not prescribed, it was generally done in the form of new shares, allocated either gratis or at a reduced price to the shareholders. These measures contributed greatly to the improvement in the financial structure of enterprises and facilitated the supply of capital to corporations.

At the same time, measures were taken to protect the investor. In March 1950, the Securities Transaction Law was partially amended and the Securities Commission was given power to fix uniform standards for listing liabilities and for improving the audit system. The commission published rules concerning the listing of corporate liabilities but failed to make the auditing of corporate reports by independent certified public accountants obligatory. This deficiency has not yet been remedied.

All these factors combined to activate the stock market. As mentioned earlier, the funds raised through the emission of new shares were increasingly channeled into equipment investment. A survey by the Ministry of Finance, which included the capital increases under reorganization plans, showed the use of funds from the emission of shares:

	Total ¥ mill.	Equipment investment ¥ mill.	Working capital ¥ mill.	Repayment of loans ¥ mill.
1949	80,794	21,757	21,709	37,327
1950	48,831	17,750	19,332	11,747
1951	77,800	34,310	24,149	19,340
1952	130,646	59,688	37,773	33,184
1953 1st half	105,957	47,340	39,309	19,302

By industries, manufacturing showed the largest increase, but in the beginning of 1953 bank and shipping firms also strengthened their capital structure through new issues.

Stock Issues by Industrial Groups

(In millions of yen)

	1950	1951	1952	1953 1st half
Mining	2,737	2,540	5,808	3,262
Construction	396	597	945	646
Manufacturing	24,569	43,986	66,276	39,169
Wholesale & retail	7,397	9,262	9,789	8,464
Banking & insurance	5,831	9,848	11,455	23,671
Transportation, communications & public utilities	7,176	10,288	27,643	26,550

Source: Ministry of Finance.

4 STAGNATION AND REACTIVATION OF THE BOND MARKET

1) Stagnation of the Bond Market under the Monetary Stringency—The demand for funds caused by the Korean War boom brought an increase in the issue of industrial debentures, while issues of financial debentures after June 1950 rose because of the capital increases in five special institutions. As stated above, in March 1950 a law abrogating the organic laws of the old special banks (Industrial Bank, etc.) had been passed, so that the Industrial Bank, Kangyo Bank, Hokkaido Takushoku Bank, and the banks for agriculture and industry (which had already gone out of existence during the war) lost their character as special banks and were treated as ordinary banks. At the same time, the Law Concerning the Issuance of Debentures by Banks was passed, and the government diverted funds from the counterpart funds for investment into the preferred stocks of the five institutions.

Another step taken to increase the issue limit of industrial debentures allowed companies to add successively to the capital by one-fourth of the revaluation fund in the first year, two-fourths in the second, and three-fourths in the third for computing the issue limit of debentures (limited to the amount of capital plus reserves or the net worth of the enterprise under Article 297 of the Commercial Code). An amendment to the Revaluation Law in April 1951 authorized the immediate addition of three-fourths of the revaluation fund.

These measures enlarged the debenture offerings, but the market was unable to absorb them. Demand for loans and other funds waned, but deposits did not grow correspondingly. The difference between the increase in loans and that in deposits in the year 1951 came to about ¥65 billion, which was covered by a ¥68 billion increase in bank borrowing from the central bank. The tight-money policy of the Bank of Japan and the decrease in government bonds held by the city banks led to a shrinkage of the open-market operations of the Bank of Japan, which were entirely suspended in October 1951. After June 1949 the bond market had relied on the investment purchases of financial institutions, and when these institutions lost their liquidity the bond market dried up. In the latter half of 1950, the proposed amounts of bond issues had to be drastically reduced and, from September 1950 to September 1951, only about 30 percent of the planned amounts of industrial debentures could actually be floated.

In order to alleviate the situation, the Deposits Bureau resumed its purchases of bonds. (In April 1951, this institution was reorganized in conformity with the Dodge line and renamed the Trust Fund Bureau.) Initially, the occupation authorities had prohibited the Deposits Bureau from investing directly in industrial enterprises, and its operations were restricted to investments and loans related to national and local governments. But, in November 1950, Mr. Dodge agreed to have the Deposits Bureau take over industrial debentures so that the huge increase in postal savings (the chief source of funds of the Deposits Bureau) would be made available for industrial financing. Since January 1951 the Deposits Bureau has also bought outstanding financial debentures, which has enabled the banks to unload their holdings and take over new issues. Financial debentures, therefore, showed a much better absorption rate than industrial debentures.

The shrinkage in the flotation of industrial bonds led to a concentration on issues of selected industries: electric power, iron and steel, shipping, and railroads. Funds raised through bond issues served largely for the repayment of loans through which equipment investment had been financed. Besides the Trust Fund Bureau, individuals accounted for a larger part of the purchases of financial debentures. In August and November of 1951, the Trust Fund Bureau took over bonds of the Tokyo Transit Corporation, thus entering again the field of industrial financing. Due to the monetary stringency, some maturing debentures could not be refunded by new issues.

Use of Actual Net Funds from Industrial Bond Issues (1949–51)

(In millions of yen)

	1949 First half	%	1949 Last half	%	1950 First half	%	1950 Last half	%	1951 First half	%	1951 Last half	%
Amount issued	1,910	—	14,645	—	21,465	—	24,297	—	20,565	—	18,537	—
Net funds received	1,854	100	14,284	100	19,990	100	22,783	100	19,302	100	17,393	100
New industrial funds	544	29.3	6,844	47.9	10,659	53.3	10,653	46.8	12,376	64.1	8,429	48.5
Equipment funds	514	27.7	5,927	41.5	7,700	38.5	8,570	37.6	11,763	60.9	7,765	44.7
Working capital	30	1.6	917	6.4	2,959	14.8	2,082	9.2	612	3.2	664	3.8
Repayment of advances on company bonds & loans	1,170	63.1	7,288	51.0	9,261	46.3	12,079	53.0	6,926	35.9	8,857	50.9
Equipment funds	1,147	61.9	4,244	29.7	4,793	24.0	7,871	34.5	5,856	30.4	7,477	43.0
Working capital	23	1.2	3,045	21.3	4,468	22.3	4,207	18.5	1,069	5.5	1,379	7.9
Old bonds exchanged	140	7.6	152	1.1	70	0.4	50	0.2	—	—	106	0.6

Note: "Net funds received" for 1949 shows amount paid in.
Source: Industrial Financing News, Sept. 1950 and Feb. 1952, issued by the Japan Industrial Bank.

Absorption of Industrial & Financial Bonds
Last half 1950-1951

(In millions of yen)

	Industrial Bonds						Financial Bonds					
	1950 Last half	%	1951 First half	%	1951 Last half	%	1950 Last half	%	1951 First half	%	1951 Last half	%
City banks	7,965	32.8	8,554	41.6	6,954	37.5	10,456	35.3	7,031	18.6	6,136	18.6
Local banks	9,564	39.4	7,025	34.2	7,058	38.0	10,088	34.1	5,129	13.6	4,014	12.2
Trust banks	304	1.3	361	1.7	314	1.6	141	0.5	57	0.1	93	0.1
Insurance companies	1,049	4.4	921	4.5	677	3.6	84	0.3	50	0.1	95	0.1
Central Cooperative Bank of Agriculture and agricultural cooperatives	4,743	19.5	3,040	14.8	2,543	13.7	772	2.6	530	1.4	1,013	3.2
Central Bank for Commercial and Industrial Co-operatives, credit associations, & credit cooperatives	130	0.5	177	0.9	328	1.7	398	1.4	505	1.3	555	1.7
Mutual banks & mutual financing associations	14	0.1	48	0.2	286	1.5	275	0.9	328	0.9	493	1.6
Individuals & others	524	2.1	435	2.1	174	0.9	5,349	18.2	6,459	17.1	7,364	22.3
Trust Fund Bureau	—	—	—	—	200	1.0	2,000	6.8	17,700	46.9	13,290	40.2
Total	24,297	100	20,565	100	18,537	100	29,566	100	37,793	100	33,057	100

Source: "Public and Corporate Bonds Statistics Monthly," March 1951 and Feb. 1952 issued by the Japan Industrial Bank.

2) Increase in Bond Issues—Toward the end of 1951, economic stagnation became apparent, fund demand decreased, and certain sectors, such as textiles, curtailed their operations. The government took anticyclical measures and increased its spendings. In 1952, bank loans went up by ¥600 billion, a not too large increase over the ¥500 billion of the preceding year. Bank deposits, on the contrary, recorded a very substantial rise of ¥700 billion, while the increase had come to only ¥450 billion in 1951. This helped the banks to reduce their borrowings from the Bank of Japan.

This change in conditions favored the flotation of bonds and, in the latter half of 1952, bond issues increased by about 40 percent. In the first half of 1953, however, the situation worsened again, and political complications together with a deteriorating balance of payments situation added to the difficulties. The increase in bank loans in the first half of 1953 amounted to ¥242 billion against a ¥73 billion increase in deposits. Nevertheless, the amount of bond issues grew. Not including government bonds, bond and debenture issues came to about ¥17.8 billion; if issues for refunding maturing bonds were deducted, the net increase came to ¥15.6 billion. Public offerings of bonds also showed a tendency to increase, rising from ¥2.8 billion in the first half of 1952 to ¥8 billion in the latter half and coming to about ¥7 billion in the first half of 1953. Public offerings of local bonds, which had been resumed in August 1952, contributed to this increase.

In June 1952, the flotation of convertible bonds started again with a ¥20 million issue of Kayaba Kogyo underwritten by Yamaichi Securities Co., Ltd. In the latter half of the year, three issues, involving ¥400 million, followed, and another three issues amounting to ¥950 million were offered for public subscription in the first half of 1953. In December 1952, the law authorizing the issuance of debentures by banks was abrogated and the Long-Term Credit Bank Law was enacted. The Industrial Bank of Japan was reorganized under this law, and the Kangyo, Hokkaido Takushoku, and local banks cooperated in setting up the Long-Term Credit Bank. Later, in 1957, a third bank, Nippon Fudosan Ginko (Japan Hypothec Bank), was organized under this law. These banks were authorized to issue debentures up to twenty times the aggregate of their capital and reserves (thirty times in the first five years after their foundation). Of the other four institutions which, at the time of the enactment of the law, issued debentures, the Central Cooperative Bank of Agriculture and Forestry and the Central Bank for Commercial and Industrial Cooperatives continued to do so on the basis of their organic laws, while the debenture ceiling was raised to twenty times capital and reserves. The Kangyo and the Hokkaido Takushoku banks discontinued the issuance of debentures and operated as deposit banks in accordance with the policy adopted at the time of their reorganization.

More bonds were offered to the public in 1952 and absorbed by individuals. At the same time, the Trust Fund Bureau increased its purchases. Although the share taken up by banks decreased, they still absorbed about 70 percent of the ¥2 billion in local bonds put on the market. Banks took up more industrial bonds, their share going up from 75.7 percent in the latter half of 1951 to 77.7 percent in the first half of 1952 and to 80.1 percent in the second. But in the first half of 1953, the money market became tight, and the Trust Fund Bureau and other government institutions played a more active role in the absorption of debentures.

Through this period, a large difference remained between the planned amounts of bond issues and the actual sales, indicating the continuous scarcity of investment capital. Despite

Public and Corporate Bond Issues
Last half 1950—First half 1953

(In millions of yen)

	Last half 1950			First half 1951			Last half 1951			First half 1952			Last half 1952			First half 1953		
	(A)	(B)	(C)	(A)	(B)	(C)	(A)	(B)	(C)	(A)	(B)	(C)	(A)	(B)	(C)	(A)	(B)	(C)
Financial bonds	51 (19)	29,566 (6,435)	5,500	52 (24)	37,793 (4,513)	5,950	55 (29)	33,057 (7,664)	6,690	51 (25)	33,847 (5,235)	7,620	59 (26)	47,295 (13,236)	9,475	66 (33)	60,640 (17,089)	12,890
Kogyo bonds	19 (18)	15,781 (6,035)	2,800	21 (20)	18,158 (3,813)	2,800	23 (23)	18,067 (6,464)	4,200	19 (19)	18,067 (3,885)	4,900	21 (20)	26,400 (11,136)	6,000	26 (26)	30,817 (14,599)	7,100
Long-Term Credit bonds	—	—	—	—	—	—	—	—	—	—	—	—	3	2,820	200	13	18,243	2,100
Kangyo bonds	7	7,385	—	7	10,785	—	6	7,500	—	6	7,500	—	5	7,500	—	—	—	—
Hokkaido Takushoku bonds	2	1,100	—	3	950	—	6	900	—	6	900	—	5	750	—	—	—	—
Agri. & Forest bonds	10 (1)	2,700 (400)	300	7 (3)	3,300 (500)	—	8	3,050	—	8	2,900	—	13	3,950	600	15	4,600	850
Comm. & Ind. bonds	13	2,600	2,400	13 (1)	3,600 (200)	2,150	12 (6)	3,540 (1,200)	2,490	12 (6)	4,480 (1,350)	2,720	12 (6)	5,875 (2,100)	2,675	12 (7)	6,980 (2,490)	2,840
Tokyo Bank Foreign Trade bonds	—	—	—	1	1,000	1,000	—	—	—	—	—	—	—	—	—	—	—	—
Industrial bonds	144 (2)	24,279 (50)	24,297	186	20,565	20,343	181 (4)	18,537 (106)	18,160	187 (29)	20,448 (1,735)	20,065	205 (25)	25,121 (1,868)	24,250	194 (4)	27,410 (310)	26,930
Local bonds	1	200	—	1	12	—	—	—	—	4	1,093	—	20	2,544	2,000	59	4,804	2,950
Public & company bonds	—	—	—	—	—	—	—	—	—	—	—	—	—	—	—	6	3,051	—
Total	196 (21)	54,063 (6,485)	29,797	239 (24)	58,370 (4,513)	26,293	236 (33)	51,594 (7,770)	24,850	242 (54)	55,388 (6,970)	27,685	284 (51)	74,960 (15,104)	35,725	319 (37)	92,854 (17,399)	42,770

Notes: Figures in parentheses show amount refunded.
(A) Number of descriptions
(B) Amount
(C) Amount raised publicly
Source: "Industrial Financial News," February 1952 and July 1953, issued by the Japan Industrial Bank.

prior consultations among the underwriters, the actual amounts raised came to only 60 percent of the planned amounts. Industries such as electric power, chemicals, iron and steel, textiles, and mining accounted for the largest issues, and only the leading firms were able to place debentures.

Amount of Industrial Bonds Issued by Type
1952—First half 1953

	First Half 1952		Last Half 1952		First Half 1953	
	Cases	¥ million	Cases	¥ million	Cases	¥ million
Industries	95	9,634	109	13,268	98	14,040
Food industry	—	—	5	500	4	520
Textile industry	33	3,125	28	3,760	26	3,455
Chemical industry	21	2,010	34	3,198	28	2,870
Ceramic industry	5	475	4	450	2	300
Metal industry	22	2,880	23	3,550	20	4,200
Machine & tool industry	12	1,120	14	1,710	18	2,695
Other industries	2	24	1	100	—	—
Agriculture, forestry, and marine industries	—	—	2	83	—	—
Mining industry	10	1,000	11	1,200	12	2,150
Transportation	25	2,440	24	2,580	24	3,030
Land transportation	22	2,040	20	1,880	18	1,980
Marine transportation	3	400	4	700	6	1,050
Communications	2	200	3	300	4	400
Electric and gas industries	53	7,090	52	7,000	53	7,550
Electric industry	44	6,260	44	5,800	45	6,250
Gas industry	9	830	8	1,200	8	1,300
Trade	1	4	1	100	—	—
Miscellaneous	1	80	3	590	3	240
Total	187	20,448	205	25,121	194	27,410

Source: "Public and Corporate Bonds Statistics Monthly", October 1952 and April 1953, issued by the Industrial Bank.

Use of Actual Net Funds of Industrial Bonds Issued
1952—First half 1953

	First Half 1952		Last Half 1952		First Half 1953	
	¥ million	%	¥ million	%	¥ million	%
Amount issued	20,448	—	25,121	—	27,410	—
Net funds received	19,200	100	23,618	100	25,779	100
New industrial funds	6,090	31.7	7,815	33.1	7,566	29.4
Equipment funds	5,821	30.3	7,015	29.7	6,840	26.6
Working capital	268	1.4	800	3.4	726	2.8
Repayment of advances on corporate bonds & loans	11,374	59.3	13,933	59.0	17,902	69.4
Equipment funds	9,898	51.6	11,502	48.7	14,698	57.0
Working capital	1,475	7.7	2,431	10.3	3,204	12.4
Old bonds exchanged	1,735	9.0	1,868	7.9	310	1.2

Source: "Industrial Financial News" July 1953 issued by the Industrial Bank.

2 ECONOMIC
REHABILITATION

2 ECONOMIC NORMALIZATION

▲1 PROGRESS OF ECONOMIC NORMALIZATION

In 1953, the economy was deteriorating; exports declined while imports showed a large expansion due to investment and consumption demand. At the same time, the special procurement orders, which had been of great help to Japan, particularly in view of the stagnation of the world's economy, tapered off. Japan's international payments situation further deteriorated, and the favorable balance of $94 million achieved in fiscal 1952 turned into a deficit of $313 million in fiscal 1953. The index of mining and manufacturing production went up by 24 percent in fiscal 1953, and this rise was entirely due to internal demand. In order to bring imports down, their preferential financing was discontinued, and, in September 1953, the Bank of Japan adopted a tight-money policy. In October, the application of the penalty rates was made stricter, and, in March 1954, more stringent measures for compressing fund demand and reducing imports were taken. A deflationary budget was drawn up for fiscal 1954 which limited public investments but remained on the same scale as the budget of the preceding year (general account expenditures: fiscal 1953, ¥1,017.2 billion; fiscal 1954, ¥1,040.8 billion). Tight money, therefore, became the most important instrument of contraction, resulting in an unprecedented number of dishonored bills and numerous bankruptcies, particularly among textile traders. Prices started to fall in February 1954 and production turned downward in March. Inventories had accumulated and required special financing.

At this time, however, the outlook for the world economy brightened. The European economy began to expand, world prices stopped falling, and Japan's exports increased. Since the monetary stringency left enterprises short of funds, imports remained low. The balance of payments situation improved and fiscal 1954 closed with a surplus of $344 million, an improvement of $657 million over the previous year. The export excess and fiscal disbursements contributed to a relaxation of the monetary stringency, and the increase in bank loans came to only ¥230 billion as against ¥430 billion in the preceding year, while deposits increased by ¥360 billion as against ¥290 billion in 1953. At the same time, advances by the Bank of Japan could be reduced by about 40 percent.

In 1955, the prosperity spread from Europe to the U.S., which gave Japan an opportunity for a large expansion of her exports. In September 1954, industrial output began to go up again, and, in March 1955, the highest postwar marks were being eclipsed. In 1955, the production index for mining and manufacturing reached 180.7, as against 166.9 in the preceding year. Inventories shrank, and exports in fiscal 1955 came to $2,100 million, up $490 million over the level a year earlier. For the first time, the trade accounts could be balanced independently of special procurement orders, leaving a surplus of about $140 million, while the overall balance came to $530 million.

A bumper rice crop and the favorable export situation led to a surplus of government payments over receipts of ¥277 billion (payments excess from the foreign exchange fund, ¥170 billion; from the food control special account, ¥170 billion). The increase in bank deposits reached ¥680 billion, almost double the amount in the preceding year, while the increase in loans was of about the same order as in the previous year. This led to a great relaxation of the money market, so that actually an excess of liquid funds appeared and interest rates declined. Banks lowered their rates for the discount of drafts by 1 *rin* in May 1955, and the insurance companies followed suit by reducing their loan rates in June. After a reduction in the call rate, the decline spread to long-term rates. Despite higher production and greater demand, prices remained stable and gave the economy the advantages of volume prosperity. The monetary liquidity continued into 1956, but in May money became tighter. Loans in 1956 rose to ¥1,042.8 billion, 3.1 times the amount in the previous year. The rise in deposits could not keep pace with this increase; banks resorted again to borrowing from the central bank and the overloan situation reappeared.

Together with consumer demand stimulated by the prosperity, equipment investment increased sharply and, in 1956, the production index of mining and manufacturing rose 23.4 percent. Machinery production scored a gain of 58.5 percent, the best in postwar years, and a manifestation of the 70 percent increase in equipment investment. The sudden expansion created bottlenecks in iron and steel, electric power, and coal, which in turn spurred an expansion of imports. The pressure of domestic demand reduced export propensity; nevertheless, the 22 percent increase was only slightly below the 24 percent expansion in the preceding year. But the rise in imports came to a record 39 percent, far above the 15 percent of a year previously. The balance of payments situation worsened, and the last quarter of fiscal 1956 witnessed a deficit of $130 million. Prices started to rise in 1956; fiscal receipts exceeded payments by ¥160 billion and the fund demand was very pressing. In March and May 1957, the Bank of Japan increased the discount rate in order to curb excessive bank borrowing, and, in June, a full-fledged deflationary policy was put into effect.

 2 THE STOCK MARKET

The tight-money policy of the Bank of Japan, enforced in 1953, and the economic stagnation naturally depressed the stock market, and the numerous business failures deepened the gloom. Corporate earnings shrank, and a strike by the staff of the exchange did not improve the situation. Stock prices fluctuated, but the general trend was downward, while the volume of transactions decreased. The Dow-Jones average fell to a low of ¥295.19 in April 1953, while the lowest point, after the boom, was reached on November 30, 1954, with the simple average declining to ¥94.85. Steels, shipbuilding, and trading firms lost about two-thirds from their high prices, while the average decline came to about one-half.

Various measures were discussed to shore up the market and even the resumption of term trading was proposed. Investment trusts suffered a great setback; new trusts set up in 1954 amounted to ¥24.1 billion, only half of the preceding year's figure. No additions could be made to the open trusts.

A maturity of five years was proposed for new trusts, but this proposal was only put into execution in March 1956. In the meantime, the period of maturity was extended by one year to three years. Investment trusts with share certificates of ¥1,000 were also started in January 1955.

The recession hit bottom in September 1954 as far as corporate settlements were concerned. In December, the stock market showed signs of revival and the formation of the Hatoyama cabinet raised expectations that the tight-money policies would be revised. The good showing of the Socialists in the election in February 1955 dampened the optimism of the market, but, in August, the prospects of an excellent rice crop activated the market and the liquidity achieved through fiscal payments brought some investment in stocks. Portfolio purchases of banks grew in 1956 and led to the so-called monetary bull market lasting from about June 1955 to June 1956. The Dow-Jones average rose from ¥352.47 on June 30, 1955, to a June 1956 high of ¥512.25. The most heavily traded stocks were in shipbuilding; they were followed by shipping, mining, steels, and chemicals.

In the three months following the June high the market remained dull, but the favorable corporate settlements at the end of September revived the market in the middle of October. Corporate earnings increased by 43.5 percent over the level a year earlier, and the shares of automobile, shipbuilding, and shipping companies became the market favorites. Fishing companies also became popular, since relations with Russia seemed to be improving, which would help fishing in the North Pacific. The Suez crisis sent stock prices up, with shipping taking the lead. A new record for trading volume was set on November 2, 1956, when 89 million shares changed hands on the Tokyo Stock Exchange. The rise continued in the first half of 1957; on May 4, the Dow-Jones average reached a new high of ¥595.46, but the Bank of Japan's raise of the discount rate reversed the trend and put an end to the bull market, which had lasted for almost two years.

The recovery of the stock market also helped the investment trusts. New trusts increased

Market Prices per ¥50 shares on the Tokyo Stock Exchange

	February 2, 1953	November 1, 1954
Banks, insurance	¥172.47	¥ 84.03
Railways, land transportation	117.54	83.11
Marine transportation	96.41	44.58
Gas, electric power	66.86	46.85
Mining	156.72	77.28
Shipbuilding, machinery mfg.	196.03	65.56
Iron & steel, metals	130.29	45.93
Textiles	149.81	97.75
Food industry	220.19	143.58
Marine products	116.70	70.92
Chemical industry	133.62	73.39
Other industries	223.24	122.57
Trading	351.78	132.45
Industrial enterprises	207.62	112.67
Total average	158.14	78.34

Source: Tokyo Stock Exchange.

Issuance of Stocks

	Amount of stocks issued	Amount handled by Capital Increase Adjustment Council	
	¥ million	Number of issues	¥ million
1953 First half	108,375	351	75,530
Last half	87,649	189	45,201
1954 First half	77,960	212	65,228
Last half	70,202	101	36,132
1955 First half	59,205	90	43,454
Last half	47,261	53	23,720
1956 First half	108,114	112	63,678
Last half	204,387	249	115,439
1957 First half	102,308	195	81,021

Source: Ministry of Finance and Yamaichi Securities Co., Ltd.

Use of Net Funds Received on Stock Issues

	Investment funds ¥ million	%	Working capital ¥ million	%	Repayment funds ¥ million	%	Total ¥ million	%
1953 First half	47,340	44.6	39,309	37.1	19,302	18.3	105,957	100
Last half	46,904	54.6	22,140	25.7	17,108	19.7	86,159	100
1954 First half	39,067	51.3	24,386	31.9	12,788	16.8	76,246	100
Last half	26,811	39.3	19,540	28.5	21,979	32.2	68,339	100
1955 First half	24,915	43.0	14,026	24.1	19,035	32.9	57,982	100
Last half	18,872	43.5	13,636	31.4	10,909	25.1	44,488	100
1956 First half	41,543	39.5	47,746	44.4	17,334	16.1	106,628	100
Last half	111,108	55.0	49,647	24.6	41,173	20.4	201,936	100
1957 First half	70,744	69.9	20,797	20.5	9,561	9.4	101,104	100

Source: Ministry of Finance.

Amount of Stocks Issued by Major Types of Business (In millions of yen)

	Mining	Construction	Mfg. industry	Wholesale & retail	Finance & insurance	Transportation, communications & other public services
1953 First half	3,262	646	39,169	8,464	23,671	26,550
Last half	1,278	660	39,030	4,166	6,665	30,049
1954 First half	557	1,024	46,206	5,041	4,133	16,135
Last half	2,498	8,617	28,414	16,878	1,876	16,070
1955 First half	401	6,089	23,658	6,308	1,560	15,936
Last half	2,734	449	16,657	5,188	6,179	8,022
1956 First half	4,508	3,231	33,007	9,343	33,611	20,058
Last half	5,210	1,521	92,000	20,841	20,390	56,784
1957 First half	3,352	1,951	51,506	8,527	3,055	26,384

Source: Zaisei Kinyū Tōkei Geppō ("Financial Statistics Monthly") by the Ministry of Finance.

from the ¥25 billion level in 1954 and 1955 to ¥50 billion in 1956. The rise in stock prices pushed the trust values up, and, on March 30, 1957, with the Dow-Jones average at ¥587, the share values of the 153 outstanding unit trusts (face value per share ¥5,000) averaged ¥7,024.45, the highest reaching ¥10,608.95, the lowest standing at ¥4,983.38. The favorable development of the investment trust business naturally influenced the stock market, and the two bid each other up.

The two groups which had suffered most from the collapse of the Korean boom, shipbuilding and shipping, led the advance and became extremely popular through the Suez crisis, although shipping shares had formerly been quoted below face value.

3 EXPANSION OF THE ISSUE MARKET

The recession starting in 1953 led to a decrease in fund demand, so that stock issues in 1954 and 1955 declined. Of the funds raised through new issues, a smaller part was used for equipment investment, and larger sums served for repaying loans. Besides the unfavorable business situation, the fact that a large number of the leading enterprises in banking, shipbuilding, machinery, and textiles had finished a round of capital increases should not be overlooked. Despite the dullness of the market, issues remained above the ¥100 billion level and stocks of shipping firms, electric power companies, steel manufacturers, and chemical firms were among the offerings in 1955. The issues handled by the Capital Increase Adjustment Council exceeded ¥50 billion.

An amendment to the Antimonopoly Law passed in September 1953 greatly relaxed the restrictions on corporate stock ownership; only the acquisition of stocks of other firms which would actually restrict competition remained prohibited. Banks were allowed to hold up to 10 percent of the issued shares of a single company, and the Fair Trade Commission could sanction even larger holdings. This made issuance of stocks much easier, since it enabled financial institutions and other firms to take over shares of related enterprises.

The government sought to improve the financial structure of enterprises through a revision of the tax law by which 10 percent of the dividends paid on capital increases (if the capital was increased by a transfer from the revaluation reserve, 5 percent) was exempted from the corporation tax for a period of two years. Another law sought to speed up the incorporation of the revaluation reserve in to the capital of enterprises. Both measures stimulated the issuance of new shares.

In 1956, stock issues reached unprecedented proportions. In the beginning, the demand for working capital was very strong, due to the upsurge in business, but soon equipment investment became the prime mover. Issues in the first half of 1956 were double those of the preceding six months, and the amount doubled again in the latter half of the year, bringing the total for the year to ¥312 billion, the highest since the end of the war.

4 NORMALIZATION OF THE BOND MARKET

Despite the monetary stringency, bond issues in 1953 and 1954 remained fairly high, partly due to the issuance of debentures, guaranteed by the government, of the National Railways and the Telegraph and Telephone Corporation. A law guaranteeing principal and interest of these bonds had gone into effect on August 1, 1953. These debentures were floated at an issue price of ¥98, bore 7 percent interest, and matured in seven years. The underwriting syndicate comprised eighteen banks, six trust banks, and four securities companies. Issues of local bonds and industrial debentures declined in 1953 and 1954, and only about 50 percent of the planned amounts could be raised. Industrial debentures were practically limited to electric power, metals, mining, railroads, chemicals, shipbuilding, and machinery. Banks took over about 75 percent of the issues. Issues of financial debentures rose, but the increase was almost entirely accounted for by the purchases of the Trust Fund Bureau and individuals. The end of the inflation heightened the interest of individuals in bonds.

In the latter half of 1954, conditions improved and public offerings exceeded ¥53.7 billion. The favorable development continued in the following year when they reached ¥67 billion in the first and ¥83.4 billion in the second half. Thus the absorption of bonds and debentures became much smoother, many issues were fully subscribed, and issue conditions became easier, which led to a wave of bond flotations for converting outstanding loans. The average amount of a single issue rose to about ¥180 million in the latter half of 1955, and Tokyo Electric Power Co. floated an issue amounting to ¥1 billion in December of that year. The relaxation of the money market made it possible to expand the issues beyond the first-rate companies. Individuals took up an increasing part of the debenture issues, and in particular the debentures of public corporations, whose interest payments were exempt from income tax, became only too popular. The increase in bond purchases by banks and individuals diminished the reliance on the Trust Fund Bureau. In January 1956, the Bank of Japan discontinued the system of prior approval of debenture issues as acceptable collateral, which was another step toward the normalization of the bond market.

At about this time, the consultative committee entrusted with discussing bond issues was reorganized and its procedure simplified, but actually the committee had lost its meaning. Interest rates declined in 1956, so that issue conditions of most debentures were modified, and a general revision of interest rates and other conditions went into effect in August 1956. The system of government-guaranteed debentures was enlarged, and issues of Japan Air Lines, the Road Corporation, the Electric Power Sources Development Corporation, the Northeast Development Corporation, the Hokkaido Development Corporation, the Housing Corporation, and the Public Enterprises Finance Corporation were included. This brought issues of government-guaranteed debentures in 1956 to sixteen, amounting to ¥35.3 billion.

The favorable situation continued until May 1957, when the shift in monetary policy brought about a tightening of the market. Interest rates were raised in July and the bond market entered a new phase.

Amount of Public and Corporate Bonds Issued

	Financial bonds		Industrial bonds		Local bonds		Public & corporate bonds		Total	
	Number of descriptions	¥ million	Number of descriptions	¥ million	Number of descriptions	¥ million	Number of descriptions	¥ million	Number of descriptions	¥ million
1953 Last half	66 (27)	68,150 (16,980)	156 (147)	20,833 (20,050)	42 (23)	3,435 (3,170)	14 (7)	14,537 (9,500)	278 (204)	106,955 (49,700)
1954 First half	79 (31)	74,498 (20,180)	142 (132)	16,050 (15,650)	120 (20)	7,581 (2,250)	13 (7)	13,128 (8,900)	354 (190)	111,257 (46,980)
Last half	96 (30)	72,148 (23,160)	183 (160)	21,697 (21,405)	45 (21)	3,020 (2,390)	13 (6)	11,249 (6,750)	337 (226)	108,114 (53,705)
1955 First half	101 (35)	77,413 (27,040)	229 (213)	32,383 (30,890)	120 (20)	9,773 (2,400)	15 (6)	9,922 (6,750)	465 (274)	129,491 (67,080)
Last half	102 (36)	94,920 (28,537)	221 (204)	41,571 (39,730)	57 (30)	5,436 (4,660)	12 (6)	14,621 (10,500)	392 (276)	156,548 (83,427)
1956 First half	73 (30)	98,865 (25,883)	180 (164)	42,769 (41,330)	536 (36)	34,929 (10,015)	15 (6)	20,402 (16,000)	804 (236)	196,965 (93,228)
Last half	81 (37)	11,679 (31,143)	144 (125)	58,862 (57,130)	115 (1)	10,766 (1,500)	14 (4)	18,635 (13,000)	354 (167)	199,942 (102,773)
1957 First half	76 (36)	107,935 (32,875)	210 (194)	65,454 (63,850)	433 (34)	20,988 (8,910)	19 (10)	20,910 (16,600)	738 (274)	215,287 (122,235)

Note: Figures in parentheses show amount raised publicly.

Source: "Industrial Financial News," February 1955, and July & August 1956, issued by the Industrial Bank; and "Public and Corporate Bonds Statistics Monthly," March and June 1957 issues.

Use of Actual Net Funds of Industrial Bonds Issued

(In millions of yen)

	1953 Last half	%	1954 First half	%	1954 Last half	%	1955 First half	%	1955 Last half	%
Amount issued	20,833	—	16,050	—	21,697	—	32,381	—	41,571	—
Net funds received	19,625	100	15,117	100	20,474	100	30,650	100	39,674	100
Net industrial funds	5,783	29.5	4,329	28.6	2,172	10.6	1,259	4.1	3,284	8.3
Equipment funds	5,783	29.5	4,264	28.2	2,071	10.1	965	3.1	2,792	7.0
Working capital	—	—	65	0.4	100	0.5	294	1.0	492	1.3
Repayment of advances on corporate bonds & loans	13,716	69.9	10,565	69.9	10,914	53.3	14,981	48.9	20,469	51.6
Equipment funds	11,853	60.4	8,855	58.6	9,423	46.0	13,322	43.5	16,689	42.1
Working capital	1,862	9.5	1,710	11.3	1,490	7.3	1,659	5.4	3,780	9.5
Old bonds exchanged	125	0.6	222	1.5	7,388	36.1	14,409	47.0	15,920	40.1

Source: "Industrial Financial News," July and August 1956, issued by the Industrial Bank.

Sources of Industrial Equipment Funds

	Stocks		Industrial bonds		Loans by general financial institutions		Government funds		Total
	¥ million	%	¥ million	%	¥ million	%	¥ million	%	¥ million
1954	42,156	9.8	3,646	0.8	253,133	58.9	130,330	30.3	429,265
1955	33,142	6.8	6,705	1.3	305,611	63.4	136,355	28.3	481,813
1956	134,358	15.3	53,551	6.1	530,043	60.4	159,507	18.1	877,459

Source: "Japan Economic Statistics," by the Bank of Japan (by fiscal year).

2 ECONOMIC REHABILITATION

3 POSTWAR PROGRESS OF THE SECURITIES BUSINESS

▲1 IMPROVEMENT IN THE POSITION OF SECURITIES DEALERS

The initial postwar legislation put all business connected with securities under the regulations of the Securities Transaction Law, which applied to the stock exchanges, dealers, underwriters, and all other businesses connected with buying and selling securities, except banks and trust banks.

This law still permitted individuals to engage in the securities business. The old Japan Securities Exchange Law had made joint-stock companies compulsory, but the end of the war came before the period fixed for the change expired, although actually almost all members of the exchange had already completed this reorganization. An amendment to the Securities Transaction Law in 1953 made the corporate form obligatory for the securities business, irrespective of membership in the stock exchange. The chief intent of this amendment was the protection of the investor, but it also contributed to the improvement of the profession, which had, in the past, been in disrepute.

The same law laid down certain capital requirements. The original version of the law required that the capital should be equal to at least one-twentieth of all liabilities. In March 1950, a flat minimum requirement of ¥500,000 in net business funds was added, and the business period of the securities companies was revised from six months to one year, in order to give these firms a more stable earnings position. Another amendment, passed in August of the same year, laid down minimum capital requirements for nine different categories of firms engaged in the securities business, including underwriters and members of the exchanges, and ranging from ¥500,000 to ¥30 million. The amounts were changed later, and the highest raised to ¥50 million.

In the beginning, the prewar system which made a government license necessary had been replaced by a system of registration. In 1948, when the Securities Transaction Law went into effect, over eight hundred firms were registered. The number to over one thousand in 1949, but the recession brought it down to 958 in 1950, and, at the end of June 1957, registered securities firms numbered 615, which operated 1,233 branches or other offices. The number of offices increased chiefly through the numerous branch offices of the large securities companies. The competition led to considerable friction, and, in order to police the business, the Federation of Japanese Securities Business Associations was founded. New branch offices were to be approved by the association of the respective locality, but this approval could not be withheld without good reason. In case of disagreement, the federation was to mediate the dispute. But sometimes the agreement was disregarded, and stricter rules were adopted in November 1953. About twenty-five thousand persons were engaged in the securities business in the middle of 1957, and yearly transactions involved 33 billion shares.

Under the new regulations, the stock exchange was organized on the basis of the membership principle, and the general assembly of the members was the highest organ of the exchange. The general assembly chose the president, the board of directors, and the auditors; three-fourths of the directors and two-thirds of the auditors had to be members of the exchange. The board of directors was the executive organ of the exchange. Membership in the exchange was based on the consent of the exchange. The number of regular members was initially limited to 130; the highest actual number of members was reached in September 1949 with 129; it had dropped to 100 by June 1957. The members trade on their own account as well as on commission; broker specialists (*saitorinin*) can only act as go-betweens for the regular members and cannot accept customer orders. On the Tokyo Stock Exchange, these *saitorinin* were twelve firms called *jitsuei shōken k.k.*; there were also twelve firms in Osaka and eight in Nagoya. The minimum capital required of regular members in Tokyo and Osaka was ¥30 million, while *saitori* members had to have a capital of ¥500,000. The actual capital of some firms was much greater, and, on June 30, 1957, the average per member of the Tokyo Stock Exchange came to ¥39.2 million.

Due to pressure from SCAP officials, a new amendment was made to the Securities Transaction Law in 1948 which prohibited financial institutions from acting as underwriters, so that the underwriting business became the exclusive field of securities companies. Capital requirements for the underwriting of bond issues were fixed in August 1950 and were revised in July 1954. Only firms with a capital of more than ¥50 million could act as original underwriters.

2 SECURITIES BUSINESS AND DEALERS ASSOCIATIONS

The wartime control associations were dissolved after the war and replaced by associations of the members of the old stock exchanges. These associations prepared for the reopening of the stock exchanges. However, different organizations had been set up by the securities firms, and these organizations remained in existence and took charge of the group trading.

But, with the enactment of the Securities Transaction Law, the dual system became meaningless, and, at the end of March 1948, the old stock exchange associations were dissolved and their business transferred to the securities associations. The Tokyo securities association was called Tokyo Shoken-gyo Kyokai. Since the Tokyo Stock Exchange reopened in 1949, the post of president of this association has usually been held by the chairman of the Tokyo Stock Exchange. Similar associations were founded elsewhere, and these associations together form the Federation of Japanese Securities Business Associations mentioned above. These associations are not organized under the Securities Transaction Law but are voluntary associations of firms engaged in the securities business. Another organization is the Securities Investment Trust Association, founded in July 1957, which comprises firms engaged in the securities investment trust business.

II

INSTITUTIONAL

DEVELOPMENTS

1 THE BANKING SYSTEM

1 BANKING STRUCTURE

The history of modern Japanese banking dates back to 1872 when the first National Bank Ordinance was promulgated. But it took about twenty years for the banking system to take on a definite shape, and its present form was fixed only after the Second World War. Banks played a very important role in the industrial and commercial development of the country, and they continue to occupy a central position in the economy. Although similar in many respects to the banking systems of Western countries, the structure of banking, as well as the business practice of Japanese banks, shows some notable peculiarities.

Significant for Japan's entire financial system is the large part played by the government and governmental institutions in the field of money, credit, and investment. Government influence extends far beyond the formulation of monetary policy or the determination of interest rates to the extension of credit to individual firms or the financing of particular projects.

In addition to the Bank of Japan, governmental financial institutions comprise a great variety of banks and so-called finance corporations (*kōko, kinko*) set up for special purposes or a special clientele. The private banking system is organized on the basis of different business fields. According to their legal status, Japanese banks are divided into ordinary banks, long-term credit banks, and foreign exchange banks. Among the ordinary banks, those which formerly specialized in the trust business are now distinguished as trust banks. Ordinary banks are commonly divided into city banks and local banks. This distinction, originally purely factual, has gained quasi-legal significance through administrative practice, and the latest additions to the number of city banks, Taiyo and Saitama banks, gained this status through approval by the Ministry of Finance. The only bank organized under the Foreign Exchange Bank Law (the Bank of Tokyo) is often classified together with the city banks which it resembles in operations and size.

The most important institution in the field of banking and credit, however, is the Ministry of Finance which shapes fiscal and monetary policies, supervises not only all credit institutions but also the financial behavior of all corporations, collects taxes and customs duties, controls foreign exchange, and has a decisive voice in the approval of foreign investment in Japan and Japanese investment overseas. The Ministry of Finance directly administers the trust fund. The Trust Fund Bureau (*Shikin Unyōbu*; literally, Fund Management Division), organized in 1951 to take over the functions of the prewar Deposits Bureau, is in charge of the surplus funds of the special accounts and the funds accumulated through the postal savings system (including postal transfer savings). Legally, the trust fund can be used for loans to, and investment in bonds issued by, national and local governments, the National

Railways, and other public enterprises, and financial institutions of the government and other agencies possessing a public character; further for investment in financial debentures issued by banks, the Central Cooperative Bank for Agriculture and Forestry, and the Central Bank for Commercial and Industrial Cooperatives (the official English style of the last institution is the Shoko Chukin Bank, but, since this appellation is unintelligible to the uninitiated, the English translation of the name of this agency has been retained). Investments in financial debentures are not to exceed one-third of the total funds, nor 50 percent of the total bond issues of one institution, nor 60 percent of any single bond issue. Actually, the Trust Fund Bureau supplies the largest part of the funds dispensed each year by the government through the fiscal loan and investment program (*Zaisei Tōyūshi*; in the fiscal 1971 budget, funds of the Trust Fund Bureau provided ¥3,133.4 billion out of ¥4,280.4 billion).

For economic aid, the government uses the overseas economic cooperation fund, which was originally established in 1958 as the Southeast Asia development cooperation fund and administered by the Japan Export-Import Bank. Its name was changed and its management made independent in 1960; its purpose is to finance investments in developing countries for longer terms and at lower interest rates than would be possible for private financial institutions and the Export-Import Bank.

Japan's Financial Institutions

	Number of institutions	Number of offices & branches
1. Bank of Japan	1	49
2. Commercial banks	86	7,040
Ordinary banks	75	6,744
City banks	15[1]	2,409
Local banks	61	4,335
Long-term credit banks	3	34
Trust banks	7	262[2]
3. Financial institutions for small business[3]	1,156	9,250
Mutual loan & savings banks	72	2,844
National Federation of Credit Associations	1	(1)
Credit associations	502	3,871
The Shoko Chukin Bank (Central Bank for Commercial & Industrial Cooperatives)	1	74
National Federation of Credit Cooperatives	1	(1)
Credit cooperatives	532	2,098
National Federation of Labor Credit Assns.	1	(1)
Labor credit associations	46	363

(continued)

Notes: 1. The Bank of Tokyo, although not an "ordinary" bank, is usually listed with the city banks.
2. Number of offices as of the end of 1970; foreign branches are not included.
3. Excluding government organizations (listed under 7).

4. Financial institutions for agriculture, forestry, and fisheries[3]	7,761	33
Central Cooperative Bank of Agriculture & Forestry	1	33
Prefectural federations of agricultural credit cooperatives	46	(46)
National mutual insurance federation of agricultural cooperatives	1	(1)
Prefectural mutual insurance federations of agricultural cooperatives	46	(46)
Agricultural cooperatives	6,026	(6,026)
Credit federations of fisheries cooperatives	34	(34)
Fisheries cooperatives	1,607	(1,607)
5. Securities finance institutions	273	1,851
Securities finance companies	3	(3)
Securities companies	270	1,851
6. Insurance companies	41	4,075
Life insurance companies	20	1,479 (17,965)[4]
Nonlife insurance companies	21	2,596 (215,494)[4]
7. Government financial institutions	11	251
The Japan Development Bank	1	7
Export-Import Bank of Japan	1	10
The People's Finance Corporation	1	113
The Housing Loan Corporation	1	13
The Agriculture, Forestry, & Fisheries Finance Corporation	1	15
The Small Business Finance Corporation	1	37
The Hokkaido & Tohoku Development Corporation	1	3
The Local Public Enterprise Finance Corporation	1	(1)
The Small Business Credit Insurance Corporation	1	52
The Medical Care Facilities Finance Corporation	1	1
Personal Services Finance Corporation	1	(1)
8. Trust Fund Bureau	1	(1)
Postal Savings System		
Post offices handling postal money orders and postal savings	1	17,209

4. Agencies (including individuals).

Principal Accounts of Financial Institutions

(In billions of yen)

End of year	All banks Banking accounts	Trust accounts	Government financial institutions	Central coop. Bank of Agr. & For.	Agric. cooperatives	Shoko Chukin	Mutual banks
Deposits							
1963	15,648.1	2,923.9	—	419.7	1,568.5	99.8	2,373.2
1964	17,846.2	3,295.9	—	618.2	2,066.3	118.5	2,780.0
1965	20,653.1	3,536.2	—	1,007.5	2,432.6	139.3	3,220.0
1966	23,790.0	3,881.9	—	1,069.6	2,985.9	148.0	3,728.3
1967	26,667.1	4,346.7	—	1,154.0	3,653.9	177.4	4,403.8
1968	31,012.3	4,973.9	—	1,276.5	4,314.5	206.9	4,453.3
1969	35,978.9	6,039.9	—	1,706.5	5,301.0	261.4	5,398.3
1970	41,308.8	7,231.4	—	1,710.7	6,186.6	329.7	6,366.4
Loans							
1963	14,562.6	1,496.5	2,394.0	412.5	695.7	335.0	2,000.5
1964	16,829.7	1,796.3	2,846.7	568.5	905.6	417.5	2,277.1
1965	19,217.9	2,192.7	3,363.3	823.1	1,049.2	509.0	2,642.6
1966	22,046.0	2,479.2	4,015.0	855.7	1,290.9	612.7	3,080.5
1967	25,323.0	3,000.0	4,747.0	945.6	1,629.8	726.2	3,637.2
1968	29,032.8	3,607.9	5,628.9	1,113.4	2,047.0	856.7	3,630.4
1969	33,784.4	4,312.3	6,651.5	1,370.5	2,536.6	1,016.5	4,393.2
1970	39,479.3	5,155.0	7,657.6	1,837.4	3,112.2	1,204.0	5,242.2
Securities							
1963	2,356.5	1,231.0	9.3	66.8	24.9	7.5	145.8
1964	3,007.0	1,200.9	15.1	73.9	28.0	8.7	177.9
1965	3,962.1	1,008.4	26.4	367.9	32.1	10.1	255.3
1966	4,766.9	945.0	20.2	427.4	79.9	11.2	315.0
1967	5,218.8	923.7	27.5	430.5	125.6	13.4	380.2
1968	5,962.3	994.6	23.1	483.5	156.6	16.2	386.5
1969	6,531.8	1,188.8	25.6	464.0	192.7	19.2	465.2
1970	7,147.4	1,391.7	30.8	538.1	223.4	22.4	544.0

Principal Accounts of Financial Institutions (cont.)

(In billions of yen)

End of year	Credit assoc.	Life insurance	Nonlife insurance	Trust Fund Bureau	Post Office life ins.	Total (incl. others)	Net total
Deposits							
1963	2,189.8	1,370.3	291.4	3,288.3	1,071.6	33,005.4	30,515.0
1964	2,655.7	1,699.9	356.7	3,844.6	1,119.6	38,727.0	35,524.5
1965	3,113.8	2,094.3	397.6	4,705.0	1,204.4	45,546.6	41,381.4
1966	3,688.4	2,562.9	477.1	5,849.5	1,370.0	53,205.4	48,405.4
1967	4,457.1	3,109.8	573.0	7,271.5	1,533.6	62,234.8	56,658.8
1968	5,221.1	3,757.1	670.6	9,052.9	1,769.0	72,373.8	65,930.7
1969	6,408.3	4,564.0	825.0	11,148.5	2,050.9	86,534.6	78,723.9
1970	7,739.5	5,522.7	1,125.1	13,710.2	2,410.9	107,884.8	95,699.3
Loans							
1963	1,809.6	858.2	50.8	2,587.2	791.6	29,251.2	27,204.3
1964	2,202.1	1,057.8	63.9	3,254.3	850.8	34,693.1	32,009.9
1965	2,407.0	1,334.2	65.1	4,075.7	870.6	40,450.1	37,516.0
1966	2,903.1	1,488.2	49.2	4,958.7	911.9	46,853.8	43,381.7
1967	3,579.1	1,775.6	58.2	5,892.0	991.1	54,934.7	50,653.1
1968	4,346.0	2,260.5	111.7	7,147.2	1,095.5	64,137.9	58,782.8
1969	5,430.0	2,883.8	166.6	8,574.6	1,254.5	76,564.0	69,953.6
1970	6,614.1	3,705.1	336.7	10,333.7	1,461.8	91,364.4	83,630.2
Securities							
1963	142.1	339.6	145.2	736.3	195.0	5,599.5	4,456.9
1964	153.5	415.8	171.9	632.4	241.3	6,313.9	4,853.0
1965	263.0	489.2	185.7	677.1	266.0	7,909.1	5,871.3
1966	328.7	742.3	233.3	944.2	336.8	9,774.5	7,718.2
1967	389.9	958.9	286.5	1,434.6	419.4	11,665.0	9,349.7
1968	469.1	1,075.2	322.4	1,963.2	492.8	13,557.1	10,921.8
1969	562.2	1,190.3	374.2	2,638.0	585.7	15,529.6	12,654.3
1970	637.4	1,259.5	437.6	3,444.9	675.8	17,759.3	14,191.5

Source: Bank of Japan.

Notes: 1. "Others" included in the total are credit cooperatives, labor credit associations, National Federation of Labor Credit Associations, fisheries cooperatives, credit federations of fisheries cooperatives, National Federation of Credit Associations, and, for securities only, the securities finance companies.

2. Overlapping accounts deducted from the total to obtain the net total are deposits and beneficiary certificates deposited with other financial institutions excluding deposits with the Bank of Japan; borrowings from other financial institutions except borrowings from the Bank of Japan; beneficiary certificates and bank debentures held by financial institutions.

Bank Deposits by Depositor
March 31, 1971

| | Total | | Demand deposits | | | | | | | |
| | | | Current deposits | | Ordinary deposits | | Deposits at notice | | Special deposits | |
	Number of accounts	¥ million	Number of accounts	¥ million	Number of accounts	¥ million	Number of accounts	¥ million	Number of accounts	¥ million
Total	66,213,679	18,655,970	5,499,332	4,657,567	56,956,938	7,141,797	873,335	5,056,262	2,884,074	1,800,344
City banks	36,438,352	10,864,113	2,943,911	2,915,225	31,475,402	4,000,276	520,008	2,788,316	1,499,031	1,160,296
Local banks	28,442,099	5,855,232	2,487,293	1,324,837	24,403,710	2,829,349	239,285	1,149,444	1,311,811	551,602
I. Corporations										
All banks	5,990,359	14,496,045	1,709,211	4,431,386	3,109,569	3,451,973	673,254	4,889,742	498,325	1,722,944
City banks	3,094,166	8,578,957	1,050,336	2,798,405	1,347,627	1,965,166	400,564	2,683,059	295,639	1,132,327
Local banks	2,665,429	4,069,855	612,727	1,216,489	1,695,652	1,248,659	167,294	1,096,289	189,756	508,418
1. General corp.										
All banks	5,732,463	11,412,497	1,683,675	3,970,730	2,967,787	2,055,407	641,878	4,390,369	439,123	995,991
City banks	2,984,379	6,781,870	1,038,335	2,493,627	1,298,757	1,200,016	384,184	2,413,236	263,103	674,991
Local banks	2,524,452	2,847,532	599,589	1,068,828	1,604,730	627,575	153,905	885,666	166,228	265,463
2. Financial institutions										
All banks	119,083	2,071,170	14,172	415,368	67,843	1,085,790	12,359	150,366	24,709	419,646
City banks	52,706	1,321,631	7,961	284,447	28,224	661,523	4,361	87,374	12,160	288,287
Local banks	61,907	719,189	5,880	126,525	38,093	415,639	7,421	54,729	10,513	122,296
3. Government and finance corp.										
All banks	138,813	1,012,378	11,364	45,288	73,939	310,776	19,017	349,007	34,493	307,307
City banks	57,081	475,456	4,040	20,331	20,646	103,627	12,019	182,449	20,376	169,049
Local banks	79,070	503,134	7,258	21,136	52,829	205,445	5,968	155,894	13,015	120,659
II. Individuals										
All banks	60,223,320	4,159,925	3,790,121	226,181	53,847,369	3,689,824	200,081	166,520	2,385,749	77,400
City banks	33,344,186	2,285,156	1,893,575	116,820	30,127,775	2,035,110	119,444	105,257	1,203,392	27,969
Local banks	25,776,670	1,785,377	1,874,566	108,348	22,708,058	1,580,690	71,991	53,155	1,122,055	43,184
III. Anonymous										
All banks	—	—	—	—	—	—	—	—	—	—
City banks	—	—	—	—	—	—	—	—	—	—
Local banks	—	—	—	—	—	—	—	—	—	—

Bank Deposits by Depositor (cont.)
March 31, 1971

	Total		Time deposits				Other deposits		All deposits	
			Time deposits		Installment deposits					
	Number of accounts	¥ million	Number of accounts	¥ million	Number of accounts	¥ million	Number of accounts	¥ million	Number of accounts	¥ million
Total										
All banks	54,195,595	23,639,414	50,139,681	23,030,456	4,055,914	608,958	118,979	388,252	120,528,253	42,683,636
City banks	26,265,116	13,830,376	26,009,204	13,790,331	255,912	40,045	118,289	374,564	62,821,757	25,069,053
Local banks	27,619,525	8,880,288	23,834,808	8,314,913	3,784,714	565,375	226	859	56,061,850	14,736,379
I. Corporations										
All banks	11,434,065	3,907,602	11,157,238	422,960	276,827	4,983	372,900	10,325,904	26,303,010	4,330,562
City banks	7,170,289	2,112,823	7,154,335	22,391	15,954	4,528	360,203	5,233,908	16,109,449	2,135,214
Local banks	3,391,609	1,704,625	3,132,991	398,191	258,618	142	746	4,768,387	7,462,210	2,102,816
1. General corp.										
All banks	10,530,220	3,797,238	10,253,825	422,602	276,395	4,206	120,214	9,956,509	22,062,931	4,219,840
City banks	6,754,765	2,069,284	6,738,818	22,387	15,947	3,791	110,853	5,079,841	13,647,488	2,091,671
Local banks	2,915,578	1,639,500	2,657,385	397,837	258,193	129	436	4,561,918	5,763,546	2,037,337
2. Financial institutions										
All banks	319,566	57,539	319,284	293	282	669	35,079	177,584	2,425,815	57,832
City banks	211,193	25,676	211,186	4	7	638	33,884	79,024	1,566,708	25,680
Local banks	99,616	30,959	99,341	289	275	12	268	93,167	819,073	31,248
3. Government and finance corp.										
All banks	584,279	52,825	584,129	65	150	108	217,607	191,811	1,814,264	52,890
City banks	204,331	17,863	204,331	—	—	99	215,466	75,043	895,253	17,863
Local banks	376,415	34,166	376,265	65	150	1	42	113,302	879,591	34,231
II. Individuals										
All banks	11,471,145	45,457,752	11,139,014	3,632,954	332,131	113,996	15,352	109,428,022	15,646,422	49,090,706
City banks	6,183,939	23,413,381	6,159,848	233,521	24,091	113,761	14,361	57,104,849	8,483,456	23,646,902
Local banks	5,234,595	21,842,809	4,927,838	3,386,526	306,757	84	113	51,006,089	7,020,085	25,229,335
III. Anonymous										
All banks	734,204	774,327	734,204	774,327	—	—	—	—	734,204	774,327
City banks	476,148	483,000	476,148	483,000	—	—	—	—	476,148	483,000
Local banks	254,084	287,374	254,084	287,374	—	—	—	—	254,084	287,374

Notes: 1. All banks includes city banks, local banks, long-term credit banks, and the banking accounts of the trust banks.

2. Special deposits include deposits for tax payments.

Source: Bank of Japan, Economic Statistics Monthly.

Fund Volume of Financial Institutions
September 30, 1970

	Number of institutions	Fund volume ¥ billion	% of total
Commercial banks	86	49,340.0	55.7
City banks	15	23,370.3	26.4
Local banks	61	13,564.6	15.3
Trust banks	7	7,182.2	8.1
Long-term credit banks	3	5,222.9	5.9
Financial institutions for small business	1,112	16,004.0	18.1
Mutual banks	72	5,908.9	6.7
Credit associations	505	7,160.0	8.1
Credit cooperatives	534	1,848.6	2.1
Central Bank for Commercial & Industrial Cooperatives	1	1,086.5	1.2
Financial institutions for agriculture, forestry, and fisheries	7,832	10,684.1	12.1
Labor credit associations	46	326.6	0.4
Insurance companies	41	6,290.7	7.1
Government financial institutions	11	5,985.8	6.8
Total	9,128	88,631.2	100.0

Note: Fund volume: deposits, securities, trusts; for governmental financial institutions, government loans are included.

Outstanding Balances of Deposits, Loans & Discounts
June 1971

(In billions of yen)

	All banks	City banks	Local banks
Deposits, total	45,308.2	27,063.7	15,196.0
Private deposits, total	41,063.1	24,636.1	13,450.2
Demand deposits	17,169.7	10,485.2	4,717.1
Time deposits	23,893.3	14,150.9	8,733.0
Public deposits	1,697.2	637.1	1,044.5
Deposits by financial institutions	2,061.5	1,317.6	698.6
Loans & discounts, total	43,202.9	23,855.1	12,490.2
Bills discounted	12,013.1	7,622.2	3,919.2
Loans on bills	21,852.6	14,147.5	6,708.0
Loans on deeds	8,992.8	1,821.9	1,806.1
Overdrafts	344.3	263.3	56.6

Notes: 1. "All banks" also includes trust banks and long-term credit banks.
  2. "Demand deposits" includes current deposits, ordinary deposits, deposits at notice, special deposits, and deposits for tax payment.
Source: Bank of Japan, Economic Statistics Monthly.

1 BANK OF JAPAN

The Bank of Japan was established on October 10, 1882, on the basis of the Bank of Japan Regulations promulgated in June of the same year. Originally, it was licensed for a period of thirty years, and one-half of its capital was supplied by the government. The charter of the bank was extended for another thirty-year term in February 1910, and, in February 1942, the present Bank of Japan Law was enacted, which transformed the bank from a joint-stock company into a special corporation. There is nothing like a general meeting of stockholders, who (except for the government) are entitled only to a yearly dividend between a minimum of 4 percent and a maximum of 5 percent. In case of dissolution, the shareholders are not entitled to any portion of the assets over and above the face value of their capital shares. The so-called subscription certificates, therefore, are more like debentures than shares of stock. Foreigners may not become owners of these certificates.

The officers of the bank are a governor, a vice-governor, three or more executive directors, two or more auditors, and several advisors (who are to express their views to the governor on problems submitted to them). The government appoints and dismisses these officers, and the employees of the bank have the status of government officials.

The supervisory powers of the government were greatly strengthened by the 1942 legislation. The minister of finance was given authority to approve the official discount rate and to fix the note issue limit. He was empowered to direct the bank, if deemed necessary for the attainment of its purpose, to undertake any business, to change its statutes, or to take any other necessary action. He could demand reports, investigate the bank, issue orders, or take other measures required for the supervision of the bank. Government officials were appointed comptrollers for the actual supervision.

An amendment to the Bank of Japan Law enacted in 1949 established a policy board, separate from the board of directors of the bank, for the formulation of monetary policies. The board consists of seven members: the governor of the Bank of Japan and one representative each of the Ministry of Finance, the Economic Planning Agency, the city banks, local banks, commerce and industry, and agriculture. The last four members are appointed by the cabinet with the approval of both houses of the Diet for a term of four years. The board elects a chairman from among its members (actually, the governor of the Bank of Japan has invariably held this post). All matters are settled by majority decision, but the representatives of the Ministry of Finance and the Economic Planning Agency have no voting power.

Regarding the note issue, the 1942 law only stated that the Bank of Japan could issue notes and said nothing about their convertibility, so that the currency system no longer implied the obligation of converting notes into specie. The bank was to maintain a reserve equivalent to the amount of the notes issued; this reserve could comprise commercial paper, bankers' acceptances, other bills, private and government drafts, government bonds, corporate debentures approved by the minister of finance, foreign balances, gold, and silver. With the permission of the minister of finance, the bank's note issue could temporarily exceed the issue limit.

The bank was authorized to make advances secured by bills, government bonds or other securities, gold or silver bullion, or merchandise; and to purchase and sell commercial paper, bankers' acceptances, other bills, and government bonds and corporate debentures approved by the minister. The bank's open market operations are based on these provisions.

The law empowered the bank to buy and sell foreign exchange, to contribute capital funds or make loans to foreign financial institutions, and to enter into correspondent relations with them. In today's actual practice, however, the role of the Bank of Japan in the field of foreign exchange is largely supervisory (approval of exchange transactions), whereas the actual business is carried on by the foreign exchange banks and the Export-Import Bank, but the operations of the foreign exchange fund, a financing organ, are carried out by the Bank of Japan.

The law stated that, with the approval of the minister of finance, the bank could undertake any business necessary for maintaining and fostering the credit system. This meant that in times of financial crisis the bank could engage in rescue operations through relief financing. The law stated explicitly that the bank, as part of its business, was to make unsecured advances to the government and subscribe to or underwrite government bonds; it also circumscribed the bank's duties in managing the state's business in the fields of currency and financing, and its role as a financial control organ.

The postwar amendment mentioned above entrusted some of the powers formerly exercised by the minister of finance to the policy board, which exercises the following functions: to formulate the basic policies for the management of the business of the Bank of Japan; to determine and change the official discount rate; to regulate market operations; to determine and change the interest rates of financial institutions; to regulate the required ratios of payment reserves; and to regulate advances to securities dealers by financial institutions.

As may be seen from this enumeration, the Bank of Japan is entrusted with the administration of the three principal instruments of monetary policy: the official discount rate, reserve requirements, and open market operations. In actual practice, however, the bank is not independent in its manipulation of those instrumentalities and is practically bound by the decisions of the government, i.e., the Ministry of Finance. In 1956, a Financial System Research Council was set up in order to prepare a revision of the Bank of Japan Law, but the council remained divided on the crucial issue of the relations between the government (Ministry of Finance) and the central bank. An interim report of the standing planning committee of the council was strongly in favor of the neutrality of the central bank, but the report met with sharp opposition on the part of the Ministry of Finance which began a determined rollback operation. Thereupon, the council split into two factions, and its recommendations submitted to the minister of finance on September 20, 1960, included two alternatives concerning the neutrality of the central bank (they were called relative recommendations). The first gave the competent minister the right to issue the necessary directives to the Bank of Japan if consultations with the governor failed to produce a solution; the draft added, however, that these directives were not to contravene the management principles of the bank. (This recommendation did not specify who would decide the compatibility of the directives with the management principles and how a dispute over this problem would be solved.) The second stipulated that the minister could demand the postponement of measure contemplated by the Bank of Japan if consultations remained inconclusive.

On February 13, 1965, the Ministry of Finance published its own draft for the revision of the Bank of Japan Law. It imposed on the Bank of Japan the duty to cooperate closely with the government and to consult with the minister of finance: "If the minister of finance considers it necessary to adjust an important matter in the management of the Bank of Japan with the policy of the government and informs the Bank of Japan accordingly, the

Bank of Japan must immediately consult with the minister of finance and adjust its views." In emergencies (natural disasters, crises), the minister of finance can order the Bank of Japan to take the measures which the minister of finance deems necessary for the maintenance of the credit order. The draft further proposed to transform the Bank of Japan into a special corporation without capital, to replace the present policy board by a management committee whose members would be appointed by the cabinet without confirmation by the Diet, and the abolition of the ceiling on the note issue.

The point of view of the Ministry of Finance received great support from the Radcliffe Report (on the working of the British monetary system) which espoused the view that the central bank ought to be subordinate to the government. The report based its position on two main arguments, the integration of economic policies and the responsibility of the government to Parliament for its economic policies. According to the Radcliffe Report, complete independence of the central bank from the government is inappropriate "because it seems to us that it contemplates two separate and independent agencies of government of which each is capable of initiating and pursuing its own conception of what economic policy requires." The report propounds the view that "the policies pursued by the central bank must be from first to last in harmony with those avowed and defended by Ministers of the Crown responsible to Parliament."

The reasons cited by the Ministry of Finance (and the Radcliffe Report) assert, negatively, that the neutrality of the central bank would permit a monetary policy unrelated or even opposed to the economic and fiscal policies of the government and, positively, that the efficiency of economic policy requires the coordination of all sectors of the economy and their integrated and comprehensive direction through the government. The not only unproven but basically wrong assumption underlying these arguments is that the government is competent for everything in the life of the nation and that everything can and should be regulated by governmental fiat. The economic policy of the nation must operate within the constitutionally guaranteed framework of private property, freedom of occupation, and freedom of association, and even an integrated economic policy should respect the limits of the constitution and the laws as well as the way of life of a democratic society. In view of the proneness of official economic policy to inflation and the importance of a sound currency not only for the national economy but also for the welfare of society, it would be highly desirable to remove the maintenance of the currency value from the sphere of political manipulation and make it the constitutional task of the central bank. This would also dispose of the second argument advanced for the subordination of the central bank to the Ministry of Finance, viz., the responsibility of the government for its economic policies to the Diet. The government is only responsible for the functions within its competence; if the constitution or the law entrusts monetary policy to a different and independent organ, the government is absolved of all responsibility. The notion that different functions are discharged by different and possibly independent organs should meet with no opposition in a democratic society. It would be no loss if planned inflation and inflationary credit expansion were banned as instruments of economic policy.

The draft of the Financial System Research Council had entrusted the Bank of Japan with handling the traditional instruments of credit policy, discount rate, reserve rate, and open market operations; they were to be used for the regulation of credit and the currency. The revision proposed by the Ministry of Finance enumerated the determination of the discount

rate and reserve requirements among the functions of the management committee but careful-
ly avoided mentioning the Bank of Japan in connection with credit or monetary policy, thus
creating the impression that the central bank was to have no part in shaping these policies.
The functions of the Bank of Japan in financing the securities market and foreign trade,
expressly stated in the recommendations of the Financial System Research Council, were
likewise omitted by the Ministry of Finance. Both drafts, however, apparently shared the
conviction that the supervision of the central bank could be made effective by requiring ministerial approval for numerous relatively unimportant details, thus replacing supervision,
which is aware of what is going on, by interference, which determines what has to be done.
These proposals show that the ministry places very little confidence in the bank's managers
as they would require specific approval for selecting collateral (to serve as a temporary
guarantee for a currency issue) other than that stipulated in the law.

The Liberal-Democratic party showed little interest in the revision of the Bank of Japan
Law, and, in March 1965, the Ministry of Finance decided not to introduce the bill in the
Diet. The ministry tried to revive the issue in May 1968 but found that the moment was not
propitious.

For the time being, therefore, the Bank of Japan retains a threefold function: it is the
country's sole note issuing institution, the government's bank, and the bankers' bank. In
practice, these functions often coincide, and it is particularly in its role as the central credit
institution that the bank implements the government's monetary policy and regulates the
currency supply. Although the official discount rate has been used in recent years to emphasize official determination to enforce a tight-money policy, the most effective method of the
central bank for regulating the money market was based on its supply of short-term credit
to financial institutions. Most city banks were chronically overloaned and relied on central
bank credit for making up the insufficiencies of their own funds. Every month, each bank
dealing with the Bank of Japan was given a credit line which implied a ceiling for the application of the lowest interest rate. This ceiling was based chiefly on the deposit balance of the
respective bank. If the bank's borrowings exceeded this ceiling, a higher (penalty) rate was
applied. In August 1947, the penalty rate was divided into steps ranging from 0.1 *sen* to
0.3 *sen* per diem (0.365–1.095 percent) above the official discount rate. By lowering or raising
the ceiling, modifying the method of its computation, enlarging or reducing the scope of
its application (rediscounts of commercial paper, for example, were often not counted in,
but at other times were included in the loans to which the ceiling applied), and by mani-
pulating the penalty rates, the Bank of Japan could enforce a much more differentiated
quantitative and qualitative credit regulation than would be obtainable through changes in
the official discount rate. In 1963, the authorities decided, in the interest of a normalization
of the money market, to discontinue the direct regulation of credit to city banks (although
credit lines were retained) and rely on open market operations for adjusting bank liquidity
and regulating currency supply (in practice, advances to banks are the most important
mechanism for expanding or—through the repayment of these advances—contracting the
currency volume). But soon this attempt had to be abandoned and the old system of "window controls" was revived. Every month, the Bank of Japan not only fixed the overall
credit ceiling of each individual bank but also reviewed its entire credit and investment
program. Although there was no legal foundation for this procedure, the banks could not
disregard the "advice" of the Bank of Japan.

In July 1967, the Bank of Japan adopted a new control formula called "position guidance" based on the ratio of loans to deposits. In order to prevent large increases in bank lending, the new method of fixing credit lines was based on the total of internal funds and borrowings of each bank whereas, until then, actual deposits and borrowings from the Bank of Japan had formed the basis. In August, the window controls were reimposed and applied to thirteen city banks, the three long-term credit banks, the banking accounts of the seven trust banks, twenty-three local banks whose deposits exceeded ¥150 billion, and the mutual banks. The Bank of Japan fixed a rate of increase in new loans (including renewals) for each quarter on the basis of the outstanding loan balances of each bank.

In November 1970, the Ministry of Finance proposed to extend the credit regulation through position guidance to other financial institutions since the city banks accounted for only 30 percent of all loans. At the same time, the ministry extended the reserve deposit system (which applied to ordinary banks, long-term credit banks, the banking accounts of trust banks, most mutual banks, credit associations, and the Central Cooperative Bank of Agriculture and Forestry) to all agricultural institutions, the trust accounts of trust banks, and insurance companies. In January 1971, however, the Bank of Japan discontinued its position guidance and removed all credit restraints.

In December 1964, Masamichi Yamagiwa resigned as governor of the Bank of Japan and was succeeded by Makoto Usami, then president of Mitsubishi Bank. It was the first time since the Meiji era that a private banker had been appointed to this post. But he served only one term and, in December 1969, Takashi Sasaki was promoted from vice-governor to governor. Michikazu Kono, president of the People's Finance Corporation and a former official of the Ministry of Finance, became vice-governor, thus virtually assuring that the long-standing tradition of awarding the post alternately to somebody from the Bank of Japan and a man from the Ministry of Finance would be upheld.

The note issue rose from ¥422 billion at the end of 1950 to ¥1,234 billion at the end of 1960, equivalent to an average yearly rate of increase of 13.1 percent. Since then, the expansion has become faster. At the end of 1970, it stood at ¥5,556 billion; the average yearly rate of increase for the decade was 16.3 percent. Actually, the note issue reached ¥5,439.5 billion on December 30, 1969, and ¥6,233.9 billion on December 30, 1970. The statutory ceiling on the note issue was last raised on November 27, 1971, when it was fixed at ¥5,700 billion. The ceiling has lost its significance as a means of regulating the currency supply.

The basic money rates of the Bank of Japan, which went into effect on December 28, 1971, were as follows:

Discounts of commercial bills and loans secured by government bonds, specified local government bonds, specified corporate and other debentures and agricultural bills	4.75%
Export usance bills in yen	4.75%
Loans secured by bills for preexport financing	4.75%
Loans secured by other collateral	5.00%
Loans from the foreign exchange fund	4.75%

2 COMMERCIAL BANKS

Apart from the Bank of Japan and the other governmental institutions, Japan's present banking system is based on the following laws: the Bank Law of 1927 (often amended but not yet replaced), the Long-Term Credit Bank Law of 1952, and the Foreign Exchange Bank Law of 1954. All ordinary banks are organized under the provisions of the Bank Law. All city banks have their head offices in one of the large cities, but their branch network covers all important cities in the country. Many city banks maintain overseas branches. In 1943, ordinary banks had been allowed to engage in the trust business, but the business of the old trust companies was ruined through the postwar inflation, and the Securities Transaction Law of 1948 prohibited trust companies from issuing, underwriting, and dealing in securities. The trust companies, therefore, were reorganized as trust banks combining trust business with ordinary banking. Besides accepting deposits and receiving money in trust, they raise funds through loan trusts and also act as trustees for the securities companies, which operate the securities investment trusts.

Before the war, long-term financing was chiefly provided by the so-called special banks, which were based on special laws and enjoyed a privileged position. They were allowed to combine the acceptance of deposits with the emission of debentures, which was not only inconsistent with sound management principles but also gave them an unfair advantage over other banks. The occupation authorities, therefore, insisted on the abolition of this system. A number of special banks were liquidated, while three of the remaining institutions —the Industrial Bank of Japan, Nippon Kangyo Bank, and Hokkaido Takushoku Bank— were reorganized as ordinary banks. Since the supply of long-term funds to industry remained insufficient, a Law Concerning the Issuance of Debentures by Banks was passed at the same time that the organic laws of the special banks were abrogated. Although the real intention of the law was to make the emission of debentures possible for institutions that had actually been emission banks, there were no restrictions on the type of banks that could issue debentures, since the regulation was based on the premise of equal treatment of all banks. But blind adherence to this principle would have led to an anomalous combination of debentures and deposits, so another solution to the problem of long-term financing had to be found. It was provided through the enactment of the Long-Term Credit Bank Law. The Industrial Bank of Japan was transformed into a long-term credit bank in December 1952, but the Kangyo and Hokkaido Takushoku banks discontinued the issuance of debentures and preferred to become ordinary deposit banks. They cooperated, however, in the establishment of the Long-Term Credit Bank, founded in December 1952 as a joint-stock company in which the government may own up to one-third of the authorized capital in preferred stock. Another bank organized under the Long-Term Credit Bank Law is the Japan Hypothec Bank set up in 1957, in which the government also holds preferred stock, while ¥1 billion of the original capital came from the assets of the liquidated Bank of Chosen (Korea). Different from the other long-term credit banks, the chief business of this bank is the supply of equipment funds and long-term working capital secured by mortgages to small enterprises.

After the war, the foreign exchange business was largely in the hands of the Japanese branches of foreign banks. When foreign exchange transactions assumed greater proportions, the Foreign Exchange Bank Law was enacted. It embodies the policy of establishing a special foreign exchange bank in order to facilitate foreign exchange transactions and export financing. The Bank of Tokyo, the successor institution to the old Yokohama Specie Bank, was recognized as the institution provided for in this law. The bank was not given a monopoly in the field of foreign exchange but, as a matter of administrative practice, it was favored in the establishment of foreign branches.

Because the Bank of Tokyo has relatively few domestic branch offices, it finds it difficult to accumulate sufficient funds. In 1962, the Foreign Exchange Bank Law was amended to authorize the bank to issue debentures up to five times its capital. Since then, the bank has issued interest-bearing bonds with a maturity of three years, a nominal interest rate of 7 percent, and a yield of 7.121 percent to the subscribers. In addition to banks and securities companies, the bank relied on its customers for selling its bonds but was still unable to raise enough funds. In 1970, therefore, it began to issue discount debentures with a maturity of one year and a yield of 6.213 percent.

In another attempt to secure larger funds, the Bank of Tokyo, in September 1969, entered into an agreement with the National Federation of Credit Associations under which the Bank of Tokyo handles the foreign exchange business of the credit associations, which, in their turn, provide the Bank of Tokyo with yen funds. Based on this agreement, individual credit associations signed contracts with the bank making it their sole agent in foreign exchange transactions. The city banks are less than happy over this unfair restriction of their business but can do nothing about it because the Bank of Tokyo enjoys the support of the bureaucracy.

Japan has no savings banks in the strict sense. During the war, a large scale merger of savings banks had been enforced, and only four institutions were left at the end of the war. They were all reorganized as ordinary banks. The largest, the Japan Savings Bank, became Kyowa Bank, one of today's city banks. The institutions now often called loan and savings banks (mutual banks) developed from the old Japanese *mujin* (a kind of mutual loan and savings association).

Japan's present banking system shows a strong concentration. In the beginning of the country's modernization, there was a great proliferation of banking institutions and, at year-end 1918, banks and savings banks numbered 2,033. But since the period between World War I and II, the government has pursued the policy of reducing the number of banks by encouraging bank mergers. The enforcement of the Bank Law of 1927 brought the number of banks down from 1,445 in 1928 to 663 at the end of 1932. During the Second World War, mergers became compulsory and only 69 banks were left at year-end 1945. Among them were eight city banks: Teikoku, Mitsubishi, Yasuda (now Fuji Bank), Sanwa, Sumitomo, Kobe, Tokai, and Nomura (the present Daiwa Bank). Later on, Teikoku was divided into Mitsui and Dai-Ichi (which, together with the Peers' Bank, had been its component parts). Besides Kyowa Bank, three of the former special banks joined the ranks of the city banks, bringing their number to thirteen; Taiyo Bank was given the status of a city bank in December 1968 and Saitama Bank in April, 1969. On October 1, 1971, Dai-Ichi Bank merged with Nippon Kangyo Bank to form Dai-Ichi Kangyo Bank, reducing the number of city banks to fourteen.

1) City Banks (Toshi Ginko)—As stated, city banks are distinguished from local banks by their actual position in the banking world. They control about one-third of the financial resources of all financial institutions and 60 percent of the funds of commercial banks. All large enterprises are clients of one or more city banks, and over half of their outstanding loan balances are loans of over ￥100 million. About 60 percent of their deposits come from corporations and, of these deposits, 90 percent exceed ￥1 million. Although the number of individual depositors is very considerable (in number of accounts as well as deposit balances, the city banks and local banks are about equal), the business of city banks is predominantly with large-scale enterprises and in large-scale transactions.

Due to their position, the city banks are the recognized leaders of Japan's financial world. Customarily, the president of the Tokyo Bankers Association (which also operates the Tokyo Clearing House) is concurrently president of the Federation of Bankers Associations of Japan, so that one of the presidents of the big banks always acts as official spokesman of the banking world.

From a legal point of view, the board of directors, elected by the shareholder's meeting, represents the highest organ of the executive structure. But, in practice, the executive committee largely replaces the whole board. In Japanese bank management, the board of directors is much more intimately involved in the day-by-day business of the bank than in the United States, and ordinarily most or all of the directors are full-time officers of the bank (not only in banking but generally in Japanese corporations, outside directors are in the minority, hardly one-fourth on the average).

The executive committee is made up of the president (*tōdori*), the vice-president (*fuku-tōdori*), if any, and the managing or executive directors (*senmu* or *jōmu*). The other directors often double as department or branch managers. Besides taking care of the routine business, the executive committee actually constitutes the highest decision-making organ for all problems concerning the management of the bank.

The head offices of the large banks are organized into a number of departments such as personnel, general affairs, operations, investigation, foreign business, research, etc. The first-line operational units of the large banks are their branches (although the head offices also comprise business offices for transactions with the public). The authority of the branch manager is limited with regard to loans, funds on hand, etc. In order to ensure an efficient overall management of funds, the flow of funds between head and branch offices is regulated through the operation of an interest account system. Furthermore, personnel and cost control and branch office inspection are practiced. For all decisions exceeding the authority of the branch manager, the approval of the head office must be obtained for each single case (this is known as the consultation system). In recent years, the mechanization and rationalization of the banking business has made remarkable progress, and the large banks have installed centralized data processing systems.

2) Local Banks (Chiho Ginko)—With offices in provincial cities, usually the seats of prefectural government, local banks are often concentrated in one prefecture. Some equal the smaller city banks in size of deposit balances, but the majority consists of small institutions; their customers, too, are medium-sized or small local enterprises, and more than half of their loans are given to businesses with a capital of less than ￥10 million. Almost half of their deposit balances represent individual deposits, and almost three-fourths of them are time deposits. This gives the local banks a strong resemblance to savings banks.

Due to the prevalence of relatively long-term funds and the nature of their clients, local

Administrative Organization of City Banks

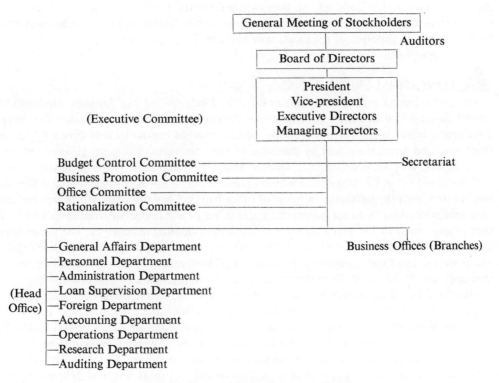

Deposit and Loan Balances of City Banks

	March 31, 1971		September 30, 1971	
	Deposits ¥ billion	Loans ¥ billion	Deposits ¥ billion	Loans ¥ billion
Fuji	2,784.8	2,490.4	3,272.1	2,777.5
Sumitomo	2,750.5	2,408.2	3,239.2	2,693.7
Mitsubishi	2,683.3	2,420.9	3,139.9	2,704.5
Sanwa	2,580.0	2,402.6	2,954.6	2,643.5
Tokai	1,933.9	1,783.4	2,252.7	1,948.0
Dai-Ichi	1,799.0	1,696.7	2,125.6	1,839.0
Mitsui	1,784·2	1,667.6	2,055.5	1,831.2
Nippon Kangyo	1,654.7	1,563.9	1,930.8	1,708.0
Kyowa	1,420.8	1,154.6	1,635.4	1,326.3
Daiwa	1,143.0	1,076.1	1,336.0	1,169.8
Kobe	1,066.7	914.7	1,262.8	1,024.5
Saitama	1,007.6	848.9	1,125.8	941.7
Taiyo	884.0	745.6	1,002.8	825.1
Hokkaido Takushoku	884.0	704.8	945.8	745.0
Tokyo	711.0	837.6	922.9	911.7
Total	25,068.9	22,716.8	29,202.3	25,179.5

Note: Actual deposits, excluding checks, bills, and government deposits.

banks invest relatively more in securities than city banks. They are very active as lenders in the call market and seldom rely on borrowings from the Bank of Japan. Monetary stringency affects them less than the city banks and, on such occasions, large enterprises may turn to local banks to supplement the funds they can borrow from city banks.

3. LONG-TERM CREDIT BANKS

The Long-Term Credit Bank Law, enacted in 1952, revived the Japanese tradition of special banks which had been interrupted by the occupation. The law provided that long-term credit banks could furnish working and investment capital to enterprises by loans, discounts, and guarantees, and by purchase of (but not subscription to) government and other bonds, corporate debentures, stocks, and other securities. Other long-term loans (collateralized by real estate) or short-term loans are only allowed to the extent that they do not interfere with the legitimate business of other banks. They can issue debentures but can only accept deposits from the government and other public bodies or from firms to which they extend credit or for which they act as trustees in floating debentures. The issuance of debentures by long-term credit banks is limited to twenty times the aggregate of their capital and reserves. The Law Concerning the Issuance of Debentures by Banks was abrogated so that ordinary banks could no longer raise funds by issuing financial debentures.

The three banks organized under this law are the Industrial Bank of Japan (*Nippon Kōgyo Ginkō*), the Long-Term Credit Bank (*Nippon Chōki Shinyō Ginkō*), and the Japan Hypothec Bank (*Nippon Fudōsan Ginkō*). The Industrial Bank of Japan, which had been founded as a special bank in 1902, was reorganized as an ordinary commercial bank after the war but reorganized a second time on the basis of the Long-Term Credit Bank Law. The debentures issued by these banks (which used to be referred to as financial debentures) are either in the form of interest-bearing or discount debentures. As a rule, they are issued in bearer form, but the owner may have them inscribed. For each bond flotation, the long-term credit banks must consult the Ministry of Finance on amounts and issuance conditions. Bank debentures are also issued by the Central Cooperative Bank of Agriculture and Forestry, the Central Bank for Commercial and Industrial Cooperatives, and the Bank of Tokyo. The interest-bearing bank debentures (maturity five years) are issued by the bond issuance syndicate, and the largest part is taken over by commercial banks, while the discount bonds (maturity one year) are issued directly by the long-term credit banks and largely offered to individual investors through the securities companies.

4. TRUST BANKS

Trust business made its start in Japan when, in 1900, the Industrial Bank of Japan Law empowered this bank to engage in the business of dealing in local bonds, debentures, and shares of stock. The Secured Debenture Trust Law of 1905 allowed banks to manage collateral securing corporate debentures on behalf of the owners of securities. In the following years, numerous trust companies were founded; they numbered 488 by 1921. Because abuses became rampant, strict regulations were enforced through the Trust Law and the Trust Business Law enacted in 1922. Up to 1927, 39 trust companies had been organized under the new rules; they included the trust companies connected with the *zaibatsu*: Mitsui, founded in 1924; the Mutual Trust Co. (its name was changed to Yasuda Trust Co. in the following year) and Sumitomo, formed in 1925; and Mitsubishi, set up in 1927. Due to the restrictive policies incorporated in the legislation, concentration in the trust business was great. At the end of the twenties and the beginning of the thirties, those trust assets held by the four *zaibatsu* trust companies mentioned above came to 70 percent of all trust assets.

The merger policy of the government pursued throughout the prewar and war periods reduced the number of trust companies to seven (one of them specialized in securities investment trusts). Moreover, in 1943, ordinary banks were allowed to engage in trust business. The postwar inflation completely ruined the money trust business which had been the most important line of the trust companies, and the Securities and Transaction Law promulgated in 1948 prohibited trust companies from issuing, underwriting, and dealing in securities. In order to provide the trust companies with more business, the occupation authorities proposed that they should be allowed to combine banking operations with trust business. The trust companies, therefore, were reorganized as ordinary banks (with the exception of the securities investment trust company which merged with another firm) and therefore called trust banks (*shintaku ginkō*). The four former *zaibatsu* firms, which had borne the names of Mitsubishi, Mitsui, Sumitomo, and Yasuda, were rechristened but resumed their old names after the peace treaty went into effect.

In 1951, securities investment trusts were set up again, but the business was taken over by the securities companies. A new field of business opened to the trust banks with the enactment of the Loan Trust Law in 1952. After December 1954, the government, by "administrative guidance," tried again to separate the trust from the banking business, although the trust banks could continue to engage in banking operations. At present, only one city bank, Daiwa Bank, retains a trust department. Trust banks now number seven; in addition to the four former *zaibatsu* institutions (Mitsui, Yasuda, Mitsubishi, and Sumitomo), there are Nippon Trust & Banking Co. (founded as Kawasaki Trust Co. in 1927, renamed Nippon Trust Co. in 1947), Toyo Trust & Banking Co. (formed in 1959 by consolidating the trust departments of Sanwa and Kobe banks and the securities transfer agency business of Nomura Securities Co.), and Chuo Trust & Banking Co. (established in 1962 to take over the trust business of Tokai Bank and Dai-Ichi Trust Bank—which was then reorganized as an ordinary bank under the style of Asahi Bank and later merged with Dai-Ichi Bank—and the transfer agency business of the Industrial Bank and Dai-Ichi Bank).

Trust banks continue to engage in banking business, but they have to keep the trust business and the banking business separate. Their balance sheets distinguish between banking accounts and trust accounts, and in the statistics compiled by the Bank of Japan, the former are counted among the banking accounts of all banks, while the trust accounts of all banks include also the trust accounts of Daiwa Bank.

Money trusts constituted the chief business of Japanese trust companies prior to the Second World War, but the inflation wiped out most large fortunes and this line of business did not regain its old importance. For designated money trusts, the general mode of managing the trust funds is fixed beforehand but the actual investment decisions are left to the discretion of the trust bank. Ordinarily, the trust funds are pooled and used by the trust banks without distinguishing the individual trusts (referred to as jointly operated trusts). Profits are distributed on the basis of the overall profit of the pool; they may be applied to special purposes (schooling, housing, pensions, retirement payments) if so stipulated in a special contract attached to the trust agreement. Actually, the trust banks have agreed on a uniform dividend rate.

Trust period	Maximum dividend rate (% p.a.)
1 year	5.75
2 years	6.30
5 years	7.03

Individual operation of trust funds was practiced for large sums. While the principal of the trust fund was guaranteed by the trust bank for joint operations, this was not the case for individually managed money trusts. But the profits were usually much higher than in joint operations since they were not subject to the restrictions of the Temporary Money Rates Adjustment Law. Since the expansion of the economy made extremely high yields possible, the Ministry of Finance regarded these trusts with disfavor. The trust banks, therefore, had to agree to a fixed maximum interest rate (1.7 *sen* per diem = 6.205 percent per annum); the trust term is at least one year, the minimum amount, ¥5 million. For specified money trusts, the settlor himself fixes the mode of operation; no guarantee of principal or interest is allowed, nor is there any limitation to their duration. This kind of trust was largely used for the accumulated yen funds of American film companies.

The first pension trusts were started in 1962 when an amendment to the Tax Law removed the tax drawbacks that had obstructed the adoption of pension plans. In order to be eligible for the tax benefits, enterprises must conclude trust or insurance contracts with trust banks or insurance companies and have the pension funds invested outside their own business. These so-called qualified retirement pension plans must be approved by the minister of finance. The contributions (employer alone or employer and employees) are managed by the trust banks according to very restrictive provisions aimed at protecting the capital. At least 50 percent of the pension fund must be invested in some ten investment objects for which principal is guaranteed or otherwise safe; 30 percent may be invested in stocks and 20 percent in real estate or real estate trust certificates. The consolidated (or combined) pension plans link a private pension plan set up by an individual company (or a group of companies) with the government's welfare pension system. The old-age pension provided for in the government system comprises the basic pension and additional payments; the basic pension is again divided into a fixed part (i.e., the payments are the same for all insurants) paid by the Treasury, and a variable part which provides for pension payments proportional to remuneration.The consolidated pension plan combines the variable part of the basic pension (of which the Treasury pays 20 percent) with a private pension plan, and the contributions of employer and employees to the government welfare pension are managed together with the contributions to the private pension plan.

A feature peculiar to the Japanese pension trust business is the great number of joint trusts in which one trust contract is concluded between a number of trust banks and one enterprise showing many enterprises maintain business relations with several trust banks.

In 1963, pension investment fund trusts were inaugurated. They are patterned after the common trust funds in use in the United States. Since stock investment for each individual pension fund did not allow efficient management, diversification of risks, or reduction of costs, a common trust fund for the purpose of investment in stock was set up (involving the legal complication of a double trust).

The most successful operation of the trust banks has been the loan trust business. Loan trusts, which are based on the Loan Trust Law of 1952, constitute a kind of time deposit with guaranteed principal and interest. They are accepted in units of ¥10,000 for terms of two or five years. The maximum interest rate (interest—the trust banks call it dividends—is paid semiannually) is 6.45 percent for two-year trusts and 7.27 percent for five-year trusts. Uninscribed (bearer) certificates are issued in ¥10,000, ¥100,000, ¥500,000, and ¥1 million denominations; inscribed certificates in multiples of ¥10,000. The certificates can be transferred during the trust period and cashed in after one year. Theoretically, the yield depends on the profit realized by the investment of the funds; actually, it has often been fixed. The Ministry of Finance has advised the trust bank to change this practice. The funds raised by the trust banks through loan trusts are given as loans to key industries. Originally, they were restricted to shipping, electric power, coal, and steel, but an amendment passed in 1971 substituted "sectors necessary for a sound development of the national economy" in place of the enumeration of particular industries. The trust banks wanted a further relaxation of the restrictions so that the funds could be used for the purchase of corporate debentures and the financing of homebuilding. Another kind of trust which the trust banks want to adopt for their own employees would be based on an installment saving plan. The accumulated funds should be usable not only for retirement benefits but also for the purchase of a home or employee shares and similar purposes; the trust assets would be invested in securities, real estate, deposits, or call loans. The contributions of the employer (trust bank) would be deductible as business expenses and those of the employees, tax-exempt.

Money in trust other than money trusts means trust assets that the trust bank receives in money but that are to be invested in property (to be turned over to the beneficiary on the termination of the trust without being reconverted into money).

Equipment trusts were set up for the first time in 1957 in the form of car trusts based on agreements between the trust banks and the electric railway companies. In the following years, the objects covered by these trusts were extended to cover all rolling stock, trucks, and vessels. Under the Secured Debenture Trust Law mentioned above, banks acting as trustees for the owners of securities are given a floating mortage covering the assets of a firm pledged as security for the debentures issued by that firm. Besides the trust banks, the city banks are engaged in this type of business.

The stock transfer agency business, which was started in Japan in 1954, is modeled after the American system. In addition to stock transfers, the trust banks also handle the business connected with the stockholders' meeting and the payment of dividends. The trust banks cannot execute orders for the purchase or sale of securities directly but must deal through securities companies; they are, however, entitled to commissions on these orders (which the city and local banks cannot claim).

Trust banks have taken up investment consulting. Toyo, Mitsubishi, and Sumitomo trust banks are already engaged in these activities, Mitsui and Yasuda trust banks as well as Dai-Ichi Kangyo Bank are expected to enter this field in the near future. Toyo and Sumitomo aim chiefly at domestic customers while Mitsubishi Trust stresses investment programs for foreign investors and custody of shares. Union-Nippon Management and Research, an affiliate of Union Bank of Switzerland, is likewise preparing to start investment consulting services which, at present, are not under special legal restrictions.

5 FINANCIAL INSTITUTIONS FOR SMALL ENTERPRISES

1) Mutual Banks (Sogo Ginko)—Mutual (loan and savings) banks are based on a 1951 law but go back to a Japanese institution known as *mujin*. Typical for this institution was the combination of installment savings and mutual loans; the loans were distributed through drawings or biddings (bids which offered the highest discounts were given preference). They first came under legal regulation in 1915 and were reorganized in 1949; but under the law of 1951, they were converted into mutual loan and savings banks and authorized to accept deposits and installment savings and give loans and discount bills. In 1953, domestic exchange, i.e., checks, drafts, and money orders, was added to their business. Originally, the mutual banks were assigned a particular business district. Their payment reserve is fixed by law at 10 percent of their time deposits and 30 percent of other deposits. This reserve must be held in the form of cash deposits with other institutions, call loans, government bonds, or other specified securities. Credit to one individual is limited to 10 percent of capital or reserves of ¥200 million, whichever is lower (in November 1970, the Ministry of Finance decided to raise the limits on individual loans to ¥500 million for mutual banks, ¥200 million for credit associations, and ¥100 million for credit cooperatives). In addition to the ordinary savings and loan business, the mutual banks are allowed to engage in the *mujin* business.

2) Credit Associations and Similar Institutions

i) Credit Associations (Shinyō Kinko)—The immediate predecessors of today's credit associations were the credit cooperatives created under the Small Enterprise Cooperative Association Law of 1949. With the exception of the cooperatives covered by other legislation (e.g., farmers, fishermen, and consumers), almost all associations in the credit business were reorganized on the basis of this law. Subsequently, the Law Concerning Financial Business by Cooperative Associations enabled them to engage in banking operations. Among the credit cooperatives, however, were many such as the former urban credit associations, which held large deposits from nonmembers and bore a strong resemblance to financial institutions, and others whose cooperative character was very pronounced and which, on principle, did not accept deposits from nonmembers. Since it was unreasonable to apply the same regulations to all these institutions, those of the first type were reorganized into credit associations (*Shinyō Kinko*; the expression *kinko* is used for the German *Kasse*) under the Credit Association Law of 1951. Institutions of the latter type were treated as genuine cooperative associations; their supervision was simplified and they were allowed more autonomy.

The credit associations are organized as nonprofit cooperatives whose capital is subscribed by their members who must be residents of, entrepreneurs engaged in business in (only enterprises with a capital of less then ¥100 million and less then 300 workers), or employees working in a certain district. The credit associations may receive deposits and installment savings from members and nonmembers without limitation but, as a rule, loans, discounts, and other credit operations are restricted to members. In exceptional cases, loans may be granted to nonmembers who are depositors with the association. In order to protect depositors, credit associations must keep 1.8 times the aggregate of 10 percent of time deposits and 20 percent of other deposits in cash, deposits with other financial institutions, call loans, government-guaranteed bonds, or financial debentures. For the same purpose, the maximum

Deposits of Mutual Loan and Savings Banks
March 31, 1971

	Number of accounts	¥ million
Total	28,066,802	6,298,575
Corporations	1,893,611	2,706,005
General corporations	1,822,563	2,397,878
Financial institutions	40,341	251,711
Public agencies	30,707	56,416
Individuals	26,014,583	3,469,779
Anonymous	158,608	122,791
Demand deposits, subtotal	13,967,582	2,043,994
Corporations	933,800	1,308,253
Individuals	13,033,782	735,741
Current deposits	1,060,486	640,259
Corporations	287,185	573,405
Individuals	773,301	66,854
Ordinary deposits	11,734,196	878,807
Corporations	462,734	284,389
Individuals	11,271,462	594,418
Deposits at notice	110,264	369,903
Corporations	59,476	331,325
Individuals	50,788	38,578
Special deposits	1,062,636	155,025
Corporations	124,405	119,134
Individuals	938,231	35,891
Time deposits, subtotal	14,099,220	4,254,581
Corporations	959,811	1,397,752
Individuals	12,980,801	2,734,038
Anonymous	158,608	122,791
Time deposits	12,151,629	4,024,673
Corporations	808,040	1,317,267
Individuals	11,184,981	2,584,615
Anonymous	158,608	122,791
Installment deposits	1,947,591	229,908
Corporations	151,771	80,485
Individuals	1,795,820	149,423
	Number of certificates	¥ million
Mutual finance contracts	796,797	117,241

Source: Bank of Japan, Economic Statistics Monthly.

limit of credits to one member (except that part of the credit secured by deposits) is fixed at 20 percent of the association's own capital and reserves or ¥100 million, whichever is lower. To the extent that it does not interfere with credit extension to members, credit associations may loan their funds to local public bodies, banks, or other financial institutions, but the aggregate of such loans (except the amounts secured by deposits and call loans) is limited to 15 percent of the loan total to members plus loans secured by deposits. Interest rates fall under the regulation of the Temporary Money Rates Adjustment Law, but, in view of the nature of their business, credit associations can pay somewhat higher interests than banks, but the maximum interest rate they can charge on loans is somewhat lower than that allowed to banks. When, however, eighteen-month deposits were introduced in February 1971, the credit associations decided not to add the usual 0.1 percent interest to the 6.0 percent interest on such deposits because it would make fund costs too high.

Together with the reorganization of the credit associations in 1951, a new overall organization, the National Federation of Credit Associations, was formed. The purpose of the federation is the pooling of resources in order to balance supply and demand of funds of the local associations. The federation accepts deposits from its member associations as well as from local public bodies and other nonprofit organizations. Temporary surplus funds of the credit associations are accepted in the form of short-term borrowings. The federation can lend money to its member associations and, with the permission of the minister of finance, to nonmembers as well; but the latter type of lending is subject to various restrictions.

The National Federation of Credit Associations decided to create a special fund (¥50 billion) for emergency help to member associations. The fund will be collected by assessments on the single associations; initially, each association will contribute three-thousandths of its outstanding deposits as of March 31, 1971; the contributions will be raised to four-thousandths by March 1972 and five-thousandths by March 1973. The federation will pay interest at a rate of 6.1 percent to the associations. The main reason for establishing the fund was the uncertainty of the economic situation; another consideration was the absence of any provisions for the credit institutions as such in the new deposit insurance system (which protects only individual investors). The special reserve fund administered by the federation can provide emergency financing in case of disasters or financial assistance to credit associations that lack sufficient capital.

In recent years, the federation has emerged as a major supplier of funds to city banks, and these loans usually exceed the loans to member associations.

ii) Credit Cooperatives (Shinyō Kyōdō Kumiai)—Institutions of a pronounced cooperative character were allowed more independent management than the credit associations under the Small Enterprise Cooperative Association Law of 1949. But the Law Concerning Financial Business by Cooperative Associations of the same year laid down certain standards of fund management, fixed a reserve ratio, regulated loans, and provided for administrative guidance.

Credit cooperatives can accept deposits and installment savings from their members as well as from people belonging to the households of their members. Furthermore, they can accept deposits from the government, local public bodies, and other nonprofit organizations. Their rates are subject to the provisions of the Temporary Money Rates Adjustment Law but, as a matter of practice, are slightly higher than the rates paid by banks.

Credit in the form of loans or discounting of notes can be given to members (and members of their households). Credit to one individual member is limited to one-tenth of the cooperative's own capital. Interest charged must remain below 18.25 percent per annum.

The National Central Association of Credit Cooperatives serves as the central credit organ for credit cooperatives. At the same time, however, they are affiliated with the Central Bank for Commercial and Industrial Cooperatives.

iii) Central Bank for Commercial and Industrial Cooperatives (Shōkō Kumiai Chūō Kinko; the Shoko Chukin Bank)—This institution, based on a special law, was established in

1936 to extend credit to cooperatives of small enterprises, manufacturers, merchants, and exporters, created under the Cooperative Association Law of 1900. The affiliated associations contributed to the capital of the bank, and a certain part was provided by the government. The membership of the institution changed in the course of time; it is now made up of the cooperatives based on the Small Enterprise Cooperative Association Law, such as trade and business cooperatives, particularly associations of barbers, saké brewers and dealers, salt manufacturers, and skippers of small vessels mainly engaged in coastal transportation. These cooperatives exercise certain regulatory and supervisory functions, establish manufacturing and warehousing facilities, and engage in banking activities for the benefit of their members. They grant short-term loans for seasonal business needs and medium-term loans for the purchase of capital equipment and for refunding high-interest loans. Other institutions associated with the Central Bank for Commercial and Industrial Cooperatives are the credit cooperatives, the central associations of the various cooperatives, and the export and import associations.

The central bank operates under the supervision of both the minister of finance and the minister of international trade and industry. It can accept deposits from affiliated associations, their members, nonprofit organizations, public bodies, and financial institutions. Another source of funds is the issuance of debentures. The bank can give loans, discount drafts, and guarantee liabilities of its affiliated associations and their members.

iv) Agricultural Financing—Financial institutions to meet the special needs of farming were set up as early as 1900. In 1923, the Central Bank for Industrial Associations was founded as the central credit organ of agricultural and other cooperatives, later becoming the Central Bank for Agriculture and Forestry; finally, after the enforcement of the Agricultural Cooperative Association Law of 1947, it was reorganized as the Central Cooperative Bank of Agriculture and Forestry (*Nōrin Chūō Kinko*). Its capital is subscribed by the agricultural cooperatives and their federations as well as by fisheries and forestry cooperatives. The bank can issue debentures and is also provided with funds from the government's Agriculture, Forestry, and Fisheries Finance Corporation. It plays an important role in agricultural financing because the payments for the rice purchased by the government under the Food Control Law are channeled through the Central Cooperative Bank and its affiliated associations.

In 1966, the Central Cooperative Bank abolished the special premium (0.2 percent) on funds deposited by member cooperatives, but there remain incentive rates depending on deposit balances.

In addition to the local agricultural cooperatives, there are forty-six credit federations of agricultural cooperatives organized on a prefectural basis. The fisheries cooperatives are likewise grouped in thirty-four prefectural credit federations which, however, only exist in prefectures with an important fishing industry. There are also a number of credit federations of marine products processing cooperatives.

v) Labor Credit Associations (Rōdō Kinko)—Through the initiative of the labor unions and consumer cooperatives, workers' credit cooperatives were established around 1950. They were reorganized under a special law enacted in 1953. By 1955, one such institution had been set up in each prefecture.

6 FINANCIAL INSTITUTIONS OF THE GOVERNMENT

1) Central Financial Institutions

i) Trust Fund Bureau (Shikin Unyō-bu)—Under the occupation, the precursor of the Trust Fund Bureau, the Deposits Bureau, was limited to handling government bonds and bonds of local public bodies, and only in 1951 did the Fund Management Division Law give it its present organization and functions. (Fund Management Division is the literal meaning of *Shikin Unyō-bu*.) This law mentions postal savings, accumulated funds of special accounts, etc., which the bureau should manage for the advancement of the public good by an integrated, reliable, and profitable administration. Of the funds lent out by the bureau, the loans to governmental financial institutions and other public agencies under the yearly fiscal loan and investment program, drawn up together with the budget, are of particular importance, since they serve largely to support the economic policies of the government.

All deposits accepted by the Trust Fund Bureau are time deposits; the interest rates paid by the bureau are fixed by law and vary with the terms of the deposits, which range from one to three months to over seven years.

Principal Assets of the Trust Fund Bureau
December 31, 1970

	¥ million
Assets	
Cash	580
Securities, total	3,444,908
Long-term government securities	355,513
Short-term government securities	1,458,447
Corporate bonds	1,630,947
Bank debentures	333,998
Loans, total	10,333,763
Loans to general & special accounts	465,696
Loans to local public bodies	2,258,569
Loans to government-affiliated institutions	6,021,547
Other	1,587,950
Total assets＝Liabilities	13,779,252
Liabilities	
Deposits of postal savings & postal transfer savings	7,345,833
Deposits of postal life insurance & annuities	272,921
Deposits of Welfare Insurance Special Account	4,054,275
Deposits of national annuities	655,732
Other deposits	1,404,882
Other funds	45,609

Source: Bank of Japan

ii) Industrial Investment Special Account (Sangyō Tōshi Tokubetsu Kaikei)—This account, administered by the Ministry of Finance, was set up in 1953 in order to make funds available to industry and trade in the form of capital investment and loans. A large part of the initial funds was derived from the counterpart funds for American aid (GARIOA and EROA), which played an important role in Japan's postwar reconstruction. Total help came to about $2 billion, and negotiations for repayment were arduous and time consuming. Besides some doubts concerning the character of the debt (there never was any formal agreement regarding the aid and no promise of repayment), the amount was disputed. MITI said that it possessed no accurate figures for the help received. Records left by SCAP's economic and scientific section showed a total of $1,197,458,000 ($1,131,346,000 in civilian goods and $66,112,000 in military supplies) from September 1945 to March 1951. From April 1951 to March 1956, when MITI kept its own records, total aid came to $853,776,000 (civilian goods $847,315,000 and supplies released by the Army $6,460,000) which would have brought the aggregate to $2,051,234,000. According to figures released by MITI in June 1961, American aid under GARIOA, EROA, and other civilian programs came to $1,717 million, and sales from army stocks to $78 million, for a total of $1,795 million. Foodstuffs accounted for the largest part of this sum, $1,050 million, while $511 million was for raw materials and fuels. If the value of goods for which Japan disclaimed liability is subtracted, the aid came to $1,746 million.

The U.S. government wanted Japan to repay according to the terms on which West Germany's debt was settled: repayment of one-third (about $650 million) over thirty years with $2\frac{1}{2}$ percent interest. Japan asked for cancellation of the interest payment and reduction of the total amount to $550 million. The United States refused the first request since this would constitute a fundamental departure from the original formula; Japan thereupon reduced its offer to $430 million payable in twenty years and further asked that the money be used for economic aid to developing countries.

The last request was largely for political reasons. The repayment of the debt became a domestic issue when, during the deliberations on the 1961 budget, the Socialists warned the government against subjecting the people to "double payment." What they meant was that the people, having paid for the commodities sold under the aid program, would be forced to pay once more if the debt were repaid by appropriations from the general accounts (i.e., taxes).

Under an agreement reached in the beginning of June 1961, Japan promised to pay $490 million in fifteen years and $2\frac{1}{2}$ percent interest on the outstanding balance of the principal, which was to raise total payments to $579,230,000. The amortization plan foresaw twenty-four half-yearly payments of $21,959,125 and six half-yearly payments of $8,701,690, but Japan could accelerate the payments. The Ministry of Finance declared that the payments would be made from the funds of the industrial investment special account and that no appropriations from the general accounts would be needed, but it soon had to replenish the capital of the special account by transfers from the general accounts.

Up to 1955, available funds of the industrial investment special account were directed to the Japan Development Bank, the Japan Export-Import Bank, and the Electric Power Sources Development Co. Since 1956, when direct investments from the general accounts came almost to an end, finance corporations (*kōko*), public bodies (*kōdan*), and special corporations (*tokubetsu gaisha*) have been added to the institutions that the special account can supply with funds. Besides the counterpart fund (¥229,413 million, which would correspond to $637,250,000), the government's investments (from the general accounts) in the Japan Development Bank and the Export-Import Bank, the former emergency commodity import fund, and the receipts from the specially designated commodities payments disposal special account were transferred to the industrial investment special account. Moreover, funds were added through appropriations from the general accounts, issues of special tax-exempt government bonds, and a number of bond issues in the United States and Europe.

iii) Postal Savings and Postal Life Insurance—Important for national saving and as a government fund source is the postal savings system. The Ministry of Postal Services operates a series of enterprises connected with money; besides the postal savings system, money orders, postal transfers, and postal transfer savings (patterned after the European giro system), postal annuities and postal life insurance are handled at post offices. For internal administrative purposes, money orders, postal transfers, and postal transfer savings come under the postal business special account, while postal savings are administered separately and postal annuities together with postal life insurance form a third special account.

The postal transfer system is widely used by industrial and commercial enterprises, less by individuals. Although the accumulated funds of the system are officially called "postal transfer savings," they rather represent working capital and other liquid funds. The other systems, however, may largely be regarded as savings.

Postal savings are operated in three forms, current (ordinary) deposits, time deposits, and installment savings. Ordinary deposits may be deposited and withdrawn at any time upon presentation of the passbook, but only at the post office which issued the passbook. Whereas banks calculate interest on deposits on a day-by-day basis, the post office pays tax-exempt interest (3.6 percent per annum) each month on the month-end balance.

Savings deposits (called savings certificates because a certificate for a definite amount is issued) may be withdrawn after six months; interest accrues semi-annually and may be left to bear compound interest. Since February 1, 1971, time deposits with a term of over two and a half years and an interest rate of 6 percent have been added to offset the new eighteen months deposits of ordinary banks. For installment savings, a fixed amount is paid each month; the whole deposit matures in two years.

Postal life insurance may be taken out at any post office without medical examination; premiums are payable monthly. A special discount is given for group insurance.

Postal annuities provide yearly payments ranging from ¥3,000 to ¥240,000 for various periods and starting at a certain age of the beneficiary. Premiums may be paid monthly, semiannually, annually, or in a lump sum.

Outstanding balances of postal savings and postal transfer savings at the end of December 1970 are given below:

	¥ million
Postal savings	7,405,008
Ordinary deposits	1.944,774
Savings certificates	5,163,545
Postal transfer savings	37,918
Total	7,442,926

Source: Ministry of Posts and Telecommunications.

On December 21, 1971, the outstanding balance on postal savings reached ¥9,003.3 billion. The interest rates presently paid on postal savings are as follows:

	% p.a.
Ordinary deposits	3.6
Installment savings	4.08
Saving certificates	
under 1 year	4.25
over 1 year	4.75
over 1½ years	5.50
over 2 years	5.75
over 2½ years	6.00
Time deposits, 1 year	5.50

Principal Assets of Postal Life Insurance and Postal Annuities
December 31, 1970

	¥ million
Securities	675,864
Government securities	21,644
Local government bonds	27,360
Corporate bonds	626,740
Bank debentures	193,147
Loans	1,461,811
Loans to government	41,497
Loans to local public bodies	859,430
Loans on policies	114,934
Loans to government-affiliated institutions	416,766
Deposits with Trust Fund Bureau	272,921
Total	2,410,947

Source: Bank of Japan

Postal Savings and Postal Annuities

(In billions of yen)

Fiscal year	Postal savings			Balances at end of fiscal year		
	Deposits	Withdrawals	Balance end of fiscal year	Postal transfer savings	Postal life insurance	Postal annuities
1962	1,485.8	1,257.1	1,539.3	12.6	868.2	14.7
1963	1,773.1	1,475.0	1,837.4	14.4	999.1	16.3
1964	2,089.4	1,697.1	2,229.7	18.0	1,090.5	17.9
1965	2,444.1	1,971.3	2,702.5	17.7	1,133.5	19.3
1966	2,905.1	2,297.7	3,309.9	17.7	1,233.1	20.9
1967	3,540.6	2,741.2	4,109.3	17.1	1,396.0	22.3
1968	4,344.3	3,350.9	5,102.7	24.0	1,576.7	21.5
1969	5,278.6	4,064.8	6,316.5	26.6	1,824.9	21.4
1970			7,743.9	28.9	2,109.2	

Source: Ministry of Posts and Telecommunications.

iv) Foreign Exchange Fund Special Account (Gaikoku Kawase Shikin Tokubetsu Kaikei)—
This account was set up under a special law passed to this effect in 1951 to handle the
government's purchases and sales of foreign exchange. Naturally, most of the business of
the account is done with the foreign exchange banks, and the account's position is intimately
connected with the developments in the international payments situation. An export surplus
means that the government must pay out yen funds in order to absorb the inflow of foreign
exchange while the yen funds of the account increase with increasing imports. Not only the
size of foreign trade and the international payments balance, but also settlement methods
and payment conditions, particularly the usance system, are of importance to the position
of the fund.

To finance its transactions, the account issues bills which carry an interest rate of about
6 percent per annum. These bills are usually taken over by the Bank of Japan. The account
keeps the amounts needed for ordinary transactions in current accounts whereas the remainder is held in time deposits or in American treasury notes. The special account is under the
jurisdiction of the Ministry of Finance.

2) Special Financial Institutions—Many prewar and wartime institutions were dissolved
under the demilitarization program. The only remaining ones were the People's Bank, the
Pension Bank, and the Deposits Bureau of the Ministry of Finance. Under the provisions of
the Financial Institutions Reconstruction and Reorganization Law, which regulated the
liquidation of the wartime losses of all financial institutions with the exception of the Bank of
Japan, the People's Bank lost its entire capital and that of the Pension Bank was reduced by
90 percent. Since the business of these institutions was deemed socially desirable, their operations were taken over by the People's Finance Corporation (*Kokumin Kinyū Kōko*) set up in
1949. In the following year, the Housing Loan Corporation (*Jūtaku Kinyū Kōko*) was
established as a corporation based on public law in order to grant loans at low interest rates
for home building in cases in which financing through banks or other financial institutions
proved difficult. In the course of time, new agencies have been set up for a great variety of
purposes; in many cases, the main purpose of organizing a special institution was to create
new jobs for the upper crust of the bureaucracy, while the work of these agencies could have
been carried out just as well or even better by existing institutions. Of real significance for the
economy (particularly for the support of private industry by public funds) are the two
institutions discussed below.

i) Japan Development Bank (Nippon Kaihatsu Ginkō)—The Japan Development Bank was
founded in 1951 on the basis of a special law passed to this effect. It was a successor to the
Reconversion Finance Bank set up in 1947 in order to supply capital—created by the printing press—to Japanese industry. (This institution was largely responsible for the runaway
inflation and the complete failure of the currency reform of February 1946).

The business program of the bank comprises: (1) loans for equipment investment; (2) subscription to industrial debentures; (3) guarantee of financial obligations; (4) other business
connected with the foregoing purposes. Of eventual profits, a certain percentage is retained
as reserve while the rest must be paid into the Treasury. In practice, the Japan Development
Bank initially supplied funds to large enterprises, chiefly to the electric power industry
and shipping, but now also does to hotels and car dealers; the so-called medium-sized

and small enterprises turn to the Small Business Finance Corporation, and little businessmen, artisans, and shopkeepers rely on the People's Finance Corporation. The bank cannot raise money by domestic borrowing but is empowered to contract loans in foreign currency. Since 1953, the Japan Development Bank has played an important role in securing foreign capital, first from the World Bank and later from bond issues in the United States and Europe.

In the past, the electric power industry and the shipping companies have been the chief beneficiaries of the bank's activities. Since the loans given by the bank imply not only a considerable saving in interest but also very favorable terms of repayment, they have been of no little help to these industries. In the reconstruction period, the electric power companies made solid progress, but, despite the more than generous government subsidies, shipping as well as coal mining went from bad to worse. In order to rebuild Japan's merchant marine, virtually destroyed by the war, the government organized yearly shipbuilding programs for which government subsidies were given in two forms: long-term, low-interest credits extended through the Japan Development Bank, and grants-in-aid, which paid part of the interest on commercial loans (differential between ordinary interest rates and preferential Japan Development Bank rates). Moreover, under the government's reorganization plan for the shipping industry enforced in 1963, the government financed a moratorium on the interest arrears (i.e., the government paid the accrued interest to the commercial banks and canceled the arrears payable to the Japan Development Bank). The share of the bank's loans for ships built under the government's programs varied between 50 percent and 90 percent with the programs and the type of vessel built.

As of September 30, 1970, total outstanding long-term borrowings of NYK (*Nippon Yusen Kaisha*), Japan's largest shipping line, amounted to ¥127,760 million; 78.1 percent of this sum had been advanced by the Japan Development Bank. At the same time, special legislation enabled the shipping lines to increase internal reserves by accelerated depreciation and thus decrease taxable profits. The effects of these measures are illustrated below:

(NYK, accounting year October–September)	1967	1968	1969
Operating profit to net sales	10.8%	7.3%	9.8%
Profit before special depreciation to net sales	8.3	5.7	7.6
Pretax profit to net sales	1.1	1.4	2.3

In 1966, the cabinet decided to assist urban renewal and the modernization of the distribution system as well as the construction of private railroads and public parking by loans from the Japan Development Bank; the loans were to finance 30–50 percent of the costs; the interest rate was fixed at 8.4 percent and maturity at twenty years with a three-year grace period. In 1970, MITI proposed to establish a special credit category for regional development and assign priorities to the lending of the Japan Development Bank and the Tohoku Development Finance Corporation. In line with an overall reduction of long-term interest rates effected in August 1971, the standard loan rate of the Japan Development Bank was reduced from 8.5 percent to 8.2 percent. The Construction Ministry wanted the bank to finance housing projects; an amendment to the organic law of the bank authorizing loans (interest rate 8.2 percent, maturity seven to ten years) to private developers was passed by the Diet in the fall of 1971.

ii) Export-Import Bank of Japan (Nippon Yushutsunyū Ginkō)—This institution was set up on December 28, 1950, to supply funds for export financing. Its original name, Japan Export Bank, was changed to its present form when, in 1952, the financing of imports was added to its functions. In export financing, the chief emphasis of the bank's operations is on exports of plant and equipment (including ships) by extending loans to or discounting drafts of domestic manufacturers and by granting credit to foreign customers. For imports, the bank makes advances to importers and manufacturers whose imports have been approved or by rediscounting drafts discounted by ordinary commercial banks for import financing. In May 1953, capital export financing, which up to then had to take the form of exports of plant and equipment for the purpose of investing in foreign firms, was extended to include capital investment in or the acquisition of stock of foreign corporations by Japanese exporters or manufacturers; loans could also be given to foreign partners who founded a joint enterprise with Japanese firms either abroad or in Japan. The same revision canceled the limitation of the bank's existence to five years. The bank may also lend funds to domestic manufacturers for equipment required in their overseas manufacturing operations. Another amendment in 1957 enlarged the framework of the bank's activities and made it possible to grant credits for technical services and advance loans to foreign governments or other agencies for economic development projects. In all the cases listed the bank can also guarantee the debtor's liability to the same parties who are entitled to be given credit by the bank.

The Export-Import Bank is supposed to adjust its fund supply to the conditions of the money market. It negotiates, therefore, in cooperation with the city banks involved in a given transaction, and its share in the fund supply varies with the conditions of the money market, the situation in international trade, the general business outlook, and the availability of funds from the client's own resources. The Japan Export-Import Bank Law provides that the bank supply funds if it is difficult to obtain them through ordinary financial institutions and the repayment of the loan and the fulfilment of all other obligations appear certain. The loan share of the bank should generally remain below 70 percent, but it may be increased if special circumstances make it desirable. In export financing, the bank has advanced up to 80 percent of the required funds and has supplied up to 70 percent of foreign investment and working capital. In the case of credit extended to foreign governments, the bank can subscribe the entire amount; this can also be done in other cases, especially if a loan runs for longer than five years and the transaction appears of particular importance. For overseas investments and enterprises, the bank may supply up to 70 percent of capital needs without the cooperation of commercial banks.

Six months is the shortest term of maturity for the bank's loans and five years the longest, but, in special cases, shorter and longer terms may be agreed on. Usually, ten years is the ultimate limit, but, in extraordinary cases, the bank may extend the maturity to up to fifteen years. Repayment may be effected in installments or in toto and must be made to the Export-Import Bank and the other banks involved proportionally to the outstanding balances. The beginning of repayment may be deferred up to three years. Usually, collateral in the form of a mortgage, a lien, or some equivalent security is required. Ordinarily, the bank demands the guarantee of a foreign government or a foreign bank. The interest rate is determined in each individual case and depends on the importance of the enterprise for Japan's export trade, the kind of investment, the maturity of the loan, etc. The interest rate on advances to foreign governments is the same as that of the World Bank.

1 THE BANKING SYSTEM

2 BANKING BUSINESS

The business of ordinary banks corresponds more or less to that of commercial banks in America and Europe. It comprises general banking operations such as acceptance of deposits, advances (loans and discounts), domestic and foreign exchange, settlement of drafts and checks drawn against current accounts, etc. Ordinary banks are in addition engaged in what may be considered as savings bank business and accept small savings deposits.

The Bank Law limits the business of ordinary banks to acceptance of deposits, lending of money, discounting of bills, remittances, and ancillary operations. By law, banks are not permitted to underwrite securities; by administrative guidance, the trust business has been separated from banking. There is no legal definition of ancillary operations; according to administrative practice, they comprise settlement of drafts and checks drawn against current accounts, custodial deposits, safekeeping, money exchange, payment of dividends, collection of debts, guarantee of liabilities, acceptance of drafts, letters of credit, and purchase, sale, and lending of securities. In recent years, banks have diversified into leasing, credit cards, and consulting, but they established separate companies to engage in these activities.

1 DEPOSITS

Deposits constitute the most important source of loanable funds and form the basis of the entire banking business. With regard to origin, primary and secondary deposits may be distinguished; the first represent funds derived immediately from the currency in circulation; the others already belonged in one form or another to the bank deposit system. From the point of view of liquidity, the distinction between demand and time deposits is important. In Japan, demand deposits are either checking accounts (called current deposits in the statistics of the Bank of Japan), ordinary deposits, which may be withdrawn at any time upon the presentation of the depositor's passbook, and deposits at notice, which must be left intact for one week and then may be withdrawn usually at two days' notice (but banks often make special arrangements for large depositors). No interest is paid on checking accounts, while the interest rate on deposits at notice is slightly higher than on ordinary deposits. Interest is calculated on a daily basis and credited to the depositor's account semi-annually. Time deposits and fixed deposits (which cannot be withdrawn during a specified period) are not renewed automatically, i.e., the customer must sign a new agreement. But the banks have introduced time deposits with automatic renewal; interest is either added to the capital or paid out to the customer. Deposits at notice are rarely used by individuals; they are mainly used for business funds not immediately needed.

Some new forms of demand deposits have come into use with the development of consumer credit in recent years, e.g., in connection with checking accounts in department stores, credit cards, and similar credit arrangements. Time deposits must be left untouched for a stipulated period (three months, six months, one year, eighteen months), but every bank will accommodate a customer who finds himself suddenly in need of funds. Although the postal savings system, mutual banks, and credit cooperatives are serious competitors, time deposits still absorb a large portion of popular savings. Rising incomes brought a spectacular increase in securities investment, particularly in the form of investment trusts, in the wake of the Iwato Boom, but the slump in the stock market which began in 1961 disillusioned the small investors, and it was only in 1970 that investment trusts showed signs of recovery. In prewar days, time deposits constituted about one-half of all bank deposits and thus enabled the banks to invest a sizeable part of their funds in long-term loans. The share of time deposits in the deposits of all banks, which dropped from 52.3 percent in 1962 to 48.3 percent in 1963, gradually rose again and averaged about 56 percent in 1970. About 70 percent of all time deposits for one year are renewed when they mature.

Anonymous time deposits were popular in the immediate postwar period, largely because they could be used for tax evasion. They were abolished on the recommendation of the Shoup Tax Mission but reintroduced in 1952. These deposits were entered under code numbers or fictitious names and the depositor was not required to inform the bank of his true identity. The Ministry of Finance advised the banks to discontinue this practice. In January 1968, all banks, credit associations, agricultural credit cooperatives, and post offices put up notices informing their customers that deposits under fictitious names would no longer be accepted; on the other hand, the banks are under no obligation to ascertain the identity of the depositor.

In the beginning of 1971, the Ministry of Finance estimated fictitious deposits at about ¥250 billion, 0.6 percent of all deposits. The ministry announced that it would punish banks for accepting fictitious deposits, e.g., by not allowing the relocation of branches (the Bank Law does not provide for such penalties). According to the National Tax Administration Agency, 10,825 deposits under fictitious names with deposits amounting to ¥11.9 billion were discovered in fiscal 1970 (fiscal 1969, 10,134 deposits with ¥10.4 billion). These deposits were found at 390 branches of city banks (fiscal 1969, 224) and 122 branches of local banks (fiscal 1969, 145).

Installment savings are another kind of time deposit. The depositor pays fixed amounts at fixed times (e.g., ¥10,000 on or before the twenty-fifth of each month); withdrawals require previous notice (e.g., thirty days); all payments and withdrawals are entered into a passbook. The same form of saving is also used by the postal savings system. Banks often combine installment savings with a particular savings purpose or consumer credit. Installment savings plans are in use for housing (homebuilding, purchase, or remodelling), car purchases or purchases of other consumer durables (e.g., pianos), education, marriage, foreign travel, etc. Another form combines installment savings with accident insurance.

Deposits for tax payments cannot be used for other purposes; the interest paid on these deposits is tax-exempt. Since practically all banks act as fiscal agents (agents of the Bank of Japan) and accept payments of national as well as local taxes, the system is advantageous and expeditious for the banks. (Deposits of government agencies constituted the most important part of the funds in the first years of the modern Japanese banking system, and employees of private banks work as tellers in some offices of public bodies.) Although no special deposits are required, banks also handle other recurrent payments on behalf of their depositors, (e.g., telephone bills and utility charges) and collect periodic payments for private institutions (e.g., tuition fees).

The so-called special deposits largely represent bank liabilities against cashiers' orders. Part of these deposits serve as window dressing for month-end reports (as do certain other items), and Japanese statistics often distinguish between "nominal" and "actual" deposit balances. For deposits placed by other banks, the banks pay the same interest rate as that paid to ordinary depositors on ordinary deposits and deposits at notice, but on deposits for longer than three months banks paid a uniform rate of 6 percent to other banks.

Mitsui Bank initiated a new type of account called "discount deposits." The deposits are for a definite period of time and the interest is subtracted beforehand when the deposit is made. (Actually, the depositor is paid a flat sum, e.g., ¥50,000, at the end of the period.) Local and mutual banks soon imitated Mitsui Bank. The Ministry of Finance had some misgivings about the system (because it was similar to discount bonds) and issued the following instructions: (1) the banks have to avoid appellations which might give the impression that these deposits are similar to discount bonds; (2) the document given to the customer must retain the nature of a receipt; (3) the amount of the deposit, the date of deposit, and the amount at maturity must be inscribed in letters of the same size; (4) in the case of automatic renewal, the amount cannot be rounded.

Mitsubishi Bank planned to introduce a system of deposits under which fixed amounts (units of ¥10,000) would be left for periods from three months to five years and the interest rate would depend on the actual period of deposit. Withdrawal would require one month's notice. Mitsubishi proposed the following interest rates:

over three months	3%
over one year	5.75%
between one and a half and five years	6%

The Ministry of Finance turned down the proposal on the ground that the categories did not correspond to those of the Temporary Money Rates Adjustment Law and would require a revision of the guidelines. But the same system is already in force for the savings certificates of the post office.

The city and local banks introduced "time deposits with overdrafts" in October 1969. In fact, the banks lend against the security of the deposit; eligible are time deposits of one year or eighteen months with a minimum balance of ¥50,000. The loan can be as high as the deposit; ¥500,000 is the ceiling. Initially, the interest rate was 6.5 percent but with the introduction of eighteen month deposits, the interest rate was raised to 6.75 percent.

Another new kind of account proposed by the banks was called "premium deposits." These were installment deposits. The plan foresaw monthly payments of a fixed sum (up to ¥50,000) during five years. The interest rate was to be 5.75 percent but, after five years, a premium of 4 percent would be paid on the balance; part of the premium was to be paid by the banks, and part by the government. On February 1, 1971, time deposits with a maturity of eighteen months were introduced; the interest rate was fixed at 6 percent. The city banks want to add time deposits with an indefinite maturity on which the applicable interest rate would vary with the actual time the deposit was left untouched, but this proposal is still under study.

In practice, the distinction between the various types of deposits is less sharp than in the government's regulations. Banks may arrange to transfer funds automatically from one account to another (e.g., from ordinary to current deposits or vice versa) as soon as a certain ceiling is reached—this practice has been reprimanded by the Ministry of Finance—or pay higher interest rates on deposits than authorized under the Temporary Money Rates Adjustment Law (banks could do this because call money was in great demand).

As shown in the following table, the share of the city banks in deposits has decreased in the last ten years.

Structure of Deposits by Type of Financial Institution

(In percent)

	Share in outstanding deposit balances, year-end			Rate of change		
	1959	1964	1969	1959–64	1964–69	1959–69
City banks	33.6	28.9	24.3	−4.7	−4.6	−9.3
Local banks	18.8	17.6	17.1	−1.2	−0.5	−1.7
Long-term credit banks	6.2	6.2	6.2	0.0	0.0	0.0
Trust banks	6.7	7.8	8.5	1.1	0.7	1.8
Mutual banks	6.9	8.1	7.6	1.2	−0.5	0.7
Credit associations	6.0	8.1	8.6	2.1	0.5	2.6
Credit cooperatives	1.1	1.9	2.3	0.8	0.4	1.2
Agricultural financial institutions	7.2	8.3	9.5	1.1	1.1	2.3
Life insurance companies	4.4	5.3	6.2	0.9	0.9	1.8
Nonlife insurance companies	1.2	1.1	1.1	−0.1	−0.1	−0.1
Postal savings	8.0	6.8	8.3	−1.2	1.5	0.3

Notes: 1. Adjusted for the change in status of Taiyo and Saitama banks.
2. Trust banks: total of banking and trust accounts with the exception of loan trusts.
Source: The Fuji Times.

The main reasons for the decrease in the deposit share of the city banks were: (1) individuals have become more familiar with other forms of investment such as loan trusts, life insurance, and bonds (as mentioned already, the popularity of investment trusts slipped badly after the stock market slump which began in 1961); (2) greater competition on the part of other financial institutions (mutual banks, trust banks, agricultural credit institutions, postal savings, and life insurance companies); (3) the flow of funds away from the cities and into the country through taxes and government spending; (4) the concentration of the increase in bank note circulation in the large cities (which implies lower deposits); (5) the

	Ratio of deposits Jan.–Mar. 1970	Average yearly rate of increase in deposits 1963–70	Average yearly rate of increase in loans 1963–70
	%	%	%
Large enterprises	28.1	20.4	17.4
Small enterprises	42.6	21.9	21.9

Note: Large enterprises, capital of at least ¥50 million.

restrictions on new branch offices. Another factor is the preponderance of large enterprises among the clients of the city banks (the increase in bank deposits of large enterprises has been slower than in those of small enterprises, as illustrated above).

Nevertheless, the share of individual deposits rose from 27.4 percent at the end of September 1964 to 34.2 percent at the end of September 1970 in the deposit total of the city banks, while it went up in the same period from 45.5 percent to 48.0 percent for the local banks.

In the three months from May to July 1971, deposits showed a large increase; Fuji Bank became the first Japanese bank with deposits exceeding ¥3 trillion (end of May, ¥3,026.7 billion) and four banks (Sumitomo, Mitsubishi, Sanwa, and Tokai) had deposits exceeding ¥2 trillion. By the end of August, Sumitomo's and Mitsubishi's deposits had also risen to ¥3 trillion. Altogether, the deposits of the fifteen city banks increased by ¥3,056.8 billion from April to August 1971 (during the same period of 1970, the increase amounted to ¥680.3 billion). Prepayments for exports played an important role in the rapid increase, which enabled the city banks to reduce their borrowings from the Bank of Japan by ¥1,035.8 billion (April–August 1970, increase of ¥535.5 billion in borrowings from the Bank of Japan).

 LOANS

Until very recent times, the basic function of Japanese banks was to collect deposits from the public and to channel the funds thus accumulated into industry and commerce. Consumer credit now plays a somewhat larger role than before but business loans remain the most important way in which banks use their funds. Due to the readiness of the Bank of Japan to give credit to the commercial banks, liquidity is of little practical significance in Japanese bank lending. Hence, the financial managers of the country permitted the so-called overloan situation not only to arise but also to continue for long periods without fear of panic or insolvency.

Lending takes four forms: discounts of bills, loans on bills, loans on deeds, and overdrafts. At the end of 1970, bills discounted constituted 33.6 percent of all advances; loans on bills 56.5, percent; loans on deeds, 9.0 percent; and overdrafts, 0.9 percent. Loans on bills serve mainly to provide working capital for enterprises; the bills usually have a maturity of two or three months, but they are often renewed and the loans thus become long-term loans not only for working capital but also for equipment investment. Most of the bills discounted are commercial bills issued against shipment of merchandise; they are mostly short-term (three months) instruments. First-class commercial bills are eligible for rediscount by the Bank of Japan.

The most important factor influencing the Japanese loan system is the capital structure of Japanese enterprises. In the second half of fiscal 1970, the average ratio of net worth to total capital employed of 565 corporations listed on the First Section of the Tokyo Stock Exchange was 18.5 percent. The enormous expansion of the postwar period could not be financed by the funds available through depreciation and retained earnings, and the capital market could not have absorbed the issues of stocks and debentures which would have been necessary to raise sufficient capital. Bank credit, therefore, was the most important means of financing the expansion. This method offered the additional advantage of allowing enterprises to deduct interest payments as business expenses, while dividends have to be paid out of profits after taxes. Although interest rates are high, they remain below the dividend rates many Japanese companies try to maintain as a matter of prestige. Moreover, loans can be scheduled closely to needs.

Very important for the loan structure are the industrial groupings in which certain firms are connected with particular banks. In prewar times, the firms belonging to one of the large *zaibatsu* would rely almost exclusively on financing through the financial institutions of the group, and as a rule the *zaibatsu* banks refrained from central bank credit and allowed none of the government institutions to break into their circle. It was only after the China incident that the greatly increased fund demand of industry forced the *zaibatsu* to finance their enterprises with the help of government funds, borrowing from the Industrial Bank, joint financing with other banks, or offerings to the public. Although the postwar dissolution of the *zaibatsu* was accompanied by a number of drawbacks, it gave the former *zaibatsu* enterprises greater freedom of action. The reconstruction of the old groups has restored many of the old ties, but it could not reestablish the exclusive reliance on intragroup financing. Two factors were decisive for this development: first, the tremendous increase in fund demand and, second, the insufficiency of bank funds. Together with the rehabilitation and modernization of the old industries, the postwar period brought the expansion of many sectors hitherto neglected and the induction of new technologies. Most of the new facilities, such as oil refining and petrochemical plants, required huge funds, and no bank was in a position to finance these projects single-handedly. Moreover, banks compete with one another just as fiercely as enterprises in other sectors, and each bank tries hard to line up as many first-class firms as possible. City banks, therefore, find it difficult to apportion their funds among their numerous important customers, the more so because these funds have not grown proportionally with fund demand.

As a result, although almost all large Japanese enterprises belong to a group clustered around a certain bank, they do business with a number of banks on which they rely for a good deal of their funds. There is no immediate connection between this development and the emergence of the so-called *kombinats*, enterprise groups based on technological integration, but both phenomena point to the disappearance of the old exclusiveness. The *kombinats* are most numerous in the petrochemical industry, and the banks played a leading role in the formation of these enterprise clusters. In the beginning, competition between the various groups led to a costly and foolish duplication of facilities, and the government's attempt to prevent overcapacity restricted installations in many new sectors (synthetic fibers, oil refining, petrochemicals, liquified petroleum gas) to uneconomical small-scale plants. The pressure for a more rational use of funds was an important factor in bringing enterprises of different and often competing groups together on the same site for the utilization of certain raw materials (naphtha, petroleum gas, coke oven gas), but a few *kombinats* have been formed by enterprises belonging exclusively to a certain group (Mitsui at Iwakuni, Mitsubishi at Yokkaichi, etc.).

The second reason that forced enterprises to rely on more than one bank for their funds was the monetary stringency prevailing most of the time after the inflation. There were a few isolated periods of monetary relaxation (in 1955–56, for example, when the banks could repay most of their borrowings from the Bank of Japan), but, as a rule, money remained tight even during the contracting phase of the business cycle. Enterprises often found it more expedient to finance inventories than to curtail production during the periodic recessions, so that bank loans showed no actual decrease.

The banks found it increasingly difficult to satisfy the pressing fund demands of industry out of their own resources. As mentioned above, central bank credit made up the deficiency, and the situation became exceedingly tight in 1961 when, despite the various credit controls, borrowing from the Bank of Japan increased by one and a half times over the preceding year. The urgency of the fund demand may be illustrated by the fact that the city banks used the Eurodollars and pounds secured by their overseas branches to bolster their domestic lending capacity, a practice which prompted the Ministry of Finance to enforce a number of restrictions on the use of these funds and to order banks to keep a minimum liquid balance of 20 percent of specified short-term foreign liabilities.

Net Supply of Funds to Industry

				(In billions of yen)
	Fiscal 1967	Fiscal 1968	Fiscal 1969	Fiscal 1970
Total	7,060.1	7,847.2	10,591.2	13,449.8
Stock issues	355.5	486.2	804.5	1,009.3
Industrial debentures	203.1	273.2	281.2	406.2
Loans & discounts, total	6,501.3	7,087.6	9,505.4	12,038.2
Loans & discounts by private financial institutions	5,838.2	6,273.8	8,589.8	10,985.7
Banking accounts of all banks	2,995.5	3,126.8	4,360.6	5,807.0
Trust accounts of all banks	534.1	588.8	671.3	825.4
Financial institutions for small business	1,359.4	1,406.9	2,073.8	2,139.9
Mutual banks	458.5	505.5	671.9	762.2
Credit associations	526.8	532.4	950.1	908.1
Credit institutions for agriculture, forestry, & fisheries	656.8	687.6	877.8	1,305.0
Insurance companies	292.2	463.6	606.1	908.1
Loans by government financial institutions	559.2	683.9	803.1	944.1
Japan Development Bank	133.7	167.3	177.0	207.4
Export-Import Bank	138.6	142.5	193.4	255.5
Small Business Finance Corporation	91.3	103.0	136.0	147.5
Loans by special accounts	103.9	129.8	112.3	108.4
Foreign funds	58.8	197.6	105.6	99.1

Note: Foreign funds are not included in the total.
Source: Bank of Japan.

Because the individual banks found it impossible to accommodate their customers to the full extent of their requisites, large enterprises were forced to establish working relationships with a number of banks; they have to use these banks for current transactions if they want to rely on them for major loans (the necessity for maintaining compensating balances is another reason). The banks coordinate their lending to large customers although they do not organize formal syndicates for this purpose. But in a reversal of its former policies, Mitsubishi Bank, toward the end of 1969, curtailed lending to nongroup enterprises and compiled a list of enterprises to which no loans would be given. In the beginning of 1970, Sumitomo Bank gave notice to Marubeni-Iida that no new loans would be forthcoming and that out of about ¥20 billion in outstanding loans, ¥6 billion was to be repaid within one year.

The overall result of postwar developments has been a remarkable expansion of the scale of Japanese banking. For the ten-year period from the end of 1951 to the end of 1961, the ratio of increase was 685 percent for deposits, 645 percent for loans and discounts, and 1,078 percent for securities holdings. From 1960 to September 1970, deposits increased 3.8 times, loans 4.1 times, discounts 3.4 times, and securities holdings 3.7 times.

The traditional distinctions between short- and long-term loans, loans for capital investment (usually called equipment loans), and working capital remain important, but they may often be disregarded in practice, Due to the strict supervision of bank lending by the Bank of Japan, loans are often arranged for short terms (up to six months) with the understanding that they will be renewed. Loans officially labeled as working capital may be used for equipment investment. These practices accounted for the phenomenon that loans for equipment investment continued to grow even when equipment investment declined.

The share of the city banks in outstanding loan balances has been slipping in the last ten years, as shown in the following table.

Structure of Loans by Type of Financial Institution

	Share in outstanding loan balances, year-end %			Rate of change %		
	1959	1964	1969	1959–64	1964–69	1959–69
City Banks	37.1	33.7	28.0	−3.4	−5.7	−9.1
Local banks	17.2	16.7	16.9	−0.5	0.2	−0.3
Long-term credit banks	6.9	6.6	6.5	−0.3	−0.1	−0.4
Trust banks	7.1	8.1	8.6	1.0	0.5	1.5
Mutual banks	6.8	7.7	7.9	0.9	0.2	1.1
Credit associations	4.9	6.9	8.1	2.0	1.2	3.2
Credit cooperatives	1.1	1.8	2.2	0.7	0.4	1.1
Agricultural financial institutions	3.6	4.7	5.9	1.1	1.2	2.3
Life insurance companies	3.1	3.7	4.6	0.6	0.9	1.5
Nonlife insurance companies	0.2	0.2	0.3	0.0	0.1	0.1
Government financial institutions	12.0	10.1	10.0	−1.9	0.8	−1.1

Notes: 1. Adjusted for the change in status of Taiyo and Saitama banks.
     2. Trust banks: total of banking and trust accounts with the exception of loan trusts.
Source: The Fuji Times

Only the largest firms can obtain unsecured credit, while some form of collateral is required for most borrowers. Securities (stocks and bonds), mortgages, or the guarantee of a third party constitute the usual forms of collateral but in the sixties the practice of demanding substantial compensating balances as partial collateral became widespread. Complaints over this practice led to investigations by the Fair Trade Commission, and the issue was discussed in the Finance Committee of the House of Representatives. The bankers associations promised to take remedial action and instructed their member banks to reduce obligatory deposits (i.e., which cannot be withdrawn at will) to 20 percent of the deposits of their debtors by May 1965. Although the group relations mentioned above constitute the chief reason why banks prefer to lend to large enterprises, the low credit rating of small firms and the impossibility for them to provide acceptable collateral are also important considerations.

INTEREST RATES

After the First World War, the large banks concluded an agreement concerning the interest rates on call loans and overdrafts and a conventional minimum rate on general loans was established. After World War II, the first agreement was concluded in May 1946 and concerned the minimum rates on loans (fixed at 1.30 *sen* per diem = 4.75 percent per annum) and discounts (1.10 *sen* = 4.02 percent). On July 5, 1947, the Tokyo Bankers Association agreed on a maximum limit of 2.30 *sen* (8.4 percent) for loans and discounts, and the various provincial bank associations followed suit. But the Fair Trade Commission ruled that such an agreement contravened the Antimonopoly Law which had gone into effect just a few days prior to the agreement, on July 1. On October 23, therefore, the agreement was canceled.

The government, however, deemed it inadvisable to leave interest rates to themselves and, in December 1947, the Temporary Money Rates Adjustment Law (*Rinji Kinri Chōsei-hō*) was passed, which imposed state controls on interest rates. The law applies not only to ordinary banks but, with the exception of the financial institutions of the government, to practically all banks. According to this law, the minister of finance entrusts the governor of the Bank of Japan (when the policy board was established, this function was transferred to the board) with determining, altering, and abolishing the maximum interest rates of financial institutions. (This arrangement gives the initiative for all changes to the minister of finance.) The banks are free to fix their interest rates within the limits of the maximum rates. Not subject to regulation under the Temporary Money Rates Adjustment Law are interest rates on loans for longer than one year and short-term loans of less then ¥1 million. The governor of the Bank of Japan has to consult the Money Rates Adjustment Council before taking any action; with the exception of three ex officio members (one bureau chief each from the Ministry of Finance and the Economic Planning Agency and the vice-governor of the Bank of Japan), the fifteen members of the council are appointed by the minister of finance. The interest rates fixed by the policy board are published by the Ministry of Finance. The official discount rate of the Bank of Japan is not subject to the deliberations of the Money Rates Adjustment Council but is fixed by the policy board; in practice, however, since the official discount rate is of basic importance for all money rates, all changes are coordinated.

The first direct link between the official discount rate and the interest rates charged by banks was established in May 1957, when the discount rate for drafts eligible for rediscount by the Bank of Japan was fixed at the same level as the official discount rate. In the preceding year, the Federation of Bankers Associations had voluntarily lowered one part of the interest rates on loans below the maximum rates fixed under the Temporary Money Rates Adjustment Law. (Rates thus lowered are referred to as "voluntary" rates.) On March 2, 1959, another voluntary reduction was carried out in conformity with the lowering, on February 19, 1959, of the official discount rate from 2.00 *sen* (7.3 percent) to 1.90 *sen* (6.935 percent). On that occasion, the standard (prime) rate was introduced. Since the successive reductions of interest rates had narrowed the margins between the various rates so that they did not sufficiently reflect differences of credit rating and the nature of the loans, this occasion was used to rectify the interest structure by lowering only the discount rate for drafts eligible for rediscount by the Bank of Japan and the discount rate for drafts (as well as the interest rate on loans) that, according to the newly established categories, had the same credit rating. Together with widening the spread between these and the other rates, the new arrangement established the usage of changing the standard and other rates in conformity with the changes in the official discount rate.

Interest rates of mutual banks, credit associations, and credit cooperatives are regulated under the organic laws of these institutions. Mutual banks, for example, need the approval of the minister of finance for their rates which, in practice, are fixed in their business instructions. Since their fund costs are high and their risks greater, their interest rates are higher than those of commercial banks.

The interest rates of trust banks on loans and discounts are also subject to regulation under the Temporary Money Rates Adjustment Law; they used to be 2 *rin* higher than those of the city and local banks and have been 0.5 percent higher since April 1970. In June 1955, the Trust Bank Association decided to keep the interest rates based on an agreement of the association (within the limits fixed under the law) 2 *rin* higher than those agreed upon by the Federation of Bankers Associations; the difference was reduced to 1 *rin* in April 1956 and 0.25 percent in September 1969.

Prior to April 1970, the rates of credit associations were 1 *rin* or 0.365 percent higher than the maximum rates fixed for banks under the Temporary Money Rates Adjustment Law; since April 1, 1970, they have been 0.1 percent higher on fixed deposits and 0.25 percent higher on deposits for tax payments and other deposits.

Interest rates charged by insurance companies on loans are likewise subject to the Temporary Money Rates Adjustment Law; they were 2 *rin* higher than those for commercial banks until April 1970 and have been 0.5 percent higher since then. The rates agreed upon by the insurance associations were 2 *rin* higher than those of the Federation of Bankers Associations; the difference was reduced to 0.75 percent in September 1969 and 0.5 percent in November 1970.

Interest paid on deposits by banks, and practically all other private financial institutions, is subject to the maximum limits fixed under the Temporary Money Rates Adjustment Law. The interest rates of mutual banks are the same as those of commercial banks, but those of credit associations and credit cooperatives are 0.25 percent higher. Of great importance for all private financial institutions are the interest rates of the postal savings system, which are based on the Postal Savings Law. They are appreciably higher than the rates of commercial banks in order to encourage popular saving.

A number of detailed rules apply to the calculation of interest in special cases. If time deposits, fixed deposits (which cannot be withdrawn during a specified time), and installment deposits are withdrawn prior to maturity, the rate on ordinary deposits on the day of withdrawal or a lower rate is applied. After maturity, the interest rate on time deposits or fixed deposits is calculated as follows: (1) in case of payment in cash or transfer to other deposits, the interest rate on ordinary deposits on the day of payment or a lower rate is applied for the period from maturity to the day of payment; (2) if the time deposit or fixed deposit is renewed, the interest rate on time or fixed deposits on the day of renewal applies. If deposits at notice are withdrawn during the period for which they have to be left intact (usually ten days), the interest rate on ordinary deposits or a lower rate applies. If deposits for tax payment are withdrawn for other purposes, interest for the time up to withdrawal is calculated on the basis of the interest rate on ordinary deposits or a lower rate.

As adopted in March 1959, the standard rate had two steps: (1) discounts of commercial bills rediscountable with the Bank of Japan and loans collateralized by such bills; (2) discounts of bills of the same credit rating and loans collateralized by such bills. The first step was equal to the official discount rate; the system was part of the low interest policy intended to further economic growth and the reason was that the Bank of Japan supplied the bulk of the "growth currency" through its advances to the city banks.

As a result of the growth of the economy, the industrial structure underwent a considerable change. The position of the electric power companies and the steel manufacturers (considered first-rate enterprises) was no longer so prominent as it had been and the banks applied the highest credit rating to a much smaller percentage of their loans (March 1969, only 2 percent of all loans). The Federation of Bankers Associations wanted to unify the standard rate when the official discount rate was raised in September 1969 but the enterprises that would be affected opposed the plan. The Bank of Japan considered the distinction obsolete; there had been a reason for the preferential treatment of commercial bills in the postwar era, but the reason was no longer valid; there was little difference between discounts of commercial bills and loans collateralized by national bonds. The Bank of Japan abolished the difference between the two last named categories on September 1, 1969, and the Federation of Bankers Associations discontinued the division of the standard rate into two steps on October 31, 1970. Henceforth, the standard rate was 0.25 percent higher than the official discount rate.

In October 1966, the Federation of Bankers Associations announced rules regulating deposits of bank employees (like many other enterprises, the banks run a special deposit system for their own employees). Interest rates on employee deposits up to ¥1 million should not exceed 7.5 percent; and interest rates on installment savings deposits for homebuilding should not exceed 8.5 percent, and payments into such a deposit category should be limited to 15 percent of the monthly salary and 50 percent of the semiannual bonus.

The traditional Japanese way of calculating interest was on a daily basis (*sen* per ¥100). When the Bank of Japan switched to yearly rates, the private banks followed suit. In February 1969, the Federation of Bankers Associations adopted the complete conversion of the interest rate system from daily to yearly rates. Differentials in short-term rates were to be in steps of 0.25 percent and in long-term of 0.1 percent. All years, including leap years, were to be counted as 365 days—actual interest calculation: (capital × number of days × yearly interest rate)÷365; all figures were to be rounded to yen. The new system went into effect for new loans subject to standard interest rates and for export trade bills on

September 8, 1969, and for all other items on November 7. Adaptation to international usage was the main reason for the change.

Effective April 1, 1970, the Ministry of Finance decreed what was described as a "liberalization" of interest rates. Until then, the interest rates on deposits had been divided into ten different categories (by kind and term of deposit); the new regulation distinguished four categories: time deposits, ordinary (demand) deposits, deposits for tax payment, and other deposits. Maximum interest rates were fixed for each of the four categories (without distinguishing between time deposits for three months, six months, and one year), and the banks were free to set their own interest rates within these limits; however, in order to avoid confusion, the Bank of Japan was to fix guidelines. Actually, the ceiling fixed by the Ministry of Finance and the guidelines announced by the Bank of Japan are identical. The banks want to have the Temporary Money Rates Adjustment Law changed so that the ceiling or the guidelines would not set maximum rates but a standard rate that would allow higher or lower rates fixed by each bank within a certain band. (Probably all banks would pay the highest possible rates.)

On April 20, 1970, the interest rate on one-year deposits was raised from 5.5 percent to 5.75 percent, the first change in the interest rates on deposits since April 1961. The main reason for the change was the increase in consumer prices; the rate of increase in the consumer price index for Tokyo has been higher than 5.5 percent in six out of the last ten years (consumer price index for Tokyo, 1965 = 100: 1961, 77.9; 1970, 130.4).

One of the most difficult problems in the postwar era has been the adjustment of the long-term interest structure. Actually, the so-called long-term rates also include medium-term rates, which are not treated as a separate class. (The problem of medium-term credit became acute with the attempts of the city banks to tap medium-term funds by the issuance of certificates of deposit and the introduction of two-year time deposits; both proposals were turned down by the Ministry of Finance.) These rates comprise the interest rates (usually called "dividends") on money trusts and loan trusts, on bonds, and on long-term loans. Some of these rates are actually short-term rates (one-year trusts, one-year discount debentures), while the two-year savings certificates of the postal savings system reach into the medium-term field. The periodic decline in bond prices became an obstacle to the flotation of new bonds, while the rise of the call money rate in times of monetary stringency diverted large funds from the capital market into the money market. Prior to October 1965, short-term interest rates were higher than long-term rates. A major overhaul of long-term rates was carried out in the months of March and April 1970 and another adjustment was decided upon in July 1971.

Japanese interest rates have little effect in regulating fund demand and supply, one of the chief functions interest rates should fulfill. Theoretically, changes in the banks' standard rates should precede changes in the official discount rate rather than follow them, because the standard rate should reflect the actual conditions of the money market. Japanese rates are fixed by monetary policy and therefore related to general economic conditions and not to the day-by-day market situation. Due to the lack of a liberal tradition, Japanese banks are not accustomed to independent action and are not willing to take the risk involved in acting on their own. The artificial controls on interest rates have been at least partly responsible for some of the distortions in Japanese financing: the underdevelopment of the capital market, the excessive reliance on indirect financing, the enormous demand of the city banks for call money, and the tendency of the call money rate to rise above the official discount rate and long-term interest rates.

Despite the very stringent regulation of interest rates, there are a number of differences, particularly in the rates charged by banks on loans. The so-called nonregulated rates are higher because long-term interest rates are higher. The share of long-term loans in the lending of city banks is small, so that their average interest rates are lower than those of the local banks; the prevalence of large loans in the lending of city banks and of smaller loans as well as loans to small enterprises (greater credit risk) in the lending of local banks has the same effect. The possibility of having eligible commercial bills rediscounted by the Bank of Japan keeps the average discount rates well below the average interest rates on loans.

Customarily, the maximum standard interest rate fixed by the Federation of Bankers Associations within the limits set by the Bank of Japan changes with the changes in the official discount rate, but this does not mean that all interest rates change. The new rates apply to new loans, but the lowering of the interest rates charged by banks generally is less than the reduction in the official discount rate. Between October 1970 and June 1971, the official discount rate was reduced by 0.75 percent, but the decline in the average rate on loans was only 0.075 points, 10 percent of the reduction in the official discount rate. This contrasted sharply with a decline of 45 percent in the official discount rate for the period from August 1968 to May 1969 and a ratio of 28 percent between January and September 1965. Two main reasons explain this situation. In 1970 and in the first months of 1971, fund demand remained strong because the effects of the slowdown in the economy were not felt at the same time in all sectors. The second reason was the change in the composition of bank loans; there had been a substantial increase in long-term loans. The share of long-term (over one year) loans in total bank lending at the end of June 1971 was 32.3 percent (city banks 21.6 percent) as against 24.9 percent in September 1970, 29.1 percent in June 1970, and 17.7 percent in September 1965. The "regulated" rates of all banks declined by 0.174 points from October 1970 to June 1971, equivalent to 23.2 percent of the reduction in the official discount rate; for the city banks, the decline was 0.208 points, or 27.7 percent. In August 1971, the average interest rate of city banks dropped to 7.263 percent and that of local banks to 7.766 percent.

The reduction in the official discount rate brings a reduction in the rates the banks can charge on loans, but no lowering of the rates they must pay on deposits. Hence, the profit margin of the banks is put under pressure by a reduction in the official interest rate, and in September 1971, the Federation of Bankers Associations opposed a fifth reduction of the official discount rate because it would bring the official discount rate down to the level of one-year deposits (5 percent). In order to ease the squeeze on their profits, the banks proposed that the interest rates on demand deposits should be lowered (those on time deposits were to remain unchanged), but the Ministry of Finance showed little interest in the proposal. The banks even requested corporate customers to change one-year deposits into three-month deposits so as to lessen the interest burden.

This request is not so strange as it sounds. If an enterprise borrows from a bank, a certain percentage of the loan must be deposited with the bank, and these so-called debtor's deposits may amount to 30 percent or 40 percent of the loan. Hence, the real rate of interest paid on the loan is much higher than the nominal interest rate. If a company borrows ¥100 million at 7.3 percent, it may be asked to deposit ¥40 million in the form of a one-year time deposit (on which it receives 5.75 percent interest) and ¥5 million as a current deposit (no interest). Hence, the real rate of interest is near to 10 percent. Because these deposits are made at the request of the banks, the banks may ask to change them.

Interest Rates on Bank Deposits

Deposit	February 1, 1971	Planned rates
Time deposits		
3 months	4 %	4 %
6 months	5 %	5 %
1 year	5.75 %	5.75 %
18 months	6 %	6 %
Installment deposits	3.9 %	3.9 %
Current deposits	no interest	no interest
Ordinary deposits	2.25 %	2 %
Deposits at notice	2.5 %	2.25 %
Deposits for tax payment	3 %	2.75 %
Other deposits	2.25 %	2 %

Interest Rates on Trusts

(In percent p.a.; parentheses indicate no change)

1. Maximum rates under Temporary Money Rates Adjustment Law

Date of change	Designated money trusts			Loan trusts	
	Over 1 year	2 years & longer	5 years & longer	2 years	5 years
Jan. 1948	4.2	4.4	4.8		
July	4.4	4.6	5.0		
Aug. 1949	4.7	5.5	6.0		
Jan. 1951	5.0	6.0	7.0		
May	5.4	7.0	9.0		
Sept.	6.0	(7.0)	(9.0)		
Apr. 1961	regulation rescinded				

2. Interest rates fixed by banks

Date	Over 1 year	2 years	5 years	2 years	5 years
June 1952				8.8	9.5
Aug. 1955				8.5	9.2
Nov.				7.7	8.4
Mar. 1956		6.8	7.5	7.1	7.8
May		(6.8)	(7.5)	6.6	7.3
Sept.		6.4	7.1	(6.6)	(7.3)
July 1957		(6.4)	(7.1)	7.0	7.8
Sept.		6.8	7.5	(7.0)	(7.8)
Apr. 1961	5.5	6.3	7.07	6.5	7.37
Sept. 1966	(5.5)	6.2	6.98	6.35	7.22
	Over 1 year	2 years	5 years	2 years	5 years
Mar. 1968	(5.5)	(6.2)	7.03	(6.35)	(7.22)
Apr.	(5.5)	(6.2)	(7.03)	(6.35)	7.27
Mar. 1970	(1 year & longer)	6.3	7.23	6.45	7.47
Apr.	5.75	(6.3)	(7.23)	(6.45)	(7.47)

Interest Rates on Bank Deposits

1. Maximum rates under Temporary Money Rates Adjustment Law

(Parentheses indicate no change)

Date of change	Time deposits 3 months	Time deposits 6 months	Time deposits 1 year	Fixed savings	Fixed installment savings	Current deposits	Deposits for tax payments	Ordinary deposits	Deposits at notice	Other deposits
Jan. 1948	3.7% p.a.	4.0% p.a.	4.2% p.a.	Same as time deposits	3.0% p.a.	No interest		0.5 *sen* p.d.	0.6 *sen* p.d.	0.6 *sen* p.d.
July	3.8	4.2	4.4					(0.5)	(0.6)	(0.6)
May 1949	(3.8)	(4.2)	(4.4)	(3.0)	(3.0)		0.7 *sen* p.d.	(0.5)	(0.6)	(0.6)
Aug.	(3.8)	4.4	4.7		(3.0)		(0.7)	(0.5)	(0.6)	(0.6)
Jan. 1951	(3.8)	4.6	5.0		(3.0)		(0.7)	(0.5)	(0.6)	(0.6)
May	(3.8)	4.9	5.4		(3.0)		(0.7)	(0.5)	(0.6)	(0.6)
Sept.	4.0	5.0	6.0		(3.0)		0.8	0.6	0.7	0.7
Oct. 1952	(4.0)	(5.0)	(6.0)		4.0		(0.8)	(0.6)	(0.7)	(0.7)
May 1957	(4.0)	(5.0)	(6.0)		(4.0)		0.9	0.7	0.8	0.8
July	4.3	5.5	(6.0)		(4.0)		(0.9)	(0.7)	(0.8)	(0.8)
Apr. 1961	4.0	5.0	5.5		3.9		0.8	0.6	0.7	0.7
Apr. 1, 1970	Deposits for fixed terms: 5.5% p.a.						3.0%	Other deposits: 2.5% p.a.		
Apr. 20	Deposits for fixed terms: 5.75% p.a.									

2. Maximum rates under guidelines of Bank of Japan

	Deposits for fixed terms — Time deposits 3 months	6 months	1 year	1½ years	Fixed savings	Fixed installment savings	Current deposits	Deposits for tax payments	Ordinary deposits	Deposits at notice	Other deposits
April 1, 1970	4.0	5.0	5.5		Same as time deposits	3.9	No interest	3.0	2.25	2.5	2.25
April 20	(4.0)	(5.0)	5.75			(3.9)		(3.0)	(2.25)	(2.5)	(2.25)
Feb. 1971	(4.0)	(5.0)	(5.75)	6.0		(3.9)		(3.0)	(2.25)	(2.5)	(2.25)

Changes in Principal Interest Rates

I. Interest Rates on Short-Term Loans   (Parentheses indicate no change)

1. Maximum rates on bank loans fixed under the Temporary Money Rates Adjustment Law

(sen p.d. unless otherwise indicated)

Date of change	(1) Discount of commercial bills eligible for re-discount by the BoJ	(2) Discount of & loans on export bills eligible for re-discount by the BoJ	(3) Discount of & loans on export bills not eligible for re-discount by the BoJ	(4) Discount of & loans on import bills	(5) Discount of & loans on "stamp" bills	(6) Discount of & loans on other bills	(7) Over-drafts	(8) Call loans (over-night)
Jan. 1948						2.5	2.7	9.0
July "						2.8	3.0	1.0
Aug. "						(2.8)	(3.0)	1.1
Aug. 1949		2.6				(2.8)	(3.0)	(1.1)
Sept. "		(2.6)				2.7	(3.0)	(1.1)
Feb. 1950		2.4				2.5	2.8	(1.1)
Apr. "	2.3	2.2			2.4	(2.5)	(2.8)	(1.1)
Nov. "	2.2	2.0			(2.4)	(2.5)	(2.8)	(1.1)
Oct. 1952	2.1	1.9			2.3	2.4	2.7	(1.1)
Jan. 1954	(2.1)	(1.9)		1.9	(2.3)	(2.4)	(2.7)	(1.1)
July "	(2.1)	(1.9)	2.1	(1.9)	(2.3)	(2.4)	(2.7)	(1.1)
Aug. "	(2.1)	(1.9)	(2.1)	2.1	(2.3)	(2.4)	(2.7)	(1.1)
May 1957	2.3	(1.9)	(2.1)	2.3	abolished	2.5	2.8	abolished
Apr. 1970	9.5%	9.5%	9.5%	9.5%		9.5%	10.25%	

Notes: 1. From February 1950 to January 1954, import bills were included in (2).
2. Stamp bills were used for financing the production of specially designated commodities and commodity imports; also included in this category were trade bills other than those eligible for rediscount by the Bank of Japan (abolished July 1954), bills certified by public corporations, and agriculture and fishery bills.
3. From February to March 1950, the interest rate was 1 *rin* (0.1 *sen*) higher for loans and discounts under category (6) below ¥5 million, and from April 1950 to March 1970, the interest rate was 1 *rin* higher for loans and discounts under categories (1), (5), and (6) below ¥3 million.

I. Interest Rates on Short-Term Loans (cont.)   (Parentheses indicate no change)

2. Maximum "voluntary" rates agreed upon by the Federation of Bankers Associations
(*sen* p.d. unless otherwise indicated)

Date of change	(1) Discount of commercial bills eligible for re-discount by the BoJ	(2) Discount of & loans on bills of similar credit rating	(3) Discount of & loans on export bills eligible for re-discount by the BoJ	(4) Discount of & loans on export bills not eligible for re-discount by the BoJ	(5) Discount of & loans on import bills	(6) Discount of & loans on other bills	(7) Over-drafts	(8) Call loans
June 1955						2.3		
May 1957						abolished		
June "			1.8	2.0				
July "			(1.8)	(2.0)				3.5
June 1958	2.1		(1.8)	(2.0)	2.1	2.3	2.7	2.6
Sept. "	2.0		1.7	1.9	2.0	2.2	2.6	2.5
Mar. 1959	1.9	1.95	1.6	1.8	(2.0)	(2.2)	2.5	2.4
July "	(1.9)	(1.95)	(1.6)	(1.8)	(2.0)	(2.2)	(2.5)	2.3
Dec. "	2.0	2.05	1.7	1.9	2.1	2.3	2.6	(2.3)
Aug. 1960	1.9	1.95	1.6	1.8	2.0	2.2	2.5	(2.3)
Jan. 1961	1.8	1.85	1.5	1.7	1.9	2.1	2.4	2.2
July "	1.9	1.95	1.4	1.6	2.0	2.2	2.5	2.3
Oct. "	2.0	2.05	(1.4)	(1.6)	2.1	2.3	2.6	2.4
Oct. 1962	1.9	1.95	(1.4)	(1.6)	2.0	2.2	2.5	2.3
Nov. "	1.8	1.85	(1.4)	(1.6)	1.9	2.1	2.4	2.2
Mar. 1963	1.7	1.75	1.3	1.5	1.8	(2.1)	(2.4)	2.1
Apr. "	(1.7)	(1.75)	(1.3)	(1.5)	(1.8)	2.0	2.3	(2.1)
Apr. "	1.6	1.65	(1.3)	(1.5)	1.7	(2.0)	(2.3)	2.0
Mar. 1964	1.8	1.85	(1.3)	(1.5)	1.9	2.2	2.5	2.2
Jan. 1965	1.7	1.75	(1.3)	(1.5)	1.8	(2.2)	(2.3)	2.1
Apr. "	1.6	1.65	(1.3)	(1.5)	1.7	2.1	2.4	2.0
June "	1.5	1.55	(1.3)	(1.5)	(1.7)	2.0	2.3	(2.0)
Sept. 1967	1.6	1.65	(1.3)	(1.5)	regulation discontinued	2.1	2.4	regulation discontinued
Jan. 1968	1.7	1.75	(1.3)	(1.5)		2.2	2.5	
Aug. "	1.6	1.65	(1.3)	(1.5)		2.1	2.4	
Sept. "	6.25%	6.50%	5.00%	5.50%		8.25%	9.25%	

Changes in Principal Interest Rates (cont.)

I. Interest Rates on Short-Term Loans (cont.) (Parentheses indicate no change)

2. Maximum "voluntary" rates agreed upon by the Federation of Bankers Associations (cont.)

Date of change	(Previous chart) (1) (2)	Discount of & loans on export usance bills in yen eligible for rediscount by the Bank of Japan	Discount of & loans on bills for preexport financing — Eligible for rediscount by the Bank of Japan	— Others	Loans secured by other bills or discounts thereof	Over-drafts
May 15, 1970	(6.25% 6.50%)	5.75%	6.00%	6.25%	8.25%	9.25%
	Discount of & loans on commercial bills eligible for rediscount by the Bank of Japan & bills of the same credit rating					
Oct. 31, 1970	6.25%	5.75%	6.00%	6.25%	8.00%	9.00%
Jan. 23, 1971	6.00%	(5.75%)	(6.00%)	(6.25%)	7.75%	8.75%
May 11, 1971	5.75%	(5.75%)	(6.00%)	(6.25%)	7.50%	8.50%
July 31, 1971	5.50%	(5.75%)	(6.00%)	6.00%	7.25%	8.25%
			Discount of & loans on bills for preexport financing eligible for collateral by the Bank of Japan			
Aug. 10, 1971	5.50%	6.00%	6.00%		7.25%	8.25%

Notes: 1. Starting with March 1959, (1) and (2) were standard interest rates.
2. Until Jan. 1968, the interest rates on category (1), and until Sept. 1969, interest rates on categories (2) and (6) were 1 *rin* higher for loans and discounts below ¥3 million.
3. Rates under (8) were initially arranged by agreement among banks; the rate was changed to 3.0 *sen* in Oct. 1957 and 2.8 *sen* in April 1958.
4. A higher rate (+0.5%) is charged on category (6) for bills of a lower credit rating.

3. Other rates

Date of change	Maximum interest rates on loans of mutual banks	Maximum interest rates on loans of trust banks
June 1951	3.5 *sen* p.d.	4.5 *sen* p.d.
Dec. 1958	(3.5 *sen* p.d.)	3.5 *sen* p.d.
July 1961	(3.5 *sen* p.d.)	3.0 *sen* p.d.
Mar. 1970	12.75% p.a.	11.00% p.a.

Changes in Principal Interest Rates (cont.)

(In percent p.a.; in parentheses: *sen* p.d.; brackets indicate no change)

II. Interest Rates on Long-Term Loans

Date of change	Long-term credit banks (prime rate)	Trust banks (loan trust funds: prime rate)	Cent. Bank for Commercial & Industrial Coops. (general loans, loans to coops.) (1-2 years)	(over 2 years)	Cent. Coop. B. of Ag. & For. (loans to other than ag. credit insts.)	Life insurance companies (prime rate)	Japan Development Bank (basic rate)	Small Enterprises Finance Corporation (basic rate)	People's Finance Corporation (basic rate)	Hokkaido & Tohoku Dev. Finance Corporation (basic rate)
May 1951	11.32(3.1)	n.a.	n.a.		n.a.	n.a.			n.a.	
Sept. 1953	[11.32(3.1)]									
Oct.	[11.32(3.1)]						10.0	10.0	9.96	
Jan. 1955	[11.32(3.1)]	11.32(3.1)				11.32(3.1)	[10.0]	[10.0]	[9.96]	
July	10.95(3.0)	10.95(3.0)				10.95(3.0)	[10.0]	[10.0]	[9.96]	
Aug.	[10.95(3.0)]	[10.95(3.0)]				[10.95(3.0)]	9.0	9.6	9.6	
Nov.	10.22(2.8)	10.22(2.8)	12.0	12.5		10.22(2.8)	[9.0]	[9.6]	[9.6]	
Jan. 1956	9.49(2.6)	9.49(2.6)	[12.0]	[12.5]		[10.22(2.8)]	[9.0]	[9.6]	[9.6]	
Feb.	[9.49(2.6)]	[9.49(2.6)]	[12.0]	[12.5]		9.49(2.6)	[9.0]	[9.6]	[9.6]	
Apr.	9.13(2.5)	[9.49(2.6)]	11.0	11.5		9.13(2.5)	[9.0]	[9.6]	[9.6]	
May	[9.13(2.5)]	9.13(2.5)	[11.0]	[11.5]		[9.13(2.5)]	[9.0]	[9.6]	[9.6]	
July	[9.13(2.5)]	[9.13(2.5)]	[11.0]	[11.5]		[9.13(2.5)]	[9.0]	[9.6]	[9.6]	9.0
Apr. 1957	[9.13(2.5)]	[9.13(2.5)]	10.0	10.5		[9.13(2.5)]	[9.0]	[9.6]	[9.6]	[9.0]
May	[9.13(2.5)]	[9.13(2.5)]	[10.0]	[10.5]	11.5	9.49(2.6)	[9.0]	[9.6]	[9.6]	[9.0]
Aug.	[9.13(2.5)]	[9.13(2.5)]	[10.0]	[10.5]	[11.5]	9.59(2.6)	[9.0]	[9.6]	[9.6]	[9.0]
Sept.	[9.13(2.5)]	[9.13(2.5)]	10.5	11.0	[11.5]	9.49(2.6)	[9.0]	[9.6]	[9.6]	[9.0]
July 1958	[9.13(2.5)]	[9.13(2.5)]	10.0	10.5	[11.5]	9.13(2.5)	[9.0]	[9.6]	[9.6]	[9.0]
Apr. 1959	[9.13(2.5)]	[9.13(2.5)]	9.7	9.9	11.0	[9.13(2.5)]	[9.0]	[9.6]	[9.6]	[9.0]
Jan. 1961	[9.13(2.5)]	[9.13(2.5)]	9.4	9.6	[11.0]	[9.13(2.5)]	[9.0]	9.3	9.3	[9.0]
Feb.	[9.13(2.5)]	[9.13(2.5)]	[9.4]	[9.6]	10.22(2.8)	8.7	[9.0]	9.0	9.0	[9.0]
Apr.	8.7	8.72(2.39)	[9.4]	[9.6]	[10.22(2.8)]	[8.7]	8.7	[9.0]	[9.0]	8.7
Apr. 1962	[8.7]	[8.72(2.39)]	9.3	9.5	[10.22(2.8)]	[8.7]	[8.7]	[9.0]	[9.0]	[8.7]
June 1964	[8.7]	[8.72(2.39)]	9.0	9.2	[10.22(2.8)]	[8.7]	[8.7]	[9.0]	[9.0]	[8.7]
Sept. 1965	[8.7]	[8.72(2.39)]	8.9		[10.22(2.8)]		[8.7]	8.7	8.7	[8.7]
Jan. 1966	8.4	8.43(2.31)	[8.9]		9.86(2.7)	8.4	8.4	[8.7]	[8.7]	8.4
Apr.	[8.4]	[8.43(2.31)]	8.6		[9.86(2.7)]	[8.4]	[8.4]	8.4	8.4	[8.4]
Oct.	8.2	8.21(2.25)	[8.6]		9.8	8.2	8.2	[8.4]	[8.4]	8.2
Jan. 1967	[8.2]	[8.21(2.25)]	8.4		[9.8]	[8.2]	[8.2]	8.2	8.2	[8.2]
Sept. 1969	[8.2]	8.2	[8.4]		[9.8]		[8.2]	[8.2]	[8.2]	[8.2]
Apr. 1970	8.5	8.5	[8.4]		[9.8]	8.5	[8.2]	[8.2]	[8.2]	[8.2]
Aug.	[8.5]	[8.5]	8.6			[8.5]	[8.2]	[8.2]	[8.2]	[8.2]
Sept.	[8.5]	[8.5]	[8.6]			[8.5]	8.5	[8.2]	[8.2]	8.3
Sept. 1971	[8.5]	[8.5]	8.2-8.4	8.4-8.6		[8.5]	[8.5]	[8.2]	[8.2]	[8.3]

Interest Rates on Postal Savings

(In percent p.a.; parentheses indicate no change)

Date of change	Ordinary deposits	Installment savings	Savings certificates				Fixed savings (1 year)
			under 1 year	1 year & over	1½ years & over	2 years & over	
Dec. 1947	2.76	3.12	Under 2 years		3.00	3.10	
June 1949	(2.76)	(3.12)	2.90	3.00	(3.00)	(3.10)	
June 1951	(2.76)	(3.12)	3.00	3.15	(3.00)	3.30	
Apr. 1952	3.96	4.20	4.20	4.80	5.40	6.00	
Dec. 1957	(3.96)	(4.20)	4.50	5.00	5.50	(6.00)	
Apr. 1961	3.60	4.08	4.20	4.70	5.00	5.50	
Oct. 1961	(3.60)	(4.08)	(4.20)	(4.70)	(5.00)	(5.50)	5.00
Apr. 1970	(3.60)	(4.08)	4.25	4.75	5.25	5.75	5.25

Notes: 1. Prior to April 1957, savings certificates were issued also for periods over 3 years, over 4 years, and over 5 years.

2. Prior to April 1970, savings certificates were issued for periods under 1 year, over 1 year, over 1½ years, and over 2 years.

Interest Rates of Central Bank for Commercial and Industrial Cooperatives (general loans; loans to cooperatives)

(Parentheses indicate no change)

Date of change	Maximum interest rates reported to minister of international trade and industry and minister of finance	Interest rates fixed by bank president
Aug. 1948	3.10 *sen* p.d.	
Mar. 1949	(3.10)	3.00 *sen* p.d.
Sept. 1957	3.00	(3.00)
Mar. 1956	2.75	(3.00)
Apr. "	(2.75)	2.75
Mar. 1957	2.65	(2.75)
Apr. "	(2.65)	2.65
Sept. "	2.70	2.70
July 1958	2.65	2.65
Apr. 1959	2.60	2.60
Jan. 1961	2.50	2.50
May 1963	(2.50)	2.45
June 1964	(2.50)	2.40
Sept. 1965	(2.50)	2.35
Apr. 1966	(2.50)	2.30
Jan. 1967	(2.50)	2.25
Dec. 1969	(2.50)	8.20% p.a.
Mar. 1970	9.00% p.a.	(8.20% p.a.)
Aug. "	(9.00% p.a.)	8.30% p.a.

Average Interest Rates on Loans and Discounts of Mutual Loan and Savings Banks
January–June 1971

(In percent p.a.)

	Loans	Discounts
1971, January	8.492	8.228
February	8.489	8.225
March	8.483	8.226
April	8.491	8.222
May	8.495	8.211
June	8.491	8.195

Source: National Association of Mutual Loan and Savings Banks.

Interest Rates of Central Cooperative Bank of
Agriculture and Forestry
(loans on bills to other than agricultural credit institutions)

Date of change	Maximum interest rates based on Temporary Money Rates Adjustment Law	Maximum interest rates reported to minister of agriculture & minister of finance
Jan. 1948	2 *rin* higher than bank loans	n.a.
Oct. 1952	1 *rin* higher than bank loans	
May 1957		2.7 *sen* p.d.
Apr. 1959		2.6
Feb. 1961		2.5
Aug. 1961		2.6
Sept. 1969		9.25% p.a.
Apr. 1970	0.25% higher than bank loans	

Average Interest Rates on Bank Loans

(As of end of December of year indicated)

	sen p.d.				% p.a.	
	1965	1966	1967	1968	1969	1970
All banks	.2.084	2.019	2.013	2.021	7.605	7.693
City banks	1.982	1.912	1.918	1.930	7.369	7.455
Local banks	2.155	2.099	2.083	2.089	7.789	7.852
Trust banks	2.062	1.946	1.904	1.926	7.308	7.491
Long-term credit banks	2.408	2.335	2.291	2.280	8.320	8.438
Mutual banks	2.431	2.353	2.303	2.317	8.365	8.418

Note: Mutual banks are not included in all banks.
Source: Bank of Japan.

Average Regulated and Nonregulated Interest Rates on Bank Lending

(In percent p.a.)

	Regulated rates					Nonregulated rates				
	All banks	City banks	Local banks	Trust banks	Long-term credit banks	All banks	City banks	Local banks	Trust banks	Long-term credit banks
1969 September	6.939	6.807	7.296	6.740	6.350	8.150	7.944	8.137	7.705	8.440
December	7.245	7.132	7.542	7.084	6.705	8.234	8.087	8.235	7.812	8.449
1970 March	7.270	7.156	7.571	7.108	6.717	8.248	8.107	8.253	7.860	8.449
June	7.290	7.177	7.588	7.125	6.763	8.296	8.170	8.267	8.011	8.500
September	7.317	7.205	7.604	7.139	6.781	8.383	8.197	8.286	8.092	8.536
December	7.305	7.183	7.606	7.121	6.756	8.346	8.235	8.295	8.131	8.554
1971 March	7.237	7.104	7.568	6.062	6.627	8.355	8.235	8.289	8.236	8.582
June	7.143	6.997	7.510	6.953	6.523	8.429	8.383	8.383	8.383	8.604

Note: Regulated rates: subject to the Temporary Money Rates Adjustment Law.
Nonregulated rates: not subject to the Temporary Money Rates Adjustment Law; lending for longer than one year or short-term lending of less than ¥1 million.

Average Interest Rates on Loans and Discounts of All Banks
January–June 1971

(In percent p.a.)

	All banks		City banks		Local banks		Trust banks		Long-term credit banks	
	Loans	Discounts	Loans	Discounts	Loans	Discounts	Loans	Discounts	Loans	Discounts
1971, January	7.757	7.516	7.468	7.391	7.864	7.813	7.688	7.149	8.468	6.859
February	7.754	7.492	7.459	7.362	7.859	7.803	7.713	7.123	8.474	6.820
March	7.747	7.457	7.444	7.319	7.852	7.784	7.762	7.083	8.488	6.751
April	7.746	7.430	7.434	7.289	7.857	7.765	7.799	7.053	8.491	6.724
May	7.734	7.400	7.415	7.255	7.853	7.741	7.789	7.019	8.497	6.688
June	7.719	7.359	7.390	7.208	7.846	7.710	7.784	6.980	8.504	6.635

Source: Bank of Japan.

Composition of Bank Lending by Interest Rate

(Percentage of outstanding loan balances as of end of year indicated)

Interest rate *sen* p.d.	1965	1966	1967	1968	Interest rate % p.a.	1969	1970
Outstanding loan balance (¥ bill.)	19,020.1	21,831.0	25,071.6	28,737.2		33,472.0	39,089.9
below 1.5	1.15	1.24	1.33	1.41	below 5.5	1.56	0.68
1.5–1.6	5.32	6.48	0.65	0.55	5.5–6.0	2.22	1.38
1.6–1.7	5.91	7.48	12.10	11.90	6.0–6.25	2.15	2.93
1.7–1.8	6.58	9.19	10.13	9.55	6.25–6.5	2.00	5.39
1.8–1.9	6.94	8.81	9.65	9.22	6.5–6.75	10.40	6.39
1.9–2.0	7.60	8.83	8.86	8.54	6.75–7.0	7.63	6.85
2.0–2.1	10.67	10.52	9.97	8.78	7.0–7.25	6.77	6.82
2.1–2.2	11.93	10.40	10.09	10.06	7.25–7.5	8.00	7.38
2.2–2.3	8.89	8.73	11.33	13.95	7.5–7.75	7.15	6.95
2.3–2.4	10.95	11.21	12.21	12.73	7.75–8.0	5.84	6.14
2.4–2.5	9.36	7.63	6.91	7.15	8.0–8.25	11.80	10.21
2.5–2.6	6.85	4.90	3.89	3.68	8.25–8.5	12.58	10.53
2.6–2.7	4.53	2.67	1.57	1.30	8.5–8.75	7.51	12.46
over 2.7	3.32	1.91	1.31	1.18	8.75–9.0	6.07	5.77
					9.0–9.25	4.06	4.97
					9.25–9.5	2.08	2.23
					9.5–10.0	1.30	1.88
					over 10.0	0.88	1.03

Notes: 1. Loans of all banks.

2. Not included are overdrafts, loans to financial institutions, bank acceptances, and notes held by the Bank of Japan for repurchase.

Source: Bank of Japan.

Discounts at Standard Interest Rate

	Standard interest rate %	Percentage of outstanding balance of discounts discounted at standard interest rate
October 1959, monetary relaxation	7.12	22.5
July 1960, credit restraints	7.48	26.2
June 1961, monetary relaxation	6.75	22.3
January 1962, credit restraints	7.5	23.6
February 1964, monetary relaxation	6.02	8.2
October 1964, credit restraints	6.75	10.9
June 1967, monetary relaxation	5.66	9.3
February 1968, credit restraints	6.39	14.8
June 1969, monetary relaxation	6.02	12.8

Notes: 1. The periods selected represent the time at which the standard interest rate was most widely used during the respective period of monetary relaxation or credit restraints.

2. The standard interest rate has been converted into percentage p.a. from the customary *sen* p.d. rates.

Source: Nihon Keizai Shimbun.

**Ratio of Decline in Interest Rates on Loans to Reduction
in Official Discount Rate**

Date of reduction in official discount rate (beginning of monetary relaxation) (A)	Extent of reduction in official discount rate eight months after A % (B)	Extent of reduction in interest rate on all bank loans eight months after A % (C)	C/B %
June 18, 1958	1.46	0.453	31.0
August 24, 1960	0.73	0.394	54.0
October 27, 1962	1.46	0.588	40.3
January 9, 1965	1.095	0.420	38.4
August 7, 1968	0.365	0.208	57.0
October 28, 1970	0.75	0.183	24.4

Source: Nihon Keizai Shimbun.

4 PORTFOLIO INVESTMENT

Although investment in securities by Japanese banks is not inconsiderable, it seems of less importance both as an investment method and as a source of income. In prewar times, the *zaibatsu* banks owned a considerable portion of the shares of enterprises belonging to or affiliated with the respective concerns, but they had to divest themselves of their holdings, and the Antimonopoly Law, enacted in 1947, prohibited financial institutions with more than ¥5 million in assets from acquiring more than 5 percent of the stock of any other company. The revision of the Antimonopoly Law in 1953 raised the limit of allowed stock ownership to 10 percent and empowered the Fair Trade Commission to authorize larger percentages in individual cases. As a matter of fact, most banks own blocks of shares in the enterprises belonging to their group. In some cases, the banks took part in the foundation of these enterprises or acquired the shares in connection with other financial transactions, but, as a rule, stock ownership serves to emphasize the group relationship rather than to establish it. Nevertheless, it sometimes happens that the acquisition of large blocks of stock accompanies changes in group allegiance but both may have been previously arranged together. Since the largest part of the stock portfolio of banks is made up of shares of related enterprises, the yield of these shares is of no consequence in their selection. On the other hand, because their stock portfolios consist mainly of this type of stocks, no bank will even consider the liquidation of its stock portfolio as a means of increasing loanable funds.

While the Antimonopoly Law limits the stock ownership of individual banks, there is no restriction on the ownership of financial institutions as a group, and financial institutions have become the leading stockholders in many, if not most, major Japanese enterprises. Japanese managers regard stockholding by financial institutions as a stabilizing factor and consider individual ownership as volatile. Hence, in releasing the stocks bought up by the emergency organs created in 1963 and 1964, the companies tried to persuade banks or insurance companies to take over their shares.

Generally speaking, the concentration of stock ownership in financial institutions has been growing. This applies especially to the stocks of large enterprises, while the shares of small firms are usually held by their parent companies.

The situation is completely different for bonds. Banks are the most important buyers of certain bond issues, particularly bank debentures. Government bonds and government-guaranteed bonds are eligible for the open market operations of the Bank of Japan; the Bank of Japan may add first-rate commercial paper held by the banks, financial debentures, debentures issued by the electric power companies, and bonds of local public bodies sold by public subscription to the securities eligible for open market operations. Banks sometimes agree to take over a certain portion of the issues of financial debentures on the understanding that the issuing bank (one of the long-term credit banks) will give a corresponding loan to one of its clients.

5 AUTOMATION

In the beginning of the fifties, Japanese banks began to change from disconnected and partial mechanization of banking operations to a systematic and integrated reorganization. Prior to 1955, banks used calculating machines, electric calculators, accounting machines (for ordinary deposits and checking accounts), and coin counting machines. Microfilm was used on a limited scale. In the second phase of automation (1955–1960), punch card systems were adopted for the calculation of salaries and dividends and the compilation of statistics. Banks began to install medium-sized computers in 1959 and 1960; they were first used for off-line operations. In a related development, banks improved the telecommunication facilities connecting their branches with the head office and built nationwide teletype systems. The city banks then moved on to on-line, real-time systems. Mitsui Bank began to operate an on-line system for ordinary deposits in May 1965 and Fuji Bank in February 1967. In July 1967, Sumitomo Bank started to use the on-line system for deposits, loans, and domestic remittances, and, since then, all leading banks have adopted the on-line system. Of 7,933 all-purpose computers (value ￥738.6 billion) installed at the end of September 1970 in Japan, 620 units (value ￥102.0 billion) were installed in financial institutions. As of March 1971, the banks were using 7,900 on-line terminals (out of a total of 14,000). The teller terminals are usually connected with the main computers through branch controllers, which are fitted with a magnetic core memory so that they can function as buffers and lessen the load on the computers; they can also be used for batch processing. The main computers are located in a special computer center (or centers, e.g., one center for eastern Japan and another for western Japan). The ledger now takes the form of a computer memory. Lamps on the indicator panel of the terminal notify the operator of errors, insufficient funds, or accounts for which loss or theft of the passbook or similar contingencies have been reported; in such cases, the machine locks automatically until corrective action is taken. The system makes it possible to have customers deposit or withdraw money at any branch office (this had been tried before but only in a limited way) and allows the almost instantaneous remittance of funds. Information concerning customers or business activities is readily available and provides the basis for a comprehensive management information system.

The most fundamental reason for automation is the reduction in operating costs, in particular, personnel costs; another reason is the reliability and efficiency of the operations.

The Financial System Research Council undertook a study to evaluate the economies achieved by the adoption of a real-time, on-line system. For this study, the council divided the city banks into two groups, the larger banks with funds exceeding ¥2 trillion, over 200 branches, and 15,000 employees and the smaller banks with funds of ¥700 billion, 150 branches, and 7,000 employees. The council's calculations showed that the investment in an on-line system would start to pay off in the third year for the first group and in the fourth for the second group. A summary of the calculations for the first group is given below.

Profitability of Adoption of On-Line System

Year of operation	1st	2nd	3rd	4th	5th	6th	Total
Saving in personnel & office expenses							
Saving in personnel							
Number of persons	960	1,200	1,800	1,872	1,947	2,025	
¥ million (A)	2,109	2,591	3,784	4,199	4,676	5,233	22,595
Increase in expenditures necessitated by investment							
¥ million (B)	1,957	2,616	2,683	1,982	1,512	1,139	11,889
Increase or decrease in operating profit by increase or decrease of expenditures							
¥ million (C)	−220	−296	−231	25	318	670	266
Net loss or saving (A−B+C)							
¥ million	−68	−321	870	2,242	3,485	4,764	10,972
% of operating expenses	−0.4	−1.8	4.5	10.5	14.9	18.5	

The local banks installed a data processing system that permits the automatic transfer of remittances between all branches of the member banks. The Federation of Bankers Associations decided to extend the system to all commercial banks (including the Central Bank for Commercial and Industrial Cooperatives) so that remittances between the sixty-seven hundred offices of the eighty-six banks will becom pletely automatic by 1973. The processing center will be installed in an annex of the Nippon Telegraph and Telephone Corporation; the costs of installing the system are estimated at ¥30 billion, and yearly operating costs at ¥3 billion. A further application of the system is the installation of auto-matic cash dispensers ("autoteller service"). The first Japanese cash dispenser was developed by Tateishi Electric and installed in the Shinjuku branch (Tokyo) and Umeda branch (Osaka) of Sumitomo Bank; it uses a plastic card and a dial cipher. Mitsubishi Bank uses a magnetized card which contains the customer's bank code, account number, and the maximum amount the customer can withdraw; the machine holds up to ¥11 million in cash. The machine developed by Fuji Bank is to be linked with the computerized on-line deposit system; withdrawals are possible up to a maximum of ¥539,000 in any combination of ¥10,000 and ¥1,000 bills. At present, all eleven automatic cash dispensers installed in Japan are off-line machines, but on-line machines may be used in the future.

6 OPERATING METHODS

In October 1966, the Federation of Bankers Associations adopted common standards of bank financing, commonly referred to as the financing rule, which the Ministry of Finance expected to stop the overheating of the economy. The marginal ratio of deposits to loans (i.e., the ratio of the increase in deposits to the increase in loans) was to be reduced from 100 percent to 90 percent; each bank was to report the actual ratio each quarter to the secretariat of the bank presidents' conference (until then, only the changes in the ratios had to be reported semiannually). For each industrial sector in which the adjustment of equipment investment presented difficulties, a committee was to be organized, which was to include representatives of the respective industry, the financial institutions, and, if required, of MITI and the Japan Development Bank.

In September 1967, the Banking Bureau of the Ministry of Finance issued instructions on accounting to the effect that all banks should follow uniform standards of reporting. The bureau noted that it had found large differences in the profits as stated in the reports of the banks to the Ministry of Finance and as stated in their tax returns. Henceforth, the accrual method should be used for both income and expenses; bad loans were to be written off as soon as collection became doubtful. For the valuation of listed stocks, the low-price method should be followed; the valuation of movables should be based on the Tax Law and for immovables, the depreciation charges should not exceed 160 percent of the standard depreciation of the Tax Law. The reserve for bad debts was to remain within eighteen-thousandths of the outstanding loan balance at the end of the term; the reserve for price fluctuations was to be based on the assets standards of the Tax Law and both reserves were to be made continuous. The reserve for retirement allowances had to be equal to 100 percent of the benefits payable under the rules for voluntary retirement.

As indicated by the bureau, the banks were reluctant to disclose their true profits, all the more so because, until fiscal 1970, the Ministry of Finance had pegged their dividend rate at 9 percent per annum. (For the April–September 1970 term, the leading banks increased their dividend rate to 14 percent per annum.) For the first time since 1954, profits of the city banks showed a decline in the settlement for the April–September 1966 term, and, since then, the profit situation has been less bright; but compared with other enterprises the Japanese banks are rather profitable. In addition to the Bank of Japan (which traditionally used to be Japan's top corporate moneymaker), eight banks were among the thirty enterprises with the highest profits for the April–September 1970 term.

In this term, income from advances (discounts, loans) accounted for 74.3 percent of the operating profits of ordinary banks, and income from securities (interest, dividends), 13.4 percent. Interest paid on deposits constituted 52.1 percent of all operating expenditures; interest paid on borrowed funds made up 17.3 percent of the operating expenses of the city banks (see page 150).

In the October 1970–March 1971 term, operating income of the city banks increased by 6.9 percent, operating profits by 13.2 percent, and net profits by 12.7 percent. It was the twelfth consecutive term for which the city banks had been able to report higher profits (see page 150).

Total profits of the sixty-one local banks for the October 1970–March 1971 term amounted to ¥66.6 billion, an increase of 5 percent over the preceding term. It was the lowest rate of

Revenues and Expenditures of Ordinary Banks
April–September 1970

(In billions of yen)

	City banks	Local banks	Total
Operating income	1,074	520	1,594
Income from loans	765	411	1,176
Income from securities	139	74	213
Other income	170	35	205
Operating expenses	910	396	1,306
Interest paid on deposits	431	249	680
Interest paid on borrowed funds	56	2	58
Interest paid on call money	106	1	107
Administrative & general expenses (personnel, materials)	216	123	339
Other expenses	101	21	122
Operating profit	164	125	289
Extraordinary profit or loss	−12	—	−12
Net profit for the term before taxes	152	125	277
Corporation tax	66	62	128
Net profit for the term	86	63	149

Operating Income of City Banks
October 1970–March 1971

	Operating income ¥ million	Operating profit ¥ million	Net profit ¥ million	Dividend rate % p.a. Actual	Dividend rate % p.a. Potential
Fuji Bank	125,250	22,317	12,722	12	13.38
Sumitomo Bank	121,817	22,578	13,397	12	14.48
Mitsubishi Bank	120,874	20,857	11,738	12	13.13
Sanwa Bank	120,440	17,338	10,109	12	12.58
Tokai Bank	87,624	12,118	6,571	12	10.25
Mitsui Bank	82,435	11,759	6,379	10	10.53
Tokyo Bank	81,485	6,291	3,242	10	11.92
Dai-Ichi Bank	80,420	9,937	6,044	10	10.44
Nippon Kangyo Bank	78,909	11,724	6,426	10	11.11
Daiwa Bank	57,384	6,714	3,441	10	9.06
Kyowa Bank	54,898	8,282	4,747	10	9.29
Kobe Bank	46,915	6,361	3,084	10	8.73
Saitama Bank	39,106	7,525	3,905	10	11.04
Taiyo Bank	33,427	4,781	2,402	12	8.61
Hokkaido Takushoku Bank	32,931	4,392	2,397	10	8.42

Notes: 1. Potential dividend rate: highest rate under the rules laid down by the Ministry of Finance on the basis of business results.
2. The dividend rates of Tokai Bank and Taiyo Bank include a special dividend of 2 percent.

Cost and Profit Ratios of Banks

(In percent)

1. City Banks

Business year	Interest paid on deposits & bonds	Operating costs Total	Operating costs Personnel costs	Operating costs Cost of materials	Taxes	Cost of deposits & bonds (a)	Income from loans & call loans Total	Income from loans & call loans Loans	Income from loans & call loans Call loans	Income from securities	Income from loans, call loans & securities (b)	Profit margin (b)−(a)	Interest paid on borrowed money	Cost of deposits, bonds & borrowed money (c)	Profit margin (b)−(c)
1965 I	4.022	2.532	1.122	0.828	0.582	6.554	7.550	7.553	5.476	7.016	7.457	0.903	6.918	6.642	0.815
II	3.994	2.503	1.029	0.810	0.664	6.497	7.233	7.235	5.221	7.045	7.199	0.702	6.028	6.395	0.804
1966 I	4.106	2.529	1.125	0.773	0.631	6.635	7.131	7.132	5.688	7.148	7.134	0.499	5.961	6.503	0.631
II	4.121	2.395	1.011	0.757	0.627	6.516	6.994	6.995	6.077	7.234	7.037	0.521	5.997	6.417	0.620
1967 I	4.116	2.386	1.060	0.738	0.588	6.502	6.965	6.966	5.368	7.110	6.991	0.489	6.209	6.449	0.542
II	4.116	2.295	1.033	0.730	0.532	6.411	7.116	7.116	6.330	7.155	7.123	0.712	6.991	6.514	0.609
II	4.116	2.093	1.130	0.831	0.132	6.209	7.116	7.116	6.330	7.155	7.123	0.914	6.991	6.348	0.775
1968 I	4.138	2.140	1.177	0.816	0.147	6.278	7.337	7.337	6.780	7.163	7.306	1.028	7.297	6.451	0.855
II	4.112	2.042	1.121	0.801	0.120	6.154	7.162	7.162	7.206	7.176	7.165	1.011	6.821	6.264	0.901
1969 I	4.164	2.088	1.163	0.789	0.136	6.252	7.215	7.214	8.462	7.230	7.217	0.965	6.897	6.355	0.862
II	4.128	2.041	1.119	0.809	0.113	6.169	7.454	7.453	8.565	7.270	7.424	1.255	7.425	6.389	1.035
1970 I	4.189	2.082	1.164	0.796	0.122	6.271	7.600	7.600	8.415	7.283	7.550	1.279	7.471	6.478	1.072

2. Local Banks

Business year	Interest paid on deposits & bonds	Operating costs Total	Operating costs Personnel costs	Operating costs Cost of materials	Taxes	Cost of deposits & bonds (a)	Income from loans & call loans Total	Income from loans & call loans Loans	Income from loans & call loans Call loans	Income from securities	Income from loans, call loans & securities (b)	Profit margin (b)−(a)	Interest paid on borrowed money	Cost of deposits, bonds & borrowed money (c)	Profit margin (b)−(c)
1965 I	4.091	2.910	1.292	0.669	0.949	7.001	8.070	8.097	7.624	7.155	7.928	0.927	7.161	7.002	0.926
II	4.084	2.749	1.215	0.663	0.871	6.833	7.853	7.898	6.879	7.036	7.720	0.887	6.171	6.827	0.893
1966 I	4.121	2.656	1.254	0.624	0.778	6.777	7.803	7.860	6.730	6.979	7.662	0.885	6.145	6.772	0.890
II	4.104	2.696	1.197	0.634	0.865	6.800	7.688	7.715	6.892	7.348	7.630	0.830	6.325	6.793	0.836
1967 I	4.111	2.656	1.216	0.584	0.856	6.767	7.673	7.701	7.060	7.214	7.597	0.830	6.480	6.763	0.834
II	4.089	2.681	1.173	0.587	0.921	6.770	7.747	7.738	7.978	7.210	7.661	0.891	7.204	6.776	0.885
II	4.089	2.073	1.266	0.736	0.071	6.162	7.747	7.738	7.978	7.210	7.661	1.499	7.204	6.175	1.486
1968 I	4.103	2.153	1.345	0.716	0.092	6.256	7.893	7.852	8.713	7.094	7.764	1.508	7.256	6.264	1.500
II	4.076	1.986	1.210	0.703	0.073	6.062	7.724	7.710	8.115	7.210	7.641	1.579	6.876	6.072	1.569
1969 I	4.106	2.060	1.304	0.668	0.088	6.166	7.772	7.754	8.141	7.143	7.670	1.504	6.324	6.167	1.503
II	4.057	1.931	1.183	0.679	0.069	5.988	7.879	7.850	8.780	7.323	7.791	1.803	7.290	5.997	1.794
1970 I	4.130	2.026	1.297	0.646	0.083	6.156	7.993	7.952	8.928	7.440	7.907	1.751	7.015	6.162	1.745

Notes: 1. Ratios on basis of balance sheet data; ratio of operating costs to total loans and discounts.
2. I=first half of business year (April–September), II=latter half of business year (October–March).
3. Some accounting rules were changed effective 1968; data in the sections for the latter half of 1967 have been recalculated on the basis of the new rules for the sake of comparison. These sections are indicated by the addition of a line.

increase since the latter half of fiscal 1967, when the rate of increase was 4.9 percent. Deposits held by local banks increased by 8.3 percent (as against 9.3 percent in the previous term) and loan balances were 9.9 percent higher (as against a gain of 11.1 percent in the preceding term).

In 1959, the Ministry of Finance had pegged the yearly dividend rate of city banks, trust banks, and long-term credit banks at 9 percent, and that of local and mutual banks and credit associations at 10 percent. On February 20, 1970, the ministry announced new standards: (1) as a rule, the dividend rate of the financial institutions mentioned above will be 10 percent per annum; (2) if a bank wishes to pay a higher dividend rate, it must justify this rate on the basis of the ratio of net worth to total capital employed and the ratios of operating costs and profits to capital; (3) the maximum dividend rate will be 15 percent.

In recent years, there have been a number of cases of fraud and embezzlement by bank employees. The most spectacular incident involved an assistant branch manager of the Fuji Bank who "lent" ¥1.9 billion against fictitious foreign drafts. In September 1970, the Federation of Bankers Associations urged its member banks to improve surveillance and to use restraint in the development of new business (e.g., no exaggerated campaigns to increase deposits for the celebration of anniversaries or by fixing goals—¥2 trillion in deposits— which induce bank employees to resort to undesirable tactics; in such campaigns, bank employees are often assigned quotas, i.e., a certain number of new accounts or a certain amount of new deposits which they should procure). The federation also renewed its warning against the tendency to demand larger compensating balances in times of credit restraints. As a means of preventing fraudulent manipulations, the banks plan to have all employees take an uninterrupted one-week vacation a year. In this way the work of all employees will temporarily be taken over by a substitute; this will facilitate the discovery of irregularities. All employees are entitled to at least twenty days of paid vacations, but many employees, particularly supervisory personnel, rarely take off more than a couple of days at a time.

7 CLEARING SYSTEM

The first clearing house was established in Osaka in 1879; the Tokyo Clearing House was organized in 1891 by ten banks belonging to the Tokyo Bankers' Club. It became independent of this organization in 1900 but was absorbed by the Bank of Japan during the Second World War. In 1946, the clearing business was again transferred to the Tokyo Bankers' Association which operates the Tokyo Clearing House. Clearing houses have been established in numerous cities throughout the country (number at the end of 1970: 121). In 1903, the National Clearing House Federation was founded. The Federation of Bankers Associations had adopted uniform forms for promissory notes (the banks were to sell these forms only to depositors and supervise the conditions stated in the drafts) and transfer by check, but new forms became necessary for the adoption of the magnetic ink character recognition system. The federation established a committee on the unification of clearing rules; as a long-range goal, an integrated on-line, real-time system linking all banks has been under consideration.

The various clearing houses operate more or less in the same way. Weekday business hours of the Tokyo Clearing House are from 10 A.M. to 11 A.M. (Saturdays from 9.30 A.M.

to 10.30 A.M.), and banks are supposed to settle their balances through transfers on their current accounts with the Bank of Japan by 1 P.M. (Saturdays 11.30 A.M.) of the same day. The clearing houses try to eliminate dishonored bills by suspending their drawers from all transactions involving bills and checks with all member banks for a period of three years.

In July 1965, the Central Bank for Commercial and Industrial Cooperatives was admitted to the clearing system which, until then, had been restricted to commercial banks.

Clearing of Checks and Bills
(Number in thousands; value in billions of yen)

	1965	1966	1967	1968	1969	1970
Bank clearing						
All clearing houses						
number	302,975	327,352	346,690	368,011	379,264	394,166
value	151,097.0	164,670.2	188,592.2	225,298.9	262,032.4	318,980.5
Tokyo Clearing House						
number	117,474	126,216	132,197	139,264	142,812	147,144
value	76,294.2	82,698.0	94,845.1	115,296.7	134,525.9	164,198.3
Osaka Clearing House						
number	59,201	62,445	64,977	67,945	68,769	71,114
value	30,568.6	33,268.9	37,896.1	44,361.0	51,635.6	63,439.3
Dishonored checks & bills						
All clearing houses						
number	4,077	3,830	3,746	3,752	3,274	3,407
value	557.4	554.0	643.5	737.1	621.8	787.8
Tokyo Clearing House						
number	1,304	1,251	1,315	1,206	1,031	1,054
value	215.6	220.3	264.6	290.3	252.5	343.9
Osaka Clearing House						
number	856	857	839	762	581	573
value	125.9	132.2	146.9	160.5	116.5	141.6
Suspension of transactions						
All clearing houses						
number	197	138	98	102	95	97
value	2,854.9	2,655.9	2,868.8	3,205.1	2,737.9	3,208.9
Tokyo Clearing House						
number	46	32	26	23	19	18
value	1,031.4	1,028.7	1,121.7	1,151.0	1,042.5	1,182.3
Osaka Clearing House						
number	30	21	15	12	9	8
value	550.3	490.6	513.5	517.1	411.7	454.3

Source: Tokyo Clearing House

MERGERS

Most of the city banks have a nationwide network of branches. Immediately after the war, the government encouraged the establishment of new branch offices although through most of the fifties and sixties it allowed virtually no new branches. As a result, branch offices were clustered together in old locations with a shrinking population but were relatively sparse in the new suburban population centers. Strategically located branches are indispensable for Japanese city banks since their basic mode of operation consists in collecting deposits from a large number of customers and lending the funds thus accumulated to relatively few borrowers. This is the reason why the diversification in individual financial assets created a serious problem for city banks.

Prewar government policy had encouraged bank mergers in order to reduce the number of local banks. At various times, the slogan "One prefecture, one bank" reflected the actual trend, and although it was never literally enforced, it was not far from realization at the end of the war. With a few exceptions, the branches of local banks are located exclusively in the prefecture in which their head office is located. The number of local banks has hardly changed in the last twenty years, and the nationwide networks of the city banks and the proliferation of credit associations and similar institutions have put local banks in a less enviable position. On the other hand, their liquidity has generally been higher than that of the city banks and, together with mutual loan and savings banks and credit associations, they supply the city banks with call money.

In June 1966, the Financial System Research Council formed a special committee to study the credit problems of small enterprises. After reviewing the situation, the council, in October 1967, submitted the following recommendations: (1) the presently existing credit institutions for small enterprises, viz., mutual loan and savings banks, credit associations, and credit cooperatives, are to be retained, but the regulations concerning the respective business spheres and minimum capital requirements should be revised to conform to the changes in the economy; (2) mergers between institutions of different kinds should be allowed and institutions should be able to change from one category to another.

The council proposed the following differentiation between the credit institutions for small enterprises: (1) mutual banks should be joint-stock companies; the mutual banks in Tokyo and other large cities should have a minimum capital of ¥300 million, those in other areas one of ¥200 million; they should accept deposits from and give loans to enterprises with a capital of less than ¥200 million and less than 300 employees; (2) credit associations in the twenty-three wards of Tokyo and other designated cities should have a capital of ¥100 million, those in other locations ¥50 million; they should be empowered to accept deposits from nonmembers as well as members, but loans should be restricted to members, except for small loans (the total of these loans not to exceed 20 percent of all loans); eligible as members should be enterprises in the district apportioned to the particular credit association with a capital of less than ¥100 million and less than 300 employees, inhabitants of the district, and people working there; (3) credit cooperatives in the twenty-three wards of Tokyo and designated cities should have a mininum capital of ¥20 million, in other areas ¥10 million; in addition to the acceptance of deposits from and loans to members, their business should be expanded to include domestic remittances, safekeeping of securities, and loans as agents of the National Federation of Credit Associations; a grace period of three years should be given for bringing the capital to the new minimum. Apart from the new loan limits and capital requirements, these proposals left the institutions almost entirely unchanged.

In February 1968, two laws were passed which closely followed the recommendations of the council. The first law, called Law Concerning Mergers and Changes of Status of Financial Institutions, opened the way to mergers of financial institutions organized under different laws and permitted existing financial institutions to change into a different kind of financial institution. The second law adapted the organic laws of mutual banks, credit associations, and credit cooperatives to the new system.

In November 1967, the Financial System Research Council formed a special committee which was to study a possible reorganization of financial institutions. In July 1968, the council published a report entitled "Problems Concerning Interest Rates and Size of Financial Institutions," which made the following recommendations: (1) in order to increase competition among financial institutions, interest rates controlled by the government should be liberalized; (2) the official discount rate should be fixed in percent per annum, and interest rates on deposits should be changed in accord with the changes in the official discount rate; (3) interest rates on loans should be reduced; banks should put less emphasis on unnecessary frills (referred to in Japan as "service") and help their customers in a more substantial way; (4) in view of domestic and international developments, the size of banks should be increased to match the increase in size of other enterprises. To this effect, mergers and tie-ups among banks should be encouraged.

The council cited the following reasons for a complete reorganization of the banking system: (1) the present financial system was organized in the beginning of the fifties, and in the intervening years some features were found ill adapted to the actual situation originally, special institutions were created for long-term financing and others to provide credit to small enterprises, but gradually the boundaries have become blurred—the various institutions now look very much alike: their activities overlap and they compete in about the same fields (this situation was referred to as "homogenization" or "assimilation" of financial institutions; what was meant was the extension of long-term credit by commercial banks and the development of the mutual banks and the larger credit associations which have become ordinary banks in everything but name); (2) chronic fund dislocation—fund demand concentrates on the city banks whose funds are usually insufficient to satisfy the needs of their large corporate customers, whereas other financial institutions dispose of ample funds but lack suitable opportunities for their efficient placement (fiscal operations are largely responsible for this dislocation; the government collects most of its taxes from urban areas but pays out a large part of its funds in rural districts); (3) with the exception of some city banks, the expansion of financial institutions has been lagging behind the growth pace of the economy making them small-scale, high-cost operations; (4) financial institutions must offer new facilities and services to meet the needs of the times, but this kind of adaptation is obstructed by the obsolete demarcation of business lines.

For the solution of these problems, the council made the following proposals: (1) the parceling out of business fields to the various financial institutions by administrative regulation seems inappropriate; the excessive administrative guidance of financial institutions should be discontinued and administrative controls limited to the absolutely necessary; (2) all banks should be given freedom to compete under the same conditions so as to stimulate cost reduction; (3) for this purpose, interest rates must be liberalized and the interest mechanism allowed to function properly; (4) protection of depositors should not be effected by the administrative protection of financial institutions but by deposit insurance or similar measures; (5) concentration by mergers or tie-ups should be promoted so as to achieve thoroughgoing economies of scale. Such mergers should not be restricted to financial institutions of the same kind, but mergers between different kinds of financial institutions should also be taken into consideration.

In this connection, two developments deserve attention, namely, the increase in bank mergers and the increase in branch offices. A few bank mergers had been approved before the recent change in policy. In 1963, Dai-Ichi Bank took over Asahi Bank; in the following year, Sumitomo Bank absorbed Kawachi Bank, and, in 1968, Mitsui Bank merged with Toto Bank. These mergers, in which city banks swallowed up local banks with which they already had close connections, did not change the banking structure, but the merger of Dai-Ichi Bank and Mitsubishi Bank, which was announced on January 1, 1969, would have greatly upset the balance among the city banks. Due to opposition from inside Dai-Ichi Bank as well as on the part of the bank's clients and shareholders (above all, the enterprises of the Furukawa and Kawasaki groups), the merger plan had to be abandoned.

In his address to the New Year meeting of the Federation of Bankers Associations, on January 7, 1964, the then minister of finance, Kakuei Tanaka, indicated a change in government policy by stating that he considered bank mergers desirable.

The Ministry of Finance laid down the following guidelines for bank mergers: (1) mergers of local banks will be approved only if they do not create regional economic problems and if they strengthen the business of the merging banks; (2) mergers of city banks will be approved if they eliminate excessive competition, but no single bank should become too strong and the merger should have no adverse repercussions on the economy; (3) mergers between city banks and local banks are inadvisable because they will lead to excessive competition among city banks, but mergers between banks with traditional connections will be approved if the local bank cannot expect further growth.

Until 1969, the Ministry of Finance allowed merging banks to retain only one branch in a certain location; other branches in the same neighborhood had to be closed down. Following the mergers of Dai-Ichi Bank with Asahi Bank and Sumitomo with Kawachi, ten branches had to be shut down. In 1967, the ministry began to allow the transfer of branches, i.e., banks could obtain permission to relocate branches from unprofitable locations to more promising neighborhoods. In 1967 and 1968, the number of branches which banks were allowed to relocate was restricted to two for each bank, but, in February 1969, the

Ministry of Finance announced a change in its rules. No restrictions were put on the number of branches which could be moved, but the ratio of the book value of the real estate used for business purposes to the net worth of the bank must be lower than the standard established by the Ministry of Finance for each kind of bank (the basic ratio for ordinary, longterm credit, and trust banks is 50 percent; for mutual banks, 70 percent).

The city banks were particularly anxious to set up branches in the new residential developments, which are often far from the old population centers. In fiscal 1969, the Ministry of Finance authorized the opening of fourteen new branches and the relocation of thirty-two, and, in fiscal 1970, consent was granted to set up thirteen new branches and relocate forty-seven. For fiscal 1971, the total of new branch offices to be opened by city banks rose to eighty-one, including the relocation of sixty-eight branches.

A large number of the new branch offices was established in the prefectures adjacent to Tokyo where housing developments have contributed to a substantial increase in population (according to the national census of 1970, the rate of increase in population from 1965 to 1970 was 4.9 percent for Tokyo, 28.2 percent for Saitama Prefecture, 24.6 percent for Chiba Prefecture, and 23.5 percent for Kanagawa Prefecture; the nationwide average was 5.5 percent). In fiscal 1969, eight new bank branches were opened in Saitama, four in Chiba, and fifteen in Kanagawa; in fiscal 1970, the number of new foundations was thirteen in Saitama, eight in Chiba, and fifteen in Kanagawa. For fiscal 1971, the Ministry of Finance approved the establishment of fifty new branches in these prefectures: twenty in Saitama, seventeen in Chiba, and thirteen in Kanagawa.

The mergers among financial institutions for small enterprises made possible by the law mentioned above have increased: in fiscal 1968, there were eight mergers between institutions belonging to the same category and three between those belonging to different categories; the figures were nine and eight in fiscal 1969. From 1968 to May 1971, thirty-eight mergers took place between institutions of the same kind and sixteen mergers between institutions belonging to different categories; three banks became a different kind of financial institution. As a result of these changes, the number of mutual banks, credit associations, and credit cooperatives decreased from 1,134 in May 1968 to 1,093 at the beginning of 1971. The first mutual bank to take advantage of the new law was the Japan Mutual Bank (the largest mutual bank, with a capital of ¥10 billion and operating funds—as of May 1968—of ¥550,953 million), which became an ordinary bank, changed its name to Taiyo Bank, and was given the status of a city bank—as far as funds were concerned, it placed between twelfth-ranked Kobe Bank (¥656,323 million) and thirteenth-ranked Hokkaido Takushoku Bank (¥506,357 million); it had been second to the largest local bank, Saitama Bank (¥630,330 million), which became a city bank in April 1969. In June 1969, the National Federation of Credit Cooperatives (with which 534 credit cooperatives are affiliated) merged with the Tokyo Federation of Credit Cooperatives.

On March 11, 1971, Dai-Ichi Bank and Nippon Kangyo Bank announced that they would merge on October 1, 1971. The merger was formally approved by the stockholders' meetings of the two banks on May 28, 1971. Dai-Ichi Bank increased its capital by ¥3 billion to bring it up to Kangyo's capital (¥27 billion) so that the merger could be effected on a fifty-fifty basis. Dai-Ichi Bank ranked sixth among the city banks in terms of deposits, while Kangyo ranked eighth. The new bank, called Dai-Ichi Kangyo Bank, is Japan's largest with ¥4,056.4 billion in deposits, ¥3,547.0 billion in outstanding loans (September

30, 1971), 278 offices, and 23,200 employees. About sixty offices were located in the same locations and the Ministry of Finance had already allowed the new bank to relocate 15–20 offices in fiscal 1971. The merger may start a new phase in the reorganization of Japanese banking. The Fair Trade Commission approved the merger because the combined share of the two banks in the business of the fifteen city banks (as measured by deposit balances) was 13.8 percent, and their share in the deposit balances of all banks 8.3 percent.

A series of mergers may accompany the reversion of Okinawa. At present, there are two enterprises in each category of financial institutions, the Bank of Ryukyu (capital $1.5 million, 51 percent owned by the U.S. Civil Administration) and the Bank of Okinawa (capital $1.3 million); Nanyo Mutual Bank (capital $837,500) and Chuo Mutual Bank (capital $700,000); Ryukyu Fire & Marine Insurance Co. (capital $180,000) and Kyowa Fire & Marine Insurance Co. (capital $300,000); Ryukyu Life Insurance Co. and Okinawa Life Insurance Co. Moreover, the Bank of America N.T. & S.A. and the American Express International Banking Corporation have branch offices in Okinawa, and the Central Trust of China has a representative office (see Fuji Bank Bulletin, March 1970, on the financial institutions on Okinawa). The Ministry of Finance has decided that, through administrative guidance, the number of institutions will be reduced to one in each category.

2 COOPERATION

The abortive fusion of Mitsubishi Bank and Dai-Ichi Bank temporarily worked as a deterrent to merger attempts between city banks, but there has been a growing tendency toward tie-ups, which allow closer cooperation without the difficulties involved in a merger. Mitsubishi Bank, Tokai Bank, and Nippon Kangyo Bank concluded an agreement for the settlement of domestic remittances in the form of an open correspondence contract, and a similar arrangement was worked out among Sanwa, Mitsui, and Kyowa banks. Saitama Bank and Chubu Mutual Bank agreed on cooperation covering domestic remittances and "business guidance"; in January 1969, Saitama Bank, Yokohama Bank, and Chiba Bank concluded a cooperation agreement under which deposits with each of the banks are accepted and can be withdrawn at all offices of the three banks. In another move to tap the resources of the smaller banks, Sumitomo Bank in March 1971 asked the approval of the Ministry of Finance and the Bank of Japan for a plan under which Sumitomo Bank would guarantee loans by local and mutual banks to its clients (e.g., Sumitomo Metal Industries and Asahi Chemical). The loans would generally have a maturity of three years and an interest rate of 9 percent.

A limited form of cooperation has developed in connection with the payment of salaries and wages into bank accounts. The city banks try to persuade their corporate customers to replace the cash payment of wages by automatic transfer to an account opened for each employee with the bank. To make the system sufficiently convenient, the city banks want to supplement their own network of branches by concluding cooperation agreements with other banks. The first group of this kind was formed by Fuji Bank, which signed up Taiyo, Suruga, and Chiba Kogyo banks. Another group comprises Sumitomo, Kyowa, and Taiyo banks, and a third one the banks cooperating with the Japan Credit Bureau, i.e., Sanwa, Mitsui, Kyowa, Daiwa, and Kobe banks. In the development of joint deposit cards, the Heiwa Mutual Bank played a leading role because it was the only bank with late business hours (its offices stay open until 7 P.M.—other banks close at 3 P.M.). Heiwa had tie-ups with Mitsui, Dai-Ichi, Sumitomo, Sanwa, Nippon Kangyo, Tokai, Kobe, Daiwa, Yokohama, Fuji, and Tokyo banks, creating a network of 840–860 offices in the Tokyo Metropolitan area. In January 1970, Sanwa Bank concluded agreements with twenty banks for the mutual payment of time deposits; agreements for the mutual payments of deposits exist between the sixty-one member banks of the National Association of Local Banks and the seventy-two mutual banks belonging to the National Association of Mutual Banks. Fuji Bank reached an agreement with the Central Cooperative Bank of Agriculture and Forestry under which the computer centers of the two institutions will be linked by telex and their on-line systems used for domestic remittances. Settlement will be made on the basis of an open correspondence contract. The tie-up is important because it will prepare the way for linking the Central Cooperative Bank of Agriculture and Forestry with the nationwide on-line real-time system planned by the Federation of Bankers Associations for 1973 which will connect all city, local, and trust banks. It may also indicate the intention of the Central Cooperative Bank to seek a revision of its status (removal of restrictions on its operations) when the present law on which it is based expires (October 30, 1973).

Another field in which interbank cooperation has made significant progress is credit cards. The credit card business started in Japan in 1960, when, under a franchise agreement with American Diners International and the cooperation of Fuji Bank, the Japan Diners Club was established. In addition to credit cards issued independently by a few banks (Mitsubishi's Diamond Credit, Sumitomo Credit Service, and the Million Card Service of Tokai Bank), there are two large systems: Union Credit, a credit card company established jointly by Fuji, Mitsubishi, Dai-Ichi, Kangyo, Taiyo, and Saitama banks in June 1968, and the Japan Credit Bureau supported by eight banks (Sanwa, Mitsui, Kyowa, Daiwa, Kobe, Hokkaido Takushoku, Yokohama, and Chiba). Membership in the Union Credit system supposes an acceptable credit rating, but cards are also issued to wives, and to children over eighteen years of age. Purchases at stores honoring the credit cards (department stores, specialty shops, hotels, restaurants, bars, clubs, golf courses, gas stations) are limited to ¥100,000 per purchase and ¥300,000 per month; cash loans can be obtained at all offices of the member banks up to ¥50,000 a month (a fee of 2 percent is charged on these loans). Accounts are closed on the tenth of each month and settled on the fifth of the following month by debiting the account of the member with one of the member banks.

Another development which led to interbank cooperation was the introduction of bank-guaranteed checks, first used by Dai-Ichi Bank in April 1969 under the name Bancard Check, and later taken up by Kofuku Mutual Bank (Kofuku Guarantee Check) and Nippon Kangyo Bank (Kangin Guarantee Check). Agreements for mutual acceptance cover Dai-Ichi Bancard Check and Kangin Guarantee Check, Kangin Guarantee Check and Tokai Million Card, Kangin Guarantee Check and Kofuku Guarantee Check, and Dai-Ichi Bancard Check and Kofuku Guarantee Check. The banks connected with Union Credit issue a uniform guarantee check. On its part, the Japan Credit Bureau group offered personal loans in the form of overdrafts. Eligible are employees of the companies listed on the stock exchanges (both sections) and independent proprietors of similar credit rating; loans are limited to one-fourth of annual income and are given in six amounts (from ¥100,000 to ¥500,000); the interest rate is 9.25 percent per annum.

International credit cards are issued by the Japan Diners Club, the Japan Credit Bureau (in cooperation with American Express), Diamond Credit (Mitsubishi Bank and American Interbank Card Association), Sumitomo Credit Service (under a tie-up with Bank of America, Barclays Bank, and the Royal Bank of Canada), and Nippon Shimpan (under an agreement with the Interbank Card Association and Euro-Card).

The six banks making up the Union Credit group (Fuji, Mitsubishi, Dai-Ichi, Kangyo, Taiyo, and Saitama) submitted a proposal to the Ministry of Finance calling for a joint system of mortgage bonds. The Japan Credit Bureau group (Sanwa, Mitsui, Kobe, Toyo Trust & Banking, and Mitsui Trust & Banking), together with Tokai and Kyowa banks are considering a similar arrangement.

3. DIVERSIFICATION

In recent years, the banks have shown great eagerness in branching out into peripheral business lines. The credit card business, leasing, consulting, information, computer services, and the travel agency business have been the favorite fields chosen by the banks for diversification. The banks consider their participation in leasing as a substitute for financing equipment investment and, like credit cards, an adaptation of banking to modern conditions. Information began to be stressed with the introduction of computers, and the organization of "think tanks" became a fad, just as the formation of atomic energy groups had been the fashionable thing to do in the fifties. The restrictions on the use of the public telephone, telegraph, and teleprinter network prevent a general information and data processing service and until September 1, 1971, even leased circuits (rented on a long-term or temporary basis) could be used "jointly" only by "two or more persons jointly conducting the same business or two or more persons who find it necessary to communicate with each other by reason of their closely connected business" (Article 66 of the Public Telecommunications Law). Banks, for example, could use leased lines for data processing between their computer centers and their branch offices, but not for data processing for other banks, for customers, or for central data processing by the clearing house. A wishy-washy amendment, a compromise between the business organizations pressing for the free use of the public communications system and the control-hungry bureaucracy, made the joint use of leased circuits by certain groups possible (production, sales and inventory control, arrangements for the handling of deposits between financial institutions, seat reservations by travel agencies). But the use of general circuits for data processing remains prohibited (the restrictions are scheduled to be lifted on September 1, 1972). The amendment, as originally drafted by the Telecommunications Ministry, required specific approval of each application and all terminal equipment; the cabinet had sense enough to change this requirement to "automatic" approval if certain standards are met but not enough sense to put the entire field of communications on a business basis (what Nippon Telegraph and Telephone Corporation was meant to do but never did).

The banks have begun to offer computer services in order to find something to do for their unused computer capacity. In 1967, Sanwa Bank reorganized its Business Control Department into a separate company called Toyo Computer Service and in a similar way, Japan Hypothec Bank set up Fugin Keisan Center. In 1971, Toyo Computer Service was transformed into Toyo Information System. In October 1967, the Mitsui group founded Computer Systems Service; in November 1970, when the capital of the company was increased, its name was changed to Mitsui Information Development. In December of the same year, Nippon Kangyo Bank established the Kangin Management Center, which combines management consulting with computer services. Japan Information Service was set up by Sumitomo Bank in February 1969.

The year 1970 saw the foundation of a number of enterprises by bank groups. Mitsubishi merged three organizations: the well-known Mitsubishi Economic Research Institute, the Mitsubishi Atomic Industry General Computation Center, and Technico Economic Information into the Mitsubishi General Research Institute. In July, Mitsubishi Bank and five other companies set up the Diamond Computer Service. Together with fifty-two companies, Fuji Bank established Fuyo Information Center in May 1970; the company undertakes computations and information processing and develops software. Further foundations were: General System Research Institute (Daiwa Bank group and Kozo Keikaku Kenkyusho, July 1970), Central Systems (Tokai Bank, July 1970), Showa Computer Service (Kyowa Bank and three other firms, February 1971), Saigin Computer Service (Saitama Bank, July 1971), Sumitomo Business Consulting (March 1971), and Century Research Center (C. Itoh & Co. with the Dai-Ichi Kangyo Bank group).

Closely connected with their activities in the field of information are the banks' efforts in consulting. The banks engaged in management consulting on a limited scale for the benefit of their customers, particularly small enterprises, but with the growing complexity of business management a number of specialized companies were founded for these services. In May 1970, a group of banks (Industrial, Taiyo, and Saitama) set up the consulting firm, Japan Management Systems. In July of the same year, Fuji Bank established a joint venture for management consulting with First National City Bank called Fuji National City Consulting, in which two subsidiaries of the principals, Nihonbashi Kogyo Real Estate and City Coop Consultants, also participated.

Effective October 1, 1971, Fuji National City Consulting absorbed the marketing consulting firm Coral (Japan). In addition to Kangin Management Center mentioned above, the Mitsui group organized Mitsui Consultants Co., which undertakes industrial and development consulting.

4 THE NEW BANKING SYSTEM

The reorganization of Japan's banking system is far from over. No decision has been reached on the basic problems of the kind of credit which should be available and the type of credit institutions which should provide it. The postwar system was based on the distinction between commercial banking (short-term deposits, short-term loans) and long-term banking, but long-term banking took the form of long-term loans and not of emission banking. The long-term credit institutions can raise only a small portion of the funds they need directly (mainly the loan trusts of the trust banks), while most of their funds are derived from the short-term credit institutions. Moreover, under the Securities Transaction Law, which restricts underwriting to securities companies (except underwriting of government-guaranteed debentures, local bonds, and industrial mortgage bonds), banks are virtually excluded from the emission business. The counterpart of the prevalence of indirect financing is the so-called underdevelopment of the capital market.

Japan's adherence to the principle of commercial banking goes back to the times of the great panics (1920 and 1927). Its relevance in the era of managed currencies and anticyclical policies and under a system of readily available central bank credit is rather doubtful. The Ministry of Finance, the Financial Structure Research Council, the committee on the reorganization of financial institutions (usually called the Iwasa committee) of the Japan Economic Research Institute, and the various banking organizations have discussed numerous particular aspects of the actual situation without coming to grips with the real problem (the respect for the status quo prevents everybody from calling a spade a spade).

In September 1968, the Financial System Research Council set up a special committee on private financial institutions, which, in June 1970, submitted the following recommendations: (1) strengthen the function of interest rates for economic adjustment and consider linking the interest rate to the official discount rate; (2) improve the efficiency of the monetary system by promoting mergers and tie-ups between financial institutions; (3) strengthen the foreign exchange system in view of the internationalization of the economy; (4) establish a system of deposit insurance.

One of the problems discussed in the report was the supply of medium-term (one to five years) credit. Medium-term financing had not been considered in the original organization of the banking system but had become important because many enterprises relied on medium-term loans for their equipment investment. As mentioned above, ordinary banks, mutual banks, and credit associations supplied these funds by the periodical renewal of short-term loans called *tanki no korogashi* ("rolling over of short-term credit"). In order to develop medium-term financing, the city banks wanted to introduce time deposits with a maturity of two years and an interest rate of 6.25 percent, the issuance of certificates of deposits, and the revision of Article 65 of the Securities Transaction Law restricting underwriting to securities companies. The city banks hoped that, through these new forms of deposits and the so-called department-store banking, they could arrest the downtrend in their shares in deposits and loans. The trust banks (which feared the impact on their loan trusts) opposed the first two demands and the securities companies balked at the extension of underwriting to the banks. The presidents of the four large securities companies sent a letter to the finance minister, Takeo Fukuda, urging him not to touch Article 65, "the lifeline of the securities companies." The committee of the Financial Structure Research Council was divided on the desirability of medium-term credit; many of the members feared an adverse repercussion on the bond market and the fund sources of the long-term credit banks. Certificates of deposits were deemed inconsistent with the actual conditions of the money market. The practical result of the discussions was the introduction of time deposits with a maturity of eighteen months and an interest rate of 6 percent.

A survey carried out by the Ministry of Finance showed that between 11 percent and 38 percent of all loans given by ordinary banks were for terms between one and five years. The committee found that there was little relation between the length of credit and the interest rates charged and came to the conclusion that the long-term credit market was too expensive, too stereotyped, and too little adapted to the real needs of the economy. It was critical of the system of agency loans practiced by the long-term credit institutions (which do not have enough branches and entrust their business to other banks as agents), which negates the proper function of long-term credit institutions. In addition to providing funds to industry, these institutions should also supply a larger part of "social capital" and finance housing, urban renewal, and regional development.

A point which was often stressed in the discussions was that there should be more real competition between financial institutions (although the committee, like the Ministry of Finance, deplored the "excessive" competition of the banks for deposits), that financial institutions should act on their own responsibility and not just obey the orders of the Ministry of Finance, and that interest rates should be allowed to exercise their proper function of regulating the fund supply. Actually, competition is restricted by official regulations not only of such basic conditions as interest rates and number of offices but also by restrictions on the kind of promotion banks can undertake (e.g., newspaper ads cannot exceed the size of 15 × 4 inches and the value of gifts to customers must remain below ¥50). As a preliminary step to relaxing administrative control over banking, a deposit insurance system went into effect on July 1, 1971. The committee proposed that a single system should include banks, mutual banks, credit associations, and credit cooperatives; that individual deposits should be covered up to ¥1 million; and that a uniform premium rate should be adopted. The draft prepared by the Ministry of Finance foresaw the establishment of a special corporation with a capital of ¥450 million, contributed in equal shares (¥150 million) by the government, the Bank of Japan, and the private financial institutions. Membership is obligatory for city, local, and mutual banks, credit associations, and credit cooperatives. The vice-governor of the Bank of Japan is chairman of the board of trustees and also chairman of the management committee, which includes eight representatives of private financial institutions. The management committee fixes the premium rates at a level percentage of the deposits of each institution. In case of failure, each depositor is indemnified up to ¥1 million.

In order to increase efficiency, freedom in the relocation of branch offices, more elastic interest rates, and relaxation of the restrictions on dividend rates were proposed. In February 1970, the Ministry of Finance, which had already changed its policy on the relocation of branch offices, raised the general ceiling on bank dividend rates to 10 percent, and announced accounting standards on which the calculation of higher dividend rates had to be based. Like many "temporary" laws, the Temporary Money Rates Adjustment Law enacted in 1947 has proved very durable and there is no indication that all controls will be removed. Another suggestion of the committee taken up by the Ministry of Finance was the abolition of the distinction between Class A and Class B foreign exchange banks.

The committee seems to have been intrigued by the relation between size and efficiency. It reached the conclusion that in each category of financial institution, the larger enterprises operated more efficiently. Operating costs (personnel and materials) of the four largest city banks (with deposits over ¥1.5 trillion) were 1.48 percent of deposits; those of the next four (deposits between ¥1–1.5 trillion), 1.75 percent, and those of the seven smaller banks (deposits under ¥1 trillion), 1.86 percent. Although, admittedly, there are differences in the cost structure of city and local banks, their business is more or less the same and the committee thought there should be less difference in their costs. The question of size was also taken up in relation to international competition and the ability of financial institutions to supply the funds their customers need. In 1970, the then largest Japanese bank in terms of deposits, Fuji Bank, ranked nineteenth in *Fortune*'s list of the fifty largest banks; in 1968, its deposits, ¥6.2 billion, were only 27 percent of those of the Bank of America ($22.5 billion). With $11.6 billion in deposits the new Dai-Ichi Kangyo Bank is the world's tenth largest; on the basis of total assets the bank rates sixth in the world. The enormous expansion of the Japanese economy has increased the fund demand of enterprises much faster than was foreseen ten years ago. Since 1961, industrial production has grown about 3.3 times, bank loans over 3.8 times, and issues of bank debentures 4.7 times (about one-third of the increase is due to inflation). Even more remarkable than the quantitative growth of the economy has been the evolution of Japan's productive apparatus into one of the most advanced industrial systems of the world (there remain immense differences between individual enterprises), but the financial system is basically the same that was organized for an economy which was struggling to get out of the postwar confusion. The problem, therefore, is far more complicated than increasing the size of financial institutions; the system needs much more flexibility and a good deal less bureaucracy. Under present conditions, the banks often have to trim the needs of their clients to available funds instead of supplying the funds needed by their clients. The city banks assert that the same institution should be in a position to render all financial services the customer wants, unhampered by artificial fences. On the other hand, the basic function of the banks, to borrow money at a low rate and lend it at a higher rate, becomes problematic when the banks borrow the money from the Bank of Japan—the problem is not that the banks distribute the funds but that they make a profit on it. And sometimes the question is asked whether the borrower really needs the money or the banks just want to hike their profits.

The Ministry of Finance has reshuffled the personnel of the Financial System Research Council and appointed Makoto Usami, the former governor of the Bank of Japan, chairman of the council, which will next consider the internationalization of banking and the inflow of short-term funds.

In a report entitled "Corporate Fund Supply in the Seventies," the Japan Economic Research Council made the following proposals: (1) long-term credit banks should be allowed to underwrite corporate debentures; (2) the government should amend the Commercial Code and the Tax Law to promote the division of companies; and (3) the emission of workers shares should be encouraged through tax privileges. The council advocated more emissions of new shares at market prices and a limitation on the expansion of trade credit.

2 SECURITIES COMPANIES

1 BUSINESS OF THE SECURITIES COMPANIES

Securities companies, Japan's most important institutional investors, are organized under the Securities Transaction Law which, until the revision effected in 1967, provided that only a joint-stock company registered with the Ministry of Finance may engage in the securities business. (The amendment of 1967 replaced the registration system by a license system.) The work *shōken* ("securities") must appear in the corporate name of these firms. Best known are the "big four" securities companies: Nomura, Nikko, Yamaichi, and Daiwa. Eighty-three securities companies are members of the Tokyo Stock Exchange; the Tokyo-based companies are organized in the Tokyo Securities Dealers Association; and the overall national organization is the Federation of Securities Dealers Associations of Japan.

Roughly speaking, the postwar securities firms exercise three functions: (1) brokers—earning commissions by buying and selling securities at the request of customers; (2) dealers—selling or buying securities on their own account (these two functions are based on their membership in the stock exchange); (3) underwriters—emission of corporate stock or debentures offered for public subscription. But the most important factor in the growth of the securities companies was their investment trust business.

Investment trusts, used by the securities companies to raise funds from the investing public were regulated by the Securities Investment Trust Law of 1951, which defined them as "trusts for the purpose of using the trust property for investment in specially designated securities based on the directions of the settlor or for the purpose of dividing the beneficiary rights and giving them to a number of indefinite persons" (Article 2). The original conception was that the securities companies would act as settlors, and trust banks as trustees; the former were to handle the offerings to the public and the latter to invest the funds thus raised in securities selected by the former. But since this procedure was not expressly stated in the law, it was practically ignored until 1959, when the Ministry of Finance ruled that the securities companies could not act as settlor and trustee at the same time for the same contract.

The beneficiary rights of the investment trusts must be divided into equal shares evidenced by beneficiary certificates. Beneficiaries have an equal right to repayment of the principal and to dividends according to the number of beneficiary certificates. The permission of the minister of finance is required to act as settlor; the trust contract form and the dissolution of contracts also need approval. The Finance Ministry further ruled that no guarantee of principal is permissible.

Investment trusts are operated in two forms: closed- and open-end trusts. For the first type, also called "unit trust," a definite sum of money (e.g., ¥4 billion) is raised by public subscription and invested for a definite period of time (e.g., five years). With the approval

Principal Accounts of Securities Companies
December 1970

	¥ million		¥ million
Cash & deposits	182,473	Deposits received	71,809
Short-term loans & advance payments	83,338	Payable to customers	73,286
Receivables from customers	397,189	Securities borrowed	220,674
Securities owned	155,867	Guarantee-money received (incl. securities)	573,782
Stocks	80,093	Long-term borrowing	38,902
Customers securities held	742,790	Capital	102,521
Investment in affiliated companies	50,557		
Short-term borrowing	474,213		
from banks	151,436		
from securities finance companies on margin transactions	193,616		

Note: 247 companies
Source: Bank of Japan

Investment Trusts

(In millions of yen)

	New trusts			Fund management					
	Unit trusts	Open-end trusts	Total assets	Unit trusts			Open-end trusts		
				Total	Call loans	Stocks	Total	Call loans	Stocks
1951	13,300	—	13,300	—	—	—	—	—	—
1952	32,550	1,094	53,178	52,219	—	45,911	959	—	772
1953	59,700	282	85,012	84,341	1,300	70,657	671	—	489
1954	24,110	0	81,079	80,484	1,370	73,774	595	—	527
1955	25,510	871	62,782	61,553	2,440	55,366	1,228	135	1,063
1956	51,230	201	75,252	73,996	14,001	57,489	1,256	145	1,103
1957	73,060	19,484	149,483	127,958	27,796	94,837	21,525	11,891	9,506
1958	99,070	7,342	228,466	199,039	38,971	152,804	29,426	10,013	18,654

Source: The Investment Trust Association.

of the minister of finance, the term may be lengthened or shortened, if necessary, to protect the interests of the investors. Once a year, the income of the fund is divided among the investors. A certain portion of the bulk of these gains is retained in order to increase the redemption value of the fund.

In an open-end trust, no definite ceiling is set on the amount of the fund and certificates can be bought at any time. Dividends are paid twice a year, and a larger portion of the capital gains is distributed than in the closed-end type. This keeps the price of the certificates low and ensures greater marketability.

The investment trust business expanded favorably in the boom year 1956. The expansion continued into 1957 despite a rather dull market, and average monthly sales were about ¥6,000 million. In September, ¥15,800 million in trust funds were placed, reflecting the entry into the field of two new open-end type trusts and, by the end of the year, ¥73 billion unit type and ¥19.4 billion open-end type trusts had been placed, for a total of ¥92.5 billion or 1.8 times the amount in the previous year. Furthermore, after redemptions and cancellations, the remaining principal reached ¥116.3 billion for unit type and ¥20.5 billion for open-end trusts, a total of ¥136.8 billion for all trusts. This was more than twice the balance in the previous year.

The favorable conditions continued into 1958 with ¥22.7 billion placed by March (a 13 percent increase over the first quarter of 1957) and, in April, the amount sold exceeded the ¥10 billion level. In May, the market weakened and placements declined somewhat, but, even so, it was obvious that the investment trust method of saving and investment had obtained public understanding and support. By the end of 1958, new issues of closed-end type trusts had risen to ¥99 billion and those of open-end types to ¥6.5 billion.

In 1958, seven "new" securities companies, Tamazuka, Kangyo, Okasan, Kakumaru, Yamazaki, Eguchi, and Yamakano, were given permission to establish investment trusts. This doubled the number of firms in the investment trust business, the seven "old" firms being Yamaichi, Nomura, Nikko, Daiwa, Daisho, Osakaya, and Oi. Yamazaki handled only open-end trusts, while the other new firms set up unit type trusts. The big four, however, continued to dominate the business and their sales accounted for 90.4 percent of all trusts established in 1958. For June and July 1959, the Ministry of Finance provisionally raised the ceiling of the investment trusts to be established by the big four by ¥1 billion to ¥4 billion, and this expansion was made permanent for all securities companies in August 1959. One reason for the enlargement of the investment trust framework was the rapid growth of open-end type trusts. Up to this time, the unit type had been by far the preponderant form of investment trust, but the growing popularity of this form of saving and the appearance of a large number of very small investors (who accounted for 57.7 percent of all subscribers in 1959) favored the growth of the open-end type.

In view of the increasing importance of the investment trust business for the stock market, the Ministry of Finance urged the separation of the investment trust business from the other activities of the securities companies at the first meeting of the Securities Investment Trust Association in April 1959. The reason was because of the possible conflict of interest within the management of the trusts. When setting up an investment trust, the stock department of the securities companies will buy the necessary shares on the market. But since it is impossible to obtain large blocks of shares at once, the buying operations are usually started well in advance of the trust establishment. In the interest of the beneficiaries, the shares should be bought at the lowest possible prices, but the stock department of the securities company would earn more by selling the shares at the highest possible prices to the investment trust department. After an exhaustive study of the issue, the big four decided, in November 1959, to reorganize their investment trust departments and their trust fund management departments as independent companies, and the other ten companies followed suit. One company was to engage in the sale of investment trust certificates (beneficiary certificates) to the public, the second company was to manage the trust funds collected by the sale of trust certificates (a function which the Investment Trust Law had intended to be exercised by the trust companies). The securities companies remained in charge of buying and selling the stocks in which the trust funds were to be invested. The new system went into effect on April 1, 1960, but the separation was more nominal than real.

Investment trusts continued to grow through 1959 and 1960 and to the end of 1961. The trusts gradually increased their holdings of bonds, while the weight of stocks declined as stock prices rose. This development favored the absorption of public bonds and corporate debentures. In January 1961, investment trusts made up exclusively of government-guaranteed debentures of public corporations were inaugurated. They were open-end type trusts; the par value of one unit was ¥10,000; the investment period was one year. In the beginning, the high yield (7.8 percent per annum) and the guarantee of the principal proved a great attraction.

Commission on Sales and Purchases of Investment Trusts

	Unit trusts	Open-end trusts		
		Ordinary	Installment	Cumulative
Trust certificate unit	¥10,000	¥1,000	¥1	¥1
Number of certificate units per minimum trading unit	1	10	initial purchase 50,000 additional purchases 1,000	initial purchase 100,000 additional purchases 10,000
Commission per trading unit Commission payable by purchaser	¥500	under 5,000 units ¥30 over 5,000 units ¥20	¥30	¥300–500 depending on size of purchase
Commission payable by seller	0	¥20	¥20	0

Note: The minimum purchase of open-end trusts is ten trading units at market prices.

Investment trusts achieved a large expansion in 1960, and twice the Ministry of Finance raised the ceiling on new issues. For the first half of the fiscal year, the regulations limiting new investments were changed by stipulating that the principal of outstanding investment trusts established by one company should not exceed ￥200 billion and that new trusts should be limited to ￥30 billion for the first half (April–September) of fiscal 1960. For the latter half, the addition of trusts invested exclusively in government-guaranteed bonds was authorized.

With the recession starting in the fall of 1961 and the lethargic state of the stock market, the investment trust business suffered a severe setback. Profits declined, subscriptions tapered off, and cancellations increased. For bond trusts, in particular, cancellations outstripped new subscriptions in most of the months of the year 1962. Six leading securities companies inaugurated a new type of open-end trust, distributing only the income from dividends and interest while reinvesting capital gains, but capital gains were hard to come by in the next seven years. The balance of outstanding capital had risen from ￥330 billion at the end of 1959 to ￥604.2 billion at the end of 1960 and exceeded ￥1 trillion (￥1,192,865 million) at the end of 1961. But the growth slowed down in 1962 when the establishment of the trusts dropped to almost half of the amount in the previous year (1961, ￥832,695 million; 1962, ￥430,935 million; outstanding balance at the end of 1962, ￥1,263,306 million). In 1963, open-end trusts fared particularly badly; in all months but March cancellations exceeded new trusts, and dividends, which had been as high as ￥200, dropped to ￥20 and even ￥10. Only funds made up of stocks of large companies were able to pay ￥70–80 on a ￥1,000 certificate. Despite the slump in the stock market, the securities companies continued to invest trust funds in stocks (the chief reason being their large stock inventories) and the share of stocks in investment trusts rose from 76 percent at the end of October 1962 to 82.5 percent at the end of September 1963. With the end of the business term, the securities companies began to sell stocks (in October, such sales amounted to about ￥5 billion), which was not without influence on the ailing stock market.

Bond trusts, which had made a favorable start in 1961 (outstanding balance at year-end ￥156,020 million), suffered a setback in 1962 when cancellations exceeded new trusts (balance at the end of 1962, ￥132,679 million). But they attracted more investors in 1963 when their outstanding balance increased to ￥171,515 million.

2 SECURITIES COMPANIES

2 THE 1965 CRISIS

The position of the securities companies became critical in 1964. Their overextension, induced through their aggressive business practices, led to substantial losses. For the settlement of accounts in September 1964, Yamaichi reported losses amounting to ¥3,455 million, Nikko's losses were ¥2,431 million, and those of Daiwa ¥2,175 million; of the four large securities companies, only Nomura could report a profit (¥570 million). Of the ten smaller securities companies managing investment trusts, only one (Yamazaki) had made a profit; Oi Securities lost about ¥2 billion and Daisho ¥1.3 billion.

Following the September settlement, Konosuke Koike retired as chairman of Yamaichi Securities; Hajime Ogami became chairman and was succeeded as president by Teru Hidaka (formerly managing director of the Industrial Bank, at that time president of Nissan Chemical). Similar changes were made in other securities companies (Nikko, Daiwa, Daisho, and Osakaya). The companies closed numerous branch offices and cut down on personnel; many small companies went out of business. In June 1964, a new securities bureau was organized in the Ministry of Finance which was to be responsible for the capital market. The ministry also began to prepare an amendment to the Securities Transaction Law which was to be revised on the following lines: (1) adoption of a licensing system for securities companies (replacing the registration system); (2) stricter qualifications for customers' men of securities companies; (3) separation of the broker business (buying and selling for customers) from the business of the dealer (buying and selling on own account); (4) unification of the associations of securities companies (at that time, thirty-four).

Moreover, the ministry wanted to strengthen the influence of representatives of the public interest on the board of directors of the stock exchanges, to make the stock exchanges more responsive to the directives of the Ministry of Finance, and to prevent fictitious transactions, particularly on the small exchanges. The Tokyo Securities Dealers Association proposed to establish a college providing four-year courses on securities and finance in which the employees of securities firms would be enrolled.

However, the financial position of the securities companies had deteriorated to such an extent that purely administrative measures could not save them. Yamaichi Securities, in particular, was practically bankrupt. Losses for the term ending March 1965 amounted to ¥3,454 billion, those for the September term to ¥4,145 billion, bringing total accumulated losses to over ¥10 billion. At the end of April, the company's outstanding investment trusts amounted to about ¥250 billion, its borrowings to over ¥70 billion, and its liabilities on the so-called *unyō azukari* to over ¥50 billion. (*Unyō azukari*, literally "use trust," a kind of securities deposit; the securities companies borrowed the securities owned by their customers against a fee, 1 *rin* per diem, and used these securities as collateral for bank loans or stock purchases—nineteen securities companies, including the big four, engaged in this practice.) In the boom years 1960 and 1961, Yamaichi did more trading on its own account than for customers, relying more on capital gains than on fees. The company had bought large blocks of shares in "growth companies" particularly those traded over the counter or on the Second Section (in many cases, Yamaichi had been the original underwriter). When the stock market declined, the firm was unable to sell these stocks because their sale would have involved enormous losses, but, since they had been purchased with borrowed funds (for which the shares the company had borrowed through *unyō azukari* constituted the collateral), Yamaichi had to pay interest, and the difference between the dividend income from stocks and the interest payable to banks became increasingly larger. In the beginning of 1965, the deficit resulting from this differential amounted to ¥300–500 million a month, and the company's total interest burden was over ¥8 billion.

Yamaichi's position became unmanageable and the firm asked its main debtor banks for a moratorium on its interest payments. On May 21, 1965, the presidents of Fuji Bank and the Industrial Bank, the vice-president of Mitsubishi Bank, and the president of Yamaichi Securities jointly published a rehabilitation plan agreed upon by the banks (in addition to those named above, Yasuda Trust & Banking and Mitsubishi Trust & Banking). As rationalization measures, Yamaichi was to cut its employees by about two thousand and close about twenty branch offices (actually, twenty-six branches were shut down). Interest payments to the eighteen banks from which Yamaichi had borrowed were to be suspended or reduced so that monthly interest payments would not exceed ¥150 million.

The disclosure of Yamaichi's desperate situation gave a great shock to the already weakened investor confidence; distress sales of shares, cancellation of investment trusts (which reached ¥32 billion in May) and of *unyō azukari* (no definite figures are available but the decrease in Yamaichi's holdings on this account between May and September is said to have amounted to ¥23 billion) increased, and the Dow-Jones average sank below ¥1,100. The political and economic leaders became apprehensive and on May 28, 1965, the Bank of Japan asked the consent of the minister of finance for relief financing for Yamaichi on the basis of Article 25 of the Bank of Japan Law. On the following day, the policy board of the Bank of Japan decided to grant Yamaichi unsecured and unlimited loans through the city banks. It was the first time since the 1931 panic that financing on the basis of Article 25 had been resorted to. On June 7, Oi Securities stopped its interest payments (about ¥30 million a month) and the relief financing of the Bank of Japan was extended to this firm.

Altogether, the Bank of Japan lent ¥28.2 billion to Yamaichi and ¥5.3 billion to Oi Securities Co. On June 11, 1966, a plan for the rehabilitation of Yamaichi was announced, the main features of which were as follows: (1) a new company, K.K. Yamaichi, was to take over the business of the existing Yamaichi Securities Co.; the new company (renamed Yamaichi Securities Co. after the business cessation) was founded with a capital of ¥9 billion and started operations on September 1, 1966; (2) the existing Yamaichi Securities Co. (called Yamaichi Co. after the business cessation) leased offices and equipment to the new company; the sole function of the old company was the repayment of the special loans to the Bank of Japan; (3) the Bank of Japan loans were to be repaid within eighteen years at a rate of ¥214 million a month; repayment to the nineteen other banks was to be deferred for three years; Yamaichi was to pay interest at a rate of 1 *sen* (3.65 percent per annum) on the outstanding balances of the loans of the three main banks (Fuji Bank, Industrial Bank, and Mitsubishi Bank), and at a rate of 1.1 *sen* (4.015 percent) on the balances due to the other fifteen banks. Actually, Yamaichi and Oi were able to repay the special loans much earlier than anticipated, Wako Securities Co. (the successor firm to Oi Securities) making the last payment in July 1969, Yamaichi in September 1969. At that time, the two Yamaichi firms were amalgamated (legally, the old firm absorbed the new firm and changed its name to Yamaichi Securities Co.); outstanding balances of the loans given by the three main banks amounted to ¥1.8 billion and those of the other fifteen banks to ¥1.4 billion.

2 SECURITIES COMPANIES

3 REORGANIZATION OF THE SECURITIES COMPANIES

Yamaichi and Oi were not the only securities companies which had difficulties. The number of securities dealers sank from about six hundred at the end of 1962 to 430 at the end of 1965; between October 1964 and September 1965, the securities companies reduced the number of their offices from 2,424 to 2,166 and their personnel from 87,000 to 69,000. Of great importance for the reorganization of the securities business was an amendment to the Securities Transaction Law passed by the Diet on May 24, 1965, which went into effect on October 1, 1965. Under this amendment, the securities companies, which, until then, could engage in all types of securities business simply by registering with the Ministry of Finance, were obliged to obtain a license which was given in four different forms: for brokers, dealers, underwriters, and distributors. The amendment laid down standards for approval including sufficient financial resources, sound earnings prospects, qualified personnel, and suitable local conditions in the place of business. Supervision by the Ministry of Finance became stricter. Customers' men had to be registered with the Ministry of Finance and the securities companies had to assume full responsibility for their actions. The regional offices of the Ministry of Finance were to investigate the local securities firms. As a transitory measure, the existing securities companies were allowed to remain in business until March 31, 1968, but they had to apply for a license before the end of September 1967 if they wanted to stay in business. Moreover, all losses had to be written off. Of the 359 securities companies registered at the end of September 1967, 302 applied for licenses and 277 had been licensed by April 1, 1968 (including the new Yamaichi Securities Co., which was the first to be licensed under the new system; mergers later reduced the number to 275). Licenses for all four functions were given to so-called general securities companies; most companies were allowed to do business as brokers, dealers, and distributors, but not as underwriters. The conditions for the general securities companies were: (1) a capital of at least ¥3 billion; (2) trading on own account not to exceed 20 percent of all transactions; (3) no *unyō azukari*; (4) no "touting" of stocks (no recommendation to buy particular issues). With the exception of the capital requirements, the conditions were the same for the other securities companies.

Partly due to the strict new rules, some securities companies merged and thus were able to qualify as general securities companies. On July 1, 1967, Daisho (capital ¥4 billion), Tamazuka (capital ¥1.5 billion), and Yamakano (capital ¥1 billion) became Shin-Nippon Shoken. The losses of the three firms equaled about one-half of their capital; two shares of the old firms, therefore, were exchanged for one of the new firm and then the capital was doubled and brought to ¥6.5 billion. Nippon Kangyo Securities Co., a subsidiary of Nippon Kangyo Bank with a capital of ¥2.5 billion, merged with Kakumaru Securities Co. (Japan's oldest securities company in the field of stocks, capital ¥800 million). Nippon Kangyo Bank wanted its securities company to retain its relative position in bond underwriting (Kangyo's share was 5 percent, that of Shin-Nippon Shoken 6 percent) and obtained the consent of Fuji Bank, Kakumaru's main bank, to the merger (Kakumaru's share in bond underwriting was 2 percent).

In the first merger after the license system went into effect, the three firms Nitto Securities Co., Eguchi Securities Co., and Daiichi-Kure Securities Co. agreed to amalgamate. The new firm, called Eguchi-Nitto Securities came into existence on October 1, 1971, and has a capital of ¥3 billion. Yamatane Securities Co. applied for permission to increase its capital (then ¥1 billion) to ¥2 billion by October 1971 and ¥3 billion by October 1973 so as to become a "full-line" securities company. Another merger, that took place on October 1, 1971, amalgamated Toichi Securities Co. (capital ¥200 million) and Hokuyo Securities Co. (capital ¥40 million). Nomura Securities Co., the parent company of Toichi, arranged the merger through which Toichi, now a member of the Tokyo Stock Exchange, will extend its operations to Osaka.

In July 1967, the Securities Investment Trust Law was amended (effective October 1967). The amendment gave legal standing to the Securities Investment Trust Association, required approval by the minister of finance of the regulations of the association, strengthened supervision by the Ministry of Finance, and sanctioned the mother fund system (joint management of several funds). The main purpose of the amendment was to protect customers by preventing abuses.

An amendment by the Ministry of Finance to its own enforcement ordinance concerning the Securities Transaction Law which went into effect on July 1, 1971, opened the way for small securities companies to act as underwriters or as leaders (managing firms) of underwriting syndicates. Because the underwriting of bond issues exceeding ¥500 million was restricted to securities companies with a capital of at least ¥3 billion, the small companies lost their customers when these firms became bigger.

The new regulations divided securities companies into three classes depending on the size of the capital: from ¥200 million to ¥1 billion, from ¥1 billion to ¥3 billion, and higher than ¥3 billion. Securities companies of the first class licensed for underwriting can handle bond issues up to ¥200 million; those of the second class, issues up to ¥500 million; and only the third class, larger issues. At present, only Nomura Securities Co. has affiliated companies with a capital of over ¥1 billion to which Nomura can divert smaller issues; the other large companies will try to create such companies by mergers.

After 1964, the Ministry of Finance had allowed neither the opening of new offices nor the relocation of old ones except in case of mergers or transfer of business; the introduction of the license system resulted in an uneven distribution of offices and, in April 1969, the Ministry of Finance announced that the opening of new offices, chiefly by the relocation of existing offices, would be allowed.

Toward the end of 1968, Nomura Securities Co. started installment investment trusts, which were soon copied by Nikko, Daiwa, Yamaichi, Shin-Nippon, and Wako. The investor added a fixed amount to his investment each month; dividends were reinvested and, after completion of the investment goal, the fund had to be left untouched for two years. A new type of unit trust, called "family fund," was set up by Nomura in June 1970; Nikko, Daiwa, and Yamaichi followed suit in July and were later joined by Nippon Asahi.

In November 1969, the board of trustees of the Securities Investment Trust Council proposed a new method for the trading of investment trusts. Formerly, sales by the investor were based on the price of the preceding day; cancellations, on the price of the current day; since April 1970, the price on the day of the transaction has been applied in all cases. Commissions used to be split; half was paid on the day of the purchase and half at the time of the sale; now, the entire commission has to be paid on the day of purchase. The board also decided that stocks listed on the Second Section could be bought for investment trusts; until then, only stocks listed on the First Section had been eligible.

At the settlement of accounts for the business year ending September 1969 (the securities companies settle their accounts once a year; they issue an interim report for the six-month period ending March), sixty-two of the eighty-three securities companies which are members of the Tokyo Stock Exchange were able to pay higher dividends, eight companies resumed dividend payments, one company reduced its dividend rate, and only two companies, Yamaichi and Wako, declared no dividend. For the accounting year ending September 1970, both Yamaichi and Wako, after a lapse of seven years, resumed dividend payments, distributing a dividend of 6 percent.

The main income sources of the securities companies are: (1) brokerage commissions on the execution of orders for the purchase or sale of stocks for customers; (2) commissions on underwriting of stock or bond issues; (3) commissions on the sale of financial debentures and investment trust certificates. In the fifties, profits from trading on their own account constituted a large source of income (until 1964, about 50 percent); in recent years, the Ministry of Finance has curbed trading on their own accounts. In the settlement of accounts for the accounting year ending September 1969, brokerage commissions accounted for 74 percent of the total commission income of the securities companies (¥176.6 billion out of ¥237.8 billion).

Income from underwriting is relatively small. Costs of bond underwriting are high while new bonds are difficult to sell; usually, the market prices of old bonds are lower than the issue prices of new ones and even higher commissions have failed to make the business profitable. Japanese securities companies derive little profit from financing the margin buying of their customers; in the September 1969 settlement, it amounted to ¥15.7 billion. Because trading slows down when the market declines, the income of securities companies is squeezed when business becomes difficult.

In order to promote individual investment, Yamatane Securities Co. introduced what it called "Yamatane Guideline Service." The company will inform investors buying on margin of the position of their portfolio if its value drops by 10 percent or more below the basic value of the investment or exceeds it by 15 percent.

Total income of all 275 securities companies for the twelve months from October 1969 to September 1970 amounted to ¥307,894 million, up 24.4 percent over the preceding year. Income from fees and commissions was ¥239,583 million (25 percent higher and almost 78 percent of the total); income from transactions on their own account ¥68,311 million (22.6 percent higher). Gross profits increased by 27.7 percent and reached ¥71,826 million.

The recovery of the stock market in 1969 brought the value of the old unit trusts to par and redemption of overdue trusts became possible; by September 1969, all matured trusts had been redeemed. For the first time in six years, the balance of outstanding trusts increased, but the cancellation rate remained high.

In an effort to discourage long-term portfolio investment of securities companies (i.e., fixation of their capital), the Ministry of Finance, in April 1970, laid down the following rules: (1) portfolio investment of securities companies should not exceed 20 percent of their net assets; (2) mutual stockholding between securities companies and companies listed on the stock exchange should not exceed 10 percent of the net assets of securities companies; (3) securities companies should not invest more than 5 percent of their net assets in shares of any single listed company. The securities companies were to reduce their holdings to these limits by September 1970.

The Ministry of Finance has drafted uniform accounting standards for the securities companies which were enforced for the business year starting October 1971. In addition to introducing uniform accounting categories, the regulations aim at strengthening the internal reserves of the companies by requiring depreciation charges and reserves for possible losses and other contingencies up to the limit allowed by the Tax Law, and by restricting dividend payments and bonuses to officers to one-third of aftertax profits.

The securities companies invariably rely to a large extent on borrowed funds. In one of the largest recent transactions, the Japan Securities Finance Co., in December 1970, lent ¥4 billion to the six largest securities companies to finance the distribution of bond issues.

The large securities companies have automated their operations by the installation of electronic computers and central electronic data processing. The small securities companies plan to install a joint on-line computer system for automating their transactions. The Tokyo Securities Computer Center may offer its facilities to the small companies, and the large securities firms may link their affiliated companies with their own systems.

On April 15, 1970, the Ministry of Finance gave the securities companies permission to acquire foreign securities for their investment funds. (Insurance companies were given similar permission.) A ceiling of $100 million was set on all acquisitions, and the four big securities companies were allocated 70 percent of the total. Foreign securities were not to exceed 30 percent of any one fund. Until October 1970, the companies had only invested $22 million. In April, 1971, the ceiling on investment in foreign securities for investment trusts was raised to 50 percent of net assets.

In February 1971, Yamaichi received permission to purchase stocks listed on the Toronto Stock Exchange for its investment trusts, and Daiwa acquired shares of seven German corporations.

In November 1969, Nomura Securities International, and, in January 1970, the American subsidiaries of Nikko, Daiwa, and Yamaichi were admitted to the Boston Stock Exchange; and they were also admitted to the Pacific Coast Stock Exchange on November 30, 1970. Nikko established a joint venture in Hong Kong in May 1970, and Daiwa in January 1971. In June 1970, Nomura founded a joint venture in Bangkok with local banks. On October 1, 1970, the four large securities companies transformed their representative offices in London into branch offices.

On April 10, 1971, Nomura Securities Investment Trust Management Co. obtained approval for setting up an international investment trust called Associated Japanese International Fund. The fund, which plans to sell ¥15 billion in certificates in the first year of operations and up to ¥50 billion in three years, will include 50 percent of foreign stocks (United States, Canada, West Germany, and the Netherlands), and, in addition to Japan, certificates will be sold in Canada, Britain, the Netherlands, and Hong Kong. Merrill

Lynch, Pierce, Fenner & Smith, N. M. Rothschild & Sons, Nomura International, and Nomura Kokusai Hong Kong will handle sales outside Japan. Merrill Lynch, Rothschild, and Bankers Trust Co. will serve as investment advisers.

In May, Daiwa Securities Investment Trust Managment Co. was authorized to establish an international investment trust called Daiwa International Fund. Dreyfus and Morgan Grenfell will act as advisers in the management of the foreign issues.

On May, 1971, the Ministry of Finance gave permission to two other securities investment trusts (a perfect example of the "me-too" way of doing business of Japanese enterprises), Nikko International Investment Trust and Yamaichi's Joint International Trust Fund.

A law embodying the regulations drafted by the Ministry of Finance for the entry of foreign securities dealers into Japan was passed by the Diet in 1971. A license will be required for engaging in the securities business which will be given for the same categories as the ones in the Securities Transaction Law, i.e., dealers, brokers, underwriters, and distributors. Individuals need no license if their transactions are exclusively with securities companies. A license will also be necessary for opening an office; such a license will only be given to corporations which have been in the securities business for at least three years. They will be required to deposit a guarantee fund. Foreign companies will not be permitted to combine banking with the securities business. As mentioned above, the Japanese banks want to have this restriction removed, but the securities companies oppose any change because they would lose all influence on large enterprises.

Under an eight-point program for decelerating the increase in the country's foreign exchange reserves, the government liberalized investment in foreign securities effective July 1, 1971. The limitation of $100 million on the investments of securities and insurance companies was removed, and individual investors were allowed to acquire foreign securities through authorized securities companies. The following rules were laid down for individual portfolio investment: (1) acquisition for portfolio investment is limited to issues listed on exchanges in the OECD countries; (2) buying and selling is to be conducted through domestic securities companies; (3) no futures or margin trading is permitted; (4) the settlement between the individual investor and the securities company is to be effected in yen (individuals will have no foreign currency account); the trading will be in the name of the securities company; (5) settlement will have to be made within four days; (6) the foreign securities purchased will be kept abroad by a custodian company for the securities company which will be the nominal holder of the securities; domestic trust companies can also arrange for the custody of the securities; the securities company delivers to the Japanese investor a certificate of deposit (JDR); if the investor wants to have the securities registered in his own name, he must conclude a custodian contract in his own name or have the securities sent to Japan; (7) reports, notices, announcements, etc., will be forwarded by the securities companies to the investors at cost; if such notices are not important, they will only be posted in the offices of the securities companies; (8) the investor can vote his stock through the securities company or the custodian company; if he wants to vote personally, he must register the securities in his own name; (9) if the investor acquires convertible debentures, the securities company or custodian company must follow the instructions of the investor; (10) interest and dividend payments will be accepted by the securities company as agent of the investor; (11) all applications in connection with the acquisition of foreign securities have to be submitted to the Ministry of Finance through the securities companies.

After consultation with the Ministry of Finance and the Bank of Japan, the securities companies agreed to the following conditions: (1) the securities companies will not engage in dealings on their own account; (2) there will be no trading in foreign securities among securities companies; (3) orders will be placed directly with securities companies having foreign accounts.

On July 1, 1971, nine securities companies (Nomura, Yamaichi, Nikko, Daiwa, Shin-Nippon, Nippon Kangyo Kakumaru, Wako, Nitto, and Osakaya) applied for permission to open foreign currency accounts for dealing in foreign securities. The other securities companies can accept orders from customers but must channel these orders through one of these nine companies. For the time being, acquisition of foreign securities is limited to those listed on eight stock exchanges: New York, London, Paris, Frankfurt, Amsterdam, Sydney, Zurich, and Toronto.

Commissions for transactions in foreign securities are based on the value of transactions (buying or selling).

Value of transaction ¥ million	Commission ¥1,000
100	14
150	16.5
200	19
250	21.5
300	26.5
400	29
450	31.5
500	34
600	39
700	44
800	49
900	54
1,000	59
1,500	75
2,000	100
2,500	125
3,000	135
3,500	157
4,000	180
4,500	202
5,000	225
6,000	240
7,000	280
8,000	320
9,000	360
10,000	400
over 10,000	400 + ¥35,000 for each ¥10 million

3 STOCK EXCHANGES

1 THE TOKYO STOCK EXCHANGE

Under the Securities Transaction Law of 1948, nine exchanges were originally organized: Tokyo, Osaka, Nagoya, Kyoto, Kobe, Hiroshima, Fukuoka, Niigata, and Sapporo. In October 1961, second sections were added to the exchanges in Tokyo, Osaka, and Nagoya for issues formerly traded over the counter. But a new over-the-counter market started on February 1, 1963, and on September 8, 1969, a trading center for over-the-counter stocks was established at the Tokyo Stock Exchange. There are different sections for shares (including investment certificates of special corporations), bonds, and, since May 1, 1970, convertible debentures.

Tokyo is by far the most active of all Japanese exchanges and accounts for about two-thirds of all transactions. The Kobe Stock Exchange, which had originally been established in 1883 following the foundation of stock exchanges in Tokyo and Osaka, was dissolved on October 31, 1967 (it was actually absorbed into the Osaka Stock Exchange). It had had twenty member firms; 237 issues of 234 corporations had been listed, but only 1 issue was exclusively listed on the Kobe Exchange. Between 1949 and 1952, the exchange had handled 2.52 percent of all transactions on Japanese exchanges, but its business had fallen below 2 percent in 1955 and, in 1966, the volume was 340,980,000 shares, 0.7 percent of the national total. In its last year, daily turnover was 758,000 shares, which was much too small to cover expenses.

Although commonly called stock exchanges, the official appellation of these institutions is "securities exchanges." Article 2 of the Securities Transaction Law lists the following classes of securities which can be traded:

1. government bonds;
2. bonds of local public bodies;
3. debentures issued by corporations set up by special law;
4. secured and unsecured corporate debentures;
5. investment certificates issued by corporations set up by special law;
6. shares of stock and certificates showing the right to receive new shares of stock;
7. beneficiary certificates of securities investment trusts and loan trusts;
8. securities or certificates issued by foreign countries or foreign corporations of the same character as the securities listed under the preceding numbers;
9. securities and certificates specified by government ordinance.

The Business Regulations of the Tokyo Stock Exchange (Article 10) distinguish four kinds of transactions:

1. cash transactions—settlement has to be effected the same day the contract is concluded but may be deferred until the next day with the consent of both parties;
2. regular-way transactions—settlement must be made within four days for stocks and fifteen days for bonds;
3. seller's option transactions;
4. when-issued transactions.

In 1962, 95.2 percent of all dealings were regular-way transactions, of which about 20 percent were margin transactions. Credit is provided through the Securities Finance Company. No margin transactions are allowed in the second sections. Blocks of 1,000 shares form the smallest trading units on the first sections, while, up to January 1972, 500 shares were the smallest unit on the second sections. Shares with a face value of ¥500 are traded in units of 100 shares. For special corporations, 100 certificates constitute the smallest amount. Bond transactions are in blocks with a face value of ¥1 million, but convertible bonds are traded in units with a contract value of ¥100,000.

Commission rates depend on the price of stock and the number of shares traded. The following list, although incomplete, illustrates the system (commission per share).

Price per share ¥	Less than 30,000 shares ¥	30,000– 50,000 shares ¥	50,000– 100,000 shares ¥	Over 100,000 shares ¥
50 or less	1.30	1.20	1.00	0.90
75 or less	1.50	1.30	1.20	1.00
100 or less	1.70	1.50	1.40	1.20
:	:	:	:	:
1000 or less	5.00	4.50	4.00	3.50
for every ¥200 over ¥1,000	1.00	0.90	0.80	0.70

The same rates are applicable to issues of new shares. For subscription rights, the commission depends on the price of the rights and the amount. For the same classes as in the preceding table, the commissions are as follows (in yen):

Price of subscription rights

less than ¥10	0.90	0.80	0.70	0.60
less than ¥25	1.10	1.00	0.90	0.80

The seller of securities has to pay a Securities Transaction Tax of 0.15 percent.

Commissions on convertible debentures are calculated as follows:

Contract value under ¥500,000	1.0%
„ „ „ ¥1 million	0.9%
„ „ „ ¥3 million	0.8%
„ „ „ ¥5 million	0.7%
„ „ „ ¥10 million	0.6%
Contract value ¥10 million and over	0.5%

Commissions on bond transactions are based on the par or contract value of the bonds.

They are fixed in yen for ordinary bonds and in percent for convertibles. Below are the rates in force early in 1971:

Value of transaction	Commission per ¥100 of par or contract value of			
	Government bonds ¥	Government-guaranteed bonds ¥	Municipals & bank debentures ¥	Corporate debentures ¥
Less than ¥5 million	0.20	0.30	0.40	0.50
Less than ¥10 million	0.15	0.20	0.30	0.40
Less than ¥100 million	0.10	0.15	0.20	0.30
¥100 million and over	0.05	0.10	0.15	0.20

Although bonds have gained more importance in recent years, the Japanese bond market remains rather restricted. Bond issues may be divided into the following classes.

1. Long-term government bonds. Except for the immediate postwar years, fiscal policy was based on budgetary balance until 1965. In January 1966, the government began to rely on long-term bond issues for raising revenues. These bonds are absorbed by the market. At present, eighteen government bond issues are traded on the Tokyo Stock Exchange.

2. Short-term government bills. Food certificates issued by the Food Control Agency chiefly for financing the government's rice buying. Foreign exchange fund notes issued through the foreign exchange fund for financing purchases of foreign exchange sold to the government under the Foreign Exchange and Foreign Trade Control Law. The bills, issued each week through the Bank of Japan, usually have a maturity of sixty days; the discount rate is 5.625 percent per annum. Financial institutions, securities companies, and short-term fund brokers entitled to central bank credit can subscribe to the bills. The public can buy them from these institutions.

3. Municipal bonds. Many issues of local public bodies are handled through private placement and a number of such issues have been underwritten by local banks.

4. Bank debentures. Six financial institutions are entitled to float debentures: the Industrial Bank of Japan, the Long-Term Credit Bank, the Japan Hypothec Bank, the Bank of Tokyo, the Shoko Chukin Bank (Central Bank for Commercial and Industrial Cooperatives), and the Central Cooperative Bank of Agriculture and Forestry. Debentures issued by these institutions are of two different types: interest-bearing and discount. Debentures of the first type are underwritten almost entirely by financial institutions and handled outside the open market, while discount debentures are offered to the public through the securities companies.

5. Government-guaranteed debentures. They are issued by government or semigovernmental agencies established for managing public services, utilities, or development projects. Trading is most active in the bonds of the Nippon Telegraph and Telephone Corpora-

tion which requires new subscribers to buy a certain amount of bonds. The corporation issues interest-bearing and discount bonds.

6. Corporate debentures. They are often subdivided into electric and general corporate debentures and often referred to as industrial debentures. At present, twenty-four issues are traded. Bonds (other than bank debentures) listed on the exchanges are issued by 223 corporations; they are divided into five classes, A, A', B, C, and D, depending on the credit rating of the companies. Class A bonds are issues of the electric power companies, the large steel manufacturers, and other key enterprises (in May 1971, the following enterprises were transferred from Class A' to Class A: Matsushita Electric Industrial, Toyota Motor, Nissan Motor, Toray Industries, Kobe Steel Works); Class A' are other first-rate enterprises (e.g., Fujitsu, Showa Denko, Mitsubishi Chemical, Mitsubishi Estate, Asahi Chemical, Toyo Spinning, Sanyo Electric); Class B are large enterprises, the other classes comprise large and medium-sized firms. In addition to the issues listed on the exchanges, there are about six thousand nonlisted bond issues which are traded over the counter. The minimum amount of one issue used to be ¥200 million; it was raised to ¥500 million effective September 1, 1971, when issue conditions were revised.

7. Convertible corporate debentures. At present, eighteen issues are traded on the Tokyo Stock Exchange.

Municipal bonds and government-guaranteed and corporate debentures are floated each month upon consultation between the depository banks and the securities companies. At present, issues of public and private debentures (including thirty-eight issues of the Nippon Telegraph and Telephone Corporation) are traded on the Tokyo Stock Exchange, but there is very little interest in these securities. Among the short-term government bonds, foreign exchange fund notes have a certain influence on the liquidity of the money market. An excess of imports leads to a tightening of money, while an export surplus makes for easier money. Since 1962, the Bank of Japan has used open-market operations to regulate the money supply, but, on the whole, loans to the city banks have been more important. Occasionally it has bought government-guaranteed debentures held by financial institutions in order to relieve a temporary fund shortage, particularly when receipts by the Treasury were expected to show a large excess over payments to the public. But since banks were required to repurchase these debentures from the Bank of Japan, the whole transaction was just a substitute for loans.

Trading posts are arranged by industries; on the First Section of the Tokyo Stock Exchange, they are: Marine Products, Mining, Construction, Foodstuffs, Textiles, Pulp & Paper, Chemicals, Oil & Coal Products, Rubber Products, Glass & Ceramic Products, Iron & Steel, Nonferrous Metals, Metal Products, Machinery, Electric Machinery, Transportation Machinery, Precision Machinery, Other Products, Commerce, Banking & Insurance, Real Estate, Land Transportation, Shipping, Warehousing & Communications, Electricity & Gas, and Amusement & Services. A separate post handles the so-called "specified" stocks: Heiwa Real Estate, Ajinomoto, Matsushita Electric Industrial, Canon, Mitsukoshi, Tokio Marine and Fire Insurance, Mitsubishi Estate, and N.Y.K. The distribution is very uneven: Marine Products covers six issues; Electric Machinery, sixty-eight.

There were 759 issues traded on the Tokyo Stock Exchange in September 1961. They represented 619 of the leading companies in Japan, but there were a very large number of other smaller companies whose shares were held by the public or who "went public." These shares were traded over the counter and as many of them seemed to be so-called growth issues, they attracted more and more investor interest so that the volume of trading over the counter grew to unusual proportions.

Recognizing this situation, both the Ministry of Finance officials and the securities dealers felt a need to create a second market where such shares could be listed and traded more efficiently. Prices would then be public, marketability increased, and the cumbersome over-the-counter system of both trading and settlement streamlined. The Ministry of Finance supported the idea, as it gave better control, plus a modicum of investor protection. The major securities dealers, who do the lion's share of the business, were in favor of the plan as it would increase their revenues and reduce their costs, and the issuing companies went along as it would improve marketability, give free advertising, and make it easier for them to increase capital.

Consequently, in October 1961, second sections, as they are called, were established on the Tokyo, Osaka, and Nagoya exchanges, with trading posts being allotted to the sections. On the opening day, 385 issues of 325 companies were listed on the Tokyo Second Section. Volume in the first month was 78,074,500 shares.

Since then, the number of companies and issues listed has steadily increased and, as from time to time investor interest veered away from the shares on the first section in favor of the higher yield and expected better growth potentials of the second section stocks, volumes of trading continually increased. In January 1971, 737 companies were listed on the First Section of the Tokyo Stock Exchange with a capital of ¥6,196,581 million, and on the Second Section 543 companies with a capital of ¥306,576 million.

One provision lacking on the exchanges is the existence of an efficient odd lot market. Round lots are either 500 or 1000 shares, and most purchases are of round lots. However, at the time of capital increases, shareholders frequently find themselves owning a multiple of less than 500. To round these out by purchase of the number required, or to sell them, is quite difficult, and even when possible it can usually only be done at a substantial price concession. The establishment of an odd-lot post or posts with automatic price protection at a fixed small price differential would be a valuable addition to investor protection.

In order to prevent too violent price fluctuations, the exchanges stop trading if the increase or decrease in the price of a particular issue during one session exceeds a certain limit. The board of directors reduced the ceilings as a result of the enormous price slumps caused by the "Nixon shock" in August 1971.

Stock price	Maximum range of price increase or decrease	
	Old ceilings	Ceilings effective August 24, 1971
below ¥200	¥ 50	¥ 30
„ ¥500	¥ 80	¥ 40
„ ¥1,000	¥100	¥ 50
„ ¥1,500	¥200	¥100
above ¥1,500	¥300	¥150

These ceilings were adopted by all Japanese stock exchanges.

Sales Volumes of All Japanese Stock Exchanges

Year	Volume 1,000 shares	Value ¥1,000
1965	50,583,157	5,782,977,895
1966	52,040,980	7,570,582,164
1967	42,159,157	6,281,407,829
1968	65,641,137	11,723,157,614
1969	68,853,144	18,674,831,221
1970	57,099,263	12,030,257,161

Source: Tokyo Stock Exchange.

Tokyo Stock Exchange, First and Second Sections

End of year	No. of companies listed	No. of issues listed	Capital ¥ million	Capital stock listed ¥ million	No. of shares listed (million)	Total market value ¥ million	Sales volume Total 1,000 shares	Daily average 1,000 shares	Sales values ¥ million	Turnover ratio %
1965	1,255	1,291	4,546,849	4,529,269	80,189	8,510,927	34,838,338	115,742	4,004,551	43.87
1966	1,246	1,296	4,730,994	4,713,414	82,847	9,389,677	35,938,158	120,598	5,266,520	44.08
1967	1,248	1,307	4,955,376	4,969,469	87,804	9,270,610	28,805,203	96,338	4,311,032	33.76
1968	1,242	1,285	5,321,804	5,338,023	93,649	12,664,542	46,885,945	155,251	8,433,629	51.68
1969	1,250	1,330	5,824,573	5,842,686	102,610	18,353,404	50,985,772	171,669	13,891,316	51.96
1970	1,280	1,381	6,520,457	6,522,075	114,436	16,235,545	42,753,117	143,950	9,152,455	39.39

Note: Since January 1970, total market value includes new shares to be issued on the basis of rights offerings or stock dividends when shares have gone ex-rights or ex-dividends although the new shares have not yet been issued.

Source: Tokyo Stock Exchange.

Tokyo Stock Exchange

Year	Num- ber of trading days	Num- ber of com- panies listed (1)	Capital of listed stock ¥ million (1)	Total market value ¥ million (2)	Average daily volume 1,000 shares	Turn- over ratio % 	Tokyo Stock Price Index (3)	Arith- metic stock price average (4)	Average yield rate % (4)
				First Section					
1955	300	596	579,299	1,057,673	8,350	26.02	33.97	108.17	7.14
1956	304	591	831,614	1,640,408	22,014	52.17	44.85	126.43	6.04
1957	302	602	1,018,325	1,674,886	25,468	45.48	49.19	114.10	6.82
1958	300	601	1,198,845	2,322,678	38,948	58.52	51.70	110.36	6.15
1959	299	603	1,469,885	3,777,018	70,906	89.79	75.49	146.39	4.10
1960	302	599	1,882,256	5,411,360	90,166	92.41	97.35	167.54	3.67
1961	301	662	2,659,158	5,462,277	103,285	77.50	112.10	187.39	3.34
1962	302	706	3,183,108	6,703,922	109,718	63.69	98.59	141.08	4.20
1963	302	676	3,593,117	6,669,382	130,383	65.64	108.20	127.27	4.09
1964	301	661	4,091,770	6,828,072	94,945	41.87	95.56	106.30	4.93
1965	301	666	4,211,570	7,901,308	112,798	45.99	91.68	99.56	5.13
1966	298	654	4,388,749	8,718,748	115,659	45.38	109.88	120.40	3.97
1967	299	672	4,642,687	8,590,107	92,635	34.78	110.48	113.43	4.32
1968	302	681	4,984,134	11,650,617	149,356	53.18	118.91	125.80	4.26
1969	297	693	5,455,565	16,716,736	162,446	52.58	151.05	171.65	3.30
1970	297	736	6,161,769	15,091,360	138,194	40.27	163.48	181.58	3.37
				Second Section					
1961		345	200,721	677,917	4,965	51.12	106.56	219.76	3.80
1962		477	240,550	957,303	9,390	80.33	135.72	258.30	2.91
1963		582	300,093	758,148	4,648	30.32	120.09	175.17	4.21
1964		609	335,968	597,059	2,546	14.09	84.30	104.81	6.37
1965		589	319,199	609,619	2,944	15.86	71.44	87.87	7.39
1966		592	324,665	670,928	4,939	26.34	97.64	143.53	4.35
1967		576	326,776	680,502	3,704	19.45	105.80	138.62	4.61
1968		561	353,888	1,013,924	3,896	30.15	129.89	156.18	4.45
1969		557	387,120	1,636,668	9,223	43.00	191.35	196.19	3.55
1970		544	360,306	1,144,185	5,756	25.81	216.39	189.42	3.81

Notes: 1. End of year.
2. Until 1958, beginning of December; 1959–1966, end of first week in December; since 1967, end of year.
3. Base date: January 4, 1968. The index covers all issues listed on the First Section; the index for the Second Section covers 300 issues.
4. Until 1967, 225 issues listed on the First Section, 50 issues listed on the Second Section; since 1968, all issues.

Source: Tokyo Stock Exchange.

The constitution of the Tokyo Stock Exchange distinguishes between regular members (limited to ninety-nine corporations) and *saitori* members (limited to twelve corporations). A regular member is defined as a securities dealer engaged mainly in the securities business; a *saitori* member is a securities dealer making a speciality of serving as a broker's broker in securities transactions and acting as an intermediary among regular members in their business on the market of the exchange. In addition to subscription (regular member, ¥5 million; *saitori* member, ¥200,000), regular members pay a fixed membership fee and a fixed rate fee, *saitori* members a fixed membership fee. Regular members must deposit a guarantee fund of ¥3 million, and *saitori* members a guarantee fund of ¥20,000. Effective from March 1971, the membership fees for the Tokyo and Osaka stock exchanges were raised; the lowest fee was raised from ¥80,000 to ¥100,000, and the ceiling of ¥400,000 on membership fees was abolished. Organs of the exchange are the general meeting, the president, twenty governors, and three auditors. Originally, fourteen of the governors were elected by the regular members out of their own number; they elected the president who, with the consent of the majority of the "member governors," appointed six "nonmember governors" (persons other than the officers and employees of the members). Two auditors are elected by the members out of their own number, while the third must be a nonmember. Out of the nonmember governors, four are appointed as "standing governors" (who may not engage in business directly connected with the securities business during their term of office); the other two are regarded as representing the public interest. Out of the standing governors, the president, with the consent of the majority of the member governors, appoints an executive vice-president. The governors constitute the board of governors.

Each member firm (out of the eighty-three) is represented at the exchange by a member representative who must be a representative director of the firm; the member representatives attend the general meeting and act on behalf of the member firm in all relations with the exchange. For its business transactions, the member firm appoints a floor representative and a number of traders (officially called "persons in charge of transactions," their number depends on the volume of business and the capital of each firm) who must be approved by the board of governors. The *saitori* members also appoint a floor representative and traders; their business is called *baikai*, i.e., serving as intermediary for the purchase or sale of listed stocks between regular members on the trading floor of the exchange.

In April 1967, Teiichiro Morinaga was appointed president of the Tokyo Stock Exchange. After retiring as vice-minister of finance, Morinaga served as governor of the Small Business Finance Corporation and governor of the Japan Export-Import Bank. Until then, the president of the Federation of Securities Dealers Associations of Japan had concurrently held the post of president of the Tokyo Stock Exchange. The Ministry of Finance used the Yamaichi affair to bring the post under its control. In July 1967, the Stock Exchange Council published a memorandum "Concerning the Organization and Improvement of the Stock Circulation System" which proposed the following changes: (1) the representatives of the public interest on the board of governors should be given a larger proportional position and their views better reflected; (2) the various committees of the exchange should not report to the board of governors but to the president of the exchange; (3) since the importance of the local exchanges (i.e., other than the Tokyo Stock Exchange) is decreasing, ways should be found of connecting them with the Tokyo Stock Exchange; (4) in order to strengthen the autonomous regulatory function of the exchange and the securities dealers associations, the respective fields subject to regulation should be clearly defined and supervision or guidance allocated (which meant the dealers associations should keep out of the affairs of the exchange).

In October 1967, the general meeting of the members of the Tokyo Stock Exchange dutifully sanctioned the following changes: (1) the number of member governors will be reduced by two; the number of nonmember governors will be increased by two governors representing the public interest and another standing governor; (2) the representatives of the public interest will take part in the election of the president of the exchange; (3) a disciplinary committee directly under the president will enforce the regulations of the exchange; the majority of the members of this committee will be nonmembers. These changes went into effect in April 1968, together with the enforcement of the license system for the securities companies. A similar reorganization was carried out in the Osaka Stock Exchange; other reforms which were debated included the abolition of the membership system for the exchanges and the requirement of approval by the minister of finance for the president of the exchange.

Another change effected in October 1967 was the abolition of *baikai* or "trading in hand" in which the same trader buys and sells directly from and to his customers and then reports the transactions to the exchange. The Ministry of Finance had always opposed this method as incompatible with the principle of fair price formation because: (1) there is no competitive buying and selling; (2) the method casts doubts on the honesty of the transaction and the integrity of the dealer; (3) the transaction is not reflected in the price formation of the exchange; (4) customers and dealers have opposing interests; (5) the interests of other customers are affected at least indirectly. The large securities dealers, however, loved this system and about half of all transactions had been through *baikai*. In the method prescribed by the Ministry of Finance, priority of price (shares should be bought and sold at the price nearest to the price indicated by the customer) and priority of time (orders first on the market should be executed first) were to replace the priorities of each institution. The actual method now used is a combination; first consideration is given to orders of members registered on the exchange (i.e., buying orders are checked against outstanding selling orders already on the exchange and vice versa), the remainder is handled by the dealer's own stock inventory.

In the same year, the Ministry of Finance also revised the rules for margin trading: the settlement date was postponed from three to six months, the so-called continuation fee was abolished, the interest rate payable by the seller was reduced, and the margin buyer had to put up a minimum deposit of ￥150,000. Margin trading is financed by the securities finance companies; there is a ceiling on the credit given to securities companies but no ceiling on the credit given by the securities companies to their customers. The stocks bought on credit are deposited with the securities companies (or the Securities Finance Co.) as collateral, but in the transactions of the securities companies with the Securities Finance Co. buying and selling involving the same stock cancel each other out—which reduces costs but encourages speculative trading.

An ordinance of the Ministry of Finance which went into effect on December 10, 1968, made the following changes: (1) if collateral for margin buying is given not in the form of cash but in securities, only 60 percent (until then 70 percent) of the value can be accepted as collateral; (2) a customer buying on margin must deposit 40 percent (until then 30 percent) of the price for all issues. New regulations went into effect in October 1970; they contained guidelines on credit volume, abolished the settlement date, and required the securities finance companies and/or the securities companies to hold a certain part of the securities given as collateral (i.e., only a certain portion of the collateral can be used for other transactions).

In November and December 1969, margin requirements were raised to 50 percent for a number of issues (in Tokyo, thirty-five issues; Osaka, twenty-four; Nagoya, nine; in February 1970, margin requirements were again uniformly set at 40 percent (the 50 percent ratio remained in effect only for Nippon Yakin Kogyo). Effective March 26, 1971, the Tokyo Stock Exchange raised margin requirements for Atsugi Nylon Industrial Co. to 70 percent and for sixteen other firms (including Sony, Matsushita Electrical Industrial Co., Toto, and Daiwa House) to 50 percent. The Osaka Stock Exchange took a similar step for twelve issues. Usually, the number of issues eligible for margin trading (i.e., which the securities finance companies will accept as collateral) is increased each year in April after consultations between the stock exchanges, the securities finance companies, and the Ministry of Finance. In 1969, the number was increased three times but in 1970, because of the overheating of the stock market, the increase was postponed until October when 40 new issues were added to the 389 eligible issues listed on the Tokyo Stock Exchange and 30 to the 362 issues listed on the Osaka Stock Exchange.

In 1966, the capital required for listing on the First Section of the Tokyo Stock Exchange was raised to ¥1 billion, but thanks to the large expansion of the economy, this requirement can be met by an increasing number of companies. In August 1971, the policy committee of the Tokyo Stock Exchange discussed a proposal to raise the minimum capital requirement for listing on the First Section. For the Second Section, the minimum capital had been raised from ¥100 million to ¥300 million in February 1970. The main reasons why enterprises want to have their stock listed are: (1) better access to the capital market; (2) enhancement of the reputation of the company, which helps not only their business relations but also their recruitment of personnel.

New listings on the Tokyo Stock Exchange, including transfers from other exchanges, in the last ten years were as follows:

Year	Number of newly listed companies	Year	Number of newly listed companies
1961	23	1966	6
1962	187	1967	5
1963	97	1968	10
1964	36	1969	22
1965	1	1970	38

Among the twenty-one companies newly listed in 1971 was Dai'Ei, Inc., the largest operator of supermarkets. According to a survey made by the Tokyo Stock Exchange, there were 305 companies with a capital of ¥1 billion or more which were not listed at the beginning of 1970 (only a few of them were newly listed in the course of 1971).

A fee of ¥1 million is charged for each new listing. In addition to a certain capital the exchanges require a certain distribution of the shares; if the shares are too closely held, no market can be expected to develop. The Tokyo Stock Exchange requires the sale of 300,000 shares, plus 5 percent of all issued shares. Two methods are used to effect these sales: shares are either offered for public subscription or shares held by the president of the company, related or affiliated companies, or other large stockholders are offered for sale (the ratio of public subscription to sales is about 7:3). The time between the sale of the shares and listing on the exchange used to be two months; the Ministry of Finance reduced the interval to twenty days in order to prevent speculative trading.

The most difficult problem involved in new listings is the price formation. In May 1970, the following standards were laid down for the determination of the price of newly listed stocks: (1) net assets per share; (2) net profit per share in the year before listing; (3) net dividends per share in the year before listing; (4) comparison with similar companies in the same field. To the theoretical price arrived at by these considerations, the securities companies add 10 percent (it used to be 20 percent) to cover the risk of underwriting. In a number of cases, the market price soon zoomed to a multiple of the price listed (some recent examples: Akai Shoji, 4.2 times; Takasago Netsugaku, 3.5 times; Fuji Denki Kagaku, 3.2 times). Effective April 1, 1971, gains from the sale of newly listed stock are taxable; under the former rules, income from stock trading was only taxable if it was business income, i.e., if there were at least fifty sales a year or if the sales involved more than 250,000 shares a year. Under the new regulations, income is taxable if derived from the sale of more than 25 percent of the newly listed stock.

In view of the difficulties of the stock market in the years following the 1959–61 boom, strict rules were laid down for capital increases. The main requirements were that the ex-rights price of the stock was at least ¥60, that the enterprise was paying a dividend of 10 percent, and that it was able to maintain the same dividend rate after the capital increase. Exceptions from the 10 percent rule have been made, e.g., for shipping companies (8 percent). In November 1970, the president of the Tokyo Stock Exchange proposed a revision of the 10 percent requirement because the large private railroad companies, in protest against the government's refusal to let them raise their fares, reduced their dividend rates from 10 percent to 9 percent and thereby became ineligible for capital increases.

The Tokyo Stock Exchange also considered the control of "insider trading," particularly, buying or selling by directors, relying on special information, of stock of their own company. Securities companies involved in such transactions should be punished by a fine or suspension of trading. The Ministry of Finance ruled that the securities companies should make pertinent inquiries if there was ground for suspicion that directors were acting on the basis of inside information and draw attention to the violation of the law; if necessary, they should refuse to execute such orders. The most common forms of insider trading on the Tokyo Stock Exchange are selling before announcing a decrease in the dividend rate or the suspension of dividend payments, and buying of shares before announcing favorable developments (usually combined with selling after the announcement).

On October 15, 1970, the Securities Transaction Council proposed a revision of the Securities Transaction Law which concerned the following points: (1) stricter disclosure requirements; (2) regulation of support buying; (3) regulation of take-over bids; (4) regulation of foreign securities dealers doing business in Japan. In particular, the council advocated the following measures: (1) not only the company, but its officers, underwriters, and certified public accountants and auditing firms should be civilly liable for any false statements in a prospectus; (2) if a prospectus for an increase in capital contains serious misrepresentations, the minister of finance can fix a period up to one year within which no application for a capital increase will be accepted; (3) not only the companies listed on the stock exchanges but also the companies whose stocks are listed with the Securities Dealers Association for over-the-counter trading must file business reports with the minister of finance.

Support buying (which may fall under the prohibition against market manipulation contained in Article 125 of the Securities Transaction Law) has become a problem with the increase in issues at market prices. In August 1970, Tsuneo Machida, a former director of Yamaichi Securities Co., filed a complaint with the Public Prosecutor for the Tokyo District Court alleging that four major securities companies and Matsushita Electric Industrial Co. had conspired to manipulate the price of Matsushita Electric Industrial Co. by buying 3,150,000 shares of stock in the company so as to raise its price from ¥627 on May 1, 1970, to ¥674 on May 2, 1970. The four securities companies had taken over 5 million shares each to sell at a price of ¥630 between May 4 and 19. Matsushita had announced the issue already in January; of the 20,000,000 new shares, 18,500,000 shares were allotted to stockholders (the allotment was to stockholders as of February 28; it was a public offering with preference given to existing stockholders at a ratio of about 40:1; Matsushita's capital was ¥37,125 million, corresponding to 742.5 million shares). Matsushita's stock had reached a high of ¥827 in January 1970; the ex-dividend high was ¥802, the low ¥730. In April, the stock slipped from a high of ¥797 on the sixth to a low of ¥595 on the thirtieth. Between April 30 and May 11, the four companies were alleged to have purchased a total of 18,330,000 shares of which they resold 11,670,000. The price of the stock rose from ¥635 on May 1 to a high of ¥678 on May 2; by May 26, it had dropped to a low of ¥520. Officials of the Tokyo Stock Exchange dismissed the allegations as groundless for other issues had also experienced wide fluctuations (the Dow-Jones average registered a high of ¥2,534.45 on April 6—the high of the entire year— and a low of ¥2,114.32 on April 30; in May, the average fell from a high of ¥2,209.61 on the seventh to a low of ¥1,929.64 on the twenty-seventh).

The law which enacted the amendments proposed by the council permits support buying provided it is reported to the minister of finance and publicly announced; the announcement will have to specify the price at which support buying will be undertaken and the name of the securities firm in charge of the operation.

The regulation of take-over bids has aroused considerable controversy. One view was against any regulation; such bids, considered pernicious, are unknown in Japan and a legal regulation might only encourage them. The other view asserted that the liberalization of inward capital investment would eventually lead to take-over bids by foreign interests. This position involved another difference of opinion. The industry, certain government agencies, and members of the Liberal-Democratic party wanted a regulation of take-over bids so as to prevent inroads of foreign capital, while the Ministry of Finance maintained that the regulation should be for the protection of investors, not of industry. *Keidanren* ("Federation of Economic Organizations") wanted a provision under which a take-over bid would need approval by the minister of finance who would have to consult with the competent minister before sanctioning such a bid. The federation also advocated a relaxation of the restrictions on the acquisition of its own stock by a company (Article 210 of the Commercial Code), and these two proposals were supported by the Automobile Industry Association, which further demanded that the minister of finance should be given authority to prohibit take-over bids by foreign capital, that the prohibition against holding companies be relaxed, that cumulative voting be prohibited in the articles of incorporation, and that a government organ for defensive buying of stocks be established. The government draft does not require approval of take-over bids although certain quarters in the government had asserted that, from the point of view of the national economy, the government should have the right to intervene and prohibit a take-over.

The proposed regulations provide that whoever offers to buy 10 percent or more of the shares of a company from present stockholders outside the stock exchange (or if he already holds 10 percent of the stock but intends to acquire more) must notify the minister of finance of his intention, state the conditions of his offer, and submit a certificate showing that the capital required for his take-over has been deposited with a bank. The take-over bid becomes effective on the eleventh day after the notification has been sent to the minister of finance, i.e., ten days have to pass between the notification and the beginning of purchases. The industry wanted a period of thirty days in which the enterprise could organize its defense against the take-over, but the Ministry of Finance was of the opinion that a week should be sufficient to ascertain the pertinent facts. The Tokyo Stock Exchange expressed the view that the take-over bid should become effective immediately because any interval would result in skyrocketing prices. Passed by the Diet, the amendments concerning disclosure, support buying, and take-over bids became effective July 1, 1971.

The Legal System Research Council (an advisory organ to the minister of justice) approved an amendment to the Commercial Code which would abolish cumulative voting and relax conditions for the issuance of convertible debentures. Both changes are contrary to the interests of the small stockholders but wanted by big business. (Defense against foreign capital is given as reason for the first change.) The Ministry of Justice drafted changes in the auditing of joint-stock companies so as to prevent fraudulent reports, but the Association of Tax Accountants objected to the revision.

These changes were among the amendments to the Commercial Code advocated by Keidanren. They included: (1) relaxation of the restrictions on the possession of the corporation's own shares (treasury stock); (2) emission of warrant bonds (bonds with a warrant entitling the holder to purchase stock at a stated price); (3) the possibility of excluding cumulative voting by the articles of incorporation; (4) regulations for splitting up a company; (5) recognition of records or files made by computer or microfilm; (6) adoption of consolidated reports; (7) increase in the ceiling on bond emissions; (8) limitation of the right to inspect the stockholders register. The general trend of these proposals is the removal of restrictions on corporate activities intended for the protection of the public.

The Ministry of Finance has asked the Council on Corporate Accounting to prepare a report on the consolidated accounting system.

Starting August 1971, the Tokyo Stock Exchange introduced the following regulations: (1) companies must announce the dividend in yen, not in percent; if accounts are settled twice a year, the dividend per share for six months must be stated; if accounts are settled once a year, the dividend payment per share for the entire year must be announced; (2) together with the dividend, earnings per share (net profit after tax per average issued share) must be reported; (3) if a stock dividend is distributed, the number of new shares per 100 shares must be stated. At the same time, the exchange announced that the sessions for specified stocks would begin at the same time as general trading, i.e., at 9 A.M. and 1 P.M.

Although, as mentioned above, take-over bids are not customary in Japan, transfers of large blocks of shares as a result of a secretly negotiated agreement are not unusual. They are particularly frequent if an enterprise becomes affiliated with another enterprise or a certain group. A recent example was the acquisition of 6,620,000 million shares of Shibaura Sugar Refining Co. by Mitsui & Co. from Hideki Yokoi, president of Toyo Yusen and Shibaura's largest stockholder. This transfer made the merger of three sugar refining companies into Mitsui Sugar Refining possible. A less controversial transaction was the increase in Kawasaki Heavy Industry's share in Japan Aircraft Manufacturing Co. from less than 10 percent to 25.9 percent. The Fair Trade Commission stated that a cease and desist order would be issued if a take-over bid should involve unfair competition.

Occasionally, the acquisition of stocks is intended to secure preferential treatment as a customer. Recently, Sanko Steamship Co. bought large blocks of shares of the leading shipbuilders (Mitsubishi Heavy Industries, 50 million shares; Ishikawajima-Harima Heavy Industries, 25 million shares; Hitachi Shipbuilding & Engineering, 15 million shares; and about 3.5 million to 10 million shares in Nippon Kokan, Kawasaki Heavy Industries, and Sumitomo Heavy Machinery), allegedly for making sure that it can carry out its shipbuilding program despite the large order backlog of the shipyards.

As far as misleading or untruthful reports are concerned, the Ministry of Finance seems to have become stricter after the failure of Sanyo Special Steel in 1965. The company had falsified its balance sheet after 1962 by reporting imaginary profits, declaring dividends, and paying directors bonuses despite heavy losses. In 1970, seven firms listed on the exchange were ordered to correct their reports. Overstatement of profits was the most common dishonesty.

The Tokyo Stock Exchange, in cooperation with Hitachi Ltd., has drawn up an automation program which will initially be adopted for the thirty most heavily traded issues. Until now, volume and market trend have been transmitted to display terminals in dealers' offices, but the new system will eventually replace floor trading and make the over 1,000 *saitori* superfluous. The exchange expects average daily volume to rise to 700 million shares in 1972, but in view of the strong concentration on certain issues (thirty issues account for about 50 percent of all trading) and certain hours (8.30–9.00 A.M. during the morning session and 12.30–1.00 P.M. during the afternoon session), a partial computerization will take care of most of the business. Another rationalization measure, proposed in November 1970 but not yet carried out, is the establishment of a Japan Securities Settlement Co., a clearing house for stock transactions. Each member of the exchange would have an account with the clearing house for the most important twenty to thirty issues and keep a deposit of a certain number of stock certificates. Transactions between member dealers of the exchange would be settled by crediting or debiting their accounts with the clearing house so that actual delivery of the certificates could be dispensed with.

A new stock price index was introduced for the First Section of the Tokyo Stock Exchange on July 1, 1969, and on August 1, 1969, for the Second Section. The new index is calculated by dividing the aggregate market value of all listed shares of the section by the aggregate market value of all issues at the close of trading on January 4, 1968 (the first trading day of the year). The base period value is adjusted for capital increases or decreases as well as new listings or delistings. This is the second attempt to replace the Dow-Jones average; the first revision, the average of all issues based on stock prices as of January 5, 1959 = 126.19, had not been successful.

Critics of the old Dow-Jones charge that it overstates and distorts price movements. The Dow-Jones is based on the price of 225 selected issues as of May 16, 1959, divided by 225 = ￥170.21. The index is adjusted for new issues and, on account of these adjustments, it is about thirteen times higher than the simple arithmetic average, so that price movements are amplified thirteen times. Moreover, the Dow-Jones does not take into account the size of the capital of the issues; Sony with a relatively small capital (￥4,038 million) has the same weight as Nippon Steel Corporation (capital ￥229,360 million). Sony frequently goes up or down ￥100 a day, moving the Dow-Jones by about ￥6; if Nippon Steel changes at all, it is by ￥1–2 which has almost no influence on the Dow-Jones. The 225 issues of the Dow-Jones represent about one-third of those listed on the First Section: food, marine products, textiles, oil, stone, clay and glass, nonferrous metals, and real estate account for about half of the selected issues, general and electrical machinery for about 20 percent. In other words, the selection no longer corresponds to the structure of Japan's economy and the importance of the stock issues. The reason why most dealers prefer the Dow-Jones is that it is more "lively," i.e., most issues covered by the index are actually traded whereas many issues in the new index are hardly traded at all.

Investment in stocks and bonds by individuals has failed to expand at the same pace as the economy so that there has been a relative decline in individual stock ownership. In addition to tax incentives (dividend income up to ￥50,000 a year per issue is taxed separately if the shares owned are less than 5 percent of the shares issued), the government amended the Commercial Code so as to increase the marketability of shares. The main changes, effective July 1, 1966, were: (1) the right to new shares was made transferable; (2) the transfer of stock becomes effective by the transfer of the stock certificate for inscribed as well as uninscribed (bearer) shares (i.e., endorsement is unnecessary); (3) par shares can be changed into nonpar shares and vice versa; (4) convertible debentures may be converted into shares even when the transfer books are closed prior to the stockholders' meeting; (5) no inscribed share certificates need be issued if the stockholder declares that their issue is unnecessary; (6) transfer of shares to a particular party can be blocked by a vote of two-thirds of all issued shares; (7) the offer of new shares at a particularly favorable price to investors other than those who already hold stock in the company requires a special resolution of the stockholders' meeting.

The reason for the first amendment, an assimilation to the American practice, was that until then stockholders who could not raise the necessary funds for "right" issues had to sell part of their old shares or forego the acquisition of the new shares allotted to them. Both alternatives might involve a substantial financial loss which can be avoided by detaching the right to new issues from the ownership of the old stock.

The simplification of the stock transfer adjusted the law to actual practice. Interlocking stockholding among corporations has increased, particularly within the old *zaibatsu* groups (20–30 percent of the shares of the enterprises of the Mitsubishi and Sumitomo groups are estimated to be held within the group). Firms afraid of take-overs by foreign capital have been trying to find "stable" stockholders, chiefly by having financial institutions acquire large blocks of their shares. The Tokyo Stock Exchange classifies stock ownership below 5,000 shares as floating shares.

At the end of fiscal 1970, the stock ownership structure of all 1,584 companies listed on the Tokyo Stock Exchange was as follows:

	Number of shares	%
Cumulative number of stockholders		
17,854,159	119,141,850,000	100.0
Corporate stock ownership	67,451 million	59.6
Financial institutions	36,881 //	30.9
Investment trusts	1,643 //	1.4
Securities companies	1,412 //	1.2
Other corporations	27,515 //	26.1
Domestic		23.1
Foreign		3.0
Individual Japanese stockholders	47,570 //	39.9
Central & local governments	4,120 //	0.3
Individual foreign investors		0.2

Structure of Stock Ownership

(In percent)

Latter half of fiscal year	Financial institutions			Other corporations	Individuals	Other
	City banks	Life insurance companies	Other			
1955	6.1	7.7	12.3	11.8	51.3	10.8
1960	7.9	7.2	17.2	17.5	44.8	5.4
1965	8.9	8.7	15.0	16.2	42.3	8.9
1969	11.0	13.0	11.0	20.8	38.7	5.5

Note: 300 companies listed on the First Section of the Tokyo Stock Exchange.
Source: Nikko Securities Co.

In January 1969, the Tokyo Stock Exchange suspended off-market transaction of securities ordered by overseas customers. Such transactions had been permitted on account of the time differential but with the increase in foreign orders, this system seemed to interfere with fair price formation. Due to the concentration of foreign interest on a few issues, buying for foreign investors was sometimes suspended because the limits on foreign stockholding had been reached. In June 1970, the Ministry of Finance announced guidelines for trading, imposing a ceiling on the daily volume of shares traded by foreign investors through Japanese brokerage houses; the main objective of these regulations was to prevent sharp drops in stock prices. For the same purpose, the ministry permitted overseas branches of Japanese securities companies to own foreign currency funds for intervening in foreign exchanges and keeping quotations of Japanese stocks from declining suddenly on foreign markets and thus triggering a slump on the Japanese exchanges.

In October 1970, the Tokyo Stock Exchange became a member of the International Federation of Stock Exchanges, an organization established in 1961 and comprising seventeen stock exchanges in sixteen countries. Its aim is to study problems of common interest such as the distribution of stocks, taxes on securities, and financial reports of corporations listed on the exchanges.

3 STOCK EXCHANGES

2 SECURITIES FINANCE COMPANIES

The postwar reorganization of the stock exchanges made regular transactions the basic type of stock exchange business. This form requires delivery of the shares and settlement on the fourth day from the date of the sales contract, but if the customer pays "earnest" money (in the West called "margin") within three days from the contract date, settlement may be deferred for ninety days. This system, modeled somewhat after American margin transactions, was introduced in June 1951.

Unlike the United States, however, Japanese banks and other financial institutions rarely provide credit for stock purchases by accepting the purchased securities as collateral. The U.S. system of brokers' loans is not practised here. This puts the burden of extending credit on the securities dealers themselves, but, with the exception of the largest securities companies, the dealers lacked the capital to take over the task of credit financing. A system was therefore established, by creation of securities finance companies, which linked the demand for funds to the demand for shares incidental to the credit transactions of the members of the stock exchanges. Ordinarily, the lending activities of the securities finance companies are restricted to members of the stock exchange. The securities finance companies were established to take the shares bought by the buyer as collateral when they lend the money needed for settlement to the buyer, and they accept the claims (money receivable) of the seller as collateral when they lend shares to the seller. Thus, out of the total volume of transactions in a particular issue, the securities finance companies can settle large volumes by mere bookkeeping operations, since funds as well as shares lent will come back as collateral to the extent that purchases and sales offset each other, so that the securities finance companies need only relatively small balances of funds and shares.

The securities finance companies were first established as a countermeasure to the stagnation of 1949–50. In Tokyo, Osaka, Nagoya, and Kyoto, they originated out of a reorganization of the old short-term settlement institutions attached to the stock exchanges. In the beginning, their chief business consisted of lending funds and shares to customers introduced by the securities dealers, but when, in June 1951, margin transactions started, they became the chief credit organs in this system. They were, at first, under the regulations for moneylenders, but, in August 1955, a chapter entitled "Securities Finance Companies" was added to the Securities Transaction Law. As a result, the nine securities finance companies, which had been set up at the various stock exchanges, were consolidated into three firms, Japan Securities Finance Co. (Tokyo), Osaka Securities Finance Co., and Chubu Securities Finance Co. (Nagoya). The securities finance companies at the other stock exchanges became branches of these three major companies.

Principal Accounts of Securities Finance Companies
December 31, 1970

	¥ million
Cash	3,157
Call loans	—
Loans, total	266,531
Loans on bills & notes	101,276
Loans on margin transactions	165,255
Borrowed money	78,192
Call money	147,810
Guarantee money for margin transactions	487
Guarantee money for lent stocks (margin transactions)	19,143
Guarantee money for lent stocks	0
Deposits	13,148
Capital	3,400
Loans to Brokers	
Money lent to brokers	
Balance 937,821,000 shares	165,255
Stocks lent to brokers	
Balance 94,064,000 shares	19,143
Outstanding balance	
843,757,000 shares	146,111

The securities finance companies need the approval of the minister of finance for their establishment. Their chief business is to lend funds or shares required for credit transactions to members of the stock exchanges (Securities Transaction Law, Article 156–3). In addition, they lend funds and shares to customers of the securities dealers, take custody of securities, in particular in connection with the transfer and settlement system of the exchanges, and act as the general credit organs of the exchanges.

The most important part of the business of the securities finance companies is to lend money and shares. The Japan Securities Finance Co. (JSF) restricts its lending to the regular members of the stock exchanges in Tokyo, Sapporo, Niigata, and Fukuoka and to issues declared eligible for margin trading. Members of the exchanges who wish to borrow from the JSF pay in a "loan collateral" up to the settlement day. This is equal to the earnest money paid by the customer to the securities dealer and presently amounts to 30 percent of the desired loan. But the collateral can also be in the form of stock instead of cash; in such cases, stock is accepted at 70 percent of its market value.

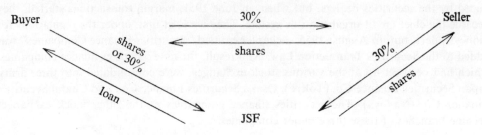

JSF tabulates all applications for financing and stock loans by issues and remits to the clearing department of the stock exchange the balances for each settlement day. On the other hand, it receives from the clearing department the stocks or sums of money serving as collateral. This cooperation with the clearing department forms one of the distinctive features of the system. If changes in stock quotations impair the value of the collateral, margin calls are made.

As a rule, loans are for twenty-four hours, but if the lender does not request repayment, they are automatically extended from day to day. Each day JSF collects the interest from the borrower and pays it to the lender (the party who loaned the stocks). The maximum interest rates for these transactions are fixed by the Ministry of Finance, but the rates actually applied vary. Effective February 1, 1971, the securities finance companies reduced interest rates as follows:

Loans for margin trading:
buyer's rate from 9 percent to 8.75 percent
seller's rate from 4.5 percent to 4.25 percent
Rate for financing of lend-lease transactions:
from 8.25 percent to 8 percent
Rate for money in place of leased stocks:
from 4.5 percent to 4.25 percent

If the value of the shares borrowed exceeds the amount of the loan, the shares received from the buyer as collateral are insufficient to cover the shares lent to the seller. In such a case JSF must procure the balance of the shares from outside, and the seller must pay a fee on the total value of the shares borrowed, which is then split proportionally between the buyer and the lender of the shares. The rate for this "fee" is very high (the maximum is 50 *sen* per share per diem) and subject to large fluctuations. The fee is determined by bidding among the members of the exchange who desire to borrow shares. The system serves to keep down the borrowing of shares and to increase the amount of loans.

Credit extended by JSF against securities as collateral does not differ from that of other financial institutions. The borrower gives a promissory note payable, as a rule, in one month, but in the case of loans for the payment of capital increases and loans backed by public bonds or corporate debentures, payable in two months; under special circumstances, renewal may be possible. Four types of credit are given by JSF.

1. General loans: funds for buying stock, or for working capital in general, advanced to securities dealers and their customers. For customers, the loan must be guaranteed by a securities dealer and is channeled through him.

2. Loans for financing payment of capital increases: if firms listed on the stock exchange increase their capital, stockholders can borrow the required funds. The new shares serve as collateral.

3. Short-term borrowing: securities dealers who want to obtain the purchase price for shares sold in regular way transactions prior to the settlement day, or who have received an order to sell from a customer and want to remit the purchase price prior to the settlement day, can borrow the money on the security of the shares sold.

4. Loans against public bonds and corporate debentures: this form of lending was introduced in February 1960 in order to foster the bond market. Securities dealers can borrow

funds, for the purchase of bonds already issued, from customers other than financial institutions; customers owning bonds can obtain loans against these bonds for temporary financial needs.

JSF can also finance the settlement of new stock issues, i.e., advance to the company, on the date fixed for the payment of the new shares, the funds equivalent to the new shares sold on the security of the newly issued shares, but the system is hardly used.

For raising the necessary funds, JSF relies on bank loans and call money. Bank loans are used for general loans but, as a rule, call money is relied on for financing stock transactions. Hence more than half of JSF's own borrowings come from the call money market. In April 1950, JSF became one of the short-term financing agencies and, with the adoption of margin transactions in June 1951, a tripartite agreement was signed between the Bank of Japan, Tokyo Stock Exchange, and JSF, through which a close link between the funds required for margin transactions and the call money market was forged. Based on this agreement, JSF deposits with the exchange the stocks received as collateral and all other stocks which it holds, and the exchange issues a certificate stating that it holds the collateral for short-term fund transactions. Against this certificate, JSF can go into the call money market through short-term fund dealers, while the Bank of Japan recognizes the draft drawn by JSF and backed up by the certificate as collateral, if the short-term fund dealers cannot meet the requirements of JSF and have to borrow from the central bank. The same system exists for the Osaka and Nagoya stock exchanges. The Bank of Japan controls this fund supply system by raising or lowering the ratio of lending against the nominal value of the certificate.

In efforts to prevent a complete collapse of the stock market, the Bank of Japan extended credit to the four large securities companies in September 1964 and to ten medium-sized securities companies in November through JSF. It was the first time that the Bank of Japan had provided direct financing to JSF, which borrowed the funds at 6.935 percent and lent them to the securities companies at 7.665 percent (call loan money to brokers about 12 percent).

Based on an agreement drawn up in October 1950, the borrowing of JSF from the city banks (which accounts for the largest part of JSF's bank loans) is, as a rule, in the form of joint financing, i.e., not from any particular city bank but from the city banks as a group. But, in addition, JSF may borrow from individual city or local banks. Usually, stocks serve as collateral.

JSF can control margin transactions and prevent excessive speculation by raising interest rates and/or collateral requirements, but these changes need the approval of the minister of finance. Other ways of controlling the volume of transactions are: (1) by establishing a loan ceiling for the members of the exchange, and raising the collateral requirements if their loan balance exceeds this ceiling; (2) to require additional collateral for certain issues determined after consultation with the exchange authorities.

With the help of funds received in trust from the Japan Joint Securities Co., the Japan Securities Finance Co. began financing purchases of public and corporate bonds in February 1971.

3 STOCK EXCHANGES

3 JAPAN JOINT SECURITIES CO. AND JAPAN SECURITIES HOLDING ASSOCIATION

In the years following the 1959–61 boom, the situation of the stock market went from bad to worse, and the securities companies, anxious to prevent a complete collapse of the market, resorted to heavy support buying. In order to supply the securities companies with liquid funds, the city banks, in June 1962 and on several occasions thereafter, extended credit against bonds as collateral. At the end of October 1962, the city banks granted additional loans collateralized by the government-guaranteed debentures held by the investment trusts. Large support buying by the life insurance companies helped to stabilize the market, but the so-called Kennedy shock, the impact of the measures announced in July 1963, caused a new slump. Due to the loss of investor confidence, the monetary stringency, and the generally unsatisfactory economic conditions, the market was unable to absorb the overhang of stocks. On January 20, 1964, twelve city banks, the Industrial Bank and the Long-Term Credit Bank, and the four large securities companies founded the Japan Joint Securities Co. (*Nippon Kyōdō Shōken*) with a capital of ¥2.5 billion. In addition to support buying, the company could loan money in the call market. The company restricted its buying to the First Section of the exchange and was not to hold more than 10 percent of any single issue. Later, local banks, trust banks, life insurance companies, and some medium-sized securities companies became stockholders, bringing the number of firms to 119. The capital was increased to ¥30 billion; at their peak, borrowings from the Bank of Japan amounted to ¥67.8 billion, other borrowed funds to ¥120 billion. During the years 1964 and 1965, the company bought a total of ¥189.6 billion in stocks (190 different issues).

Since the securities companies had bought a considerable amount of stocks listed on the Second Section, the relief buying of the Joint Securities Co. left them with an unbalanced stock inventory. On January 12, 1965, fifty-seven securities companies founded a second organ, the Japan Securities Holding Association (*Nippon Shōken Hoyū Kumiai*) which was to take over stocks held by the securities companies or the investment trusts. By July the association had taken over stocks valued at ¥182,686 million from investment trusts and about ¥50 billion from securities companies.

The release of the stocks thus taken off the market was not free from problems. Besides the inability of the market to absorb large blocks of shares, the holding association required the consent of the member firms which had transferred the stocks, and the companies whose stocks the two support organs tried to sell wanted to see them in the hands of "stable" stockholders. In March 1966, the Joint Securities Co. sold about 50 million shares valued at ¥10.7 billion in the market, and the holding association transferred almost 199 million shares (¥20,850 million) to the securities companies. In April and May, the association returned to the securities companies the ¥50 billion in stocks originally taken over from these firms. In June, the holding association sold 4,860,000, and the Joint Securities Co. 1,270,000 shares of Kansai Electric Power Co. (value about ¥4.8 billion). Purchases by the life insurance companies absorbed about ¥50 billion of the stocks released by the two organs.

The Japan Securities Holding Association was dissolved on January 11, 1969, after having established a capital market promotion foundation to which the profits from the operations of the association were given as endorsement. By December 1969, the holdings of the Joint Securities Co. were down to about ¥33 billion, but opinions on the disposition of the company (which, in the meantime, had been licensed as a securities company) were divided. The city banks wanted to have it dissolved and half of its profits transferred to the Japan Securities Finance Co. and the other half allocated to a deposit insurance fund to be created under the reorganization plans proposed by the Financial System Research Council. The Ministry of Finance and the Bank of Japan were opposed to the proposals made by the banks; the banks, they said, were not the only interested parties; since a large part of the funds used by the company had been supplied by the Bank of Japan, the bank should have a voice in the issue. The president of the company, Ryojiro Mitsumori, wanted to retain his job and remain in business in order to support the bond market. The securities companies said that they welcomed help for the bond market but that there would be trouble if the Joint Securities Co. remained in existence, and the banks thought that with ¥27 billion nothing much could be done for the bond market. Nevertheless, Mitsumori, the Ministry of Finance, and the Bank of Japan prevailed; on November 26, 1970, the stockholders' meeting agreed to the proposal to dissolve the company on January 30, 1971, and to use the remaining profits to establish a foundation to be called the Japan Joint Securities Foundation (*Nippon Kyōdō Shōken Zaidan*). The capital (¥30 billion) was returned to the original investors (banks, 66.7 percent; securities companies, 16 percent) together with ¥6,600 million in dividends (the company had not distributed a dividend since its foundation). For the business year ending September 1970, the company had reported profits of ¥12,876 million; with profits carried over, undivided profits amounted to ¥32,210 million. The stock portfolio was valued at ¥2,300 million for the end of October 1970. The foundation is to use its capital (¥28 billion) for making advances to the Japan Securities Co. (interest rate, 7 percent) and the Small Enterprise Credit Insurance Corporation (interest rate, 3.5–4 percent). The profits of the foundation are used for public purposes connected with banking and securities. Ryojiro Mitsumori became chairman of the board of directors; one director each is appointed by the Ministry of Finance and the Bank of Japan.

Part of the funds of the foundation (¥9.5 billion) was given in trust to the Japan Securities Finance Co. for promoting bond purchases by individuals. Actually, three types of transactions are contemplated: (1) loans to individuals secured by bonds; (2) loans to securities companies for buying bonds sold by individuals; (3) loans to securities companies for purchases on the stock exchange or the bond center. The Securities Finance Co. pays 7 percent interest, but the interest rate for individuals is 8.5 percent and for securities companies 7.5 percent. Loans to individuals are limited to ¥10 million per case but are given on a preferential basis; among the securities companies, those not entitled to central bank credit are to be preferred. In the financing of purchases of bonds sold by individuals, the bond certificates have to be deposited as collateral (the loans are not given if the bonds are only registered).

4 INSURANCE COMPANIES

While some forms of mutual assistance, including a kind of marine insurance, existed already in the Tokugawa era, modern insurance companies date from the Meiji era. The government operates a great variety of insurance systems. In the field of social security, Japan possesses the following insurance systems: health insurance, day laborers' health insurance, seamen's insurance, national health insurance, national annuities, welfare annuities, unemployment insurance, and workers accident compensation insurance. In addition, the government operates a special insurance system for government employees. These systems have been set up at different times and under various circumstances, and neither the systems nor their administration are integrated. National health insurance is organized along territorial lines, while other systems operate on an occupational basis. Moreover, the government has organized numerous insurance schemes for business: agricultual cooperative reinsurance, forest fire insurance, fishing vessel reinsurance, small fishing enterprise finance guarantee insurance, export insurance, wooden vessel reinsurance, automobile liability reinsurance, and machinery installment credit insurance. But most of these systems are not very important for the monetary system. Only postal life insurance and postal annuities represent fund sources which play great roles in the fiscal loan and investment programs. These systems were started in 1916, and, before the Second World War, accumulated premiums and other reserves were administered by the Insurance Bureau of the Ministry of Postal Services, but, during the war, surplus funds as well as reserves were administered by the Deposits Bureau. Under the "Law Concerning the Management of the Accumulated Reserves of Simple Life Insurance and Postal Annuities" (simple life insurance is the official name for postal life insurance) enacted in 1952, accumulated premiums remain under the jurisdiction of the minister of postal services, but surplus funds are deposited with the Trust Fund Bureau. Hence postal life in surance funds figure separately in the government's investment plans.

Japan's first private life insurance company, Meiji Life Insurance Co., was established in 1881. In the following years, a proliferation of small insurance companies led to many abuses which the Insurance Business Law (*Hokengyō-hō*) enacted in 1900 tried to bring under control. Only joint-stock or mutual companies were allowed to engage in the insurance business (under the postwar occupation, all life insurance companies were reorganized into mutual companies); a license from the minister of finance was required and strict rules regulated operations, agents, and premiums. The law laid down the basic principle that the same institution cannot engage in life and nonlife insurance. Fire insurance also started in the Meiji era. Initially, foreign companies established branches in Japan and, in 1887, Tokio

Fire Insurance Co. was founded. In 1948, a special organization for the calculation of non-life insurance premiums was established which is exempt from the application of the Antimonopoly Law. All insurance premiums must be approved by the minister of finance. Since 1965, qualifying examinations have been held for the sales staff of the life insurance companies; these examinations, however, are voluntary. Out of a total sales force of about three hundred thousand (mostly women), fifty thousand have passed this examination.

In the prewar period, the insurance companies belonging to the *zaibatsu* dominated the industry and they still remain in the forefront. In 1933, total assets of the life insurance companies exceeded ¥2 billion; loans made up ¥564 million and investments ¥1,044 million (in the same year, bank deposits amounted to ¥8,727 million). The insurance companies already were important institutional investors. They jointly founded the Life Insurance Securities Co., which successfully supported the stock market in the beginning of the thirties. This company was dissolved in 1933 but the insurance companies continued their cooperation in the form of an investment syndicate. During the war, the government's concentration policy reduced the number of life insurance companies from twenty-eight to twenty-one and that of nonlife insurance companies from forty-two to sixteen. The present numbers are twenty life insurance and twenty-one nonlife insurance companies, but as mentioned above the life insurance enterprises are all mutual companies. From among all the insurance companies, only thirteen nonlife insurance companies are listed on the stock exchange.

The life insurance companies sell three basic types of insurance: term insurance, whole life insurance, and annuities; but in recent years, special-purpose saving plans (education insurance, i.e., saving for payment of school fees; marriage insurance), various combinations (term insurance and annuities, etc.), and various forms of group insurance have been promoted. The insurance companies compete with the trust banks for the pension fund business. The main business lines of the nonlife insurance companies are marine, fire, and automobile insurance: in 1961, a form called overall home insurance that covers ten different insurance objects (fire, theft, lightning, explosion, storm, flood, etc.) was introduced.

In the fifties, the life insurance companies channeled larger funds into loans to key industries (electric power, steel, and chemicals) than into portfolio investment (the share of loans in the investable funds of the life insurance companies rose from 42 percent in 1955 to 65 percent in 1960; at the same time, the share of portfolio investment declined from 38 percent to 33 percent, and then further to 25 percent). Different from prewar conditions, their investments in bonds are small, while stocks make up the largest part of their portfolios. The low interest rates of bonds and their inferior marketability were the main reasons for this development. The situation is the same with nonlife insurance companies for which investment constitutes the chief form of fund management. On April 1, 1971, the ceiling on lending by the nonlife insurance companies was abolished, but the 30 percent limit on investment in stocks remained in force.

In the beginning of the sixties, the life insurance companies were able to achieve a significant expansion of their business. From fiscal 1961 to 1964, the average yearly rate of increase in the number of contracts was over 30 percent; the rate dropped to 25 percent in fiscal 1965 (due largely to the increase in the cost of living). On April 1, 1964, all life insurance companies started personal accident insurance (against traffic accidents, falls, overturns, drowning, gas poisoning, earthquakes, floods, storms, etc.) covering death, injuries, and hospitalization. Premiums for old-age insurance were lowered and the ceiling on tax deductible life insurance raised. Following the compilation of a new life expectancy table by the insurance companies based on their experience in the years from 1960 to 1963, premium rates were lowered by about 3 percent. Pressed by the government, the Life Insurance Association (twenty member firms) agreed to invest part of their funds in public programs (fiscal 1963, ¥43 billion; fiscal 1964, ¥54 billion; in 1964, the breakdown was as follows: Housing Corporation, ¥33 billion; purchase of government-guaranteed bonds, ¥10 billion; local bonds and bonds of the Central Bank for Commercial & Industrial Cooperatives, ¥9 billion; debentures of the Japan Hypothec Bank, ¥2 billion). Naturally, this was not the most desirable form of investment from a business point of view, particularly in view of the strong corporate fund demand, but the companies cannot disregard the "advice" of the Ministry of Finance.

In September 1966 Kyoei Life Insurance began to sell life insurance combined with home loans. If one-third of the face value of the insurance policy is paid, either in installments or a lump sum, the insured receives a home loan equal to the face value of the policy. The loan is to be repaid in fifteen years and the yearly interest rate is 9.8 percent. Only applicants under fifty years of age are eligible because repayment of the loan is canceled if the borrower dies. Initially, the company limited this type of insurance to 1,000 cases a year.

The life insurance companies also introduced travel insurance. Policies were divided into two classes: Class A for long trips and Class B for short ones. Eligible were persons between the ages of fifteen and seventy-five; validity of the policy ranged from one week to one year. Benefits were $50,000 in case of death; for injuries, the ceiling was $50,000 for Class A and $10,000 for Class B. Depending on the seriousness of the injury, 100 percent, 50 percent, or 30 percent of the ceiling would be paid for Class A, and 100 percent, 70 percent, 50 percent 30 percent, or 20 percent for Class B.

Another form of insurance which started in 1966 was sickness insurance. The policy pays ¥1 million at maturity or ¥3 million in case of death; in addition, benefits are paid if the the insured is hospitalized for longer than thirty days on account of sickness or longer than ten days on account of an accident. Benefits are paid up to 100 days of hospitalization for each case and up to 400 days during the validity of the contract.

Kobe City devised a plan which insured the life of the supporter of a crippled or disabled person. The supporter pays a monthly premium of ¥2,000 to the city; the city has concluded a collective insurance contract with the twenty life insurance companies. If the supporter of the cripple dies, the life insurance companies pay the city ¥3 million. The city accumulates these funds and pays the person who undertakes to care for the cripple a monthly stipend of ¥20,000.

This system was imitated by a number of local bodies, but it was found inadequate, mainly because no transfer of benefits was possible in case of a change in residence. In February 1970, therefore, a new system was inaugurated which is jointly handled by the Social Welfare Promotion Association and the life insurance companies. The prefectural authorities pay ¥20,000 a month to a physically handicapped person whose supporter took out this type of insurance, if the supporter dies. The insurance companies turn the insurance money over to the prefectures which accumulate these funds.

Many towns insure their inhabitants against traffic accidents. The system is voluntary; a participant pays a yearly premium of ¥360 and is entitled to benefits up to ¥100,000 in case of injury while his family is paid ¥500,000 in case of death. Larger towns handle this system independently; the smaller towns usually tie up with an insurance company. A number of agricultural cooperatives started mutual fire and liability insurance and the system spread to small towns. Since September 1970, the National Mutual Insurance Federation of Agricultural Cooperatives and the Prefectural Mutual Insurance Federations of Agricultural Cooperatives have been permitted to operate in the call money market.

With the diffusion in car ownership, the premium income of the insurance companies rose rapidly, from ¥8.8 billion in fiscal 1959 to ¥29.8 billion in fiscal 1963. In February 1964, new premium rates were introduced, and in July 1964, a new method of fixing the premium rates for fire insurance was adopted. The traditional system was based on the market value of the building; the depreciation was deducted from its value. The new system was based on the replacement (rebuilding) value, but only within the following limits: up to 30 percent depreciation, the full amount will be paid; if depreciation is between 30 percent and 40 percent, 90 percent of the insurance value will be paid; for 40–50 percent depreciation, 80 percent will be paid; if a building has been depreciated by over 50 percent, no insurance policy will be written.

In June 1966, the insurance companies began to sell earthquake insurance, not as an independent contract but as part of their comprehensive home insurance or comprehensive store insurance contracts. Coverage was limited to 30 percent of the total coverage and payments to ¥900,000 for immovables and ¥600,000 for movables. The contracts had to be concluded for at least a year; premiums were graded depending on the rating of the building and its location. In April 1971, the ceiling on earthquake insurance was raised to ¥3 million for immovables and ¥2 million for movables, but coverage remained limited to 30 percent of the insurance amount. Premium rates were reduced by 10 percent. The government provides reinsurance and reimburses the insurance companies for payments exceeding ¥30 billion up to a total of ¥270 billion.

The share of premiums for fire insurance in the premium income of the insurance companies has decreased over the years; it declined from 60.6 percent of the total in fiscal 1955, 57.6 percent in fiscal 1957, and 56.5 percent in fiscal 1958 to 34.0 percent in fiscal 1966, 31.2 percent in fiscal 1967, and 29.6 percent in fiscal 1968. The share of automobile insurance, on the contrary, rose from 13.6 percent in fiscal 1957 to 49.7 percent in fiscal 1967 and 50.8 percent in fiscal 1968. In April 1968, the insurance companies announced that 10 percent of the fire insurance premiums would be returned to the insured if a ten-year contract were kept in force over the entire ten-year period. If earnings on premiums were higher than expected, the excess would be returned to the insured. In November 1968, the companies introduced special insurance for housing developments (community insurance against fire, theft, etc.). Premiums for automobile insurance were raised to 1.9 times; benefit payments increased in case of death from ¥3 million to ¥5 million and survivors' benefits changed from a range of ¥190,000–¥3 million to ¥150,000–¥5 million. New forms of insurance covered accidents while mountain climbing, driver's insurance (accidents in borrowed or rented cars), fishing insurance for anglers (accidents and loss of equipment while fishing); the companies also introduced new combinations, such as ordinary accident and automobile accident insurance, fire and accident, and fire and theft insurance.

Japanese insurance companies were hard hit by ship disasters, including the loss of the *Bolivar Maru* in 1968 and the *California Maru* in 1970. In the last case, hull insurance alone amounted to ¥1,670 billion. The London maritime insurance companies refused to reinsure the companies unless premiums were raised; a gradual increase in premiums was agreed on.

Despite the opposition of the insurance companies, the insurance business was opened to direct foreign investment ("automatic" approval of fifty-fifty joint ventures) under the second liberalization program which took effect in March 1969. Proposals for reinsurance contracts were made by American, German, and Swiss insurance companies, but the Japanese insurance companies agreed not to accept such proposals. Since insurance companies need a license from the minister of finance to operate in Japan, the liberalization brought no change in the actual situation.

Due to the inflation, the life insurance companies wrote higher insurance policies. In July 1969, Meiji Life Insurance began to offer ¥1 million policies; Nippon, Dai-Ichi, and Sumitomo followed in September 1970 and the other companies in October and November. In January 1971, Chiyoda Life Insurance began to sell a policy which would pay up to ¥14.5 million in case of death by accident. The companies have been negotiating with the Ministry of Finance for the adoption of a policy with a changing value: part of the premiums would be invested for the account of the insured and the dividends accumulated; the benefits would be increased in accordance with the income from the investment. The companies expect such an "inflation-proof" policy would find wide acceptance. The present law provides that life insurance must be for a fixed amount and limits investment in stocks to 30 percent. For contracts with a variable amount, profits from the investment in stocks would have to be treated as a reserve, and the new type of contracts would have to be kept separate from already existing contracts. Moreover, the variable contracts would have to guarantee a certain amount in order to protect the insured against a decline in stock prices. Effective June 15, 1970, premiums for fire insurance were reduced but those for automobile insurance raised: premiums for insurance against damage to automobiles by 15 percent, personal injuries by 89 percent, and material damage by 59 percent. The premiums of compulsory traffic accident insurance were raised twice, in November 1969 and in June 1970. The Automobile Liability Insurance Law was amended effective October 1, 1970. The law had been enacted in 1955 and in the meantime, conditions had changed. The main revisions were: (1) additional premiums will be levied on drivers involved in accidents; (2) self-insurance (owners of 200 and more vehicles) is abolished; (3) compensation for loss of earnings is limited to ¥3,000 per day.

Since the life insurance companies are mutual companies, they distribute part of their profits as dividends to their policyholders. The main sources of profits are: (1) the difference between actual insurance payments and those assumed in the calculation of premium rates; (2) the difference between actual income from fund management (investments and loans) and budgeted rate of return (usually 4 percent per annum); (3) the difference between actual operating expenses and budgeted expenses. Generally speaking, the second source of income was the most important, whereas there was hardly any profit from the first and relatively little from the third. The Ministry of Finance ordered the insurance companies to transfer the largest part of the profits to reserves. Until fiscal 1968, the ministry kept the dividend rates of all companies at the same level, but, in fiscal 1969, it allowed the companies with larger reserves to distribute a larger percentage of the profits from fund management as dividends. In fiscal 1970, the accumulated reserves of five of the twenty life insurance companies were up to the permissible limit of legal reserves, and reserves of all companies had increased to such an extent that the ministry thought it safe to have the dividend rates reflect the actual profits from fund management. For fiscal 1971, therefore, the ministry "liberalized" the dividend rates of the life insurance companies so that they would reflect not only the profits from fund management but also, to a certain extent, the profits from the rationalization of management. This will make the difference between the large and small insurance companies even greater. At the end of fiscal 1970, the ratio of the assets of the largest insurance company to those of the smallest was 86:1, and the ratio of the value of outstanding insurance contracts 153:1. The dividends paid by the large insurance companies (thirty-year, ¥1 million endowment policy, issued at age thirty, held for five years) are expected to amount to ¥5,700, those by the small companies to ¥4,600.

The life insurance companies have invested an increasingly larger share of their funds in loans, and their connections with industrial enterprises have also grown stronger through their advance into pension plans. This development has changed the role of securities investment; the life insurance companies not only invest a much smaller percentage of their funds in stocks but the nature of their portfolios is gradually assuming the same significance as that of the banks, a symbol and guarantee of permanent business relations. It is this role as "stable stockholders" in which the insurance companies find themselves that explains their vehement opposition to stock issues at market prices (this problem will be discussed below) and the flotation of convertible debentures. In the freewheeling days of the Iwato boom, the insurance companies, although very active in the stock market, had already shifted the weight of their investment policy to corporate loans. But stocks held by reason of business connections cannot be sold when prices are high, which means that a not inconsiderable part of the securities portfolio of the insurance companies is practically frozen. If the companies whose shares they own issue new shares at market prices or debentures convertible at market prices, the insurance companies (and the rest of the stockholders) lose the capital gain implied in issues at face value and discounted in the stock prices; if they subscribe to the new stocks, they cannot count on a sufficient yield ratio (they need about 7.5 percent for their operations; in 1970, the highest average yield rate of all stocks listed on the Tokyo Stock Exchange was 4.1 percent, the lowest 2.73 percent). The life insurance companies, therefore, repeatedly protested against issues at market prices, issues of debentures convertible at market prices, and large new issues (which require large stockholders to mobilize considerable liquid funds). The insurance companies stressed that these issues infringed on the interests of existing stockholders and asserted that the market was still geared to allocation to stockholders at face value. They proposed that, for a transitional period, the issue price should be fixed about halfway between the face value and the market price; that stockholders should be given a preemptive right, and that the prospectus should set forth in detail how the stockholders would be reimbursed for the premium (the difference between the face value and the issue price).

The life insurance companies informed the companies that they would not subscribe to issues at market prices and that they might possibly sell the stocks of the companies offering such issues. In the beginning of 1971, representatives of the insurance companies personally met the executives of 98 companies of whose shares the insurance companies held 15 percent or more and explained their position; to 415 companies of whose shares the insurance firms owned 3–15 percent, their attitude was explained in writing.

At the end of December 1970, loans accounted for 60.8 percent of the assets of the twenty insurance companies, stocks for 20.2 percent. Although the relative share of securities investment in the funds of the life insurance companies may not decline, the future role of the companies as institutional investors looks doubtful.

The twenty life insurance companies reported net assets amounting to ¥5,854,784 million for the end of fiscal 1970, an increase of 20.5 percent. The share of stocks in total assets sank to 19.6 percent, the first time since 1948 (when the share was 15.7 percent) that it dropped below 20 percent.

The five largest life insurance companies reported the following ratios for investment in stocks.

	Assets as of March 31, 1971		Projection for fiscal 1971	
	¥ billion	Investment in stocks %	Increase in assets ¥ billion	Investment in stocks %
Nippon	1,295.0	19.95	250	17.0
Dai-Ichi	940.6	19.78	167	15.0
Sumitomo	667.1	17.94	134	19.0
Asahi	521.7	20.04	93	19.0
Meiji	495.2	25.12	86	12.5

Value of Life Insurance Policies

(In millions of yen)

Fiscal year	Value of new policies written	Value of policies in force
1958	1,289,194	4,463,963
1959	1,677,294	5,631,216
1960	2,048,094	6,997,084
1961	2,663,664	8,898,104
1962	3,569,330	11,455,251
1963	4,725,617	14,900,440
1964	6,250,341	19,492,816
1965	7,345,618	24,417,283
1966	8,867,887	30,444,488
1967	11,179,637	38,243,084
1968	13,310,311	47,424,153
1969	17,419,829	60,183,523

Source: Life Insurance Association

Investments of Life Insurance Companies

(In millions of yen)

End of fiscal year	Net assets	Investments						
		Total investable funds	Cash & deposits	Securities		Loans	Real estate
				Total	Stocks		
1951	53,053	49,289	3,283	18,560	14,896	20,643	6,803
1955	192,928	188,008	7,175	64,215	57,059	97,670	18,948
1958	450,812	445,829	8,338	118,534	107,639	280,391	35,571
1959	582,633	576,374	9,032	148,886	134,981	367,168	45,326
1960	752,804	743,508	9,940	185,269	171,477	473,024	61,474
1961	953,030	942,566	12,072	231,646	214,348	596,933	85,161
1962	1,188,167	1,173,932	15,402	285,234	264,016	747,056	108,321
1963	1,473,442	1,456,775	16,998	350,534	318,947	928,382	146,247
1964	1,820,104	1,800,874	23,307	427,195	376,865	1,150,903	171,956
1965	2,243,109	2,221,896	25,322	539,101	474,087	1,414,636	211,645
1966	2,735,524	2,712,787	31,703	811,329	688,000	1,580,830	253,957
1967	3,301,644	3,278,008	38,705	977,378	807,339	2,222,815	339,010
1968	4,000,123	3,968,807	47,598	1,115,406	917,350	2,421,426	384,376
1969	4,859,843	4,822,488	53,862	1,238,261	1,018,153	3,086,147	444,218

Source: Ministry of Finance; The Life Insurance Association.

Investments of Nonlife Insurance Companies

(In millions of yen)

End of fiscal year	Capital	Net Assets	Investments				
			Total investable funds	Cash & deposits	Securities	Loans	Real estate
1951	1,079	36,630	29,890	12,850	9,588	3,858	3,594
1955	9,535	97,499	84,903	26,004	33,876	13,096	11,918
1958	18,946	156,533	138,110	32,138	63,592	25,871	16,508
1959	19,000	175,785	153,222	33,510	76,225	25,457	18,030
1960	32,792	216,338	188,932	40,854	93,065	35,384	19,629
1961	33,552	252,464	217,557	44,359	110,686	51,574	20,938
1962	33,814	289,705	251,693	51,591	127,361	49,737	23,004
1963	44,989	347,341	301,482	63,961	148,879	61,786	26,856
1964	47,592	416,302	360,211	79,688	172,292	77,328	30,903
1965	47,582	476,790	406,164	94,664	195,655	79,217	36,627
1966	53,874	578,502	487,951	116,692	249,386	80,268	41,605
1967	55,464	707,439	588,534	140,227	294,915	105,303	48,089
1968	58,594	851,258	695,715	158,089	332,657	151,657	53,312
1969		1,080,518	880,774	188,588	386,022	194,283	60,834

Source: Ministry of Finance; The Marine & Fire Insurance Association of Japan.

Principal Assets of Life Insurance Companies

	December 1970	March 1971
	(In millions of yen)	
Value of policies in force	74,938,370	78,230,095
Cash	592	3,397
Deposits	19,583	55,842
Call loans	31,680	35,092
Loans, total	3,705,186	3,929,000
Loans secured by real estate mortgages	1,059,419	1,099,939
Loans secured by stocks & bonds	317,052	334,878
Loans secured by insurance	381,027	393,570
Loans guaranteed by banks	812,234	854,339
Others (loans to local public bodies, Housing Corporation)	1,135,453	1,246,275
Securities, total	1,259,552	1,274,530
Government securities	16,682	33,424
Local public bonds	11,049	9,797
Corporate debentures	67,307	85,315
Stocks	1,127,816	1,145,265
Other	36,696	730
Immovables	506,153	516,073
Total operating funds	5,522,745	5,813,934
Other assets	47,158	40,850
Total assets	5,569,903	5,854,784

Assets of Nonlife Insurance Companies

	December 1970	March 1971
	(In millions of yen)	
Cash	134	340
Deposits	215,278	224,985
Call loans	65,077	66,301
Loans, total	336,706	377,634
Loans secured by mortgages	38,483	41,442
Loans secured by securities	57,409	73,759
Loans secured by insurance	1,787	2,140
Other	239,026	260,291
Securities, total	437,600	499,219
Government securities	1,523	1,652
Local public bonds	11,202	12,437
Corporate bonds	53,453	50,566
Stocks	354,116	365,690
Loan trusts	7,248	7,768
Investment trusts	1,269	1,302
Immovables	70,359	72,165
Total operating funds	1,125,156	1,190,646
Other assets	228,332	242,289
Total assets	1,353,488	1,432,935

III

THE PERIOD
OF
RAPID GROWTH

1 ECONOMIC DEVELOPMENTS

1 STRUCTURAL CHANGES IN THE ECONOMY

1 THE GROWTH MECHANISM

In the immediate postwar period, latent demand was always strong so that, as a tendency, effective demand usually exceeded productive capacity. In this situation, the key to economic growth was the increase in productive capacity. In Japan's postwar economy, conditions favored technological progress and the large share of labor in primary industries provided a ready reservoir of workers for the growing manufacturing industries. The most important factor was capital accumulation for which the high rate of personal savings on the one hand and, on the other, the enormous investment activity of private enterprise (largely financed by credit) were the most important factors. Supported by strong demand, the operating rate of equipment was high; investment concentrated on direct production facilities such as factories and machinery and labor was no problem. The high investment productivity stimulated private investment activities while the heavy equipment investment in turn increased investment productivity. In short, the enormous equipment investment of private enterprise played a pivotal role in the rapid economic growth and was its prime mover.

The increase in equipment investment not only built up productive capacity but also stimulated demand. Investment as a demand factor induced new investment and led to an accelerating self-feeding boom. This mechanism was significant for the rapid expansion.

Technological progress was very fast. Technological innovation during the period of rapid growth was largely based on the induction of foreign technology. Even after the recovery of the prewar level of production around 1955, Japan's technological level remained far below the standard of the advanced industrial nations. This brought about a feverish endeavor to secure technology from abroad, and to a large extent equipment investment served both quantitative expansion and qualitative improvement of productive facilities. The large enterprises, in particular, did not want to be left behind in the race in which the protection (or enlargement) of the market share of the enterprise was an important consideration in investment decisions.

Although the main trend in the postwar development of Japan's economy was a strong expansion, the economy by no means followed a straight upward course. Compared with the periods of growth, the adjustment intervals were short. The main expansionary phases were:

Korean War boom, November 1951–January 1954, 27 months;
Jimmu boom, October 1954–June 1957, 33 months;
Iwato boom, July 1958–December 1961, 42 months;
Profitless prosperity, November 1962–October 1964, 24 months;
Izanagi boom, November 1965–August 1970, 58 months.

The mechanism underlying the cycle was as follows. The uptrend started with an increase in final demand, in consumption, exports, or fiscal expenditures. This stimulated production and, at the next stage, brought an increase in inventory investment and more active investment in plant and equipment which, in turn, had a multiplier effect on economic activities and led to a boom. At that point, the demand–supply relation became strained, domestic prices began to rise, and imports increased. In the first four of the five boom periods listed above, the large deficits in the balance of payments prompted the government to adopt a policy of credit restraints, whereas in the last boom the strong rise in wholesale prices led to the imposition of monetary restrictions. The deflationary policy brought a slowdown; production became stagnant, corporate earnings declined, and the number of bankruptcies increased. But together with these undesirable phenomena, the calming down of imports brought an improvement in the balance of payments which made it possible to relax the credit restraints and thus paved the way for a new upward push of the economy.

In this way, the changes in the balance of payments and the monetary restrictions imposed in response to the deterioration in the international payments situation, as well as the relaxation of these restraints, were of great significance for the fluctuations in the postwar economy. Compared with the prewar cycles or the cyclical phenomena in the West, the downturn in Japan's postwar cycles did not imply an absolute contraction. Thanks to the strong expansionary trend, the contracting phase of the cycle merely meant a lower rate of expansion without a shrinkage of the economy, so that Japan's so-called recessions were actually periods of less rapid growth.

2 GROWTH FACTORS

The deflationary policy enforced under the Dodge line in 1949 resulted in a contraction of demand and brought a stagnation, the paralyzing effect of which was only broken through the sudden increase in demand generated by the Korean War. On a statistical basis, output regained the prewar level in 1951, but the basic differences between the prewar and postwar economies make a comparison difficult. Before the war, defense expenditures claimed a large share of the national product, and the direct and indirect expenses connected with Japan's overseas establishment further reduced the resources available to the private sector. Naturally, the munitions industry profited from the expansion of military demand, but on balance, being unproductive, it was a burden on the economy rather than a help. In the postwar economy, the replacement demand remained unsatisfied and an enormous backlog of potential demand could not be translated into effective demand. But as long as domestic replacement demand and occupation policies kept the problem of international competitiveness out of the economic picture, the question of modernization did not become acute. Gradually, however, the necessity for increasing exports became more pressing, and with it came the realization that Japan's technological weakness was a formidable obstacle to an expansion of trade. Since it was out of the question to bridge a gap of about twenty years by indigenous research and development, the induction of foreign technology seemed the only feasible way of catching up with the advanced industrial countries. At the same time, measures had to be taken to prevent a take-over of Japanese enterprises by foreign capital. Capital transactions between Japan and foreign countries came under the regulations of the Foreign Exchange and Foreign Trade Control Law of 1949 and the Law Concerning

Foreign Capital (usually called the Foreign Investment Law) of 1950. The first law established a strict control system (actually a continuation of the wartime controls) over the entire field of foreign exchange, while the latter laid down rules for the induction of foreign capital and regulated foreign loans, investment in securities, etc. The effect was a continuation of Japan's closed economy. The laws had been drafted from the point of view of maintaining official control over all transactions with foreign countries and, until the basic reorientation of Japan's policy expressed in the "Outline of the Plan for Trade and Exchange Liberalization" adopted in June 1960, the legislative regulations were an obstacle to the inflow of foreign technology. Nevertheless, once the importance of technological innovation had been recognized, Japanese enterprises vied in securing foreign licenses and, if necessary, in concluding foreign tie-ups or in setting up joint ventures.

Prior to the Iwato boom, the expansion of the economy was basically determined by effective demand and actual market conditions. The Jimmu boom, which began with a favorable expansion of exports in 1955, got out of hand through a tremendous explosion of equipment investment (which rose from ¥960.1 billion in fiscal 1955 to ¥1,512.6 billion in fiscal 1956, an increase of 57.6 percent); a deflationary policy went into effect in May 1957, but equipment investment continued to grow (fiscal 1957: ¥1,867.3 billion, an increase of 23.5 percent). The need for modernization was the chief reason for the equipment investment. Around 1955, Japan's basic industries still lacked enough capacity for domestic demand, and none of her industries had been able to catch up with postwar technological innovations. A large part of the huge investment funds went into the plant and equipment of industries such as machinery, iron and steel, and electric power. Investment, therefore, was largely for investment goods and a not inconsiderable part of the funds constituted indirect costs. Industry moved to new sites—partly because existing sites were insufficient, partly because the switch to oil as fuel made coastal sites desirable, and partly because the *kombinats* required new locations. But even at this stage, the industry already anticipated future expansion and made preparations for later additions.

Following the Korean War, the government had channeled large funds into key industries such as electric power, iron and steel, coal mining, and shipping. Other sectors whose capacity had expanded rapidly were chemical fertilizers and textiles. Production, therefore, could be stepped up without expanding the productive apparatus (which was called volume prosperity). The availability of credit led to accelerated investment. The steel industry started a rationalization and modernization program and, in the middle of the fifties, the first petrochemical *kombinats* were built. In the investment boom which began in 1956, the main emphasis was on electronics, synthetic fibers, plastics, and petrochemicals, and the automobile industry made preparations for introducing a system of mass production. The increase in personal income strengthened demand for consumer durables, notably electric home appliances such as television sets, washing machines, and refrigerators. At the same time, the optical industry and shipbuilding, in which military demand during the war had stimulated technological progress, further improved their technologies and assumed an important role in exports.

The investment fever of 1956 resulted in a large increase in imports (42.2 percent over 1955), and in the beginning of 1957 the balance of payments deteriorated rapidly. The authorities adopted a drastic deflationary policy and the so-called saucer type recession thus induced lingered on through the following year. In retrospect, the recession of 1957–58 was ascribed to inventory adjustment. Actually, this was the chief result of the extremely tight credit policy adopted by the government in May 1957, but it was not the cause of the recession.

The expanding phase of the third cycle started in 1959. The government forecasts in the beginning of the year had been very cautious but the increase in equipment investment resulted in an unprecedented acceleration of economic growth. The buoyancy continued all through 1960, and, in September of that year, the Ikeda cabinet announced its "Plan for Doubling National Income."

The plan, drawn up by the Economic Council (*Keizai Shingikai*), has often been criticized, chiefly because of its lack of planning. But it introduced the use of a vision (a description of Japan's economy and standard of living in a not so distant future) as a tool of political propaganda and, since then, this type of planning has been in vogue (incidentally, neither the "Plan for Doubling National Income" nor any other economic plan has been carried out; actual developments made them obsolete). It allowed the government to hide the lack of a political program behind the dreams of an affluent society (consequently the public outcry against environmental pollution may have permanently impaired the value of these "visions") and evoke the mirage of a welfare society in order to distract attention from its industry first and "the-consumer-be-damned" attitude.

Since the plan aimed at a specific rate of growth and embodied target figures for 1970, Japan's business leaders engaged at once in a competitive race toward the production goals. Everybody figured out how much he would have to expand in order to secure *his* share in the larger economy, hoping that by hurrying up he could steal a march on his rivals. Nobody was troubled by any thought of the capacity of the market; the main concern was to make the necessary credit arrangements before the government shut off credit. According to the Revised Report on National Income Statistics (1951–67), equipment investment rose from ¥1,734.7 billion in fiscal 1958 to ¥2,222.1 billion in fiscal 1959, ¥3,170.6 billion in fiscal 1960, and ¥4,227.4 billion in fiscal 1961. In some industries, such as textiles, paper and pulp, and chemical fertilizers, government controls kept investment down, but in machinery, iron and steel, and petroleum refining, the expansion was tremendous. This round of investments, therefore, brought a large increase in capacity together with a high degree of rationalization. Many of the new installations were built on coastal sites where huge tankers and large bulk carriers could unload their cargoes directly into the plant. Not only agriculture but also sectors such as coal mining and textiles (except synthetic fibers) lost in relative importance. On the other hand, the expansion was not limited to large enterprises; many small firms sharply increased their investment outlays and the formation of the second sections for the Tokyo, Osaka, and Nagoya exchanges was due to the enormous growth of medium-sized and small enterprises. The demand for large quantities of goods of better quality from the subcontractors of large enterprises was the main reason for the investment rush of small enterprises. The large concerns rely greatly on small manufacturers for parts, components, and subassemblies, and the technical progress of the large enterprises required a corresponding modernization of the subcontractors. Formerly, the cheap labor available through the use of the small firms had been the most important reason for the reliance on subcontractors; it now became a secondary consideration (it retained its significance for textiles, ready-made clothing, toys, sundries, and to some extent for processed foods), and efficiency, reliability, and integration with the production program of the main enterprise made the automation of the small firms imperative. The formation of the so-called *kōjō danchi* ("industrial parks") was greatly furthered by the need of the large concerns for an efficient production system, but many of the *kōjō danchi* were organized independently by associations of small firms.

Important factors in the expansion were the general industrial and economic level of the country, a fair supply of technically competent workers and engineers (for which the high educational standard of the country must be credited), capable managers, and a credit system which retained a certain elasticity even under strict official controls. While exports where important in the so-called recessions, Japan's expansion was by no means export-led growth or the result of an undervalued currency.

A subtle change in outlook came with the overcrowding in the growth industries. Besides petrochemicals, the market potential of modern consumer goods attracted the attention of manufacturers. Radio and television sets, other electric home appliances such as fans, washing machines, vacuum cleaners, refrigerators, and room air conditioners, synthetic fibers such as nylon, polyester, acryl, and propylene, and, finally, automobiles were some of the product lines whose promising future lured more producers into heavier investment outlays than even the most optimistic demand forecast could warrant for the foreseeable future. Significant for the kind of competition resulting from this rush into new products was that, with very few exceptions, none of the competing manufacturers could rely on any special advantage which would give them a better chance in the market. Hence, as a matter of programming, each maker aimed at expanding production sufficiently to bring costs down, while in the final outcome price cuts often reduced expected profit margins and impaired the stability of the entire industry.

CONCENTRATION

Hardly less important than the tremendous expansion of the economy was the concentration which, in many ways, contributed to the new shape of Japan's economy. The conflict between fragmentation and consolidation is a basic feature of Japan's entire economy. It is often mentioned as the most urgent problem for the improvement of agriculture, but it pervades the whole economy, with some notable exceptions (e.g., electric power generation, rail transportation). The fragmentation is largely due to historical factors: topographical conditions, overpopulation (which ceased to be an employment problem but remained in the sense of a very undesirable ratio of population to the size of the economy), and the scarcity of capital may be cited as the most obvious elements. Moreover the postwar agricultural reform failed to anticipate the antinomy between the creation of about 6 million owner-farmers and agricultural productivity, and, in addition, the occupation policies embodied in the Antimonopoly Law attempted to make competition the supreme law of an economy for which harmony is the basic value.

Historically, concentration has always been the official policy, because no policy was adopted until the effects of overcrowding induced the authorities to pay attention to these developments. In the postwar economy, however, the movement toward concentration was first a rollback of the official deconcentration policy. In some respects, the groups headed by the city banks resemble the prewar *zaibatsu*, but there are also significant differences. In the prewar era, holding companies controlled the *zaibatsu* through the appointment of executives of the concerns. The postwar deconcentration broke up not only the combines but also such individual firms as Mitsui Bussan, Mitsubishi Shoji, Mitsubishi Heavy Industries, Oji Paper, and Japan Iron Works (of these firms, only Oji Paper has not been reconstituted, but also other large prewar enterprises have not been reorganized). Trying to keep in contact with one another, to pool information, and to prepare for their eventual reunification, the members of the old *zaibatsu* formed clubs, first camouflaged as social gatherings but later openly conducted as regular presidents' meetings of the heads of the key companies of the respective groups. These meetings were later supplemented by regular meetings of executives on the operating level and committees for special purposes, but today's cooperation among the different *zaibatsu* groups is a far cry from the prewar integration. There is no central direction and the meetings of the company presidents have neither legal nor actual authority over the member firms.

Despite the efforts at consolidation and integration, the cohesion inherent in a common tradition and the mutual assistance of the enterprises belonging to the *zaibatsu* groups, certain conflicts of interest remain and competition has not been eliminated. This phenomenon is due to another basic difference between today's groups and the prewar *zaibatsu*. Before the war, all enterprises of each *zaibatsu* were basically part of a whole, and their functions were coordinated and integrated by a central authority in the *zaibatsu*. The postwar groups united independent enterprises which had been going their own ways for a number of years and were not inclined to sacrifice their independence for the sake of group solidarity. The leading executives of the individual firms had arrived at their posts in their own right and had no intention of accepting restrictions on their authority from outsiders.

In addition to the three groups named after the prewar *zaibatsu* (Mitsubishi, Mitsui, and Sumitomo), a few other groups are clustered around city banks. The Fuji Bank group comprises such enterprises as Marubeni-Iida (formed in 1955 by the merger of Marubeni and Iida, originally Kansai cotton traders), Nippon Kokan, Oki Electric, Nihon Cement, and Showa Denko, and is connected with Hitachi, Ltd., Nissan Motor, Nippon Reizo, Canon, and numerous other enterprises. Dai-Ichi Bank is the main bank of both the Kawasaki and the Furukawa groups (and also of smaller groups such as Shibusawa, Meiji, Fujiyama, and the former Suzuki Shoten); Sanwa Bank cooperates with numerous firms in the Kansai area not belonging to Sumitomo, among them Hitachi Shipbuilding & Engineering, Ube Industries, Osaka Gas, Teijin, Nippon Rayon, Nichibo, Nakayama Steel, Nisshin Steel, and Maruzen. The group formation is intimately connected with the system of financing.

Other groups have been formed by private railroad companies (which usually also operate department stores): Tokyu, Seibu, and Tobu are representative for the Kanto region; Hankyu for the Kansai. From the transportation field and department stores, these groups branched out into the tourist, amusement, and hotel businesses, and are also active in food processing, real estate, construction, suburban development, sightseeing and recreational facilities, ropeways, helicopter transportation, amusement parks, movie theaters, cabarets, cafes, dance halls, skating, bowling, advertising, animal feeds, livestock, and poultry.

In addition to in-group mergers, three developments involving the *zaibatsu* groups (including to a certain extent the Fuji Bank group) are indicative of the changes connected with Japan's economic growth: (1) cooperation among the firms belonging to the same group, often in the form of establishing joint subsidiaries; (2) cooperation with or control over firms outside the group; (3) cooperation between firms belonging to different groups.

Fields in which cooperation was particularly noticeable included petrochemicals, petroleum refining, residential construction, information, and the development of submarine resources. The petrochemical *kombinats* are outstanding examples of cooperation among firms belonging to different groups, but the development of overseas raw material resources may be the field in which intergroup cooperation has made the most progress.

Cooperation with or control over firms outside the group was largely based on the system of affiliation called *keiretsuka*. Through this arrangement, a firm secures the services of a whole string of otherwise independent enterprises on a permanent basis. The usual aim of this type of affiliation lies in the direction of vertical integration, ranging from the supply of raw materials and parts to distribution and sales outlets. Usually, the affiliated firms are small outfits which receive orders, capital, credit, materials, and often management personnel, from the large companies which thus secure the services of reliable subcontractors or a constant supply of parts, an arrangement which allows a quick adaptation to business changes. For the small firms, it is by no means an unmixed blessing, since the large companies often use their position for squeezing prices while they cut back on orders as soon as business recedes. But under normal condiditons, small enterprises are happy to have steady customers whom they can trust to pay their bills and on whom they can usually rely for help. The payment of subcontractors is an extremely difficult problem, particularly in times of recession, and despite a special law enacted for the protection of subcontractors, the situation remains unsatisfactory. If the principal needed quality work, the subcontractor sometimes received part of his equipment from the bigger enterprise; also, as mentioned above, the changed conditions have shifted the emphasis from cheap labor to technological integration.

In the past, the dichotomic character of the Japanese economy has often been stressed, and the prevalence of small enterprises in certain sectors has served as a pretext for postponing the liberalization of the economy. But there has always been a basic interdependence of the dissimilar components which formed the basis of the *keiretsuka* type of affiliation. The upper crust of Japan's corporate society is made up of large establishments highly modernized and automated, with a high degree of productivity and up-to-date technology. Their wages are comparatively high and many enterprises provide company housing, medical care, recreational facilities, and other fringe benefits including retirement pay (in the form of a lump-sum payment or a pension). The vast majority of Japanese enterprises, however, are small outfits. As of July 1, 1969, 3,362,771 out of 4,649,880 establishments had 1–4 employees (72.5 percent) and only 7,745 establishments employed a force of over 300 workers (0.17 percent). The official definition of small enterprises covers businesses with a capital of less than ¥50 million and less than 300 employed in manufacturing industries, and businesses with a capital of less than ¥10 million and less than 50 employed in commerce and services. They account for over 99 percent of all establishments, 50 percent of the value of shipments, 82 percent of retail sales, and 41 percent of all exports. The productivity of the small firms is low and despite relatively larger wage increases in small enterprises, a considerable differential remains between wage rates of large and small companies as well as between the wages of men and women. There are also regional differences: according to the Ministry of Labor, in 1970 the ratio of wages of twenty to twenty-two-year-old workers in southern Kyushu to those in the Tokyo–Yokohama area was 100:155; for workers aged forty to forty-nine, the ratio was 100:188.

Official pronouncements stress the shrinking gap between the wage levels of large and small enterprises and the improvement in working conditions in the latter establishments as signs of the disappearance of the dual structure. It must be remembered that this dichotomy is not just a matter of size (capital, number of employees), although these quantitative factors are usually relied on for statistical purposes. In addition, the distinction involves certain qualitative elements, some of which may be defined (technological level, position in industry, group affiliation, banking connections, relations with the distribution system), but it also includes intangibles such as prestige (of the firm and its managers), tradition, and the general opinion of the economic world on the worth of the enterprise. The expansion has accentuated rather than obliterated the differences in these respects, and the relatively higher increase in the wage level of small enterprises has added to their difficulties without improving their status. The labor shortage produced another phenomenon which further aggravated the position of small establishments. Until the beginning of the sixties, labor mobility was very low, but the turnover of labor has climbed fantastically in some sectors and locations, and this development again affected small enterprises to a much greater extent than large establishments.

With the shift of emphasis from production to sales (which came with the 1962 recession), the large enterprises focused their attention on the affiliation of enterprises in the distribution system. As far as wholesalers are concerned, the arrangement called *tokuyakuten* has been used traditionally in many branches in which the manufacturer found it too difficult to undertake nationwide distribution. Although the name *tokuyakuten* (special agent) seems to suggest an exclusive relationship, this is usually not the case and the same *tokuyakuten* may handle the products of some or all competitors in a given line.

The efforts of the manufacturers to secure exclusive retail outlets have been particularly vigorous for brand products such as those in pharmaceuticals, cosmetics, electrical appliances, apparel, bread, etc. The affiliation of retail stores was often accompanied by the formation of special associations, but such associations are also formed for affiliated enterprises on the production side. In a number of cases, membership in such an association involved the signing of a price maintenance contract (which was lawful for pharmaceuticals and cosmetics but not for electric appliances).

It should be noted that the system of affiliation is in no way considered as something undesirable. On the contrary, MITI has recommended *keiretsuka* as an important step toward structural reform, and all companies are proud of their membership in a particular group—which is a measure of their standing in the industrial society and often of real advantage.

The degree of integration achieved by *keiretsuka* varies; it may range from product types and production schedules to credit arrangements and investment programs. The *kombinats* also require the quantitative and qualitative adjustment of products and the alignment of investment plans, but the cooperation involves no corporate subordination and the technological integration is basically the reverse of the technological coordination of the *keiretsu* enterprises. These enterprises are oriented toward the finished products of the main enterprise, while in the *kombinats*, the end products, although usually derivatives, are different.

Two kinds of mergers have attracted most attention: those giving the merged firm an important share of the market and those reuniting enterprises broken up by the postwar deconcentration, particularly the reconstruction of the former *zaibatsu* firms. Some of the mergers in the last category also involved the first aspect, but, generally speaking, mergers as such have been of little significance for the structural changes in Japan's economy. Even the much-opposed fusion of Yawata Iron & Steel and Fuji Iron & Steel left the steel industry pretty much the same, and neither the amalgamation of the three successor firms to Mitsubishi Heavy Industries nor the merger of Nissan Motor and Prince Motor had revolutionary consequences. Only the mergers involved in the government's reorganization of the shipping industry (1963–64) resulted in a complete remodeling of the industrial landscape.

As far as practical effects are concerned, the tie-ups (*teikei*) between different enterprises may be more important than mergers, for the simple reason that they are far more numerous. Such cooperation agreements may cover every conceivable aspect of business management, and the agreements concluded in the last few years have created a tangle of intercorporate relations which even the Fair Trade Commission finds difficult to unravel. These agreements are much easier to negotiate than mergers, can be changed or rescinded if they prove unsatisfactory, and impose relatively few restrictions on the freedom of corporate action. While cartels and cartellike arrangements remain to a certain extent in foreign trade and some segments of small enterprises, they seem to have become almost obsolete in big business. But production curtailments and the adjustment of investment programs are still handled on an industry-wide basis under government guidance.

In addition to the consolidation of the shipping industry, a number of other sectors were rationalized on the basis of special laws, e.g., textiles, chemical fertilizers, machinery, and electronics. In order to initiate a comprehensive reorganization of industry, the government, in 1963, submitted to the Diet a bill called law for the promotion of specified industries (the original title had been law for strengthening international competitive power). Its purpose was to exempt industries affected by import liberalization from the restrictions of the Antimonopoly Law, so as to facilitate mergers and permit the formation of cartels. The industries in whose reorganization MITI was particularly interested were machinery and equipment for electric power generation, electric wire and cable, automobiles, iron and steel alloys and carbon steel, rolled aluminum and aluminum alloys, and organic chemical products. The government considered that the smallness of enterprises (scale of production as well as size of establishments) and the excessive competition due to this situation was the chief reason for the lack of competitive strength of Japanese businesses in international markets.

The proposed bill never became law, but for a long time MITI tried to bring about a concentration which would have created large units equal in size to the giants of international business. MITI fought particularly hard to implement its blueprint for the automobile industry which foresaw the reduction of the number of automobile manufacturers from nine to three or five who were to produce only a limited number of models. Mitsubishi's tie-up with Chrysler changed the basic pattern of official thinking and Japan's automobile industry is now divided into two groups: companies affiliated with foreign manufacturers and those remaining independent.

In a number of sectors, enterprises have formed cooperative groups for the adjustment of production lines, joint sales, joint purchase of raw materials, and joint development of technology. The government subsidizes these arrangements through the so-called structural loans given by the Japan Development Bank.

4 GROWTH INDUSTRIES

Not only the structure of the Japanese economy as a whole but that of many individual sectors has changed through the expansion. Among the industries with the highest investments and the largest increases in production was the steel industry. In 1950, Japan Iron Works, one of the so-called national project companies (*kokusaku kaisha*) set up in preparation for the war, was dismembered and most of its facilities taken over by Yawata Iron & Steel Co. and Fuji Iron & Steel Co. These companies, together with Nippon Kokan, another integrated steelmaker, formed the big three of the steel industry. But in the following years, a number of other steel manufacturers, who so far had only engaged in steel making and rolling, expanded their facilities and built their own blast furnaces. In this way, Kawasaki Steel Corporation, Sumitomo Metal Industries, and Kobe Steel Works advanced into the ranks of the integrated steelmakers. In the latter half of the fifties, fierce competition developed between the big three and the newcomers. The result was a large increase in pig iron and crude steel production. In 1953, pig iron output (4,518,000 tons) already exceeded the wartime peak (1943: 4,256,000 tons) and crude steel production reached this mark a year later (1943: 7,650,000 tons; 1954: 7,750,000 tons). Crude steel output increased over 4.5 times in the fifties (from 4,839,000 tons in 1950 to 22,138,000 tons in 1960) and grew almost as fast, at an annual rate of nearly 15.5 percent, in the following decade (1970: 93,327,000 tons). At times, capacity far exceeded demand and, in the recession of 1962, the steel industry operated at 76.36 percent of crude steel capacity and 53.18 percent of hot rolling capacity. The low operating ratios made the productivity gains from rationalization and automation largely illusory, at least temporarily, while the heavy interest payments (only a fraction of the new installations could be financed by internal cash flow) and the financing of large inventories (because manufacturers kept production at a high level compared with demand in order to preserve some of the benefits resulting from their modernization) greatly impaired the profit position of the industry.

In 1970, Nippon Steel Corporation (the firm formed through the merger of Yawata and Fuji) became the world's largest steel producer (as a result of a 10.7 percent decrease in the output of U.S. Steel). The industry's forty-eight blast furnaces (five others are under construction) include some of the world's biggest. Although Japan must import almost all its iron ore and most of its coking coal, Japanese steel exports (in 1970, about 18 million tons) are so competitive that "voluntary" quotas restrict exports to the United States. Despite production curtailments in effect since the end of 1970 the five large companies planned to invest ¥793.9 billion in fiscal 1971, up 13.5 percent over fiscal 1970 (¥697.5 billion)—more than all bank loans for equipment investment in all industries during 1962 (¥766.4 billion).

A completely different development pattern prevailed in the chemical industry. The chemical fertilizer industry, which formed the core of Japan's chemical industry, recovered quickly from the wartime devastation thanks to the large investment funds channeled into the industry in the interests of food production. The Korean War boom brought a large expansion of exports and the industry enjoyed a period of prosperity. With the end of the boom, export markets began to dry up. In order to protect the farmers and to prevent the manufacturers from offsetting losses from below-cost exports by hiking domestic prices, the government, in 1953, set a new standard controlling maximum prices for domestic sales of ammonium sulfate. The price reductions imposed by these conditions forced the manufacturers to rationalize their enterprises, but large export deficits continued to accumulate and the fertilizer companies struggled with enormous difficulties. In 1964, direct official control of prices was discontinued and, at about the same time, the international price level began to rise. These changes greatly relieved the burden of the industry, which further tried to overcome the impasse by reducing costs and by diversification. But with a few exceptions, the old chemical companies were left out of the most important development, the establishment of the petrochemical industry.

MITI adopted the policy of building up the petrochemical industry in 1955. For the initial phase, four complexes were allowed to be built: Mitsui, at Iwakuni; Mitsubishi, at Yokkaichi; Sumitomo, at Niihama; and Nippon Petrochemical, a subsidiary of Nippon Oil, together with a dozen independent firms (including some enterprises of the Furukawa group), at Kawasaki. The second petrochemical program (1960) added five new *kombinats* and enlarged the first four. In order to prevent overcapacity, MITI first limited cracking plants to 20,000–25,000 tons of ethylene a year. In 1966, MITI reversed its policy and fixed 100,000 t/y (tons per year) as the minimum capacity of new olefin centers and, soon after, raised the minimum to 200,000 t/y. Ethylene capacity rose from 420,000 t/y in 1963 to 971,000 t/y in 1965 and 3,869,800 t/y at the end of 1970. But the relative narrowness of the domestic market, the large number of producers, and the impossibility of competing in international markets (chiefly on account of higher prices) made the situation of the industry extremely difficult.

As mentioned above, the requirements of technical cooperation led to the coordination of expansion programs, which often involved the adjustment of technology, production schedules, and financial arrangements. But the rapid developments in the field of petrochemicals and synthetic fibers, particularly the appearance of new products, processes, and applications, tended to disrupt existing combinations, create new areas of competition, and make products, facilities, sales channels, and distribution systems obsolete. On the other hand, cooperation among the olefin centers has made much progress and has led to the formation of so-called combined *kombinats*, i.e., complexes grouping two *kombinats* around the same olefin center.

Cotton spinning, the most representative branch of Japan's textile industry in prewar times, was forced to curtail operations soon after the Korean War boom, and, in 1956, a special law made the installation of new or additional equipment subject to official approval. At that time, the industry owned about 9 million spindles (in 1937, the prewar peak, 12.5 million spindles were counted, but the postwar equipment was considered more efficient), and there was no further increase. In the 1957–58 recession, cotton spinning as well as rayon and staple fiber experienced a bad slump, necessitating a considerable curtailment of production. The progress in the production of synthetic fibers, the expansion of cotton spinning in the developing countries, and the decline in the export of cotton products were the main causes of the difficulties experienced by the cotton industry.

Production of synthetic fibers started in 1949, but the initial difficulties were considerable, and it was only in 1955 that some progress became apparent. A more rapid expansion began in 1959, but the installation of new equipment was made subject to prior government approval, and MITI tried to prevent overcapacity by strictly rationing the facilities which could be built for the production of synthetic fibers. The firms that were first allowed to install productive facilities long retained a competitive advantage over the companies whose plants were approved later, so that, all through the sixties, the synthetic fiber industry retained a dichotomic structure, giving the "old" producers a more or less oligopolistic position. Output of cotton yarn and cotton fabrics reached a high in 1961 (cotton yarn 559,000 tons, cotton fabrics 3,383 million sq.m.) and has been fluctuating below this level since (1969: cotton yearn 527,281 tons, cotton fabrics 2,749 million sq.m.). Production of woolen yarn and woolen fabrics increased relatively slowly, but production of synthetic fabrics grew rapidly (from 116 million sq.m. in 1957 to 2,397 million sq.m. in 1969).

Until the slowdown in the fall of 1970, automobiles and electric household appliances ranked as Japan's foremost growth industries. Production of passenger cars rose from 1,593 in 1950 to 165,094 in 1960 and 3,178,311 in 1970; production of chassis for trucks and buses rose from 30,004 in 1950 to 317,162 in 1960 and 2,110,142 in 1970 (2,063,579 trucks, 46,563 buses). Of the 5,288,453 units produced in 1970, Toyota produced 1,609,190 and Nissan 1,374,000 units. The rate of increase in automobile production has slowed down in recent years (1966, 21.9 percent; 1967, 37.6 percent; 1968, 29.9 percent; 1969, 14.4 percent; 1970, 13.1 percent); manufacturers have been trying to make up for the slower growth in domestic sales by larger exports. Exports of motor vehicles rose from 39,060 units in 1960 to 1,086,776 units in 1970; the 1970 total comprised 725,586 passenger cars, 351,611 trucks, and 9,579 buses. Exports of motorcycles rose from 43,237 units in 1960 to 1,737,000 units in 1970 (total production in 1970, 2,947,000 units). The rate of increase in exports of motor cars in 1970 was 26.7 percent; that of motorcycles, 33.8 percent.

In the field of electric appliances, there has not only been a tremendous increase in output but also a remarkable diversification of products. Mass production was achieved in radio receivers, electric refrigerators, electric washing machines, and monochrome television receivers; among the new products were transistor radios, tape recorders, stereo sets, and, above all, color TV sets. Production of color TV receivers in 1970 amounted to 4,885,731 sets, an increase of 32 percent over the preceding year. The consumer boycott protesting the pricing system of the manufacturers reduced the rate of increase in domestic shipments from 95 percent in 1969 to 28.7 percent; the antidumping measures against imports of Japanese-made TV receivers reduced exports of color TV sets from 1,003,419 units in 1969 to 993,274 units in 1970. The use of integrated circuits revolutionized the manufacture of electronic equipment and made the fantastic development in electronic desk-top calculators possible. The first models were marketed in 1964, production rose from 4,100 units in 1965 to 1.4 million in 1970, and their average price declined from ¥409,000 in 1965 to ¥96,000 in 1970.

In the production of large computers, Japan has not yet overcome all problems, and the same holds true for the use of computers. As of the end of March 1970, 6,718 computers were installed in Japan, the second highest number for one country. But a survey by MITI among 2,623 computer users (March 1970) showed 90 percent used the batch system; insufficient software, inadequate terminals, and a lack of computer engineers formed the main obstacles to the use of on-line operations.

It seems hardly necessary to mention shipbuilding. For the fifteenth consecutive year, Japan was the world's largest shipbuilder in 1970 with launchings of 10,475,804 gr. t., 48.5 percent of the world total of 21,689,513 gr. t., according to Lloyd's register of shipping. At the end of the year, Japanese shipyards had an order backlog of 29,357,226 tons. Japan built eight out of the nine largest ships launched in 1970. The British firm Globtik Tankers has a 477,000 dwt. tanker on order from Ishikawajima-Harima Heavy Industries to be delivered in the latter half of 1975, and to cost about £17.4 million. The ship will be chartered by Tokyo Tanker Co., a joint venture of Nippon Oil Refining, Koa Oil, and Nippon Oil. Remarkable improvements in construction technology, particularly in welding, made the building of the supertankers possible. The latest welding method is nine times as fast as traditional welding, with a margin of error of 3 mm. The largest ships afloat were the six tankers of the Universe class (326,000 dwt.) built by Ishikawajima-Harima and Mitsubishi Heavy Industries for Daniel K. Ludwig's National Bulk Carriers; in September 1971, the 372,400 dwt. *Nisseki Maru* was delivered by Ishikawajima-Harima to Tokyo Tanker Co. The giant tankers, bulk carriers, and container ships have greatly altered the logistics of shipping.

Still small but growing is Japan's aircraft industry. During the war, Japanese plants turned out about one hundred thousand planes, including the famous Zero fighters. Production facilities not destroyed were dismantled, and not only production and repair but also specialized research and instruction were banned by the occupation. The rehabilitation of the industry started in 1952; with the organization of Japan's self-defense forces in 1955, the industry began to assemble military aircraft under license. Supported by the government, a sixty-passenger medium-range turboprop called YS-11, was developed. Despite reasonably good sales (180 units), the project was a flop (a badly drawn up agency contract alone cost Nihon Aeroplane Manufacturing Co., a semigovernmental enterprise in overall control of the undertaking, over ¥1 billion). Other civilian aircraft produced in Japan are two light planes: the MU-2 twin-engined executive type turboprop (six to nine passengers) of which Mitsubishi Heavy Industries has already sold 201 units (171 have been exported), and a single-engined plane, FA-200, manufactured by Fuji Heavy Industries. In addition to trainers and liaison planes, Japanese manufacturers have built F-86F, F-104J, and F-4EJ fighters, as well as the P2V-7 and P-2J antisubmarine patrol planes under license from foreign manufacturers and partly equipped with imported instruments. Domestically developed were the PS-1 flying boat, built by Shin Meiwa Industry, and the XC-1 cargo plane, scheduled for production in 1973. Japanese companies have also built numerous types of helicopter. The leading manufacturer of jet engines is Ishikawajima-Harima, but Mitsubishi Heavy Industries and Kawasaki Heavy Industries are also building jet engines. Military orders (including repairs) account for about 60 percent of the sales of the aircraft industry (1970, ¥167 billion).

An industry that suffered a fatal decline was coal mining. The industry had played an important role in the modernization of Japan's economy and had been one of the main supports of the development of the *zaibatsu*. Immediately after the war, the rehabilitation of the coal industry was considered the most urgent task, and coal output, which had fallen to 20 million tons in 1946, stayed on the 50 million ton level in the fifties and the beginning of the sixties. But the advance of oil created enormous problems for coal. Coal mining suffered more under the recession of 1953–54 than other industries. In 1955, the government took a number of protective measures including the closure of unproductive mines—which were bought up by the state—and restrictions on the installation of heavy boilers. A new rationalization plan was adopted in 1960 which sought to maintain demand for coal at 55 million tons. But coal simply could not compete with heavy oil. Only a small part of the coal mined in Japan can be used as coking coal (in 1969, 7,585,000 tons out of 44,124,000 tons), and the largest part (1969, 23,572,000 tons) is used for power generation. In addition to electric power and gas, steel and the National Railways were allocated amounts of coal which they had to buy, but these measures, which created a number of irrationalities in the pricing and structure of Japan's energy supply, could only delay the decline of the industry. Despite numerous rationalization measures financed by government credits, the accumulated deficits became an unbearable burden which the government finally took over.

The electric power industry was another one of the sectors given top priority in the supply of long-term funds. In the first half of the fifties, the share of fiscal loans channeled into electric power was particularly high. The debenture issues of the power industry were accorded preferential treatment and, in 1963, were made eligible for the market operations of the Bank of Japan. Imports of thermal generating equipment were financed with the help of loans from the World Bank, the U.S. Export-Import Bank, and foreign manufacturers.

The structure of the industry has remained almost unchanged. In 1951, Nippatsu (*Nippon Hassōden*), the electric power monopoly created during the war, was reorganized by setting up nine regional power companies. In order to make up for the insufficient capital investment during the war, the government, in 1952, established the Electric Power Development Company (half of the capital was contributed by the government), which was to supplement the investment activities of the power companies by constructing hydroelectric power plants. As anticipated, exploitable hydroelectric power sources became scarce and, in 1956, the emphasis shifted from hydro to thermal power (initially coal-fired plants). Another semigovernmental agency, the Japan Atomic Power Co., was founded in 1957 to construct nuclear power stations. Japan's first nuclear power station (at Tokaimura, 166,000 kw.) went into operation in July 1967; the second station (Tsuruga, 322,000 kw.) was completed in 1969. Both semigovernmental companies sell their electricity to the regional power companies. The first nuclear power station built by a private power company, Mihama No. 1 of Kansai Electric Power Co. (340,000 kw.), reached criticality in July 1970 and began commercial operations in December.

After the government realized the irrationality of restricting the use of heavy oil for power generation, the power companies began to construct large oil-fired stations on coastal sites. But electricity demand outran capacity and electric power companies increased investment, in fiscal 1971, 28.4 percent over the preceding year to ¥977.4 billion, to build 13.54 million kw. of thermal and 6.13 million kw. of nuclear power facilities. In order to avoid pollution, Tokyo Electric Power Co. will build a plant with a capacity of 1 million kw. using liquefied natural gas. The power grids in nearly all of Japan are connected and plans are now being made to connect Hokkaido with the rest of the country by a 500,000 volt undersea cable.

Generation of electric power, which had fallen to 20,982 million kwh. in 1945, surpassed the wartime high (34,526 million kwh.) in 1949 and more than doubled in the fifties (from 39,123 million kwh. in 1950 to 97,829 kwh. in 1960). As of March 1970, the country had 2,090 generating plants (including private stations) with a combined capacity of 59.5 million kw. (32.6 percent hydro, 0.08 percent nuclear power, the rest thermal); the share of hydroelectric power in actual output is about 24 percent. For electric light, Japan has a diffusion rate of 99.98 percent.

5 CONSUMPTION DEMAND

A trend which greatly contributed to the changes in Japan's industrial structure was the change in consumer demand. Higher incomes raised the consumption level, and, more than in any other field, the quantitative expansion was accompanied by significant qualitative changes. Personal consumption expenditure at current prices rose from ¥3,300 billion in fiscal 1951 to ¥10,518.3 billion in fiscal 1961 and ¥31,607.2 billion in fiscal 1969. Outlays for private house building increased from ¥111.8 billion in fiscal 1951 to ¥819.4 billion in fiscal 1961 and ¥4,337.7 billion in fiscal 1969.

Average monthly wages rose from ¥12,200 in 1951 to ¥26,626 in 1961 and ¥64,333 in 1969 (establishments with at least thirty workers; men ¥75,948, women ¥36,838; average in electricity, gas and water ¥92,000, in apparel ¥35,924). According to a preliminary report of the Statistics Bureau of the Prime Minister's Office, married salaried workers earned an average of ¥1,360,000 (monthly average ¥112,900) in 1970, a nominal increase of 15.6 percent over 1969, while the real rate of increase was 7.4 percent.

On an unadjusted basis, average total monthly expenditures of urban households increased from ¥14,389 in 1951 to ¥38,223 in 1961 and ¥80,405 in 1969. The Engel's coefficient dropped from 54.4 in 1951 to 32.2 in 1970, when monthly living expenditures amounted to ¥83,750. Between 1951 and 1969, average consumer prices have more than doubled, but in some sectors the increase has been much steeper and by far the steepest rise has been in land prices. (In March 1970, the index of urban land prices for 140 cities, March 1955 = 100, stood at 1395.) This has affected all expenditures for housing for which consumption expenditures in 1969 were 12.7 times higher than in 1951. As a matter of fact, housing constitutes a consumption sector in which the Japanese living standard leaves much room for improvement. The upper middle class owns substantially better houses compared with pre-war times, but in the large urban conglomerations the housing shortage (estimated at 3.6 million homes in 1968) remains an acute problem. According to the Ministry of Health and Welfare, 62.8 percent of the households covered in the 1969 survey on national living standards owned their own houses; the ratio was 39.8 percent in the large cities and 84.4 percent in rural areas. In 1968, floor space of owner occupied houses averaged 97.42 sq. m. but was only 41.07 sq. m. in private rented housing. Despite the adverse price picture, housing constitutes a field in which consumption expenditure as well as investment will continue to rise.

Consumer durables represent another sector in which the change has been truly revolutionary. Not only has the diffusion rate of many home appliances increased to saturation levels (February 1971: sewing machines, 84.4 percent; monochrome TV sets, 82.3 percent; electric washing machines, 93.6 percent; refrigerators, 91.2 percent; electric fans, 85.0 percent; color TV sets, 42.3 percent), but there has been a very pronounced "trade up." Sewing machine, electric irons, and bicycles were about the first Western-style consumer durables that found wide acceptance among Japanese households. Then followed radio receivers and cameras. The next wave brought electric fans and washing machines and, a little later, television sets began their spectacular invasion of the homes of all classes of society. At about the same time, ballpoint pens and wrist watches became extremely popular and transistor radios made their appearance. Record players, often combined with radio sets, tape recorders, and stereo sets were added to the audiophonic gadget market, while refrigerators and vacuum cleaners joined the arsenal of home appliances. In the latter field, besides Western-style durables such as electric, gas, and oil stoves, water heaters, kitchen ranges, hot plates, and electronic ranges, a few typically Japanese products are widely used: gas and electric rice cookers, fish broilers, sukiyaki stoves, and electric foot warmers (replacing charcoal burners in a contraption known as a *kotatsu*). In 1965, the first color television receivers appeared on the market, and sales rose from 154,000 sets in 1965 to 5,232,000 sets in fiscal 1969. As mentioned above, the dual pricing system provoked consumer resistance, and while sales had increased 69.9 percent in 1969 (the rate of increase had been even higher in the preceding years but the base had been small), they rose by less than 14.7 percent in fiscal 1970. In addition to color TV sets, appliances such as car stereos, cassette tape recorders and stereos, transistor tape recorders, car TV, and video tape recorders were put on the market (the manufacturers are now working on electronic video recording). Also in 1965, domestic manufacturers began to market room airconditioners; in the first three years, sales were disappointing and it was only in the exceedingly prosperous year of 1968 that sales reached larger proportions (888,000 units). The diffusion rate of passenger cars rose very slowly in the fifties (1960, 2 percent of all households) but rose to 26.8 percent in 1970 (number of passenger cars owned at the end of October 1970, 8.4 million). Traffic and pollution problems, tax policies, and repressive regulations may slow growth.

In the field of food, the most remarkable development has been the wide acceptance of foods of convenience and the change in food habits. To a certain extent, these two went together because many of the instant preparations were Western-style foods (e.g., instant coffee). But the change in food habits was much broader. It involved the partial replacement of the traditional diet of rice and fish by foods such as bread, macaroni, spaghetti, meat, ham, sausages, butter, cheese, and eggs, a larger consumption of fruit, the use of seasonings such as catsup and mayonnaise, the immense popularity of chewing gum, chocolate, and ice cream and, to a lesser degree, of candy and biscuits, the large increase in the consumption of fruit juices (natural and synthetic), Coca-Cola, and Pepsi Cola as well as beer (already widely drunk before the war) and whisky. The westernization of clothing is practically universal (although the ladies retain their kimonos for special occasions), but a significant change has occurred in style consciousness. Tokyo fashions are synchronized with London, New York, Paris, and Rome, and in the last few years, modishness has spread to men's wear (including the use of cosmetics and hair dryers). The so-called leisure boom helped to implant the notion of casual wear in the buying public, and the growing popularity of bowling, golf, and foreign travel has boosted sales of sporting goods and travel accessories. At the end of October 1970, Japan had 1,207 bowling establishments with 29,755 lanes (Tokyo's World Lanes has 252 alleys in one building); the 558 golf courses drew a yearly total of 7,806,000 golfers; in 1970, Japanese gamblers spent ¥1,300 billion on horse, bicycle, and motorcycle races and another ¥400 billion on motorboat races.

Of similar importance have been the changes in the distribution system. The appearance of chain stores and supermarkets has not only jolted the retail trade but has also forced new marketing methods on wholesalers and manufacturers. The industries most affected by these changes (food, textiles) have gradually adjusted themselves to the modifications demanded by the distribution revolution, but the distribution system of fresh foods remains inadequate and is partly responsible for the enormous increase in consumer prices. Also still groping for suitable forms and institutions is consumer credit. This situation is part of the general pattern of Japan's economy, which, up to now, has been production oriented. Government policies as well as banking practice have very little consideration for the consumer, while industry labored (and partly still labors) under the illusion that advertising could make up for the lack of consumer appeal in their products and marketing methods. The increase in advertising expenditures (1951, ¥24.3 billion; 1961: ¥211 billion; 1970, ¥752.4 billion) reflected the growing awareness of the importance of consumption.

1 ECONOMIC
DEVELOPMENTS

2 PROGRESS AND REVERSES

1 OVERSUPPLY AND PRODUCTION CURTAILMENTS

In 1959, the expansion of industrial production gained momentum as the year went on. The mining and manufacturing index (1955 = 100) rose from 147.3 in January to 206.5 in December, and the expansion continued all through 1960 (December 1960, 251.2). Exports, particularly to the United States, increased (rate of increase over the preceding year, 20.2 percent) so that, despite an 18.7 percent rise in imports, the balance on trade in the balance of payments remained favorable. Due to the 1960–61 recession in the United States, the increase in exports slowed down in 1960 to 17.3 percent and fell to 4.5 percent in 1961, while the increase in equipment investment pushed imports up by 24.8 percent in 1960 and 29.4 percent in 1961. While current accounts in the balance of payments still showed a surplus of $111 million in 1960, they plunged into the red to the tune of $1 billion in 1961 (on a customs clearance balance, the trade deficit was $1,574.8 million, the highest ever).

Prices remained stable in the first half of 1959; the consumer price index for all cities (1960 = 100) rose from 96.2 in July to 97.7 and reached a high of 98.1 in October. The high for 1960 was 101.7 (October), but, in 1961, the rise gained momentum and, in December, the index reached 110.2. The rise continued without significant interruption until 1971 (1965 = 100; January 1971, 136.6; September, 143.9). Wholesale prices (1960 = 100) rose from 97.8 in January 1959 to 101.8 in November; the index reached a high of 106.9 in September 1960 but was down to 105.7 by December. The completely unrelated movements of wholesale and retail prices were one of the signs of the structural distortions caused by the rapid expansion of the economy.

In an early move to prevent an overheating of the economy, the Bank of Japan, in September 1959, enforced for the first time the reserve deposit system and took another step toward tighter money in December by raising the official discount rate by 1 *rin* to 2.0 *sen* (7.3 percent). While the budget for fiscal 1959 had provided for economic stimulation, the government decided to keep the 1960 budget neutral. But the high rate of economic growth brought an unexpectedly large increase in tax revenues, and the government disposed of the largest part of the increase by creating new spending opportunities through supplementary budgets. The original budget for fiscal 1960 had foreseen expenditures on general accounts of ¥1,569.7 billion, a 10.6 percent increase over the preceding year; with the supplementary budgets, expenditures rose to ¥1,765.2 billion, an increase of 16.7 percent over the revised 1959 budget. In the following years, while credit restraints were in force in order to deflate the economy, the government compiled larger and larger budgets. (The adoption of the budget by the Diet is a mere formality; in February 1971, because he said this in an election speech Takeji Kobayashi had to resign as minister of justice and later lost his seat in the Upper House elections, but that does not change the situation.) The rate of increase in the original budget was 24.4 percent in 1961, 24.3 percent in 1962, and 17.4 percent in 1963; the rate of increase in the revised budgets was 19.4 percent in 1961, 21.6 percent in 1962, and 19.3 percent in 1963; the revised budget for 1963, ¥3,056.8 billion, was about double the original budget for 1960. This feat of doubling the budget in four years in a supposedly non-inflationary economy has found much too little attention. It certainly illustrates another characteristic of the last dozen years: the complete dissociation of fiscal policy from monetary policy and the requirements of economic policy. Naturally, fiscal policy could not remain without influence on the economy, but as far as fiscal spending was concerned, the government's actions were entirely out of line with its policy pronouncements.

In January 1961, the Bank of Japan, despite the large and growing deficit on current account in the balance of payments, lowered the official discount rate (which had been cut by 1 rin in August 1960) by 1 rin to 1.8 sen (6.57 percent). Prime Minister Ikeda, a longtime advocate of low interest rates, considered Japanese interest rates too high by international standards and wanted to bring them nearer to the international level so as to prepare for the liberalization of trade and exchange. At the same time, interest rates on bank deposits and bank loans as well as the yields of public and corporate bonds were lowered. It was the first time since the termination of the war that interest rates on bank deposits were reduced.

The announcement of the government's plan for doubling national income, the reduction of interest rates, the increase in fiscal expenditures, the large issues of new shares absorbed by the stock market and the investment trusts, and the potential increase in the flotation of corporate debentures, made possible by the establishment of investment trusts made up of public and corporate bonds, were powerful economic stimulants. In April 1960, the trade deficit in the balance of payments became larger, and, despite the continuing surplus from short-term capital transactions, the overall balance turned unfavorable in May. In July, the Ministry of Finance, the Bank of Japan, and the city banks joined in a common appeal to industry to postpone at least 10 percent of their planned investments. In the same month, the official discount rate was raised by 1 rin (to 1.9 sen, 6.94 percent; the discount rate for export bills, however, was lowered from 1.3 sen to 1.2 sen); another raise followed in September. At the same time, the penalty rates were made more stringent; instead of the surcharge of 1.09 percent in force since 1957 on loans exceeding the credit line fixed by the Bank of Japan, a two-step system was introduced with penalty rates of 1.46 percent and 2.19 percent. In October, the rate of the reserve deposits was increased. The overloan position of the city banks, which had much improved in the years 1955–56, worsened again with the rapid expansion in 1957. It was less of a problem in 1959 and 1960, but became very pronounced in 1961. The Ministry of Finance took a serious view of the situation and strengthened its "administrative guidance" aimed at reducing the overloans. On September 26, 1961, the cabinet adopted a policy for the improvement of the balance of payments which drastically changed the official guidelines of the economy, although the government emphasized that it would stick to its basic program aimed at a high rate of economic growth. The effects of the credit squeeze gradually seeped into the economy. The large enterprises kept production at a high level in order to maintain a sufficient operating rate, because they considered the financing of inventories the lesser evil (the inventory index for mining and manufacturing, 1960 = 100, rose to 117.9 in 1961, 127.6 in 1962, 141.0 in 1963, and 161.5

in 1964; in 1964, the index reached 202.7 for coal and petroleum products, 191.5 for machinery, and 176.2 for chemicals; it was 194.4 for capital goods and 173.9 for consumer durables). The large companies continued an aggressive investment policy even after the imposition of the credit restraints; the huge programs drawn up in the boom years were carried out under the changed conditions of monetary stringency and aggravated the financial difficulties of business. At ¥4,229.2 billion, equipment investment remained at the same level in fiscal 1962 that it had reached in fiscal 1961, and went up to ¥4,670.2 billion in fiscal 1963. Trade credit was increasingly relied on as a source of current funds and the accounts payable of the large enterprises showed an enormous expansion.

Generally speaking, however, 1962 was a year of indecisive fluctuations. Although the recession was not very severe and its impact was only felt gradually, the economy was stagnant. In the beginning of the year, production continued to increase and remained on a high level through most of the year. Actually, some industries, notably producers of capital goods, operated under severe production curtailments which, however, in some cases (iron and steel, paper, textiles) were as much the result of overcapacity as of a decline in demand. The steel industry was given special credits to finance its inventories. The production goal for 1962, which had been fixed at 31.4 million tons of crude steel at the beginning of the year (actual output in 1961, 28,268,368 tons), was reduced to 27.3 million tons in August and actual output was only slightly higher.

During the first half of the year, the machinery industry could still increase its production, but the decrease in orders which started in the fall of 1961 worsened in the summer of 1962 and clouded the outlook. Machinery exports, however, increased, but, besides questions of quality, the inability of Japanese manufacturers to offer payment conditions matching those of foreign competitors formed a definite obstacle to greater expansion. The increase in car production, however, was much higher than the general average and exports were favorable, but manufacturers of electric home appliances suffered from the stagnation in sales of radio and TV sets.

As on earlier occasions, credit restrictions formed the main instrument of economic adjustment, but they failed to produce an immediate change in the behavior of the economy. Although the government talked much about the necessity for decelerating the expansion, the budget for fiscal 1962 provided for expenditures of ¥2,426,801 million on general accounts, exceeding the already highly inflated original budget of the previous year by 24.3 percent. Tax revenues for fiscal 1961, which had originally been budgeted at ¥1,664,899 million, had actually reached ¥2,062,883 million, and a series of supplementary budgets had created additional spending possibilities raising outlays on general accounts from the originally budgeted ¥1,952.8 billion to ¥2,107.4 billion.

The heavy outflow of foreign exchange which started in 1960 came to an end with the new year in 1962, and, in July, the current accounts showed a surplus. In October, the government declared that the ordeal was over, but the Dow-Jones index fell to the lowest point of the year, dropping to ¥1,238.48 on October 23. Corporate results were the worst in years; although sales declined only moderately, profits were down by large percentages.

To increase exports while reducing imports was one of the key aspects of the government's program of economic readjustment. Despite an increase of 16.1 percent in exports and a decrease of 3 percent in imports, foreign trade on a customs clearance basis still showed a deficit of $720 million, but on an exchange basis the trade balance showed a surplus of

$241 million. A new factor in the balance of payments was the increasingly large deficit in services accompanying the expansion of foreign trade; invisibles had shown a surplus until 1959, but the deficit rose from $36 million in 1960 to $634 million in 1965. The Ministry of Transport used the deficit in invisibles as a pretext for drawing up larger and larger ship-building programs financed by the Japan Development Bank. Since 1961, the ministry has predicted that the increase in Japanese bottoms would increase the share of the Japanese flag in maritime transportation and wipe out the deficit. The prediction, repeated each year, is further from fulfillment than ever, the deficit in invisibles in 1970 amounting to $1,831 million, the highest ever. Generally speaking, however, the development of exports was favorable, and the large increase in exports of machinery indicated the adaptation of the export structure to the changes in the country's industrial structure. The relative increase in exports of steel and chemicals and the decrease in the proportion of textile exports were other signs of this trend.

Another noteworthy event in Japan's foreign trade relations was the conclusion of the so-called Liao-Takazaki agreement, a "private" treaty signed in December 1962 by Liao Cheng-Chih, chairman of the Sino-Japanese Friendship Association, and Tatsunosuke Takazaki, a prominent member of the Liberal-Democratic party. Trade between Japan and Communist China had practically come to a standstill in 1959 following an incident, and transactions were restricted to what the Chinese called "friendly" firms. The official position of the Japanese government was the separation of politics and economics, which the Chinese, however, did not recognize. The susceptibilities of Nationalist China naturally complicated the normalization of relations with Peking; the sale of a vinylon plant to Red China under conditions which the Nationalist government termed economic aid, and other incidents, strained relations to the breaking point. The differences were patched up, in October 1963, by the dispatch of Bamboku Ono as Prime Minister Ikeda's special envoy to Taipei, where he delivered the notorious Yoshida letter in which a former prime minister, Shigeru Yoshida, promised Chiang Kai-shek that the Japanese government would not extend official aid to Communist China (i.e., not finance exports to China by credits from the Export-Import Bank). The government's position on the letter is ambiguous; on occasion Prime Minister Sato has stated that the government is not bound by the letter but has persistently refused to repudiate it.

While official relations with the Soviet Union remain hampered by the unsolved territorial issue (return of the islands of the Kuriles next to Hokkaido: Kunashiri, Etorofu, Shikotan, and the Habomai group), private industry has displayed a keen interest in trade relations with the Soviet Union and the plans for the development of Siberia proposed by Anastas Mikoyan (then first deputy chairman of the council of ministers) during his visit to Japan in May 1964.

2 THE PRICE RISE

The continuation of the rise in consumer prices during the recession accentuated a problem which has plagued the economy ever since the Iwato boom. The wholesale price index of the Bank of Japan (1960 = 100) reached its highest point in September 1960 with 106.9 but dropped to 97.9 in October 1962 (average for the year, 99.3); after that, wholesale prices remained more or less stable until 1967. But consumer prices increased 17.7 percent in the three fiscal years from 1960 to 1962. Structural imbalances were blamed for the rise, but there is no unanimity among economists on the causes. For many years, the government took the position that the expansion of the economy made a certain increase in prices unavoidable and that the rise in incomes compensated for the rise in living costs. In recent years, the growing danger of a cost inflation has shaken the government out of its nonchalant attitude and brought proposals for the adoption of an incomes policy.

Industry blamed the large wage increases for the price spiral, a charge which the labor unions hotly denied, pointing out that wage increases remained within the limits of productivity gains and that the increase in real wages was much smaller than the rise in nominal wages. (The wage index of the Ministry of Labor, 1965 = 100, is based on wages in establishments with more than thirty regular workers; the nominal wage index rose from 61.1 in 1960 to 198.7 in 1970; the index of real wages from 79.1 in 1960 to 152.4 in 1970.) The share of the compensation of employees in national income rose from 48.7 percent in fiscal 1951 to 55.8 percent in fiscal 1961 and stood at 54.7 percent in fiscal 1969. By fiscal 1969, compensation of employees had increased 3.38 times over fiscal 1961, while income from unincorporated enterprises increased 2.61 times, property income 3.31 times, and corporate income 3.20 times. The Ministry of Labor was of the opinion that there was a connection between the increase in wages and the rise in prices, but that structural factors played an important role in the price rise whereas the increase in wages was largely caused by the conditions in the labor market. Actually, the highest price rises were for food and services, and, until 1969, prices of goods manufactured by large enterprises rose much less than those produced by small firms. As mentioned above, wages in small enterprises rose faster than those in large establishments; the shortage of young workers (caused by a decrease in the

Rice Prices

(Average prices)

Year	Producers' price unhulled, ¥ per 150 kg.		Consumers' price polished, ¥ per 10 kg.
1955	10,160		765
1956	10,070		765
1957	10,322.5	Jan.–Sept.	765
		Oct.–Dec.	850
1958	10,323		850
1959	10,333		850
1960	10,405		850
1961	11,052.5	Jan.–Nov.	850
		Dec.	955
1962	12,177		955
1963	13,204		955
1964	15,001		955
1965	16,375		1,110
1966	17,877		1,215
1967	19,521	Jan.–Sept.	1,215
		Oct.–Dec.	1,395
1968	20,672	Jan.–Sept.	1,395
		Oct.–Dec.	1,510
1969	20,672		1,510
1970	20,672		1,510
1971	21,305		1,510

entry of school leavers in the labor market) was an important factor in pushing up wages, but the Minimum Wage Law enacted in 1959 was of no significance. However, the forming of food prices is greatly influenced by the government, which fixes the price of rice, controls the prices of all grains, subsidizes a number of other agricultural products, and approves rates of public utilities and transportation charges; moreover, tariffs and taxes almost double prices of petroleum products, sugar, and bananas.

Of all distortions, the problems in the agricultural sector are the most formidable. Until the formulation of a new program for the basic principles of a comprehensive agrarian policy adopted by the cabinet in February 1970, the main features of postwar agricultural policy were: (1) owner operated small holdings; (2) assimilation of agricultural to industrial income irrespective of productivity; (3) protection of agriculture against foreign competition and self-sufficiency in food. The last objective could never be reached completely, the main exceptions being wheat and sugar (ratio of self-sufficiency in foods, 83 percent; rice, 116 percent; wheat, 20 percent; sugar, 27 percent; soy beans, 6 percent).

Following the destruction of the cities during the war, the farming population (employed in agriculture) temporarily increased (from 13.4 million in 1940 to 16.1 million in 1950) but declined slowly in the fifties (1960, 14.9 million) and rapidly in the sixties. In 1970, the farming population numbered 8,230,000, 16.2 percent of the total labor force of 51,530,000 (total population according to the national census of October 1, 1970, 104,649,107).

Employment Structure

	1965	1970
Primary industries	25.5	19.3
Secondary industries	31.6	34.1
Tertiary industries	42.8	46.6

In February 1970, the number of farming households (5,324,000) accounted for 25.6 percent of the national total, as against 46 percent in 1950. Only 832,000 households were exclusively engaged in farming; 1,802,000 were primarily engaged in farming but relied also on other income, and for 2,709,000, over half of all farm households, income from other occupations was higher than income from farming. Average farm income, however, has been rising constantly, from ¥343,386 a year per household in fiscal 1959 to ¥1,250,000 in fiscal 1969 (the average number of persons per household decreased from 5.8 in 1959 to 4.95 in 1969; national average, 3.72). Labor productivity per worker in agriculture was 35.1 percent of that in manufacturing industries. The small size of most holdings remains an obstacle to rationalization in the sense of large-scale, highly mechanized farming, but nowadays most farmers consider the small size of their farms an advantage because it allows them to work more off the farm (the average Japanese farm household cultivates 0.7 hectares of rice fields or keeps 4.4 milch cows).

3 BUSINESS FAILURES

The developments in the first half of the sixties were greatly influenced by Japan's balance of payments position. The deflationary policy adopted in 1961 was primarily motivated by the deterioration in the balance of payments, and the same difficulty cut short the uptrend which started in late 1962. The Bank of Japan reduced the official discount rate four times, in October and November 1962 and in March and April 1963. Different from the enormous increase in equipment investment during the Iwato boom, the expansion drew its main support from consumption expenditures and fiscal spending. Exports grew satisfactorily in 1962 but slowed down somewhat in the following year; imports, however, expanded much more rapidly in 1963 and, on a customs clearance basis, foreign trade registered a $1,284 million deficit.

Rate of Increase over Preceding Year

(In percent)

	1959	1960	1961	1962	1963	1964	1965
Private consumption expenditure	9.4	14.3	14.5	16.2	17.2	15.8	12.5
Current government expenditure	9.5	14.3	16.2	16.1	18.0	16.1	15.5
Government investment	17.0	20.7	28.1	32.7	15.8	10.4	14.3
Private equipment investment	17.5	44.1	41.0	3.3	5.1	21.0	−5.6
Exports (customs clearance)	20.2	17.3	4.5	16.1	10.9	22.4	26.7
Imports (″ ″)	18.7	24.8	29.4	−3.0	19.5	17.8	2.9

Sources: Economic Planning Agency, National Income Statistics; Min. of Fin., Trade of Japan

Industry, still intoxicated by the heady wine of the rapid expansion, talked about "profit-less prosperity" and "expansion without the feeling of an upswing." The production index for mining and manufacturing (1960 = 100) rose steadily (1961, 119.4; 1962, 129.3; 1963, 143.3; 1964, 166.8; 1965, 173.1), but the economy seemed to be blanketed by a feeling of emptiness and disappointment. The government grew increasingly nervous about the balance of payments. The chronic deficit on invisibles grew larger, worsening the deficit on current account, but, in most months, the surplus from capital transactions could offset the deficiency so that the overall balance showed a slight surplus. There was no substantial change in the foreign exchange reserves, which rose from a low of $1,486 million at the end of December 1961 to a high of $1,922 million at the end of October 1963. In November, the overall balance showed a deficit of $11 million, which was nothing to worry about. But the policy-makers had a bad case of jitters and, in December, the Bank of Japan switched to a policy of monetary restraints by announcing an increase in the reserve deposit ratio effective December 16. As if to confirm the fears of a new overheating, the overall balance was in the red both in January ($23 million) and February 1964 ($54 million), and, on March 18, 1964, the discount rate was raised by 2 *rin* to 1.8 *sen* (6.57 percent). In fact, the increase in imports was quite normal; the increase in production required large imports of raw materials and fuels which accounted for about $500 million of the increase in imports. Larger inventory investment added another $200 million to the import bill; about half of these imports served to replenish stocks run down in the recession year, 1962, and the other half was necessary in view of the larger scale of the economy. The bad grain harvest of 1963 made larger imports of wheat and barley necessary, and the rise in the price of raw sugar was responsible for over $100 million of the increase in imports.

The uneasiness of the Bank of Japan was heightened by the anticipation of the adverse effects of Japan's renunciation of the exceptions provided in Article 14 of the IMF agreement and the assumption of the duties of Article 8 (no direct restrictions on imports to protect the balance of payments), as well as the observance of Article 11 of GATT. Another step toward an open economy was Japan's admission to the OECD (Organization for Economic Cooperation and Development), which was approved on July 26, 1963, and took effect on April 28, 1964. In order to meet the impact of the new situation on the balance of payments, the government applied for a standby credit of $305 million from IMF (which Japan could claim unconditionally). Furthermore, measures to promote exports (particularly tax rebates for technological exports and the development of overseas markets and more favorable depreciation schedules) and to restrict imports (e.g., a "Buy Japanese" program) were taken.

The government considered the expansion too fast and the increase in imports a threat to the balance of payments. The banks generally shared the government's point of view while many economists regarded the expansion in 1963 as apparent rather than real and expressed the fear that the deflationary policy would lead to a recession. As a matter of fact, the policy decisions of the government were based on a misreading of the developments in the economy.

Following the relaxation of the credit restraints in October 1962, production slowly moved upward, but demand failed to match the increase in output and, instead of decreasing, inventories of finished goods became larger (index of producers' inventories of finished goods, MITI, 1960 = 100; average of manufacturing industry, 1961, 122.3; 1962, 161.3; 1963, 170.4; 1964, 195.9; 1965, 223.5; the increase was particularly high in machinery: 1961, 140.6; 1962, 212.0; 1963, 248.3; 1964, 313.6; 1965, 364.2). What had happened was that manufacturers, instead of reducing the accumulated inventories to meet the increase in demand (the usual procedure after a recession), pressured MITI into relaxing the production curtailments. The reason was that the excessive capacity, largely financed by bank loans constituted a heavy burden and that the low operating rate nullified the reduction in costs expected from the huge investment outlays. The increase in production reduced inventories of raw materials; and imported raw material stocks, in particular, decreased quickly in the beginning of 1963 (index of raw materials, MITI, 1960 = 100; general: 1961, 107.3; 1962, 116.4; 1963, 108.5; 1964, 113.5; 1965, 112.1; imported raw materials: 1961, 115.3; 1962, 118.4; 1963, 111.7; 1964, 116.9; 1965, 116.7). The replenishment of the raw materials inventories was one of the main reasons for the sharp increase in imports. Another result of these developments was continuing pressure on the money market. Although there were certain fluctuations, loans to industry remained more or less the same and advances of the Bank of Japan declined very little from the level reached during the boom (outstanding year-end balances: 1959, ¥337.9 billion; 1960, ¥500.2 billion; 1961, ¥1,284.5 billion; 1962, ¥1,285.1 billion; 1963, ¥1,155.6 billion; 1964, ¥1,110.4 billion; 1965, ¥1,627.7 billion). But industry's fund demand was not prompted by large investment projects. Only in a few sectors, e.g., synthetic fibers, petrochemicals, cement, oil refining, and automobiles, were investment activities of large enterprises very conspicuous, but, in fiscal 1963, investments by small enterprises rose by 30.2 percent over the preceding year. Generally, however, the economy was far from overheated. Business results for the six-month term ended September 1963 were somewhat better than in March, but most enterprises suffered from low business volume.

Two phenomena were significant for the situation, the large increase in business failures and the slump in the stock market. In 1962, the number of bankruptcies increased by 61.4 percent over the preceding year and reached 1,779 cases (involving debts exceeding ¥10 million), higher than the 1,736 cases in the recession year, 1957. The value of liabilities showed an increase of 128.9 percent over the previous year, rising to ¥1,840 billion. The number of business failures as well as the amount of liabilities involved declined in 1963 but really skyrocketed in 1964, when the number rose by 142.3 percent and the value of liabilities by 173.2 percent. Since then, the high number of bankruptcies has become chronic (the number declined only in 1969).

A study undertaken by the Tokyo Shoko Mercantile Agency (Tokyo Credit Bureau for Commerce and Industry) gave the following reasons for business failures: stagnant sales, inefficient management, uncollectible accounts, insolvency of other firms, undercapitalization, and excessive equipment investment. All these reasons may be responsible for the business failures, but the basic reason is the highly insecure credit structure on which Japan's entire economy is built.

Business Failures

Year	Number of bankruptcies	Total liabilities ¥ billion
1956	1,123	46.4
1957	1,736	76.8
1958	1,480	58.0
1959	1,166	48.4
1960	1,172	65.2
1961	1,102	80.4
1962	1,779	184.0
1963	1,738	169.5
1964	4,212	463.1
1965	6,141	562.4
1966	6,187	398.7
1967	8,192	485.4
1968	10,776	797.4
1969	8,523	548.4
1970	9,765	729.2

Source: Tokyo Shoko Mercantile Agency, Ltd.

The frailty of the Japanese credit structure can be readily understood from the importance of trade credit. The intense competition has made payment conditions extremely liberal (70 percent in notes with a maturity of 120–180 days is not unusual) and every downturn in the economy brings a worsening of conditions. Since the decline in business is usually the result of credit restrictions, enterprises find themselves deprived of credit just at the time when they need it most. Thus, the one-sided reliance on monetary policy for regulating the economy has not been without influence on the bankruptcy situation. Thanks to their close relations with the city banks, large enterprises can usually secure the funds to tide over the periods of monetary stringency, but small enterprises are in a much more vulnerable position. With the rapid expansion, the size of small enterprises and their business volume have also grown so that liabilities involved in business failures have increased faster than their number. Many small firms work as subcontractors, and this position often makes them more vulnerable to the credit contractions. It also explains the domino effect of many bankruptcies.

In 1964, two companies whose shares were listed on the First Section of the Tokyo Stock Exchange became insolvent, but the most spectacular failure was the collapse of Sanyo Special Steel Co., which applied for reorganization on March 6, 1965. Sanyo had been Japan's third largest producer of steel alloys (1963, 9.6 percent of total production) and the largest manufacturer of bearings (60 percent of total output). As of January 31, 1965, total liabilities of the firm amounted to ¥47.9 billion, ¥32.7 billion in current liabilities and ¥15.2 billion in long-term borrowing. Among the company's creditors were some of the leading city banks: Kobe, Mitsui, Mitsubishi, Fuji, and the Industrial Bank. The total due to banks amounted to ¥26.4 billion. Sanyo had also contracted loans from foreign banks, guaranteed by Japanese banks ($3 million from the Chartered Bank of London and $3 million from the Bank of London & South America), and had placed a note in the amount of £5 million in London through Banque Lambert. Of the ¥21.5 billion due to creditors other than banks Sanyo owed ¥12.1 billion to the large trading companies (C. Itoh, Mitsui and Co., Mitsubishi Shoji, Marubeni-Iida, and Tokyo Tsusho) and ¥4,344 million to about three hundred forty medium-sized and small enterprises; of these enterprises, seventy were subcontractors whose claims amounted to about ¥700 million. About forty subcontractors to whom Sanyo owed ¥560 million and the same number of other firms with claims of ¥1.7 billion were themselves in financial difficulties.

Later investigations showed that Sanyo's management had doctored the company's balance sheet for several years, had declared dividends, and paid directors' bonuses although the firm was deep in the red. Shortly before the debacle, the directors had withdrawn their deposits from the company's employees savings fund. Production of steel alloys had increased about fourfold since 1959, but stiff competition and small-lot production of a great

Borrowing and Trade Credit

(Outstanding balances in billions of yen)

End of year	Borrowing				Trade credit received	
	Corporations		Individuals		Corporations	Individuals
	From private financial institutions	From government institutions	From private financial institutions	From government institutions		
1954	3,426.2	434.6	562.5	177.7	1,754.0	560.4
1955	3,892.2	506.3	631.4	214.3	1,973.0	593.4
1956	4,832.6	582.9	830.3	259.5	2,534.2	705.4
1957	5,983.1	684.8	1,005.6	326.7	2,900.1	893.3
1958	7,021.3	783.0	1,181.1	416.5	3,232.3	1,141.6
1959	8,317.1	908.5	1,470.1	501.3	4,784.4	1,349.2
1960	10,089.0	1,055.5	1,901.8	591.3	5,715.0	1,599.0
1961	12,405.8	1,222.4	2,391.7	694.5	8,246.3	2,024.9
1962	14,990.6	1,429.7	2,962.1	814.5	9,693.5	2,701.9
1963	18,918.2	1,674.7	3,711.2	928.9	12,309.0	3,495.1
1964	24,029.0		5,612.4		14,718.5	4,227.8
End of fiscal year						
1964	24,935.4		5,726.3		15,715.7	5,726.3
1965	28.938.3		6,783.5		16,889.1	6,783.5
1966	33,100.5		8,452.0		20,946.3	8,452.0
1967	38,336.8		10,269.9		25,944.0	10,269.9
1968	44,213.8		12,252.6		28,544.7	12,252.6
1969	46,969.8	5,293.2	12,820.1	2,272.6	36,249.7	10,608.1
1970	56,315.3	6,181.3	15,694.2	2,695.7	40,580.0	11,184.6

Source: Bank of Japan, Summary of Flow of Funds.

variety of products impaired profitability and the interest burden resulting from large investments in equipment compounded the firm's financial difficulties.

In former years, small textile traders had accounted for a large number of the insolvencies, but this situation had changed. Although cyclical factors continued to influence business failures, the structural changes in industry and the changes in consumer demand became more important.

A second episode that illustrated the state of the economy was the slump of the stock market in the years from 1963 to 1965. The activities of the securities companies, in particular their investment trust business, had pushed stock prices to unrealistic heights in the boom years 1959–61 (Dow-Jones high, ¥1,829.74, July 18, 1961). The downtrend which started in 1961 continued through the following years, only interrupted by two periods of rising prices. In the beginning of 1963, prices started to rise and the Dow-Jones reached a high of ¥1,634.37. When, on July 18, 1963, President Kennedy announced the imposition of a special tax on capital exports, the Dow-Jones lost ¥123.32 in two days and plunged to ¥1,390.99. In view of Japan's dependence on the American capital market, this reaction was quite understandable, all the more since the move ended the hopes of large American investments in Japanese securities. President Kennedy's assassination completely demoralized the already weakened market and the Dow-Jones tumbled to ¥1,245.23. Despite some support buying, the market failed to recover and on December 18 fell to ¥1,200.64, the low of the year (low for 1962: ¥1,238.48, October 23, 1962).

For some nebulous reason, the government and the financial world regarded the ¥1,200 mark as some kind of Maginot line and, prompted by the government, the city banks and the large securities companies founded the Japan Joint Securities Co. (see page 199) which, with the help of central bank credit, tried to take the pressure off the stock market. The readiness of the government and the Bank of Japan contrasted sharply with the general monetary stringency that was largely responsible for the rising wave of business failures. As mentioned above, the credit squeeze was only one of the factors responsible for the increase in insolvencies, but the imposition of credit restraints for largely imaginary balance of payments difficulties in a situation that strained the financial resources of most enterprises, and the mobilization of huge funds to try to cure the symptoms of the economic malaise indicated a certain confusion in the leadership.

The depressive tendencies had already appeared in the settlement of accounts for the March–September term of 1964. Although most of the companies listed on the First Section of the Tokyo Stock Exchange could report an increase in sales, average profits of the 604 firms remained 2.5 percent below the preceding term and 56 firms reduced their dividend rates.

Production remained high, but the rising inventories revealed the growing difficulties encountered in the market. The manufacturers of electric household appliances, in particular, felt the impact of insufficient demand. Electric appliances were among the products whose growth had sparked the Iwato boom. In rapid succession, radio and television (monochrome) receivers, electric washing machines, transistor radios, tape recorders, and refrigerators had stimulated the expansion of the manufacturers of light electrical machinery (catapulting Sony and Matsushita Electric into the position of market favorites). Due to the saturation of the market, capacity in these lines far exceeded demand and the industry failed to develop a new product which could take up the slack and absorb the flood of parts and components produced by the numerous subcontractors. The hopes which the industry had set on air-conditioners were sadly disappointed; it was only during the following boom (when color television sets and stereo and cassette tape recorders were added to the stock of electrical appliances) that their sales reached sizable proportions.

An exception to the generally gloomy picture was the automobile industry whose production of four-wheeled vehicles fell somewhat short of the one million mark in 1962 but greatly exceeded it in 1963 and kept growing in the following years (production of passenger cars: 1963, 407,830; 1964, 579,660; 1965, 695,974; truck and bus chassis: 1963, 875,711; 1964, 1,123,822; 1965, 1,177,478). It was in these years that Japanese automobiles began their penetration into the export market (exports of passenger cars: 1963, 38,051 units; 1964, 77,536 units; 1965, 117,810 units).

The situation became worse in 1965. In the preceding years, the investment programs initiated in the boom period had been continued and the expansion of trade credit had met a large part of financial needs but, toward the end of 1964, the effects of the credit restraints became more pronounced and the settlements of accounts for the terms ended March and September 1965 reflected the stagnation of sales and showed a sharp decrease in profits. In the middle of the year, production curtailments became more numerous and a number of industries organized depression cartels. In addition to the lower utilization of equipment, Japanese enterprises are hurt by the impossibility of adjusting their labor force to business conditions. The system of lifelong employment traditional in most large enterprises allows them only to dismiss part-time workers and cut down on overtime but they cannot fire their regular workers. Hence, when the operating rate is low, unit labor costs rise.

The increase in business failures appeared in the losses of the large trading companies. For March 1965, Mitsubishi Shoji reported ¥2.1 billion in uncollectibles, Mitsui and Co. ¥6 billion, Marubeni-Iida ¥370 million, C. Itoh and Co. ¥2.4 billion, and Toyo Menka ¥1.4 billion; for the eleven large trading companies, uncollectibles rose from ¥3 billion for the September 1964 settlement to ¥15 billion for the March 1965 settlement and, with the exception of Marubeni-Iida, the uncollectibles exceeded profits.

In January 1965, the Japan Securities Holding Association came into being, but, despite the efforts of the authorities at supporting the stock market, the Dow-Jones index continued its downward trend. In March 1965, the index fell below ¥1,200, in May below ¥1,100, and on July 12, 1965, the Dow-Jones sank to the lowest point of the year, ¥1,020.49. In May, Yamaichi Securities Co. was practically insolvent and the government came to its rescue.

Different from private industry, the government had stuck to an optimistic view of the situation and only tried to stimulate business by reducing the official discount rate (in three steps from 6.57 percent to 5.48 percent). At the end of July, however, a fiscal program of increased spending was decided upon; although it remained without immediate effect on the economy, the stock market reacted favorably. At the end of August, the Dow-Jones climbed to ¥1,255.58 and rose above the ¥1,300 mark in November.

4 ENVIRONMENTAL POLLUTION

A problem which received only belated attention was environmental pollution. In the beginning of the sixties, cases of injuries to health caused by industrial effluents among the rural population became more numerous, but the government was more interested in whitewashing industry than in effective control of industrial waste. The occurrence of eye-trouble resulting from chemical smog and other forms of air pollution in the capital resulted in mass hysteria and pollution control became a national issue. In many cases, the local population opposed the building of new plants, particularly electric power stations, steel plants, and aluminum and oil refineries; and local governments, in addition to enforcing stricter public nuisance ordinances, concluded agreements with local enterprises stipulating standards for the sulfur dioxide content of smoke or waste gas or other industrial waste. The health hazards resulting from industrial effluents (*Minamata* disease, *Itai-itai* disease), agricultural chemicals (toxic substances found in food), the pollution of Tagonoura Bay by the wastes from paper manufacturing plants, and the exhaust fumes of automobiles became national issues.

Due to the government's basic policy of giving priority to economic growth and industrial production, existing legislation was inadequate and even the only recently (1967) enacted Basic Public Hazards Countermeasures Law stood in need of revision. In December 1970, therefore, the Diet passed fourteen laws concerned with pollution. About half of them revised earlier legislation (including amendments for preventing pollution of the sea adopted by the Inter-Governmental Maritime Consultative Organization in 1969); others introduced new controls or safeguards (including a law for preventing contamination of farmland and a law which replaced the penal provisions contained in various previous laws by the newly established crime of pollution). The original drafts prepared by the ministries in charge were considerably watered down by the Liberal-Democratic party when industry objected to provisions that would have imposed effective controls. Generally speaking, the Japanese authorities are still primarily concerned with abating and preventing pollution; they have not unconditionally adopted the principle that industry cannot omit free resources such as air and water from the pricing system and allocate the social costs of production to society. Still less are ecological considerations given priority in government and private planning, and only academic interest is accorded to the basic problem of man's existence in nature, the reconciliation of technology with the integrity of the material world, and the organization of progress along lines and in patterns that will not impair and eventually destroy the physical conditions on which human life depends.

In the fiscal 1971 budget, an amount of ¥931 billion was allocated in the general accounts for antipollution measures (an increase of 39.8 percent over the preceding year), and the fiscal loan and investment program allocated ¥170.2 billion for the same purpose (49.0 percent more than the previous year's amount). The general accounts provided ¥66.0 billion to try to prevent the sinking of the land suface. The main funds related to pollution control in the fiscal loan and investment program were ¥40.0 billion for the Pollution Prevention Corporation (which finances antipollution measures), ¥10.0 billion for the Japan Development Bank (loans to private industry for financing installation of pollution control devices), and ¥114.0 billion in local bonds. According to the settlement of accounts for fiscal 1968, local bodies spent ¥19.6 billion on antipollution measures. Expenditures to prevent water pollution accounted for the largest share in the spending of prefectural governments and the large cities, while towns and villages spent a lot of money on the minimization of noise and the abatement of vibration from airports.

Many of the government's financial institutions give special loans for the installation of equipment related to the prevention or abatement of pollution. In addition to the supplementary financing provided by local bodies in connection with modernization loans available to small enterprises (in fiscal 1968, twenty-nine prefectures and the six large and twenty-nine other cities), altogether sixty-four local bodies had independent financing programs which, in fiscal 1968, supplied ¥4.6 billion. The recipients were small enterprises, and most loans were ¥5–10 million. In many cases, local bodies provided interest subsidies in connection with their financing programs (in fiscal 1968, ¥259 million).

Private banks initiated a loan plan called the pollution prevention finance system. It was first introduced by the Bank of Yokohama in August 1970 and was later taken up by other local banks. The system is more or less the same; small enterprises that have been notified by the local authorities that they must stop pollution can obtain loans up to ¥10 million (Yoyo Bank, ¥15 million) to install antipollution equipment or relocate their factories. Interest rates are usually 0.5 percent lower than on general long-term loans, or 8.5 percent (if the Credit Guarantee Association guarantees the loans, the interest rate is 0.1–0.5 percent lower). Maturity is seven years; for the payment of interest and the beginning of repayment, a grace period of six months or one year is common.

Tax concessions for facilitating the installation of antipollution equipment comprise a special depreciation schedule that allows the writing off of one-third of the purchase price of the equipment in the initial year, exemption from property taxes or reduction of the tax rate, special concessions for the replacement of certain types of property, reduction of the registration tax and the real estate acquisition tax, shortening of the useful life of equipment, and lower taxes on desulfurized heavy oil.

Special subsidies or indemnities are provided for the abatement of noise in the vicinity of public airfields, for nuisances arising from installations of Japan's Self-Defense Forces or the U.S. Forces stationed in Japan, and for facilities installed by port authorities for the disposal of discharged oil.

5 INFRASTRUCTURAL DEFICIENCIES

During the rapid expansion of the Japanese economy in the last decade, the rate of private capital formation greatly exceeded fiscal investment and created an investment gap between the private and the public sectors. The worsening problems of environmental pollution have added a new urgency to the need for remedying the deficiencies in the infrastructure, in housing, roads, harbors, sewer systems, parks, and green belts. Private economists and government agencies are unanimous in urging the allocation of greater resources to social capital, but the present tendency to adopt inflated programs for specific needs, irrespective of the cost effectiveness of the proposals and the balanced allocation of available fiscal resources, can only lead to the same irresponsible waste that has marked past fiscal policies. The present situation actually goes back to the prewar neglect of everything not of direct importance to military preparedness, to the postwar apathy (e.g., abandoning the idea of widening the roads in Tokyo because this would have involved pulling down the shacks built by the air raid victims), to the complete absence of any system of priorities (the government spent enormous sums on prestige projects such as the 1964 Olympics, Expo '70, and the Winter Olympics 1972, new government office buildings, and luxury housing for the members of the Diet, while the publicly financed housing programs always fell short of their targets; local bodies built modern town halls and civic centers, while many schools remain housed in prewar wooden structures that are nearly all dangerous firetraps), and to fiscal rigidity. This means that programs once established receive larger allocations from year to year and remain in force long after they have outlived their usefulness. The usefulness of many of the several hundred special companies, corporations, and agencies set up by the government on the basis of special laws is open to serious doubt, but they constitute convenient channels for subsidizing industry and agriculture and provide remunerative sinecures to former government officials. Equally superfluous are the innumerable commissions attached to every ministry and the Prime Minister's Office. In short, the shortcomings are due to the absence of rational planning based on a coherent system of priorities.

The present tendency is to improve the infrastructure by wild bursts of spending. As mentioned above, most economic plans have been revised or replaced by new plans before their completion because the rapid growth of the economy made them obsolete. To obviate this necessity, the target figures are now fixed so high that they conform to the numerical proportions of the space age. Under the New Economic and Social Development Plan (1970–75) the government intends to spend ¥55 trillion on infrastructural facilities (increasing expenditures at an average yearly rate of 13.5 percent); for fiscal 1971, four new five-year plans were approved: the Fourth Harbor Construction Plan (total costs, ¥2.1 trillion), the Second Airport Construction Plan (¥560 billion), the Third Sewer Construction Plan (¥2.6 trillion), and the Second Residential Construction Plan (9.5 million housing units). In 1969, the Ministry of Construction proposed a new five-year plan for road construction that involved outlays of ¥10 trillion, a 50 percent increase over the costs foreseen in the 1967–71 program. A grandiose plan to build a network of 9,000 km. of trunk lines similar to the New Tokaido Line at a cost of ¥11.3 trillion would connect Wakkanai at the northern tip of Hokkaido with Kagoshima in the south of Kyushu by 1985. Naturally, these programs are entirely out of line with available resources; hence, after fixing excessive targets, the government raises the corresponding revenues by levying new taxes or floating more bonds. In addition to the financial aspects of these plans, the nonchalant predictions concerning the physical expansion of the economy are somewhat startling (e.g., production of 150 million tons of crude steel in 1975). The trunk line scheme is the same kind of politically inspired gambit which was one of the causes of the quandary in which the Japan National Railways find themselves at present, viz., the construction and operation of uneconomical lines to please the local constituents of dietmen (another reason was the undercapitalization of the enterprise which was forced to finance huge construction projects by loans). While the New Tokaido Line, running between the two largest cities in the country, is the most profitable of JNR's lines, it is hard to see how this plan can provide for amortization.

There can be no doubt that the country's infrastructural facilities are woefully inadequate, but some of the massive spending programs are political ploys designed to enhance the reputation of ambitious politicians and to line the pockets of government contractors, and will not benefit the people. The overcrowding of commuter trains is worse than it was fifteen years ago when it was thought inhuman; the construction of huge housing developments without adequate transportation facilities in the suburbs and prefectures next to the big cities has aggravated the commuter problem. (Since different authorities are in charge of housing and transportation, the programs in these two sectors are not coordinated.) As is often the case, the decision makers are remote from the scene, and their decisions are based on indirect information and abstract goals.

1 ECONOMIC
DEVELOPMENTS

3 THE SHIFT TO AN OPEN ECONOMY

1 TRADE AND EXCHANGE LIBERALIZATION

In order to cope with the difficulties of the postwar era Japan imposed severe restrictions on foreign trade and exchange, and her membership in the International Monetary Fund (1952) and her adherence to the General Agreement on Tariffs and Trade (1955) brought no immediate change.

Toward the end of 1958, the leading European countries restored the convertibility of their currencies. This development prompted the government to adopt the liberalization of trade and exchange as a policy goal. In the three-year period starting on January 1, 1960, the rate of liberalization of imports (i.e., abolition of quotas) was to be raised from 37 percent (based on the dollar value of imports in fiscal 1959) to 90 percent, while current transactions were to be liberalized within two years. In conformity with this policy, an "Outline of the Liberalization Plan for Foreign Trade and Foreign Exchange" was drawn up in June 1960. The basic policies for the liberalization of imports were: (1) imports of raw materials were to be liberalized as quickly as possible in order to reduce costs of domestic manufactures; (2) goods not competing with domestic products and lines in which Japanese products are competitive in international markets were to be liberalized next, and special measures were to be taken to allow an early liberalization of goods whose liberalization would procure special advantages; (3) lines in which the government had promoted technical development or rationalization by programs based on laws or other measures (i.e., industries which were not competitive) were to be liberalized upon an evaluation of the results obtained by such measures; (4) for industries whose immediate liberalization would result in difficulties an expansion of imports was to be decided upon specifically, by taking into account the demands of import partners and the effects of trade expansion, so that liberalization was to proceed to the extent that arrangements could be made for the protection of these industries.

Practically, all commodities were divided into three categories, IQ (import quota), AIQ (automatic import quota), and AA (automatic approval). For the first category, all imports had to be specifically approved; for commodities under the second category, import licenses were given "automatically" (i.e., only the usual red tape was required) up to a certain limit; and theoretically no restrictions were placed on imports of commodities falling under the third category. Since past experience was an important factor in the allocation of quotas, newcomers were practically barred from entering the import business in many lines (unless they could buy the quota "rights" from somebody wanting to get out).

The liberalization of imports was effected by transferring commodities to a different import category (from IQ to AIQ or from AIQ to AA). The government continued to use the percentage system to indicate the degree of liberalization (in April 1970, liberalization was said to have reached nearly 94 percent) which, on account of the base year and the method used (dollar value of imports in fiscal 1959), was completely misleading. The problem, however, was far from simple, not only on account of the impact of the liberalization on the domestic economy, but also because of its connection with the tariff structure (Kennedy round and preferential tariffs) and the discriminatory measures against Japanese imports on the part of other countries (United States, West Germany, France, Italy, etc.). Japan wanted to receive concessions from her trading partners for her removal of import restrictions, and negotiations to this effect were extremely arduous. Nevertheless, real progress has been made; the liberalization which went into effect on October 1, 1962, nearly halved the number of restricted commodities (previously 254 items).

Trade liberalization was the subject of a great many discussions between Japan and the United States, and the friction between the two countries has become exacerbated during the Nixon administration. The removal of the remaining restrictions on imports was taken up in November 1968 at Geneva, and the talks were continued in Tokyo without any progress. The United States stressed the liberalization of agricultural commodities, but Japan wanted to start with industrial products. In January 1969, the United States asked the Japanese government to reexamine its liberalization policy. In May 1969, Secretary of Commerce Maurice Stans visited Japan, presenting a number of demands which Japan considered ill-founded and conflicting. While pressing for the abolition of Japanese restrictions on imports and capital investment, he also insisted upon the imposition of "voluntary" restraints on Japanese exports of woolen and synthetic textile products. The reaction of the Japanese press to Stans's demands was outright hostility and the threat that the American government would take no further action on the liberalization of trade unless the textile problem was solved was branded as crude Yankee imperialism. In the United States dissatisfaction with Japan grew and the anti-Japanese sentiment evoked the memory of the time before Pearl Harbor. Despite official denials on both sides, the return of Okinawa seemed to be entangled in the trade problems. The Tokyo meeting of the joint Japan-U.S. economic committee in July 1969 emphasized Japan's favorable balance of payments position and during the consultations in Washington in November 1969, Japan's duties as an economic world power were used as an argument for extracting greater concessions. New Japanese proposals formulated in June 1969 were turned down by Washington in July as completely unsatisfactory. In September 1969, the Japanese cabinet decided on the liberalization of fifty-two items before the end of 1971, and, in October, the completion of the liberalization of inward forward investment was moved up to October 1, 1971.

By the end of March 1971, the government had reduced the number of commodities whose imports were restricted to eighty. Of these, forty-nine were agricultural products, and the liberalization of imports of agricultural products has been the most frustrating chapter in this development. The Ministry of Agriculture has persistently opposed all attempts at liberalization and, as a result of its policy, the price of wheat in Japan is double the CIF price in the United States (the same is true for rice); the wholesale price of beef is 2.3 times the CIF price abroad and the price of butter paid by large users is 2.6 times the foreign price. The liberalization of imports of grapefruit has been blocked four times by a group of politicians in the Liberal-Democratic party, *Kajitsu Shinkō Giin Renmei*, supporting the interests of fruit growers to the detriment of the consumer, and the same group has opposed the reduction of the ridiculously high duties on bananas (60 percent; changed to a seasonal duty effective April 1, 1971—a quota system remains in force for banana imports from Taiwan; liberalization had been scheduled for August 1971). The number of restricted commodities was reduced to forty by the end of September 1971 (twenty items liberalized at the end of April and another twenty at the end of September), which are now decontrolled further on a case by case basis.

Foreign exchange quotas for imports (generally fixed within 2 percent of domestic consumption) were abolished at the end of fiscal 1970 but were revived when the liberalization of grapefruit and the other twenty-five items (complete decontrol of twenty positions, partial decontrol of six), which was to have gone into effect in April, was postponed due to the opposition of the farm lobby to the liberalization of grapefruit imports. Acceleration of the removal of import restrictions was included in the eight-point program adopted by the government on June 4, 1971, in order to lessen the pressure for a revaluation of the yen. Hence, the liberalization of the twenty-six items, including grapefruit, which had been postponed, was effected immediately. Other measures envisaged were the reduction of tariffs and the adoption of preferential tariffs on imports from developing countries.

The number of items under the AIQ (automatic import quota) system was reduced from seventy-three to forty-seven at the end of June 1971, but MITI opposed the complete abolition of the system on the ground that the officials in charge of administering the system would lose their jobs. Of the remaining items, forty-four are to be transferred to the AA (automatic approval) system by the end of 1971 and only three items (lactose, uranium, and plutonium) will remain subject to the AIQ system. Under the AA system, importers are granted import licenses upon application to an authorized foreign exchange bank, but for items under the AIQ system, an application must be filed with MITI and this application is rejected if MITI deems the import undesirable (there are no published standards on what is or is not desirable). Hence, Japanese and foreign businessmen consider the system highly arbitrary. The attitudes formed in the immediate postwar period, when foreign exchange had to be husbanded, still dominate the bureaucracy and completely obsolete legal regulations remain on the statute book.

President Nixon's new economic policy and the subsequent floating of the yen provided the Ministry of Agriculture with a welcome opportunity for demanding the postponement of the liberalization of seven categories of farm products scheduled for the end of September, 1971. With the customary disregard for the consumer, Minister of Agriculture Munenori Akagi assured the general agricultural policy committee of the Liberal-Democratic party that the problem of the liberalization of farm imports would be handled "with the utmost caution." Yielding to pressure from the farm block, the government has already decided not to liberalize imports of beef, oranges, and fruit juice, items of major importance for consumers and in the liberalization of which the American government was greatly interested. In case the liberalization of products such as refined sugar, feed, and bananas is carried out, the Ministry of Agriculture intends to have tariff rates raised and to adopt guaranteed minimum prices.

Because computers were excluded from the fourth round of capital liberalization which went into effect on August 4, 1971, the government was considering a partial liberalization of imports of peripheral equipment for late in 1971 or early in 1972. On October 1, 1971, import restrictions were removed completely on twenty items and partially on five categories. Of the forty items (twenty-eight farm products, twelve industrial products) whose import remained restricted, ten were to be liberalized by the end of the year or by March 1972.

The protection of the status quo by the government's import restrictions may be exemplified by the system still in force for the importation of shoes. In order to protect the domestic shoe industry, imports of shoes are only allowed through two cartels (official wholesalers' associations), one in Tokyo (about a hundred members) and another in Osaka (forty members). The two cartels are given a dollar allocation (fiscal 1970, $2.6 million; fiscal 1971, about $4 million) which is distributed on the basis of past experience. This means that newcomers are excluded. At the end of September 1971, MITI decided to give an additional allocation of $600,000 for fiscal 1971 ($460,000 for Tokyo and $140,000 for Osaka) to be used for firms without past experience. Requests by wholesalers in Nagoya and other places for an allocation were refused on the ground that their associations were not juridical persons and were incapable of joint imports. Needless to say, the system results in higher prices, less choice, and superfluous red tape.

In connection with the liberalization of imports, a thoroughgoing revision of the tariff system went into effect on April 1, 1971, the principal objective of which was to replace import quotas as the principal instrument of import controls. It was the third revision in the postwar period. The first tariff revision, in 1951, was designed to cope with the change in Japan's economic position resulting from the war; the second, which went into effect in 1961, followed the adoption of the principle of trade liberalization by the Japanese government in 1960. With the progress in the liberalization of imports, tariff rates were raised; as a result, the ratio of tariff revenues to the total value of imports, which had been a low 1.01 percent in 1951, rose to 6.4 percent in 1961 and 7.7 percent in 1964.

Tariff rates on items which had been subject to import quotas were generally raised because they had been rather low; but, because the revision also represented the fifth and last step in the implementation of the linear tariff reductions under the Kennedy round (advanced from January 1972), tariffs were reduced on 1,923 items. A number of technical provisions were adopted in order to facilitate the prevention of market dislocations by a sudden increase in imports. Among these measures were the shift from ad valorem to specific duties, the adoption of alternative (either ad valorem or specific duties) and composite duties (a combination of ad valorem and specific duties), seasonal tariffs, and tariff quotas, and the reduction of duties on imports of raw materials.

Based on agreements between the advanced industrial countries and the UNCTAD secretariat, preferential tariffs were granted to developing countries in 1971. Effective August 1, 1971, Japan reduced tariffs on 59 agricultural products by 20–100 percent; 833 products of mining and manufacturing industries will be admitted duty-free, but 7 products will not be given preferential treatment and on 57 "sensitive" products the tariff reductions will be limited to 50 percent. For imports of manufactures, ceilings will be fixed and, if imports from a certain country exceed 50 percent of the ceiling, further imports from that particular country will not enjoy preferential tariffs. The preferential tariffs apply to ninety-six countries, including Spain, Greece, Turkey, Cyprus, Malta, and Yugoslavia, but not to countries maintaining discriminatory trade restrictions against Japan under GATT's Article 35 (Portugal, Romania, Bulgaria, Jamaica, Botswana, Lesotho, and Swaziland).

The most important measure for the liberalization of current exchange transactions was the introduction of "free-yen" accounts. Starting July 1, 1960, nonresidents could open accounts with Japanese banks licensed to engage in foreign exchange business (including Japanese branches of foreign banks). No restrictions were put on the type of account which could be opened. Monies which could be placed in these accounts were: yen received by a nonresident in settlement for commodity imports into Japan or from other current transactions; yen received by a nonresident in cases in which the remittance of foreign currency was permitted, e.g., dividend payments on stock acquired under the Foreign Investment Law or the Foreign Exchange Control Law; yen received by a nonresident through the sale of foreign currency to foreign exchange banks; yen transferred from other free-yen accounts; finally, interest accruing from free-yen accounts may be credited to these accounts. There were no restrictions on withdrawals from free-yen accounts, either for remittances abroad, for payments to residents, or for transfers to other free-yen accounts.

Interest rates on free-yen deposits were the same as those on the corresponding Japanese deposits, but, in March 1971, the Ministry of Finance authorized the foreign exchange banks to fix the interest rates on free-yen deposits at any level within the legal interest rates. The ministry wanted the banks to reduce the interest rates so as to stop the inflow of foreign funds.

By allowing the use of free-yen accounts for the settlement of transactions contracted for in yen, the so-called yen exchange system was adopted, which meant that the yen had been added to the list of designated currencies under the Foreign Exchange Control Law, (i.e., currencies that may be used in transactions involving international payments) and that settlements effected through free-yen had been recognized as standard settlements (which may be used in current business transactions), so that the yen basis could be officially used in transactions abroad.

Japanese foreign exchange banks were allowed to give short-term credits to foreign banks possessing free-yen accounts. They could also conclude free-yen forward exchange contracts with nonresidents. Export and import contracts on a yen basis were to receive preferential treatment. The Bank of Japan was to discount export usance bills drawn in yen at the same rate as export advance bills (at that time, 5.475 percent), while the rate on advances against import usance bills was the same as on import settlement bills (7.3 percent); advances were made up to 85 percent of the face value of the bills.

The control over foreign exchange largely served protectionist purposes by closing the domestic market to foreign competition; it also provided the government with a convenient means of curbing the activities of Japanese producers and traders. In particular, the foreign exchange controls served to check what the authorities labeled "excessive competition." There is no dearth of legislation and institutions which give the government a far-reaching influence on the economy, but they do not ensure the comprehensive, centralized, and efficient supervision which the control over foreign exchange made possible. The Foreign Exchange and Foreign Trade Control Law not only applied to the activities of foreigners which is quite normal but also curbed the actions of Japanese and of foreign corporations established by Japanese abroad, which is incompatible with the principle of territorial jurisdiction because it infringes the sovereignty of the countries in which the subsidiaries are located.

After the announcement of the government's liberalization policy, the economic leaders engaged in an animated exchange of views with the authorities on a new formula of economic guidance. There was some fear that in the absence of strong controls, Japan's economy would not be able to weather the onslaught of foreign competition. While some of Japan's entrepreneurs thought that the paternalistic protectionism kept the industry in too strict a tutelage and formed an obstacle to economic maturity and independence, the bureaucracy was little inclined to relinquish its power and many businessmen preferred the safety of official protection to the opportunities and risks of the free market.

Out of the quest for a system which would secure the blessings of protectionism without the odium of trade restrictions emerged the formula of a new industrial structure to be set up through a thoroughgoing rationalization of the corporate world. The plans were partly prompted by actual conditions, e.g., in the shipping industry and in coal mining, and partly by the general consideration that greater concentration of production and an increase in the size of enterprises would eliminate "excessive competition," facilitate "administrative guidance," and strengthen Japan's position in international markets. Mergers, standardization, and the formation of groups of enterprises in the same branches were the chief means advocated for the reorganization of industry, while the individual enterprises were to strengthen internal capital and lessen their reliance on outside financing.

In the Treaty of Commerce, Establishment, and Navigation, which Japan signed with the United Kingdom in 1962 after more than six years of negotiations, Great Britain agreed to grant most-favored nation treatment one month after ratification (Great Britain enjoyed most-favored treatment as a result of the war) and to cease application of GATT's Article 35 to Japan. But both parties reserved the right to impose unilateral import restrictions in case of emergencies. Moreover, Japan promised to retain limitations on exports of eighteen commodities for a period of no longer than five years and to enforce voluntary export controls on sixty-one other items.

Following the recommendations of the International Monetary Fund that Japan should conform as quickly as possible to Article 8 of the IMF agreement because her foreign exchange position no longer warranted the application of Article 14, the Japanese government decided to take appropriate steps toward that goal. On February 20, 1963, Japan declared her intention of observing Article 11 of GATT (prohibition of all quantitative import restrictions), and on April 1, 1964, Japan assumed the obligations of Article 8 of the IMF agreement; with the exception of certain restrictions on tourist travel, limitations on payments based on current transactions were removed.

In its *Economic White Book for Fiscal 1963*, which bore the subtitle *The Economy in an Open Economic System*, the Economic Planning Agency stated that Japan's industry had come of age and should be able to compete with the advanced industrial nations of the West on an equal footing. The liberalization of world trade should make it possible for Japan to increase her exports and thereby raise the standard of living. The effort to achieve self-sufficiency through import restrictions was branded as the most dangerous threat to world trade, and the agency declared that Japan would do her best to remove such restrictions.

On April 28, 1964, Japan joined the Organization for Economic Cooperation and Development (OECD). In prior negotiations, Japan had obtained reservations on nineteen of the eighty-three positions on OECD's list for liberalization. Effective November 20, 1963, the government liberalized fifty positions of services and capital transactions. Among the payments for services which could be approved by the foreign exchange banks were charter parties not exceeding one year, insurance premiums, prizes for contests, tax payments, legal costs, fines, and compensation payments and repayments. Charter parties for the shipment of exports were completely liberalized while restrictions remained on charters for the import of coal, iron ore, and crude and heavy oil. Subscriptions for foreign newspapers and periodicals were liberalized up to $500 and the same sum could be sent for the support of parents living abroad. Emigrants could take out a sum of $5,000 with the approval of the Bank of Japan or a foreign exchange bank. The same banks could approve promotion costs up to $10,000 and up to $5,000 for market surveys.

For capital transactions, the following positions were liberalized: (1) repatriation of profits of foreign corporations which started operations after July 1, 1963—a report to the Bank of Japan is required; (2) repatriation of interests and dividends on Japanese shares of stock and bonds owned by nonresidents and repatriation of the principal (in case of sale of the securities)—a report to a foreign exchange bank required; (3) leases of buildings and other real estate owned by foreigners must be approved by the Bank of Japan, but rents can be paid through exchange banks; (4) savings accounts can be transferred through exchange banks if the sum does not exceed one-fifth of the year-end balance and is not higher than $2,000; (5) foreigners leaving Japan can take Japanese securities with them but must observe customs procedures; (6) foreigners leaving Japan can change their remaining yen currency into foreign currency provided the amount remains within the limits of the foreign currency originally taken into Japan. Foreign travel had been one of the reservations obtained by Japan when joining the OECD; in April 1964, foreign travel for pleasure was allowed for the first time since the war to ordinary citizens (the privileged classes had been able to do this under various pretenses) and tourists were allowed to take out up to $500 once a year (businessmen were allowed $35 per day up to a maximum of $2,000 for each trip without limitation on the number of trips). In April 1966, the limitation to one trip per year was removed; in April 1969, the ceiling was raised to $700 for tourists and $2,000 for businessmen (one of the many examples of the inequality before the law in Japan), and, on March 1, 1970, the tourist allowance was increased to $1,000. Students who study abroad can take $1,000 with them and can receive a daily allowance of $10 for two years of foreign studies. Effective July 1, 1970, travelers returning from abroad were allowed to retain up to $100 in foreign currency (under the former regulations, all foreign currency had to be exchanged into yen except for $30 worth which could be kept as a "souvenir").

Another major step in the decontrol of foreign exchange transactions was taken on September 1, 1969, when the following measures went into effect. Japanese branches of foreign enterprises established prior to July 1, 1963, without applying for approval will be allowed to repatriate principal and earnings; the permission, until then given in exceptional cases by the Ministry of Finance, will be given routinely by the Bank of Japan. The Bank of Japan can also approve the remittance of dividends paid on shares acquired by foreign investors prior to July 1, 1963, without guarantee of remittance of principal and earnings. Foreign residents will be free to remit home their current incomes. Until then, only the remittance of living expenses for near relatives had been allowed. The ceiling on the assets which foreign residents were allowed to take with them when leaving the country was raised from $10,000 to $50,000; approval by the Bank of Japan was required. (The $50,000 ceiling was abolished in May 1970.) Nonresident foreigners having "blocked" (i.e., not transferable) yen accounts in Japan were allowed to repatriate the balances as of July 31, 1969, or convert these accounts into free-yen accounts. The ceiling on yearly remittances from "blocked" yen accounts was raised from 20 percent to 30 percent of the balance at the close of the preceding year.

Afraid of the disturbing influence on its monetary policies of the growing influx of short-term funds, in 1962, the government enforced a "foreign currency deposit reserve system." The government also imposed limits on the amounts the foreign branches of Japanese banks could lend and, until February 25, 1970, loans by foreign branches with a maturity exceeding six months were subject to specific approval. On April 1, 1966, the reserve ratio on foreign currency was reduced from 25 percent to 15 percent, but the Ministry of Finance and the Bank of Japan began to regulate more strictly the overall amounts of foreign exchange held by the city banks. In connection with the so-called yen shift (use of yen funds for import financing instead of dollar usances), the city banks were ordered to reduce their foreign exchange holdings first by 10 percent and, in October, by another 6 percent. Another sign of the change in the official treatment of foreign exchange funds (from the balance of payments point of view to the monetary policy or countercyclical policy point of view) was the addition of the rubric "short-term fund position of foreign exchange banks" to the balance of payments statistics in July 1968.

In order to facilitate foreign trade, the overseas offices of the trading companies were allowed to retain a certain portion of their foreign exchange earnings and, in December 1969, the foreign offices and branches of manufacturing enterprises were also given permission to retain foreign funds (the ceiling on the funds which could be kept by the trading companies was raised at the same time). No exact figures on the amounts involved have been published, but the total was fixed first at $100 million and later at $180 million for each group. The procedure for foreign exchange transactions of trading companies was simplified in May 1970.

Outward foreign investment, direct as well as indirect, required special permission. For the acquisition of foreign securities by residents (natural persons having their domicile or residence in Japan and juridical persons having a branch or office in Japan), approval by the minister of finance was needed. The Bank of Japan could approve applications involving less than $50,000 per case; this ceiling was raised to $200,000 in October 1969 and $1 million on September 1, 1970. Long-term loans given by residents to a foreign corporation under their control (the criterion was ownership of over 50 percent of the capital by the Japanese side or, in the case of corporations in developing countries, 25 percent ownership and participation in management by one or more permanently stationed officers) could be approved by the Bank of Japan if the maturity of the loan was longer than one year and the amount less than $50,000. Investment in real property was approved if such investment was related either to direct overseas business activities or to the business of a corporation in which investment had been made and such investment contributed to the balance of payments. Approval by the minister of finance was needed for transferring funds for the establishment or management of overseas branches of financial institutions; for other enterprises, approval could be given by the Bank of Japan.

In a major revision of the regulations effective October 1, 1969, the ceiling on cumulative investment in a foreign corporation, in which the Japanese interest was at least 25 percent, was fixed at $300,000. Approval of investments whose cumulative value remains below $200,000 is given automatically by the Bank of Japan; if the cumulative balance exceeds $200,000 but remains below $300,000, the Bank of Japan can approve the investment but the competent ministry can order a specific examination after consultation with the Ministry of Finance. Regulations concerning the acquisition of real estate and the establishment of foreign branch offices remained the same, but, since November 1970, the transfer of amounts of up to $1 million for the establishment of foreign branch offices can be approved automatically by the Bank of Japan (banks and securities companies, however, still need the approval of the Ministry of Finance for opening overseas branches or representative offices).

In April 1970, Japanese investment trusts were authorized to acquire up to $100 million of foreign securities for their portfolios and, in December, the same permission was given to life and nonlife insurance companies. In connection with the government's endeavors to prevent a too steep increase in Japan's foreign exchange holdings, the Ministry of Finance planned a number of other measures relaxing the foreign exchange restrictions. Under former regulations, individuals had to sell foreign currency brought back or received from abroad within ten days; this period was extended to one month and, during this time, the money can be used for foreign travel or remittances. The amount of foreign currency tourists can take abroad was raised from $1,000 to $3,000. There was some speculation that individuals would be allowed to open accounts in foreign currency with Japanese or foreign banks, but this seems premature. The restrictions on foreign currency holdings by corporations were also eased. Trading companies and manufacturers were allowed to keep dollars and pounds (receipts for exports or payments of imports) for twenty days; the period was extended to six months with no restrictions on the kind of currency, the kind of deposit (except savings deposits), or the amount. Airlines and shipping companies were allowed to hold income from international fares (former ceiling $28 million) without limitation. Restrictions on imports and holdings of foreign coins (except gold coins) were removed. The Ministry of Finance also plans to abolish the restrictions on the types of foreign currency (at present fifteen) in which payments for exports can be accepted; the measure was considered as a preparatory move to the use of Chinese currency in trade with the People's Republic of China.

In the middle of May 1971, restrictions were imposed on overseas lending (chiefly to overseas subsidiaries of Japanese corporations) of Japanese foreign exchange banks and on guarantees of overseas borrowings. The growing anxiety over a possible revaluation of the yen induced the trading companies to decrease their holdings of foreign exchange and, in June, the Ministry of Finance abolished the ceiling on the foreign exchange holdings of the trading companies (which actually declined from about $300 million at the end of May to $200 million at the end of June).

As part of the eight-point program for preventing a revaluation of the yen, the government, effective July 1, 1971, removed the $100 million ceiling on investment in foreign securities by Japanese securities and insurance companies. Thus, individuals and corporations were allowed to invest in foreign securities without restrictions, although purchases and sales had to be made through securities companies. At the same time, the acquisition of overseas real estate was liberalized. No limit was imposed on the value of real estate which could be bought abroad, but the Ministry of Finance declared that speculative buying and selling was prohibited. The discriminatory treatment of individuals, however, continued with regard to deposits with foreign banks (which remain prohibited). Together with the liberalization of the acquisition of foreign securities, the government also abolished the $1 million ceiling on direct outward investment by Japanese enterprises which can be approved by the Bank of Japan. The government, however, will not approve such investments if they lead to excessive competition in one particular country.

Starting fiscal 1972, Japanese will be allowed to take out insurance in yen with foreign insurance companies having branch offices in Japan; later, such insurance contracts will be allowed also with foreign insurance companies without Japanese branches. Capital investment in the insurance business (up to 50 percent of the capital of a joint venture) was liberalized in 1969, but, because a government license is required for the insurance business, no foreign firms are actually operating in Japan for Japanese; the eleven foreign insurance companies now doing business in Japan operate exclusively for foreigners and are limited to insurance contracts in foreign currency.

On August 21, 1971, the government suspended the enforcement of the ¥20,000 limit tourists were allowed to take out of the country in cash, but, in September, the restriction was again enforced, ostensibly because tourists found it difficult to use yen currency abroad (a ridiculous pretext), actually because President Nixon's new economic policy had wrought a drastic change in the international situation. But the authorities again reversed their policy and, effective October 1, travelers were allowed to take out ¥100,000 in cash. At the same time, Japanese foreign exchange banks were allowed to change yen notes accepted by foreign banks (including foreign branches of Japanese banks). After a few days of huge dollar purchases by the Bank of Japan at the fixed exchange rate, ostensibly the yen was floated on August 28. But it soon became clear that it was a managed float and that the Bank of Japan intervened so as to keep the rate of increase in the value of the yen over the old dollar parity below 6.5 percent. In order to prevent further inflows of short-term funds, foreign exchange controls were made stricter. Starting September 1, the foreign exchange banks were advised to keep the conversion of foreign currency (mainly Eurodollars) into yen at the level of August 31, not to sell dollars for delivery on the following day, and not to accept prepayment for exports ("leads") by trading companies. The reason was to prevent foreign exchange banks from selling dollars in order to lessen exchange risks and to block the inflow of short-term funds. At the same time, the Ministry of Finance ordered the securities companies accepting foreign orders (the four large securities companies, Kangyo Kakumaru, and Shin-Nippon) not to increase their "securities yen" balances. The securities companies usually receive the purchase price together with the order from abroad, but because "ordinary way transactions" are settled on the fourth day they convert the foreign currency into yen ("securities yen") when the order arrives.

Initially, the Ministry of Finance enforced these measures through "administrative guidance," but because the foreign exchange banks and the foreign banks complained of the disruptive effects of these measures (which were without legal foundation), the ministry created a semblance of legality by revising, on September 6, the "Ministerial Ordinance Concerning Control of Nontrade Transactions." By this revision the minister of finance gave himself power to regulate the acceptance of short-term funds; in particular, restrictions were imposed on the conversion of foreign currency into yen, on outstanding balances of borrowings from overseas, and on balances of free-yen accounts. On the same day, the Bank of Japan advised the foreign exchange banks that the balance of foreign funds converted into yen had to remain at the same level every day (until then, it had to be at the same level in the middle and at the end of the month), and that the balance of short-term foreign funds and free-yen accounts had to be kept at the level of September 6, 1971. Furthermore, the foreign exchange banks were ordered to pay back the direct loans from the foreign exchange fund which had been given to finance the "yen shift." While these measures blocked the inflow of short-term funds and thus enabled the Bank of Japan to prevent the yen from floating too high, they also put foreign trade financing into a straitjacket. Because the banks had to keep the balances of free-yen accounts at the same level, they could not accept regular transfers even for foreign embassies or international organs. The Frankfurt Exchange suspended yen quotations because the Japanese banks were unable to accept foreign funds, and the German authorities complained to the Japanese Embassy at Bonn about the obstacles to trade transactions created by the new controls.

For the purely notional purpose of keeping the yen at an arbitrary level, the authorities did their best to throttle Japan's foreign trade, already threatened by Mr. Nixon's sanctions. In the first ten days of September, purchases of export bills fell to one-third of the volume in the first half of August. The relapse into emergency controls, although understandable as a reaction to the antics of the foreign exchange banks and the trading companies prior to the floating of the yen, was all the more inapt since the minister of finance, appearing before the Finance Committee of the House of Representatives, justified the failure of the government to suspend foreign exchange transactions after President Nixon's announcement of the inconvertibility of the dollar into gold (a failure which may have cost the taxpayers a cool $557 million) on the ground that if the exchange market was closed Japan's foreign trade would be thrown into confusion. This is exactly what the government did by stifling foreign exchange transactions.

On September 11, Keidanren (Federation of Economic Organizations) requested the Ministry of Finance to relax the restrictions on foreign exchange transactions because they were slowly strangling foreign trade and hurting the economy. The ministry, however, refused to change its policy, one of the reasons being that it lacked experience in intervening in forward transactions.

On June 1, 1971, the Bank of Japan began to deposit funds ($200 million) from the foreign exchange fund with the foreign exchange banks in order to supply funds for trade financing. The purpose of this measure was to decrease dollar purchases from foreign banks and to stabilize the futures market. The deposits were for a period of four months. On September 27, 1971, the Ministry of Finance and the Bank of Japan decided to increase the fifth deposit (October 1) by $50 million so as to provide funds to buy export bills from small enterprises ($200 million was to replace the first deposit which fell due). Moreover, the Bank of Japan was to buy, through the foreign exchange banks, export usances up to $300 million from small enterprises.

Despite growing dissatisfaction with the retention of rigid foreign exchange controls, the Japanese bureaucracy is unwilling to change from a system of specific exceptions to comprehensive control to a system of basic freedom with specific controls.

2 LIBERALIZATION OF FOREIGN INVESTMENT

The so-called Foreign Investment Law regulates five forms of capital imports: (1) technological assistance contracts (for longer than one year); (2) acquisition of shares of stock or participation certificates; (3) beneficiary certificates (investment trusts and loan trusts); (4) bonds (in the case of corporate debentures, with a remaining maturity of at least one year); (5) loans (with a maturity of at least one year). All other capital transactions are subject to the provisions of the Foreign Exchange and Foreign Trade Control Law (1949).

Practically, the most important forms of capital induction are the following. (1) Investment for participation in management. This category also includes the foundation of joint ventures. Under the original regulations, each case was subject to specific approval and foreign ownership limited to 50 percent of the capital. The examination of each application had to be considered in the light of economic, commercial, and industrial policy; actually, the impact of the planned enterprise on existing Japanese business was the most important consideration. For approved investments, repatriation of principal and earnings was guaranteed. (2) Acquisition of stock on the stock exchange. In the beginning, two forms of acquisition of shares were possible: acquisition against foreign currency and acquisition against yen. For the first form, permission was required which was generally given by the Bank of Japan automatically, i.e., without previous approval by the Foreign Investment Council. Foreign ownership in "restricted" enterprises was not to exceed 5 percent; in other business lines foreign investors could own up to 8 percent of the issued shares of one company, but an individual investor could acquire no more than 5 percent of the shares of one enterprise. (Restricted industries are: waterworks, gas, electric power, local railroads, tramways, marine transportation, harbor express service, road transportation, forwarding, air transportation, banks, trust business, mutual banks, long-term credit banks, foreign exchange banks, fisheries, mining, and broadcasting.) Repatriation of capital and earnings was guaranteed, but the capital had to be left untouched for two years and could then be repatriated in five yearly installments. In 1960, the ceiling on the acquisition of shares of companies in non-restricted industries was raised to 15 percent and to 10 percent in restricted industries; the capital could be repatriated in three yearly installments. The second form of the acquisition of stock was against yen. This was outside the regulations of the Foreign Investment Law so that no permission was required but also no repatriation of principal or earnings possible. This form of acquisition could also be used for newly establishing a company organized under Japanese Law, and these so-called yen base companies became very popular because wholly owned subsidiaries could be set up in this way. Between October 1956 and July 1963, 289 companies with a total capital of $140 million were established on this basis. Of these, 161 were wholly owned subsidiaries. Since July 1, 1963, however, such foundations have been subject to "reporting" which practically put an end to this form of foundation (i.e., the establishment of a branch or plant need only be reported, but approval is required for the induction of funds from abroad). The "reason" for the change was that Japan's admission to OECD would necessitate the liberalization of capital transactions. In reality, Japan joined OECD under the reservation that direct inward investment (and a number of other positions) would not be liberalized. The real reason for the change was that the Japanese bureaucracy did not like these foundations because they were too "independent." As mentioned above, the remittance of earnings by enterprises established prior to July 1, 1963, without guarantee of repatriation (i.e., yen base enterprises) and the remittance of dividends paid on stock acquired against yen prior to the same date without such guarantee were made possible on September 1, 1969. (3) Acquisition of bonds and investment certificates. Permission was required which was only given when at least six months remained until maturity. Remittance of earnings was free, but, initially, permission was needed for the repatriation of the principal. (4) Long-term loans. Loans (with a maturity exceeding three years) were subject to strict scrutiny which was to examine their impact on the balance of payments, the industry involved, and the enterprise contracting the loan. One of the main purposes for which these loans were given was the import of machinery and equipment (e.g., financed by the U.S. Export-Import Bank). The World Bank (International Bank for Reconstruction and Development) provided loans for key industries (electric power, iron and steel) and public works (e.g., expressways). Important private loans flowed into oil refining and the petrochemical industry. The Ministry of Finance was particularly strict in screening applications for "impact" loans, i.e., general loans not given for financing particular projects. The ministry also insisted on low interest rates. In the beginning, loans were restricted to productive and infrastructural facilities and only with the beginning of the liberalization were loans approved for consumer industries. (5) Short-term loans. Most of these loans (maturity less than one year) serve for financing imports. Conditions for approval were about the same as those for long-term loans. The Ministry of Finance permitted only loans from first-class foreign banks. The Japanese city banks also introduced foreign capital by transferring time deposits from their foreign branches (which were deposited in free-yen accounts) and the trust banks sought foreign funds for their loan trusts (maturity two or five years). (6) Induction of foreign technology. Approval depended on a strict examination, but the approval of the licensing contract also included approval of the royalty payments. Frequently, however, the government required changes in the payment conditions (usually lower royalty payments and sometimes deferment of part of the payments). (7) Emission of foreign bonds. In addition to government and municipal bonds, government-guaranteed debentures of public corporations (Nippon Telegraph & Telephone) and the Japan Development Bank were floated. Bonds of private companies were issued in 1961 and some of the issues were in the form of convertible debentures. Government permission was required for which not only the repercussions on the balance of payments but also the position of the enterprise were taken into consideration. Private placements were frequent. (8) American Depositary Receipts (ADR). In order to facilitate the acquisition of Japanese stocks by foreign investors, the ADR system, originally devised for European issues, was adopted for Japanese stocks. After drawn-out negotiations, the Ministry of Finance approved the emission of ADR's for a few selected companies but it was only in June 1961 that the first ADR's were issued. Later adaptations were European Depositary Receipts (EDR), London Depositary Receipts (LDR), and Curaçao Depositary Receipts (CDR).

The legal regulation of foreign investment was largely inspired by the postwar situation of the Japanese economy. A large part of the productive facilities was destroyed, no capital was available, and the country had no access to world markets. Foreign currency was insufficient for the purchase of even the most essential foods and raw materials. Control of all foreign currency transactions and use of foreign currency in accordance with the requirements of the national economy were the basic goals of the postwar legislation. As a rule, all foreign investment projects or technological agreements were subject to government approval, which was only given if the transaction was deemed to contribute to the "autonomy and sound development" of the Japanese economy and the improvement of the country's balance of payments position. The government was authorized to refuse approval of new investments for protecting the balance of payments and MITI was ordered to compile a list of "desirable" technologies which was to be revised from time to time. The laws provided that the restrictions should be relaxed or discontinued as soon as their necessity disappeared, but this protestation of good intentions had no influence on the measures actually taken by the government. The enforcement provisions of the laws granted practically unlimited discretion to the administrative agencies (the Ministry of Finance and the ministries in charge of the specific branches of industry, above all MITI and the Ministries of Agriculture, Health and Welfare, and Transportation) to grant or refuse approval. These laws are not the only ones in which the lack of objective standards opens the way to administrative arbitrariness (most Japanese laws are drafted by the administrative agencies which have to enforce them and the convenience of the administrators seems to be the overriding consideration) and makes it possible to adapt the laws to changing purposes.

The administrative regulations were revised in 1960 in the sense that foreign investment in joint ventures would be approved if no adverse influence on the Japanese economy was to be expected; but the basic attitude of the government remained protectionistic, and induction of capital and technology were regarded as necessary evils to be limited as much as possible. With the growth of the Japanese economy, the prevention of foreign takeovers became the main objective of the administration of the Foreign Investment Law. Basically, it is a question of power: the bureaucracy, having secured a decisive voice in the management of the country's economy, is unwilling to agree to a diminution of its influence.

In April 1963, all limitations on the repatriation of principal and interest of portfolio investment in securities were removed, but the liberalization of capital investment in conformity with the rules of OECD only started in 1967. The basic policy underlying the liberalization was contained in a report of the Foreign Investment Council (approved by the cabinet on June 6, 1967) which was drafted in the old spirit of protectionism and in which the prevention of the possible difficulties resulting from the liberalization received more attention than the facilitation of foreign investment. The liberalization program distinguished between industries in which foreign investors could only acquire up to 50 percent of the capital and those in which foreign ownership could go up to 100 percent. The first category is considered the "normal" form of foreign investment. In liberalized industries foreign investment is approved "automatically," but the difference between automatic approval and case by case examination is hazy. In its report, the Foreign Investment Council recommended a simplification of the procedure for automatic approval so as to distinguish it from case by case examination; automatic approval is given by the competent minister and not by the Foreign Investment Council.

Some of the rules laid down in the liberalization program imposed greater restrictions than had been in effect before. The liberalization affected only newly founded enterprises (participation in existing enterprises remained subject to specific approval); a new enterprise is considered an existing enterprise: (1) if the property contributed by Japanese investors as investment in kind or the property to be transferred by an existing company to the newly established enterprise consists of plants, stores, or warehouses; (2) if, immediately upon its foundation, the newly established enterprise acquires through transfer, lease, cession, etc., the business of an existing company or the property of such a company for continuous use in its business operations or if it merges with an existing company.

A second condition for approval of fifty-fifty joint ventures is that foreign capital should not exercise a dominant influence on business management. This means: (1) there must be Japanese stockholders who also manage another enterprise in the same line of business as the newly established enterprise, the aggregate number of shares owned by them must constitute at least one-half of the total number of shares issued by the newly established enterprise, and one of the Japanese stockholders managing another enterprise in the same line of business must own at least one-third of those shares; (2) the number of Japanese (meaning Japanese representing the interests of the Japanese stockholders) among the directors or representative directors must at least be proportional to the ratio of the shares owned by the Japanese stockholders; (3) the voting procedure should conform to the ordinary method laid down in the Japanese Commercial Code, i.e., the consent of a particular director or the unanimous consent of all stockholders should not be required for the execution of business; (4) the foreign investment should have no exceptionally detrimental effect on Japanese interests.

The acquisition of shares in newly established enterprises belonging to Class 2 (foreign ownership up to 100 percent) is likewise subject to the condition that the new foundation is not a camouflaged acquisition of an existing enterprise. Approval will also be withheld if an exceptionally detrimental effect on the Japanese economy is feared from the foreign investment.

If the share of foreign capital in a newly established enterprise amounts to one-third or more, prior approval by the competent minister is required in the following cases: (1) if the enterprise intends to take up a line of business not included in the original articles of incorporation; (2) if the enterprise acquires the business or the property (except real estate other than plants, stores, or warehouses) of an existing company for continuous use in its business operations and a special resolution of a general meeting of stockholders is required for this transfer, or if the enterprise is merged with an existing company.

Foreign investment in existing enterprises or in new foundations in nonliberalized industries can be approved by the competent minister to the extent to which the acquisition of shares can be approved by the Bank of Japan for portfolio investment; beyond this limit, specific examination of each application and case by case approval is needed.

The first liberalization program (effected July 1, 1967) included 33 industries (actually, products or product groups) in which foreign ownership was limited to 50 percent and 17 industries in which foreign investors could acquire up to 100 percent of the capital. The limitation on portfolio investment was raised from 15 percent to 20 percent for total foreign investment in a single company in nonrestricted industries and from 10 percent to 15 percent for restricted industries; the ceiling on the ratio of shares which a single foreign investor could own in one enterprise was raised from 5 percent to 7 percent. The second program (March 1, 1969) raised the number of liberalized industries in Class 1 (50 percent) to 160 and those in Class 2 (100 percent) to 44.

The limitations on portfolio investment remained unchanged.

The negotiations on the numerous unsettled economic issues disturbing the relations between the United States and Japan made little progress. In June 1968, the Japanese government formulated a new set of proposals for the liberalization of car and engine imports and the reduction of tariffs on large cars, but remained unyielding on the conditions for the entry of American car manufacturers into Japan (no wholly owned subsidiaries; fifty-fifty joint ventures will be approved on a case by case basis; no joint ventures with Japanese automobile manufacturers). The United States rejected these proposals as completely unacceptable and a Japanese memorandum presented in August 1968 spelled out Japan's final position: import quotas on engines and parts would be enlarged starting in 1969 and complete liberalization effected by 1972; quotas on chassis with mounted engines would be increased in the autumn of 1968; applications for car assembly would be approved on a case by case basis; the reduction of tariffs on large cars, corresponding to the last stage of the Kennedy round (import duties reduced to 17.5 percent), would go into effect on April 1, 1969.

In the period between the first and the second liberalization programs, foreign investments in existing enterprises (case by case approval) were more numerous than those in newly established enterprises, and cases of investment in liberalized industries were only four of which two were approved "automatically." The reason was that the liberalization extended only to internationally competitive industries in which enterprises founded by foreign capital had very little chance of capturing a significant part of the domestic market. The situation remained more or less the same after the implementation of the second liberalization program. Foreign investment in existing enterprises increased more rapidly than foreign participation in newly established companies (acquisition of stock in existing enterprises: fiscal 1968, 194 cases; fiscal 1969, 300 cases; newly founded joint ventures: fiscal 1968, 88 cases; fiscal 1969, 130 cases); only 14 foundations were in liberalized industries. Nevertheless, a number of notable joint ventures was established. In the field of electronics, CBS—Sony was founded in December 1967 and Nippon Texas Instruments in April 1968, and, in 1969, a series of joint enterprises was organized to manufacture automotive parts (Aisin-Warner, transmissions; Koyo Eaton Yale & Towne, axles; Koyo TRW, steering).

In addition to the liberalization of investment, induction of foreign technology was liberalized effective June 1, 1968. The measures affected licensing agreements (use of patents), utility models, know-how, and technical information. Different from the regulation of capital transactions, seven sectors enumerated in a negative list (aircraft, weapons, explosives, nuclear energy, space exploration, electronic computers, and petrochemicals) have not been liberalized, i.e., applications for the induction of technology concerning these sectors require specific approval. With a few exceptions, the Bank of Japan can automatically approve all contracts whose value does not exceed $50,000 irrespective of the kind of technology involved. Contracts not related to the seven restricted sectors but with a value exceeding $50,000 are approved by the Bank of Japan unless the competent minister objects to the approval within one month after the filing of the application. Objections can only be raised if the planned induction of technology would constitute a serious impairment of the Japanese economy.

The reaction of foreign countries, particularly the United States, to the first two liberalization programs was decidedly negative; these programs were generally regarded as evasive maneuvers designed to gain time and to postpone a real liberalization. The Americans were particularly incensed at Japan's refusal to liberalize foreign investment in electronics and the motor industry. But capital investment was only one of the problems complicating Japan's economic relations with other countries. The frictions resulting from Japan's remaining import restrictions, the imbalances in Japan's trade with the developing countries, the growing penetration of the American market by Japanese products, and the breakdown of the negotiations with the American government on additional restrictions on Japan's textile exports into the United States, created a climate in which the Japanese government found it necessary to demonstrate its readiness "to fulfill its obligation as an advanced industrial country." The list of industries compiled by the Foreign Investment Council for the third liberalization program exceeded the proposal submitted by Keidanren (Federation of Economic Organizations). Under this program, which went into effect on September 1, 1970, the number of liberalized industries rose to 447 in Class 1 (50 percent) and 77 in Class 2 (100 percent), for a total of 524. Particularly noteworthy was the partial liberalization of restricted industries such as banking and transportation. On the other hand, sensitive industries remained excluded, in particular, automobiles, aircraft, automatic control equipment, electronic computers (including software and data processing), nuclear energy, and space exploration. The liberalization of the manufacture of small computers proposed by Keidanren and the Foreign Investment Council was postponed due to the opposition of MITI and the industry.

Together with the revision of direct investment, the ceiling on the acquisition of shares by foreigners for portfolio investment in nonrestricted industries was raised from 20 percent to "below 25 percent." For Japanese outward investment, the maximum amount which could be approved automatically by the Bank of Japan was increased from $300,000 to $1 million.

In May 1965, Yoichiro Makita, then vice-president of Mitsubishi Heavy Industries, announced that the company had reached an understanding with Chrysler Corporation on the foundation of two joint enterprises, one for the import and export and another for the manufacture of automobiles. Mitsubishi was to contribute 65 percent, Chrysler 35 percent of the joint ventures. Less than a year before, the Automobile Industry Association, in the so-called Hakone declaration, had laid down the policy that the Japanese automakers would not tie up with foreign capital, and MITI had long favored a reorganization of the motor industry to prevent the entry of foreign companies. Mitsubishi had studiously avoided informing MITI of its negotiations but, due to the tension in Japan's relations with the United States, the government found it impossible to oppose the planned tie-up. Mitsubishi's audacity cleared the way for other companies and, soon, negotiations were under way between Toyo Kogyo and Ford and between Isuzu Motors and General Motors. The government stated that the Mitsubishi-Chrysler venture (the partners abandoned the plan of establishing two enterprises) would not be approved prior to the general liberalization of the automobile industry; hence, this measure, originally scheduled for some time in 1972, was moved up first to October 1 and finally to April 1, 1971. Automatic approval of joint enterprises in the automotive industry will be given for the manufacture of motor vehicles (passenger cars as well as trucks and tractors), auto bodies, parts and accessories, piston rings, electric devices for internal combustion engines, and electric bulbs for cars. Foreign ownership will be limited to 50 percent. At the same time, the share of foreign participation that will be automatically approved was raised from 50 percent to 100 percent for the manufacture of motorcycles and fluorescent lighting.

The fourth (and last) of the liberalization programs was carried out in August 1971. The Foreign Investment Council intended to compile a negative list of industries in which foreign investment would not be allowed (mining, electric power, gas, and some branches of banking, transportation, and real estate). Also planned was a second liberalization of technology imports. A proposal drawn up by the Ministry of Finance foresaw the liberalization of five of the sectors on the negative list (aircraft, nuclear energy, space exploration, electronic computers, and petrochemicals), but MITI, in which the protectionist tendencies remain very strong, planned to retain restrictions on all industries and technologies whose strategic importance in the national economy outweighs entrepreneurial interests.

The growing conflict with the United States had a decisive influence on the formulation of the fourth liberalization program. By July, the number of industries to be put on the negative list had been reduced from about seventy to seventeen, and, in the final "recommendations" submitted by the Foreign Investment Council, only seven industries were designated as subject to specific screening: (1) agriculture, forestry, and fisheries; (2) oil refining and distribution; (3) leather and leather products; (4) computers, including peripheral equipment and parts, manufacture, sale, and rental of computer-controlled automatic equipment; (5) data processing and computer software; (6) retail chains comprising more than eleven stores; (7) real estate. In order to obviate foreign criticism, the recommendations explicitly stated that the computer industry should be liberalized within three years. For the same reason, the number of industries in which foreign investors can own up to 100 percent of the capital was increased from 33 to 228, but some of the liberalized industries seem to have been made up by the bureaucrats just for inflating the number, whereas the categories requiring special screening are broad indeed. Actually, up to September 1971, only 32 enterprises wholly owned by foreign investors had been approved "automatically." The basic conditions remained unchanged.

Foreign portfolio investment in Japanese securities was further liberalized by raising the ceiling on the percentage of stock an individual foreign investor can own from 7 percent to "below 10 percent" of the issued stock. The ceiling on ownership in one company remained at "below 25 percent" for nonrestricted and at 15 percent for restricted industries.

Number of Liberalized Industries

	Class 1 Automatic approval of foreign participation up to 50% of capital	Class 2 Automatic approval of foreign investment up to 100% of capital	Total
First Liberalization Program, July 1967	33	17	50
Second Liberalization Program, March 1969	127	27	154
Third Liberalization Program, September 1970	287	33	320
Liberalization of automobile manufacturing & related industries, April 1971	6	—	6
Subtotal	453	77	530
Fourth Liberalization Program, August 1971 Transfer from Class 1 to Class 2		141	
Change in sphere of application		+6 −6	
Additional industries	All industries except those in Class 2 & those requiring specific screening	10	
Total		228	

The worsening relations with the United States following President Nixon's shift to a new economic policy led to a relaxation of the rules applied to direct foreign investment. In the beginning of October 1972, the Foreign Investment Council approved a proposal by the Ministry of Finance to relax "to a certain extent" the requirement that investments cannot be made in kind (e.g., land, plant, or equipment) and that a joint venture must be established with a Japanese enterprise in the same line of business. At the same time, the ministry announced that only applications for investments exceeding ¥200 million will be subject to examination by the Foreign Investment Council (formerly, all investments over ¥50 million had to be submitted to the council), and the period of examination was to be shortened from six weeks to one month.

3 ECONOMIC WORLD POWER

Due to the 1964–65 recession, the nominal growth rate of GNP declined from 17.9 percent in fiscal 1964 to 10.2 percent in fiscal 1965 (real growth rate: fiscal 1964, 13.3 percent; fiscal 1965, 4.5 percent). In July 1965, the government had decided to prime the pump by fiscal expenditures; since the natural increase in tax revenues remained below expectations, government bonds amounting to ¥230 billion were issued in January 1966 in order to finance an enlarged public works program. Thus, the principle of budgetary balance that had been observed since the adoption of the Dodge line in 1949 was abandoned and deficit financing became the rule. The budget for fiscal 1966 foresaw expenditures amounting to ¥4,314,270 million, 17.9 precent higher than the 1965 budget (including supplementary budgets total expenditures on general accounts rose to ¥4,477.1 billion, an increase of 19.6 percent over the preceding fiscal year). In addition to ¥3,197,711 million in tax revenues and ¥381,258 million in other receipts, the budget planned to raise ¥730 billion through bonds. The Trust Fund Bureau was to take over ¥30 billion of the bond issues, while the banks had to purchase 70 percent and the securities companies 30 percent of the remaining ¥700 billion (the interest rate on the bonds was 6.5 percent, emission price ¥98.60, maturity seven years). The original fiscal loan and investment program amounted to ¥2,027.3 billion, 25.1 percent higher than the original program for the preceding year (the revised program, ¥2,085.4 billion, was "only" 17.3 percent higher than the revised program for fiscal 1965). In order to speed up the recovery of the economy, contracts for public works and the investment programs of the national railways, the Telegraph and Telephone Corporation, and similar public corporations were advanced and orders for 82 percent of all planned expenditures placed in the first half of the fiscal year.

Three factors were expected to contribute to a turnabout in the economy: government spending, exports, and consumption expenditures. Actually, however, the longest expansionary phase in Japan's postwar development was mainly supported by equipment investment. On a national account basis, investment in producers' durable equipment declined by 8.2 percent in fiscal 1965 (from ¥5,467.0 billion in fiscal 1964 to ¥5,012.5 billion) but rose by 25.4 percent in fiscal 1966 (¥6,285.6 billion), 28.6 percent in fiscal 1967 (¥8,081.8 billion), 22.5 percent in fiscal 1968 (¥9,903.2 billion), and 29.7 percent in fiscal 1969 (¥12,850.4 billion). The investment boom was slow in developing, for the July–September quarter of 1966 the deflationary gap was estimated at ¥3,900 billion, but, in the following quarter, equipment investment increased 20.8 percent over the corresponding period for the preceding year. The most remarkable feature of the investment activities was the trend toward large-scale facilities which was part of the rationalization or reorganization program designed to make Japan's industry more competitive. The government urged the fertilizer manufacturers to build joint ammonia plants so that capacity could be increased to 1,000 tons per day; in June 1967, MITI decided that new naphtha cracking plants would only be approved if their capacity would reach 300,000 tons of ethylene a year. The shipbuilding industry not only built larger and larger tankers but also larger and larger docks. The world's largest tanker, the *Nisseki Maru*, was delivered by Ishikawajima-Harima Heavy Industries to her owner, Tokyo Tanker Co., on September 8, 1971. The 372,400 dwt. tanker can carry 450,000 kl. of crude oil. The largest dock now completed is the shipyard of Nippon Kokan at Tsu (up to 600,000 dwt.); Mitsubishi Heavy Industries is building the first million-ton dock at Kayaki near Nagasaki. As of December 1969, Japan possessed the five largest blast furnaces in the world (the largest was Fukushima No. 3 of Nippon Kokan with a capacity of 3,016 cu. m.; in the meantime, Fukushima No. 4 with a capacity of 4,197 cu. m. has been completed). The No. 1 generator at the Anegasaki Plant of Tokyo Electric Power, which went into operation in the autumn of 1967, possesses a capacity of 600,000 kw.

In the beginning of 1966, wholesale prices began to rise and continued their upward trend until February 1967. For fiscal 1966, the rise amounted to 2.7 percent, the largest yearly increase since 1956 (6.2 percent). The sharpest increases were for nonferrous metals and lumber, whose prices reflected the influences of international market conditions.

While equipment investment expanded relatively slowly in 1966, demand for consumer durables increased by 26.9 percent in 1966 compared with the last quarter of 1965. For the four quarters in 1966, the percentage shares in the total increase of GNP over the preceding quarter were 57.0 percent, 41.2 percent, 35.5 percent, and 58.2 percent for personal consumption expenditures, 22.2 percent, 13.7 percent, 17.9 percent, and 25.7 percent for private equipment investment, −2.0 percent, 48.3 percent, 12.2 percent, and −7.6 percent for government spending, and 33.1 percent, 7.1 percent, 12.9 percent, and 15.3 percent for exports.

A survey carried out by MITI in February 1967 showed that 1,817 enterprises under MITI's jurisdiction planned to increase equipment investment in fiscal 1967 by 39.3 percent over the preceding year. An adjustment to the investment programs scaled the rate of increase down to 29.0 percent, but the rate remained very high in some of the key industries: electric machinery, 75.9 percent; petroleum refining, 54.3 percent; petrochemicals, 48.4 percent; automobiles, 46.0 percent; synthetic fibers, 44.6 percent; electronics, 39.7 percent; and, steel 34.9 percent. In shipbuilding, investments rose from ¥28.0 billion in 1966 to ¥41.8 billion in 1967 (49 percent) and ¥44.2 billion in 1968 (6 percent). The electric power industry increased its capacity by 11.4 percent in 1966, 14.2 percent in 1967, and 10.3 percent in 1968.

For the term ended March 1966, the companies listed on the First Section of the Tokyo Stock Exchange reported an increase of 3.8 percent in sales and 3.4 percent in profits, indicating the beginning of the longest expansionary trend in postwar Japan. Results for the September term were better than expected: sales were up 10 percent and profits 20 percent. The reasons given were: (1) the recovery was relatively fast; (2) the operating rate of industry was high; (3) enterprises were able to reduce inventories and loans, thus reducing financing costs; (4) because equipment investment had been low in the preceding years, depreciation charges were less of a burden. But despite the favorable development of the economy, the stock market remained depressed and the Dow-Jones average declined from a high of ¥1,583.73 on April 1 to ¥1,364.34 on December 5, 1966, and daily volume remained below 100 million shares after June.

In February 1967, the reports of the Economic Planning Agency and the Bank of Japan expressed concern over a possible overheating of the economy, citing excessive equipment investment, the rise in wholesale prices, and the deterioration of the balance of payments as danger signals. The Ministry of Finance wanted to keep the budget "neutral" so as to avoid an undesirable stimulation of the economy; the original budget for fiscal 1967 (general accounts) provided for ¥4,950.9 billion in expenditures (an increase of 14.8 percent over the preceding year), but supplementary budgets pushed the total well over the ¥5 trillion mark to ¥5,203.4 billion (76.2 percent higher than the corresponding fiscal 1966 figure). The fiscal loan and investment program was initially expanded by 17.9 percent to ¥2,388.4 billion and finally by 19.8 percent to ¥2,498.8 billion, a typical example of fiscal neutrality *à la japonaise*. Government bond issues were to raise ¥820 billion in revenues (¥790 billion to be absorbed by the market).

In March 1967, the cabinet approved the so-called Economic and Social Development Plan for fiscal 1967–71. The main objectives were: (1) average real growth rate of GNP, 8.3 percent; (2) reduce the rate of increase in consumer prices to 3.0 percent; (3) surplus in the balance of payments in fiscal 1972, $2 billion; (4) average rate of increase in equipment investment, 10.1 percent; (5) investment of ¥27.5 trillion in public works; average yearly rate of increase, 10.5 percent; (6) construction of 7.3 million homes (government financed 3 million) providing a home for each family; (7) GNP in fiscal 1970, ¥40.2 trillion (in 1960 prices; nominal value, ¥61,710 billion); (8) per capita national income in fiscal 1970, ¥470,000 (fiscal 1965, ¥250,000). The basic policies to be pursued were: (1) price stabilization; (2) efficiency in the economy; (3) social development. Increase in productivity, increase in the supply capacity, and greater mobility of the labor force were listed as the chief means for achieving price stability.

Important changes occurred in the international situation. After five years of negotiations in the Kennedy round, an accord was reached at Geneva on May 15, 1967 providing for a linear reduction of tariffs (average 30 percent on a 1969 basis) over five years. At the same time, an international grain agreement was concluded and rules laid down to prevent the abuse of antidumping tariffs. The introduction of special drawing rights (SDR), which had been discussed for four years, was decided upon by the IMF meeting at Rio de Janeiro in September 1967. And the second session of UNCTAD (United Nations Conference on Trade and Development) at New Delhi, in February 1968, adopted preferential tariffs for developing countries. The closing of the Suez Canal, following the Six-Day War between Israel and the Arabs, did not affect Japan directly, but the sharp increase in tanker demand, while pushing up prices through the rise in freight charges, triggered a flood of new orders for large tankers and brought a considerable increase in ship exports (1966, 3,972,991 gr.t.; 1967, 4,915,977 gr.t.; 1968, 5,479,206 gr.t.; 1969, 6,061,431 gr.t.).

The continued high level of economic activities worried the authorities. At the beginning of the year, the government economists had predicted an increase of 14 percent in equipment investment, but, in August, the rate was well above 20 percent. In steel, petrochemicals, and oil refining, actual investment was higher than foreseen in the original programs. Sales of consumer durables, notably color television sets, air conditioners, and motor cars, showed a large expansion. The increase in exports was slow while imports gained rapidly; in August, foreign exchange reserves fell below the $2 billion line ($1,982 million) for the first time in twenty-two months. In the latter half of the year, wholesale prices began to rise again.

In July 1967, the government ordered a decrease in the issues of government bonds and government-guaranteed debentures; and in September, budgetary expenditures amounting to ¥300 billion (= 7 percent of the budget) were deferred. The measures were much more decisive than on earlier occasions when fiscal retrenchment for deflationary purposes had been more or less nominal (¥71 billion in fiscal 1957 and ¥77 billion in fiscal 1961). On September 1, the Bank of Japan raised the official discount rate by 1 *rin* to 1.5 *sen* (5.84 percent) and imposed stricter window controls by keeping the increase in bank loans for each quarter below the increase in the corresponding quarter of the preceding year. On November 18, 1967, the English pound was devalued by 14.3 percent and international interest rates began to rise. On December 1, the call rate went up by 1 *rin* (lender's rate on over-the-month loans 2.25 *sen*, about 8.2 percent). On January 5, 1968, the policy board of the Bank of Japan decided to raise the official discount rate to 1.7 *sen* (6.205 percent).

Different from 1964, the deflationary measures failed to kill the boom. The producers of electrical machinery, the electric power companies, and oil refineries reduced their investment programs, and sensitive sectors, such as iron and steel or paper and pulp, curtailed production, but the motor industry as well as the petrochemical enterprises carried out their original programs without much change. Generally speaking, the economy continued to expand; but the pace slowed down in 1968 and inventories rose sharply.

Production Indices

(1965=100)

Year	Mining & manufacturing production		Shipments		Producers' inventories of finished goods		Ratio of inventories to shipments
	Index	Rate of increase %	Index	Rate of increase %	Index	Rate of increase %	%
1966	113.2	13.2	113.7	13.7	104.8	4.8	92.2
1967	135.2	19.4	133.6	17.5	113.3	8.1	84.8
1968	159.2	17.7	155.3	16.2	139.1	22.8	89.6
1969	185.9	16.8	181.3	16.7	169.4	21.8	93.4
1970	215.9	16.1	207.3	14.3	204.2	20.6	

In the six months from October 1967 to March 1968, sales of the 529 companies listed on the Tokyo Stock Exchange increased 9 percent over the preceding term, with profits after taxes rising 7.9 percent. The rise in sales of the companies listed on the First Section was higher than in the preceding six months but the increase in profits lower (7.4 percent as against 12.2 percent). For the companies listed on the Second Section, the increase in sales as well as in profits was lower (sales 10.0 percent as against 10.5 percent, profits 16.4 percent as against 19.1 percent). The results showed that the deflationary measures had slowed down the economy but that the expansion was still strong. It actually reached its apogee in 1968. Compared with 1958, i.e., prior to the Iwato boom, GNP was 3.8 times larger, final expenditures 4.9 times, production of crude steel 5.2 times, and the value of exports 3.7 times.

Japan had become the world's third largest economic power, behind the United States and the Soviet Union, and the nation came under increasing pressure to assume the responsibilities of a great economic power. Just what these responsibilities were was never very clear and depended a great deal on who was speaking, representatives of the advanced industrial countries of the West or of the developing countries in Asia, Africa, or Latin America. Thus the government found itself in the uncomfortable position of having to take measures for diplomatic reasons that were not only against its avowed policies but also against the interests of the establishment and therefore politically unpalatable. The government had to convince industry that Japan could no longer afford the selfish pleasure of economic growth without regard to what this did to other people and that the time for internationalization had arrived. Just as liberalization, so internationalization meant above all to get ready for international competition and, at this particular juncture, it meant that Japanese enterprises had to become comparable in size to their largest foreign competitors. "Large-scale mergers" became the catch phrase. The first attempt, the reunification of the three successor firms to the prewar Oji Paper Manufacturing Co., aborted because the Fair Trade Commission intimated that a merger application would be turned down. But the next merger plan, the fusion of Yawata Iron & Steel Co. and Fuji Iron & Steel Co., was found reconcilable with the Antimonopoly Law and, on March 31, 1970, Nippon Steel Corporation came into being. Its capital amounts to ¥229,360 million, the highest of any company in Japan. As of September 30, 1970, it counted 572,100 stockholders and a labor force of 82,046. Crude steel production in the six months from April to September 1970 amounted to 17.1 million tons, sales to ¥662.5 billion. But in the motor industry, in which MITI wanted concentration more than in any other field, all merger plans failed except the rather inconsequential fusion of Nissan and Prince in 1966.

The failure of the Oji merger plan and the controversies over the Yawata-Fuji merger touched off a debate on the Antimonopoly Law. In June 1969, Keidanren (Federation of Economic Organizations) published a report entitled "View on Mergers and Antimonopoly Policy," which came to the following conclusions: (1) the antimonopoly policy is an obstacle to the growth of Japanese enterprises within the world economy; (2) in the application of the Antimonopoly Law, the domestic economy should not be considered merely by itself, without reference to the world economy; (3) the liberalization of the economy is sufficient to prevent managed prices or market domination and abuses can be corrected after they occur; (4) the examinations of the Fair Trade Commission are too time-consuming, and teh commission is too preoccupied with legal problems. Junji Hiraga, the chairman of the federation's study committee, expressed the opinion that holding companies should be allowed because they were necessary for the modernization and rationalization of the economy.

Two committees of the Liberal-Democratic party also issued reports on the problem. In August 1969, the Economic Research Committee set forth the following views: (1) in its present form the Antimonopoly Law constitutes an obstacle to a necessary reorganization of the economy; (2) the present preventive system should be changed into a corrective system; (3) instead of amending the Antimonopoly Law, an economic guidance law should be enacted; (4) the Fair Trade Commission should be made more amenable to government policy by making the chairman of the commission a state minister and transferring part of the commission's functions to the Economic Planning Agency.

The Administrative Research Committee published a report, in October 1969, in which it proposed the following changes in the organization and functions of the Fair Trade Commission: (1) the chairman should be a state minister; (2) the guidance functions of the commission should be transferred to the Economic Planning Agency, and the commission remain in charge only of investigation, prosecution, and trial; (3) as an alternative, the trial might be transferred to the courts; (4) the Fair Trade Commission could also be transformed from an administrative into an advisory agency; (5) in order to strengthen consumer protection and price policy, the Fair Trade Commission might be merged with Economic Planning Agency. A new attempt to emasculate the Antimonopoly Law is being made in connection with Japan's effort to develop foreign raw material sources, in particular, the exploration and exploitation of petroleum. At present twenty different organizations are engaged in looking for oil (only two, the Arabian Oil Co. and the North Sumatra Oil Development Cooperation Co., are actually producing), and the industry thinks that some kind of consolidation is needed. To this end the foundation of a holding company has been proposed, which is now prohibited by the Antimonopoly Law.

The tendency toward concentration was closely related to the growing emphasis on new fields, particularly housing, seabed development, information, and environmental pollution, which were considered the most promising sectors for the seventies. Particularly noteworthy was the formation of enterprise groups for large-scale efforts in these fields: the *zaibatsu* groups, the large trading companies, and the city banks were in the forefront of these activities. At the same time, the various ministries, eager to gain control over these developments and the funds involved, were asserting conflicting jurisdictional claims.

The international money market went through some stormy weather. In January 1968, President Johnson announced new measures to protect the dollar. The March gold rush led to the suspension of the gold pool and the adoption of the two-tier price system for gold. In June and July, BIS and IMF had to provide international support for the pound and the dollar. Following the imposition of a 10 percent surtax by the United States, the international situation calmed down and international interest rates, which had reached their highest point in July, began to decline.

The economic expansion aggravated many of Japan's domestic problems. In 1968, 48 percent of the population lived in urban areas that possessed only 12 percent of the country's land surface, 58 percent of the urban population dwelling within the fifty kilometer radii of the centers of the three largest cities (Tokyo, Osaka, and Nagoya). According to the 1970 census, Japan's urban population constituted 72 percent and the rural population 28 percent of the country's total population (103,720,060, as of October 1, 1970); in 1920, the ratios had been the reverse, 24.1 percent and 75.9 percent. The Overall Development Plan, drawn up in 1962, in connection with the Plan for Doubling National Income, in order to stimulate regional development by building new industrial cities, had been a complete failure. In order to correct the excessive concentration in the large urban conglomerations and stop the depopulation of the rural areas, the Economic Planning Agency (EPA) worked out a new blueprint for regional development. The first draft was completed in October 1968; the plan foresaw expenditures of ¥500 trillion, including ¥170 trillion for public works. Even the freehanded bureaucrats had to admit that it would be "difficult" to finance this extravaganza of visionary spending. After consultation with other ministries, EPA presented a second draft in December 1968 which placed more emphasis on living conditions; a third draft was published in January 1969 and the final draft was ready in March 1969. In the meantime, the furor caused by the alarming worsening of environmental pollution has made it necessary to completely revamp all development plans.

Another problem which had been simmering for a long time and became acute in 1968 was rice production. The government's price policy had encouraged farmers to produce more and yet more rice, but demand had not increased. In October 1968, stocks of old rice (1967 crop) amounted to 2.65 million tons; in order to avoid a further increase, the Ministry of Agriculture began to formulate plans to reduce the acreage planted with rice. In November 1968, the Financial System Research Council, a consultative organ to the minister of finance, submitted a proposal for reducing the deficit in the food control special account. The consumer price of rice should be decontrolled (a step which was taken in 1971); the government should reduce the producer price paid to the farmers by 20 percent (the price had just been raised by 5.8 percent); farmers should be encouraged to convert rice paddies to other crops; and a ceiling should be imposed on the government's rice purchases. For computing the price paid to the farmers, the government should start from the consumers' price (¥20,541 per 150 kg.), deduct transportation, storage, and financing costs and dealer's margins (¥4,315) and pay the remainder (¥16,226) to the producers. The difference between the old and new producer prices should be paid out to the farmers as subsidies.

By October 1969, stocks of old rice (partly two years old) had grown to 5.6 million tons, equivalent to ten months' consumption. A "voluntary" reduction of rice production by 1.5 million tons was agreed upon by the government and the agricultural associations; to effect this reduction, 350,000 hectares (11 percent of the total acreage) were to be taken out of rice cultivation. A pension system was to be set up for farmers retiring from farming or relinquishing their land to third parties (including agricultural cooperatives).

In September 1970, the Financial System Research Council published another report which stated that the rice price would have to be reduced by 36.3 percent if it were to reflect the actual supply-demand relation and that, in order to adjust supply to demand, rice production would have to be cut back by 3 million tons to the level of 1957.

In the latter half of 1968, some soft spots had developed in the economy and the expansion slowed down between December 1968 and March 1969, the rate of increase in mining and manufacturing production falling to 9.8 percent (annual rate) while inventories of finished goods increased. The authorities were divided on the significance of the slowdown: MITI asserted that supply was exceeding demand and that the boom had reached its end; the Economic Planning Agency and the Bank of Japan were of the opinion that the expansion would continue. Actually, the clouding of the economy was only temporary and, by April, the uptrend had regained its former strength. In February 1969, wholesale prices, which had been relatively steady in 1968, began to rise sharply (the wholesale price index of the Bank of Japan, 1965 = 100, rose from 105.6 in January to 109.9 in December 1969 and continued to rise until April 1970, when it reached 111.7). This was partly the result of an increase in internal and external demand and partly a reaction to higher prices in foreign markets. But the increase in wholesale prices was the main reason for the switch to a deflationary policy which was put into effect on September 1, 1969, when the official discount rate was raised to 6.25 percent (on that occasion, the Bank of Japan changed from the old *sen* per ¥100 to the percentage system to express the discount rate). At the same time, the Bank of Japan increased the reserve deposit ratio, which had remained unchanged since July 1965; for banks with demand deposits exceeding ¥100 billion, the rate was raised from 1 percent to 1.5 percent. On September 8, the Federation of Bankers Associations announced an increase in the rates on bank loans. The enforcement of a deflationary policy despite a favorable balance of payments position did not find universal approval.

The main support for the expansion came from personal consumption expenditures, equipment investment, and exports. Higher wages made larger consumer spending possible, and the rate of increase in personal consumption expenditures in fiscal 1969 reached 15.0 percent. Higher prices, however, were responsible for a considerable part of the increase. The consumer price index (Prime Minister's Office, 1965 = 100) rose from 117.4 in January to 124.5 in December 1969. For fiscal 1969, the rate of increase was the largest since 1965 (fiscal 1966, 4.7 percent; fiscal 1967, 4.2 percent; fiscal 1968, 4.9 percent; fiscal 1969, 6.4 percent), but, in fiscal 1970, the rate of increase climbed to 7.3 percent.

Corporate earnings continued to rise which, together with a favorable expansion of exports and the sharp increase in bank lending, enabled enterprises—with a few exceptions —to continue their capital spending without losing their liquidity. In fiscal 1969, investment in producers' durable equipment grew by 29.8 percent (national accounts basis), far above the nominal rate of increase in GNP (18.9 percent, real rate 13.0 percent). Only residential construction achieved a comparable rate of increase (28.6 percent). The growth rate of exports in 1969 (23.3 percent) was much higher than that of imports (15.7 percent) so that, on a customs clearance basis, the favorable balance amounted to $966.5 million while, on an exchange basis, the surplus on trade was $3,699 million. (For fiscal 1969, the rate of increase in exports was 22.9 percent, that in imports 22.2 percent, due to a sharp rise in imports in the latter half of the fiscal year.) Exports to the United States, which had expanded by an enormous 35 percent in fiscal 1968 grew only at about half that rate and exports to Southeast Asia also increased less rapidly, but exports to Europe showed a favorable development. The share of exports in shipments of mining and manufacturing products was about 14 percent and the structure of exports closely conformed to the country's industrial structure. Very broadly speaking, the emphasis in exports shifted from nondurable to light durable consumer goods and further to capital equipment and motor cars. The share of textiles in total exports fell from 30.4 percent in 1960 to 18.7 percent in 1965 and 14.2 percent in 1969; that of food (largely fish and fruit) from 6.4 percent in 1960 to 4.1 percent in 1965 and 3.6

	Food	Industrial supplies	Capital equipment	Consumer goods nondurable	durable
1962	6.8%	45.8%	23.1%	8.6%	13.7%
1965	4.1	45.2	27.6	6.4	12.3
1969	3.6	38.7	30.1	5.2	21.6
1970	3.3	3.8	31.1	4.4	21.3

	Light industrial products	Heavy industrial products
1958	48.3%	40.6%
1960	46.5	43.2
1965	31.8	61.8
1969	25.5	69.3
1970	22.9	72.3

Source: Ministry of Finance, Trade of Japan.

percent in 1969. The basic trend is illustrated in the tables on the previous page (because enumeration is incomplete, the percentages do not add up to 100).

The growing foreign exchange reserves embarrassed the government and various measures were taken to keep them to an acceptable level. Official reserves increased from a low of $524 million at the end of 1957 to $1,824 million at the end of 1960; year-end balances ($ million): 1965, 2,107; 1966, 2,074; 1967, 2,005; 1968, 2,891; 1969, 3,496; 1970, 4,399. Strictly speaking, Japan's foreign exchange holdings were not very large relative to the country's trade volume. At the end of March 1971, official foreign exchange holdings (government and Bank of Japan) amounted to $5,458 million, equivalent to somewhat less than the average value of 3.3 months' imports in 1970 on a foreign exchange basis. The most important step taken by the government to slow down the inflow of dollar funds was the so-called yen shift, the use of yen credits instead of dollar usances to finance imports. Moreover, the authorities restricted the induction of impact loans and the flotation of foreign bonds, but the deficiency thus created was compensated by increased foreign investment in Japanese securities.

In September 1969, the general meeting of the International Monetary Fund approved the special drawing rights system and it went into effect in January 1970. An increase in the capital of the fund was sanctioned in December 1969; instead of the average enlargement of about 35 percent, Japan's share in the capital was enlarged by 65.5 percent which raised it from $725 million to $1.2 billion, the fifth largest contribution. On February 12 and March 24, 1970, the Bank of Japan gave two loans of ¥36 billion ($100 million) each to the World Bank, and, in the middle of 1970, Japan took over $250 million in loans that Italy had extended to IMF.

The devaluation of the French franc, in August 1969, and the revaluation of the German mark, in October, increased the pressure, particularly on the part of the United States, for a revaluation of the yen, but the government took the position, generally supported by the country's financial leaders, that there was no reason for revaluation.

The original budget for fiscal 1969 foresaw expenditures on general accounts amounting to ¥6,739.6 billion, 15.8 percent above the original budget for fiscal 1968. Due to what was called budgetary rigidities, the government found it increasingly difficult to finance new programs; the root of the problem, of course, had nothing to do with the budget but with the bureaucratic tradition that a program, once approved, is not discontinued, that each agency considers the increase in its budgetary appropriations as the measure of its importance, and that the success of a minister is judged by the amount of money which is restored after the original requests of his ministry (which customarily grossly overstate the real needs) have been cut by the Ministry of Finance. Total general account expenditures for fiscal 1969 rose to ¥6,930.9 billion, an increase of 17.1 percent.

In August 1969, Kakuei Tanaka, then secretary general of the Liberal-Democratic party and one of the most astute and ambitious Japanese politicians, proposed a new tax on automobiles (¥20,000-¥50,000 per car) which was to finance construction of highways, railroads, and subways. Not only the automobile manufacturers but also the Ministry of Finance opposed the new tax; they said an increase of 50 percent in expenditures for road construction would be undesirable from the point of view of economic policy and another tax on motor cars in addition to the eight already imposed (including taxes on gasoline) would be inequitable (the then Finance Minister, Takeo Fukuda, is a rival of Kakuei Tanaka and vice versa). But the politicians are much too interested in new sources of money to pass up such an opportunity and the road lobby and the railroad lobby, although at loggerheads over the division of the spoils, joined forces to push through the new tax for fiscal 1971.

One reason for the insufficiency of fiscal revenues for financing the government's programs is that the programs are largely based on what are officially described as "visions," i.e., blueprints of desirable future conditions drawn up without any thought of financial resources. The government then finds that there is not enough money to pay for the plans and imposes new taxes. The inequalities and inequities of the Japanese tax system stem partly from the failure to adapt the progressive rates of the income tax to the inflationary increase in nominal incomes and partly from questionable administrative practices. While the income tax payable by wage and salary earners is withheld at source, corporations and persons filing tax returns not only pay much later but, according to one estimate, pay only one-third of the taxes they ought to pay. Physicians and dentists, for example, can deduct 72 percent of gross income as expenses, and the Tax Administration Agency complains that there is no feasible way of checking the true receipts of bars, eating establishments, and the retail trade generally. Interest and dividend income is taxed separately from other income, supposedly to encourage saving; actually, the high-income classes are the main beneficiaries of these privileges. Corporate taxes are levied on only a fraction of the real earnings; under the pretext of strengthening the internal capital of corporations, the government allows them to salt away a large part of their profits before taxing them (in the settlement of accounts for the April–September 1970 terms, Nippon Steel Corporation could deduct ¥20 trillion for special depreciation and the development of overseas markets from ¥38 trillion in operating profits; the company set aside ¥5.6 trillion for the payment of taxes on a pretax profit of ¥18.6 trillion). In 1965 and 1966, the tax rate of the corporation tax was reduced by 3 percent as an antirecession measure; the cut remained in force when business recovered (the rate was raised in fiscal 1970). Companies can spend 0.25 percent of the amount of their capital plus ¥4 million for entertainment free of tax; of the sum exceeding the basic deduction, 50 percent was taxable until fiscal 1969; the rate was raised to 60 percent for fiscal 1969 and 70 percent for fiscal 1970. According to the Tax Administration Agency, Japanese business spent ¥915.5 billion on entertainment from February 1969 to January 1970.

The compilation of the budget for fiscal 1970 was delayed due to the dissolution of the House of Representatives in December 1969. Contrary to predictions, the general election on December 27 resulted in a notable victory for Prime Minister Sato and the Liberal-Democratic party; the Socialists were soundly defeated, but Komeito and the Communists were able to chalk up important gains. Although the credit restraints imposed in September 1969 aimed at curbing domestic demand, the government compiled a highly inflationary budget providing for an increase of 18.0 percent in general account expenditures. The supplementary budgets increased the outlays from ¥7,949.8 billion to ¥8,213.1 billion and brought the rate of increase over the fiscal 1969 total to 18.5 percent. The final fiscal loan and investment program was 18.3 percent higher than in the preceding year. In the first half of fiscal 1970, government spending was somewhat restrained, but, in the latter half, spending for public works picked up and the increase in the salaries of government employees added to fiscal outlays.

In April 1970, shipments of mining and manufacturing products showed signs of slackening and inventories of finished goods began to rise. Wholesale prices, whose rise had been the immediate occasion for the adoption of the credit restraints, continued to move upward until April, thus rising for a record period of fifteen consecutive months. The decline in commodity prices in overseas markets, the tendency of trading companies and users to restrict their purchases to actual needs, and the stagnation in sales of automobiles and electric household appliances finally led to a weakening of wholesale prices.

Until the settlement of accounts for the six-month term ended March 1970, the corporations listed on the Tokyo Stock Exchange had been able to report higher sales and higher profits, but, reflecting the weakness in demand and higher labor costs, business results for the term ended September 1970 were less favorable (figures for the March 1970 settlement in parentheses). Of the 368 companies listed on the First Section of the Tokyo Stock Exchange, sales of manufacturing companies increased by 6.2 percent (+20.0 percent) compared with the preceding term, operating profits decreased by 0.6 percent (+20.3 percent), and net profits increased by 1.3 percent (+11.6 percent). For nonmanufacturing companies, the increase in sales was 7.8 percent (+13.2 percent), operating profits grew by 1.9 percent (+ 19.3 percent), and net profits by 2.5 percent (+13.1 percent). Net profits were down for automobiles (–13.3 percent), oil refining (–5.8 percent), electrical machinery (–4.4 percent), iron and steel (–3.6 percent), stone, glass, and clay (–3.0 percent), and chemicals (–1.2 percent); among nonmanufacturing industries coal mining suffered the worst decline in net profits (–56.3 percent), followed by real estate (–24.4 percent), metal mining (–9.7 percent), and private railroads (–1.2 percent). Sales of the 177 companies listed on the Second Section increased by an average of 9.2 percent (+11.7 percent), operating profits decreased by 1.4 percent (+20.4 percent), and net profits were down by 6.4 percent (+25.8 percent). The average for all 545 companies was sales +8.8 percent (+13.1 percent), operating profits +1.7 percent (+19.3 percent), and net profits +2.1 percent (+13.7 percent). The reasons for the dramatic deterioration were: (1) the large investments in capital equipment over the last five years had created considerable overcapacity; (2) domestic demand for some consumer durables, notably for motor cars and color television sets, had declined; (3) the increase in exports of textiles and electric household appliances had slowed down; (4) the growing labor shortage had led to an accelerated increase in wages, adding to costs.

In the first half of fiscal 1970, equipment investment remained high and was still considerable in the latter half in nonmanufacturing industries. Personal consumption expenditures also remained on a high level. The rate of increase in employment was low but labor's spring offensive brought a steep increase in wages. For large enterprises, the rate of increase came to 18.3 percent as against an increase of 15.6 percent in the preceding year. Despite a slight decline in the propensity to consume, the rate of increase in personal consumption expenditures reached 17.4 percent, the second highest rate in the last ten years (fiscal 1963, 17.7 percent). Diversification of demand played an important role in this increase. As mentioned above, there was a marked sluggishness in the sales of automobiles and color TV sets due to consumer resistance, but the decrease was made up by higher expenditures for furniture and furnishings, and travel, sports, and other leisure activities. Another factor which contributed greatly to the strength of the economy was residential construction. According to the national census taken on October 1, 1970, the average number of persons per household was 3.72, the first time that this figure had sunk below 4—a clear indication that the nuclear family is becoming the prevalent social pattern. The concentration of the population in the large urban conglomerations still continues worsening the already acute housing shortage; on the other hand, the rise in incomes and the availability of bank loans for homebuilding sustained a high rate of expansion in residential construction.

In the beginning of 1970, the export situation did not look altogether favorable. The increase in exports to Southeast Asia was slowing down and exports to the United States were threatened by the rising protectionist sentiment and the charges of dumping leveled against some of Japan's leading export companies. The worldwide inflation, however, supported the expansion of world trade, which rose to $312,500 million in 1970. The smooth expansion of exports to Europe and the Communist countries raised total Japanese exports in 1970 to $19,359 million, a 21 percent increase over 1969, while imports reached $18,872 million, 23.6 percent higher than in the preceding year (customs clearance basis).

The production adjustments in the latter half of the year slowed down the increase in imports of raw materials, but imports of foodstuffs and consumer goods, stimulated by the government's policy of allowing larger imports in order to brake the rise in consumer prices, more than compensated for the deceleration. In the balance of payments, the balance on trade for 1970 amounted to $4,019 million (exports $19,021 million, imports $15,002 million), but the deficit on invisibles rose to $1,798 million, the deficit on transfers to $207 million, and the deficit on long-term capital account to $1,597 million. The short-term capital account showed a surplus of $757 million, and the overall surplus amounted to $1,374 million.

The slowdown in demand and the pressure of overcapacity resulted in a large increase in inventories and, starting with October 1970, production was cut back in steel, automobiles, color TV sets, chemicals, plywood, and fertilizers. It was the first time since the 1965 recession that production had been reduced; but, different from 1965, the production curtailments were carried out by industry without MITI's "administrative guidance."

The wholesale price index started to drop in June 1970, remained more or less at the same level during the latter half of the year, and sank again in the beginning of 1971. For fiscal 1970, the decrease came to 0.7 percent. In the first half of the year, the decline in prices of nonferrous metals in overseas markets was an important factor but also the weakness of steel prices resulting from overproduction (in the last boom, the steel industry repeated on a larger scale its performance during the Iwato boom: investment race, overcapacity, overproduction, price collapse). In the latter half of the year, the weakness in demand also affected textiles, machinery, pulp, paper, and lumber, but, due to the international situation, oil prices went up. Industry was all the more upset over the prolongation of the monetary stringency because it considered the price increases a result of a cost-push inflation which, differently from a demand-pull inflation, cannot be checked by credit restraints. Moreover, equipment investment had calmed down around June or July 1970 so that there was no longer any danger of overheating on that score.

In view of the state of the economy, the Bank of Japan, on October 28, 1970, reduced the official discount rate by 0.25 percent to 6 percent, thus virtually ending the credit restraints which had remained in force for almost fourteen months. As of September, the diffusion index was below fifty and other indicators, in particular the leading and coincident indicators, signaled the same message of a slackening economy. The government had taken a rather optimistic view of the situation, but business had urged the lifting of the monetary restrictions after their original objective, the halt of the rise in wholesale prices, had been achieved. Because the economy retained a strong expansionary thrust the authorities had been reluctant to ease the credit squeeze, but business conditions deteriorated rapidly in the last quarter. According to a revised estimate of the Economic Planning Agency, GNP reached ¥73,213.7 billion in fiscal 1970, an increase of 16.4 percent over fiscal 1969 when GNP amounted to ¥62,920.4 billion, 17.9 percent higher than in the preceding year. In real terms, GNP rose from ¥52,497.8 billion in fiscal 1969 to ¥57,493.2 billion, a rate of 9.7 percent, the lowest in four years. Compared with the preceding quarter, the real rate of growth was 2.9 percent for the first quarter of fiscal 1970 (April–June), 2.9 percent in the second, –1.0 percent in the third, and 3.0 percent in the fourth; it was –0.3 percent in the first quarter of 1971 and –0.2 percent in the second. In nominal terms, personal consumption expenditures increased in fiscal 1970 at a rate of 15.9 percent, residential construction by 15.4 percent, and investment in plant and equipment by 14.6 percent. But as a result of the 7.3 percent increase in consumer prices the real rate of increase in personal consumption expenditures was 8.1 percent.

The revised estimate of Economic Planning Agency put per capita personal income in fiscal 1970 at $1,583, which placed Japan at about the same level as Great Britain (1969, $1,509). The diffusion rate of many consumer durables was fairly high, with the exception of motor cars and air conditioners.

According to the same source, average savings per household ascertained by the same survey amounted to ¥1,286,000 held in the following forms: savings deposits, 54.9 percent; securities, 20.2 percent; life insurance 22.4 percent; others, 2.5 percent. Housing remained unsatisfactory, although the space per person has been rising constantly (1970, 5.87 *jō* per person, 17.4 sq. ft.). According to a survey of the Ministry of Labor covering 143 enterprises in seventeen different industries, the spring offensive in 1971 resulted in an average wage increase of 16.6 percent in large enterprises, while a survey by the Japan Productivity Center (covering 267 major companies) put the rate of increase at 17.1 percent. Both surveys agreed that the rate of increase was lower than in 1970 (18.3 percent or 18.9 percent). Generally, the increase in labor productivity matched the increase in nominal wages and far exceeded that in real wages.

(Indices: 1965 = 100)

Year	Index of labor productivity	Wage index	
		Nominal	Real
1959	61.3	57.2	80.1
1960	69.3	61.8	83.5
1961	76.4	68.9	88.4
1962	78.5	75.4	90.6
1963	86.2	83.2	93.0
1964	96.6	92.0	99.0
1965	100.0	100.0	100.0
1966	113.0	111.6	106.2
1967	131.7	126.3	115.6
1968	150.5	145.1	126.1
1969	173.0	168.9	139.5
1970	197.1	198.7	152.4

Sources: Index of labor productivity: Japan Productivity Center; Wage index: Ministry of Labor.

Diffusion Rate of Consumer Durables
February 1971

	(Percentage of households)
Electric washing machines	93.6%
Electric refrigerators	91.2
Electric fans	85.4
Black & white TV receivers	82.3
Oil stoves	82.0
Gas water heaters	44.0
Color TV receivers	42.3
Passenger cars	26.8
Air conditioners	8.0
Pianos	6.8

Source: Economic Planning Agency.

The income of Japanese farmers averaged ¥1,386,600 per household in fiscal 1970, an increase of 10.9 percent over the preceding fiscal year. Income from farming fell by 5 percent to ¥503,000, accounting for only 36.3 percent of their total income. Income from other activities amounted to ¥883,000, an increase of 22.6 percent. Expenditures per farm household averaged ¥1,227,000, a nominal increase of 13.3 percent over fiscal 1969, but the real rate of increase was only 5.6 percent because consumer prices in rural areas rose by 7.3 percent (the same as the national average).

The deterioration in the economy was confirmed by the business results of the companies listed on the Tokyo, Osaka, and Nagoya stock exchanges. For the six-month term ended March 1971, sales of 375 companies listed on the First Section of the Tokyo Stock Exchange increased by 4.6 percent, but their operating profits declined by 9.8 percent and their net profits by 5.4 percent. For 172 companies listed on the Second Section, the increase in sales amounted to 3.8 percent, the decrease in operating profits being 10.7 percent and that in net profits 14.2 percent. The average rate of increase in sales of all 547 companies compared with the preceding term was 4.6 percent, the rate of decrease in operating profits 9.8 percent, and the decrease in net profits 5.8 percent.

The increase in business failures also underscored the difficulties at least partly created by the credit squeeze. According to Tokyo Shoko Mercantile Agency, insolvencies of firms with debts exceeding ¥10 million numbered 10,160 cases in fiscal 1970, an increase of 21.3 percent over fiscal 1969. Total liabilities amounted to ¥775,789 million, an increase of 36.2 percent. Another credit agency, Teikoku Koshinsho, put the number of bankruptcies at 10,001 (+18.6 percent) and liabilities at ¥771,415 million (+34.9 percent). As indicated by the sharp increase in debts, the failures involved not only small but also medium-sized firms. Among them were Dai-Ichi Glass Co., Japan's largest maker of glass bottles, and Satoh Agricultural Machine Manufacturing Co., the fourth largest producer of agricultural machinery, listed on the First Section of the Tokyo Stock Exchange. For the business term ended October 1970, Satoh had reported losses of ¥680 million and, on March 5, 1971, the company filed a petition for reorganization under the Corporate Reorganization Law; with debts exceeding ¥20 billion, it was Japan's second largest bankruptcy case following Sanyo Special Steel with ¥58 billion in 1965.

The performance of the stock market in 1970 was marked by one of the largest one-day losses. In the beginning of the year, the continued expansion despite the credit restraints ordered in September 1969 supported the market, and the expectation of good corporate results for the March term pushed the Dow-Jones average beyond the ¥2,500 mark on March 26 and, on April 6, the index reached a historic high of ¥2,534.45. But, on April 30, the index declined by ¥201.11, a loss of 8.69 percent. On May 19, the index fell below ¥2,000 and, on May 27, the Dow-Jones was down to the low of the year, ¥1,929.64. On the next day, however, the index recorded the largest rise of the year, ¥79.46, or 4.12 percent. The slump was very much a matter of mood; the reasons given for the decline were: (1) the unsatisfactory state of the American economy; (2) the monetary stringency; (3) the slow-down in exports to the United States; (4) the decrease in foreign investment in Japanese securities. Foreign purchases of Japanese stocks had been brisk in 1969, but, in December of that year, the Federal Reserve Board imposed stricter controls on foreign investment. In the January–March quarter of 1970, net purchases of Japanese securities by foreign investors totaled $118 million, but, in the months from April to July, net sales amounted to $147 million.

In the beginning of 1971, the Dow-Jones average rose from a low of ¥1,981.74 on January 6 to a January high of ¥2,115.25 on the nineteenth and continued to move upward (February 28, ¥2,246.36; March 29, ¥2,405.65). The relaxation of the money market—on January 20, the Bank of Japan reduced the official discount rate a second time bringing it down to 5.75 percent—was an important factor; another reason was the renewed interest of foreign investors. The government, which only a few years previously would have delighted at any interest shown by foreign investors in Japanese securities, was then extremely annoyed, not only because these stock purchases added to Japan's foreign exchange reserves but also because much of the investment was prompted by anticipation of yen revaluation.

Since the slowdown had become more severe than expected and threatened to develop into a full-fledged recession, the government, in addition to reducing the official discount rate, compiled a stimulative budget for fiscal 1971. Expenditures on general accounts were raised to ¥9,414.3 billion, 18.42 percent higher than the original budget for fiscal 1970 (¥7,949.8 billion). The fiscal loan and investment program was expanded at an even higher rate; the total, (¥4,280.4 billion) represented a 19.6 percent increase over the previous year (¥3,579.9 billion). Spending for public works, which has a particularly strong stimulative effect on the economy, was increased by 19.7 percent over the preceding year. Provision was made to increase fiscal outlays for certain projects if the economy failed to respond to the initial measures.

Contrary to the buoyancy of the stock market, the economy showed few signs of improvement in the beginning of 1971. The index of mining and manufacturing production (1965 = 100) decreased slightly in January (from 222.9 in December 1970 to 221.8) and rose a little in February (222.0) and more strongly in March (225.9); for the entire fiscal year 1970, industrial production increased by 13.5 percent. The index of shipments declined in January and February (December 1970, 215.2; January 1971, 211.6; February: 209.7) but rose in March by 6.6 percent to 223.4. While the inventory index, which had been rising since March 1970, continued its upward trend until February (inventories of finished goods: February 1970, 184.9; March, 185.5; December, 233.1; January 1971, 235.7; February, 239.5); when compared with the same month one year earlier, the index had risen 29.5 percent. It registered its first drop in March 1971, when it fell 1.1 percent to 236.6. Private orders for machinery (except ships), which had risen in January by 24.0 percent over the preceding month to ¥232.7 billion, dropped in February to ¥191.7 billion, 17.6 percent lower than in the preceding month and 23.2 percent below the level a year previously; but they rose by 47.3 percent over the preceding month in March, when they were 9.1 percent higher than the year before. The wholesale price index for February was 0.2 percent lower than in February 1970, the first time in six years and two months that the index had fallen below the year-earlier level, and it fell another 0.2 percent in March when it sank to 110.5, 0.7 percent below the level of March 1970 (111.3). The index rose 0.3 percent in April but was still 0.8 percent lower than a year previously. In March, the diffusion index (based on twenty-five series) rose above fifty for the first time in seven months. According to a number of surveys made in the beginning of the year, equipment investment, which had played a leading role in the growth of the economy, was to be much more subdued than in the preceding five years. The decline in corporate profits dampened investment propensity though installation of labor-saving machinery and antipollution equipment and investment for the modernization of small enterprises continued. While investment was relatively low in most manufacturing sectors, it was high in electric power, shipbuilding, and shipping.

The sluggishness of the economy continued through spring and summer of 1971. Key industries such as steel and electrical machinery maintained their production restrictions, but inventories failed to come down. Wholesale prices remained more or less at the same level, while consumer prices continued to rise. In September, the consumer price index rose by 5.9 percent over the preceding month and by 10.3 percent over the same month in 1970; the jump in prices of fresh foods due to bad weather was the main cause of the rise.

Selected Indices

(All indices: 1965 = 100)

1971	Mining & manufacturing production	Producers shipments	Inventories of finished goods	Wholesale prices	Consumer prices (Tokyo)
January	222.9	210.9	235.3	110.9	136.6
February	222.9	210.0	239.8	110.7	136.1
March	227.7	222.5	238.1	110.5	135.9
April	224.1	216.8	242.2	110.8	138.5
May	213.6	211.5	238.7	110.8	138.1
June	227.7	218.1	238.7	110.6	138.0
July	229.1	221.5	235.7	110.7	139.1
August	227.8	214.8	239.6	110.9	138.1
September	233.2	226.0	238.8	110.6	146.2
October	226.7	213.7	244.4	110.0	144.2
November	231.3	221.3	245.3	109.8	141.1
December	230.6	225.5	245.1	109.8	141.1

Orders for machinery (except ships) reached a high of ¥282.3 billion in March but fell to ¥161.1 billion in May; private construction awards rose to ¥243.9 billion in March but dropped to ¥145.9 billion in April. The only bright spot in the generally gloomy economy was the strength of exports which, after a shaky performance in January and February, stayed around the $2 billion level. Validated exports in the July-September quarter amounted to $6,650,701,000, 25.4 percent higher than in the same quarter in the previous year. After rising to $1,720 million in March, imports declined steadily and were down to $1,484 million (customs returns) in August. Imports of industrial raw materials such as coal, scrap, and wood, and also imports of machinery were affected by the decrease.

Payments for past equipment investment and the financing of inventories and production curtailments kept corporate fund demand strong until March 1971. In April, the money market eased considerably; enterprises from good medium-sized firms upward disposed of large liquid funds. The situation facilitated a certain improvement in the payment conditions of subcontractors. Manufacturers of electric appliances, who had paid 10 percent cash in the beginning of 1971, paid 22 percent in August; in the machinery industry, the pattern changed from 25 percent cash and 75 percent drafts to 60 percent cash and 40 percent drafts, and the share of drafts in the payments of the steel industry declined from 80 percent to 50 percent. Generally, however, enterprises did not repay all their bank loans because they wanted to maintain their banking relations, or establish business connections with better banks. Many firms renegotiated the terms of their loans and shifted from short-term to long-term financing. In contrast to the customary lags in payment a number of firms began to make prepayments for orders and even pay on account for future orders. Also noteworthy was the tendency of large enterprises to invest their idle funds in bonds or treasury bills. The banks were keen to attract new borrowers and the city banks succeeded in increasing their loans so that the balance of outstanding loans of the city banks rose by ¥2,373.3 billion in the six months from April to September 1971, the highest increase on record. The loan balance of the trust banks increased by ¥337.8 billion, likewise a record, and outstanding bond issues of the long-term credit banks went up by ¥482.9 billion. Deposits of the city banks increased by ¥3,885.5 billion. The large payments from the foreign exchange fund resulting from the continuing export surplus played an important role in the monetary relaxation, but the relatively low level of consumption expenditure also contributed to the increase in deposits. The city banks were able to reduce their borrowings from the Bank of Japan and switched their borrowings in the call market from over-the-month to unconditional loans. The smaller financial institutions were hard pressed to find profitable investment opportunities for their idle funds and the general trend of falling interest rates cut into the profits of all financial institutions.

The availability of funds, however, did not result in what the government desired most in order to overcome the sluggishness in the economy, a strong rise in investment outlays. A survey by the Industrial Bank, undertaken in September 1971 and covering 1,204 enterprises, showed an estimated increase of 13.9 percent in the first half of fiscal 1971 and forecast an increase of 5.9 percent for the latter half, resulting in an average increase of 9.3 percent for the entire fiscal year. For fiscal 1972, the bank predicted a decrease of 1.6 percent. In the manufacturing industries (745 enterprises), equipment investment was expected to decline by 4.5 percent in fiscal 1971 and 11.7 percent in fiscal 1972; in nonmanufacturing industries, however, capital outlays were estimated to rise by 29 percent in the current and 9.6 percent in the next fiscal year.

While it is possible to regulate industrial equipment investment by monetary policy when capacity is insufficient, monetary policy cannot influence investment in times of overcapacity. Nevertheless, the government tried hard to stimulate the economy by reducing interest rates. After reducing the official discount rate to 5.75 percent on January 20, 1971, the Bank of Japan lowered it to 5.5 percent on May 8 and 5.25 percent on July 28; a general reduction of interest rates went into effect on August 10, 1971. On October 1, the call rate (lender's rate) on over-the-month loans fell to 6.0 percent, 3.25 percent lower than in October 1970, and a second reduction on October 15 of all call rates by 0.25 percent brought the overnight rate to the same level as the official discount rate (5.25 percent). But the economy continued to drift aimlessly and "stagflation" became the most overworked term in the vocabulary of economic commentators. Bankruptcies involving liabilities exceeding ¥10 million rose to 872 in March (aggregate liabilities ¥93.9 billion) but were less high in the following months (August, 682 insolvencies with a total of ¥51.3 billion in liabilities).

The uncertainty in the economic situation was intensified by the growing resistance of the public to the industry-oriented nature of society and the new awareness of the dangers of environmental pollution. The local population, often supported by militant student radicals, protested against siting new factories, new power plants, new highways, or new towns in their neighborhoods. The protests sometimes approached hysteria and, in the battle against the new Narita airport, the wild men of the new left beat three unarmed policemen to death. (The government, remembering the riots of 1960, is more afraid of the death of a demonstrator than concerned with the safety of the law enforcement officers and still refuses to provide the riot police with arms.)

The government's enormous budget, designed to stimulate the economy, failed to achieve any appreciable improvement. In view of the emphasis placed on investment in infrastructural facilities (whose effects are only felt after a year or eighteen months) and politically motivated subsidies, the lack of results was not surprising.

In contrast to the gloom in the economy, the stock market achieved its strongest advance since the Iwato boom—for no apparent reason. The volume of transactions on the Tokyo Stock Exchange registered a strong increase in the beginning of the year with average daily volume rising from 172 million shares in January to 237 million shares in February and staying well above 200 million in March (224 million) and April (234 million). The market suffered a setback in May; the Dow-Jones average, which had risen from a low of ¥1,981.74 in January to a high of ¥2,489.35 on May 4, temporarily slipped below the ¥2,400 mark and for May the average daily volume dropped to 140 million shares, but June saw another advance when the Dow-Jones index rose above the ¥2,600 line. Some hesitancy developed in July but, on August 14, one day before Mr. Nixon's announcement of his new economic policy, the Dow-Jones average reached the historic high of ¥2,740.98.

The issue which attracted most attention in the summer of 1971 was the possible revaluation of the yen. Pushed up by buoyant exports, Japan's foreign exchange reserves rose from $4,399 million at the end of December 1970 to $7,927 million at the end of July 1971. With the exception of January, the trade balance as well as the overall balance showed substantial surpluses in all months. The highest overall surplus was registered in May, when, due to large inflows of long- and short-term capital, international payments showed a favorable balance of $1,183 million.

Despite the government's insistence that it had no intention of revaluating the yen, many businessmen began to take precautions against a yen revaluation and, for the first time since the immediate postwar years, the phenomenon of "leads and lags" began to influence the foreign exchange market. Traders desired prepayment for exports in order to avoid exchange losses and postponed payments for imports in the hope of reaping exchange gains. In the face of mounting foreign, particularly American, pressure for a revaluation of the yen, the Japanese government maintained that Japan's balance of payments position did not constitute a basic disequilibrium in the sense of the articles of the International Monetary Fund and expressed its determination not to change the parity of the yen. But in order to obviate foreign criticism, the government, on June 4, 1971, adopted an eight-point program designed to prevent a too rapid accumulation of foreign reserves. The main provisions of the program were: (1) acceleration of the liberalization of imports, including larger quotas for imports which will not be entirely freed; (2) preferential tariffs on imports from developing countries, to go into effect on August 1; (3) earlier implementation of the last portion of the tariff reductions under the Kennedy round; (4) earlier implementation of the liberalization of direct foreign investment; expansion of the number of industries in which wholly owned foreign enterprises will be approved "automatically" and "automatic" approval of fifty-fifty joint ventures in all industries except those on a negative list; creation of a lending system in foreign currency to promote Japanese outward investment and abolition of the $1 million ceiling on such investments; (5) removal of nontariff trade barriers as far as possible; (6) expansion of economic aid to developing countries, promotion of the development of overseas raw material sources, and increases in Japan's contributions to international organizations; (7) gradual abolition of the preferential tax system for exports; reexamination of the operations of the Export-Import Bank; measures will be taken to ensure orderly marketing in exports; (8) flexible operation of fiscal and monetary policies.

The program, if carried out, would have mitigated some of the irritants in Japan's relations with the United States but would not have changed to any appreciable degree the basic trend in Japan's foreign trade.

In a different field, the Japan Textile Federation, with the blessing of Representative Wilbur Mills, chairman of the House Ways and Means Committee, decided to adopt voluntary curbs on textile exports to the United States for three years starting July 1, 1971. The industry first announced its readiness to restrict their exports after the long drawn-out negotiations between the two governments had failed to produce results, chiefly on account of America's insistence on item by item quotas, not to mention the failure of the American industry to prove any substantial injury attributable to Japanese imports. In view of the fact that only 8 percent of the textile products on the American market are imports and that Japanese textiles account for only one-fourth of the imports (American imports of synthetic fibers from Japan are less than 1.5 percent of total consumption) such injury may be difficult to prove. Initially, the Japan Textile Federation had made its voluntary restrictions dependent on voluntary controls on the part of three other textile exporters (the Republic of Korea, Taiwan, and Hong Kong) but later cancelled these conditions because, in the view of the Japanese manufacturers, their voluntary restraints were based on their desire to maintain friendly relations rather than on the needs of the American textile industry.

The Japanese plan divided textile products into four broad categories: cottons, woolens, synthetic fibers, and secondary products. The increase in exports was to be kept to 5 percent in the first year and 6 percent in the following two years, with actual exports in fiscal 1970 (1,259 million square yards valued at $510 million) serving as base. Shifts of quotas were to be allowed from one category to another.

President Nixon and the American textile industry denounced the program as soon as it was announced—without waiting for the results of the restrictions. However, the Japanese government, completely misjudging Mr. Nixon's tenacity, lulled itself into the naive hope that a troublesome issue had been put to rest, at least for the near future.

4 THE "NIXON SHOCK"

The Japanese mass media have used two expressions to describe the dramatic change in the world situation created by President Nixon's announcement of his new economic policy on August 15, 1971: "dollar shock" and "Nixon shock." The term "dollar shock" completely misunderstands the far-reaching nature of the measures taken by President Nixon to reinvigorate the American polity. The "defense of the dollar," which many Japanese commentators considered as an important objective of the policy shift, was only one of the means required for the basic goal of "making America strong again." The president's domestic program, the price and wage freeze for halting inflation, was influenced by the consideration that a strong economy was desirable for victory in the 1972 election, while the suspension of the convertibility of the dollar into gold and the imposition of the 10 percent tax on imports were to restore the equilibrium in America's balance of payments, or at least reduce the deficit to manageable proportions. The retreat from overcommitments and the reorientation toward national welfare, indicated in the message on the state of the union and the "Nixon doctrine," did not mean that the United States would no longer imperil her balance of payments by political and military spending abroad; on the contrary, the United States, impatient with allies who had been reluctant to cooperate with American policies, wanted to go on with the kind of spending which had caused the huge deficit in the payments balance but desired to shift some of the burden. It was a kind of self-assertion of American nationalism against attacks from within and without, a demonstration to convince the nation and the world that America would not succumb to the traumatic experiences of the disruption of her social fabric at home, the disaster of Vietnam, the growing anti-Americanism in Latin America, and the loss of military superiority.

The economic measures taken to control America's untractable inflation may have had some kind of economic foundation, but there was little economic rationale for demands made on the outside world and in particular for a revaluation of the yen. As Sanford Rose explained in his article "U.S. Foreign Trade: There's No Need to Panic" in the August 1971 issue of *Fortune*, America's position in world markets remains exceedingly strong (see also the editorial in the same issue) and America's foreign investments (valued at $75 billion, against $13.2 billion in foreign investments in the United States) underscore her position as a mature creditor country. Until 1971, the United States has always enjoyed a favorable balance on trade which, in view of the tremendous expansion of American exports (1950, $10 billion; 1960, $32 billion; 1970, $43 billion), throws in doubt President Nixon's basic assumption that the undervaluation of foreign currencies, in particular the yen and the German mark, was responsible for America's balance of payments difficulties. The total accumulated surplus of the United States on the balance of trade in the last twenty years amounts to $50 billion, while it was only in 1965 that for the first time since the end of the war (as a matter of fact, since 1931) Japan achieved a surplus in her trade with the United States. The outspoken demand of the secretary of the treasury to have other currencies revalued to the extent of achieving an improvement of $13 billion in America's balance of payments (Mr. Connally was willing to settle for $11 billion) was seemingly devoid of any financial or economic plausibility. That the IMF at least partially supported the American claim would seem to support the contention that there is a certain political bias in that institution.

There was a feeling in Japan that President Nixon's announcement of his new economic policy was a declaration of economic war. Together with the president's announcement of his visit to the People's Republic of China and the subsequent demand for an inter-governmental agreement on textile exports, it took Japan by surprise but emphasized the interrelationships of world trade in the modern era. The Japanese mass media generally avoided analyzing the political implications of President Nixon's new economic policy and the Japanese business world worried only about the economic consequences. The most striking manifestation of the impact of NEP was the precipitous slump in the stock market.

The Dow-Jones average, which had reached an all-time high of ¥2,740.98 on August 14, was down to ¥2,162.82 on August 24. In the four days from the sixteenth to the nineteenth the index lost ¥550.82. Far more serious than these paper losses was the turmoil in the foreign exchange market. Despite President Nixon's suspension of the convertibility of the dollar (which made the parity of $35 for an ounce of gold a purely imaginary equation), the Japanese government reaffirmed its determination to maintain the rate of $1 = ¥360. In view of the American insistence on a revaluation of the yen and the floating of other currencies, this position was questionable, all the more so because the dollar on which this parity was based (i.e., a dollar convertible into gold) had become a purely fictitious entity and the system which had supported this parity had died.

In the two weeks which followed Mr. Nixon's "Pearl Harbor," Japan's political and economic leadership, which had been utterly unprepared for this attack, was in complete disarray. The Bank of Japan tried to stop the inflow of dollars, but to no avail. The bank had to buy hundreds of millions of dollars at the old fixed rate, despite a ban on taking in Euro-dollar funds and a temporary suspension of spot transactions.

From August 16 to August 19, the net dollar purchases of the Bank of Japan amounted to $2.2 billion; on August 27, it bought a record $1,250.2 million. This finally convinced the authorities that they had to act. On the same day, the Ministry of Finance announced that the "present limits on the margin of fluctuation will be suspended temporarily" and the yen was set afloat. Altogether, the Bank of Japan's dollar purchases in those two weeks amounted to $3.9 billion, and Japan's official reserves, which had stood at $7,927 million at the end of July, were up to $12.514 million. Thanks to Mr. Nixon, Japan's foreign exchange holdings had increased by $4,587 million, more than one-fourth of the balance of payments deficit which the United States was attempting to cure.

Soon after President Nixon's move, many Japanese business leaders, who up to then had urged the government to maintain the old yen parity, called for an immediate revaluation of the yen. A few businessmen, such as Kogoro Uemura, president of the Federation of Economic Organizations, and Yoshizane Iwasa, board chairman of Fuji Bank, had proposed this before. But the vast majority of Japan's businessmen were concerned about the losses they would suffer from the imposition of the import tax and the yen revaluation, and there was a universal clamor from industrial organizations as well as from individual enterprises and entrepreneurs that the government should compensate them for their losses. Typical of the uncertainty created by Mr. Nixon's NEP were the numerous cancellations by large enterprises of preliminary employment arrangements for students expected to graduate in March 1972.

Even more disconcerting than the behavior of the business community was the inaction of the government. It was only on August 24 that the cabinet took up the issue and decided to go ahead with the eight-point program adopted in June in order to ease the tension between Japan and the United States and to increase government spending so as to mitigate the impact of NEP on the Japanese economy.

A large part of the dollar sales which finally forced the government to float the yen were made by the foreign exchange banks and the large trading companies. It was rumored that the Bank of Japan had put off the floating of the yen so as to give the banks an opportunity to get rid of their dollar holdings. There were also rumors that some banks had borrowed large dollar funds for conversion into yen, and a Socialist member of the House of Councillors, Shizuo Wada, charged that the exchange controls had been eased just before floating the yen on purpose and that the decision to float the yen had been leaked by Shiro Inoue, a director of the Bank of Japan and son of a financial leader in the interwar era. Naturally, these charges were emphatically denied.

Although the yen was cut from its old parity, it was not allowed to float freely. In order to facilitate the managed float, a number of new restrictions on exchange transactions were introduced which greatly hampered the financing of foreign trade. The yen gradually moved upward but it was only in the beginning of October that the Bank of Japan relaxed its intervention, and, on October 15, the dollar was quoted at ¥329.50, equivalent to a revaluation of the yen by 9.25 percent on the IMF basis (ratio of difference from old fixed rate to new value).

President Nixon had announced his NEP at a time when the Japanese economy was in the doldrums. The government as well as various economic research institutes had already scaled down their earlier predictions for fiscal 1971, and now everybody began to figure out how much of an impact a revaluation of the yen would make at rates between 5 percent and 25 percent. The obsession with keeping the expansion of the economy at a level of at least 8 percent (real rate) was typical of the conservative thinking of the government, the business world, and the economists. The actions of the American government, in particular the ultimatum demanding the conclusion of an intergovernmental agreement on restrictions on exports of textiles to the United States, clearly showed the precariousness of Japan's position in export markets. On the other hand, the victory of the OPEC (Organization of Petroleum Exporting Countries) over the major petroleum companies indicates that the procurement of raw materials from developing countries will undergo a basic change. Under these conditions, the type of quantitative expansion which has been prominent in Japan's economic growth may become impossible, and the country may have to change to an entirely different economic structure.

In order to improve Japan's relations with the United States, the Ministry of Foreign Affairs proposed the following steps: (1) a government to government agreement restricting textile exports; (2) a large revaluation of the yen; (3) large purchases of U.S. weapons; (4) restrictions on exports of TV sets and automobiles to the United States; (5) liberalization of imports from the United States. Not only the business world but even some members of the cabinet and other politicians were alarmed at this proposal for what seemed a "sellout" or "unconditional surrender" to the United States, and Prime Minister Sato was said to have been highly critical of the failure of the Foreign Office to correctly assess American intentions.

On October 13, 1971, Japan signed the 1970 extension of the international cotton textile agreement (an action which had been delayed for over a year) and two days later, on October 15 (the deadline set by the Americans), Kakuei Tanaka, Minister of International Trade and Industry, and David M. Kennedy, Mr. Nixon's special envoy for textile negotiations, initialed an agreement under which Japan will impose item by item restrictions on exports of wool and man-made fiber textiles for three years beginning October 1, 1971. This acceptance of the American terms seemed to confirm the suspicion that Mr. Sato had promised governmental restrictions on textile exports as a quid pro quo for the return of Okinawa.

The government was reluctant to admit the true nature of the crisis in Japan's relations with the United States, and the business world was equally inclined to overlook the basic issues. President Nixon's NEP ended the postwar relationship of protector and protected between the United States and Japan; while Japan's political and business leaders continued to talk of harmony, understanding, and cooperation, the United States seemed to have shifted to a stance of confrontation of interests and had caused a showdown with a "ruthless" competitor who did not observe the rules of "fair" trade. Unfortunately, there are no objective standards for such things as "ruthless" or "fair." Furthermore, there is a basic difference between American and Japanese protectionism; the United States tends to protect industries which are old and obsolete, while Japan tries to protect young and immature industries. This is no excuse for prolonging restrictions unduly, but it is a factor which is usually overlooked. The most important consideration, however, is that both sides tend to disregard the interests of the consumer who becomes the victim of the artificial restraints which hamper the basic function of the economy, that of supplying the material goods for the satisfaction of human needs.

2 FISCAL AND MONETARY POLICIES

1 FISCAL POLICIES

1 POLICY MAKING

Even before the problem of environmental pollution threw doubt on the adequacy of the policy of economic growth, the country's postwar development had been subjected to some soul-searching criticism. Occasionally, the strictures were inspired by nostalgic memories of the good old times and sentimental regrets over the disappearance of the quaint and exotic in the people's style of living, but there was also deeply felt concern over the destruction of the landscape and the traditional values, the ideological vacuum created by the defeat, and the irrelevance of the slogans and policies of the postwar parties. A few years ago, the nation's leaders became alarmed at the growing animosity against Japan, particularly in the developing countries of Southeast Asia where the Japanese "economic animal" had succeeded in replacing the "ugly American" as the villain responsible for the economic troubles and social inequities in the have-not countries. While looking with awe and envy at the Japanese achievements, they are also receptive to the charge of economic imperialism hurled at Japan by the Chinese Communists.

Given Japan's position, the country cannot afford not to grow, but there may be legitimate differences of opinion on the kind and direction of growth best suited to or most desirable for the country. Basically, Japan's postwar growth upheld the decision made in the Meiji era directing the country toward modernization and industrialization which, practically, implied westernization. Whereas the policy pursued in the Meiji era was inspired by nineteenth-century concepts of imperialistic nationalism, the postwar policy grew out of the needs of a mass society because industrial progress was the only practical way of providing food, clothing, and shelter. It would be preposterous to claim that Japan has solved the problems of poverty or social injustice but, to the casual observer, the country and the people give the impression of prosperity and affluence. Nevertheless, even the government has had second thoughts about its policies. Following suggestions abroad that GNP is hardly an indicator of human welfare and happiness and that new measures of social progress and environmental quality are needed, the planning committee of the Economic Council, in a report submitted in March 1971 proposed the formulation of an indicator of "net national welfare" (NNW). The committee pointed out that GNP failed to indicate the relevance of expenditures to national welfare because the categories used do not reveal the purposes for which the expenditures are made.

The recommendations of the planning committee were presented in connection with the revision of the government's New Economic and Social Development Plan (1970–75) to be worked out by the Economic Council. According to some officials of the Economic Planning Agency, the plan would have to be completely recast because the figures have no relation to reality. The dissatisfaction with the growth policies of the government resulted largely from their orientation toward production, the same bias which dominated the thinking of industry. The government's plans were not directed toward the satisfaction of wants but toward the attainment of targets whose significance for the national welfare was obscure. It is true that abstract notions like national welfare cannot automatically ensure clarity of direction or unity of purpose, but, with considerable understatement, it may be said that the policy-making function of the government could stand some improvement.

Actually, there has been disagreement inside the government and government agencies between the advocates of economic growth and those who wanted to give priority to the quality of life. In view of the distortions which arose under the Plan for Doubling National Income during the sixties (actually, the distortions were not the result of the plan), a Medium-Term Economic Plan was drafted for 1964–68 and approved by the cabinet in January 1965. But, because the plan was based on Ikeda's program, the Sato cabinet repudiated the plan in January 1966 and ordered a new plan to be drawn up. The Long-Term Economic Plan for 1967–71 was supposed to correct the distortions created by the rapid expansion of the economy, viz., the rise in consumer prices, the weaknesses in corporate management, and the overcrowding of the cities. The plan proposed a reorganization of industry so as to equal the economic efficiency of the advanced countries. The following measures were to contribute to greater efficiency: (1) improvement of enterprises; (2) modernization of low-productivity sectors; (3) reexamination of the financial system; (4) greater mobility of the labor force; (5) greater administrative efficiency. The Economic Council was ordered to prepare a new plan. In March 1968, the cabinet approved the Economic and Social Development Plan (1967–72). The three most important goals of the plan were: (1) price stabilization; (2) economic efficiency; (3) social development. The average real rate of increase in GNP during the period from fiscal 1967 to 1972 was to be kept to 8.3 percent (GNP in fiscal 1972 in 1960 prices, ¥40,200 billion, nominal value, ¥61,710 billion; per capita national income, ¥470,000); the increase in consumer prices was to be brought down to 3 percent by fiscal 1972; private equipment investment was to grow at an average yearly rate of 10.1 percent; over the five years, a total of ¥27,500 billion was to be invested in the infrastructure (average yearly rate of increase, 10.1 percent); the government was to finance the construction of 3 million of the 7.3 million homes to be built during the period.

The boom which started in 1966 wrought havoc with the target figures of the plan (nominal GNP in fiscal 1970 ¥73,213.7 billion), and in April 1970, the Economic Council submitted a new economic and social development plan. In May 1970, the Economic Planning Agency announced a revision of the New National Comprehensive Development Plan which contains projections up to fiscal 1985. The original overall development plan had been drafted in 1962 and had been updated in 1969. The New Economic and Social Development Plan incorporated four objectives which MITI had set forth as the basic lines of Japan's economic policy in November 1969: (1) internationalization of the economy; (2) qualitative improvement of the standard of living and the environment; (3) prevention of pollution; (4) price stability. The average real rate of growth of GNP was fixed at 10.6 percent, the nominal rate at 14.7 percent (GNP at market prices in fiscal 1975, ¥141,990 billion); the average yearly rate of increase in consumer prices was estimated at 4.4 percent.

The plan did not explicitly lay down priorities but, judging by the target figures, placed the strongest emphasis on the improvement of the infrastructure. In addition to a large increase in fiscal capital investment (total for 1970–75, ¥5.5 trillion) and private residential construction, a relatively large increase was foreseen in social security benefits (in view of the present low level of these payments, it seems doubtful that they will become sufficient). The principle of "high welfare, high burdens" is to be applied to the social sphere (the second part of the slogan will certainly be achieved while the first part will remain a vision). Social insurance premiums were to be adjusted to incomes and the financial position of all social insurance systems reexamined every five years. Compared with the Western countries, where taxes equal 30 percent of GNP, taxes were too low in Japan (about 20 percent of GNP); the corporation tax should be increased and a larger part of the revenues raised by indirect taxes.

Expenditures for environmental improvement (sewers, garbage disposal, parks) are to be expanded almost six times (from ¥430.2 billion in the years 1964–69 to ¥2,501 billion in the years 1970–75) and the private sector is to share the burden of building up the infrastructure. The users or beneficiaries will have to pay for the improvements. What the government has in mind is that private developers will have to provide the land for public facilities or even build these facilities. The plan does not mention how the impact of these requirements on the price of land will be neutralized—the construction of new roads, railroads, airports, and similar facilities has been an important factor in the enormous rise of land prices.

The plan propounds the principle—correct in itself—that less money should be spent on repairing damage ("backward-looking expenditures") and more on building new installations ("forward-looking expenditures"). Prices are to be stabilized by controlling aggregate demand, modernizing low productivity sectors, stimulating competition (abolition of cartels), enlarging the share of imports in satisfying domestic demand, and reducing prices controlled by the government.

2 BUDGET

Although the plans attempted a certain quantitative correlation between the targets of the various sectors, they were largely a collection of sectoral programs. Usually, the plans and forecasts of the various sectors are worked out by subcommittees; another subcommittee then attempts to unify and harmonize the different plans. The subcommittees are not organized on any systematic principle but according to more or less cohesive problems. In this way, the formulation of the policies incorporated in these plans duplicated one of the basic weaknesses of Japan's fiscal policy: the prevalence of particular interests and the neglect of the whole. Although the budget is compiled by the Ministry of Finance, the original requests are submitted by the individual ministries and agencies. Each ministry formulates its requests from a strictly departmental point of view, trying to get as much money as possible for the programs under its jurisdiction.

In the implementation of the overall economic plans, the operative plans for which budgetary appropriations are provided are the sectoral programs, e.g., the plans for road building, sewer construction, or housing, for which the ministry in charge puts in specific requests which may or may not be related to the overall forecasts. The Ministry of Finance attempts to reconcile the sectoral demands with available resources but does not and cannot establish an order of national priorities and, on this basis, evaluate the usefulness of the single programs or their relevance to national goals. The budget, therefore, does not reflect the public needs of the country but the power of the various governmental agencies. For each department, its own well-being is the basic consideration, then the interests of its clientele insofar as they contribute to the present or future well-being of the department or its officials. There is, of course, no guarantee that the ministries and agencies concern themselves with all the interests needing attention; on the contrary, given the evolution of the administrative structure by historical accretion, the chances are that some interests, people, and problems remain outside the jurisdictional purview of the governmental agencies. Being outside the established order, new problems or requirements may long remain unattended. Naturally, if a project involves money or power (e.g., the construction of oil pipe lines), a number of ministries may claim jurisdiction over it. Another consequence of the system is its orientation toward production, for most ministries are concerned with the producers of goods or the purveyors of services. Since no ministry took care of the consumers, they were made wards of the Economic Planning Agency which is also in charge of prices. Lacking any executive function, about all the agency can do is to make surveys.

The final approval of the budget by the Diet is a purely ceremonial matter; of real importance are the attempts by pressure groups of dietmen representing special interest groups to get more money for their clientele. The most influential pressure group is the farm bloc, and this group has repeatedly tried to intimidate the government and the Diet by having its constituents demonstrate in or around the Diet. The veterans' group is another very successful pressure group: veterans' pensions and benefit payments to survivors have risen from ¥49,999 million in fiscal 1953 (when pensions for veterans were revived) to ¥299,930 million in fiscal 1971, although the number of beneficiaries should have decreased. The pressure groups are particularly influential in restoring appropriations curtailed by the Ministry of Finance. Big business does not rely on pressure groups but on individual politicians; its influence, therefore, depends on the power constellation in each particular case. The automobile industry, for example, was unable to block Kakuei Tanaka's new automobile tax. The opposition parties have little say on the budget; they can only use the committee meetings to expose waste and corruption—of which there is a great deal.

The food control special account is only one of the expenditure categories whose growing deficits arouse much debate but where political inhibitions prevent the government from attacking the root of the evils. Government control of rice distribution should have ended in 1955 at the latest; it was kept in force to secure the farm vote for the Liberal-Democratic party. Pressure by politicians compels the Japan National Railways to keep unprofitable and unnecessary lines running and even build new ones while the deficit from current operations makes capital accumulation impossible and, in the absence of new capital contributions, obliges JNR to finance new construction by borrowing. The third account which is constantly deep in the red is national health insurance where the politically powerful Japan Medical Association complicates efforts at rationalization.

For fiscal 1968, the government adopted the principle of an "overall" budget, i.e., that all expenditures should be included in the original budget and no supplementary budget adopted. The Ministry of Finance was of the opinion that no stimulation was needed and that the emphasis in spending should be shifted to the latter half of the fiscal year since ¥300 billion for public works had been deferred from fiscal 1967 and was available for spending

National Budget and Related Indicators

| Fiscal year | Expenditures on general accounts | | | | Fiscal loan & investment program | | | | Government purchases of goods & services | | Nominal rate of increase in GNP | Ratio of general accounts to GNP | |
| | Original budget | | Incl. supplementary budgets | | Original budget | | Incl. supplementary budgets | | | | | Original budget | Incl. suppl. budgets |
	¥ billion	Rate of increase %	¥ billion	Rate of increase %	¥ billion	Rate of increase %	¥ billion	Rate of increase %	¥ billion	Rate of increase %	%	%	%
1960	1,569.7	10.6	1,765.2	16.7	606.9	13.9	625.1	11.2	2,674.0	15.8	19.1	9.7	10.3
1961	1,952.8	24.4	2,107.4	19.4	773.7	27.5	830.3	32.8	3,289.7	23.0	22.5	9.8	10.6
1962	2,426.8	24.3	2,563.8	21.6	905.2	17.0	951.3	14.6	4,053.2	23.2	9.1	11.2	11.8
1963	2,850.0	17.4	3,056.8	19.3	1,109.7	22.6	1,206.8	26.9	4,597.1	13.5	18.1	11.1	12.0
1964	3,255.4	14.2	3,340.5	9.3	1,340.2	20.8	1,430.5	18.5	5,328.0	15.8	15.5	11.0	11.3
1965	3,658.1	12.4	3,744.7	12.1	1,620.6	20.9	1,776.4	24.2	6,176.1	15.9	10.6	11.2	11.5
1966	4,314.3	17.9	4,477.1	19.6	2,027.3	25.1	2,085.4	17.3	7,060.7	14.3	16.7	11.3	11.8
1967	4,950.9	14.8	5,203.4	16.2	2,388.4	17.9	2,498.8	19.8	8,177.3	15.8	17.5	11.1	11.7
1968	5,818.6	17.5	5,917.3	13.7	2,699.0	13.0	2,784.6	11.5	9,291.5	13.6	17.8	11.0	11.1
1969	6,739.6	15.8	6,930.9	17.1	3,077.0	14.0	3,208.0	15.2	10,187.8	9.6	17.9	10.7	11.0
1970	7,949.8	18.0	8,213.1	18.5	3,579.9	16.3	3,794.0	18.3	12,252.0	20.2	16.4	10.8	11.2
1971	9,414.3	18.4	9,658.9	17.6	4,280.4	19.6	4,913.7	29.9	14,750.0	20.8	10.1	11.7	12.0

Notes: 1. Rate of increase: rate of increase over preceding fiscal year.
2. Data on government purchases of goods and services and GNP for fiscal 1971 are forecasts.

in the first half (instead of the usual ratio of four in the first and six in the latter half, the spending ratio should be three in the first and seven in the latter half). The original fiscal 1968 budget, therefore, amounted to ¥5,818.6 billion, 17.5 percent higher than the original budget for fiscal 1967. But in February 1969, a supplementary budget was approved which brought total expenditures to ¥5,917.3 billion, an increase of 13.7 percent over the preceding fiscal year. The increase in the rice price paid to the farmers was given as the reason for abandoning the principle of an overall budget; the real reason was that the natural increase in tax revenues was higher than expected.

The final 1970 budget (i.e., including the supplementary budgets) was 4.65 times larger than the final budget for fiscal 1960, an average yearly rate of increase of 16.6 percent.

In the same period, the size of the fiscal loan and investment program expanded 6.07 times, equivalent to an average yearly rate of increase of 19.8 percent. On the basis of the government's estimates for fiscal 1970, nominal GNP was 4.8 times higher than in fiscal 1960 (average yearly rate of increase 17.0 percent), investment in producers' durable equipment 5.2 times (17.9 percent), residential construction 8.25 times (23.5 percent), and personal consumption expenditures 4.2 times (15.5 percent). Comparatively speaking, therefore, the budget has just kept pace with the economy. The trouble is that the budget does not represent the most economical allocation of resources and that the increase in the size of the budget has also increased the volume of misdirected funds.

The expected natural increase in revenues forms the basis for fixing the framework of the budget. When the first half of the fiscal year is passed, the Ministry of Finance begins to collect budget requests for the coming fiscal year from the various ministries and agencies. The Ministry of Finance then plans the necessary surgical operations to cut down these requests, which usually exceed by a large margin the expected allocations, to the size of the previously established budget frame. (In 1970, the prime minister asked his colleagues to keep the increase in budget requests down to 25 percent.) When the Ministry of Finance announces the draft of the budget to be submitted to the cabinet, the tough bargaining between the Ministry of Finance and the other ministries begins; assorted political bigwigs and representatives of pressure groups haggle over the restoration of some of the cuts. If no amount of wrangling can reconcile the opposing views, the issue is usually left to the wisdom of the prime minister. It is a sad fact that the Ministry of Finance is the only organ which tries to maintain some kind of restraint in spending while the elected representatives of the people, who are supposedly the guardians of the people's interests, seem to be hell-bent on spending.

Despite the much-advertised tax cuts, the government usually had more money than it expected at the beginning of the fiscal year. It is for this reason that one or more supplementary budgets dispose of the surplus cash in the course (and sometimes shortly before the end) of the fiscal year. The higher deficit in the food control special account or salary increases for government employees provide a convenient smokescreen for obscuring the fact that the government bilked the taxpayer in the first place and that the money is being spent not because a need exists but, true to Parkinson's Law, because the money is there. All settlements of accounts in recent years have shown that the government did not succeed in spending all revenue—certainly not for lack of trying!

The general accounts allocate funds for the ordinary functions of government and transfer payments; the main categories in fiscal 1971 are shown opposite (bottom).

Settlement of Accounts: Revenues

(In billions of yen)

Fiscal year	General accounts	Special accounts	Total	Minus Duplica-tions	Minus Debt amorti-zation	Net total	Agencies connected with the government
1960	1,961.0	3,939.2	5,900.2	1,972.6	61.6	3,866.0	1,634.4
1961	2,515.9	4,431.8	6,947.7	2,256.3	31.8	4,659.5	2,048.7
1962	2,947.6	4,798.4	7,746.0	2,444.4	23.3	5,278.3	2,369.3
1963	3,231.2	5,383.3	8,614.5	2,739.0	38.1	5,837.4	2,672.0
1964	3,446.4	6,148.1	9,594.9	3,021.0	49.5	6,524.4	2,828.7
1965	3,773.1	7,216.0	10,989.1	3,526.6	20.8	7,441.7	3,303.2
1966	4,552.1	8,658.3	13,210.5	4,504.1	8.5	8,697.9	3,865.6
1967	5,299.4	10,747.6	16,047.0	5,662.1	63.7	10,321.2	4,219.1
1968	6,059.9	13,408.9	19,468.8	7,406.1	27.2	12,035.6	4,788.4

Settlement of Accounts: Expenditures

(In billions of yen)

Fiscal year	General accounts	Special accounts	Total	Minus Duplica-tions	Minus Debt amorti-zation	Net total	Agencies connected with the government
1960	1,743.1	3,555.1	5,298.2	1,967.8	61.6	3,268.7	1,429.7
1961	2,063.5	3,959.2	6,022.7	2,250.8	31.8	3,740.0	1,847.2
1962	2,556.6	4,283.6	6,840.2	2,442.5	23.3	4,374.4	2,174.7
1963	3,044.3	4,785.9	7,830.2	2,732.7	38.1	5,059.3	2,472.1
1964	3,311.0	5,557.6	8,868.6	3,019.3	49.5	5,799.8	2,695.3
1965	3,723.0	6,406.4	10,129.4	3,522.5	20.8	6,586.1	3,134.6
1966	4,459.2	7,669.9	12,129.1	4,499.7	8.5	7,620.9	3,612.1
1967	5,113.0	9,572.3	14,685.3	5,653.1	63.7	8,968.6	4,039.2
1968	5,937.1	11,902.7	17,839.8	7,398.1	27.2	10,414.6	4,544.8

	¥ million	%
Social security	1,344,080	14.2
Education	1,078,875	11.3
Debt service	319,340	3.3
Pensions	336,005	3.6
Transfer payments to local governments	2,054,424	21.8
Defense	670,902	7.1
Public works	1,665,591	17.7
Trade promotion & economic cooperation	101,103	1.7
Promotion of small enterprises	57,907	0.6
Transfer to food control special account	463,372	4.9
Transfer to industrial investment special account	80,300	0.8
Other	1,102,416	11.6
Reserve	140,000	1.4
Total	9,414,315	100.0

The special accounts handle funds for purposes beyond the scope of the government's administrative activities. The official classification is enterprise accounts, control accounts, insurance accounts, financing accounts, and accounting accounts; they cover public works (road construction, harbor construction, railroad construction, and flood control), government enterprises and services (alcohol monopoly, forest administration, postal services, and state hospitals), governmental financial and insurance systems (Trust Fund Bureau, foreign exchange fund, industrial investment, and about fifteen different insurance systems), and the government's purchases and sales of rice and other foodstuffs (the transfer to the food control special account is to offset the deficit in the account arising from the difference in the price paid to producers and the price paid by wholesalers to the extent that the deficit cannot be offset by higher prices for imported grain and flour which are also handled by the account).

The agencies connected with the government are the public corporations such as Japan National Railways, Nippon Telegraph and Telephone Corporation, the Monopoly Corporation, and the financial institutions of the government (Japan Development Bank, Export-Import Bank, etc.)

The Fiscal Loan and Investment Program provides funds for special accounts, public corporations, and special corporations (i.e., semigovernmental corporations) and organizations through which the government channels subsidies; a large part of these funds is allocated to governmental financial institutions; (in fiscal 1971: Japan Development Bank, ¥286.0 billion; Export-Import Bank, ¥379.0 billion; People's Finance Corporation, ¥277.6 billion; Small Business Finance Corporation, ¥273.6 billion; and Housing Loan Corporation, ¥282.9 billion). In fiscal 1971, total funds allocated to housing under this program amounted to ¥698.8 billion; road construction, ¥349.1 billion; small enterprises, ¥564.2 billion; the Japan National Railways, ¥427.4 billion; and local bodies, ¥710.6 billion. The fund sources for the program are shown below (fiscal 1971).

	¥ billion
Industrial investment special account	85.3
Trust Fund Bureau	3,133.4
Postal savings	1,350.0
Welfare annuities	946.6
People's annuities	194.9
Postal life insurance	495.0
Bonds & borrowing	566.7
Government-guaranteed debentures	300.0
Total	4,280.4

Expenditures of local governments in fiscal 1971 were budgeted at ¥9,717.2 billion, an increase of 19.6 percent over the preceding year. Local taxes provided ¥4,055.0 billion of the required revenues; transfer from central government revenues, ¥2,046.4 billion; share of the Treasury in local projects, ¥2,393.5 billion; issues of local bonds, ¥447.1 billion; fees, ¥137.1 billion; and miscellaneous revenues, ¥503.3 billion.

The government feared that the Nixon shock might lead to a full-fledged recession and the business world clamored for increased government spending to prop up sagging demand. Although revenues fell behind the expected increase, the government included a cut of ¥165 billion in the income tax as an additional antirecession measure. Bond issues were to provide for the largest part of the revenues required for the supplementary budget submitted to the Diet in October 1971. Expenditures under the supplementary budget amounted to ¥230 billion for public works, ¥124 billion to cover pay raises of government employees, and ¥7.5 billion in subsidies for small enterprises. The deficiency in budgeted revenues resulting from lower tax income was estimated at ¥380 billion which, together with the tax cut, created a deficit of ¥545 billion. Through a reshuffling of accounts, the net increase in the supplementary budget was kept to ¥245 billion on general accounts; the required additional revenues of ¥790 billion were to be raised by bond issues.

The government expected to have an exchange gain of about ¥20 billion on imports of wheat, feed, and weapons from the revaluation of the yen.

Like the government's overall policies, the budget is industry oriented and seriously biased in favor of industry. Direct subsidies to industry (coal mining, shipping) are not as high as those paid to the farmers (the cumulative deficit in the food control special account —which is only a part of the costs of the economic nonsense incorporated in the government's agricultural policies—amounts to about ¥2.5 trillion, and the loss from the surplus stock of rice may come to another ¥1 trillion), but a large part of the funds channeled through the government's financial institutions is for the benefit of business, particularly big business. The problem of malinvestment or misinvestment of savings forced from taxpayers or borrowed from individual savers and frozen into shapes decided by the state is not peculiar to Japan, but it is critical here because the scarcity of capital requires stricter adherence to investment worthiness.

The sad truth is that cost effectiveness is of no concern in budgetary planning. The government's spending decisions are political and not economic decisions. This does not mean that there are no economic needs or that all budgetary expenditures are uneconomical. Economic rationality is not the yardstick measuring a good many budgetary allocations but political expediency and the benefit accruing to the Liberal-Democratic party. The inadequacies of the infrastructure provide ample opportunities for spending whatever money is available, but the government has never figured out what the country can afford to spend for these purposes. The official programs or "visions" are not based on an analysis of present conditions, alternative ways of improvement, and selection of the most effective method. They invariably represent abstract solutions to abstract problems and the plans selected for execution offer political bait or pay political debts.

A few years ago, the question whether Japan was becoming a socialist state was seriously debated. There is no reason to expect Japan to imitate the social or economic policies of Soviet Russia or Sweden, to say nothing of the People's Republic of China, but it is certainly true that the degree of direct and indirect state control over the economy in general and the country's capital resources in particular is far greater than in Western countries. The funds collected from the private sector through postal savings and life insurance as well as the other governmental insurance systems are channeled into state enterprises, financial institutions of the government, agencies for public works, and special corporations. These funds and those raised through public bond issues are subject to financing and investment decisions which are politically biased and of doubtful economic value.

3 TAXES

Japan's tax system has remained basically unchanged since the reforms adopted as a result of the Shoup mission in the summer of 1949. The central government collects about double the amount of tax revenues of local governments; the tax income of prefectures is somewhat higher than that of municipalities and other local authorities. In order to supplement local revenues, the central government shares a certain part of its revenues with the local authorities and takes over a certain part of their expenditures (salaries of school teachers and costs of public works, particularly roads). In addition, local governments raise revenue through various enterprises; local transportation services (chiefly bus lines) are seldom profitable but local authorities can license races (horse, cycle, and motorboat races) and many municipalities manage establishments connected with tourism, recreation, or amusement. In Tokyo, Governor Minobe renounced the income from racing on account of the social and moral problems involved in gambling. The composition of tax revenues is given below.

Tax Receipts of National Government (fiscal 1969)

	¥ million
Total tax revenue	6,023,857
Income tax	2,005,616
Corporation tax	2,008,713
Inheritance tax	103,086
Liquor tax	557,754
Gasoline excise	438,982
Commodity excise	302,498
Local road tax	79,487
Customs & tonnage duty	331,252

If income from revenue stamps and the profit from government monopolies is included, the total tax burden amounted to ¥6,455,384 million. Taxes not specified in the above list are the sugar excise, tax on petroleum gas, playing cards tax, transaction tax, securities transaction tax, transit tax, and admission tax.

Local Taxes (fiscal 1969)

	¥ billion
Total tax revenue of prefectures	1,727.6
Prefectural inhabitants' tax	326.1
Business tax	779.5
Tobacco consumption tax	79.9
Consumption tax	107.4
Automobile tax	141.1
Total tax revenue of cities, towns & villages	1,362.6
Municipal inhabitants' tax	562.2
Municipal property tax	491.9
Tobacco consumption tax	140.1
Electricity & gas tax	85.8

The inhabitants' tax is based on the income tax; the tobacco tax is turned over to local governments from the revenues of the Monopoly Corporation; the consumption tax is levied on food and drink consumed in eating and drinking establishments.

The ratio of the tax burden to national income is given below.

Fiscal year	National income ¥ billion	Tax burden			Ratio of tax burden to national income	
		Total ¥ billion	National ¥ billion	Local ¥ billion	Total tax burden %	National taxes %
1960	13,269.1	2,547.7	1,801.5	744.2	19.3	13.6
1961	15,755.1	3,134.2	2,227.7	906.5	19.9	14.1
1962	17,729.8	3,447.4	2,390.7	1,056.7	19.4	13.5
1963	20,607.2	3,944.6	2,731.7	1,212.7	19.1	13.3
1964	23,329.3	4,558.8	3,159.2	1,399.6	19.5	13.5
1965	25,977.4	4,829.1	3,279.7	1,549.4	18.6	12.6
1966	30,326.4	5,431.6	3,663.0	1,768.6	17.9	12.1
1967	35,913.9	6,546.3	4,396.8	2,149.5	18.3	12.3
1968	42,467.0	7,903.9	5,323.8	2,580.1	18.8	12.6
1969	49,319.3	9,545.6	6,455.9	3,090.2	19.3	13.1

The national taxes include revenue stamps and profit from government monopolies.

According to the Ministry of Finance, Japan's income tax is low compared with abroad because the ceiling on tax exempt income is relatively high while rates are lower. The ministry published the following table which compares minimum taxable wage or salary income in the leading industrial countries.

(In yen)

	Single	Married couple	Married couple with 1 child	Married couple with 2 children	Married couple with 3 children
Japan 1970	347,919	587,528	741,329	900,185	1,059,041
Average year under 1971 Tax Law	393,416	646,281	812,814	984,908	1,153,846
United States (1969 amendments to Internal Revenue Act)	621,000	846,000	1,071,000	1,296,000	1,521,000
United Kingdom (1970 Finance Law)	361,152	516,672	644,544	772,416	927,936
West Germany (1969 amendments to Tax Law)	336,391	501,636	619,668	784,913	961,961
France (1970 amendments to tax system)	450,110	702,195	937,215	1,008,275	1,170,325

Note: For Japan, deductible social security payments have been deducted; for West Germany, deductions also include social security payments. Premiums for social security insurance have not been deducted for the United States, the United Kingdom, and France. Foreign currencies have been converted at the following rates: $1=¥360; £1=¥864; 1DM=¥98.36; 1 Fr.frc.=¥64.82.

The revision initiated by the Shoup mission had shifted the direction of Japan's tax policy from reliance on indirect taxes to greater emphasis on income taxes (which had already become the main source of revenue through the 1940 reform of the income tax system). A stiff progressive rate started with a 20 percent tax on a taxable yearly income of ¥50,000 and went up to a rate of 55 percent on a taxable income of ¥500,000 (the basic deduction was ¥25,000; deduction for each dependent ¥12,000). As a result of these high rates, revenue from income taxes accounted for 38 percent of all tax revenue in fiscal 1950. From fiscal 1951 on, the Income Tax Law has been revised every year (with the exception of 1960), but no revision of the tax rates was carried out between 1962 and 1969. In 1957, a tax revision raised the basic tax-exempt income from ¥80,000 to ¥90,000; the rate for the lowest income tax bracket was fixed at 10 percent instead of 15 percent applicable to a taxable income of ¥50,000. The highest tax class was made to start at ¥50 million (tax rate 70 percent) instead of at ¥5 million (tax rate 65 percent). The ceiling of the lowest bracket was raised to ¥100,000 in 1959 and to ¥150,000 in 1961. In 1962, the basic exemption was fixed at ¥100,000 and the rate on taxable incomes lower than ¥100,000 was set at 8 percent; the highest rate was changed to 75 percent and made applicable to incomes above ¥60 million. In December 1968, the Taxation System Council recommended that the lowest rate be fixed at 10 percent on a taxable income of ¥300,000 and the highest at 75 percent on a taxable income of ¥80 million; this recommendation was carried out in two steps in fiscal 1969 and 1970. In order to encourage capital accumulation, deduction of premium payments for life insurance was introduced in 1951 (partially extended to nonlife insurance), separate taxation of interest and dividend payments started in 1963 (a tax credit for dividends had already been allowed in 1948), and, in 1965, the taxpayer was given the choice of having dividend income taxed separately or of including it in his tax return.

The adjustment of the income tax to the inflationary rise in incomes, therefore, was chiefly in the form of raising the level of the lowest taxable income and increasing deductions (in fiscal 1971, the lowest taxable income of a single wage earner was ¥382,042; the basic deduction for a wage earner ¥190,000, deduction for spouse ¥190,000, deduction for other dependents ¥130,000). This exempted families with incomes below the average expenditure level from income taxes, but the bulk of Japan's wage and salary earners moved rapidly into higher income brackets and tax classes so that a large part of the increase in nominal wages was canceled by higher prices and higher taxes. Hence, from fiscal 1959 to fiscal 1969, national tax revenue increased 5.0 times and revenues from corporation taxes 5.1 times, but revenues from income taxes 7.2 times. In fiscal 1969, revenues from income and corporation taxes were almost equal and represented an identical 33.2 percent of total tax income, but, in fiscal 1959, the share of income taxes had been 23.1 percent and that of corporation taxes 32.6 percent. As mentioned above, the government's so-called tax reductions are merely a publicity ploy; they reduce only a part of the natural increase in tax revenues (the Tax System Research Council once recommended 25 percent of the anticipated natural tax increase as a desirable proportion of the tax reduction, but the actual reductions always remained below this ratio). The progressive tax rate has produced a significant shift in the burden.

In 1966, Professor Masashi Oshima of Doshisha University filed suit against the Tax Administration Agency and asked for nullification of the income tax because it violated the rule of equality and nondiscrimination laid down in Article 14 of the Constitution. The professor based his claim on the following reasons: (1) the deductions allowed under the Tax

Percentage Distribution Fiscal 1968 of Income Tax Revenues by Income Classes

(In percent)

Income classes Taxable income	Share in number of taxpayers	Share in income	Share in income tax revenues
Over ¥5 million	1.5	17	43.5
¥2 – 5 million	9.5	24.5	32
¥1 – 2 million	22.5	25	16.5
¥700,000 – 1 million	23	16	5
¥500,000 – 700,000	22.5	11	2
Under ¥500,000	21	6.5	1

Law do not cover the actual expenses incurred by the wage and salary earner in the course of his employment; (2) the tax privileges accorded medical practitioners, farmers, and the recipients of interest and dividend income put a relatively heavier burden on wage earners; (3) the tax "bite" is higher for wage income earners than for those filing income returns. The state (Ministry of Finance) had this rebuttal: (1) everything wage earners need for their work is provided by the employer; (2) a large part of commuting expenses is borne by the employer and is tax-exempt; (3) the deductions allowed under the Tax Law greatly exceed necessary expenses and also compensate for the early payment involved in withholding at source; (4) it is practically impossible to distinguish between general consumption expenditures and expenditures required for work. The suit is still winding its way through the courts.

A popular saying has it that a wage earner pays 90 percent of the taxes he ought to pay, a doctor 60 percent, and a farmer 40 percent. A survey in the latter half of 1970 (September 14–18), covering 6,000 persons in 674 different localities, revealed a fairly widespread dissatisfaction with the existing tax system. A few of the results of the survey are summarized below.

	Office workers	Super-visory employees	Blue collar workers	Professionals, individual proprietors	Engaged in agriculture, forestry & fisheries
Tax burden heavy	61%	64%	61%	52%	50%
Tax burden unequal	82	84	74	52	35
Tax burden fair	9	7	12	26	32

Of all respondents, 23 percent thought that the tax system was fair but 60 percent considered it unfair; 68 percent thought that the system favored certain classes. Tradespeople were suspected by 14 percent of the respondents of being unduly privileged and 13 percent asserted the same of politicians (68 percent thought that politicians cheated in their tax returns, only 10 percent believed that they were honest); other classes the respondents singled out as being "given a break" were managers, doctors, other professional people, "the rich," actors, farmers, and corporations.

The corporation tax, first adopted in 1899 and completely revised in 1940, was again reformed in 1950. Profits in each accounting period were taxed at a rate of 35 percent; the rate was raised to 42 percent in 1952 so as to tax the high profits gained in the Korean War boom; at the same time, however, special tax measures (e.g., the tax-deductible reserves for price fluctuations introduced in that year) kept the actual tax burden low. The tax rate was reduced to 40 percent in 1955; 38 percent, in 1958; 37 percent, in 1960; and 35 percent in 1966. Accelerated depreciation, reserves for market development, and tax deductible expenses for entertainment are a few of the special tax privileges granted to corporations. Thanks to the enormous expansion of the economy, the share of revenues from the corporation tax rose from 15 percent in 1950 to over 30 percent. Industry often pleads for a reduction in the corporation tax rate; the low ratio of equity capital (17.4 percent at the end of 1970) is given as the main reason for this demand. Industry also favors a return to the pre-Shoup policy, of deriving a relatively larger share of revenue from indirect taxes, which is being considered by the government and may be implemented with the change to a value added tax system.

Cases of tax evasion or tax fraud by individuals and corporations are numerous. Between July 1969 and June 1970, the Tax Administration Agency discovered about 67,000 cases of tax fraud by the self-employed, who had concealed ¥203.3 billion in income and failed to pay ¥33.7 billion in taxes and penalties. Doctors, money-lenders, operators of pinball parlors, real estate brokers, actors, and actresses were numerous among the tax delinquents. In the same period, a random survey of 151,000 corporations revealed that 71,000 firms had failed to pay ¥10.7 billion in taxes.

The actual way tax collection from individual proprietors, members of the free professions, artists, writers, baseball players, and cabaret hostesses is handled indicates the approach the tax officials take for detecting fraud or evasion. Each tax office has a "super-secret" set of lists known as *tora no maki* (literally "Tiger Roll," i.e., secrets of the trade; crib). These lists give the sales and average rates of return (ratio of profits to sales) for the various stores and establishments and the tax rates applicable to them as well as the tax rates on the income of individuals. Annual sales of a high-class bar (i.e., in which a large bottle of beer sells for more than ¥300) are estimated at ¥1,301,000 per employee or ¥556,000 per chair; the tax rate applicable to bars in large cities is 59.5 percent. In the case of corporations, the situation is similar; the tax office figures out what the company should pay and, if the return of the firm remains below this estimate, it will investigate.

4. BOND ISSUES

For a long time following the end of the postwar inflation, the principle of fiscal balance had been adhered to. During the period of rapid expansion, the natural increase in tax revenue permitted a steep increase in government spending. But the slowdown of the economy brought a deceleration in the increase in tax revenue expected for fiscal 1965 which would have necessitated a revision of the government's spending plans. The issue of bonds to stimulate the economy as well as safeguards to prevent unrestrained deficit financing had already been discussed in 1965, and opinions were divided on such problems as their effects on monetary policy and the money market, interest rates, management guidelines, and amortization. For the first time since 1951, long-term government bonds were issued in the beginning of 1966. Since existing legislation forbade the issuance of bonds for general expenditures, the bonds were called "construction bonds" and, officially, the proceeds were to be used for financing special projects. In order to prevent an inflationary expansion of the money supply, the bonds were not to be taken over by the Bank of Japan but to be absorbed by the market. For the months from January to March 1966, bonds amounting to ¥230 billion were to be floated; the Trust Fund Bureau was to take over ¥120 billion and the market (banks and securities companies) ¥110 billion. Actual sales started on January 28, 1966. For fiscal 1966, flotations were raised to ¥730 billion of which the Trust Fund Bureau was to buy ¥30 billion, while sales on the market were to dispose of ¥700 billion. The bonds were issued in monthly quotas fixed after consultation between the Ministry of Finance, the Bank of Japan, and the national bond underwriting syndicate comprising the commercial banks and securities companies organized in the National Bond Underwriters Promotion Association. Beginning with October 1966, the bonds were traded on the stock exchanges. Issues in fiscal 1966 actually amounted to ¥675 billion, providing 14.87 percent of the revenue on general account. Originally, the government had advocated bond issues because other sources of revenue were insufficient and bond issues were to be reduced if tax revenues became higher, but this policy was soon discarded and, for fiscal 1967, bond issues were increased to ¥810 billion (¥30 billion to be taken over by the Trust Fund Bureau), equivalent to 16.16 percent of the budgeted revenues.

In a report published on December 26, 1966, the Fiscal System Council discussed some of the problems involved in the flotation of bonds. The council expressed the opinion that the establishment of a sinking fund would have some undesirable features and would not constitute the most efficient use of funds; the flotation of new bonds should be relied on at least partially for amortization. According to existing legislation (Finance Law, Article 6), one-half of surplus funds had to be used for the amortization of outstanding bonds or other debt and an amortization plan had to be laid before the Diet (Article 4, Paragraph 2). This was interpreted to mean that the government had to state how much would be amortized in each fiscal year but that it would not be necessary to indicate how the money would be raised.

In order to facilitate the absorption of the bond issues, the Bank of Japan, on December 14, 1965, advanced ¥16 billion to short-term moneylenders (bill brokers) in Tokyo, Osaka, and Nagoya. Sales of the bonds floated in fiscal 1966 were as follows:

	¥ million	%
City banks	273,099	40.5
Local banks	134,708	19.9
Long-term credit banks	65,313	9.7
Trust banks	23,656	3.5
Mutual banks	23,656	3.5
National Federation of Credit Associations	23,656	3.5
Central Cooperative Bank of Agriculture and Forestry	23,656	3.5
Life insurance companies	23,656	3.5
Securities companies	83,600	12.4
(Individual investors	74,099	11.0)

At an issue price of ¥98.60 and an interest rate of 6.5 percent (maturity seven years), the yield of the bonds amounted to 6.795 percent. The underwriting syndicate received a 48 *sen* commission per ¥100; the securities companies charged a 68 *sen* handling fee per ¥100.

Under the rules laid down by the Bank of Japan, government bonds had to be held for one year before becoming eligible for open market operations; in 1967, therefore, the Bank of Japan began to buy bonds from the city banks. The arrangement was much criticized because it seemed an indirect way of having the Bank of Japan take over government bonds. Difficulties in marketing the bonds began in the summer of 1967. In June 1967, the call rate was raised by 1 *rin* which brought the borrower's rate of over-the-month call money to 7.483 percent. The agricultural credit institutions, which had been large bond buyers, found the call market more attractive. The expectation of a switch to a tight-money policy (the official discount rate was raised by 1 *rin* in September 1967 and window controls reintroduced) was another factor. As part of the fiscal measures taken to cool off the economy, the total of the national bonds to be sold on the market was reduced by ¥70 billion from ¥760 billion to ¥690 billion and the total of government-guaranteed debentures by ¥50 billion from ¥510 billion to ¥460 billion. In February 1968, the Chosei Nenkin pension fund took over ¥38 billion of national bonds. While the budget had counted on bond issues to provide 16.16 percent of the necessary revenues, they actually contributed 14.76 percent, less than in the preceding fiscal year. In August, the price of government bonds (issues maturing November 1973) traded on the market fell to ¥98 which made new emissions difficult. The issue target for fiscal 1967 was reduced to ¥700 billion and the underwriters as well as the Bank of Japan tried to convince the Ministry of Finance that the issue conditions had to be improved, i.e., that the issue price should be reduced. The securities companies were also dissatisfied with the government's failure to take stronger support measures. They also wanted to have the tax exemption granted to deposits (in order to promote saving, interest on deposits not exceeding ¥1 million and meeting the requirements of the National Savings Association Law is not taxed) extended to national bonds—a proposal which drew fire from the banking world.

For the bonds issued in February 1968, the issue price was lowered by 50 *sen* to ¥98.10, raising the yield to 6.90 percent. The Bank of Japan and the underwriting syndicate had urged a reduction by 60 *sen* whereas the Ministry of Finance wanted to keep the decrease to 40 *sen*; so a compromise price was adopted. Together with the adjustment of the price of national bonds, interest rates on government-guaranteed debentures, bank debentures, and loan trusts were revised.

Beginning April 1968, bonds with a face value of ¥50,000 were issued so as to facilitate sales to individual investors. Until then, denominations ranged from ¥100,000 to ¥10 million.

The Ministry of Finance considered the issuance of bonds with a maturity of ten years; these issues started in January 1972. On account of the difficulties in marketing bonds, issues were reduced to ¥640 billion in the budget for fiscal 1968 (about 11 percent of total revenues) and to ¥490 billion for fiscal 1969 (7.2 percent of total revenues); the Trust Fund Bureau took over ¥50 billion in fiscal 1968 and ¥30 billion in fiscal 1969. In recent years, the Ministry of Finance has usually fixed the amount of government-guaranteed debentures to be floated together with the national bond issues (fiscal 1969, ¥36 billion; fiscal 1970, ¥30 billion; fiscal 1971, ¥30 billion). The fiscal 1970 budget provided for the flotation of ¥430 billion in national bonds, but, when a supplementary budget for fiscal 1970 amounting to ¥230,320 million was drawn up in January 1971, the issues were reduced by

¥50 billion. For fiscal 1971, the original budget included ¥430 billion in bond issues (Trust Fund Bureau, ¥30 billion), but, on account of the prolonged business stagnation and the impact of the Nixon shock, revenues remained below the budgeted level and the government anticipated a deficiency of ¥380 billion. Moreover, in order to forestall a recession, income taxes were to be reduced by ¥165 billion and expenditures increased by a net ¥245 billion

National Government Debt
Outstanding Balances

(In millions of yen)

End of fiscal year	Total	Domestic bonds	Foreign currency bonds	Short-term bills		Short-term borrowing	
				Total	Food bills	Total	Special accounts
1959	1,252,970	459,803	81,655	578,263	328,178	132,747	83,678
1960	1,340,283	446,820	74,076	679,606	351,020	139,280	90,409
1961	1,222,946	436,353	56,334	581,163	307,107	149,044	100,382
1962	1,280,664	413,647	48,182	667,160	312,061	151,545	109,086
1963	1,184,564	424,501	46,356	551,615	270,556	162,091	119,869
1964	1,349,211	433,217	60,796	655,545	330,485	199,382	157,411
1965	1,766,562	688,331	57,331	718,554	406,090	302,345	260,641
1966	2,662,273	1,421,839	54,211	823,449	503,904	362,773	321,351
1967	3,818,406	2,155,011	58,471	1,205,645	840,051	399,278	357,856
1968	4,785,834	2,674,809	57,951	1,584,586	1,186,500	468,487	427,065
1969	5,479,362	3,077,523	57,973	1,825,455	1,368,391	518,410	476,988
1970	6,226,660	3,597,462	54,469	1,941,434	1,293,169	633,295	—

Source: Ministry of Finance

National Government Debt by Holder and Lender

(In millions of yen)

	March 1971	August 1971
Total	6,226,660	6,182,718
Government, total	2,437,909	2,999,831
Domestic bonds	1,189,739	1,729,249
Short-term bills	691,230	707,987
Borrowing (incl. temporary)	556,940	562,595
Bank of Japan, total	1,881,980	1,124,481
Domestic bonds	1,203,422	583,654
Short-term bills	678,558	540,827
Others, total	1,906,771	2,058,406
Domestic bonds	1,204,301	1,403,065
Foreign bonds	54,469	52,649
Short-term bills	571,646	526,619
Borrowing	76,355	76,073

Note: Government includes the Trust Fund Bureau, industrial investment special account, Postal Life Insurance, etc.
Source: Bank of Japan.

under a supplementary budget sent to the Diet in October 1971. The resulting deficit of ¥790 billion was to be covered by additional bond issues, so that total issues of national bonds in fiscal 1971 were to rise to a record ¥1,220 billion. This brought reliance on bond issues for budgetary revenues from 4.6 percent in the original budget to almost 13 percent. The market was to absorb ¥550 billion of the additional issues while the Trust Fund Bureau was to take over the remainder. Conditions were to remain the same for the ¥300 billion floated in the last months of 1971 but, starting with January 1, 1972, national bonds were to have a maturity of ten years and the underwriter's commission was to be raised from ¥0.50 per ¥100 to ¥0.55.

As shown in the above table, Japan's indebtedness has increased significantly in the last six years, and the flotation of bonds was the most important factor in this development. In itself, the debt is nothing to worry about but the change from a rather conservative to a less responsible fiscal policy is significant.

2 FISCAL AND MONETARY POLICIES

2 CREDIT POLICIES AND MONEY SUPPLY

1 CREDIT POLICIES

In the beginning of 1959, the economic outlook seemed not very promising and the government did not expect a large expansion. The monetary restraints, imposed in 1957 in order to restore equilibrium in the balance of payments, were gradually relaxed in the latter half of 1958 when the Bank of Japan lowered the official discount rate (first in June 1958, then again in September). In February 1959, the official discount rate was lowered for the third time, and, as on previous occasions, the Federation of Bankers Associations of Japan followed suit and, at the same time, replaced its "autonomous money rates" by the "standard money rate" system. In the course of the year, business became more active, but money remained readily available and the average interest rates on bank loans continued to fall until September.

On September 11, 1959, the Bank of Japan announced the enforcement of reserve deposit requirements. The adoption of this system had been under discussion for a long time and legislation to this effect had already been passed in 1957, but it had never been enforced.

Under the regulations announced by the Bank of Japan, banks were divided into two categories: those whose deposit balances exceeded ￥20 billion (as of March 31, 1959), and those under ￥20 billion. Banks of the first class were required to deposit a sum corresponding to 1.5 percent of their demand deposits and 0.5 percent of their time deposits with the central bank, while the rates were 0.75 percent and 0.25 percent for banks of the second class. These regulations were revised in October 1961, when the government again pursued a deflationary policy. This time, three categories were established: (1) banks with deposit balances exceeding ￥100 billion, for which the deposit requirements were fixed at 3.0 percent of demand deposits and 1.0 percent of time deposits; (2) for banks with deposits between ￥20 billion and ￥100 billion, the rates were set at 2.25 percent and 0.75 percent; (3) the rates remained the same, 0.75 percent and 0.25 percent, for banks with less than ￥20 billion in deposits.

Fund demand grew rapidly during the latter half of 1959, and the trend was accelerated by the need for repairing the typhoon damage in the Nagoya area (Ise Bay typhoon) on the one hand and, on the other, by rising prices. On December 1, 1959, the Bank of Japan raised the official discount rate—more as a warning signal than as an effective measure for curbing fund demand. The expansion was reflected in the note circulation of the Bank of Japan, which, for the first time, exceeded the ￥1 trillion mark at the end of the year. But despite the increase in bank loans (up ￥989.9 billion), outstanding loans of the Bank of Japan to city banks at the end of 1959 were below the level of a year earlier.

The expansion of the economy continued in 1960 (real growth of GNP: fiscal 1959 over fiscal 1968, 11.7 percent; fiscal 1960 over fiscal 1959, 13.3 percent; fiscal 1961 over fiscal 1960, 14.4 percent). Until the middle of the year, the Bank of Japan held to its line of checking a sudden expansion of the money supply and stressing preventive policies. Governor Masamichi Yamagiwa pursued two basic objectives: (1) elasticity of money rates, which would enable the money market to fulfill its function of adjusting supply to demand; (2) removal of the obstacles to the automatic supply-demand adjustment through elastic money rates, the most serious obstacles being the lack of bank liquidity, the high rate of external funds in the industrial capital structure, and the undeveloped securities market. But with the installation of the Ikeda cabinet, monetary policy underwent a drastic change. Ikeda's fundamental policies were: (1) an ample supply of funds to make a high rate of economic growth possible; and (2) lowering of money rates to reduce capital costs of enterprises and to improve their competitive position in world markets. Whereas Governor Yamagiwa and the bankers had envisaged lower interest rates as the effect of improved monetary elasticity, Ikeda, whose economic thinking was largely influenced by the patterns of a wartime, controlled economy, considered them as a means of implementing his short-term objectives. Consequently, the Ministry of Finance urged the city banks to lower their interest rates on deposits. Neither the Bank of Japan nor the city banks wanted to take this step, not only because the proposed reduction was contrary to the actual situation of the money market, but also because it would adversely affect their accumulation of deposits, which were already feeling the effects of the shift to direct investment. The Ministry of Finance, however, soon overcame the opposition of the banks by intimating, in the form of a proposal submitted by the Tax System Research Council, that (1) the tax privilege for income derived from interest would be allowed to expire at the end of March 1961, and that (2) the tax exemption for small deposits under the National Savings Association Law would be abolished. These measures would have hurt the banks even more than a reduction of the interest rates on deposits. On January 25, 1961, the official discount rate was lowered to 1.8 *sen* (6.57 percent per annum), and, on April 1, a general reduction of interest rates was effected. The rate of interest on postal savings was lowered to 5 percent on six-month time deposits and 5.5 percent on one-year time deposits, while the rate of interest on current deposits was set at 3.6 percent. The interest rates paid by the banks on time deposits were set at 4 percent for three months, 5 percent for six months, and 5.5 percent for one year. Rates on demand deposits were lowered by 0.1 *sen* per diem. Interest rates on trust deposits for two years were lowered by 0.5 percent to 6.3 percent, and those for five years by 0.43 percent to 7.07 percent; those on loan trusts were reduced to 6.3 percent and 7.37 percent, for two and five year trusts respectively. Yields on government bonds remained unchanged (long-term obligations, 6.432 percent; short-term bills, 6.023 percent), but returns on new debenture issues were lowered. The interest rate on long-term loans by the Industrial Bank or the Long-Term Credit Bank to electric power companies was reduced from 9.125 percent to 8.7 percent.

Despite the official policy of monetary relaxation, the call market remained very tight through 1960. After a period of relative calmness in the beginning of 1961, the demand for funds, not only on the part of city banks but also by securities companies increased sharply. Insurance companies, mutual banks, and credit cooperatives were the chief suppliers of these funds.

The large deficits on current account in the balance of payments at the beginning of 1961 created worry in some circles over the course of the economy. Governor Yamagiwa counseled caution and expressed the view that equipment investment was excessive. He contended that it was unsound to rely on the overall balance of international payments (the stand taken by the government) and stressed that an adjustment of current accounts was needed. In the course of May, Japan's representative business organizations expressed concern over the tempo of the expansion and the country's foreign exchange position. By June, the view that the investment fever was running too high and that an adjustment was necessary had found universal acceptance. Characteristically, the government did not cut back its own plans, but MITI brought pressure upon industry to reduce its investment programs. Unwilling to make money tighter by canceling the untimely lowering of the interest rates, the Ministry of Finance and the Bank of Japan urged the city banks to cut investment loans by 10 percent. On July 21, 1961, the Bank of Japan announced a raise of 0.1 *sen* in the official discount rate, bringing it to 1.9 *sen* per diem (6.935 percent per annum). At the same time, the discount rate for export bills was reduced to 1.2 *sen* per diem (4.38 percent per annum), the lowest since 1948. A second raise (again by 0.1 *sen*) announced on September 28 brought the official discount rate to 2 *sen* (7.3 percent). At the same time, the reserve ratio of the banks was increased. Interest rates on bank deposits and long-term loans were not raised, so that the difference between long-term and short-term rates widened and the bond market became less active.

The tight-money policy failed to slow down the economy immediately and it was only in 1962 that its effects were actually felt. But fund demand remained very pressing, because industry, instead of financing new investment, now found it necessary to finance large inventories, despite drastic cutbacks in production and a severe curtailment of operating rates.

The enforcement of the tight-money policy was tempered by some measures designed to relieve the friction caused by the deflation. In particular, efforts were made to prop up the sagging stock market. The Ministry of Finance increased the ceiling on new investment trusts to be set up by securities companies, allowing each firm a net increase of ¥20 billion instead of the former ¥18 billion. It also removed the ¥9 billion limitation on investments in call loans and bonds, so that these transactions were no longer held down to a certain limit.

Three times the Bank of Japan came to the help of the four major securities companies by extending loans secured by government bonds and corporate debentures.

For the same purpose of bolstering sagging stock prices, the Securities Finance Company raised the ceiling on some of its credits, while the regulations for credit transactions on the securities market were relaxed. The government similarly increased its help to small enterprises; ¥35 billion was channeled into the three public finance corporations serving small businesses, and the government took up ¥20 billion in financial debentures issued by these institutions. An additional ¥30 billion was made available to small enterprises between June and September 1962.

The banks found it increasingly difficult to satisfy the pressing fund demand of industry out of their own resources. As mentioned above, central bank credit made up the deficiency, and the situation became exceedingly tight in 1961, when, despite the various credit controls, borrowing from the Bank of Japan increased by one and a half times over the preceding year (advances of the Bank of Japan: end of 1960, ¥500.2 billion; end of 1961, ¥1,284.6 billion). In February 1962, loans and discounts of the Bank of Japan actually exceeded the note issue (¥1,318.2 billion as against ¥1,272.1 billion), and this situation lasted until October.

The balance of payments regained its equilibrium in June 1962 and, in October, some steps were taken to relax the monetary stringency. The official discount rate was lowered by 0.1 *sen*; and the penalty rates on bank borrowings from the central bank were reduced. Up to then, the penalty rate had been divided into two steps. For the first step, an additional 0.4 *sen* above the normal discount rate had been charged on loans above the ceiling fixed each month for each bank; for the second step, this additional rate had been 0.6 *sen*. The Bank of Japan now reduced the penalty rate to a uniform 0.3 *sen*. The ratio of reserve requirements was also lowered, effective November 1. For banks with deposits over ¥100 billion, the reserve ratio was reduced to 0.5 percent for time deposits and 1.5 percent for demand deposits; and the same ratios were adopted for banks holding deposits in excess of ¥20 billion but less than ¥100 billion. At the same time, the Bank of Japan decided to regulate the money supply in future by open-market operations. Up to then, additional currency was supplied almost exclusively through advances by the central bank to city banks, so that an expansion in the circulation of bank notes coincided with increased bank borrowings. From then on, the Bank of Japan endeavored to meet the credit requirements of the city banks by market operations (buying of bonds), which brought the system of currency supply more in line with the practice observed in the United States and elsewhere. But the system of direct borrowing from the central bank was not entirely discarded. The Bank of Japan fixed a ceiling for each bank based on its quarterly fund position. For loans in excess of this ceiling, the banks were charged an additional (punitive) rate of 1.0 *sen* per diem (the ordinary surcharge of 1.095 percent was applicable to a certain portion within the credit line).

Through the new arrangement, called the new financial adjustment system, the Bank of Japan hoped to correct some of the shortcomings in the money supply system. Because money had been supplied in the form of loans to the city banks, the result had been spiraling loan balances. This situation became chronic and made it impossible to adjust fund supply through the limitation of central bank credit. The use of market operations was expected to restore the initiative to the Bank of Japan. Buying operations were carried out with ordinary banks, long-term credit banks, and the foreign exchange bank; eligible paper was initially restricted to government-guaranteed debentures and buying was conditional on repurchase within three months (the term could be extended to one year). In January 1963, the definition of eligible paper was extended to include long-term government bonds, interest-bearing bank debentures, debentures of the electric power companies, and specified bonds of local governments.

On November 27, 1962, the Bank of Japan again lowered the discount rate by 0.1 *sen*, bringing it down to the level prevailing before the tight-money policy was put into effect (1.8 *sen*, 6.57 percent per annum). At the same time, the government resumed its drive for cheap money and, in quick succession, the official discount rate was lowered twice, on March 19, and on April 19, 1963, by 0.1 *sen* each time, so that the rate came down to 1.7 *sen* per diem (6.205 percent per annum), the lowest since 1955. The rate on export trade bills was reduced to 1.1 *sen* per diem (4.015 percent per annum) and the penalty rate (old system) by 0.2 *sen* to 0.1 *sen*.

In order to prevent its low-interest policy from unduly inflating credit and worsening the already precarious capital structure of industrial enterprises, the government proposed to apply the so-called World Bank formula to domestic bank credit. The plan foresaw fixing a certain standard for the ratio of liabilities to internal capital and the liquidity ratio (ratio of short-term liabilities to liquid assets). In this way, enterprises would be forced to increase their own capital and banks would be stopped from granting new loans to heavily indebted companies. The new method was to be enforced for the 301 largest corporations with a capital of over ¥3 billion and yearly sales in excess of ¥10 billion (the formula was not to apply to enterprises in the fields of shipping, chemical fertilizers, and coal mining, nor to road construction and other public works). Lending by the thirteen city banks, the Industrial Bank, and the Long-Term Credit Bank was to be subject to the new formula. At the same time the government hoped to rectify the overloan situation of the big banks and reduce the ratio of loans to deposits to 85:100 in the next five years. Tax incentives were contemplated to promote the incorporation of revaluation reserves into the capital while reducing the dividend rate. Further plans aimed at inducing enterprises to issue new shares at prevailing market prices rather than at par value.

In the beginning of 1963, signs of an economic recovery became discernible. The government had decided to liberalize foreign trade and thought it desirable to bring the Japanese system of interest rates more in line with overseas conditions. To this end, a normalization of the financial system was deemed necessary, which meant the lowering of short-term interest rates. In March, the Bank of Japan reduced the official discount rate by 1 *rin* and cut the surcharge on the standard penalty rate from 3 *rin* to 1 *rin*. Another reduction by 1 *rin* in April brought the official discount rate down to 1.6 *sen* (5.84 percent) and, in July, the application of the penalty rate within the credit line was discontinued. The window guidance of the Bank of Japan came to an end in May.

As a result of the buying operations carried out under the new financial adjustment system, the increase in advances of the Bank of Japan fell to ¥0.6 billion in 1962, as against ¥78.4 billion in 1961, but net purchases of government bonds and other debentures rose from zero to ¥99.5 billion. In 1963, the balance of outstanding loans decreased by ¥176.5 billion, but net additions of securities to the portfolio of the central bank amounted to ¥379.7 billion, which meant that the former supply of funds by loans had been replaced by the supply of funds through the purchase of securities.

In 1963, bank deposits showed the highest rate of increase since 1952; they rose from ¥12,119 billion at the end of 1962 to ¥15,648 billion at the end of 1963 (city banks, from ¥7,237 billion to ¥9,543 billion). Loans grew at the highest rate since the 1956–57 boom; outstanding loan balances were ¥11,495 billion at the end of 1962 and ¥14,563 billion at the end of 1963 (city banks 1962, ¥6,511 billion; 1963, ¥8,347 billion). Money had become more stringent due to the increase in tax revenues, the decrease in the excess of payments from the foreign exchange fund resulting from the decrease in the surplus in the balance of payments, and the increase in industrial production. But the fierce competition among banks led to a large increase in bank lending. In the fall of 1963, the Bank of Japan, by adjusting the volume of its market operations and lowering the credit lines, switched to a policy of monetary restraint, and, in December, the rate of reserve requirements was raised on all deposits except time deposits. Window controls were reimposed in January 1964 and, on March 18, the official discount rate was raised by 2 *rin* to 1.8 *sen* (6.57 percent). At the same time, the government increased the rate of import guarantee deposits, and the banks were ordered to redeposit these deposits with the central bank. In the spring of 1964, the Bank of Japan borrowed $80 million under a swap agreement for $150 million which had been concluded with the Federal Reserve Bank of New York in October 1963.

On January 10, 1964, the Bank of Japan revived its window guidance. In the quarter from January to March 1964, the city banks had to keep the increase in their loans to ¥233.3 billion, i.e., 10 percent lower than the increase in their loans in the January–March quarter of 1963. For the following quarters, the ceilings were as follows: April–June, ¥228.4 billion (−12 percent); July–September, ¥297.6 billion (−22 percent); October–December, ¥375.9 billion (−22 percent). The three long-term credit banks were allowed to increase their advances by ¥70.5 billion in the first quarter, 15 percent higher than the increase in the corresponding quarter of 1963, but, for the following quarters, the increase was to remain below the increase in the corresponding quarter of the preceding year: April–June, ¥65.5 billion (−4.5 percent); July–September, ¥73.5 billion (−3.7 percent); October–December, ¥71.5 billion (−6 percent). Similar restrictions were imposed on local banks with deposits exceeding ¥100 billion.

This method of limiting the expansion of credit seems to have given rise to a new yardstick referred to as "rate of marginal increase in borrowing," i.e., the rate of increase or decrease in the increase in borrowing compared with the same period of the year before.

In September 1964, the Ministry of Finance imposed stricter limitations on large credits of mutual banks and credit associations, but, in the same month, the Small Business Finance Corporation was given permission to raise additional funds by floating bonds (¥3 billion), the first time that this institution had recourse to the bond market. The budget for fiscal 1965 provided for a 20 percent increase in the lending of the three institutions for small enterprises to be used for unsecured small loans. All these measures were prompted by the sharp increase in business failures. The Federation of Bankers Associations announced that its member banks would provide ¥300 billion in year-end financing to small enterprises; for the same purpose, the National Association of Local Banks pledged ¥200 billion, the mutual banks ¥165 billion, and the credit associations ¥210 billion.

Following the increase in the official discount rate, the Federation of Bankers Associations, on March 19, 1964, announced an increase in the interest rate on loans (2.4 *sen* on loans over ¥3 million, 2.5 *sen* on those under ¥3 million; the rates remained the same for export financing, for which the Bank of Japan had not changed the discount rate). The trust banks and insurance companies also raised their interest rates on loans; the mutual banks and credit associations left their rates on loans to small enterprises unchanged but raised their interest rates on loans to banks.

In addition to the increase in the official discount rate, the Bank of Japan compressed the loanable funds of the city banks by enlarging the scope of its selling operations while restricting the scale of its buying (securities purchased by the Bank of Japan from city banks on condition of repurchase within a stipulated time). This restriction resulted in a sharp rise in the call money rates which had temporarily declined, and, in August of 1964, the rate on unconditional call money climbed to 11.31 percent, and the over-the-month rate to 13.14 percent. Unable to obtain central bank credit beyond their credit lines, the city banks greatly increased their borrowings from other financial institutions and relied heavily on call money; this shift in fund sources severely reduced their earnings.

The trade balance became favorable in July, thanks to the large increase in exports, but production and imports also remained high and it was only in autumn that output leveled off. The number of bankruptcies increased sharply; their number rose from 711 in the first quarter to 1,563 in the fourth quarter, while the number for the entire year (4,212) was more than double that in the preceding year (1,738). Despite the credit restraints, the rate of increase in the note issue remained high, chiefly on account of strong consumption demand; the increase slowed down in November and December.

In October 1964, the Bank of Japan decided on a gradual easing of the monetary squeeze (it was dubbed "installment plan relaxation") and advanced ¥32 billion to the short-term moneylenders (Tokyo call brokers, ¥26 billion; Osaka, ¥5 billion; Nagoya, ¥1 billion). It was the first time since July 1957 that the Bank of Japan had provided direct financing for the call market, under the so-called system of special financing, in the form of general loans. On December 16, the reserve deposit ratio was reduced and the official discount rate was lowered three times in succession, in January, April, and June 1965, dropping from 1.8 sen (6.57 percent) to 1.5 sen (5.48 percent). This brought the discount rate down to the lowest level since 1951. In the immediate postwar period, however, the official discount rate had been of no significance for monetary policy. The reserve deposit ratio was cut again in July 1965.

With the lifting of the credit restrictions, the unconditional call money rate dropped to 1.6 sen (5.84 percent). The low interest rates made it difficult to regulate the fund supply by the buying and selling of securities as foreseen in the new fund adjustment system. Actually, the Bank of Japan's purchases of securities conditioned on repurchase by the seller were similar to borrowings from the central bank collateralized by securities. In the absence of an effective bond market, the price of the purchases and sales of the Bank of Japan was based on a theoretical price, calculated on the higher of two rates: either the interest rate on borrowings from the Bank of Japan collateralized by securities (1 rin=0.365 percent higher than the discount rate for commercial bills) or the yield to bond subscribers. Following the lowering of the official discount rate in June 1965, the rate on loans collateralized by securities was 1.6 sen (5.84 percent). Thus, the Bank of Japan would apply the yield to subscribers to government-guaranteed debentures (7.053 percent). In such a situation, it was cheaper for the city banks to borrow in the call market than to procure funds by the sale of securities to the central bank, and, in August 1965, the Bank of Japan suspended its purchases of securities conditioned on repurchase by the seller.

Together with the reduction of the official discount rate in June 1965, the policy board of the Bank of Japan decided to abolish the window controls. The banks lowered the "agreed" interest rate on loans. Rates on export bills had remained unchanged, but those on imports bills had been reduced from 1.8 sen to 1.6 sen by the Bank of Japan, so that the banks lowered their rates from 1.9 sen to 1.7 sen. At the same time, the banks strongly urged the government to abolish the legal restrictions on maximum interest rates laid down in the Temporary Money Rates Adjustment Law.

The monetary relaxation allowed an increase in bank deposits and, at the end of December 1965, deposits of all banks topped the ¥20 trillion mark. Demand for loans was slow; only in March, June, July, and September was the increase in loans higher than in the same month a year previously. The increase in bankruptcies made financial institutions more cautious in lending.

In April 1965, the maturity of export advance bills was extended from six months to one year for exports of ships, rolling stock, and machinery. Effective January 1966, the Japan Development Bank and the Hokkaido and Tohoku Development Finance Corporation reduced their long-term interest rates on loans by 0.3 percent to 8.4 percent; the Japan Long-Term Credit Bank, the trust banks, and the insurance companies reduced their preferential rates by 0.3 percent to 8.4 percent. With the reduction of the official discount rate in January 1965, interest rates on loans began to decline, although very slowly; the decline continued for twenty-three months, the longest period of decrease since the recession preceding the Iwato boom when interest rates stayed low from June 1958 to November 1959. The reason was the sluggish fund demand because equipment investment was slow to pick up. The situation was particularly difficult for the long-term credit institutions, but the short-term money market was also stagnant. There was no change in the call money rates for fifteen months from October 1965 until the end of 1966, longer than the former periods of stability (April 1954–May 1955, fourteen months, rate on unconditional loans 2.2 *sen*; November 1961–September 1962, eleven months, unconditional loans 2.4 *sen*). Lenders' rates were: overnight money, 1.5 *sen*; unconditional, 1.6 *sen*; and over-the-month, 1.8 *sen*. Generally, the Bank of Japan tried to keep the call money rates steady and below the interest rates on bonds. This policy became more important with the beginning of bond issues in January 1966.

Despite the monetary relaxation, business conditions were unfavorable in 1965, and the number of bankruptcies continued to rise. In March 1965, Sanyo Special Steel applied for reorganization (liabilities ¥47.9 billion), and, in December, two other relatively large firms became insolvent: Harima Steel (capital, ¥150 million; liabilities, ¥8.5 billion) and Showa Metal Industry (capital, ¥200 million; liabilities, ¥1.5 billion). Particularly noteworthy was the large number of construction firms which became bankrupt. The Ministry of Finance used the Sanyo Special Steel incident to advise all organizations of financial institutions that it was necessary to improve lending practices; the confidence of the public in the integrity of the banks, the ministry said, had been severely impaired.

In a rather strange development, the Bank of Japan, in January 1966, began buying short-term treasury bills from call brokers while buying operations of bonds remained suspended. It was the first time that the bank had undertaken operations involving short-term bills.

In January 1966, the Bank of Japan temporarily stopped loans against import bills. The decline in domestic interest rates led to the so-called yen shift: importers used yen loans instead of dollar usances because the Japanese interest rates had fallen below the international level. Because the yen shift caused a drain on the country's reserve holdings, the Bank of Japan had the city banks stop accepting import bills, but in later years, when the increase in official reserve holdings led to international pressure for the revaluation of the yen, the Bank of Japan encouraged the yen shift.

In February 1966, the Bank of Japan switched to unconditional market operations. Different from the former practice, repurchase was not made a condition of the bank's bond purchases; the price was to be based on actual market quotations, and only government-guaranteed debentures were declared eligible for market operations (in particular, debentures of the electric power companies were no longer accepted). In addition to banks, the four large securities companies could also participate in market operations and, in March, sixteen mutual banks having no accounts with the Bank of Japan were included in the market operations, in addition to the fifty-six mutual banks with accounts.

The lull in equipment investment, in 1965, provided enterprises with greater liquidity, and fund demands of the large enterprises in Tokyo, Osaka, and Nagoya were relatively low. Small enterprises in sectors such as wholesale, retail, real estate, and tourism, however, required larger funds and demand was exceptionally brisk in underdeveloped regions such as Tohoku and Kyushu. Private equipment investment in 1965 remained 5.6 percent below the level of 1964 (1964, ¥5,387.5 billion; 1965, ¥5,086.4 billion), but personal consumption expenditures increased by 12.5 percent (the lowest rate of increase since 1960; the real rate of increase was 5.2 percent; in real terms, the decrease in equipment investment was 6.4 percent). Agricultural income rose 14.0 percent in 1965, 12.9 percent in 1966, and 22.1 percent in 1967, which brought a marked improvement in the rural standard of living.

In May 1966, the Bank of Japan adopted a neutral policy: no stimulation, no restriction. But the situation was somewhat unstable; wholesale prices showed a large increase (they rose 2.4 percent in 1965 and 1.9 percent in 1966) and, in spite of the large surplus on trade account (1965, $1,901 million; 1966, $2,275 million), the authorities remained concerned over the balance of payments. The high foreign interest rates were one of the reasons for their uneasiness, but the outflow of capital was relatively modest (long-term capital: 1965, $415 million; 1966, $808 million; 1967, $812 million; short-term capital: 1965, $61 million; 1966, $64 million; in 1967, the balance showed a net inflow of $506 million in short-term funds). In addition to foodstuffs, the increase in wholesale prices was mainly in textiles (1967), nonferrous metals (1966, +23.2 percent), and timber.

In August, the Ministry of Finance and the Bank of Japan announced a reduction in long-term interest rates, which was put into effect in October. On October 31, 1966, the Ministry of Finance, in a notice sent to the presidents of the various bankers' associations, fixed new norms for compensating balances. The city banks, whose ratio of compensating balances to loans had been 8.6 percent at the end of May 1966, were to reduce the ratio above 4 percent by 30 percent. For the first time since the war, the Bank of Japan, in October 1966, resorted to unconditional selling of government-guaranteed debentures in order to soak up liquid bank funds. For the year-end 1966, the city banks had not to pay penalty rates even if their borrowings exceeded the ceilings; it was the first time since the enforcement of the ceiling in November 1962 that the penalty rates had not been applied. As a result there was no demand in the call market.

The expansion, which had been fairly moderate in 1966, picked up steam in 1967. GNP increased by 15.0 percent in 1966 and 17.7 percent in 1967 (in real terms: 1966, 10.0 percent; 1967, 12.9 percent); investment in producers' durable equipment rose 14.7 percent in 1966 and 28.7 percent in 1967. At the beginning of the year, the government had forecast an increase of 14 percent in equipment investment, but, by the middle of the year, it was clear that investment was growing at a much faster rate. In July, therefore, the government moved to prevent overheating and reduced the issues of national bonds and government-guaranteed debentures. The government also deferred ¥300 billion in fiscal expenditures. A temporary deterioration in the balance of payments further disturbed the authorities and, on September 1, 1967, a series of restrictive measures was put into effect. The official discount rate was raised to 1.6 *sen* (5.84 percent) and window controls were reintroduced.

Called "position guidance," the controls applied to the city banks, the three long-term credit banks, the banking accounts of the trust banks, and twenty-three large local banks (with deposits exceeding ¥150 billion). The Bank of Japan did not want to see the funds available through the decrease in issues of national bonds and government-guaranteed debentures (altogether ¥120 billion) diverted to loans. The ratio of loans to deposits, which serves as the basis for the credit ceiling of individual banks, was calculated by a new method. Up to then, actual deposits and borrowings from the Bank of Japan had been considered; this was changed into each bank's own funds and all borrowings. The credit lines were fixed on the basis of average loan balances in the six months from January to June 1967 minus borrowed funds and funds used for the yen shift; export financing in cooperation with the Export-Import Bank was treated separately. For local banks, the loans given to local bodies were taken into consideration. For the September–December 1967 quarter, the city banks had to keep the increase in loans 15 percent below the increase in the same 1966 quarter; for 1968, the "marginal rate of increase" was −29.3 percent for the January–March quarter; −22.2 percent, for April–June; and −25.4 percent, for July–September.

In January 1967, *Sanmeikai* (organ of the city banks for problems concerning the call market) recommended raising the lender's rate for over-the-month loans by 0.05 *sen* to 1.85 *sen* but leaving the other rates unchanged (overnight 1.5 *sen*, unconditional 1.6 *sen*). In February, however, the rates were raised; over-the-month 1.9 *sen*, unconditional 1.7 *sen*, overnight 1.5 *sen*. This brought the yield rate of unconditional over-the-month loans to 6.935 percent, higher than the yield of national bonds to subscribers (6.795 percent). In April, the rates were lowered to the January level but they went up again after the increases in the official discount rate on September 1, 1967, and the over-the-month rate rose to 2.25 *sen* (about 8.2 percent). In September 1967, the Federation of Bankers Associations agreed to an increase in interest rates on loans and abolished the agreed rate on call loans. It was the first increase in thirty-two months. With the increase in the official discount rate in January 1968 (up to 1.7 *sen* = 6.21 percent), the Federation of Bankers Associations raised interest rates on new loans starting January 10 (except export bills and commercial bills rediscountable with the Bank of Japan); the difference of 1 *rin* between the rates on loans over ¥3 million and below ¥3 million was abolished. The trust banks and insurance companies also increased their interest rates on loans.

Although the actions had no direct effect on the Japanese money market, the devaluation of the pound, on November 18, 1967, and the raise in the American discount rate following an increase in the bank rate heightened the uneasiness of the Japanese authorities. In April 1968, the balance of payments became favorable and, at the end of July, foreign exchange reserves regained the $2 billion level. The international currency situation had calmed down thanks to the support of the pound by the Bank for International Settlements and of the franc by the European Economic Community. In the United States, both the TB (treasury bills) and the BA (bankers' acceptance) rates were lowered. On August 7, the Bank of Japan, therefore, reduced the official discount rate by 1 *rin* to 1.6 *sen* (5.84 percent); two days later, the banks, trust banks, and insurance companies lowered their interest rates on loans. On September 20, 1968, the Bank of Japan's policy board decided to discontinue the window controls starting from October. The improvement in the balance of payments, the favorable economic situation abroad, and the calmer behavior of the domestic economy were given as reasons for the relaxation.

A temporary clouding of the economy, in the last months of 1968 and the beginning of 1969, soon disappeared. For a while, the balance of payments looked less reassuring, but, thanks to the favorable growth of exports supported by the inflationary expansion in overseas markets and a sharp increase in the acquisition of Japanese securities by foreign investors, the overall balance yielded a large surplus.

On February 28, 1969, the trustees of the Federation of Bankers Associations decided to replace the traditional system of calculating interest on a daily basis (*sen* per ¥100 per day) by a yearly percentage system. The new system went into effect on September 8.

In the first half of the year, bank lending increased very rapidly; equipment investment was at a high level and wholesale prices were rising. The seasonal increase in government disbursements scheduled for the latter half of the year (mainly payments for the new rice crop) were expected to increase effective demand. On the other hand, the American economy was expected to slow down in the fall. The authorities reached the conclusion that it was imperative to prevent an acceleration of the expansion. In an extraordinary meeting, on August 30, 1969, the policy board of the Bank of Japan decided to raise the official discount rate effective September and to increase the deposit ratio effective September 5. At the same time, the Bank of Japan adopted the system of calculating interest on a percent per year basis. On September 1, therefore, the official discount rate was raised from 1.6 *sen* (5.84 percent) to 6.25 percent. The deposit ratio, which had not been changed since July 1965, was raised from 1 percent to 1.5 percent on deposits of banks with demand deposits exceeding ¥100 billion. The discount rate for export bills, which had been left unchanged since March 1963, was raised from 1.1 *sen* (4.015 percent) to 4.25 percent, and the interest rate on loans from the foreign exchange fund (unchanged since November 1964) was raised from 1 *sen* (3.65 percent) to 4.0 percent. On September 8, the Federation of Bankers Associations announced a raise in the maximum interest rates on loans and, at the same time, put into effect the system of interest calculation based on annual percentage rates instead of on a daily basis. The new system went into effect for all new loans made after September 8 to which the standard interest rates applied, and for export trade bills; for all other loans, the change was made on November 7.

The Bank of Japan used the change in the official discount rate to abolish the difference between the discount rate on commercial bills (prior to the revision 1.6 *sen*) and the interest rate on loans secured by national bonds, specified bonds of local public bodies, and corporate debentures (prior to the revision, 1.7 *sen*). The city banks wanted to avail themselves of this occasion for eliminating the two steps in the standard rate, but the enterprises which would have been affected by such a measure (electric power companies, steel manufacturers, and the large trading companies) strongly opposed the "unification" of the standard rate, which was postponed until October 31, 1970.

The objective of the government's tight-money policy was said to be a reduction in the real rate of economic growth to 11 percent, but the credit restraints did not cause an immediate slowdown of the expansion and, until August 1970, business retained considerable optimism, so that fund demand remained strong. In November 1969 and again for two periods in 1970 (February–March, July–September), the call rate (lender's over-the-month rate) rose to 9.25 percent. Investment plans for fiscal 1970 foresaw an increase of 18.4 percent, lower than the actual rate of increase of 25.1 percent in fiscal 1969, but still very high. The share of funds for equipment investment in the total industrial fund supply rose from 35.3 percent in 1969 (¥46,806 million out of ¥103,224 million) to 44.8 percent in 1970 (¥56.614 million out of ¥126,259 million). But, when inventories began to pile up and numerous industries were forced to curtail production, the business mood changed. The downturn began in

September 1970; the increase in inventories of finished goods was the most conspicuous sign of the stagnation. In the January–March 1971 quarter, the inventory accumulation was worse than in the recession years 1962 and 1965. For the term ended March 1971, corporate profits, which had risen for eleven consecutive terms, were down on an all-industry basis by 5.8 percent.

Under the Bank of Japan's position guidance, the increase in the lending of the city banks, for the period from October to December 1969, was fixed at ¥469 billion, about 30 percent higher than the increase in bank lending in the corresponding year-earlier period, but, for the January–March 1970 quarter, the marginal rate of increase was held down to 6.5 percent; it was raised to 9.5 percent for April–June; 11 percent, for July–September; and 16 percent, for October–December. Business had shown little enthusiasm for the government's tight money policy and, on several occasions, business leaders called for a discontinuance of the credit restraints. But the Bank of Japan upheld its controls until the end of October 1970. On October 27, 1970, the policy board of the Bank of Japan decided to reduce the official discount rate by 0.25 percent, effective October 28. The Federation of Bankers Associations fixed the standard rate uniformly at 6.25 percent (which meant that only the most preferential rate was lowered), and reduced the discount rate for ordinary bills and the rate on ordinary loans to 8.00 percent and that on overdrafts to 9.00 percent.

For the year-end 1970, the fund shortage (excess of fund demand over supply) was expected to reach ¥1,600 billion, and the Bank of Japan leaned to the opinion that the new fund supply system adopted in November 1962 (supply of "growth" funds through open market operations) had reached the limits of its capacity and that an extension of buying operations was necessary. In January 1971, plans to add bank debentures and commercial bills to the securities eligible for open market operations were discussed and out of these discussions grew the proposal to organize a market for commercial bills that would provide the basis for free price formation and, at the same time, relieve the pressure on the call market. The plan to extend market operations to commercial bills was abandoned, but the bill market was organized in May 1971.

The call rate, which had been lowered by 0.5 percent at the end of October 1970, was raised again by 0.25 percent at the beginning of December but lowered by 0.5 percent on December 31. In November, the average interest rate on bank loans showed the first decline (0.001 percent, down to 7.699 percent) since June 1969. On January 20, 1971, the Bank of Japan reduced the official discount rate by 0.25 percent to 5.75 percent for commercial bills and lowered the interest rate on loans collateralized by ordinary commercial bills by 0.5 percent to 6.0 percent. On January 23, the Association of Bankers Associations reduced the standard rate by 0.25 percent to 6.0 percent; the discount rate for ordinary bills, to 7.75 percent; and the rate on overdrafts, to 8.75 percent. Although the easing of the money supply undoubtedly played a role in the decision to reduce the official interest rate, the timing, one day after the reduction of the discount rate in the United States, pointed to another consideration, the relation of Japanese interest rates to foreign interest rates. On January 18, 1971, the Federal Reserve Board decided to reduce the discount rate by 0.25 percent to 5 percent. It was the fourth reduction since November 1970, and the Bank of Japan feared that it might lead to a "dollar shift" in the financing of Japanese imports.

International interest rates, which had been high since the pound devaluation in November 1, 1967, began to fall in 1970. In addition to the reduction of the official rates in many countries, the Eurodollar rate, which had been around 12 percent in the fall of 1969, was down to 6.8 percent in November 1970 and, on February 16, 1971, the one-month rate dropped from 5 3/16–5 5/16 to 4 13/16–4 15/16 and the three-month rate from 5 7/16–5 9/16 to 5 1/4–5 3/8. As mentioned above, the authorities had promoted a yen shift so as to decelerate the increase in foreign exchange reserves. The interest rates on dollar usances are based on the Bankers' Acceptance (B/A) rate of American banks, while the costs of yen financing depend on the Bank of Japan's rate for loans on oridinary commercial bills. With the B/A rate at 4.75 percent and a commission of 1.5 percent payable to the foreign bank the cost was 6.25 percent, the 6 percent on ordinary bills plus the swap cost of 0.25 percent.

Generally speaking, until recently, the Bank of Japan could disregard developments in foreign money markets in fixing the official discount rate. Until 1955, the discount rate had no real significance in the monetary policies of the bank. Even after that date, the changes in the official discount rate had more symbolic than actual value, because the direct credit controls of the central banks were far more effective than the Bank of Japan's interest policy could be. The importance of the discount rate grew with the adoption of the new fund supply system in 1962, but it was fixed on the basis of purely domestic considerations. The reduction in January 1971 was the first time that the external balance (prevention of the inflow of foreign capital) was taken into consideration, and it was the most important factor in the reduction of the discount rate by another 0.25 percent, which went into effect on May 8, 1971. The decision was delayed by one week on account of the squabble inside the government and the Liberal-Democratic party about the rice price. At 5.5 percent, the official discount rate was at its lowest since the 1965 recession when it stood at 1.5 *sen* (5.48 percent).

In the beginning of April, the Ministry of Finance and the Bank of Japan had urged the banks to reduce their rates on loans by 0.25 percent and, in an unprecedented move, the managers in charge of loans in the city and local banks had been called individually to be appraised of the views of the authorities. A few days earlier, on April 1, the call rate had been reduced by 0.5 percent, bringing the lender's over-the-month rate down to 7.5 percent, the overnight rate to 6.5 percent, and the unconditional rate to 6.75 percent. This, together with the reduction in the discount rate at the start of May, reduced the over-the-month rate by 0.5 percent and the other rates by 0.25 percent.

The Ministry of Finance had proposed a reduction of 0.5 percent in the official discount rate, but the Bank of Japan had resisted such a large slash, which would have contravened its long-standing policy of moving the official discount rate upward in large steps but bringing it down only gradually. As a matter of fact, the authorities faced the dilemma of conflicting demands for the internal and external balances. The domestic fund supply was ample, and the actual situation of the economy made its stimulation by lower interest rates seem unnecessary and ineffective. Furthermore, the lower interest rates on loans put the banks under considerable pressure since they could not reduce interest rates on deposits. But the developments in overseas money markets and the instability in the international currency situation made it imperative to take precautionary steps against the inflow of large foreign funds that could aggravate the pressure for the revaluation of the yen.

Domestic demand remained sluggish during the summer but exports stayed high, and the large increase in payments from the foreign exchange fund resulted in an unusual relaxation of the money market. Enterprises heavily engaged in foreign trade, such as trading and shipbuilding companies, and manufacturers of automobiles, electrical machinery, and steel, bought large amounts of short-term treasury bills in order to invest liquid funds. Bill sales rose from an average of ¥50 billion to ¥140–150 billion a month; in July 1971, the market absorbed ¥207.1 billion of treasury bills and in August ¥305.4 billion. But the economy did not respond to the availability of money; investment outlays, in particular, hardly expanded. At the end of July, therefore, the government decided on a reduction of interest rates to stimulate the economy. The official discount rate was reduced from 5.50 percent to 5.25 percent effective July 28, 1971. On August 10, in connection with the abolition of the preferential financing of exports, the discount rate of bills for preexport financing was consolidated with the interest rate on loans collateralized by bills for preexport financing. The main emphasis, however, was on the reduction of long-term interest rates; the standard rate of the Japan Development Bank was lowered from 8.5 percent to 8.2 percent and that of the Hokkaido and Tohoku Development Finance Corporation from 8.3 percent to 8.2 percent. At the same time, interest rates on bank loans were reduced. The call money rate was reduced on September 1, 1971, and, together with an adjustment of the issue conditions of bonds, the dividend rates on five-year money trusts and loan trusts were lowered.

President Nixon's announcement of his new economic policy created an entirely new situation. Actual exports were not immediately affected, but many enterprises were unable to conclude new export contracts. The adjustment of the cost and price differentials, resulting from the imposition of the 10 percent tax on imports into the United States and the flotation of the yen, was extremely difficult, and enterprises with large claims denominated in dollars (deferred payments for exports and other receivables) were bound to suffer heavy losses. The government's imposition of stricter foreign exchange controls (which nearly stopped the financing of exports) worsened the already bad situation, and, on September 23, 1971, the government adopted a relief program for small enterprises. The main provisions of the plan were: (1) the three governmental financial institutions for small business (Central Bank for Commercial & Industrial Cooperatives, Small Business Finance Corporation, People's Finance Corporation) will give long-term, low-interest loans to export-related small enterprises; the total framework of these loans was fixed at ¥150 billion, of which ¥100 billion was to be given at the special rate of 6.5 percent (7 percent after three years) with a maturity of three to five years; (2) the Bank of Japan will purchase from small enterprises (through the foreign exchange banks) export usance bills denominated in foreign currency; furthermore, the government will deposit funds from the foreign exchange fund with the foreign exchange banks in order to facilitate such purchases; the government will also take measures to cover the exchange risk from the time of the conclusion of an export contract to the time of shipment of the merchandise; (3) the capital of the Small Business Credit Insurance Corporation will be increased; the coverage of the credit insurance will be extended to 80 percent and the premiums reduced by one-third; (4) special loans will be given by the Small Enterprise Promotion Corporation and the Small Business Finance Corporation to assist small enterprises changing to other business lines; (5) tax relief by allowing retroactive exchange losses, shorter depreciation periods for enterprises changing to different business lines, and deferment of tax payment.

In the first six months of fiscal 1971 (April–September), disbursements of the Treasury exceeded receipts by ¥2,410.2 billion, the largest six-month excess of payments ever recorded. The large outflow of funds from the foreign exchange fund due to the dollar purchases of the government was the main reason for the imbalance.

Treasury Accounts with the Public

(In billions of yen)

	April–June 1970	April–June 1971
General account receipts	3,880.7	4,403.4
Tax revenues	3,418.6	3,863.8
General account expenditures	−2,851.6	−3,452.6
Balance on general accounts	1,029.1	950.8
Balance on special accounts	−415.4	−152.7
Balance on food control s.a.	108.1	159.1
Errors & omissions	−25.9	−31.0
Balance on foreign exchange fund	63.9	−3,177.3
General balance	651.7	−2,410.2

2 MONEY SUPPLY

The rapid expansion of Japan's industry required a corresponding expansion of the financial sector and what is usually described as the supply of "growth" funds. The main supply routes were: (1) the buying of foreign currency by the Bank of Japan (through the foreign exchange fund special account); (2) excess of payments by the government to the private sector; (3) central bank credit financial institutions. The supply of funds through foreign currency depends on a surplus in exports. Thanks to the very favorable development of foreign trade, the current balance has shown a large surplus since 1965 (with the exception of 1967) but was in the red through most of the postwar era. Between 1949 and 1966, the government kept to the principle of budgetary balance; moreover, due to the rapid growth, the natural increase in tax income usually exceeded the original budget figures. Under these conditions, central bank credit became the most important source of growth funds. The credit supplied by the Bank of Japan largely served to cover the fund insufficiency involved in the overloans of the city banks which, moreover, borrowed heavily in the call market. Due to the chronic nature of the overloans, the function of the call market became distorted; instead of relieving short-term fund shortages, the call market served as the main instrument for correcting the so-called fund dislocation, i.e., the lack of funds of the city banks and the relative abundance of funds in local banks and the financial institutions for agriculture.

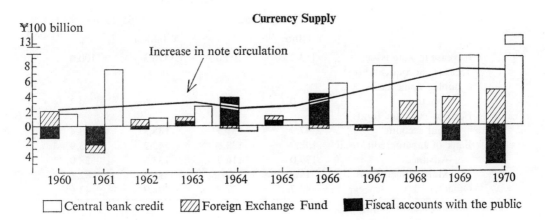

Currency Supply

¥100 billion

Increase in note circulation

☐ Central bank credit   ▨ Foreign Exchange Fund   ■ Fiscal accounts with the public

Money Supply

(In billions of yen)

	Fiscal 1969	Fiscal 1970
Total money supply at end of fiscal year	17,798.2	21,187.3
Currency in circulation	3,872.9	4,545.1
Deposit money	13,925.3	16,642.2
Increase during fiscal year	2,981.2	3,389.1
Currency in circulation	682.1	672.2
Deposit money	2,299.1	2,761.9
Time & savings deposits		
Balance at end of fiscal year	28,814.5	33,814.7
Increase during fiscal year	4,196.4	5,000.2
Total increase in currency & deposits	7,177.6	8,389.3
Increase or decrease by borrower		
Foreign assets	743.0	670.9
Claims on government	448.1	−702.6
Claims on local bodies	171.2	288.9
Claims on private business	7,352.9	9,159.2
Claims on financial institutions	−1,537.6	−1,027.1
Increase or decrease by type of fund		
Treasury funds	131.1	−144.7
Foreign exchange fund	428.6	675.5
Advances	6,959.1	8,671.5
Securities	793.6	232.2
Government bonds held by banks	27.7	−358.1
Bank debentures	−603.6	−563.5
Other accounts of banks	−102.6	143.8

Source: Bank of Japan, Economic Statistics Monthly.

Change in Pattern of Money Supply

	Yearly average			
	1956–1962		1963–1970	
	¥ billion	%	¥ billion	%
Increase in note issue	153.2	100.0	476.3	100.0
Treasury accounts with public, domestic transactions	−51.0	−33.3	1.6	0.3
Foreign exchange fund special account	47.9	31.3	135.3	28.4
Bank of Japan credit, total	198.9	129.9	542.2	113.9
Advances	179.0	116.9	133.5	28.0
Market operations	14.2	9.3	394.4	82.8
Other	−42.7	−27.9	−202.9	−42.6

Source: Nihon Keizai Shimbun.

Monetary Survey
March 31, 1971

(In billions of yen)

	Net monetary balances	Bank of Japan	Deposit banks
Assets	65,624.6	7,807.6	67,879.5
Foreign assets	2,269.9	1,964.9	2,260.6
Cash & deposits with BoJ			1,253.9
Domestic credit	63,354.7		
Claims on government	2,984.9	1,951.6	1,712.1
Government securities	1,871.1	1,447.4	425.7
Claims on local public bodies	1,526.7		1,526.7
Local public bonds	1,035.8		1,035.8
Claims on private business			
& individuals	58,843.1		58,843.1
Advances	54,215.7		54,215.7
Securities	3,783.7		3,783.7
Claims on banks		2,635.5	
Advances		2,295.2	
Other assets		1,255.6	2,283.1
Liabilities	65,624.6	7,807.6	67,879.5
Money supply	21,187.3		
Currency in circulation	4,545.1	5,303.5	
Deposit money	16,642.2		16,642.2
Time & savings deposits	33,814.7		33,814.7
Deposits from deposit banks		495.5	
Government deposits		678.8	
Due to central bank			2,635.5
Bank debentures issued			3,993.2
Foreign liabilities			1,948.9
Other liabilities	10,622.6	1,329.8	

Source: Bank of Japan.

Money Supply, 1969-70

(In billions of yen)

	1969	1970
Increase in note issue	769.4	744.8
Treasury accounts with public	117.0	−191.0
General accounts	−213.1	−517.1
Food control special account	419.4	201.9
Foreign exchange fund special account	349.4	446.6
Long-term national bonds	−378.7	−322.4
Other	−293.0	−399.4
Increase in Bank of Japan credit	885.4	1,335.2

Note: Minus sign (−) indicates excess of receipts from overpayments to the public.
Source: Nihon Keizai Shimbun.

Fund Surplus or Deficiency by Sector

(In billions of yen)

Calendar year	1957	1958	1959	1960	1961	1962
Corporate enterprises	1,072.6	−521.9	−947.7	−1,409.4	−2,429.5	−1,692.2
Individuals	761.6	714.1	1,176.2	1,372.4	1,909.0	1,882.8
Government	228.1	109.2	34.1	249.1	481.8	336.6
Public corporations	−140.3	−142.6	−132.5	−160.5	−315.1	−544.7
Domestic fund surplus or deficiency	−223.2	158.8	130.1	51.6	−353.7	−17.5
Rest of the world	223.2	−158.8	−130.1	−51.6	353.7	17.5
Total fund deficiency	−1,212.9	−823.3	−1,210.3	−1,621.5	−2,744.6	−2,236.9

Fiscal year	1963	1964	1965	1966	1967	1968	1969
Corporate enterprises	−1,959.3	−1,919.7	−1,162.6	−1,850.9	−3,017.6	−2,791.6	−3,765.0
Individuals	1,906.0	2,581.3	2,589.4	3,482.7	4,270.4	4,474.5	5,354.7
Government	357.5	119.0	85.1	−191.5	−60.5	183.7	476.3
Public corporations	−689.0	−770.4	−1,134.3	−1,082.8	−1,305.0	−1,336.3	−1,325.8
Domestic fund surplus or deficiency	−385.4	10.2	337.6	357.5	−112.7	530.3	740.2
Rest of the world	385.4	−10.2	−337.6	−357.5	112.7	−530.3	−740.2
Total fund deficiency	−2,648.9	−2,700.3	−2,674.5	−3,482.7	−4,383.1	−4,658.2	−5,841.0

Notes: 1. Minus sign (−) indicates fund deficiency.
   2. Individuals includes individual businesses.
Source: Bank of Japan, Flow of Funds.

Corporate fund demand remained invariably strong; the periods of rapid expansion were usually marked by a competitive race in equipment investment, while during the so-called recessions enterprises needed large sums for financing inventories and production curtailments. All industrial enterprises had to rely on external funds for their postwar reconstruction, and the dynamism of the expansion allowed them little respite for financial consolidation. Even under favorable conditions, therefore, internal cash flow provided only one-third of corporate fund requirements and the supply capacity of the capital market fell far short of the needs. Hence, there was no basic change in the pattern of corporate financing which evolved in the fifties. External funds accounted for the largest part of the capital supplied to industry, and bank loans constituted the bulk of these funds. The banks were able to channel these funds into industry because bank deposits remained the prevalent form of individual saving, and central bank credit fed the marginal funds into the system. Thus the expansion became possible. Import and foreign exchange controls protected the dynamic equilibrium of the system because they prevented outside claims from disturbing the domestic credit balance. Japan was able to put off negotiations on reparations and other foreign claims until the country's economy had grown sufficiently to assume these burdens without impairing the substance of its productive apparatus, and, since reparations usually took the form of exports of capital goods, they often proved of considerable benefit to Japan's foreign trade.

The new fund supply system of 1962 restored the function of central bank credit to its original purpose (that of providing an ultimate credit cushion) and the role of the call money market to covering short-term fund shortages. It also aimed at correcting the overloan position of the city banks by setting up a credit line for each of the city banks and containing bank lending within the limits of each bank's own resources. The ratio of loans to deposits (based on average balances during the six-month term), which had been 107.2 percent in the first term of fiscal 1962, declined to 96.9 percent in the first term of fiscal 1970; so that, in the sense of an excess of loans over deposits, the overloan situation has disappeared. But the city banks continue to depend greatly on borrowed funds and the dependency is actually greater than the statistics indicate. During the credit restraints in force from September 1969 to October 1970, for example, the city banks sold large amounts of bank debentures in their portfolios, even at considerable losses, in order to procure liquid funds.

Reliance of City Banks on Borrowed Funds

End of	Balance of borrowed funds		Borrowed from Bank of Japan		Borrowed in money market	
	¥ billion	Ratio to deposit balance %	¥ billion	Ratio to deposit balance %	¥ billion	Ratio to deposit balance %
March 1961	806.1	15.8	573.0	11.2	233.1	4.6
,, 1962	1,494.0	27.2	1,230.6	22.4	263.4	4.8
,, 1963	1,682.2	24.0	1,228.4	17.5	453.8	6.5
,, 1964	1,894.4	22.5	1,105.2	13.1	789.2	9.4
,, 1965	2,435.6	25.3	975.4	10.1	1,460.2	15.2
,, 1966	2,337.3	20.5	1,124.1	9.9	1,213.2	10.6
,, 1967	2,399.5	18.8	1,305.2	10.2	1,094.3	8.6
,, 1968	2,613.3	18.6	1,194.0	8.5	1,419.3	10.1
,, 1969	2,784.9	17.6	1,328.7	8.4	1,456.2	9.2
,, 1970	3,704.1	20.3	1,731.9	9.5	1,972.2	10.8
Sept. 1970	4,227.9	21.8	2,134.8	11.0	2,093.1	10.8

Notes: 1. Ratio to deposit balance: actual deposits (i.e., not including checks and bills).
      2. Data for thirteen city banks.
      3. "Borrowed from Bank of Japan" includes funds for foreign trade financing which do not fall under the credit controls of the Bank of Japan.
Source: Nihon Keizai Shimbun.

With the increasing surplus in the balance of payments, the foreign exchange fund became more important for the supply of funds and, in recent years, the excess in payments from the fund has been about half the size of the increase in bank note circulation (1968, ¥300.8 billion = 47.7 percent of the increase in bank notes; 1969, ¥349.4 billion = 45.4 percent; 1970, ¥446.6 billion = 59.9 percent; the yearly rate of increase in currency has been 17–18 percent). The unusual relaxation was largely the result of the large payments excess of the foreign exchange fund. The banks were able to repay a considerable part of their borrowings from the Bank of Japan and, in July 1971, the outstanding balances of central bank loans fell below ¥2 trillion (they had reached a high of ¥2,476.1 billion in January 1971). (The previous lows in Bank of Japan lending were ¥437 billion at the end of March 1954 and ¥27 billion at the end of March 1956.) About 75 percent of the lending of the Bank of Japan is

Treasury Accounts with the Public

(In billions of yen)

	Fiscal 1970		April–June 1971	
	Receipts	Payments	Receipts	Payments
General account	7,625.6	5,722.7	2,143.1	2,053.0
Taxes	7,198.2		1,971.5	
Government monopolies	290.7		111.5	
Revenues other than taxes	136.7		60.2	
Social security		804.3		246.9
Defense		559.3		203.3
Public works		487.6		86.9
Grants to local governments		1,914.0		964.7
Contribution to compulsory education		462.9		153.9
Other		1,494.6		397.0
Special accounts, public corporations, etc.	11,221.5	13,258.1	2,517.0	3,843.1
Food control	969.7	1,174.3	234.0	53.5
Industrial investment	35.0	105.3	6.0	62.7
Road construction	66.8	592.5	18.0	206.7
Flood control	40.9	188.2	6.2	51.9
Harbors, airports, land improvement	45.3	124.1	14.0	52.0
Insurance	2,665.3	1,164.1	753.1	306.4
Post Office	553.5	222.3	96.5	127.0
Japan National Railways	1,419.0	1,656.1	406.4	458.9
Nippon Telegraph & Telephone Corporation	1,422.8	1,439.5	371.6	344.9
Housing Loan Corporation	66.7	201.0	24.1	43.0
Agriculture, Forestry & Fisheries Finance Corp.	112.0	205.0	16.0	67.7
Small Business F.C.	392.2	479.9	103.7	126.3
Hokkaido & Tohoku Development F.C.	73.8	81.3	15.3	15.8
Small Business Credit Insurance Corp.	9.0	16.5	2.3	1.0
Medical Care Facilities F.C.	20.4	35.0	5.6	8.9
Personal Services F.C.	1.1	22.7	0.0	4.3
Trust Fund Bureau	2,308.1	2,963.8	239.0	442.8
Others	1,019.8	2,586.4	205.3	1,469.3
Long-term national bonds	317.2	43.8	126.9	11.4
Total	19,164.3	19,024.5	4,787.0	5,907.7
Balance of receipts & payments of Treasury funds except foreign exchange fund		+815.3		−136.2
Balance of receipts & payments of foreign exchange fund		−675.5		−984.5
Adjustments	61.7	56.8	2.6	32.9
Japan Development Bank, Export-Import Bank, etc.[1]	47.3	44.8	—	30.2
U.S. Forces deposits, etc.[2]	14.4	12.0	2.6	2.7
Grand total	19,226.0	19,081.3	4,789.6	5,940.6
Balance		+144.7		−1,150.9
New issues & redemptions of short-term treasury bills[3]	708.0	458.0	413.2	194.7
Total Treasury transactions with public	19,872.3	19,482.6	5,200.1	6,102.1
Balance		+389.8		−902.0

See next page for notes.

322 *A FINANCIAL HISTORY OF THE NEW JAPAN*

Transactions of Treasury with Bank of Japan

(In billions of yen)

	Fiscal 1970		April–June 1971	
	Receipts	Payments	Receipts	Payments
Current payments	551.3	199.6	276.7	186.4
Sales & purchase of foreign exchange	96.1	77.2	69.6	63.6
Cost of manufacturing bank notes	16.0	—	5.3	—
Issue tax	0.8	—	—	—
Amortization & interest payment on external bonded debt	—	7.0	—	1.1
Amortization & interest payment on national bonds	39.6	40.3	11.6	9.4
Interest or discount charges	−68.5	25.1	−18.0	21.7
Subsidiary coins	52.8	2.0	18.7	—
Others	414.5	48.1	189.5	90.6
Short-term funds	13,298.7	7,615.2	4,907.9	3,741.1
Treasury bills	918.0	918.0	499.0	499.0
Food bills	8,479.0	4,648.5	2,123.1	1,900.5
Foreign exchange fund bills	3,512.7	1,868.6	1,412.8	1,341.4
Outright	389.0	180.1	873.0	0.1
Borrowings	—	—	—	—
Investment & withdrawal of surplus funds	10,808.7	17,170.2	2,413.7	3,153.0
Trust Fund Bureau	9,714.9	15,442.5	2,016.2	2,559.1
Postal life insurance & postal annuities	246.4	357.7	76.9	144.5
Debt service fund	57.4	467.9	17.4	121.0
Japan National Railways	627.0	691.6	248.8	265.6
Finance corporations	163.0	210.6	54.3	62.9
Total	24,658.8	24,985.0	7,598.3	7,080.4
Balance		−326.3		+517.8

Notes (re chart on previous page):
1. The Japan Development Bank, the Export-Import Bank of Japan, the People's Finance Corporation, the Local Public Enterprise Finance Corporation, and the overseas economic cooperation fund do not deposit cash with the Treasury, and capital contributions of the government or fiscal loans to these institution are included in payments to the public. But increases or decreases in the balances of current deposits of these institutions with the Bank of Japan and in the balances of short-term treasury bills held by these institutions are treated as receipts or payments by the Treasury.
2. Payments entered in the payments to the public but not yet actually paid (U.S. Forces deposits remaining in the Bank of Japan and Treasury remittances in transit) and receipts entered in the receipts from the public but not yet actually received (uncollected bills & checks) are adjusted by negative entries.
3. Issues and redemptions of short-term treasury bills represent transactions of fiscal management and not basic financial transactions.

connected with foreign trade financing. In August 1971, the excess of payments from the foreign exchange fund amounted to about ¥1,600 billion. Consequently, when the government began payments for the new rice crop, the monetary relaxation became alarming. On August 20, 1971, political and economic uncertainties dampened fund demand, and the Bank of Japan began to sell three-month notes on the call market to provide an investment opportunity for short-term funds. In some instances, however, the income from these notes of local banks, credit associations, and mutual banks remained below their fund costs.

Consolidated Receipts and Payments of the Treasury

(In billions of yen)

	Fiscal 1970	April–June 1971
Balance of current receipts & payments	+484.6	−1,034.3
with the public	+132.9	−1,124.4
with the Bank of Japan	+351.7	+90.2
Balance of short-term funds	+324.7	+804.8
Treasury bills	—	0.0
Food bills	−75.2	−187.0
Foreign exchange fund bills	+191.0	+119.0
Outright	+208.9	+872.9
Borrowings	—	—
Balance of investment & withdrawal of surplus funds	−745.8	−154.7
Trust Fund Bureau	−674.7	−245.5
Postal life insurance & postal annuities	+18.3	−0.9
Debt service	−57.4	+17.6
Japan National Railways	−32.5	+56.4
Finance corporations	+0.5	+17.8
Total	+63.5	−384.1

Note: This table contains intraagency transactions involving Treasury accounts (e.g., redemption of government securities held by individual accounts) so that the data under "Balance of short-term funds" and "Balance of investment & withdrawal of surplus funds" does not agree with the other tables.

Source: Bank of Japan.

3 THE CAPITAL MARKET

1 CAPITAL ACCUMULATION

The expansion of the Japanese economy involved a significant increase in fixed assets. The preference for fixed assets was shared by both the corporate and the personal sector and although it was lower in the government sector, the rate of fixed capital formation was still higher than the growth rate of GNP. Particular remarkable was the increase in investment in private residential construction which, in the ten years between fiscal 1959 and fiscal 1969, rose at an average yearly rate of better than 23 percent. But a large part of this increase was due to higher prices; the Economic Planning Agency calculated the implicit deflator (calendar year 1965 = 100) for private dwellings at 72.3 for fiscal 1959 and 131.8 for fiscal 1969, while the deflator for GNP was 75.7 for fiscal 1959 and 119.7 for 1969.

The increase in fixed capital formation of private households was much faster than the increase in consumption expenditure. Compared with a 5.36 times increase in the savings of households and nonprofit institutions (average annual rate of increase 18.3 percent), private consumption expenditure increased 3.94 times (average annual rate of increase 14.7 percent). Noteworthy is the much faster growth of spending on consumer durables (7.85 times increase from fiscal 1959 to fiscal 1969; average annual growth rate 22.8 percent) than expenditures for nondurables (3.37 times; 12.9 percent). Price rises were largely responsible for the high rate of increase in outlays for services (4.91 times; 17.3 percent).

With an average annual rate of 19.1 percent, the expansion in plant and equipment was somewhat faster for corporate enterprises than for individual businesses (18.4 percent), but, different from the private sector, a large part of the formation of fixed capital was financed by credit, and the rate of obsolescence was much higher.

Together with the increase in fixed capital formation, the accumulation of financial assets proceeded at a very high rate. With the exception of the two years 1966 and 1967, the actual increase in savings always exceeded the official target. Individual financial assets (which include assets of individual proprietors) grew at an average annual rate of 19.0 percent. Their composition showed a slight increase in long-term assets (time deposits, trusts, and insurance) and a decline in securities holdings.

Outstanding loans and discounts of all banks (banking accounts) rose from ¥8,166.5 billion at the end of 1960 to ¥39,173.3 billion at the end of 1970; loans for equipment investment, which amounted to ¥1,344.7 billion at the end of 1960, stood at ¥8,339.1 billion. While all loans and discounts increased 4.7 times in this period, loans for financing of investment in plant and equipment rose 6.2 times. The development in the loans on the trust accounts of all banks is even more indicative of the trend. At the end of 1960, outstanding loans amounted to ¥723.0 billion of which ¥466.5 billion was for equipment funds;

at the end of 1970, the total had risen to ¥5,155.0 billion (7.1 times), equipment funds accounting for ¥4,014.9 billion (8.6 times).

The savings target for fiscal 1971 was fixed at ¥13,700 billion. Additions to savings in the two months April and May 1971 reached 19.2 percent of that total. Particularly rapid was the increase in postal savings which rose from ¥7,000.7 billion on December 3, 1970, to ¥8,010.3 billion on June 22, 1971; the balance reached ¥9,003.3 billion on December 21, 1971. Until then, about one year had been necessary for achieving an increase of ¥1 trillion.

On a national accounts basis, property income of individuals amounted to ¥5,302.0 billion in fiscal 1969, including ¥1,765.4 billion in rents, ¥2,853.6 billion in interest, and ¥683.0 billion in dividends. This agrees with the relatively small share of stocks in personal financial assets.

The 1969 national survey of family income and expenditures, which covered 42,564 households of two or more persons and 3,590 one-person households, reported an average savings ratio of 13.1 percent for households with either no one or only one person gainfully employed and 17.8 percent for households with two or more gainfully employed. According to this survey, Japan's high savings ratio had been strengthened by two factors: the decrease in the number of persons per household (which sank from 4.33 in 1959 to 3.85 in 1969) and the increase in the average number of gainfully employed per household (which rose from 1.46 in 1959 to 1.59 in 1969). In the ten-year period, the income of the household head increased 1.7 times; the income of housewives grew 3.8 times but other income decreased. In 1969, married women workers numbered 4.7 million, equal to 14 percent of nonagricultural employment. Married women workers were more numerous than unmarried ones; somewhat less than 20 percent of the married women workers were household heads. About 1.6 million women were employed on a daily basis and about half worked in enterprises employing less than thirty workers. This means that the absolute level of the earnings of women remained low.

Workers' households kept relatively more of their financial assets in postal savings and life insurance than households of individual proprietors, but the latter's bank deposits were higher. Workers' households in the highest income group showed a marked preference for stocks, investment trusts, loan trusts, and bonds (i.e., long-term, high-yield assets).

As was to be expected, the survey showed considerable regional differences in incomes and savings. The ward area of Tokyo (i.e., the twenty-three city wards, excluding the outlying areas of Tokyo metropolis) reported the highest average income and the highest average savings for both workers' households (income ¥1,371,000, savings ¥1,230,000) and households of individual proprietors (income ¥1,930,000, savings ¥2,418,000). For workers' households, the lowest average income and savings was reported from Tohoku (income ¥1,020,000, savings ¥698,000), but for households of individual proprietors the region with the lowest average income was Chugoku (¥1,116,000) and the region with the lowest savings Kyushu (¥1,104,000). Among workers' households, the rate of house ownership (national average 51.2 percent) was highest in the Hokuriku region (69.4 percent) and lowest in Hokkaido (30.6 percent).

According to Professor Milton Friedman, the propensity to save is higher for extraordinary income than for ordinary income. In Japan, the increase in extraordinary income, i.e., in midyear and year-end bonuses, has been more rapid than the rise in regular pay. Furthermore, the growing custom of paying salaries into bank accounts (not in cash) has encouraged saving. If employees receive their salaries or wages in cash, the money is gone until the next payday; if salaries are paid into a bank account, only half of the households withdraw 80 percent or more of the salary. A survey carried out by Nippon Univac among its employees showed the following:

Withdrawals immediately after payday:

% of salary withdrawn	% of households
80% & more	53%
50%–80%	31%
under 50%	14%
no withdrawals	2%

The same survey reported that the bank passbook is kept by the husband in 36 percent of the families and by the wife in 61 percent. Another factor which has encouraged saving is the companies' custom of accepting the savings deposits of their employees (companies usually pay a somewhat higher rate of interest than the banks).

According to preliminary data on workers' households, the average yearly income per household (3.9 persons) amounted to ¥1,390,000 in fiscal 1970 (monthly average ¥115,900). This corresponded to a nominal rate of increase of 15.7 percent over the preceding year, but, since consumer prices rose by 7.3 percent, the real rate of increase was 7.8 percent. Disposable income averaged ¥1,280,000 (monthly ¥106,300), 15.3 percent higher than in the preceding year. Average household expenditures amounted to ¥1.2 million (monthly average ¥84,800); the capacity to consume sank from 82.0 percent in 1968 and 81.0 percent in 1969 to 79.8 percent in 1970. (Engel's coefficient declined from 32.8 percent in 1969 to 32.2 percent in 1970.)

A survey conducted by Fuji Bank on the savings of single individuals showed that 98.7 percent of all unmarried people own some kind of savings. Of all respondents, 67.4 percent had ordinary deposits; 47.6 percent, time deposits; 36.2 percent, company deposits; and 13.9 percent, postal savings. Men usually save about 15 percent of their salaries; women, 22 percent.

In the recession following the Iwato boom, the share of securities in personal financial assets declined sharply due to the decline in stock holding and the large cancellations in investment trusts; the preponderance of savings deposits indicates that indirect financing retains its importance.

Generally speaking, saving for definite purposes plays a relatively important role in Japan and provides a link between saving and consumer credit. Home ownership is the goal of many Japanese savers; savings are used for the purchase of land or a house or the financing of construction. Education and marriage are other common purposes. Relatively few households depend on the income from savings for living expenses. Many large companies have adopted a retirement pension system; if a lump-sum payment is made at retirement, it is often used for financing the acquisition of a home. As a result of these conditions, the yield of savings, although not without influence, is not the most important consideration in the selection of individual financial assets.

The still unfilled demand for housing and consumer durables is given priority by the saving public. Due to the large increase in the price of land and rising construction costs, homes have become more and more expensive, absorbing the entire savings capacity of many households. Renting of an apartment is still usually considered to be temporary; in time, permanent renting may become acceptable, but, at present, people are unwilling to give up the dream of an independent house.

As of March 31, 1971, savings accumulated under company savings plans amounted to ¥1,334.3 billion, of which installment savings for homes accounted for 21.8 percent (¥290.2 billion). The number of savings accounts which employees had with the companies for which they worked was 5.6 million, composed as follows: ordinary deposits, 3.78 million; time deposits, 0.56 million; installment savings for homes, 0.92 million. The average interest rate paid on company deposits was 7.76 percent, the average rate on installment savings for homes 8.56 percent. The average interest rate varied with the size of the enterprise: it was 7.65 percent in enterprises with less than 30 employees, 7.80 percent in those with a work force of 30–299, and 8.30 percent in larger enterprises.

The shock from the slump in stock prices after the Iwato boom has not yet been healed and so investor confidence remains shaky. This applies not only to stocks but also to investment trusts. An important factor is the lack of investor education; in their sales campaigns the securities companies had stressed capital gains from rising stock prices, which created an overly speculative image of securities investment. The ordinary investor remained rather unfamiliar not only with the mechanism but also with the meaning of securities investment. The greatest obstacle, however, may be the inflationary trend in the economy. The market slumps destroyed the myth that the role of stock investment is to be a hedge against inflation, and the erosion of the value of money was little conducive to long-term investment in monetary assets. Life insurance was an exception; the life insurance companies organized a huge sales force oriented toward the general public and appealing to the popular yearning for security.

The government has taken a number of measures to encourage saving. The most important was the tax exemption for postal savings and small savings accounts, initially up to ¥500,000. With the increase of the tax rate on interest from 5 percent to 10 percent in fiscal 1965, the ceiling on savings accounts on which interest was tax-exempt was raised to ¥1 million. In fiscal 1967, the tax rate on interest was raised to 15 percent; to compensate for the discouraging effect on saving, the restriction of tax-exempt savings deposits to one account (one form of savings at one office) was lifted and savings in all forms up to total of ¥1 million were made tax-exempt. For fiscal 1971, the Ministry of Finance planned to raise the ceiling of tax-free savings to ¥2 million, largely because, at the end of fiscal 1969, average savings per household had risen to ¥1,417,000. But such an increase would have exempted interest on ¥4.5 million per household (postal savings ¥2 million, savings deposits ¥2 million, national bonds ¥500,000), so the only change was the addition of stock investment trusts to the tax-exempt savings categories. Effective January 1972, however, the ceiling was raised to ¥1.5 million.

Gross Saving and Capital Formation

	1959			1960			1961			1962		
	¥ billion	Change %	Share %	¥ billion	Change %	Share %	¥ billion	Change %	Share %	¥ billion	Change %	Share %
Gross domestic fixed capital formation	3,765.8	25.3	86.1	5,047.8	34.0	88.5	6,687.8	32.5	87.3	7,266.6	8.7	96.0
Increase in inventories	520.1	81.1	11.9	661.5	27.2	11.6	1,336.8	102.0	17.5	307.1	−77.0	4.1
Net lending to rest of world	85.4	−9.5	2.0	−4.9	−105.8	−0.1	−365.3	7,290.9	−4.8	−5.9	−98.0	−0.1
Gross capital formation	4,371.2	29.0	100.0	5,704.4	30.5	100.0	7,659.2	34.3	100.0	7,567.9	−1.2	100.0
Provision for consumption of fixed capital	1,361.4	18.4	31.1	1,676.9	23.2	29.4	2,165.9	29.2	28.3	2,465.6	13.8	32.6
Saving of private corporations	617.5	66.1	14.1	989.4	60.2	17.3	1,111.5	12.3	14.5	907.3	−18.4	12.0
Saving of households & private nonprofit institutions	1,485.3	18.6	34.0	1,906.5	28.4	33.4	2,392.0	25.5	31.2	2,674.3	11.8	35.3
Saving of government	842.7	34.5	19.3	1,248.6	48.2	21.9	1,697.1	35.9	22.2	1,769.4	4.3	23.4
Statistical discrepancy	64.4	−595.1	1.5	−116.9	−281.6	−2.1	292.7	−350.3	3.8	−248.7	−185.0	−3.3
Gross saving	4,371.2	29.0	100.0	5,704.4	30.5	100.0	7,659.2	34.3	100.0	7,567.9	−1.2	100.0

Gross Saving and Capital Formation (cont.)

	1963			1964			1965			1966		
	¥ billion	Change %	Share %	¥ billion	Change %	Share %	¥ billion	Change %	Share %	¥ billion	Change %	Share %
Gross domestic fixed capital formation	8,290.8	14.1	92.2	9,611.8	15.9	92.3	9,915.5	3.2	89.3	11,997.1	21.0	87.6
Increase in inventories	1,089.3	254.7	12.1	789.3	−27.5	7.6	816.3	3.4	7.3	1,343.6	64.6	9.8
Net lending to rest of world	−385.4	6,462.5	−4.3	10.0	−102.6	0.1	377.2	3,675.6	3.4	357.8	−5.1	2.6
Gross capital formation	8,994.7	18.9	100.0	10,411.3	15.7	100.0	11,109.0	6.7	100.0	13,698.4	23.3	100.0
Provision for consumption of fixed capital	3,000.8	21.7	33.4	3,667.1	22.2	35.2	4,195.9	14.4	37.8	4,959.9	18.2	36.2
Saving of private corporations	1,059.2	16.7	11.8	1,062.7	0.3	10.2	972.7	−8.5	8.8	1,718.3	76.7	12.5
Saving of households & private nonprofit institutions	2,968.0	11.8	33.0	3,307.0	11.4	31.8	3,792.7	14.7	34.1	4,546.3	19.9	33.2
Saving of government	1,929.5	9.1	21.5	1,999.0	3.6	19.2	1,956.2	−2.1	17.6	2,139.9	9.4	15.6
Statistical discrepancy	37.2	−114.9	0.4	375.0	910.9	3.6	191.4	−49.0	1.7	333.9	74.4	2.4
Gross saving	8,994.7	18.9	100.0	10,411.3	15.7	100.0	11,109.0	6.7	100.0	13,698.4	23.3	100.0

Gross Saving and Capital Formation (cont.)

	1967 ¥ billion	1967 Change %	1967 Share %	1968 ¥ billion	1968 Change %	1968 Share %	1970 ¥ billion	1970 Change %	1970 Share %
Gross domestic fixed capital formation	14,860.7	23.9	87.5	17,939.1	20.7	85.9	22,251.1	24.0	87.1
Increase in inventories	2,235.4	66.4	13.2	2,423.2	8.4	11.6	2,556.8	5.5	10.1
Net lending to rest of world	−112.8	−131.5	−0.7	530.5	−570.5	2.5	740.7	39.6	2.9
Gross capital formation	16,983.3	24.0	100.0	20,892.8	23.0	100.0	25,548.6	22.3	100.0
Provision for consumption of fixed capital	5,844.3	17.8	34.4	6,952.5	19.0	33.3	8,479.9	22.0	33.2
Saving of private corporations	2,413.9	40.5	14.2	3,522.1	45.9	16.9	3,888.5	10.4	15.2
Saving of households & private nonprofit institutions	5,803.6	27.7	34.2	6,961.5	20.0	33.3	7,959.6	14.3	31.2
Saving of government	2,819.0	31.7	16.6	3,635.9	29.0	17.4	4,691.7	29.0	18.4
Statistical discrepancy	102.5	−69.7	0.6	−179.2	−274.8	−0.9	528.9	−395.1	2.1
Gross saving	16,983.3	24.0	100.0	20,892.8	23.0	100.0	25,548.6	22.3	100.0

Notes: 1. At current prices; fiscal years.
2. Change: rate of increase or decrease compared with preceding fiscal year.
Share: percentage distribution.
Source: Economic Planning Agency, Annual Report on National Income Statistics.

Financial Savings

	Total savings balance ¥ billion	Actual increase in fiscal year ¥ billion	%	Savings target ¥ billion	Attainment of target %	Increase in fiscal year — Banks ¥ billion	%	Mutual banks ¥ billion	%	Credit associations ¥ billion	%	Agricultural cooperatives ¥ billion	%	Postal savings ¥ billion	%
1962	20,581.3	4,385.9	27.1	2,800	156.6	2,501.3	28.3	435.5	31.2	433.6	34.0	231.5	23.8	228.6	17.5
1963	25,107.3	4,525.9	22.0	3,800	119.1	2,474.8	21.8	381.8	20.9	458.0	26.8	297.1	24.6	298.0	19.4
1964	29,589.0	4,481.7	17.9	4,300	104.2	2,220.1	16.1	332.5	15.0	440.9	20.4	411.2	27.4	392.2	21.4
1965	35,189.3	5,600.2	18.9	4,800	116.7	3,026.6	18.9	394.0	15.5	460.4	17.7	399.2	20.9	472.7	21.2
1966	41,373.7	6,184.3	17.6	6,300	98.2	3,062.2	16.1	446.0	15.2	556.2	18.1	497.3	21.5	607.3	22.5
1967	48,300.6	6,926.9	16.7	7,200	96.2	3,038.0	13.7	565.0	16.7	694.7	19.2	620.9	22.1	799.3	24.2
1968	56,587.8	8,287.2	17.2	8,000	103.6	3,837.2	15.3	539.8	13.7	792.7	18.4	617.1	18.0	993.3	24.2
1969	67,503.6	10,915.7	19.3	9,600	113.7	4,939.3	16.8	795.2	19.9	1,177.5	23.0	929.0	22.9	1,213.8	23.8
1970	80,203.4	12,699.8	18.8	12,000	105.8	5,984.8	17.4	928.7	19.4	1,260.6	20.0	904.7	18.2	1,428.3	22.6

Notes: 1. The total includes actual deposits (general deposits less checks and bills) of all financial institutions, trusts, and life insurance.
2. "Banks" includes trust accounts.
Source: Bank of Japan.

Accounts of Households and Private Nonprofit Institutions

	1959			1960			1961			1962		
	¥ billion	Change %	Share %	¥ billion	Change %	Share %	¥ billion	Change %	Share %	¥ billion	Change %	Share %
Private consumption expenditure	7,994.4	11.0	77.4	9,065.2	13.4	75.3	10,518.3	16.0	73.8	12,136.4	15.4	73.7
Direct taxes & charges	376.1	5.8	3.6	492.9	31.1	4.1	625.1	26.8	4.4	789.2	26.2	4.8
Social insurance contributions	329.5	15.3	3.2	408.4	24.0	3.4	516.6	26.5	3.6	617.9	19.6	3.8
Other current transfers to government	137.7	13.1	1.3	164.5	19.4	1.4	198.8	20.9	1.4	239.7	20.6	1.5
Transfers to rest of world	1.0	41.0	0.0	2.3	124.2	0.0	2.9	25.3	0.0	4.5	58.8	0.0
Savings	1,485.3	18.6	14.4	1,906.5	28.4	15.8	2,392.0	25.5	16.8	2,674.3	11.8	16.2
Disbursements	10,324.0	12.0	100.0	12,039.8	16.6	100.0	14,253.6	18.4	100.0	16,462.0	15.5	100.0
Compensation of employees	5,685.8	11.8	55.1	6,639.2	16.8	55.1	7,957.0	19.8	55.8	9,404.8	18.2	57.1
Income from unincorporated enterprises	3,055.2	7.7	29.6	3,486.3	14.1	29.0	3,978.9	14.1	27.9	4,333.2	8.9	26.3
Income from property	1,061.2	25.3	10.3	1,308.8	23.3	10.9	1,606.8	22.8	11.3	1,890.5	17.7	11.5
Current transfers from private corporations	20.2	34.3	0.2	25.1	24.3	0.2	29.3	16.9	0.2	29.5	2.3	0.2
Less interest on consumer debt	−30.0	8.7	−0.3	−32.6	8.5	−0.3	−43.7	34.4	−0.3	49.1	12.3	0.3
Current transfers from government	511.6	14.9	5.0	590.6	15.4	4.9	702.0	18.9	4.9	829.4	18.2	5.0
Transfers from rest of world	19.9	24.9	0.2	22.5	12.7	0.2	23.4	4.1	0.2	23.4	−0.1	0.1
Receipts (personal income)	10,324.0	12.0	100.0	12,039.8	16.6	100.0	14,253.6	18.4	100.0	16,462.0	15.5	100.0
Disposable personal income	9,479.7	12.1	91.8	10,971.7	15.7	91.1	12,910.3	17.7	90.6	14,810.8	14.7	90.0
Saving ratio (%)	15.7			17.4			18.5			18.1		

Accounts of Households and Private Nonprofit Institutions (cont.)

	1963			1964			1965			1966		
	¥ billion	Change %	Share %	¥ billion	Change %	Share %	¥ billion	Change %	Share %	¥ billion	Change %	Share %
Private consumption expenditure	14,287.3	17.7	74.2	16,432.4	15.0	74.2	18,469.0	12.4	73.4	20,948.2	13.4	72.7
Direct taxes & charges	969.3	22.8	5.0	1,157.4	19.4	5.2	1,345.3	16.2	5.8	1,500.2	11.5	5.2
Social insurance contributions	753.8	22.0	3.9	887.0	17.7	4.0	1,141.2	28.7	4.5	1,359.7	19.1	4.7
Other current transfers to government	265.7	10.8	1.4	330.2	24.3	1.5	390.9	18.4	1.6	437.0	11.8	1.5
Transfers to rest of world	15.1	232.5	0.1	23.9	58.7	0.1	20.1	−15.8	0.1	30.1	49.8	0.1
Savings	2,968.0	11.0	15.4	3,307.0	11.4	14.9	3,792.7	14.7	15.1	4,546.3	19.9	15.8
Disbursements	19,259.1	17.0	100.0	22,138.0	14.9	100.0	25,159.2	13.6	100.0	28,821.5	14.6	100.0
Compensation of employees	11,005.0	17.0	57.1	12,764.7	16.0	57.7	14,698.6	15.2	58.4	16,921.8	15.1	58.7
Income from unincorporated enterprises	5,021.8	15.9	26.1	5,563.3	10.8	25.1	6,059.2	8.9	24.1	6,823.4	12.6	23.7
Income from property	2,219.5	17.4	11.5	2,602.5	17.3	11.8	2,976.1	14.4	11.8	3,422.9	15.0	11.9
Current transfers from private corporations	36.3	21.1	0.2	39.5	8.9	0.2	44.4	12.5	0.2	48.2	8.5	0.2
Less interest on consumer debt	60.1	22.3	0.3	71.5	19.0	0.3	86.8	21.5	0.3	105.1	21.0	0.4
Current transfers from government	1,013.0	22.1	5.3	1,213.9	19.8	5.5	1,446.2	19.1	5.7	1,686.5	16.6	5.9
Transfers from rest of world	23.6	1.0	0.1	25.5	8.0	0.1	21.5	−15.6	0.1	23.8	10.4	0.1
Receipts (personal income)	19,259.1	17.0	100.0	22,138.0	14.9	100.0	25,159.2	13.6	100.0	28,821.5	14.6	100.0
Disposable personal income	17,255.3	16.5	89.6	19,739.4	14.4	89.2	22,261.7	12.8	88.5	25,494.5	14.5	88.5
Saving ratio (%)	17.7			16.8			17.0			17.8		

Accounts of Households and Private Nonprofit Institutions (cont.)

	1967 ¥ billion	Change %	Share %	1968 ¥ billion	Change %	Share %	1969 ¥ billion	Change %	Share %
Private consumption expenditure	23,892.6	14.1	71.2	27,440.0	14.8	70.3	31,690.6	15.5	70.2
Direct taxes & charges	1,742.7	16.2	5.2	2,137.2	22.6	5.5	2,596.8	21.5	5.8
Social insurance contributions	1,609.6	18.4	4.8	1,868.7	16.1	4.8	2,224.2	19.0	4.9
Other current transfers to government	496.2	13.5	1.5	584.1	17.7	1.5	636.7	9.0	1.4
Transfers to rest of world	34.1	13.2	0.1	36.1	5.9	0.1	39.7	10.0	0.1
Savings	5,803.6	27.7	17.3	6,961.5	20.0	17.8	7,959.6	14.3	17.6
Disbursements	33,578.8	16.5	100.0	39,027.8	16.2	100.0	45,147.7	15.7	100.0
Compensation of employees	19,625.6	16.0	58.4	22,836.9	16.4	58.5	26,993.4	18.2	59.8
Income from unincorporated enterprises	8,124.0	19.1	24.2	9,445.5	16.3	24.2	10,342.3	9.5	22.9
Income from property	3,922.7	14.6	11.7	4,534.2	15.6	11.6	5,302.0	16.9	11.7
Current transfers from private corporations	62.2	29.2	0.2	69.7	12.0	0.2	92.7	33.0	0.2
Less interest on consumer debt	134.4	27.9	0.4	163.9	21.9	0.4	202.8	23.7	0.4
Current transfer from government	1,953.7	15.8	5.8	2,279.5	16.7	5.8	2,590.6	13.7	5.7
Transfers from rest of world	24.9	4.8	0.1	25.9	3.9	0.1	29.4	13.5	0.1
Receipts (personal income)	33,578.8	16.5	100.0	39,027.8	16.2	100.0	45,147.7	15.7	100.0
Disposable personal income	29,696.2	16.5	88.4	34,401.6	15.8	88.1	39,650.2	15.3	87.8
Saving ratio (%)	19.5			20.2			20.1		

Notes:

1. At current prices; fiscal years.

2. Change: rate of increase or decrease compared with preceding fiscal year. Share: percentage distribution.

3. Saving ratio = Saving / Disposable personal income

Source: Economic Planning Agency, Annual Report on National Income Statistics.

Growth and Composition of Personal Financial Assets

End of year	Personal financial assets	Savings deposits	Trusts	Insurance	Stocks	Investment trusts
	¥ billion	%	%	%	%	%
1960	12,711.6	44.2	3.0	9.8	11.0	4.3
1961	15,444.1	42.6	2.9	9.9	11.8	6.9
1962	18,702.5	40.8	3.4	9.9	11.8	6.2
1963	21,925.1	41.5	3.8	9.9	12.4	5.5
1964	25,416.0	42.9	4.3	9.9	12.5	4.9
1965	30,816.4	42.3	4.7	11.7	10.7	3.5
1966	35,621.9	43.9	5.2	12.5	9.6	2.6
1967	42,352.7	44.3	5.4	12.2	8.2	2.0
1968	49,351.6	45.2	5.6	12.6	7.5	1.7
1969	58,900.0	45.5	5.6	12.7	6.7	1.7
1970	69,016.4	46.1	5.7	13.1	6.4	1.8

Note: Stocks and investment trusts: face value.
Source: Nihon Keizai Shimbun.

Outstanding Balances of Personal Financial Assets

	End of 1959		End of 1969	
	¥ billion	%	¥ billion	%
Cash	777.6	7.8	3,791.2	6.7
Current deposits	34.4	0.3	203.9	0.4
Short-term deposits	1,384.5	13.9	7,355.7	12.8
Time & savings deposits	4,716.3	47.2	26,788.4	46.7
Trusts	298.5	3.0	3,308.1	5.8
Insurance	1,007.7	10.1	7,492.1	13.1
Securities	1,764.4	17.7	8,366.4	14.6
Total	9,993.4	100.0	57,305.8	100.0

Structure of Increase in Individual Financial Assets

	January–June 1969		January–June 1970	
	¥ billion	%	¥ billion	%
Total increase	2,910.2	100.0	3,252.0	100.0
Cash & demand deposits	−252.6	−8.7	−516.5	−15.9
Savings deposits	1,781.5	61.2	2,072.9	63.7
Trusts	262.1	9.0	315.8	9.7
Insurance	597.8	20.6	750.2	23.1
Securities	521.4	17.9	629.6	19.4
National bonds	39.3	1.3	34.4	1.0
Bonds of public corporations	91.0	3.1	123.0	3.8
Bank debentures	252.3	8.7	143.4	4.4
Corporate debentures	10.7	0.4	4.0	0.1
Stocks	67.0	2.3	191.8	5.9
Investment trust certificates	61.1	2.1	133.0	4.1

Source: Bank of Japan

Increase in Personal Financial Assets

(In billions of yen)

Fiscal year	1963	1964	1965	1966	1967	1968	1969
Cash & demand deposits	643.3	663.3	755.9	900.0	1,009.7	1,265.9	1,881.3
Cash	108.7	242.9	261.0	319.1	396.2	392.1	600.8
Demand deposits	534.6	420.4	494.0	580.9	613.5	873.8	1,280.5
Savings deposits	2,067.1	2,543.3	3,143.1	3,868.9	4,485.9	5,346.0	6,563.2
Savings deposits	1,549.6	1,879.1	2,221.2	2,667.9	3,179.7	3,741.1	4,637.1
Trusts	157.8	285.0	317.5	435.2	433.0	501.6	572.3
Insurance	359.7	379.2	604.4	765.2	873.2	1,103.3	1,353.8
Securities	580.1	512.5	268.6	429.0	488.3	724.9	978.0
Long-term government bonds	—	—	12.7	74.8	15.0	8.2	22.8
Bank debentures	104.6	156.6	228.1	286.7	253.5	328.9	346.7
Other debentures	23.8	78.6	119.1	113.0	180.2	200.7	199.3
Shares of stock	366.1	313.8	94.9	65.2	113.2	191.4	210.3
Investment trusts	85.6	−36.5	−186.2	−110.7	−73.6	−4.3	199.0
Total financial assets	3,290.5	3,719.1	4,167.2	5,197.9	5,983.9	7,336.8	9,422.5
Structure (%)							
Cash & demand deposits	19.6	17.8	18.1	17.3	16.9	17.3	20.0
Savings deposits	62.8	68.4	75.4	74.4	75.0	72.8	69.7
Securities	17.6	13.8	6.5	8.3	8.1	9.9	10.3

Source: Bank of Japan

Saving Ratio by Number of Gainfully Employed, Income and Savings

Number of gainfully employed per household	Average saving ratio				
	General average	Monthly income ¥50,000–100,000		Monthly income over ¥ 100,000	
		Savings ¥500,000–¥1 million	Savings over ¥1 million	Savings ¥500,000–¥1 million	Savings over ¥1 million
	%	%	%	%	%
0–1	13.1	12.2	10.6	20.9	22.7
2 and more	17.8	16.1	14.4	22.4	21.6

Note: Saving ratio $= \left(1 - \dfrac{\text{Consumption expenditure}}{\text{Actual income}}\right) \times 100$

Source: Office of the Prime Minister, Bureau of Statistics, National Consumer Survey, 1969.

Savings by Kind of Financial Assets

	Workers' households			Households of individual proprietors		
	¥1,000	% of house-holds	% of savings	¥1,000	% of house-holds	% of savings
Total savings	1,051	97.8	100.0	1,721	97.6	100.0
Postal savings	141	63.1	13.4	165	56.8	9.6
Savings certificates	93	41.3	8.9	109	37.6	6.3
Ordinary deposits	48	48.3	4.6	56	39.5	3.3
Banks	355	77.4	33.7	890	86.1	51.7
Time deposits	252	57.3	24.0	640	71.5	37.2
Ordinary deposits	103	62.1	9.8	251	70.8	14.6
Life insurance	229	83.6	21.7	342	84.2	19.9
Loan trusts, bonds	108	19.8	10.3	98	18.6	5.7
Stocks & investment trusts	144	19.1	13.3	211	17.3	12.2
Other	79	28.1	7.5	15	7.1	0.9
Liabilities	198	42.6	100.0	445	48.6	100.0
From purchase of land or house	165	21.2	83.5	240	22.0	54.0
Other	33	26.2	16.5	205	34.4	46.0

Source: Office of the Prime Minister, Bureau of Statistics, 1969 National Survey of Family Income and Expenditures, Volume 7, Savings.

Savings by Quintile Income Groups: Households of Individual Proprietors, National Average

Annual income	Average		I ¥695,000 & lower		II ¥696,000– 963,000		III ¥964,000– 1,265,000		IV ¥1,266,000– 1,864,000		V ¥1,865,000– & higher	
	¥1,000	%	¥1,000	%	¥1,000	%	¥1,000	%	¥1,000	%	¥1,000	%
Total savings	1,721	100.0	606	100.0	859	100.0	1,250	100.0	1,873	100.0	4,018	100.0
Postal savings	165	9.6	90	14.9	103	12.0	139	11.1	195	10.4	299	7.4
Savings certificates	109	6.3	59	9.7	66	7.7	91	7.3	124	6.6	204	5.1
Ordinary deposits	56	3.3	32	5.2	37	4.2	48	3.8	71	3.8	95	2.4
Banks	890	51.7	278	45.9	415	48.3	652	52.1	980	52.3	2,126	52.9
Time deposits	640	37.2	188	31.1	289	33.6	456	36.5	718	38.4	1,546	38.5
Ordinary deposits	251	14.6	90	14.8	127	14.7	195	15.6	262	14.0	580	14.4
Life insurance	342	19.9	168	27.8	239	27.8	288	23.1	381	20.3	634	15.8
Loan trusts, bonds	98	5.7	28	4.6	38	4.4	56	4.5	99	5.3	270	6.7
Stocks & investment trusts	211	12.2	35	5.8	60	7.0	105	8.4	198	10.6	655	16.3
Other	15	0.9	6	1.0	5	0.6	10	0.8	20	1.1	34	0.8
Liabilities	445	100.0	181	100.0	264	100.0	378	100.0	501	100.0	902	100.0
From purchase of land or house	240	54.0	98	54.2	137	51.7	203	53.5	263	52.5	501	55.5
Other	205	46.0	83	45.8	127	48.3	176	46.5	238	47.5	401	44.5

Source: Office of the Prime Minister, Bureau of Statistics, 1969 National Survey of Family Income and Expenditures, Volume 7, Savings.

Consumption Expenditure of Households and Investment in Dwellings

(In billions of yen)

Fiscal year	Consumption expenditures of households				Investment in dwellings	
	Total	Durable goods	Nondurable goods	Services	Total	Households
1959	7,844.5	306.0	5,563.2	1,975.4	554.9	443.1
1960	8,882.4	380.7	6,126.4	2,375.3	706.1	529.9
1961	10,303.5	501.2	6,959.8	2,842.5	886.2	657.9
1962	11,898.4	649.2	7,905.9	3,343.3	1,039.4	796.0
1963	14,012.3	868.7	9,101.4	4,042.1	1,345.3	1,019.8
1964	16,066.6	1,018.4	10,254.4	4,793.8	1,675.9	1,263.2
1965	18,053.7	1,048.7	11,537.0	5,467.9	2,021.9	1,666.8
1966	20,455.4	1,249.6	12,858.6	6,347.2	2,343.2	1.922.3
1967	23,306.4	1,518.7	14,705.3	7,082.3	2,986.8	2,407.4
1968	26,750.5	1,928.1	16,503.2	8,319.2	3,595.4	2,878.1
1969	30,864.5	2,401.7	18,736.5	9,726.3	4,472.8	3,561.1

Source: Economic Planning Agency, Annual Report on National Income Statistics.

Savings by Quintile Income Groups: Workers' Households, National Average

Annual income	Average		I ¥773,000 & lower		II ¥774,000– 966,000		III ¥967,000– 1,167,000		IV ¥1,168,000– 1,508,000		V ¥1,508,000– & higher	
	¥1,000	%	¥1,000	%	¥1,000	%	¥1,000	%	¥1,000	%	¥1,000	%
Total savings	1,051	100.0	408	100.0	603	100.0	851	100.0	1,157	100.0	2,238	100.0
Postal savings	141	13.4	85	20.9	113	18.8	132	15.5	162	14.0	213	9.5
Savings certificates	93	8.9	55	13.4	73	12.1	88	10.3	109	9.5	141	6.3
Ordinary deposits	48	4.6	30	7.5	40	6.7	45	5.2	53	4.6	72	3.2
Banks	355	33.7	155	38.1	220	36.4	295	34.6	385	33.3	718	32.1
Time deposits	252	24.0	108	26.6	153	25.4	210	24.7	272	23.5	516	23.0
Ordinary deposits	103	9.8	47	11.5	66	11.0	84	9.9	114	9.8	203	9.0
Life insurance	229	21.7	112	27.4	161	26.7	204	24.0	265	22.9	401	17.9
Loan trusts, bonds	108	10.3	23	5.6	37	6.1	74	8.7	127	11.0	279	12.4
Stocks & investment trusts	140	13.3	14	3.4	32	5.3	76	8.9	120	10.4	459	20.5
Other	79	7.5	19	4.6	41	6.7	70	8.2	97	8.4	168	7.5
Liabilities	198	100.0	64	100.0	110	100.0	175	100.0	246	100.0	395	100.0
From purchase of land or house	165	83.5	39	60.9	81	73.8	142	81.1	213	86.3	353	89.2
Other	33	16.5	25	39.1	29	26.2	33	18.9	34	13.7	43	10.8

Source: Office of the Prime Minister, Bureau of Statistics, 1969 National Survey of Family Income and Expenditures, Volume 7, Savings.

Capital Formation

	FY1959 ¥ billion	FY1969 ¥ billion	Ratio 1969/1959	Average yearly rate of increase %
GNP	13,608.9	62,433.3	4.57	16.4
National income	11,023.3	49,319.3	4.46	16.1
Gross saving (=gross capital formation)	4,371.2	25,548.6	5.84	19.3
Gross domestic capital formation	4,285.9	24,807.9	5.79	19.2
Gross private capital formation	3,212.4	19.571.7	6.09	19.8
Gross government capital formation	1,073.5	5,236.1	4.88	17.2
Gross private fixed capital formation	2,728.0	17,189.1	6.30	20.2
Dwellings	554.9	4,472.8	8.06	23.2
Investment in dwellings by households	443.1	3,561.1	8.04	23.1
Individual enterprises	401.0	2,170.9	5.41	18.4
Plant & equipment of corporate enterprises	1,882.3	10,831.9	5.75	19.1
Gross government fixed capital formation	1,037.8	5,062.0	4.88	17.2
Savings of households & private non-profit institutions	1,485.3	7,959.6	5.36	18.3

Source: Economic Planning Agency.

3 THE CAPITAL MARKET

2 THE ROLE OF INDIRECT FINANCING

In the immediate postwar period, Japanese enterprises were unable to finance reconstruction out of their own resources and had to rely for the largest part of their capital needs on external funds. Funds available in the capital market were utterly insufficient for financing the strong expansion in equipment investment, while secondary advantages connected with borrowing (different from dividends, interest payments are deductible as business expenses; loans can be scheduled according to actual needs) further encouraged the reliance of enterprises on external funds. As mentioned above, until recent years, the increase in money supply required for the expansion came mostly from central bank credit. Fiscal policy was based on the budgetary balance, and, since there was no export surplus, no capital accumulation in the form of foreign exchange took place. Credit creation by the banks, mainly the city banks, made the expansion of physical equipment and economic activities possible, while the Bank of Japan issued the currency to match this expansion.

But the bulk of the funds which the banks funneled into industry came from deposits. This made the collection of deposits the key operation for the banks and was the main reason for the fierce competition, among the city banks on the one hand and between the city banks, the mutual banks, and the credit associations on the other.

At the end of March 1971, individual deposits accounted for 36.6 percent of all outstanding deposits, while those of general corporations made up 54.0 percent; but a not inconsiderable part of the corporate deposits represented compensating balances. The share of individual deposits in time deposits amounted to 48.5 percent, that of deposits of general corporations to 44.5 percent; a large part of the deposits of general corporations constituted working capital. Basically, the banks act as intermediaries, collecting funds from individual savers and transmitting these funds to industry. In the last ten years, the overall increase in deposits was slightly lower than that in loans (all banks, deposits: end of 1960, ¥8,872.2 billion; end of 1970, ¥41,308.8 billion; average yearly rate of increase, 16.6 percent; loans: end of 1960, ¥8,182.6 billion, end of 1970, ¥39,479.3 billion; average yearly rate of increase, 17.1 percent); although it was somewhat higher than the growth rate of GNP, the rate of increase in deposits was considerably lower than the rate of increase in gross private capital formation. Until recently, the banks paid little attention to consumer credit, so that the largest part of bank loans went to the corporations; the banks, therefore, contributed little to financing the capital formation in the personal sector.

A considerable part of the external funds which the city banks borrowed in order to supplement their own resources (one aspect of the overloan situation) came from the call market, and represented savings originally deposited with local banks, mutual banks, credit associations, or agricultural credit cooperatives. Thus, two or more banks acted as intermediaries between the saver and the user of these funds. To a certain extent, therefore, the high interest rates of which industry often complained can be attributed to the increase in fund costs connected with the indirect system of financing.

Because Japanese enterprises relied on bank loans for their rapid expansion, they found themselves in a heavily overborrowed position. In their capital structure, the share of equity capital was extremely low. In the first half of fiscal 1970, the ratio of equity capital to total capital employed (476 companies capitalized at ￥1 billion and higher) was 19.28 percent; the share of internal funds in total fund supply was 41.97 percent, that of borrowings 40.37 percent; in the latter half of fiscal 1970, the ratio of equity capital to total capital employed (575 companies listed on the First Section of the Tokyo Stock Exchange) was 18.5 percent.

The main reason responsible for the heavy reliance of enterprises on external funds was the insufficiency of internal cash flow. In the context of the growing economy, enterprises could not afford to stand still; because each enterprise had to increase its size constantly and rapidly, its fund requirements were always ahead of available resources. If any enterprise had waited until it could finance its equipment investment by internal funds, it would have fallen behind in the competitive race.

The dependence on bank loans created strong bonds between banks and enterprises. These ties are particularly close between the city banks and the companies belonging to their particular groups, but they are by no means restricted to them. In many instances, the city banks form the center of three concentric circles. The first is composed of the leading enterprises of the bank's group, the second is formed by the other firms belonging to the group, and the third by the companies for which the bank is the chief supplier of funds. In many cases, mutual shareholding has further strengthened the ties of the banks with the large enterprises of their group, and city banks have made the relations with their leading corporate clients even closer by placing their officers with them as executives.

Small enterprises are practically excluded from the capital market and have to rely on the banks for the largest part of their capital needs. The special financial institutions for small enterprises, such as mutual banks and credit associations, supply the bulk of the funds required by small enterprises, but the role of the ordinary commercial banks is by no means negligible. Demand for business loans on the part of small enterprises became very brisk in 1966 when these enterprises began to improve their facilities. Large manufacturers, such as Hitachi and Mitsubishi Heavy Industries, arranged for bank loans for air conditioning and refrigerating equipment, vending machines, and dry cleaning equipment. The same system was used by local banks for the improvement of shopping streets, barber shops, and other businesses in the service sector. In the last five years, lending of city banks to small enterprises has become relatively larger; the share of loans to small businesses in the total outstanding loan balance of city banks rose from 23.7 percent at the end of 1965 to 25.8 percent at the end of 1970; the ratios were 30.3 percent and 33.1 percent, respectively, for all banks; 53.3 percent and 55.5 percent, for the local banks; and 10.7 percent and 16.0 percent, for the long-term credit banks. Of the net funds supplied to industry in 1970, private financial institutions for small enterprises provided 15.2 percent; the government's Small Business Finance Corporation, 1.1 percent; and the People's Finance Corporation, 0.8 percent. On the basis of the flow-of-funds accounts of the Bank of Japan, government funds constituted 8.3 percent of all loans given to corporations in fiscal 1969.

New stock issues increased rapidly during the Iwato boom, but since 1965 their role in corporate fund supply has again been marginal, despite a relative increase in 1967 and 1968. Corporate debentures contributed even less to corporate funds. In 1970, the recovery of the investment trusts and large individual purchases of bonds brought a certain improvement in direct financing. Nominally, the funds raised by stock and bond issues constitute direct financing (funds raised in the capital market), but a large part of the stock and bond issues are taken over by banks, so that, in view of their origin, these funds can be considered as indirect financing. (At the end of fiscal 1969, the banks held ¥1,586.9 billion in industrial debentures and ¥1,478.6 billion in stocks; of the ¥495.1 billion in industrial bonds issued in fiscal 1969, financial institutions purchased 30.9 percent.) The structure of corporate fund supply from the point of view of the origin of the funds is given in the table "Financing Channels," which shows that 90.6 percent of the funds supplied to corporate enterprises in fiscal 1969 represented indirect financing. Noteworthy is the relatively large share of government funds in this analysis.

Trade credit has played an increasingly large role in corporate financing. Accounts payable and bank borrowing supplement each other, and their aggregate share in the composition of corporate liabilities is fairly constant (about 65 percent). The ratio of trade credit to sales rose very rapidly at the beginning of the sixties; the large increase in supply capacity resulting from very active equipment investment and the ensuing fierce competition led to a deterioration in payment conditions (longer payment terms, larger part paid in bills). A lower rate of increase in equipment investment, greater ability in self-financing, and easier bank credit lessened reliance on trade credit in the latter half of the sixties, but, in 1970, the ratio of accounts payable to sales rose above the 1964 level (October–December quarter 1970, 0.83; based on the Bank of Japan's short-term economic survey of key enterprises). At the end of fiscal 1969, outstanding trade credit extended by corporate enterprises amounted to ¥46,857.8 billion; trade credit received by corporate enterprises stood at ¥36,249.7 billion and trade credit received in the personal sector at ¥10,608.1 billion.

Foreign issues of government bonds and corporate debentures were important for the induction of foreign capital, but these funds were of greater significance for the balance of payments than as additions to the country's capital resources.

Direct government financing and funds supplied by semigovernmental agencies continue to play an important role in Japanese industrial financing. While the Bank of Japan is immediately responsible for the regulation of the money market, the Trust Fund Bureau of the Ministry of Finance, a variety of special accounts, and numerous government financed banks and finance corporations supply funds to government and private enterprises. A large part of the funds channeled through the Trust Fund Bureau comes from the postal savings system. Accumulated capital, either in the form of internal reserves of enterprises or of savings, was insufficient to finance the rapid postwar growth of the economy. Central bank credit (the origin of the often-discussed overloan situation of city banks) was an important factor for fund supply during the expansion phases and, perhaps, even more important for preventing deflationary tight-money policies from shaking out the economy.

The reliance of enterprises on banks for financing their expansion programs presents a variety of aspects. One of the reasons often cited for this method is that interest payments can be deducted as a legitimate business expense, while dividends have to be paid out of profits after taxes. Undoubtedly this is true, but it does not tell the whole story. The close connections between industrial enterprises and banks seem to be a rather important factor. Japanese banks have traditionally been engaged in industrial financing, and they put much more emphasis on this part of their business than, for example, on consumer credit. Financing through loans is readily adjustable to the various phases of an expansion program and depends less on the state of the capital market. Futhermore, Japanese dividend rates are relatively high, and the maintenance of a traditional dividend rate is part of the "face" of an enterprise and therefore of importance, not only for the quotation of the company's stock but because of a need to save that face. The borrowed money adds substantially to the capital working in the enterprise, accelerates the acquisition of new equipment, and thus makes increased sales and earnings possible. When the foundations for maintaining the dividend rate have been laid, firms increase their capital and repay their bank loans with the proceeds.

According to established Japanese practice, new share issues are allocated to existing stockholders at par value or below (the difference between par and issue price being paid out of capital reserves). In recent years, some firms offered part of their new shares to the general public at current market prices or slightly below. The favorable market conditions prevailing until the summer of 1971, made this procedure possible and, in some cases, the firms could realize handsome premiums. But, in general, reaction toward this method was critical, and the firms which adopted it lost much of the goodwill of their stockholders.

The reason for this negative reaction is clear. Although dividend rates are not without influence on stock prices, growth anticipation plays a much more important role, and market prices preempt the increase in the stockholders' equity through new issues purchasable at par.

Net Supply of Industrial Funds

(In billions of yen)

	1965	1966	1967	1968	1969	1970
External funds, total	4,971.2	5,606.1	7,040.9	7,434.4	10,320.5	12,623.8
Stock issues	262.6	335.1	332.3	491.4	754.2	1,002.7
Issues of industrial debentures	219.3	225.2	278.0	159.4	298.6	358.7
Loans, total	4,489.2	5,045.8	6,430.6	6,783.5	9,267.7	11,262.4
Loans by private fin. insts.	4,044.4	4,505.0	5,803.1	5,994.1	8,379.0	10,248.2
All banks, banking accounts	2,215.2	2,629.6	3,151.7	2,857.8	4,323.9	5,107.1
All banks, trust accounts	417.8	274.7	500.1	574.8	658.4	776.9
Financial institutions for small enterprises	894.8	1,167.8	1,378.7	1,355.1	2,009.3	2,194.4
Agric. fin. insts.	289.3	358.1	539.6	744.1	831.2	1,318.3
Insurance companies	227.1	74.6	232.9	462.1	556.2	851.5
Loans by gov. fin. inst.	372.5	459.9	534.2	675.8	774.6	910.6
Special financing accounts	72.1	80.7	93.2	113.5	114.1	103.6
Foreign financing (not included in total of external funds)	2.1	−42.8	17.4	164.5	144.2	86.3
Internal financing	4,075.3	5,118.9	6,585.7	8,240.0	9,831.3	
Depreciation	3,120.7	3,669.9	4,293.2	4,965.3	6,130.4	
Retained earnings	954.6	1,449.0	2,292.5	3,274.7	3,700.9	

Indirect Financing:
Composition of Corporate Fund Supply

	Fiscal 1967	Fiscal 1968	Fiscal 1969
Total corporate fund supply (¥ billion)	6,175.0	6,826.5	9,334.2
	100.0%	100.0%	100.0%
Indirect financing	84.8	86.1	86.2
Borrowing in money market	75.2	75.8	77.9
Borrowing from banks	46.2	43.1	44.0
Borrowing from other financial insts.	29.1	32.6	33.9
Borrowing from governmental financial insts.	9.6	10.3	8.3
Direct financing	8.8	9.2	8.5
Corporate bonds	3.2	3.9	2.9
Stock issues	5.6	5.3	5.6
Foreign borrowing	6.4	4.7	5.3

Based on Flow of Funds Accounts of Bank of Japan.

Structure of Sources and Application of Funds

(In percent)

	Fiscal 1959–64	Fiscal 1965–68
Cash & deposits	10.4	12.0
Accounts receivable	31.6	28.6
Inventory investment (a)	8.5	10.1
Equipment investment (b)	44.5	45.2
Additions to fixed assets	29.0	26.4
Provision for consumption of fixed capital	15.5	18.8
Other	5.0	4.1
Sources=applications	100.0	100.0
Accounts payable	23.2	22.6
Borrowing from financial institutions	31.8	32.4
Discounts	9.2	7.6
Short-term loans	12.5	12.8
Long-term loans	10.0	12.0
Stock issues	8.7	4.3
Bond issues	2.1	1.4
Total external funds	65.8	60.7
Depreciation (c)	15.5	18.9
Retained earnings (d)	5.6	6.7
Total internal funds	20.1	25.6
Other	14.2	13.7
Ratio of self-financing	37.4	45.7

Note: Ratio of self-financing $=\dfrac{c+d}{a+b}$

Source: Fuji Bank Bulletin.

Financing Channels

	Fiscal 1967	Fiscal 1968	Fiscal 1969
Fund total (¥ billion)	10,601.5	11,374.8	14,903.0
	100.0%	100.0%	100.0%
Indirect financing (money market)	92.4	91.3	90.6
Banks	43.2	38.4	37.6
Other financial institutions	32.7	34.2	35.9
Governmental financial institutions	16.5	18.7	17.1
Direct financing (capital market)	3.7	5.7	6.2
Foreign financing	3.9	3.0	3.2

Based on Flow of Funds Accounts of Bank of Japan.

Sources and Allocation of Funds

(In billions of yen)

	Fiscal 1968 latter term 496 companies	Fiscal 1969 first term 488 companies	Fiscal 1969 latter term 484 companies	Fiscal 1970 first term 476 companies
Fund requirements	2,841.9	3,477.0	3,848.0	4,175.2
Equipment investment	1,533.6	1,631.6	1,946.4	1,964.8
Inventory investment	304.2	446.3	647.8	665.2
Finished goods (manufacturing)	114.3	100.7	175.5	215.6
Raw materials (manufacturing)	46.5	46.1	67.6	106.0
Net surplus in trade credit granted (incl. discounted bills)	332.4	493.9	463.7	371.5
Fund supply	2,841.9	3,477.9	3,848.0	4,175.2
Internal capital	1,135.1	1,471.2	1,513.5	1,752.2
Ratio of internal capital to total fund supply (%)	39.94	42.30	39.33	41.97
Depreciation	692.7	744.8	815.3	874.6
Retained earnings, reserves	357.2	499.4	567.9	659.8
Increase in capital	85.2	227.0	130.3	217.8
External capital	1,706.8	2,006.7	2,334.5	2,423.0
Borrowings (incl. discounted bills)	1,165.3	1,321.7	1,584.6	1,685.5
Ratio of borrowings to total capital supply (%)	41.01	38.00	41.18	40.37
Long-term loans (contract basis)	741.1	797.7	904.4	1,035.4
Bond issues	186.2	164.5	162.9	174.3
For reference				
Net sales	20,661.5	22,753.6	25,695.0	27,501.9
Net profits	812.1	909.3	1,057.7	1,078.4
Accounts receivable (incl. disc. bills)	993.7	1,495.7	1,854.9	1,574.9
Accounts payable	661.3	1,001.8	1,391.2	1,203.3
Ratio of equity capital to total capital employed (%)	20.80	20.34	19.57	19.28

Note: Companies capitalized at ¥1 billion and higher and listed on the First Section of the Tokyo Stock Exchange.

Source: Bank of Japan.

Structure of Sources and Applications of Fund

	Fiscal 1969 %
Fund applications	
Equipment investment	48.8
Inventory investment	14.9
Other investment	8.9
Net excess of trade credit granted	13.1
Cash & deposits	8.5
Portfolio investment	0.9
Other	4.8
Fund sources	
Internal funds	40.7
Retained earnings, addition to reserves	14.6
Depreciation	21.3
Increase in capital	4.9
External funds	59.3
Borrowing (incl. discounted bills)	39.7
Short-term loans & discounts	16.4
Long-term loans	23.2
Bond issues	4.5
Other	15.1

Note: Long-term loans: maturity 1 year and longer.
Source: Bank of Japan.

Ratio of Equity Capital

	Ratio of capital to total capital employed %	Ratio of retained earnings to total capital employed %	Ratio of equity capital to total capital employed %
1959	13.3	15.7	29.0
1960	13.2	13.9	27.1
1961	14.1	12.1	26.2
1962	14.9	10.7	25.6
1963	14.3	9.9	24.3
1964	13.8	9.1	23.0
1965	13.3	8.7	22.0
1966	12.7	8.8	21.4
1967	11.3	8.6	20.0
1968	10.6	8.7	19.2
1969	9.5	8.7	18.2
1970 (estimate)	8.8	8.6	17.4
1971 (forecast)	8.3	8.7	17.0

Note: Total capital employed: capital accounts plus liabilities.

International Comparison of Corporate Fund Supply

(In percent)

	Japan	United States	United Kingdom	West Germany
Internal funds	29.2	71.1	47.7	63.5
Retained earnings	4.4	25.7	19.1	8.9
Depreciation	24.8	45.4	28.6	54.6
External funds	70.8	28.9	52.3	36.5
Securities	9.2	10.9	23.2	10.2
Stock issues	4.7	1.2	9.7	8.4
Bond issues	4.5	9.7	13.5	1.8
Borrowing	32.0	9.6	6.3	20.4
Other	29.6	8.4	22.8	5.9
Ratio of self-financing	56.5	90.0	97.0	84.5

Notes: 1. 1963–67 average.
2. Ratio of self-financing: ratio of internal funds to equipment investment.
Source: Bank of Japan.

Lending of Japanese and American Banks

(Percentage of outstanding loans)

	Japanese ordinary banks Dec. 31, 1970	American commercial banks June 30, 1970
Loans to enterprises	93.3	37.9
Loans to agriculture	1.0	3.9
Loans for securities financing	0.4	2.6
Loans to financial institutions	0.7	5.9
Home loans (mortgages) }	4.6	24.7
Consumer (personal) loans }		22.5
Other	—	2.5

Structure of Small Business Credit

	End of 1955	End of 1970
Outstanding balances of loans to small enterprises	¥1,941.2 billion	¥29,720.3 billion
Composition by share of credit institutions	% 100.0	% 100.0
All banks	58.5	43.7
Trust accounts of all banks	1.1	1.5
Private financial institutions for small enterprises	32.0	44.8
Mutual banks	19.0	17.3
Credit associations	10.9	22.0
Credit cooperatives	2.1	5.5
Governmental financial institutions for small enterprises	8.2	9.9
Shoko Chukin Bank	3.4	4.1
Small Business Finance Corporation	2.3	3.0
People's Finance Corporation	2.5	2.4
Environmental Hygiene Finance Corporation	—	0.4
Japan Development Bank	0.3	0.1
Japan Export-Import Bank	—	0.1

3 THE CAPITAL MARKET

3 THE STOCK MARKET

1 OVERALL DEVELOPMENTS IN THE SECURITIES MARKET, 1957-63

In early 1957 the market was very active, but the increase in interest rates by the Bank of Japan, effective in May, caused a decline which continued throughout the year. At year-end, the lowest point for the year was reached with the index down to 471.53.

However, in 1958, the market recovered, influenced by the Suez Canal crisis which brought about a strong demand for ship construction.

In 1957, new issues were more numerous than ever, despite the decline in share prices. As money was tight and there was a great need for capital for new plant investment, corporations resorted to capital increases. Investment trusts also found a bigger following and, by the end of 1957, their size had about doubled.

As mentioned above, the Bank of Japan raised the interest rate and, on 8 May, the market fell sharply, down 22.9 percent in one day. The decline continued, affected further by the decision taken by the Ministry of Finance in June to increase the import guarantee rate and to raise interest on long-term contracts, so that, by July, the market was down to the level of May 1956. The volume of trading similarly dwindled, and, while there seemed a firmer tone than in summer, the market declined further when, on October 4, the USSR announced the launching of the Sputnik. The downtrend continued until the end of the year.

However, in early 1958, there was a slight recovery reflecting the cut in the interest rate, an improvement in the balance of payments, and an enlarged government budget for fiscal 1958. Investment trust buying came in, and there was a tax reduction on savings, so that, in July, the market moved towards higher ground. Volume of trading increased, with buying centering on consumer goods industries, but, when, on July 16, the U.S.A. sent troops into Lebanon, shares of shipping, petroleum, and nonferrous metal companies took the lead in the advance. Except for a lull in September, the stock market went up all through the year 1958, advancing from an average of ¥475.20 on the opening day to ¥666.54 on the last day, which, incidentally, was the highest for the year. The difference of ¥191.34 meant an increase of 40 percent in the Dow-Jones average. The reason for this active tone was the anticipation of an overall improvement in the economy. The recession seemed to have touched bottom in the latter half of the year and the expectation of a recovery became general.

With the lowering of the official discount rate in February, the financial stringency eased and, because of good corporate results expected for the March settlement, the market started to move up. On February 11, prices broke through the ¥700 average and, on May 30, the index reached the ¥800 level. The average yield of 225 representative stocks traded on the Tokyo Stock Exchange, which was around 0.07 in January 1958, became less than

0.06 in August and fell to the 0.04 level at the end of December; finally, on July 15, 1959, it sank even below the 0.04 level. In this way, the "reverse gap" between the yield from equities and the fixed interest rates on bonds made its appearance in Japan.

The large increase in investment trusts was a powerful factor in pushing up stock prices. During 1958, newly established unit and open-end trusts came to more than ¥160 billion and, even after subtracting cancellations and redemptions, the net increase reached ¥73 billion. The issue market, however, was dull, because the deflation kept capital increases down. Companies, both listed on the stock exchanges and not listed, which increased their capital during the year 1958 numbered 1,917, a 40 percent decrease as against the preceding year, and the paid-in amount of ¥280 billion remained 25 percent below the previous year.

From the depression low of April-June 1958 the economy quickly became more buoyant. The index of industrial production which had reached a low in March 1958 rose sharply and, by December 1959, it was 46.2 percent higher than the March 1959 low. The expansion of production enabled corporate profits to reach an all-time high. Investment in equipment, which had remained fairly high even in 1958, began to increase particularly in the second quarter of 1959. Large backlogs developed in orders for industrial machinery and, at the same time, there was a sharp increase in demand for durable consumer goods. There naturally developed an increasing demand for funds, which gave rise to the so-called overheating of business. To check this overheating, restrictive measures were taken by the Bank of Japan. The reserve deposit system was announced on September 11, and, on December 2, the discount rate was raised.

The stock market, which had participated in the business improvement, continued strong throughout the year and, despite a heavy break in June and a series of minor fluctuations, the Dow-Jones average, which stood at ¥671.28 on the opening in January, climbed over ¥900 on September 30. The strength was attributed by the Ministry of Finance to an abnormal scarcity of blue chip stocks, and the eight large dealers were warned to prevent the irrational boosting of prices. A similar warning was made to the general public. Despite some calming down, prices continued to advance and volume increased to 168 million shares on October 14. The balance of outstanding loans at the Japan Securities Finance Co. also grew spectacularly. Consequently, the Ministry of Finance raised the margin requirement from 60 to 70 percent. The impact of the warnings and the margin increase caused some weakness in November and, due partly to a further raise in the official discount rate in December and a discouraging outlook for the balance of payments, stock prices declined, the Dow-Jones average standing at ¥874.88 on the last trading day in 1959.

The setback was, however, temporary, and a quick recovery developed in 1960. The year's first session, on January 4, started with an average of ¥864.34, which turned out to be the year's low. The year's high was reached in the closing session on December 28, when the Dow-Jones average climbed to ¥1,356.71 for a 56 percent gain over the year. The strong expansion of the economy seemed to promise a bright future, and investor confidence became contagious, so that the volume of trading assumed larger and larger proportions.

The business cycle reached a peak in 1961 and then turned sharply downward. The year opened with an average of ¥1,366.74 and, with the exception of two slight breaks in May and June, continued upwards until July 18, when the Dow-Jones average rose to a high of ¥1,829.74, which was only reached again (and surpassed) in October 1968. The cheap money policy of the Ikeda cabinet and the growing attention of foreign investors, stimulated by the removal of some of the restrictions on capital transactions and the issuance of the first American depository receipts for Japanese stocks, were some of the factors accounting for the bullish tone of the market. But the growing imbalance in international payments aroused apprehension, and after a raise in the Bank of Japan's official discount rate in July and some half-hearted warnings against the excessive expansion of the economy, the government switched to a strict deflationary policy in September.

On June 7, 1961, the Stock Exchange Council submitted a report to the Ministry of Finance recommending the systematization of over-the-counter transactions through the organization of a second section of the stock exchanges. The ministry approved the proposal and authorized the establishment of second sections for the exchanges in Tokyo, Osaka, and Nagoya. The conditions for listing on the second sections are somewhat easier than those for the first sections. The new sections opened on October 2, 1961. The number of firms listed at that time were as follows: Tokyo—First Section 661, Second Section 325; Osaka—First Section 568, Second Section 171; Nagoya—First Section 359, Second Section 58. The Dow-Jones average for the Second Section of the Tokyo Stock Exchange rose from the initial ¥257.50 to ¥265.05, an increase of 2.9 percent, although, during these three months, the average of the First Section declined from ¥1,486.52 on October 2 to ¥1,432.60 on December 28 (with a low of ¥1,249.00 on December 19). The deflation, however, was not the only cause of the decline in stock prices. Capital increases by 653 companies listed on the stock exchange amounting to ¥685.452 million increased the volume of shares by over 12.1 million, which was almost double the increase in the preceding year (1961: 451 companies, ¥383.607 million, 6.9 million shares).

1962 was a year of indecisive fluctuations. Although the recession was not very severe and its impact was only felt gradually, the economy was stagnant. In the beginning of the year, production continued to increase, and it remained on about the same level for the rest of the year. Actually, some industries, notably producers of capital goods, operated under severe production curtailments which, however, in some cases (iron and steel, paper, textiles) were as much the result of overcapacity as of a decline in demand. Corporate results were the worst in years; although sales declined only moderately, profits were down by large percentages. The economy continued to mark time in the beginning of 1963, and, although some quarters expected an early recovery, the chief support came from government outlays and consumer spending, while equipment investment failed to pick up.

2 THE TOKYO STOCK MARKET

In the beginning of the year 1958, the market was not very active, but a steady upturn set in due to money becoming readily available through larger fiscal payments, a 0.02 *sen* reduction in the call rate, and the open-market operations of the Bank of Japan. In May, however, the attitude changed to caution, for which certain factors, such as the failure of the Japanese-Chinese trade negotiations, an expected decrease in exports, the rapid fall of prices on the New York Stock Exchange, and the increase in outstanding loans of the Japan Securities Finance Company, were responsible. The victory of the Liberal-Democratic party in the general elections and the expectation of a reduction in the official discount rate brought a slight animation. In June, quotations rose following the formation of the Kishi cabinet on the twelfth; and the lowering of the official discount rate on the eighteenth—

which brought a general reduction in bank interest rates—pushed prices up to an average of ¥584.59 on June 19. After a high of ¥586.50 on July 1, the market slipped, but due to the increasing tension in the Middle East, where American marines landed in Lebanon and, on the fourteenth, General Kassem came to power through a bloody coup d'état, the decline was temporarily halted by heavy trading in issues such as shipping, petroleum, and nonferrous metals. But, after the twenty-first, tension subsided and the market weakened. Encouraged by the prospects of a bumper rice crop, an increase in exports, and easier financing anticipating another reduction in the official discount rate, the market rallied in August. Stocks of large, first-rate companies, textiles, oils, and chemicals were particularly active. The Dow-Jones average regained the ¥580 level on the ninth and reached the ¥590 mark on the nineteenth. But, in September, the market softened again despite the lowering of interest rates, including a 0.02 *sen* reduction in the standard rate of the Japan Securities Finance Co. The uncertainties disappeared in October; on the sixth, the average broke through the ¥600 barrier and, on the following day, transactions achieved a record volume with 120 million shares, the largest since the establishment of the stock exchange. Outstanding loans of the Japan Securities Finance Co. jumped to ¥16 billion on the eleventh, and the authorities thought that the speculative fever was running too high. The guarantee deposit on credit transactions was raised from 30 percent to 40 percent effective October 16, and the first in a series of financial control measures increased the ratio of collateral by 10 percent. The money market, however, remained relatively easy, and the second financial control measure announced on November 4 proved ineffective. When the loan balance of the Securities Finance Co. reached ¥19 billion, the Ministry of Finance, on November 10, issued a warning to the securities companies. The guarantee deposit rate was raised to 50 percent and the collateral ratio another 10 percent. This measure only temporarily set the market back, and it soon resumed its upward march, pushing the average to ¥632.80 on the twenty-fourth. Notwithstanding a fourth control regulation, quotations rose steadily all through December and, on the closing day, the Dow-Jones index reached the highest point of the year, ¥666.54. Investment trust buying was an important factor in the sustained upward trend; new trusts set up in December amounted to ¥13.4 billion. The scarcity of available material constituted another major cause of rising prices, which became even more important in the following year.

Business sentiment in the beginning of 1959 was not particularly buoyant, and the government's economic predictions were rather diffident. But as the year went on, the expansion gathered momentum, and the year marked the turning point to a completely new pattern of economic growth. But since the expansion was chiefly financed through bank borrowings (which are replaced by share issues once the foundation for larger dividend payments has been laid), capital increases remained on the same level as the preceding year (they almost doubled in 1960). The difference between the year's lowest average of ¥666.69 on January 9 and the year's high of ¥976.93 on November 30 meant an increase of 45.5 percent in share prices, while the average yield dropped to an inconceivable low of 3.6 percent. This again marked a shift in investment attitude. Investors, including the securities companies, counted on capital gains through stock appreciation much more than on dividend income, and this expectation contributed much to the speculative sentiment which prevailed in the market in the following years.

After opening with an average of ¥671.28 on January 4, 1959, the market experienced a somewhat shaky start but stiffened in the latter half of the month. Toward the end of the month, professionals circulated rumors that some of the blue chips were going to reach a ceiling on *setsubun* (close of the winter by the old calendar, February 4; the date varies each year), but the rising trend continued and, on February 11, the average reached ¥704.30. Textile, paper and pulp, and petroleum stocks led the advance, being credited with recovery from the depression. The bullishness of the market aroused fears of overspeculation, and restrictions were placed on transactions in certain issues: Yokohama Sugar, Calpis, Hayakawa Electric, Hattori Clock, Taisei Construction, Dai-Nihon Ink, Iwaki Cement, Sony, Matsushita Electric, Honda Giken, Mitsui Real Estate, and Nisshin Transportation. Buying then moved to the stocks of large companies. Toward the end of the month, transactions assumed a dizzy pace and turnover exceeded the 100 million mark for three successive days, amounting to 137,784,000 shares on April 2. But after reaching a high of ¥773.39 on April 7, profit taking and a general feeling that prices had soared too high caused a break. The shares of chemical fiber companies, trading companies, shipbuilding, automobiles, electrical machinery, and chemical companies began to fall; the average went down by ¥9.19 on the ninth and ¥9.96 on the sixteenth, almost all sectors, with the exception of oils and precision machinery, being affected.

The business results for the March settlement, which were announced in May, provided an encouraging note: sales were up 6.5 percent and profits 14 percent over the preceding term. At the same time, the Kishi cabinet discussed a possible redenomination of the currency, which the public immediately associated with a devaluation. This led to a precipitate flight into equities and a rapid rise in stock prices, which jumped from ¥749.94 on the first to ¥783.62 on the fifteenth (the rise during the five days from the ninth to the fifteenth being particularly steep). Buying extended to all stocks except coal, shipping, and chemical fertilizers (Japan's "declining" industries) and, on May 30, the Dow-Jones average reached 803.08. On June 1, trading came to over 143 million shares, after having hovered around the 80 million to 100 million continuously since May 20. The big volume trading of 130 million to 140 million continued for three days, and, on June 11, the average reached a high of ¥821.38. On the twelfth, however, Nomura Securities Co., Ltd. put a substantial block of shares from their investment trusts on the market, and their selling dominated the scene for three days. Furthermore, on the seventeenth, rumors to the effect that the government would tighten controls on investment trusts sent prices tumbling for a loss of ¥30.77, the biggest drop since the sterling slump of March 5, 1953. The rumor was later denied, and prices had almost regained the previous level by the twenty-second. The leading gainers in the first half of the year were petroleum and coal products (up 50.3 percent), electrical appliances (45.7 percent), machinery (40.2 percent), paper and pulp (37.5 percent), and primary metals and precision machinery (both 28.5 percent). Shipping showed the greatest loss with 20.8 percent.

In July, active trading again sent prices up; the June high was surpassed on the fourth with ¥823.40 and a new peak of ¥854.91 was reached on the last day of the month. Sony recorded an increase of ¥117 in two days, but some large companies, such as Toshiba, and the big steel makers (Yawata, Fuji, Kawasaki), were inactive. The reason was that some of the large companies planned capital increases through public subscription (instead of the customary method of allocating new shares to existing stockholders on a par basis). Investors, therefore, were shy of these issues. On August 20, the Ministry of Finance warned the eight major securities companies, dealing chiefly in scarce blue chip issues, to prevent irrational price increases, and the chairman of the Tokyo Stock Exchange repeated the warning to investors in general. Ceilings had been put on advances and limits on declines, and trading had to be suspended if a stock hit these levels. For Sony, the span of fluctuation was fixed at ￥100 per diem; the stock reached the advance limit price on August 17, fell to the decline limit price on the twentieth, regained the advance limit price on the twenty-first, and hit the decline limit price again on the twenty-sixth. Restrictions were also imposed on Honda Giken, which reached these limits three times.

The market quietened down in September; and, although a new high of ￥902.48 was reached on the last day of the month, the spread between the highest and lowest prices came to only ￥20.58. Because the securities companies settle their accounts at the end of September, they try to avoid sharp price fluctuations. For business in general, the September settlement was very favorable, and October saw another big advance, with the Dow-Jones average reaching ￥955.64 on the thirty-first, volume having set a new record of 168,180,000 shares on the fourteenth, after exceeding the 100 million level for fourteen consecutive days. Only the shares of services, shipping, and land transportation companies were weak. The balance of outstanding loans of the Japan Securities Finance Co. grew from ￥22.2 billion at the beginning of the month to ￥28.2 billion at the end.

The Ministry of Finance raised the margin requirement from 60 percent to 70 percent on October 27, and, after the turn of the month, the market grew weaker, the average declining to ￥920.39 on the tenth. But in the latter part of the month, more credit became available; industrials, particularly precision and electrical machinery, primary metals, and above all shipbuilding, were very active, and large-volume trading flared up again. On the thirtieth, the average rose to ￥976,93, while volume came to 178,745,000 shares. On December 1, the Bank of Japan announced a raise of 0.1 *sen* in the official discount rate, and the balance of payments situation showed some signs of deterioration. Sentiment suddenly became bearish, and, on December 21, the Dow-Jones average slipped to ￥854.45, a slump of ￥122.48.

The dullness was still noticeable on the opening day (January 4) of 1960, when the average stood at ￥869.34, the lowest in six years. But the year saw one of the steepest and most sustained rises in the history of the stock market, as the Dow-Jones average finished at ￥1,356.71 in the closing session (December 28), marking a gain of 56 percent for the year. Besides the actual performance of the economy, the expectation of rapid growth, spurred on by the expansionary policies of the government, contributed greatly to the optimistic mood of the market.

The average broke through the ￥900 level on January 9 and rose above the ￥1,000 mark on February 20. The most active stocks in the first quarter were electrical and precision machinery, glass, real estate, and trading, while textiles, paper and pulp, and utilities remained weak. Particularly firm were Nippon Electric, Oki Electric, and Hokushin Electric, and the manufacturers of light electrical appliances, such as Matsushita, Yokokawa, Toshiba, were actively traded. In April, interest shifted to heavy electrical machinery (Yasukawa, Meidensha, Mitsubishi); the big gainers during the first quarter declined while chemical fibers, warehousing, and fishery shares became active.

In May and June, political uncertainties (rupture of the Paris summit meeting, the U2 incident, agitation against the Japan-U.S. Security Treaty, the cancellation of President Eisenhower's visit to Japan) clouded the scene; the average fell from ￥1,109.47 on May 7 to ¥984.47 at the end of the month and to a low of ¥967.22 on June 2. The market remained uneasy all through June and the first part of July, although it regained the ¥1,000 level. But with the installation of the Ikeda cabinet on July 18, the lowering of the official discount rate on August 25, and the selection of stocks to be sold in the U.S. in the form of ADRs (American depository receipts), the tone of the market firmed, and August ended with a high ¥1,175.75. The upward tendency also dominated the month of September, which closed at another high of ¥1,226.47. Only petroleum and coal issues were listless, while marine products gained about 60 percent in the July–September period, due chiefly to the expansion of the fishery companies into other fields of the food business.

The announcement of the government's plan for doubling national income in the following ten years provided the key note for market sentiment in the closing months of the year. Despite some minor fluctuations, the average remained above the ¥1,200 level all through October and rose to a high of ¥1,321.70 on November 14. The measures taken by the U.S. government for the defense of the dollar temporarily turned the tide of the market, but, after a low of ¥1,277.17 on December 13, confidence prevailed again, and the year ended with a highly optimistic mood. Besides the so-called international issues (blue chip stocks selected for ADRs), leisure stocks became the market favorites, particularly land transportation, real estate, fisheries, foods, and services. The volume of transactions, which had risen to over 100 million shares in October 1958, reached 226,459,000 shares on September 30, 1960, the yearly turnover rising to 27,217 million (more than double the 1958 figure). But with the record high of quotations on December 28, the average yield of 225 pivotals fell to a low of 3.25 percent.

In the beginning of 1961, the stock market retained its optimism. Despite some oscillations (two major setbacks occurred in the middle of May and the early part of June), the average rose all through the first half of the year, eclipsing the ¥1,400 mark on January 11, soaring above the ¥1,500 level on January 30, crossing the ¥1,600 level in April and the ¥1,700 mark in May, and reaching a historic peak of ¥1,829.74 on July 18, 1961. The gain during this period came to ¥463 or 33.9 percent. The main factors which accounted for the bull market were: (1) the cheap money policy of the government, which included another reduction of the official discount rate (January 26) and a general lowering of interest rates (April 1); (2) the partial relaxation of restrictions on capital transactions effected May 1, which facilitated the repatriation of the principal invested in securities by foreign investors; (3) the issuance of the first ADRs for Japanese stocks (Sony, June 7). Enthusiasm for stock investment spread through all classes of society, with investors' interest concentrating on growth stocks and the expectation of capital gains. Prices, therefore, were highly speculative, and not even the most favorable economic developments could have justified the price level.

A number of contributory factors pushed prices up, particularly announcements of new technical achievements enhancing the competitive position of the respective companies (Ishikawajima-Harima, In steel; Kokusaku Pulp, polystyrene paper; Nippon Sanso, desiccated foods; Sankyo Pharmaceuticals, a drug for cerebral hemorrhage). However, not all achievements were as claimed, and a case of fraud, involving the alleged invention of a revolutionary color television tube by Toyo Electric, received much publicity.

The rapid economic expansion that started in 1959 led to a serious deterioration in the balance of payments. At first, the government was unwilling to discontinue its policy of high growth, but a change became inevitable in the middle of 1961, and as a first step, on July

21, the Bank of Japan raised the discount rate. The deflationary policy became firmer in September, when the government urged a curtailment of investment, and the Bank of Japan announced another raise in the discount rate together with a stricter enforcement of the penalty rates on bank borrowings. Stock prices continued on their downward trend almost without interruption, and the Dow-Jones average reached a low of ¥1,299.76 on October 23. The authorities then became alarmed, and a series of measures was taken to shore up the market: the loan ceiling set by the Securities Finance Company was raised, margin requirements were lowered to 40 percent and capital increases, notably of Yawata Iron & Steel, Fuji Iron & Steel, and Tokyo Shibaura Electric (Toshiba) postponed for two months. The reason for the last measure was that many stockholders sold their shares, if they were selling above par, in order to pay for the new shares which would be issued at par.

The market recovered in November, but the Dow-Jones average fell to the lowest point of the year, ¥1,258.00, on December 19. In the last ten days of the year, however, active trading brought the average up again to ¥1,432.60 on December 28. The volume of transactions in 1961 increased by 14.1 percent over the preceding year and reached 31,091 million shares. Besides the firms listed on the newly organized Second Section, 158 firms were added to the First Section in the course of the year, bringing the number of firms to 662, the number of issues to 790, and the number of shares listed to 47,126 million.

Due to the recession and the disappointing corporate results, a bearish tone prevailed all through the year 1962, with a few rallies, sparked by artificial intervention, soon fading out. In the beginning of the year, the average rose briskly and reached ¥1,589.76 on February 14, but it declined in a series of fluctuations to ¥1,342.30 on April 25. The recovery in the balance of payments, and the supply of funds to the securities companies, through the purchase by the Trust Fund Bureau of financial debentures held by these companies (¥3 billion from the postal life insurance), provided some incentives, but the dubious business outlook

Tokyo Market Statistics

	Number of companies listed	Number of issues	Capital (¥ mill.)	Amount paid-in on listed stocks (¥ mill.)	Number of shares listed (1,000 shrs.)	Current price total (¥ mill.)	Current price per ¥50 (¥)
Jan. 1951	581	605	118,698	114,882	2,343,579	157,049	68.35
Jan. 1952	556	600	162,332	156,709	3,067,018	282,592	90.16
Jan. 1953	577	616	252,743	248,099	4,614,611	681,105	137.26
Jan. 1954	589	626	376,366	373,030	6,849,744	763,573	102.35
Jan. 1955	595	626	498,415	494,054	8,822,821	838,514	84.86
Jan. 1956	592	620	584,611	579,973	10,369,314	1,166,849	100.59
Jan. 1957	596	722	839,972	837,022	15,298,522	1,754,584	104.80
Jan. 1958	601	635	1,023,130	1,020,314	18,558,955	1,647,040	80.71
Jan. 1959	599	616	1,199,966	1,199,286	21,352,533	2,503,166	104.36
Jan. 1960	599	646	1,493,432	1,493,226	26,106,044	3,677,885	123.15
Jan. 1961	599	654	1,904,622	1,904,472	33,351,706	5,592,938	146.84
Jan. 1962	665	781	2,688,163	2,688,134	47,705,000	5,845,765	108.73
Jan. 1963	706	770	3,184,843	3,184,844	56,392,000	6,577,957	103.27

Source: Yamaichi Securities Co., Ltd.

prevented a sustained recovery. The slump in the New York stock market on May 28 produced only a minor ripple, and some good news in July (victory of the Liberal-Democratic party in the House of Councillors elections on July 1; a receipt surplus of $126 million on the trade account for the month of June) lifted the average to ¥1,487.20 on July 9. But tight money and the expectation of bad corporate results (key enterprises such as Yawata Iron & Steel, Fuji Iron & Steel, Toshiba, Hitachi, and Mitsubishi Electric were forced to cut their dividend rates) caused the market to weaken again; the average dropped below the ¥1,300 mark on September 26 and fell to ¥1,216.04 on October 29. Particularly severe was the decline in the shares of large enterprises; the simple average of twenty-seven corporations capitalized at over ¥20 billion sank to ¥57, and the quotations of fourteen companies (including large steel makers, electric power, electrical machinery, shipbuilding, and automobiles) slipped below their par values.

The government again came to the rescue. Margin requirements were reduced to the legal minimum of 30 percent (October 5), the official discount rate was lowered twice (October 26 and November 27), and city banks induced to loan ¥10 billion to securities brokers (November 6).

The Dow-Jones average regained the ¥1,300 mark on November 2 and reached a high of ¥1,457.11 in December.

 ### 3 THE STOCK MARKET IN THE PERIOD OF RAPID GROWTH

On account of the deteriorating balance of payments position, the authorities adopted increasingly stringent credit restraints, starting with an increase in the reserve deposit rate in December 1963, the reimposition of window controls in January 1964, and a raise in the official discount rate from 5.84 percent to 6.57 percent in March 1964. The credit squeeze further depressed the already bearish stock market. In the beginning of 1964, the Dow-Jones index for the First Section of the Tokyo Stock Exchange stood at ¥1,204; due to the favorable development of exports (which produced a surplus in the balance of payments as early as July), the index rose to a year high of ¥1,369.00 in July. But the monetary tightness depressed the market, whose lethargy led to an increasing volume of cancellations of investment trust contracts. In the period of rapid growth, the investment trust companies (practically identical with the securities companies) had become the most important institutional investors, and when the investment trusts stopped their buying, and even began to unload their excessive stock holdings, the market faltered. The Dow-Jones average fell to the year's low of ¥1,202.69 on September 17.

In January 1964, the Japan Joint Securities Co. was founded for the sole purpose of stabilizing the stock market. This organization intervened on numerous occasions in March and April, and resumed its support buying in August in order to prevent the Dow-Jones index from slipping below the ¥1,200 line. The loss of investor confidence following the collapse of the stock market in 1961 and the decline in corporate earnings were largely responsible for the sluggishness of the market; moreover, liquidation sales by corporations strapped for cash added to the volume of unsalable stocks depressing the market. After August 1964, the Joint Securities Co. was almost the only buyer; the stock exchange became a managed market. The Second Section, in particular, was in very bad shape. A special post was organized for the companies whose bills had been dishonored, among them Japan Special Steel and Sun Wave. Between October and the end of the year, the Joint Securities Co. was extremely active; in addition to funds provided by the banks, central bank credit was made available through the Japan Securities Finance Co., which also acted as intermediary for loans given by the Bank of Japan to the securities companies. The first loans of the Bank of Japan were given to the four large securities companies and ten investment companies through the Japan Securities Finance Co., on September 4, 1964. Their maturity was two months, but they could be extended. They were secured by bonds eligible as collateral by the Bank of Japan or stocks acceptable by the Japan Securities Finance Co. On October 23, the Bank of Japan accepted notes of the Japan Joint Securities Co.; on November 21, loans were given to ten medium-sized securities companies, and, on December 4, the Japan Joint Securities Co. received a loan of ¥40 billion from the Bank of Japan through the Japan Securities Finance Co. Securities (up to 80 percent of their value) served as collateral, but, because the interest payable on the loan (1.9 *sen* on the portion secured by bonds, 2 *sen* on the note) was higher than the expected yield from stocks (5.7–5.8 percent, 1.6 *sen*), the part of the interest payments exceeding 1.4 *sen* was deferred. Thanks to these relief measures, the Dow-Jones average stood at ¥1,216 at the end of the year.

A second support organ, the Japan Securities Holding Co., was established in January 1965 and, with the help of funds made available by the Bank of Japan, took over stocks (including issues listed on the Second Section) from investment trusts and securities companies. Despite these efforts, the index dropped below the ¥1,200 line in March 1965, and the volume of transactions continued to shrink. On a yearly basis, the daily average of stock transactions on the Tokyo Stock Exchange was lower in 1964 (97,491,000) than in 1965 (115,792,000), but, in June 1965, the actual volume on the Tokyo Stock Exchange sank to 1,300,740,000 shares (equal to a daily volume of about 50 million shares).

The slump on the stock market, in June 1965, was largely a reaction to the reorganization plans for Yamaichi Securities Co., announced on May 21, and the emergency financing by the Bank of Japan, under Article 25 of the Bank of Japan Law, decided upon on May 28. These events not only frightened investors but also convinced the government of the sad state of the economy and the necessity for taking more effective measures than lowering the official discount rate. On July 12, the Dow-Jones average was down to its lowest point since February 1960, ¥1,024.49, and not far from sinking below the ¥1,000 mark. The four large securities companies made concerted efforts to avert what they considered a major disaster. On July 27, the government announced a strong antirecession policy, including the flotation of bonds (effected in the beginning of 1966). The government policy statement found a favorable reception; the Dow-Jones regained the ¥1,100 level on July 31 and rose above ¥1,200 on August 27. Volume also was better; not only the securities companies but also credit associations and life insurance companies purchased large blocks of stocks. The government's measures for the stimulation of the economy, particularly the flotation of bonds, were bound to produce inflation, and buying of stocks was recommended as a hedge.

After the August recovery, the market weakened again. Business results for the April–September term were worse than expected. The companies listed on the First Section of the Tokyo Stock Exchange suffered a 20 percent decline in profits; electrical appliances, chemical fibers, industrial machinery, machine tools, and steel were particularly bad, reflecting the downturn in personal consumption expenditures as well as in equipment investment. Some of Japan's most prestigious enterprises had to reduce their dividend rates.

Trading on All Stock Exchanges

Year	Number of companies listed	Number of issues listed	Capital stock listed ¥ million	Number of shares listed 1,000	Total market value ¥ million	Total sales Volume 1,000 shares	Total sales Value ¥ million	Tokyo Volume 1,000 shares	Tokyo Value ¥ million
1964	1,591	1,710	4,585,904	81,591,197	7,694,330	41,789,148	4,829,527	29,344,698	3,429,791
1965	1,577	1,605	4,704,330	83,438,413	8,804,457	50,483,157	5,782,977	34,838,338	4,004,551
1966	1,562	1,615	4,895,863	86,257,481	9,736,971	52,040,980	7,570,582	35,938,158	5,266,520
1967	1,561	1,630	5,168,919	91,667,933	9,639,180	42,159,157	6,281,407	28,805,203	4,311,032
1968	1,552	1,605	5,546,698	97,697,391	13,133,818	65,641,137	11,723,157	46,885,945	8,433,629
1969	1,556	1,652	6,070,263	106,970,722	19,030,232	68,853,144	18,674,831	50,985,772	13,891,316
1970	1,580	1,698	6,756,247	118,998,368	16,824,701	57,099,263	12,030,257	42,753,117	9,152,455

Year	Osaka Volume 1,000 shares	Osaka Value ¥ million	Nagoya Volume 1,000 shares	Nagoya Value ¥ mill.	Fukuoka Volume 1,000 shares	Fukuoka Value ¥ mill.
1964	9,734,195	1,096,217	1,475,951	173,856	192,428	20,764
1965	12,406,632	1,425,113	1,602,551	174,466	203,779	20,421
1966	12,859,563	1,831,885	1,664,700	248,767	149,850	20,637
1967	10,668,789	1,554,335	1,636,321	252,281	109,547	14,043
1968	15,528,819	2,715,679	2,144,859	393,696	154,782	25,785
1969	14,719,216	3,987,619	2,247,054	582,762	149,061	34,694
1970	11,777,929	2,397,307	1,793,971	348,306	102,713	18,267

Year	Kyoto Volume 1,000 shares	Kyoto Value ¥ mill.	Hiroshima Volume 1,000 shares	Hiroshima Value ¥ mill.
1964	246,065	25,881	352,310	36,297
1965	419,064	48,499	439,792	46,979
1966	415,932	61,998	400,129	55,759
1967	375,518	74,921	224,476	30,144
1968	358,480	64,219	329,165	53,782
1969	261,737	70,600	281,045	61,078
1970	217,712	39,250	247,333	41,647

Year	Niigata Volume 1,000 shares	Niigata Value ¥ mill.	Sapporo Volume 1,000 shares	Sapporo Value ¥ mill.
1964	148,184	16,607	45,311	4,585
1965	186,762	20,441	54,642	5,268
1966	186,353	25,498	60,422	7,891
1967	105,985	14,028	46,522	6,333
1968	165,003	25,299	74,081	11,065
1969	140,663	31,650	68,592	15,110
1970	135,442	21,373	71,484	11,648

Notes: 1. Totals have been adjusted to avoid duplication of issues listed on more than one exchange.
2. Totals include sales on Kobe Stock Exchange until October 31, 1967.
3. Tokyo, Osaka, and Nagoya: totals for first and second sections.

Source: Tokyo Stock Exchange, Monthly Statistics Report.

Transactions by Principals

	All transactions		For customers' account				For members' accounts			
	Volume	Value	Volume		Value		Volume		Value	
	1,000 shares	¥ million	1,000 shares	% of total	¥ million	% of total	1,000 shares	% of total	¥ million	% of total
1964	58,686,070	6,859,566	29,744,886	50.7	3,392,158	49.5	28,941,184	49.3	3,467,381	50.5
1965	69,674,460	8,008,112	39,554,656	56.8	4,489,612	56.1	30,119,804	43.2	3,518,500	43.9
1966	71,873,660	10,533,051	41,954,607	58.4	6,080,710	57.7	29,919,053	41.6	4,452,335	42.3
1967	57,608,746	8,622,058	35,322,191	61.3	5,186,178	60.2	22,286,555	38.7	3,435,921	39.9
1968	93,770,170	16,867,246	61,375,733	65.5	10,666,398	63.2	32,394,437	34.5	6,200,842	36.8
1969	101,970,134	27,782,630	65,622,698	64.4	17,513,822	63.0	36,347,436	35.6	10,268,808	37.0
1970	85,504,633	18,304,988	55,093,976	64.4	11,497,526	62.8	30,410,657	35.6	6,807,426	37.2

Notes: 1. Tokyo Stock Exchange, first and second sections.
2. Sales and purchases are treated as separate transactions.
Source: Tokyo Stock Exchange, Monthly Statistics Report.

Spot and Margin Transactions

	Spot transactions			Margin transactions			When-issued transactions		
	Volume		Value	Volume		Value	Volume		Value
	1,000 shares	% of total	¥ million	1,000 shares	% of total	¥ million	1,000 shares	% of total	¥ million
1964	44,134,449	75.2	5,103,639	13,736,110	23.4	1,655,089	815,511	1.4	100,838
1965	49,644,196	71.3	5,540,659	19,631,588	28.2	2,407,888	398,676	0.6	59,564
1966	55,170,851	76.8	7,699,886	16,224,673	22.6	2,690,362	478,135	0.7	142,791
1967	41,064,772	71.3	5,667,207	16,428,748	28.5	2,929,239	115,226	0.2	25,615
1968	63,960,567	68.2	10,957,808	29,369,827	31.3	5,807,269	439,776	0.5	102,158
1969	73,167,166	71.8	18,495,973	27,695,340	27.2	8,979,671	1,107,628	1.1	306,985
1970	61,290,933	71.7	12,245,107	23,403,804	27.4	5,845,229	809,896	0.9	214,651

Note: Spot transactions comprise "regular way" transactions (cash on delivery), and cash and seller's option transactions.
Source: Tokyo Stock Exchange, Monthly Statistics Report.

Sales Volume of Borrowed Stocks

(Tokyo Stock Exchange, First Section)

| | Total "regular way" sales | Sales of borrowed stocks | | | | | | Seller's own stocks | |
| | | Subtotal | | Specified issues | | Other issues | | | |
	1,000 shrs.	1,000 shrs.	% of total	1,000 shrs.	% of total	1,000 shrs.	% of total	1,000 shrs.	% of total
1964	28,170,117	24,657,286	87.5	1,914,456	6.8	22,742,830	80.7	3,512,830	12.5
1965	33,741,934	29,488,846	87.4	3,249,133	9.6	26,239,713	77.8	4,253,088	12.6
1966	34,222,932	28,897,123	84.4	3,742,048	10.9	25,155,075	73.5	5,325,808	15.6
1967	27,623,747	24,318,191	88.0	2,029,862	7.3	22,288,329	80.7	3,305,555	12.0
1968	44,872,146	41,389,903	92.2	4,872,229	10.8	36,517,674	81.4	3,482,242	7.8
1969	47,696,575	43,709,447	91.6	3,629,010	7.6	40,080,437	84.0	3,987,128	8.4
1970	40,632,738	37,242,685	91.7	3,063,018	7.6	34,179,667	84.1	3,390,052	8.3

Notes: 1. The table includes sales for correcting errors in "regular way" transactions on the First Section of the Tokyo Stock Exchange so that figures differ from those in other tables.
2. Specified stocks are eight issues for which special trading posts have been set up (Heiwa Real Estate, Ajinomoto, Matsushita Electric Industrial, Canon, Mitsukoshi, Tokio Marine & Fire Insurance, Mitsubishi Estate, and Nippon Yusen Kaisha).

Average Daily Volume on Tokyo Stock Exchange

(In thousands of shares)

| | First Section | | | Second Section | | |
	1969	1970	1971	1969	1970	1971
January	171,463	191,196	172,157	7,135	10,278	6,856
February	116,714	168,565	237,597	11,289	6,825	7,393
March	141,350	223,875	224,675	11,319	7,984	6,620
April	188,538	132,019	234,013	8,978	9,151	7,229
May	219,904	113,015	140,905	12,321	4,481	6,195
June	184,456	148,950	207,875	6,676	3,343	8,916
July	94,361	118,523	195,176	6,025	3,954	7,093
August	89,366	100,389	214,749	3,538	4,310	5,477
September	169,289	122,907	139,332	7,047	3,381	3,403
October	166,145	131,814	116,920	10,178	4,950	3,013
November	192,868	113,294	181,759	15,676	6,321	4,464
December	224,142	99,201	263,265	11,188	4,338	4,832

Source: Tokyo Stock Exchange, Monthly Statistics Report.

Off-Market Transactions in Listed Stocks

(In thousands of shares)

Year	Total	Odd-lot trans-actions	Foreign resi-dents	Trans-actions with out-of-town dealers	Secondary distri-bution for listing	Baikai
1964	251,156	90,015	85	99,838	2,592	58,005
1965	258,780	77,529	1,361	77,087	—	179,692
1966	199,082	78,875	1,253	72,700	2,850	136,341
1967	187,066	88,782	5,109	49,606	8,950	111,803
1968	437,789	231,696	100,440	102,339	3,312	105,485
1969	303,325	245,043	4,126	49,265	4,890	114,958
1970	270,810	246,117	—	22,052	2,640	74,421

Notes: 1. Totals include sales under the block transaction system (i.e., transactions involving large blocks of stock), abolished October 2, 1967.
2. Off-market transactions for foreign residents were abolished February 10, 1969.
3. *Baikai*, i.e., transactions between members of the exchange through the *saitori* ("brokers' broker") members are not included in the totals.

Source: Tokyo Stock Exchange.

Prominent Price Movements on Tokyo Stock Exchange

		Dow-Jones average	% rate of change	Date	TSE stock price average	% rate of change	Date
Iwato boom	low	¥471.53		Dec. 27, '57	37.80		Dec. 27, '57
	high	¥1,829.74	+288	July 18, '60	126.59	+234	July 14, '60
1962 decline	low	¥1,216.04	−34	Oct. 22, '62	83.39	−34	Oct. 22, '62
1963 rise	high	¥1,634.37	+34	Apr. 5, '63	122.96	+47	Mar. 10, '63
1965 recession	low	¥1,020.49	−37	July 12, '65	81.29	−34	July 15, '65
1966 rise	high	¥1,588.73	+55	Apr. 1, '66	114.51	+40	Mar. 6, '66
1967 slump	low	¥1,250.14	−21	Dec. 11, '67	99.17	−13	Dec. 11, '67
1968–1970 expansion	high	¥2,534.45	+102	Apr. 6, '70	185.70	+87	Apr. 8, '70
April–May 1970 slump	low	¥1,929.64	−31	May 27, '70	148.81	−25	May 27, '70
1971 rise	low				147.08		Dec. 9, '70
	high	¥2,740.98	+40	Aug. 14, '71	209.00	+42	Aug. 14, '71
Nixon shock	low	¥2,162.84	−21	Aug. 24, '71	168.16	−19	Aug. 24, '71
1971 year-end rally	low	¥2,224.52		Nov. 6, '71	171.05		Nov. 6, '71
	high	¥2,713.74	+22	Dec. 28, '71	199.45	+17	Dec. 28, '71

Largest Declines in Dow-Jones Average prior to the Nixon shock of August 16, 1971

Date	Loss of Dow-Jones index
April 30, 1970	¥201.11
January 8, 1970	¥111.28
June 12, 1969	¥88.63
May 19, 1970	¥84.80
April 28, 1970	¥70.63
November 20, 1967	¥67.30
April 20, 1971	¥65.28
July 19, 1963	¥64.41
May 25, 1970	¥62.30

Largest Declines in Dow-Jones Average including Losses in August 1971

Date	Loss of Dow-Jones index
August 16, 1971	¥210.50
April 30, 1970	¥201.11
August 19, 1971	¥138.12
August 23, 1971	¥114.65
August 18, 1971	¥112.54
January 8, 1970	¥111.28
August 17, 1971	¥89.66
June 12, 1969	¥88.63

Tokyo Stock Exchange: Ten Largest One-Day Stock Price Rises

Date	Rate of increase based on TSE Stock Price average %	Rate of increase based on Dow-Jones average %
April 16, 1953	6.39	6.41
March 6, 1953	5.39	6.31
June 3, 1960	3.94	4.06
March 7, 1953	3.73	4.42
April 15, 1953	3.63	4.25
October 31, 1962	3.44	3.49
November 1, 1962	3.20	2.10
November 2, 1962	3.13	2.77
December 7, 1954	3.06	3.26
December 22, 1959	3.04	2.97

Tokyo Stock Exchange: Ten Largest One-Day Stock Price Losses

Date	Rate of decrease based on TSE Stock Price average %	Rate of decrease based on Dow-Jones average %
March 5, 1953	8.75	10.00
April 30, 1970	7.47	8.69
March 30, 1953	5.99	6.73
August 16, 1971	5.90	7.68
August 17, 1971	5.18	5.93
July 19, 1963	4.33	4.25
August 23, 1971	4.19	5.04
June 12, 1963	4.05	4.40
January 8, 1970	4.00	4.65
November 20, 1969	3.94	5.02

In November, a speculative rally began to push stock prices upward; on November 10, the Dow-Jones average surpassed the ¥1,300 mark and the year closed with a high of ¥1,417.83 on December 28. In order to stop the speculative trading, margin requirements were raised from 30 percent to 40 percent on November 20; for seventeen issues in which trading was particularly heavy the down payment was raised by another 10 percent, which had to be deposited in cash. The 50 percent margin requirement was then extended to all issues while the value of the securities deposited was reduced from 70 percent to 60 percent. This actually forced traders to put up 80 percent in cash for spot purchases and stopped the speculative buying.

Stock prices continued their advance in the first three months of 1966, and the Dow-Jones average reached a high of ¥1,588.73 on April 1. Volume also increased from a daily average of 157,930,000 in January to 181 million in February and 202 million in March. But the recovery of the economy made funds available for stock investment scarcer, and the partial release of the stocks held by the Japan Joint Securities Co. and the Japan Securities Holding Co. also had an adverse influence. On the other hand, corporate results for the term ended March 1966 showed an increase of 3.8 percent in sales and 3.4 percent in profits, and results were even better for the April–September term, with an average increase of 10 percent in sales and over 20 percent in profits. The only sustained buying in the stock market came from life insurance companies whose net stock purchases in the April–September term amounted to ¥119.1 billion. Because enterprises were still hesitant about equipment investment, the insurance companies had large liquid funds available for investment. In the latter half of 1966, the Dow-Jones average remained below the ¥1,500 mark and it was only on March 1, 1967, that it rose above this level. But large sales sent stock prices down again. The business results for the term ended March 1967 were much better than expected and the balance of payments was stable; the economic situation looked reassuring and, on May 31, the Dow-Jones reached ¥1,505.98. Automobiles, electrical machinery, and general machinery provided most of the lift. On June 6, the Six-Day War added a new problem to the already troubled international situation. Oils, marine transportation, and nonferrous metals went up, but the spurt was short and limited, and soon a downtrend set in which dominated the market for the rest of the year. The situation was very different from the Suez crisis of 1956. Shipping was expected to profit little from the closing of the Suez Canal on account of the great number of long-term contracts (actual developments were different from the predictions at that time). The increase in freight rates affected prices of raw materials. In August, a fairly strong downtrend sent the Dow-Jones index below the ¥1,400 line. Rumors that the official discount rate would be raised by 2 *rin* added to the nervousness of the market; it came as a kind of relief when the actual increase (August 31) came to only 1 *rin*.

In June, the city banks requested the Joint Securities Co. to adjust its sales, which were practically suspended in August. In September, the Joint Securities Co. applied for a license as a securities company; in October, the Securities Holding Co. decided to extend its activities for another year. At the end of September 1967, the market value of the holdings of the Joint Securities Co. was estimated at ¥185 billion, and that of the Securities Holding Co. at ¥176.5 billion.

In October, the good business results reported for the April–September term, particularly the increase in dividend rates and stock dividends (e.g., Sony increased its capital by 20 percent through a gratis allocation of new shares), pushed stocks up, but, in November, the devaluation of the pound and the increase in the bank rate in Britain and in the discount rate in the United States depressed the market. On a single day, November 20, the Dow-Jones slumped by ¥67.30 and, on December 11, the index fell to its lowest point of the year, ¥1,250.14, (the lowest level since October 1965). Since trading on the exchange is dominated by professionals, bad economic news has a far stronger impact than it has on the general public. Actually, the slowdown in exports was only temporary, and, although the overall balance of payments showed a deficit of $571 million in 1967 (current balance, $190 million), the trade balance remained favorable (surplus of $1,160 million).

The government's decision to implement the liberalization of inward foreign investment prompted companies, afraid of the acquisition of their stock by foreigners and foreign takeovers, to find "stable" stockholders willing to buy their "floating" shares coming on the market. Enterprises in the machinery and automobile industries, in particular, appealed to insurance companies and trust banks to cooperate in their "countermeasures" against the "foreign invasion." Since 1968, over 600 firms listed on the Tokyo Stock Exchange have adopted employee stock ownership plans for the same purpose; these plans usually restrict the resale of the stock to outsiders, and often the management of such plans is in the hands of trust banks. According to a ruling of the Ministry of Finance, employee stock ownership plans can be set up for stocks and convertible debentures but not for ordinary debentures.

On October 5, 1967, the Ministry of Finance and the Tokyo Stock Exchange issued an admonition to Nikko Securities Co. and Yamaichi Securities Co. and suspended the two firms from trading on their own accounts for one day. The two firms had, through support buying, artificially kept the price of Yamashita Shin-Nihon Kisen and Showa Kaiun (both shipping companies) on the ¥65 level from February to September. Both firms had announced capital increases (by 50 percent) for the end of September 1967 and, according to the regulations of the securities companies, capital increases could only be handled by the securities companies if the stock price was above ¥65. For the same reason, Daiwa Securities Co., the secondary underwriter, was fined ¥50,000. A number of smaller securities companies were also involved in these maneuvers; they were not punished, but the authorities generally denounced their behavior as "undermining investor confidence."

The worldwide deflationary trend, in the beginning of 1968, had a depressing effect on the stock market; stock prices slipped and trading volume was down. On January 1, President Johnson announced stronger measures for the protection of the dollar, and, on the sixth, the Bank of Japan raised the official discount rate by 1 *rin* to 1.7 *sen* (6.205 percent). The gold rush, erupting in Europe in March on account of the international currency instability, triggered a boom on the Tokyo Stock Market. Stocks were bought as a hedge against inflation; real estate, loss insurance, and nonferrous metal mining companies were the preferred issues. The good corporate results reported for the term ended March encouraged investors, and foreign purchases of Japanese securities provided additional momentum. In 1967, the monthly average of foreign buying orders had been about $12 million; in July 1968, buying orders reached $60 million. The net increase in foreign investment in Japanese securities in fiscal 1968 amounted to $319,430,000. The stability of the yen, the strong expansion of the Japanese economy, and the relatively low level of Japanese stock prices (measured by the price-earnings ratio) were the main reasons for the interest in Japanese stocks. In addition to foreign institutional investors, individuals began to add Japanese issues to their portfolios.

On May 20, the Dow-Jones regained the ¥1,500 level; the reduction of the official discount rate on August 7 (back to 1.6 *sen*, 5.8 percent) provided a further stimulus. Despite the increase in margin requirements (on August 20, margin requirements were raised from 30 percent to 50 percent for twenty-six issues, and for another forty issues on August 31), the market remained very active. The Dow-Jones average rose over ¥1,700 at the end of August, and, in September, the average daily trading volume amounted to 237,620,000 (against a daily average of 59,361,000 shares in January). On September 11, 1968, the Ministry of Finance published new regulations on margin requirements which went into effect on December 10; securities given as collateral could only be accepted for 60 percent of their value (until then 70 percent), and customers buying on margin had to deposit 40 percent (instead of 30 percent) of the price for all issues.

The large trading volume pushed stock prices up, and, on September 30, 1968, the Dow-Jones average rose to ¥1,839.81, exceeding the previous high of ¥1,829.74 recorded on July 18, 1961. The high of the year was reached on October 2 with ¥1,851.49; on October 1, 574 million shares had been traded, the fourth-largest volume in the history of the Tokyo Exchange. On October 2, the Ministry of Finance and the Bank of Japan published very cautionary appraisals of the state of the economy. On the following day, large-scale selling sent the Dow-Jones average tumbling ¥41.88, and, on October 9, large sales by the Japan Joint Securities Co. caused a drop of ¥56.74, bringing the average down to ¥1,770.93. The Joint Securities Co. and the Japan Securities Holding Co. had resumed the release of their holdings in March 1968; the largest part of their portfolios was sold to city banks and life insurance companies, but a certain part was sold on the market. At the end of December 1968, the Securities Holding Co. had reduced its inventory to ¥3 billion; the Joint Securities Co. still owned ¥33 billion in stocks. A profit of ¥43.7 billion reported by the Securities Holding Co. in September 1968 was distributed among the eleven companies that had contributed to its capital. These companies refunded the profits to endow the Capital Market Promotion Foundation established on January 7, 1969. The Japan Securities Holding Association was dissolved on January 11, 1969, while, as related above, the windup of the Japan Joint Securities Co. took another year.

From October to December 1968, the trading volume on the Tokyo Stock Exchange dropped considerably and was below 100 million shares on certain days. Investor interest shifted from large firms to industries connected with housing and the prevention of environmental pollution.

The international situation, in particular France's refusal to devalue the franc, gave a certain lift to the market, and the Dow-Jones average, which had dropped to ¥1,658.45 on November 11, was back to ¥1,716.69 on November 29. But the general public showed little interest in stocks, and, on December 23, the Dow-Jones fell to ¥1,686.74.

Despite the weak finish, the securities companies had a profitable year. If the average daily volume traded on the Tokyo Stock Exchange comes to 85–90 million shares, the securities companies can break even; after March 1968, the daily average was about 175 million shares. For the September 1968 settlement, seventy-three of the eighty-three member companies of the Tokyo Stock Exchange were able to distribute a dividend. Of the twenty-seven companies which had paid a dividend in September 1967, twenty-five increased the dividend rate (by 2–6 percent); forty-six securities companies resumed dividend payments. Yamaichi Securities Co. was able to repay one-half of the special loans received from the

Bank of Japan (¥28.2 billion) and originally repayable in eighteen years; Wako Securities Co. (the former Oi Securities Co.) made similar progress in its recovery. Nomura Securities Co. reported an aftertax profit of ¥7,333 million, 2.4 times higher than in September 1967.

The year 1969 brought the most dramatic rise in stock prices in the history of the Tokyo Stock Exchange, and, for the year as a whole, the largest trading volume (50,985,772,000 shares) and the highest daily average (171,669,000). The value of all sales was ¥13,891,316 million, 64.5 percent higher than in 1968, and four times the value of the recession year 1964. The Dow-Jones average topped the ¥1,900 mark on April 14, went over ¥2,000 on May 31, rose to ¥2,100 on October 18, surpassed ¥2,200 in November, and reached ¥2,358.96 on December 27, the last trading day. But the going was far from smooth, and the general rise involved a number of wild ups and downs.

Toward the end of 1968 and in the beginning of 1969, the expansion had seemed to slacken, and there was much talk (backed up by MITI's analysis of the situation) about the clouding of the economy. The Dow-Jones, which had regained the ¥1,800 level toward the end of January (from a low of ¥1,733.64 on the opening day of the year), fell below this mark on February 20 and, with the increase in the British bank rate in the beginning of March, it sank to ¥1,748.88; but the Bank of Japan and the Economic Planning Agency came out strongly in support of the view that the clouding was merely temporary and that there was no ground for alarm. Trading began to pick up on a selective basis; prices of market favorities soared to over ¥1,000. Until March 1969, Sony had been the only stock listed on the First Section with a ¥50 face value to rise above ¥1,000 (on December 28, 1968, Sony was quoted at ¥1,411); on the Second Section, Makita, Chichibu Cement, and Kyushu Matsushita (now on the First Section) had been traded at prices exceeding ¥1,000. On October 20, 1969, Sony recorded a high of ¥5,850, and high-flying issues were numerous among the electricals: Alps (¥2,097), Hitachi Koki (¥1,510), Japan Electron Optics Laboratory (¥1,325), Kyushu Matsushita (¥1,970), Matsushita Communications (¥3,850), Matsushita Electric Works (¥1,280), Mitsumi (¥1,790), Tateishi Electric (¥2,090), TDK Electronics (¥2,960), and Victor (¥1,085). But there were also a number of issues in other fields: National Cash Register (Japan) (¥1,010), Daifuku Machinery Works (¥1,330), Shiseido (¥1,378), Daiwa House (¥1,847), Japan Gasoline (¥1,380), Nakayama Steel Works (¥1,397), Sankyo Seiki (¥1,270), Matsushita Trading (¥2,770), and Eidai Sangyo (¥1,011). The Second Section also produced issues priced higher than ¥1,000: Akai Electric, Chichibu Cement, Daiwa Danchi, Fuji Denki, Itoki, Kakuei Kensetsu, Makita, Mizuno, Mochida Yakuhin, Okamoto Kogyo, Takasago Netsu, Teitsuko, and Toda Kensetsu.

The Tokyo Stock Exchange demanded a report on the twelve most heavily traded issues from the securities companies, and, on April 17, the three securities finance companies announced that the securities companies that had borrowed beyond their credit limit would have to pay an additional 1 *rin* per diem (0.365 percent) on the excess amount.

The heavy concentration on favorite issues produced what was called a "limping" market; there was a large spread between the prices (and the trading volume) of the actively traded and the inactive stocks. The securities companies, much interested in sales to foreign investors, had given more play to the price-earnings ratio as the measure of investment worthiness and deemphasized the old Japanese measure of yield plus expectation of capital gains. Actually, with dividend rates based on face value, the price-earnings ratio is completely irrelevant to the profitability of the investment, and the tendency of the market favorites to issue new shares at market prices (which involves a deception similar to the evaluation by the price-earnings ratio) adds to the confusion. Japanese dividend rates are rather rigid; the only company which links dividends to profits is Toto (Toyo Kiki) which earmarks at least 20 percent of earnings for distribution as dividends. Usually, when corporate profits rise, the ratio of distribution sinks; when profits decline, the distribution ratio goes up. The basic reason is that the dividend rate remains fixed as a percentage of the face value of the stock. Reflecting the drop in earnings, the distribution ratio (percentage of net profits distributed as dividends) for the October 1965–March 1966 term was 81.7 percent; for the term from October 1969 to March 1970, a period of rising profits, the distribution ratio was 44 percent. During the Iwato boom (1959–61), however, the distribution rate increased despite the expanding economy, because enterprises maintained their dividend rates while increasing their capital. Because the capital of the firms listed on the Second Section is much smaller, not only absolutely but also in relation to their sales and profits, than that of the enterprises listed on the First Section, their distribution ratio is much lower (average First Section: September 1969, 50.4 percent; March 1970, 47.8 percent; September 1970, 48.5 percent; March 1971, 53.0 percent; Second Section: September 1969, 30.8 percent; March 1970, 24.1 percent; September 1970, 29.3 percent; March 1971, 35.3 percent). For Japanese managers, the strengthening of internal reserves is much more important than giving stockholders a fair share of the earnings of the company. To buy Japanese stocks on the basis of the price-earnings ratio or per share earnings, therefore, is inconsistent with the financial management of Japanese corporations.

Although the rise in stock prices was supported by the strong expansion of the economy, the favorable growth of exports, the increase in the country's foreign exchange reserves (which, at the end of March 1969, amounted to $3.2 billion, $1.2 billion higher than the level the previous year), and the large purchases of foreign investors, the prices of the market favorites were clearly speculative and unrelated to their actual value. The Dow-Jones index, which passed the ¥2,000 mark on May 31, continued to climb until June 10; on June 12, the average plummeted by ¥88.63, larger than any previous drop until then (it was going to be surpassed in 1970). The occasion was the increase in the prime rate of the American banks, but the real reason was the overpricing of the favorite issues. In ten days, from June 12–21, the Dow-Jones lost ¥162.94, and the decline was followed by a period of market uncertainty. Average daily volume decreased from 220 million shares in May to 184 million shares in June, 94 million shares in July, and 89 million shares in August. The devaluation of the franc on August 8 created only a light ripple, but when the Japanese government announced an increase in the official discount rate (from 5.84 percent to 6.25 percent) in order to check the increase in wholesale prices, investors seemed to regain confidence. Contrary to former occasions, when a rise in the discount rate triggered a wave of selling, buying picked up. The deposit ratio for margin trading had been reduced from 40 percent to 30 percent on August 27, and investors expected a beneficial influence from the government's "preventive" credit restraints. On September 14, the Dow-Jones index regained the ¥2,000 level; then the revaluation of the German mark on October 24, which was expected to improve Japan's competitive position in world markets, stimulated renewed interest in market favorites, and a certain amount of speculative money moved from German marks into Japanese securities. On November 13, the Tokyo Stock Exchange raised the deposit margin for the sixteen most heavily traded issues from 30 percent to 50 percent but buying continued, particularly of stocks of undercapitalized companies. On November 17, 1969, the value of transactions reached ¥118.1 billion, the first time in the history of the Tokyo Stock Exchange that trading exceeded the ¥100 billion mark. The Dow-Jones rose from ¥2,096.90 on November 8 to ¥2,230.58 on November 27, but then slumped again to ¥2,170.15 on December 5. Nevertheless, buying remained active and spread to more issues, with particular interest on real estate, construction, banks, and small steel companies. On December 27, the last trading day of the year, the Dow-Jones average reached a new high of ¥2,358.96.

The high degree of activity on the stock market led to a growing number of applications for listing on the stock exchange. New listings, which had already risen from five in 1967 to ten in 1968, increased to twenty-two in 1969. In addition to the general economic factors, the increase in business profits, the rise in commodity prices, and the large buying of foreign investors contributed to the stock market boom. The term ended September 1969 was the eighth successive term with higher sales and profits. For the March 1969 settlement, only Mitsubishi Heavy Industries could report sales exceeding ¥300 billion; for the first half of fiscal 1969, four companies (Mitsubishi Heavy Industries, Toyota Motor, Hitachi, Ltd., and Nissan Motor) were in this class. According to the corporate reports to the National Tax Agency, fifty-six companies earned more than ¥10 billion in 1969, against forty-one in 1968 and thirty-three in 1967. In the first half of fiscal 1969 (April–September), the net increase in foreign portfolio investment in Japanese securities amounted to $320.75 million, slightly higher than in all of fiscal 1968. Validated securities purchases by foreigners (gross buying) rose from $159.8 million in fiscal 1968 to $2,462,897,000 in fiscal 1969. The slump on the New York stock market and the reduction of the American equalization tax from 18.75 percent to 11.25 percent, in April 1969, contributed to the increase in foreign investment in Japanese securities.

The favorable market greatly benefited the securities companies. Of the eighty-three member companies of the Tokyo Stock Exchange, sixty-two increased their dividend rates, eight resumed dividend payments, and only two, Yamaichi and Wako, paid no dividends. But these two companies were able to repay entirely the special loans (¥28.2 billion and ¥15.3 billion) they had been given in the 1965 crisis by the Bank of Japan.

Encouraged by the good showing of the Liberal-Democratic party in the general elections of December 27, 1969, the Tokyo Stock Exchange opened the new year with a gain of ¥43.89 of the Dow-Jones average on January 5, 1970. On January 6, trading on the First Section reached 419,314,000 shares, the highest volume of the year. But on the eighth, the index slumped by ¥111.28, chiefly on account of the new regulations for American outward foreign investment adopted by the Federal Reserve Board on December 7, 1969, which found belated attention in Japan. The rules had not only become stricter, but investment in Japan had been made subject to the same restrictions as in other advanced countries. On the two following days, however, the mood of the market changed; the new regulations were discovered to be less restrictive than had first been thought and the Dow-Jones went up by ¥95.41. Thus opened another year of violently fluctuating stock prices.

The market was relatively calm in February and March. The favorable prospects for the March settlement encouraged buying, and, in March, the average trading volume reached 223,875,000 shares. On March 26, the Dow-Jones average rose above the ¥2,500 mark and reached the year-high of ¥2,534.45 on April 6. But then the market turned sour. On the domestic scene, the credit restraints imposed in September 1969 began to affect industry, and, although the economic expansion had hardly slowed down, the increase in corporate profits was expected to decelerate in the April–September term. The international situation, however, was a much more depressing factor. The economic difficulties of the United States had turned out to be much more deep-seated and intractable than had been thought, and Japanese exports to the United States, in particular exports of electronic products and textiles, seemed greatly endangered. Foreign investment in Japanese stocks tapered off; in the first quarter (January–March) net purchases still registered a surplus of $118 million, but, in the second quarter, sales exceeded purchases by $147 million. In addition to the stricter official limitations imposed by the Federal Reserve Board on foreign investment, the slump in the New York stock market had greatly reduced the value of mutual funds, and the growing cancellations forced the fund managers to sell a large part of their portfolios.

The IOS debacle was already casting its shadows on the world's capital markets, and the Tokyo Stock Exchange went through a stormy stretch in April and May. On April 30, 1970, the Dow-Jones average plunged by ￥201.11, equivalent to a decline of 8.69 percent. Trading was stopped for twenty issues; until then, the largest number had been twelve, back in 1953, when the death of Stalin had sent the stock market into a tailspin. In the last months of 1969, trading had been particularly brisk in stocks of medium-sized and small companies, and speculators began to doubt the profitability of these investments. Moreover, the settlement for the heavy margin purchases in November 1969 was drawing near, and, at the same time, payment had to be made for some of the new issues at market prices (e.g., Daiwa House and Sony). On May 19, the Dow-Jones fell to ￥1,963.10 and sank to the low of the year, ￥1,929.64, on May 27. On the following day, however, the market rebounded, sending the index up ￥79.46, a gain of 4.12 percent. The deposit rate for margin trading, which had been raised to 40 percent in March, had been reduced to 30 percent on May 1, but this measure had no effect on the market.

Throughout the summer months, trading was rather dull. Investors showed some interest in stocks related to pollution control, and stocks such as Mitsubishi Metal Mining, Kurita, and Dai Nippon Toryo were bought, but the trading volume declined, the average trading volume for August being slightly above 100 million shares. Purchases by foreign investors increased again in August, but the general tendency was downward (gross portfolio purchases of foreign investors in 1970: January–March, $543.5 million; April–June, $362.5 million; July–September, $340.7 million; October–December, $295.4 million) and foreign buying lacked sufficient strength to buoy up the market. In October and November, shipping, shipbuilding, and oil stocks attracted some interest, but generally speaking, trading was slow and tended to concentrate on a few issues.

The settlement of accounts for the six-month term ended March 1970 had been highly satisfactory for the vast majority of enterprises. For 368 companies listed on the First Section of the Tokyo Stock Exchange, the average increase in sales over the preceding term amounted to 13.2 percent, the increase in operating profits to 19.3 percent and that in net profits to 13.1 percent. The oil companies reported a 24.0 percent increase in sales and a 73.7 percent increase in net profits. Only two companies in the field of services reported a decrease in sales and profits, and the manufacturers of rolling stock suffered a 58.8 percent decline in net profits. The rate of increase in sales of the 182 companies listed on the Second Section (11.3 percent) was somewhat lower than for the September 1969 term (12.7 percent), but the increase in operating profits (19.9 percent) and net profits (19.2 percent) was higher.

Rate of Increase or Decrease in Sales and Profits by Industry

	Sales					Profits				
	Sept. 1964	March 1965	Sept. 1965	Sept. 1970	March 1971	Sept. 1964	March 1965	Sept. 1965	Sept. 1970	March 1971
Textiles	12.4	2.7	7.2	8.5	3.3	−5.6	−30.5	−15.5	2.4	−18.5
Pulp & paper	4.9	−1.0	−1.0	6.8	−2.9	7.6	−14.0	−12.2	10.1	−21.7
Chemicals	5.8	7.3	−0.5	5.9	4.1	−5.4	14.9	−33.6	1.2	−13.0
Oil refining	−3.0	19.1	−4.3	−4.6	25.1	−31.5	96.6	48.0	−5.8	30.2
Iron & steel	7.2	2.9	1.3	6.3	−2.8	0.3	0.3	−43.4	−3.6	−18.9
Nonferrous metals	8.3	6.5	−0.3	4.5	−9.4	2.7	4.6	−6.2	3.5	−16.9
General machinery	8.9	1.6	−1.0	13.4	4.1	−8.8	−8.9	−17.0	7.7	−1.4
Electrical machinery	2.9	2.4	−3.3	9.8	−0.6	−4.7	−8.6	−56.4	−4.4	−21.0
Automobiles	7.0	2.3	0.2	9.1	7.0	2.3	−3.5	3.6	−13.3	23.1
Average, manufacturing	5.6	5.5	−0.3	6.2	2.2	−3.0	−7.2	−29.0	1.3	−9.5
Construction	10.7	5.7	1.4	10.2	7.8	8.9	5.8	−0.9	16.9	10.9
Trading companies	7.0	5.9	2.1	11.3	6.5	3.3	−18.2	−3.2	9.1	5.1
Average, all industries	6.2	5.8	1.7	8.8	4.6	−2.0	−3.8	−20.5	2.5	−5.4

Notes: 1. Companies listed on the First Section of the Tokyo Stock Exchange.
2. Percentage rate of increase or decrease in six-month term ended at date indicated over preceding six-month term.
Source: Nihon Keizai Shimbun.

The September settlement, however, clearly reflected the slowdown in the economy. For 375 companies listed on the First Section, the average rate of increase in sales dropped to 8.8 percent, the increase in operating profits to 1.4 percent, and the increase in net profits to 1.9 percent. For the Second Section (177 companies), the average rate of increase in sales was 9.2 percent; operating profits were down by 1.4 percent and net profits 6.4 percent. The coal mining companies listed on the First Section suffered the largest decline in net profits (−56.3 percent); other industries whose profits decreased were real estate (−24.4 percent), automobiles (−13.3 percent), metal mining (−9.7 percent), oil refining (−5.8 percent), electrical machinery (−4.4 percent), iron and steel (−3.6 percent), ceramics (−3.0 percent), chemicals (−1.2 percent), and private railroads (−1.2 percent). The deterioration in profits was even more pronounced for the firms listed on the Second Section; iron and steel companies showed a decline of 49.0 percent, ceramics of 48.4 percent, land transportation of 12.7 percent, electrical machinery of 12.4 percent, general machinery of 10.9 percent, chemicals of 2.1 percent, and nonferrous metals of 1.7 percent. But the picture was far less bleak than the averages seem to suggest. Of the companies listed on the First Section, 265 reported an increase in profits, 97 a decline; of the firms on the Second Section, 107 had higher profits, those of 61 companies were down.

A survey by Nihon Keizai Shimbun, based on the first term of fiscal 1970 (April–September or equivalent) and covering 685 companies listed on the First Section of the Tokyo Stock Exchange (not including banks and insurance companies), found that the per share earnings of 104 companies exceeded ¥30 and those of 31 companies were higher than ¥50. The highest per share earnings (¥99.40) were reported by Nakayama Steel Works; the market favorites Makita, Matsushita Communications, Pioneer, and TDK Electronics were among the top ten. Of 66 electrical machinery manufacturers listed on the First Section, 17 were among the top 100 companies (there had been 20 in the latter part of fiscal 1969). In the same group were 14 construction companies (including the big four—Shimizu, Ohbayashi, Taisei, and Kajima, but also small firms such as Japan Gasoline, Nippon Hodo, and Chugai Ro Kogyo), 11 manufacturers of pharmaceuticals, and 2 producers of cosmetics. Two hundred and fifteen companies had earnings of less than ¥10 per share, 67 less than ¥5, and 15 companies (including four coal mining companies) had losses.

Of the 538 companies listed on the Second Section, three companies reported earnings exceeding ¥100 per share (Chichibu Cement ¥190.60, Kewpee ¥130.33, Okamoto Kosakuki Seizosho ¥108.21). Companies whose earnings were higher than ¥50 numbered 38, those with earnings of ¥30 and more, 97. One hundred and thirty-one companies earned less than ¥10 per share, 48 less than ¥5, and 21 suffered losses.

A similar survey carried out for the latter half of fiscal 1970 (October 1970–March 1971 or equivalent) found that of 692 companies listed on the First Section of the Tokyo Stock Exchange, 87 companies had earnings exceeding ¥30 per share, 28 companies higher per share earnings than ¥50; the per share earnings of 265 companies were lower than ¥10 and those of 70 companies lower than ¥5; losses were reported by 17 companies. Only three electric machinery manufacturers (Pioneer, Matsushita Communications, and Sony) were among the top ten; of the 100 companies with the highest per share earnings, 18 were construction companies, 16 manufacturers of electrical machinery, and 12 each of pharmaceuticals and general machinery. Some of the electrical machinery makers who had been among the top hundred in the first half of fiscal 1970 had dropped out of that group, among them Alps, Clarion, Victor, and Mitsumi; Nitto Electric, Sansui Electric, and Tateishi Electric had moved up. The top per share earner in the first term, Nakayama Iron Works, had fallen to 112th place (¥26.90) while the top earner for the latter term, Dai-Nippon Sugar Mfg. Co. (¥98.48), occupied that place only because the company had a nonoperating income of ¥3,355 million from the sale of real property. The companies with high per share earnings had the lowest distribution rates. Kinki Denki Koji, a construction company with ¥90.29 per share earnings, distributed only 10.0 percent of its net profit, Pioneer (¥83.89) 11.9 percent, Matsushita Communications (¥74.90) 13.4 percent, Matsushita Electric Industrial (¥55.84) 17.9 percent, Kyushu Matsushita (¥52.20) 19.2 percent, Matsushita Electric Works (¥52.01) 19.2 percent, and Sony (¥73.53) 20.4 percent, and the situation was more or less the same for other market favorites mentioned above.

Of the 533 companies listed on the Second Section, the per share earnings of five companies exceeded ¥100. The per share earnings of the leader, Ricoh Watch Co. (¥547.75), had been boosted by the sale of real estate. Earnings higher than ¥50 per share were reported by 34 companies, while 89 companies had per share earnings of ¥30 or higher. Excluding the 28 companies reporting losses and one company which just broke even, 247 companies had per share earnings of less than ¥10 and 147 less than ¥5. Among the top 100 group were 15 manufacturers of electrical machinery, 13 manufacturers of general machinery, 13 manufacturers of steel and metal products, and 13 companies engaged in the construction industry.

For the last six months of 1970, the share of the sixty most active stocks in the total volume of transactions on the Tokyo Stock Exchange was as follows:

1970	First Section %	Second Section %
July	51.46	58.08
August	57.53	67.30
September	63.33	60.15
October	65.27	70.31
November	62.26	69.64
December	60.24	67.04

The tempo quickened at the start of 1971. The daily average had been 138 million shares in 1970; it had dropped to 99 million shares in December and 87 million between January 4 and 7. But from January 8 to January 19, the daily average rose to 220 million shares. Much of the trading involved low-priced stocks, indicating a development which was significant for the entire first half of 1971. In 1970, the lowest daily average price per share had been ￥121, the highest ￥381; on January 19, the daily average per share was ￥111. The Dow-Jones index dropped to ￥1,981.74 on January 4 but rose to a monthly high of ￥2,115.25 on the nineteenth. It was below the ￥2,100 line at the end of the month but rose steadily in February from ￥2,104.88 on the first to ￥2,246.36 on the twenty-seventh. The process went on almost without interrruption in March; the Dow-Jones rose above ￥2,300 on the tenth and reached ￥2,404.65 on the twenty-ninth. The expectation of large fiscal expenditure was the most important stimulus; further support came from the continuing favorable expansion of exports. Foreign purchases also became more active; net foreign buying was only $2 million in January but rose to $83.4 million in February, $132.9 million in March, and $144.4 million in April; net investment decreased to $77.7 million in May.

Average daily volume rose from 180 million in January to 250 million in February and 300 million in March; on April 14, the value of transactions on the First Section of the Tokyo Stock Exchange rose to ￥127,525 million, the highest in the history of the exchange. The only other time that turnover had exceeded ￥100 billion had been on November 17, 1969, when it reached ￥118,100 million. Four hundred and forty million shares changed hands, including 80 million shares of NYK. On April 13, the deposit rate for margin trading was raised from 30 percent to 40 percent (for certain issues to 50 percent); on April 19, a second raise, from 40 percent to 50 percent, went into effect. The Japan Securities Finance Co. raised the fee for borrowed shares to ￥3 per share per day. Between January and March, the Finance Co. borrowed 56,217,600 shares, 85 percent from securities companies and 15 percent from life insurance companies.

The settlement for the six months from October 1970 to March 1971 revealed a considerable deterioration in corporate performance. For 275 companies listed on the First Section of the Tokyo Stock Exchange, the average rate of increase in sales was 4.6 percent (down from 8.8 percent in the preceding term); operating profits declined by 9.8 percent. The situation of the firms listed on the Second Section was even worse; sales had grown by 3.8 percent, but profits had declined by 10.7 percent and net profits by 14.2 percent. The profits squeeze was particularly severe for pulp and paper, electrical machinery, iron and steel, nonferrous metals, textiles, chemicals, and pharmaceuticals. Despite eleven successive terms of rising profits, the ratio of net worth to total capital employed was down from 23.8 percent in the latter half of fiscal 1965 to 18.8 percent in the first half of fiscal 1970 (average of all industries, First Section of the Tokyo Stock Exchange); it sank to 18.5 percent in the second half of fiscal 1970. The ratio of capital to total capital employed declined from 14.5 percent in the latter half of fiscal 1965 to 10.2 percent in the first half of fiscal 1970.

Compared with 1965, the beginning of the great boom, nonferrous metals, automobiles, and real estate showed the largest decline in profitability (measured by the ratio of net profits to sales). For nonferrous metals, the worldwide stagnation in demand was chiefly responsible for the decline. In the automobile industry, the shift in demand from the more profitable medium-sized cars to the less profitable small cars played an important role, while the real estate companies had large sums tied up in land yet to be developed.

A number of manufacturing industries, notably steel and electrical machinery, had become trapped in the typical boom pattern of overcapacity-overproduction-excessive inventories-production curtailment and the pressure on prices as well as higher financing costs involved in this process. But for other sectors, such as foods, oil refining, and shipbuilding, and for nonmanufacturing industries such as construction, trade, transportation, and warehousing, the situation was much more favorable, thanks at least partly to the uninterrupted growth of exports.

An important factor in the 1970-71 recession was the shift in investment. In the sixties, investment had been mostly for enlarging capacity, although the improvement of technology usually went hand in hand with the increase in productive capacity. Recently, however, a considerable part of investment has been for the prevention of pollution and laborsaving machinery, which have contributed less to the quantitative growth of the economy.

The financial ratios showed a worsening tendency. For 575 companies listed on the First Section of the Tokyo Stock Exchange, the development is illustrated below.

	Fiscal 1969	Fiscal 1970	
	latter half	first half	latter half
Current ratio	110.0	110.8	112.1
Fixed ratio	221.4	224.2	229.1
Net worth to total capital employed	19.3	18.8	18.5
Turnover of total capital employed	1.24	1.23	1.18
Ratio of gross profit to sales	6.64	6.40	5.86
Ratio of operating profit to sales	4.20	4.03	3.53
Ratio of net profit to sales	2.29	2.21	1.98
Ratio of gross profit to total capital	8.27	7.85	6.93
Ratio of operating profit to total capital	5.22	4.95	4.18
Ratio of net profit to total capital	2.85	2.71	2.34
Ratio of net profit to net worth	26.3	26.6	23.7
Ratio of prime costs to sales	85.3	85.5	86.04

Nevertheless, most of Japan's leading enterprises improved their position in 1970. Of the fifty corporations with the highest sales (excluding banks, and insurance and trading companies), only one, Mitsubishi Heavy Industries, reported a decline in sales, and some of these companies achieved spectacular increases. Honda Motor's sales, in fiscal 1970, rose 29.2 percent over the preceding year; other companies with high growth rates were Kajima Construction (29.0 percent), Kawasaki Steel Corporation (27.3 percent), Nippon Electric (27.2 percent), Mitsubishi Chemical (25.1 percent), and Mitsukoshi (25.1 percent). Of the large trading companies, Mitsubishi Corporation increased its yearly sales to ¥4,069.9 billion, 25.5 percent higher than in the preceding year (Sumitomo Shoji hiked its sales by 29.6 percent). Of the fifty corporations with the highest profits (excluding banks and insurance companies), thirteen experienced a drop in profits in fiscal 1970 compared with 1969 (the sharpest loss, 43.4 percent was reported by Toshiba), but others had large gains: Kawasaki Steel Corporation, 59.7 percent; Shimizu Construction, 43.8 percent; Taisei Construction, 42.6 percent; Ohbayashi Construction, 41.8 percent; Kajima Construction, 36.6 percent, Daiwa House 32.6 percent; Tohoku Electric Power, 30.8 percent; Fuji Photo Film, 29.6 percent; Matsushita Electric Works, 29.5 percent; and Fujitsu, 28.6 percent. On the basis of tax returns, the number of corporations (with a capital of at least ¥100 million, including corporations not listed on the stock exchange) reporting profits exceeding ¥10 billion rose from thirty-three in (calendar year) 1967 to forty-one in 1968, fifty-six in 1969, and seventy-three in 1970.

The change in the buying pattern became more pronounced in the April–June quarter of 1971. Stocks of large companies were bought, particularly in shipbuilding, steel, electric power, and heavy electrical machinery. (In the usage of the Tokyo Stock Exchange, of the companies listed on the First Section, large companies are those with a capital exceeding ¥10 billion, medium-sized companies those with a capital between ¥2 and 10 billion, and small companies those with a capital under ¥3 billion.) Financial institutions, whose net stock purchases had amounted to 87 million shares in the first (January–March) quarter, bought 247 million shares in the second quarter. Life insurance companies, local banks, mutual banks, and credit associations were the main buyers. Net purchases of the insurance companies rose from 58 million shares to 99 million in the second quarter, those of other financial institutions increased from 29 million shares in the first to 149 million in the second quarter. The main reason for these purchases was the monetary relaxation, which had caused an abundance of loanable funds and brought the call rate down. The call rate (over the month) sank from 8.0 percent in March to 7.5 percent in April and 6.75 percent in July; the share of over-the-month loans declined from 95 percent at the end of February to 71 percent at the end of June. The city banks and the nonlife insurance companies were not interested in portfolio investment; large enterprises still borrowed from the city banks because they had to pay for past investments, and many borrowers changed from small institutions to the city banks when the latter became able to take care of their financial needs.

The stock purchases of the financial institutions were concentrated on low-priced issues whose yields were rather attractive; occasionally, they would invest for capital gains in stocks such as Matsushita Electric Industrial, Kirin Beer, Toyota Motor, or Taisei Construction. A good deal of the purchases of institutional investors involved cross trading by the securities companies, which had the financial institutions buy large blocks of stocks (e.g., Nippon Steel Corporation) sold by foreign investors. Nomura Securities Co. was particularly active in this kind of trading.

Compared with April 1970, average weighted stock prices were higher in June 1971 for transportation (including shipping and air transportation), warehousing, trade, banking, insurance, real estate, communications, electricity, gas, services, mining, transportation machinery, and oil refining. All other industries were down. In the beginning of May, the mark crisis brought a swing away from export related industries to consumer related goods.

In the middle of April, the upward trend was interrupted by a sharp temporary setback;

on April 20, the Dow-Jones average fell by ¥65.28; the slump was even deeper on the Osaka Stock Exchange, where the index lost ¥93.40, the third-largest decline on the Osaka Exchange. In May, the index sank to a low of ¥2,365.92 on the nineteenth, but regained the ¥2,400 level on the twenty-fifth. On June 7, the Dow-Jones climbed to ¥2,506.06 and eclipsed the previous high of ¥2,534.45 (reached on April 6, 1970) on June 15. On the twenty-fifth, the index rose to ¥2,600.32 and pressed toward the ¥2,700 mark during July. On July 19, the Dow-Jones reached ¥2,692.63, but slipped badly during the next two days. In the morning session of July 29, the Dow-Jones temporarily topped the ¥2,700 mark but lost ground in the afternoon, the day ending with the index at ¥2,699.18.

The rise in stock prices contrasted sharply with the general economic situation. The recovery predicted for the middle of 1971 failed to materialize, and unsolved international problems, particularly the mounting American pressure for a revaluation of the yen and restrictions on Japanese exports, intensified the gloom. In the latter half of July, the government decided on another reduction of the discount rate and an additional dose of fiscal stimulation, which reinforced the market's reliance on issues related to public works.

The Ministry of Finance took a rather detached view of market activities and seemed to regard the rise in stock prices as less speculative than the wild gyrations in the preceding year. The rise was fairly broadly based; in the middle of June, 89 percent of all issues were being traded and the turnover rate of the First Section was 55.4 percent. Outstanding credit for margin trading was estimated at ¥550 billion, only 2.7 percent of the market value of all listed stocks.

The business of the securities companies was booming. The interim settlement for the October 1970–March 1971 period had been somewhat disappointing. Income from securities transactions amounted to ¥9,782 million, higher than the ¥6,844 million for the entire year from October 1969 to September 1970, but, at ¥100,988 million, commissions were only 45 percent of the ¥224,675 million in the preceding year. The profit situation was even worse; the aftertax profits of ¥15,851 million represented only 37 percent of earnings during the previous business year. By July, however, the situation had changed completely; profits already exceeded those of the entire previous year, and there was every indication that the securities companies would have an enormously prosperous year.

In the first two weeks of August 1971, market sentiment was firm; on August 12, the Dow-Jones index rose above the ¥2,700 mark, and it reached ¥2,740.98 on the fourteenth. Institutional investors, in particular the nonlife insurance companies, disposed of large funds, and the government's measures for accelerating the economic recovery encouraged selective buying. Issues related to public works, particularly roads and harbors, and construction and dredging were bought, but oils also rose steeply (on the assumption that a revaluation of the yen would facilitate repayment of large dollar debts). At 10 A.M. on August 16 (Japan standard time), President Nixon broadcast an outline of his new economic policy. The announcement of a 10 percent tax on all imports and the suspension of the convertibility of the dollar into gold sent stock prices crashing down. The Dow-Jones index plunged ¥210.50, the largest loss for a single day in the history of the Tokyo Stock Exchange (although not the largest loss percentagewise); volume reached 282.2 million shares. The nose dive continued through the following three days, bringing the total drop to ¥550.82, a decline of 21 percent in four days. On the twentieth, a rally supported by active buying of electrical machinery, automobiles, construction, and nonlife insurance issues restored ¥93.72 to the Dow-Jones index, but oils continued to decline. The market weakened again on the following day. The new week started with a large decline of ¥114.65, which wiped out the gain made on the twentieth. Although trading was light, the downturn engulfed almost all fields; constructions suffered the largest losses, but oils, chemicals, general and electrical machinery, banking, insurance, transportation, shipping, and services also declined. The massive slump in stock prices prompted the exchange to reduce, by about half, the maximum increase or decrease in the price of a particular issue during one trading session; if the change in price exceeds this limit, a stop order is issued.

The decline reached its lowest point on August 24 when the Dow-Jones average sank to ¥2,162.82. Strangely enough, the decision of the Japanese government to float the yen, announced on August 28, had almost no effect on the stock market; the Dow-Jones index went up by ¥8.48 to ¥2,275.67. In September, an upward trend prevailed, and, on the last day of the month, the Dow-Jones stood at ¥2,428.25, a gain of over 22 percent compared with the August low. The Dow-Jones average declined from ¥2,432.50 on October 2, 1971, to a low of ¥2,227.25 on the twentieth; prices improved in the latter half of November, and a vigorous uptrend in the eight trading days of December pushed the Dow-Jones index up to ¥2,713.74 on December 28. The market value of all issues listed on the First Section of the Tokyo Stock Exchange at the end of 1971 amounted to ¥21,387,760 million, the value of those listed on the Second Section to ¥1,185,800 million. Total transactions on the Tokyo Stock Exchange in 1971 amounted to 60,813,414,000 shares (First Section, 59,028,027,000 shares; Second Section, 1,785,397,000 shares).

Dow Jones Index, August 14-24, 1971

August 1971	Dow-Jones Index	Difference		
14	¥2,740.98			
16	¥2,530.48	−¥210.50		
17	¥2,440.82	−¥89.66	−¥550.82	
18	¥2,328.28	−¥112.54		
19	¥2,190.16	−¥138.12		−¥578.16
20	¥2,283.88	+¥93.72		
21	¥2,278.44	−¥5.44		
23	¥2,163.79	−¥114.65		
24	¥2,162.82	−¥0.97		

The ups and downs of the Tokyo Stock Exchange are greatly influenced by a few issues. In 1969, twenty issues with the largest price increases accounted for 8.9 percent of all transactions; of the twenty, nine were electrical machinery manufacturers. Seven of the nine electrics were among the twenty largest losers in 1970. The swings in the prices of the market leaders are extremely wide. In 1968, Matsushita Electric Industrial moved between a low of ¥431 on February 3 and a high of ¥990 on November 17. On June 9, 1970, Matsushita rose to ¥827 (the charge of illegal support buying has been mentioned above); the stock was down to ¥458 on September 29. The ex rights high was ¥393 on November 18, 1970; the low, ¥317 on December 21.

The violent price changes are linked to the most characteristic features of the Japanese stock market; it is a short-term market in which the rate of change is very high for individual issues. One of the main reasons is the absence of large institutional investors, the weakness of the securities companies, and the structure of stock ownership. Although about 55 percent of all shares are held by corporations (34 percent by financial institutions), these corporations can hardly be considered as investors and their holdings are largely based on mutual business relations. In order to prevent foreign takeovers, Japanese companies try to have "stable" stockholders, i.e., large financial institutions, and regard reciprocal holdings of 20–30 percent of the stock as a desirable arrangement. In the 1962–63 credit squeeze, corporations sold between ¥3–4 billion in stocks in order to obtain liquid funds, which was a not unimportant factor in the stock market slump. The pension funds have joined the insurance companies and the investment trusts as institutional investors, but, compared with the size of the market, their funds available for investment in stocks are not large. Moreover, as a result of mutual corporate stockholding, about half of all shares are frozen in one way or another, thus restricting investment selection and contributing to the concentration of trading on relatively few issues.

Another basic factor in the behavior of the stock market is the absence of a large body of individual investors. The Iwato boom aroused widespread interest in stock investment, but the reverses of the market in the following years snuffed out investor interest, and the badly shaken investor confidence has not been fully restored. Stocks have not regained the attractiveness as an investment medium that they enjoyed during the Iwato boom. On the part of the investors, the reasons for the lagging accumulation of financial assets explained above apply to investment in stocks, while corporations as well as the securities companies are not too enthusiastic about individual investors. Corporations regard individual stockholders as unreliable (on the Tokyo Stock Exchange, holdings of less than 5,000 shares are called "floating shares"), and, for the securities companies, small-lot transactions are expensive.

The general tendency on the Tokyo Stock Exchange is for volume to shrink when prices go down, although Japanese institutional investors tend to sell when prices go up and to buy when prices go down. The average monthly trading volume in the period from April 1966 to November 1967 was 45 percent lower than in the period from July 1965 to March 1966; the monthly average for the period from April to November 1970 was 27 percent lower than the average from January 1968 to March 1970.

In recent years, the authorities have begun to pay attention to illegal price manipulation. In June 1970, the Ministry of Finance investigated the transactions in Mitsui Mining & Smelting Co. The stock had gone up from a low of ¥60 on January 5, 1970, to a high of ¥99 in March; it was down to ¥66 on April 30 and ¥64 on May 20. In the beginning of June, an announcement suggested that the company had developed a catalyst for the prevention of pollution by automobile exhaust gas. On June 10, of 176,040,000 shares traded, 49,450,000 (=28 percent) were shares of Mitsui Mining & Smelting Co. The price went up from ¥65 on June 1 to ¥116 on June 24.

In 1971, Toyama Securities Co. was found guilty of having manipulated the price of Dai-Nippon Sugar Mfg. Co., the first time that such a finding had been made since the licensing system was adopted. The firm was suspended from trading for three days and fined ¥300,000. On May 26, 1971, "cross orders" (the term the securities companies now use for buying and selling by the same dealer) involving 1 million shares jerked the price from ¥54 to ¥80. The

Ministry of Finance and the Tokyo Stock Exchange have also become more alert to window dressing in corporate reports.

In March 1971, the Ministry of Finance ordered Yashica to correct its reports for the three business years ended from March 1968 to March 1970 (which had been rigged by officers who had embezzled ¥847 billion from corporate funds). In June, Daiei Motion Picture voluntarily submitted an amended report for the term ended January 1971, because public accountants had pointed out irregularities in its original report. The Tokyo Stock Exchange, however, came to the conclusion that Daiei's original report did not amount to a deception punishable by delisting. The firm became insolvent in December 1971.

On August 16, 1971, the Tokyo Stock Exchange announced that, effective November 17, 1971, Ando Iron Works would be delisted. The company, which was traded on the Second Section, had overstated its profits by ¥357 million in its report for the business year ended April 1971. Based on the rules of the exchange drawn up in February 1970, the board of directors ordered the delisting because the falsification of the report had been deliberate and not merely the result of differences in accounting methods. The decision of the exchange was backed up by the Securities Bureau of the Ministry of Finance. Until November, the stock was traded at a special post to permit an orderly disposal of the stock (34 percent of the shares are held by the family of the company's president).

3 THE CAPITAL MARKET

4 THE EMISSION MARKET

In 1957 the emission market handled the highest number of shares issued either in prewar or postwar years. This was partly due to the enactment of special measures for tax exemptions on capital increases in January. By July, capital increases had reached ¥32,000 million and, by September, ¥32,700 million. This trend continued, and total capital increases during the year came to ¥205,181 million. Of the 355 firms involved, 275 were listed on the stock exchanges; their increases accounted for ¥193,792 million.

The issuing market became dull in 1958; the number of firms increasing their capital fell to 197 and the value to ¥172,800 million. The reasons for the decline were: (1) a decrease in equipment investment; (2) a shrinkage of corporate earnings; and (3) a shortage of funds in the money market. The stagnation continued through the first half of 1959, but when the expansion began to accelerate, issues became more frequent and involved larger amounts. An additional incentive was amendments to the laws regulating the revaluation of assets and the transfer of revaluation reserves. These revisions stimulated capital increases with part of the increases covered by transfers from the revaluation reserves (so that stockholders could buy new shares at a premium, e.g., for ¥40 or ¥45). The total for the year, however, rose only slightly above the previous year's level, due to the dullness during the first half; but the number of shares distributed gratis to stockholders almost doubled. Of the firms listed on the Tokyo Stock Exchange, 140 increased their paid-in capital by ¥148,873 million (2,227,214 new shares), while 171 firms added ¥41,418 million to their capital through the issuance of 655,387 gratis shares. In 1958, the number of firms distributing free shares was 109; the capital addition thus effected was ¥21,487 million and the number of gratis shares issued 345,759. Although there was a slight increase in gratis allocations in the following years (1960–62), the general prosperity engendered by the booming economy in 1959–61 caused some companies to change their issuing methods. Public offerings became more frequent, and were sometimes used in addition to allocations to stockholders. Nippon Toki Noritake, a leading maker of chinaware, allocated new shares at a rate of two old to one new at par, but also put shares on the market at a price of ¥430. Toshiba made an allocation of 1:0.7 to its stockholders, but also offered 30 million shares to the public through securities companies in blocs of 500 shares. Over 70 percent of this offer was taken up by existing stockholders. Yawata and Toyo Rayon also offered shares to the public, which were sold over the counter by securities companies. Toyo Kogyo gave the users of their products priority in buying shares offered to the public. A number of new issues were sold in the form of ADRs while other ADRs were covered by old shares purchased by the underwriters of the ADRs.

The number of firms increasing their capital as well as the amount of capital increases grew rapidly in 1960 and 1961, but, in 1962, the recession slowed down the pace and a number of planned increases had to be postponed, partly due to the financial stringency, partly because of the slump in the stock market, and partly on account of the poor corporate results. Nevertheless, the capital raised through new issues has assumed added significance in the past few years. Although the Capital Increase Adjustment Council sometimes cuts down on the plans proposed by the companies, the basic policy of the government favors a higher capitalization in order to strengthen the internal funds of enterprises and diminish their reliance on bank loans and other short-term borrowing.

On account of the depressed condition of the stock exchange, all capital increases of listed companies were, as a rule, suspended from February to October 1965. The number of issues therefore, decreased from 247 in 1964 to 58 in 1965, and it was only in 1969 that the number rose again over 200. As mentioned above, the securities companies adopted the rule that they would only underwrite issues of companies whose stocks were quoted at least at ¥60 and whose dividend rate of at least 10 percent could be maintained at that level after the increase in capital. In 1971, 277 companies increased their capital by ¥442,644 million (First Section, 148 companies, ¥395,989 million; Second Section, 129 companies, ¥46,655 million).

The two problems which attracted most attention were the issues of convertible debentures

Subscription Payments for Stocks

(In millions of yen)

| | Subscription payment for stocks | | | | | New capitalization by listed companies | | |
| | | | By use | | | | | |
	Assessment for stock	Total of proceeds	Equipment funds	Operating funds	Repayment funds	No. of companies	Capital increases	No. of issued shares (1,000 shrs.)
1949	82,158	80,794	2,175	21,709	37,327	—	—	—
1950	40,342	48,935	17,754	19,433	11,747	—	—	—
1951	73,884	77,801	34,311	24,149	19,340	257	43,690	817,012
1952	127,238	130,122	61,211	37,555	31,355	385	86,478	1,480,533
1953	180,112	192,021	94,249	61,456	36,316	355	115,035	2,094,818
1954	153,668	144,689	65,982	43,932	34,776	286	110,407	1,833,503
1955	111,629	101,454	43,809	27,686	29,960	226	83,220	1,485,314
1956	245,427	309,554	153,644	97,397	58,513	522	202,358	3,840,970
1957	293,680	288,071	196,581	57,777	33,712	427	228,401	4,178,243
1958	246,333	241,917	154,521	42,353	45,042	277	188,383	3,014,940
1959	287,504	283,219	162,705	78,069	42,444	334	197,947	3,031,832
1960	521,817	516,285	331,406	136,982	47,896	451	383,607	6,913,832
1961	995,774	977,968	661,894	213,153	102,920	653	672,073	12,109,228
1962	793,222	780,658	535,883	188,939	55,834	749	577,758	11,422,109
1963	676,100	664,765	358,892	218,531	87,341	403	398,386	n.a.

Note: "New capitalization by listed companies" refers only to companies listed on the First Section of the Tokyo Stock Exchange.

Source: 1949–56: Tokyo Stock Exchange, Monthly Statistics Report: 1957–63: Ministry of Finance.

and issues at market prices (bond issues will be discussed below). Issues of convertible debentures began in 1966. In April 1966, Nittsu (Nippon Express) announced an issue of convertible debentures with a fixed conversion price. The issue triggered a large sale of Nittsu's shares, but the issue was sold. In December 1967, Komatsu Manufacturing Co. floated $15 million in convertible debentures in the United States, the first such issue since August 1963, when Kubota had issued convertible debentures there.

In October 1966, Oki Kensetsu (listed on the Second Section) planned to issue stock at market prices, but the securities companies opposed the plan on the grounds that it would have a bad influence on the stock market. Oki Kensetsu did not go through with its plan, but the securities companies engaged in a lively discussion on the pros and cons of issues at market prices. The securities companies proposed that the existing stockholders should be compensated for the premium (i.e., the difference between the face value and the issue price) by a higher dividend rate or stock dividends.

In October 1968, Nippon Gakki announced a capital increase offering 6 million shares for public subscription at market price (to be paid in by January 31, 1969) followed by a gratis distribution of 12 million shares. The company contended that it was not an issue at market prices because the shareholders were going to be reimbursed by the gratis allocation of shares, but the securities companies did not agree.

In 1969, six companies whose stocks were traded at prices much higher than the face value issued new shares at market prices; they were Alps Electric, Mitsumi, TDK Electronics, Eida Sangyo, Toyo Toki, and Yoshitomi Pharmaceuticals. Issues at market prices in 1970 included Matsushita Electric Industrial (20 million shares), Daiwa House Industry Co. (12 million shares), and Sony Corporation (3 million shares). The Sony issue was announced on February 28; the issue price, ¥3,200, was fixed on April 13, and payment had to be made by the end of the month. Sony's price reached a monthly high of ¥4,000 on April 6 but was down to ¥2,950 on the thirtieth (closing price ¥3,060). In September, Toyo Toki announced its second offering at market prices (9.5 million shares). As mentioned above, not only individual stockholders but also the insurance companies strongly opposed issues at market prices. Their main reasons were: (1) the market price discounts the expectation of capital gains from new issues allocated to stockholders at par value; (2) dividend rates are based on the face value and not on the actual earnings of the companies; if stock is issued at market prices, dividend payments ought to be made on the basis of per share earnings. The insurance companies further stressed that issues at market prices would absorb too large a portion of their available funds and force them to sell off part of their portfolios.

The governor of the Tokyo Stock Exchange, Teiichiro Morinaga, proposed a compromise: (1) the exchange would suggest an adjustment of the issues to the underwriters and the issuing companies if too many companies issued new shares at market prices at the same time; (2) in order to facilitate issues at market prices, nonpar shares should be used and dividends should be expressed in yen. This plan was made binding by a new regulation of the Tokyo Stock Exchange, which went into effect on August 1, 1971; it prescribed that dividends be stated in yen and that the announcement of the dividend should contain a statement of earnings per share. This regulation may constitute the first step in the change to nonpar value shares.

To corporate managers, issues at par seem to involve a gift to stockholders for which the stockholders have done nothing. Issues at market prices, on the contrary, constitute an

Issues of Convertible Debentures

Company	Amount of issue ¥ billion	Interest rate %	Date of issue	Conversion period
Nippon Express	10	7.5	Aug. 1, '66	Apr. 1, '67–Mar. 31, '76
Hitachi Metals	3	7.7	July 15, '69	Oct. 1, '69–Mar. 31, '79
Japan Gas Chemical	1.5	7.7	Aug. 8, '69	Apr. 1, '70–Mar. 31, '79
Ajinomoto	4	7.7	Jan. 22, '70	Apr. 1, '70–Jan. 31, '80
Furukawa Electric	4	8.0	Feb. 17, '70	Oct. 1, '70–Feb. 28, '80
Bridgestone Tire	6	7.9	Apr. 28, '70	July 1, '70–Apr. 30, '80
Mitsukoshi	6	7.9	June 10, '70	Sept. 1, '70–May 31, '80
Toray Industries	10	7.9	July 14, '70	Oct. 1, '70–July 19, '80
Oki Electric	4	7.9	July 17, '70	Oct. 1, '70–July 30, '80
Honshu Paper	2.5	7.9	July 27, '70	Nov. 1, '70–July 31, '80
Mitsubishi Estate	10	7.9	July 24, '70	Oct. 1, '70–July 31, '80
Asahi Chemical	7	7.9	Aug. 1, '70	Nov. 2, '70–Aug. 12, '80
Sumitomo Heavy Machinery	3.5	7.9	Aug. 18, '70	Apr. 1, '71–Sept. 10, '80
Ishikawajima-Harima H. I.	6	8.0	Sept. 4, '70	Apr. 1, '71–Aug. 31, '80
Oji Paper	3.5	7.9	Aug. 20, '70	Apr. 1, '71–Aug. 31, '80
Nippon Seiko	4	7.9	Sept. 24, '70	Jan. 1, '71–Sept. 30, '80
Sumitomo Metal Mining	3.5	7.9	Sept. 19, '70	Apr. 1, '71–Oct. 1, '80
Kansai Paint	1.5	7.9	Oct. 13, '70	Jan. 1, '71–Oct. 17, '80
Nissan Motor	12	7.9	Oct. 1, '70	Apr. 1, '71–Sept. 30, '80
Shimazu Seisakusho	2	7.9	Nov. 5, '70	Apr. 1, '71–Sept. 30, '80
Hitachi Metals	3.5	7.9	Dec. 4, '70	Mar. 1, '71–Dec. 10, '80
Koyo Seiko	3	7.9	Dec. 15, '70	Mar. 1, '71–Dec. 19, '80
Nippon Light Metal	4.552	7.9	Jan. 21, '71	Oct. 1, '71–Feb. 9, '81
Mitsubishi Paper	2.5	7.9	Feb. 2, '71	Apr. 1, '71–Jan. 31, '81
Hitachi, Ltd.	12	7.8	Feb. 8, '71	May 1, '71–Jan. 24, '81
Japanese Geon	2.5	7.9	Feb. 23, '71	June 1, '71–Mar. 2, '81
Sharp	5	7.8	Mar. 23, '71	June 1, '71–Mar. 30, '81
Nippon Electric	10	7.8	Apr. 9, '71	Oct. 1, '71–Mar. 31, '81
Nippon Denso	3	7.8	Apr. 23, '71	July 1, '71–Apr. 28, '81
Kubota	8	7.7	May 10, '71	Aug. 2, '71–Apr. 15, '81
Daikin Kogyo	2.5	7.8	May 17, '71	Dec. 1, '71–May 12, '81
Nissan Diesel	2	7.8	May 7, '71	Oct. 1, '71–Mar. 31, '81
Gunze	2.5	7.7	May 27, '71	Dec. 1, '71–June 3, '81
Matsuzakaya	3	7.7	June 19, '71	Sept. 1, '71–June 26, '81
Hitachi Cable	5		July 22, '71	Oct. 1, '71–July 31, '81
Japan Air Lines	14		July 23, '71	Oct. 1, '71–July 30, '81
Yasukawa Electric	2		Aug. 2, '71	Nov. 1, '71–July 31, '81
Daimaru	4		Aug. 24, '71	Nov. 1, '71–Aug. 30, '81
Ricoh	2.5	7.5	Aug. 26, '71	Dec. 1, '71–Sept. 2, '81
Niigata Engineering	3.5		Sept. '71	Apr. 1, '72–Aug. 31, '81
Mitsubishi H. I.	13		Nov. 13, '71	Feb. 1, '72–Nov. 19, '81
Daiwa Spinning	1.5		Nov. '71	Feb. 1, '72–Nov. '81

Capital Increases:
Companies Listed on the Tokyo Stock Exchange First Section

	1964	1965	1966	1967	1968	1969	1970
Total increase in capital (¥ million)	507,677	127,076	206,870	193,938	333,095	468,247	591,797
Issues against payment							
Number of issues	247	58	142	123	186	265	414
Capital paid-in (¥ mill.)	463,897	104,362	179,400	156,486	279,022	414,371	516,152
Offerings to shareholders							
Number of issues	192	40	65	62	87	118	160
Paid-in (¥ mill.)	461,106	102,400	173,659	153,187	271,644	399,520	490,883
Private placement							
Number of issues	4	3	9	2	2	2	1
Paid-in (¥ mill.)	1,318	1,927	3,981	316	1,035	1,081	650
Public offerings							
Number of issues	51	15	24	23	33	47	110
Paid-in (¥ mill.)	1,472	34	713	1,776	3,057	7,935	18,734
Convertible debentures							
Number of issues	—	—	44	36	64	78	143
Paid-in (¥ mill.)	—	—	1,047	1,206	3,285	6,834	5,884
Share dividends (gratis distribution of new shares)							
Number of distributions	153	63	58	36	43	49	92
Value (¥ mill.)	36,274	16,491	23,234	12,034	27,803	13,007	50,467
Other							
Number of issues	24	15	18	17	51	71	81
Value (¥ mill.)	7,505	6,222	4,233	25,417	26,269	40,868	25,177

Note: Issues for which two or more different methods of financing are used, are counted under each of those methods.

Source: Tokyo Stock Exchange, Monthly Statistics Report.

Capital Increases

	Paid-in capital ¥ million	Gratis allocation ¥ million	Other ¥ million	Total ¥ million
1964	500,998	38,792	8,705	548,497
1965	113,940	16,820	6,566	137,327
1966	200,009	24,441	5,258	229,709
1967	183,876	13,842	25,813	223,531
1968	303,674	22,895	41,738	368,307
1969	450,174	14,802	43,931	508,908
1970	548,840	54,239	27,390	630,471

Capital Increases (cont.):
Companies Listed on the Tokyo Stock Exchange Second Section

	1964	1965	1966	1967	1968	1969	1970
Total increase in capital (¥ million)	40,820	10,251	22,839	29,593	30,432	40,661	38,674
Issues against payment							
Number of issues	187	48	91	116	121	179	182
Capital paid-in (¥ mill.)	37,101	9,578	20,607	27,390	24,669	35,802	32,688
Offerings to shareholders							
Number of issues	160	41	80	87	78	120	107
Paid-in (¥ mill.)	34,291	9,181	19,578	25,805	23,144	33,542	28,193
Private placement							
Number of issues	5	3	4	5	8	6	14
Paid-in (¥ mill.)	545	290	928	1,142	922	1,140	2,609
Public offerings							
Number of issues	22	4	7	24	35	53	61
Paid-in (¥ mill.)	2,264	106	100	442	602	1,120	1,885
Convertible debentures							
Number of issues	—	—	—	—	—	—	—
Paid-in (¥ mill.)	—	—	—	—	—	—	—
Share dividends (gratis distribution of new shares)							
Number of distributions	48	14	22	35	46	45	51
Value (¥ mill.)	2,518	328	1,206	1,807	2,423	1,794	3,772
Other							
Number of issues	17	8	14	6	25	44	26
Value (¥ mill.)	1,200	344	1,025	396	3,339	3,063	2,212

attractive source of funds for management. Behind the trend to issues at market prices lie the changes in the conception of the corporation; the legal principle that the stockholders are the owners of the corporation has lost most of its practical significance while the corporate managers not only behave as de facto owners but regard the stockholders only as (rather obnoxious) suppliers of (expensive) funds. Financial institutions, the most important class of stockholders in Japan, do not interfere as long as management does not make major blunders; after all, the bank managers belong to the same class of corporate managers. and their main interest concerns the profitability of their transactions with the companies whose stocks their institutions' own. They fully support the policy of limiting dividends to the "traditional" level and transfering as much as possible of the company's earnings to reserves. If a stockholder is dissatisfied with such a policy, he has the right to sell his shares.

Due to the dividend policy of Japanese enterprises, average internal cash flow in the five years from 1965 to 1969 was 2.29 times higher than in the preceding five years, so that enterprises felt less need for capital increases. The share of capital increases in corporate fund supply amounted to 20.3 percent in the latter half of fiscal 1961 and 21.1 percent in the first half of fiscal 1962; it was 6.5 percent in the first half of fiscal 1969 and 3.3 percent in the latter half, but it rose to 8.5 percent in the first half of fiscal 1970.

For all listed companies, funds raised through capital increases in 1970 amounted to ¥681,276 million, second only to the ¥712,175 million raised in 1961. The composition of the capital was as follows: allotment to stockholders, ¥538,045 million; public offerings, ¥138,079 million (including ¥115,921 million in premiums), and allotment to third parties ¥5,148 million (¥1,535 million in premiums). The lessened importance of capital increases in corporate financing is apparent in the following comparisons: share of capital increases in total investment capital: 1970, 4.6 percent; 1961, 17.4 percent; ratio of new capital to listed capital: 1970, 10.6 percent; 1961, 30 percent.

Following Nittsu's issue of domestic convertible debentures in 1967, four companies announced issues of debentures convertible at market prices in 1969, twenty-six in 1970, and eleven up to May 1971. Actual issues amounted to twenty-one during 1970, and thirteen issues were offered before the end of July 1971. Three methods have been used for issuing convertible debentures: (1) issues offered to existing stockholders on a preferential basis; (2) issues for which existing stockholders are given the right of preemption, i.e., the debentures are first offered existing stockholders; debentures not subscribed to by stockholders are offered to the general public; (3) public offerings. About half of the convertible debentures issued so far were offered to existing stockholders by one of the first two methods, half were public offerings. Total funds raised by convertible debentures in fiscal 1970 amounted to ¥114,550 million.

In accordance with the instructions of the Ministry of Finance, the securities companies had limited the issuance of convertible debentures to companies whose stocks were quoted above ¥100. This rule, however, excluded many large enterprises, and, when Mitsubishi Heavy Industries wanted to issue convertible debentures, the securities companies, with the approval of the Ministry of Finance, changed the rule so that, exceptionally, they will handle convertible debenture issues of a company whose stock is quoted below ¥100 if the business of the company is stable and no inconvenience to investors is to be feared. Mitsubishi Heavy Industries originally planned to float an issue of ¥20 billion, but the securities companies cut the issue down to ¥13 billion, issued in November 1971.

The popularity of convertible debentures is largely due to the fact that they allow speculation on a rise in stock prices without the risk of a drop in the market. The holder can always count on the fixed interest income and may realize a considerable capital gain, either on account of the rise in stock prices or because of an increase in the prices of the debentures. In the first half of 1971, prices of convertible debentures quoted on the Tokyo Stock Exchange rose in accord with the general trend of stock prices. If the price increase was added to the interest rate, the yield rate for the period from the date of issue until May 20, 1971, was 87.426 percent for Kansai Paint, 78.339 percent for Hitachi, 50.859 percent for Koyo Seiko, 46.440 percent for Nissan Motor, 38.459 percent for Mitsubishi Estate, and 32.221 percent for Oki Electric; all these debentures had been issued less than one year previously.

For a number of issues, the conversion period has already started and the rate of conversions was relatively high (e.g., for Kansai Paint, for which the conversion period started January 1, 1971, the conversion rate stood at 40 percent at the end of February). Thanks to the strong rise in stock prices in the first half of 1971, prices were higher than the issue price. Moreover, a few companies increased dividend rates and distributed stock dividends to make the conversion even more attractive. But for a number of issues, the conversion rate was rather low, chiefly because large investors preferred the fixed income, and the basic trend of rising stock prices seemed to continue.

3 THE CAPITAL MARKET

5 THE BOND MARKET

The tight money policy enforced since 1957 made the flotation of bonds rather difficult. In the beginning of 1958, the Federation of Bankers Association decided to take over ¥5 billion in debentures for the January–March period, and the Trust Fund Bureau also agreed to special bond investment operations, buying ¥6.8 billion of government-guaranteed bonds in March, and ¥10 billion of financial debentures and ¥8.7 million of government-guaranteed bonds in April and May. The National Railways, the Telegraph and Telephone Corporation, and power and steel companies were the main sectors supplied with funds through these transactions. A few other issues were put on the market in May, and when the financial stringency eased and new issues were allowed in August and in November, nine different issues totaling ¥4.7 billion were floated. Bank debentures, in particular, experienced a large expansion, their issues reaching ¥317.4 billion, an increase of ¥8.6 billion. The city banks took over ¥130.3 billion of the new issues.

The Securities Exchange Deliberation Council, at the meeting on November 17, 1959, drafted the following proposals for cultivating the debenture market: (1) industrial bonds shall be included in the media utilized by the National Savings Association; (2) measures shall be taken to incorporate industrial debentures into investment trusts to the extent that they will not affect the mobility and the management of the investment trust assets; (3) measures shall be taken to financially to assist securities dealers so that individual investors can purchase industrial debentures (the Japan Securities Finance Co. might be used for this purpose); (4) the usual practice of consultation at the time of bond flotations shall be abolished, and bonds shall be issued freely.

The bond market was active in the first quarter of 1959, but, because of the tight money, absorption slowed down until September, when large issues of government-guaranteed bonds were successfully floated. Also, the debentures of the big three steel firms were listed as grade A (issue price: ¥100 sold at ¥98.50) and four other companies, Hitachi, Tokyo Shibaura, Tokyo Gas, and Osaka Gas were added to the list. However, the bond issuance market remained dull and absorption difficult, so that various measures were taken to overcome this depression. In November, the Ministry of Finance approved the lowering of the registration fee to be paid by subscribers from 15 *sen* per ¥100 to 10 *sen*, effective December 1, 1959. By this means, plus more aggressive selling, the market witnessed a fair increase in the rate of absorption.

While the market remained dull in the first four months of 1960 and new issues had to be curtailed, a large increase in the demand for industrial funds led to an expansion of the market from May to September. During this period, government-guaranteed debentures

National Bonds

(In millions of yen)

Fiscal year	National bonds			Foreign exchange fund bills			Food bills			Outstanding amounts of national bonds
	Issue	Redemption	Balance	Issue	Redemption	Balance	Issue	Redemption	Balance	
1954	19,448	23,572	440,893	317,000	222,000	140,000	588,000	589,000	194,140	869,657
1955	4,799	19,860	425,833	692,000	687,000	145,000	1,163,000	1,047,000	310,140	969,805
1956	30,372	46,901	409,304	780,657	854,576	80,081	1,613,254	1,593,585	329,809	903,642
1957	45,458	49,004	405,758	239,082	219,160	100,003	1,424,870	1,491,618	263,061	849,557
1958	45,145	50,778	400,125	858,100	780,103	178,000	1,376,913	1,350,638	289,336	954,351
1959	89,650	29,971	459,804	1,426,549	1,354,462	250,085	1,832,667	1,793,825	328,178	1,119,722
1960	72,614	85,598	446,820	1,978,904	1,900,403	328,586	1,704,599	1,681,757	351,020	1,200,502
1961	38,869	49,335	436,354	1,300,602	1,355,132	274,056	1,194,464	1,238,377	307,107	1,073,852

Source: Bank of Japan.

Corporate Debentures

(In millions of yen)

	Bank debentures			Industrial bonds			Total		
	Issue	Redemption	Balance	Issue	Redemption	Balance	Issue	Redemption	Balance
1954	146,646	91,040	302,929	37,752	19,318	200,807	184,398	100,358	503,736
1955	172,333	113,777	361,485	73,984	46,819	227,355	246,317	160,596	588,840
1956	210,544	162,266	409,764	101,639	43,241	284,935	312,183	205,507	694,699
1957	231,400	157,884	483,280	97,101	44,630	337,361	328,501	202,514	820,641
1958	317,470	169,058	631,692	103,776	46,155	394,982	421,246	215,213	1,026,674
1959	353,557	161,880	823,369	188,003	42,143	540,805	541,510	204,023	1,364,174
1960	490,891	260,251	1,054,009	206,427	54,305	692,745	697,318	314,555	1,746,754
1961	691,225	480,646	1,264,588	406,647	20,971	1,078,406	1,097,872	501,617	2,342,994
1962	788,811	520,001	1,533,392	177,023	43,947	1,211,482	965,834	563,948	2,744,879

Source: Industrial Bank of Japan.

and local bonds were most actively issued due to the start of the new fiscal year, but this activity kept the flotation of industrial debentures down. In August, the buying operations of the Bank of Japan brought some animation to the market, and the announcement that the term of redemption would be extended from five to seven years was favorably received. In the latter part of October, the securities companies set up investment trusts incorporating public bonds and corporate debentures exclusively, and this again stimulated the market. The number of issues (industrial debentures, and government-guaranteed and public bonds), in 1960, rose to 711, totaling ¥290 billion. The share of government-guaranteed bonds in the new issues rose from 18.8 percent in 1958 and 19.5 percent in 1959 to 23.9 percent in 1960. The share of subscriptions by private individuals increased from 13.7 percent in the first half of 1960 to 16.9 percent in the latter half of the year, while the share of bonds taken over by financial institutions decreased from 79.7 percent to 75.2 percent.

In January of 1961, bond flotations came to ninety-six issues amounting to ¥66.5 billion, which was more than double the highest month in the past. The increase continued in the following two months: ¥91,380 million in February and ¥92,530 million in March. But a downward revision of the issuance terms in April dampened the market. The interest rate for electric power debentures was reduced and the issue price increased, which lowered the yield from 7.831 percent to 7.408 percent. Similar reductions were effected for other bonds.

In the second half of the year, the increases in the official discount rate of the Bank of Japan and the higher call rates kept bond issues down, and the change to a deflationary policy reduced the number of new issues. But, thanks to the very brisk tone in the beginning of the year, the total amount of new issues (industrial debentures, and government-guaranteed and local bonds) increased 68.1 percent over the preceding year and reached ¥487.6 billion. Industrial bonds saw the largest expansion with 94.4 percent. New issues of financial debentures reached ¥691.2 billion, redemptions came to ¥480.6 billion, and the outstanding balance of industrial debentures rose to ¥1,264.6 billion, 20.2 percent over 1960. Investment trusts absorbed 49.5 percent of the local bonds and government-guaranteed debentures floated in 1961, while city banks took over 27.6 percent. Individual investors accounted for ¥9.8 billion (2.0 percent) of the bond purchases.

The deflation kept the bond market down all through 1962. The government gave priority to government-guaranteed and electric power debentures, so that the flotation of other industrial debentures proved increasingly difficult. Altogether, only 23.2 percent of the original target figures of bond issues could be sold in the first half of fiscal 1962. Conditions improved, however, in the second half, and government-guaranteed bonds, in particular, showed a large increase in the last quarter of the fiscal year (January–March 1963).

On April 1, 1962, trading in bonds was suspended on the Tokyo, Osaka, and Nagoya exchanges with the exception of user bonds issued by Nippon Telegraph and Telephone public corporation. Trading was resumed in Tokyo and Osaka on February 7, 1966; 30 issues were quoted on the Tokyo Exchange and 25 issues in Osaka. Actually, however, a considerable part of trading in bonds is over the counter and trading between banks is usually done directly. An important reason for this is that only 115 of the 6,000 bond issues are listed. Purchases of listed bonds by foreign investors are very small, but, in May 1971, purchases of nonlisted bonds by foreigners were suspended. In August 1965, the underwriting syndicates for public and corporate bonds began to announce each week, on Thursday, the prices of the bonds underwritten in the course of the week; publication of prices of over-the-counter transactions in government-guaranteed bonds, bank debentures, and local bonds started in December. Bond issues listed on the Tokyo Stock Exchange increased from 11 in 1960 to 104 in 1970, sales (par value) from ¥7,928 million in 1960 to ¥159,980 million in 1970. Interest-bearing debentures of the Nippon Telegraph and Telephone Corporation account for the largest part of the transactions.

Contradictory tendencies influenced new bond issues. Corporations in need of funds wanted to issue more debentures, all the more so because new stock issues had been stopped; the Bank of Japan considered it undesirable to increase bond issues while credit restraints were in force, and the Ministry of Finance gave priority to issues of government-guaranteed debentures and local bonds. New issues of industrial bonds fell from ¥406,647 million in 1961 to ¥177,023 million in 1962; in 1963, new issues rose to ¥281,219 million and remained on the same level (¥282,713 million) in 1964. Issues rose again in 1965 and continued to increase in 1966 and 1967, reaching ¥544,293 million in the latter year. In the following two years, however, issues remained below this level but rose to ¥671,558 million in 1970 and ¥858,530 million in 1971.

Different from industrial debentures, issues of bank debentures increased without interruption, rising from ¥691,225 million in 1961 to ¥2,967,704 million in 1970; the growth corresponded to an average yearly rate of increase of 19.7 percent. Bank debentures are largely taken over by the city and other banks, which facilitates their absorption. Reflecting the enormous inflation of government investment programs, the flotation of government-guaranteed debentures rose from ¥196,509 million in 1961 to ¥1,199,578 million in 1970 (average yearly rate of increase over 24 percent). The slump in the stock market in the beginning of the sixties stimulated the interest of the securities companies in bonds, and the development of the bond investment trusts was an additional factor contributing to the absorption of bond issues.

The monthly volume of bond issues rose from about ¥30 billion in 1964 to ¥40 billion in the beginning of 1965 and ¥82 billion in December. The reduction in the official discount rate (January, April, and June 1965) and the decline of the call money rate prompted financial institutions with liquid funds (mutual banks, local banks, credit associations, and financial institutions for agriculture) to invest more in bonds; the share of the city banks in bond purchases became smaller.

Because bond yields declined, the yield rate of bond investment trusts was reduced from 7.77 percent to 7.45 percent; this caused a certain number of cancellations, but, for 1965 as a whole, new contracts exceeded cancellations.

A great change in the whole atmosphere of the bond market came with the emission of national bonds. For underwriting national bonds, a new syndicate was formed, larger than the syndicate for underwriting government-guaranteed debentures (which includes city and local banks, trust banks, and securities companies). The syndicate comprised thirty institutions, i.e., the thirteen city banks and three long-term credit banks, the five largest local banks, one institution each (the institution whose president served as president of the organization of the respective group) from the trust banks, mutual banks, and life insurance companies, the four large securities companies, the National Federation of Credit Associations, and the Central Cooperative Bank of Agriculture and Forestry. The underwriting ratios were fixed as follows: city and long-term credit banks, 51.5 percent; local banks, 20.5 percent; securities companies, 10 percent; the other five groups, 3.6 percent each. The contract for the emission of national bonds is concluded between the governor of the Bank of Japan and the president of the Federation of Bankers Associations as representative of the syndicate. Conditions for the first issue of national bonds were: interest rate 6.5 percent, maturity seven years, and issue price ¥98.60; this made the yield rate for subscribers 6.795 percent.

The emission of government bonds in fiscal 1965 was based on a special law allowing their flotation for supplementing budgetary revenues for fiscal 1965, as an exception to the Finance Law of 1947. Bonds issued during the fiscal year amounted to ¥230 billion of which the underwriting syndicate took over ¥110 billion and the Trust Fund Bureau the remainder. Actual sales began on January 28, 1966. The bonds issued in fiscal 1966 conformed to the provisions of the Finance Law by being earmarked for financing public works.

For the emission of bonds underwritten by the securities companies, the four large securities companies take over 80 percent and Kakumaru Kangyo and Shin-Nippon 13 percent, while the remaining forty-nine small securities companies take the remaining 7 percent. Each month, one of the four large companies acts as manager of the group; this company takes over 29 percent of all issues, and the others 17 percent each.

The emission of local bonds is regulated by the Home Ministry, which schedules the issues on the basis of the public works undertaken in each prefecture. Until 1971, the transfer payments to local governments (tax revenues of the national government paid out to local bodies) were deducted from public works expenditures and a certain percentage of the remainder could be raised by bond flotations. This method treated the transfer payments as a subsidy for public works, whereas they were meant to supplement the general revenues of local entities. For fiscal 1971, therefore, the subsidies of the national government for public work were subtracted from total expenditures for this purpose, and a certain percentage of the remainder was raised by bonds. The percentage varies for different types of public works. Newly added in fiscal 1971 were expenditures for the disposal of industrial waste of which 70 percent can be raised by bonds; also added were expenses for the acquisition of land for schools (for compulsory education) and for parks (until now, bonds could only be issued to buy land for highways, roads, and river regulation).

Private placements of bonds have become quite common in recent years; they amounted to ¥1.7 billion in fiscal 1968, ¥3.2 billion in fiscal 1969, and ¥5,750 million in fiscal 1970; for fiscal 1971, issues totaling about ¥10 billion were planned, but actual issues may remain below this figure. The main reasons for the increase in private issues were: public offerings are restricted to companies meeting certain qualifications (minimum requirements: capital, ¥4 billion; net assets, ¥7.5 billion; dividend rate, 10 percent p.a. for the previous six consecutive terms; ratio of net worth to total capital employed, 25 percent; ratio of total assets to net worth, 1.5 times); the securities companies are unwilling to add to the number of companies offering public bond issues because absorption of bonds is already difficult. For private offerings, a simple notification to the Ministry of Finance is sufficient, while public offerings require an application to the ministry and the publication of a prospectus. In private placements, no commission is paid to the securities companies so that the return on the bonds is better. The banks consider private placements a welcome opportunity to get a slice of the securities business. The volume of each issue was raised from ¥300 million to ¥500 million, which is about the same as that of grade B and C bonds; the yield rate is about 8.5 percent (grade D bonds, 8.483 percent), maturity is seven years. A private issue of Morinaga Confectionery was taken over by eight financial institutions, including Nippon

Kangyo Bank, Mitsui Trust & Banking, and Meiji Life Insurance; the amount of the issue was ¥400 million, the issue price ¥98.50, the coupon 8.2 percent, bringing a yield of 8.54 percent.

Financing of bond transactions is largely in the hands of the securities companies that, in turn, rely on funds provided by the Bank of Japan through the Japan Securities Finance Co. (outstanding balance: end of April 1971, ¥26.4 billion), the city banks, and the Japan Joint Securities Foundation (outstanding balance: end of April 1971, ¥22.5 billion). Of the funds made available, the four large securities companies are each given 20 percent and Kangyo Kakumaru and Shin-Nippon each 10 percent; the interest rate is 6.5 percent for market transactions and 7.5 percent for bond issues. The Japan Securities Finance Co. gives loans to individual investors for the acquisition of public and corporate bonds collateralized by industrial debentures; these funds come at least partly from the Japan Joint Securities Foundation. These loans are given either directly to individuals or to the securities companies for transactions involving individuals. For direct loans, individuals must be introduced by a securities company, which is also required to guarantee the loan; the ceiling on such loans is ¥5 million, the interest rate 8.5 percent, and maturity six months with the possibility of renewal. The securities companies are given loans for buying public and corporate bonds from individuals, for carrying bonds purchased from individuals, and for transactions between securities companies involving such bonds.

With the resumption of trading of bonds on the exchange, conditions for listing bonds were revised; firms whose bonds were to be listed were required to have a capital of at least ¥30 billion (until then, ¥8 billion); the balance of outstanding issues was raised from ¥4 billion to ¥7 billion and the amount of each issue from ¥400 million to ¥1 billion.

In May 1966, the securities companies began to announce the volume of national bonds traded over the counter; in June, prices based on these transactions were published and, on October 1, 1966, the bonds issued between January and March were listed on the exchange. Subsequent issues were listed as soon as the first interest payment on the respective issue had been made. The securities companies not only sold national bonds to individual investors but also bought bonds from investors who wanted to sell. Of the first issue, the securities companies were able to sell 12.6 percent to individual investors, more than their 10 percent quota; in the first nine months of 1966, the number of purchases of national bonds by individuals reached 146,320; the average amount per purchase was ¥324,100.

The bond market weakened in 1967; the city banks sold large amounts of bonds because they were short of funds, while the financial institutions for small enterprises and the agricultural credit institutions anticipated stronger fund demand and higher interest rates on loans and were reluctant to commit their liquid funds. In June, the Bank of Japan "advised" the city banks not to sell bonds whose prices had declined. With the shift to a tighter monetary policy in August, the price of the first national bond series sank to ¥98.15; that of the fourth series, to ¥98.00. Due to other depressing factors such as the devaluation of the British pound and the increase in the American discount rate in November 1967, bond prices sank by 10–20 *sen*; for debentures of the Nippon Telegraph and Telephone public corporation and other long-term bonds, trading was stopped because the decline exceeded the limit fixed by the exchange (¥1.50 per ¥100). Of the ¥4 billion in bonds the securities companies had taken over for public offerings in November, ¥448 million (11.2 percent) remained unsold.

In December, the Bank of Japan bought ¥10 billion of national bonds from the securities companies, thus actually intervening to support bond prices.

Together with the reduction of the issue price of national bonds in February 1968 (from ¥98.60 to ¥98.10, which increased the yield to subscribers from 6.795 percent to 6.902 percent), other long-term interest rates were revised.

The interest rate on bank debentures (coupon issues) was raised from 7.2 percent to 7.3 percent and the dividend rate on five-year loan trusts from 7.22 percent to 7.27 percent; the issue price of government-guaranteed debentures was reduced from ¥99.75 to ¥99.35, which increased their yield rate from 7.053 percent to 7.139 percent. In April, issue conditions were improved for local bonds (issue price 40 *sen* lower to ¥99.35) and industrial bonds (issue price of grade A bonds 50 *sen* lower to ¥99.00). But the emission market of bonds remained unfavorable, and, in November 1968, Keidanren (Federation of Economic Organizations) proposed a series of measures to make issues of industrial debentures more elastic and to close the gap between issue and market prices: (1) a band for the yield to subscribers should be fixed (e.g., for grade A bonds between 7.3 percent and 8.0 percent) and issue conditions should be adjusted in view of the market within this band; (2) as a rule the adjustment should be effected through a change in the issue price; changes in the other conditions should only be considered as secondary measures; (3) the adjustment in the issue price should be effected in steps of 25 *sen*; (4) the adjustments should be agreed upon by the issuer, the underwriters, and the trust companies (which act as trustees for the property securing the debentures).

On November 19, 1968, the Bank of Japan abolished the ceiling of ¥5 billion to which advances to the Securities Finance Corporation for financing bond transactions had been limited. Collateral had been restricted to industrial debentures; now, public bonds and other corporate debentures became acceptable.

The bond market was generally weak throughout the year 1968 with a slow erosion of bond prices. The reduction in the official discount rate in August brought a temporary firming of prices, but the downtrend reappeared in October, when an expected third reduction in the official discount rate did not materialize and the city banks began to sell large quantities of bonds. Purchases by agricultural credit institutions anticipated for November likewise failed to come off. Ordinarily, these institutions invest a large part of the funds paid by the government for the rice deliveries of the farmers, but because these institutions feared that the government would revise the rice distribution system (a fear which proved groundless because the revisions were only superficial), they did not want to tie down their funds. The downtrend in bond prices came to a halt in December. The city banks, however, refrained from large purchases, partly on account of the scarcity of funds and partly because of the restrictions resulting from the "position guidance" of the Bank of Japan.

In February 1969, grade A industrial debentures (yield to subscribers, 7.518 percent) brought a yield of 8.418 percent if bought on the market, and bank debentures (yield to subscribers, 7.3 percent) brought a return of 8.86 percent if bought on the market. Governor Usami of the Bank of Japan proposed to reduce issue prices of industrial debentures by ¥1, but the Ministry of Finance considered such a reduction too large because it would cause confusion in the long-term money market. Industry likewise opposed a decrease in the issue price. Finally Keidanren agreed with the securities companies on a reduction of 50 *sen* (which the Ministry of Finance thought appropriate). This lowered the issue price of grade

A bonds from ¥99.00 to ¥98.50 and increased the yield to subscribers by 0.11 percent to 7.628 percent. The change went into effect on March 3, 1969, but it brought no relief to the underwriters, who found it impossible to float the amounts of bonds desired by enterprises. In order to avoid large balances of unsold bonds, the securities companies tried to scale down bond issues.

The slump in bond prices gave rise to a new method of retiring bond issues. It has been customary to amortize bond issues by calling 3–5 percent of each issue each year (usually by drawing lots); but the companies now found it cheaper to buy up their bonds on the market. Toyo Rayon, Toshiba, and Kansai Electric were some of the firms using this method.

In order to facilitate bond transactions between different securities companies, a bond exchange center was established in July 1969.

The shift to a tight money policy in September 1969 brought new pressure on bond prices. Banks began to sell more bonds; on September 3, national bonds lost 5 *sen*, and, on the following day, prices of government-guaranteed debentures likewise suffered a large decline. On December 18, 1969, the yield rate of bank debentures rose to 9.1 percent, the highest since March 1966.

On November 27, 1970, the Asian Development Bank issued bonds denominated in yen. It was the first international issue offered to Japanese investors. Of the total issue of ¥6 billion, the underwriters reserved ¥2 billion for individual investors. The coupon rate was 7.4 percent, issue price ¥99, maturity seven years, and yield rate to subscribers 7.619 percent (between the yield rate of government-guaranteed debentures, 7.434 percent, and that of local bonds, 7.831 percent). Actually, financial institutions bought about 80 percent of the issue. The bonds are not tax-exempt, but, unlike domestic issues, the tax is not withheld at source and the investor must declare the interest income in his tax return. To invest part of the proceeds of the bond issue, the bank bought ¥2,880 million ($8 million) of government-guaranteed bonds. A second issue amounting to ¥11 billion was floated in June 1971.

For fiscal 1970, the government had originally scheduled bond issues amounting to ¥409.8 billion; in December 1970, the amount was reduced to ¥358.6 billion (face value). Up to March 1971, ¥305.0 billion had been floated, and an issue of ¥20 billion was planned for March. The Ministry of Finance wanted to have the remaining ¥33.6 billion issued in April because tax income was deemed insufficient. But the Federation of Bankers Associations strongly opposed this plan and demanded the cancellation of the remaining portion of the fiscal 1970 issues. In April, the first installment of the fiscal 1971 national bond issues, ¥80 billion, was floated which put heavy pressure on the capital market.

The budget for fiscal 1971 foresaw revenues of ¥430 billion from national bond issues (face value ¥445 billion), equivalent to 4.5 percent of budgeted revenues (fiscal 1966, 15.6 percent). The Trust Fund Bureau took over ¥30 billion and the underwriting syndicate ¥400 billion (face value ¥409.8 billion). Issues amounting to ¥200 billion were to be floated in the first half of the fiscal year (April–September), ¥209.8 billion in the second half. In July, Keidanren urged the government to increase its bond issues so as to provide additional stimulation to the economy, and, in August, the government decided to accelerate bond issues by increasing issues scheduled for September by ¥100 billion and those in October and November by ¥150 billion each, thus paving the way for additional bond issues in the last quarter of the fiscal year. Following President Nixon's announcement of his new economic policy, industry clamored for fiscal stimulation to offset the probable decline in exports, and Kakuei Tanaka, minister of international trade and industry, proposed to draw up a supplementary budget of ¥1,200 billion, to be financed largely by bond issues (¥800 billion). This is perfectly in line with the traditional preference of Japan's big business for inflationary growth. Finance Minister Mikio Mizuta intended to limit bond issues in fiscal 1971 to 16.92 percent of the initial budget but, at the same time, compile a new budget for a fifteen-month period starting January 1, 1972, which would provide for issues of national bonds amounting to ¥1 trillion. In this connection, the city banks proposed, first to issue national bonds with a maturity of ten years that would be more acceptable to small credit institutions, and, second, to allow city banks to sell national bonds over the counter, a proposal which immediately drew fire from the securities companies as a violation of Article 65 of the Securities Transaction Law. Issues of national bonds floated in the calendar year 1971 amounted to ¥720.6 billion.

Issues of local bonds authorized for fiscal 1970 amounted to ¥1,311.5 billion, an increase of 16.3 percent over the preceding year. Originally, issues of ¥966.2 billion had been planned, but additional revenues were needed to finance the cutback in rice production (purchase of rice paddies by local bodies). The amount of government-guaranteed debentures and local and corporate bond issues purchased in fiscal 1970 amounted to ¥960,860 million, ¥81.2 billion higher than in fiscal 1969; corporate bond issues amounted to ¥608,250 million. City and long-term banks bought ¥144.3 billion of these bonds; the share of all banks in bond purchases was 44.5 percent (as against 57.3 percent in fiscal 1969). Individual purchases (¥261.3 billion) accounted for 42.9 percent, a sharp increase from the preceding year (29.5 percent). The electric power companies, which issued a total of ¥308 billion in bonds, set ¥27.8 billion apart for individual investors; 90 percent of these special issues were actually bought by individuals.

According to a survey of the bond underwriting syndicate undertaken in March 1971, corporate bond issues (310 companies) planned for fiscal 1971 amounted to ¥1,092.3 billion, 79.6 percent higher than in fiscal 1970. The funds raised by bond issues were to be used as follows: new projects, ¥844.1 billion (77.3 percent); amortization of maturing bond issues ¥214.8 billion (19.7 percent); repayment of loans, ¥33.3 billion (3 percent).

Over-the-counter sales of bonds in fiscal 1970 amounted to ¥8,588,150 million, 43 percent higher than in the preceding fiscal year. Sales of interest bearing bank debentures amounted to ¥3,709.9 billion, 43 percent of the total; sales of user bonds of Nippon Telegraph and Telephone public corporation amounted to 18.6 percent, those of privately placed issues to 17.5 percent, and those of other corporate bonds to 9.1 percent (bonds of the electric power companies, 5.4 percent). The highest monthly sales were recorded in March 1971 at ¥1,106,550 million.

Transactions in convertible debentures expanded rapidly. These transactions started in May 1970 with a volume of ¥128 million (Tokyo ¥104 million); in June 1971, purchases on the three exchanges, Tokyo, Osaka, and Nagoya, amounted to ¥15,415 million (Tokyo, ¥10,483 million). Foreign investors showed very great interest in convertible debentures, but they were also popular with domestic investors. Prices went up considerably in the first half of 1971 but came tumbling down when the Nixon shock hit the market in August. Overleaf are the highs and lows as well as the conversion prices of the convertibles listed on the Tokyo Stock Exchange.

Highs and Lows of Convertible Debentures, 1971

	High ¥	High date	Low ¥	Low date	Conversion price ¥
Ajinomoto	136.00	Mar. 4	106.30	Aug. 19	255.00
Asahi Chemical	121.00	Aug. 13	97.00	Jan. 7	118.40
Bridgestone Tire	125.00	Aug. 14	98.00	Jan. 4	325.00
Daikin	121.95	Aug. 14	102.00	Oct. 19	130.00
Daimaru	110.60	Dec. 11	103.20	Nov. 1	
Furukawa Electric	120.55	Aug. 16	97.00	Jan. 6	85.00
Gunze	121.00	Aug. 11	103.20	Nov. 1	160.00
Hitachi Cable	112.00	Oct. 2	101.00	Nov. 5	
Hitachi, Ltd.	135.00	July 1	104.00	Aug. 19	110.00
Hitachi Metals	120.00	Aug. 14	101.00	Jan. 7	234.50
// // 2nd ser.	121.00	Aug. 14	100.00	Feb. 1	242.90
Honshu Paper	121.00	Aug. 13	97.00	Jan. 5	138.00
Ishikawajima-Harima H.I.	122.00	Aug. 14	101.50	Jan. 5	85.00
Japan Air Lines	114.00	Sept. 16	102.00	Oct. 19	
Japanese Geon	121.00	Aug. 14	102.00	Apr. 20	108.00
Kansai Paint	160.00	Apr. 23	100.00	Jan. 7	133.70
Kohjin	124.00	Dec. 28	103.10	Nov. 6	
Koyo Seiko	128.00	Apr. 22	104.50	Mar. 24	125.00
Kubota	121.00	Aug. 14	104.00	Aug. 19	170.00
Mitsubishi Estate	174.00	Aug. 10	108.00	Jan. 21	172.40
Mitsubishi Gas Chemical*	119.50	Aug. 13	101.00	Apr. 23	98.00
Mitsubishi Paper	121.00	Aug. 13	100.90	Apr. 1	111.00
Mitsukoshi	148.00	July 1	103.10	Jan. 7	307.00
Niigata Engineering	108.90	Dec. 24	102.00	Nov. 1	
Nippon Denso	142.00	June 30	109.00	Aug. 19	495.00
Nippon Electric	121.00	Aug. 13	101.50	Oct. 19	238.00
Nippon Light Metal	130.00	Aug. 13	101.00	Mar. 25	126.50
Nippon Seiko	121.00	Aug. 13	99.50	Jan. 6	
Nissan Diesel	125.00	Aug. 9	102.00	Nov. 8	150.00
Nissan Motor	158.00	Dec. 25	100.50	Feb. 2	155.80
Oji Paper	147.00	Dec. 24	99.00	Jan. 4	123.00
Oki Electric	129.00	Apr. 8	104.60	Nov. 22	205.90
Ricoh	124.00	Dec. 28	102.00	Nov. 4	
Sharp	123.00	June 10	103.00	Oct. 26	257.30
Shimazu Seisakusho	121.00	Aug. 14	99.50	Jan. 12	104.00
Sumitomo Heavy Machinery	121.00	Aug. 13	99.00	Jan. 5	119.00
Sumitomo Metal Mining	122.00	Aug. 16	99.00	Jan. 9	90.00
Toray Industries	122.00	Aug. 14	97.30	Jan. 7	135.30
Yasukawa Electric	111.00	Oct. 1	101.00	Oct. 19	

Note: * formerly Japan Gas Chemical.

In June 1971, the market price of three corporate bonds (Fuji Electric, Hokkaido Electric Power, and Hokuriku Electric Power) rose above the face value of ￥100; at the same time, the price of short-term bank debentures (Shoko Chukin, bonds maturing January 1972) reached ￥100.15, but the yield rate was down to 6.93 percent (interest rate 7.2 percent). In 1966, some corporate bonds had been quoted above face value, but the yield rate had remained at 7.3 percent.

In July 1971, ￥207.1 billion in short-term treasury bills were offered for public subscription, the highest amount so far; the amount corresponded to 22 percent of the entire issue for the month (usually, about 10 percent of long-term bonds are sold to the public). The maturity of these bonds is two months; because the discount rate was reduced in July, the yield rate, which had been 5.423 percent, went down to 5.168 percent. Nonfinancial corporations bought ￥148.7 billion of these short-term bills. The amount of treasury bills sold to the public rose to ￥305.4 billion. Particularly noteworthy were the large purchases by trading companies. On account of the uncertainty in the international currency market, the trading companies collected large advance payments for exports, converted the dollars into yen, and bought short-term bills with a yield of somewhat higher than 3- or 6-month time deposits. Usually, manufacturers of electric appliances, automobiles, and steel are the largest nonfinancial corporate buyers of short-term bills.

The credit restraints imposed in September 1969 led to large sales of bonds by financial institutions; hence, bond prices declined and the yield of bonds bought on the market became significantly higher than that of new issues. In January 1970, the yield to subscribers of grade A industrial bonds was 7.628 percent, but bonds purchased on the market brought a return of over 9 percent. Hence, the demand for a revision of issue conditions reappeared, and, in February, a readjustment of long-term interest rates was decided upon. The revisions were as follows:

	Issue price		Nominal interest rate %		Yield to subscriber %		New conditions in effect 1970
	New	Old	New	Old	New	Old	
National bonds	97.60	98.10	6.5	6.5	7.011	6.902	April
Government-guaranteed debentures	98.00	99.35	7.0	7.0	7.434	7.139	//
Local public bonds	98.50	99.35	7.5	7.3	7.831	7.441	//
Grade A industrial debentures	98.00	98.50	7.6	7.3	8.046	7.628	March
Interest-bearing bank debentures	99.50	100.00	7.5	7.3	7.638	7.300	//
Discount bank debentures	94.15	94.32	(5.83)	(1.55 sen =5.5575%)	6.43	6.022	May

At the same time, interest rates on loan trusts, money trusts, time deposits, and post office savings deposits were revised.

Bond prices came again under pressure with the reduction of the official discount rate in October and, until December 1970, sales of corporate bonds were slow, so that securities companies were left with large amounts of unsold bonds. In 1971, however, sales picked up and, in April and May, buying orders received by the securities companies exceeded the available supply of bonds. The slowdown of the economy caused a sharp shrinkage of fund demand, and the small financial institutions, which are important lenders in the call money market, found themselves with an excess of loanable funds. Due to the relaxation of the money market, the call rate declined; the lender's rate of over-the-month money went down from 8.5 percent in November 1970 to 8.25 percent in December, 8.0 percent in January, 1971, 7.5 percent in April, 7.0 percent in May, and 6.5 percent in July. This made investment in bonds more attractive and bond purchases by local banks, credit associations, credit cooperatives, and agricultural credit institutions increased (credit associations, for example, which used to buy about ¥10 million of bonds a month, increased their purchases to ¥1 billion). Demand was particulary strong for bonds with short remaining maturities (one to two years). Market prices, therefore, went up, causing a decline in the yield rate of bonds traded on the exchange. In the beginning of April 1971, the yield rates of bonds were as follows: Short-term bonds (bank debentures with less than two years until maturity), 7.3–7.4 percent; medium-term bonds (bank debentures with a maturity of two to five years), 7.9–8.0 percent; long-term bonds (debentures of Nippon Telegraph and Telephone Corporation with a maturity of five years), 8.1–8.2 percent.

The development in the prices of long-term bonds is illustrated below.

	Yield to subscriber	Dec. 1970	Jan. 1971	Feb. '71	Mar. '71	Apr. '71	May '71
Bank debentures	7.638%	8.87%	8.6%	8.4%	8.2%	7.9%	7.7%
Grade A industrial debentures	8.046%	8.89%	8.64%	8.45%	8.29%	8.13%	8.09%

The difference between the yield rate of issues traded on the market and that of new issues, therefore, almost disappeared, and this prompted Keidanren to press again for lower long-term interest rates. In response to Keidanren's request, the Ministry of Finance in cooperation with the financial institutions, worked out a new long-term interest structure which was announced on August 11, 1971, and went into effect on September 1, 1971. The Ministry of Finance intended to raise the issue price of national bonds by 30 sen, from ¥97.60 to ¥97.90, but the financial institutions which absorb a large part of these issues (fiscal 1970: city, local, trust, and long-term credit banks, 74 percent), opposed such a large raise, and a compromise limited the increase to 15 sen. The changes are set forth opposite.

The interest (dividend) rate on loan trusts (five years) was reduced from 7.37 percent to 7.27 percent and that on money trusts (five years) from 7.07 percent to 7.03 percent.

No progress has been made toward a solution of the much-discussed problem of greater flexibility in the conditions of bond issues, particularly the adoption of a margin of 0.25 percent in yield rates and variable maturities. The emission market for bonds remains strictly regulated and, without official pressure, not only issues of national bonds and government-guaranteed debentures but of other bonds as well would often remain unsold.

While the Nixon shock sent stock prices tumbling down, the bond market remained firm. Due to the sluggish fund demand, small financial institutions had large idle funds, and other enterprises, too, were looking for investment opportunities. The strong demand for

	Issue conditions starting Sept. 1, 1971			Issue conditions until Aug. 1971		
	Issue price ¥	Interest rate %	Yield rate %	Issue price ¥	Interest rate %	Yield rate %
National bonds	97.75	6.5	6.978	97.60	6.5	7.011
Government-guaranteed debentures	98.90	7.0	7.236	98.00	7.0	7.434
Local public bonds	98.90	7.3	7.540	98.50	7.5	7.831
Industrial debentures, grade A	98.50	7.4	7.730	98.00	7.6	8.046
„ „ A'	98.00	7.4	7.842	97.50	7.6	8.161
„ „ B	97.75	7.4	7.899	97.25	7.6	8.218
„ „ C	98.00	7.6	8.046	97.50	7.8	8.366
„ „ D	97.50	7.6	8.161	97.00	7.8	8.483
Interest-bearing bank debentures	100.00	7.3	7.300	99.50	7.5	7.638

bonds pushed prices up, and, in the first week of September, prices of all bank debentures were above their face value, the first time that this had happened since the Tokyo Securities Dealers Association began to publish bond prices in 1966. Yield rates, therefore, sank below the coupon rate, and contrary to the situation that had prevailed through most of the past years, for many issues the yield of bonds bought on the market was lower than the yield to subscribers. The monetary relaxation made it unnecessary for the larger city banks to liquidate their bond portfolios, while some of the smaller city banks sold bonds, whose market prices were higher than their book value, in order to improve their fund position.

In connection with the large increase in the issues of national bonds in order to cover the deficit in fiscal 1971, the government decided to increase the maturity of national bonds from seven to ten years starting January 1, 1972. This induced the Ministry of Finance to accede to the long-standing demand of industry and approve industrial bonds with a maturity of ten years and a coupon rate of 7.5–7.6 percent (yield to subscribers 7.9 percent). The electric power companies are greatly interested in these issues; given the long depreciation period of most of their equipment (twenty to twenty-five years), they must float three issues of seven-year bonds to finance a single investment program but need only two issues of ten-year bonds.

Issues of National Bonds and Government-Guaranteed Debentures
(In billions of yen)

Fiscal year	1966	1967	1968	1969	1970
National bonds	675.0	590.0	446.0	390.0	325.0
Government-guaranteed debentures	434.9	411.8	323.2	302.3	263.2
Total	1,109.9	1,001.8	769.2	692.3	588.2
Ratio of total to GNP (%)	2.9	2.2	1.5	1.1	0.8

Issue Conditions and Yields of Bonds

Description	Date	Issue price ¥	Discount rate % p.a.	sen p.d.	Interest % p.a.	Yield % p.a.
National bonds, 7 years	Jan. 1966	98.60			6.5	6.795
	Feb. 1968	98.10			6.5	6.902
	Apr. 1970	97.60			6.5	7.011
	Sept. 1971	97.75			6.5	6.978
Government-guaranteed bonds (public corporations), 7 years	Apr. 1955	98.00			7.0	7.434
	July	98.50			7.5	7.831
	Dec.	99.50			7.5	7.609
	Apr. 1956	99.00			7.0	7.215
	Aug.	100.00			7.0	7.000
	July 1957	98.75			7.0	7.269
	Apr. 1960	99.75			7.0	7.053
	Feb. 1968	99.35			7.0	7.139
	Apr. 1970	98.00			7.0	7.434
	Sept. 1971	98.90			7.0	7.236
Local public bonds, until Sept. 1955 5 years, later 7 years	Apr. 1955	99.50			8.5	8.643
	Oct.	99.50			8.5	8.614
	Dec.	99.50			8.0	8.111
	Apr. 1956	100.00			7.5	7.500
	Aug.	100.00			7.3	7.300
	July 1957	99.00			7.5	7.720
	Apr. 1960	99.75			7.3	7.354
	Apr. 1968	99.35			7.3	7.441
	Apr. 1970	98.50			7.5	7.831
	Sept. 1971	98.90			7.3	7.540
Industrial debentures, grade A; until Sept. 1955 5 years, later 7 years	Apr. 1955	98.50			8.5	8.934
	Oct.	99.00			8.5	8.730
	Dec.	99.00			8.0	8.225
	Apr. 1956	99.50			7.5	7.609
	Aug.	99.75			7.3	7.354
	July 1957	98.50			7.5	7.831
	Apr. 1960	99.50			7.3	7.408
	Apr. 1968	99.00			7.3	7.518
	Mar. 1969	98.50			7.3	7.628
	Mar. 1970	98.00			7.6	8.046
Bank debentures, interest-bearing, until Oct. 1955 3 years, later 5 years	Sept. 1971	98.50			7.4	7.730
	Jan. 1972	99.50			7.4	7.508
	Apr. 1955	100.00			8.5	8.500
	Dec.	98.50			7.5	7.918
	Apr. 1956	98.50			7.0	7.411
	Aug.	99.25			7.0	7.204
	July 1957	97.75			7.0	7.621
	July 1960	99.60			7.5	7.610
	Apr. 1961	100.00			7.3	7.300
	Oct. 1966	100.00			7.2	7.200
	Feb. 1967	100.00			7.3	7.300
	Mar. 1970	99.50			7.5	7.638
	Sept. 1971	100.00			7.3	7.300
Bank debentures, discount, 1 year	Apr. 1955	93.41			1.8	7.055
	Dec.	93.77			1.7	6.643
	Apr. 1956	94.14			1.6	6.224
	July 1957	93.77			1.7	6.643
	May 1960	94.14			1.6	6.224
	Oct. 1966	94.32			1.55	6.022
	May 1970	94.15	5.83			6.213
Treasury bills, 60 days	Apr. 1955	99.10			1.5	5.524
	Apr. 1956	99.13			1.45	5.338
	Dec. 1957	99.07			1.55	5.710
	Sept. 1958	99.01			1.65	6.082
	June 1963	99.07			1.55	5.710
	Apr. 1968	99.04			1.6	5.896
	Aug.	99.07			1.55	5.710
	Sept. 1969	99.0342	5.875			5.932
	Nov. 1970	99.0548	5.75			5.804
	Jan. 1971	99.0753	5.625			5.677
	May		5.5			5.423
	July		5.375			5.168

Bond Market

	1964	1965	1966	1967	1968	1969	1970
Number of trading days	301	301	298	299	302	297	297
Number of bond issues	11	11	31	31	31	32	47
Number of issues listed	35	38	61	78	75	83	104
Amount issued (¥ million)	268,463	422,011	850,410	1,706,706	2,675,593	3,401,837	4,215,031
Amount outstanding (¥ million)	266,220	419,006	843,513	1,690,412	2,643,441	3,325,372	4,097,275
Sales, par value							
Total (¥1,000)	14,392,500	18,727,900	48,930,800	51,448,000	58,969,000	94,758,000	159,980,500
Daily average (¥1,000)	47,816	62,219	164,197	172,067	195,262	319,051	538,655
Sales, market value							
Total (¥1,000)	9,942,780	14,093,556	43,796,222	44,787,571	51,668,560	82,782,026	138,713,681
Daily average (¥1,000)	33,032	46,822	146,967	149,791	171,088	278,272	467,049
Average total market value (¥ mill.)	151,000	289,656	725,136	1,508,440	2,416,190	3,059,956	3,783,592

Source: Tokyo Stock Exchange, Monthly Statistics Report.

Off-Market Transactions in Listed Bonds

(In millions of yen)

	Total volume			National bonds		Municipal bonds		Bonds of public corporations	
	Total	Sales	Purchases	Sales	Purchases	Sales	Purchases	Sales	Purchases
1966	432,314	218,585	213,755	804	878	207	177	263	251
1967	615,247	309,707	305,539	46,694	45,070	171	181	570	570
1968	800,028	414,800	385,228	95,110	71,569	92	90	415	493
1969	972,729	495,036	477,692	117,206	102,393	299	299	540	526
1970	1,575,270	786,461	788,808	154,091	143,915	356	476	226	241

	Industrial debentures		Bank debentures		Nippon Telegraph & Telephone public corp.			
					Coupon bonds		Discount bonds	
	Sales	Purchases	Sales	Purchases	Sales	Purchases	Sales	Purchases
1966	2,413	2,470	5,113	5,584	169,313	165,317	39,795	39,335
1967	1,359	1,265	7,099	6,895	202,793	199,381	51,125	51,869
1968	2,216	1,831	12,296	11,715	244,626	236,973	60,482	61,839
1969	2,510	2,424	7,410	7,882	295,673	293,183	70,890	71,417
1970	2,809	2,960	25,112	28,064	484,647	493,570	115,124	121,647

	Other special bonds		Convertible bonds	
	Sales	Purchases	Sales	Purchases
1966	203	211		
1967	97	99		
1968	140	134		
1969	34	36	1,081	
1970	59	57		826

Source: Tokyo Stock Exchange, based on weekly reports by exchange members.

Changes in Yield Rates of Bonds Following
Removal of Credit Restraints

	High		Low		Difference in percentage points
	Date	Yield rate	Date	Yield rate	
Electric debentures	Dec. 1964	8.60	Aug. 1966	7.27	1.33
DDK debentures	Dec. 1964	9.56	Aug. 1966	7.54	2.02
Electric debentures	June 1968	8.81	Sept. 1968	8.06	0.75
DDK debentures	June 1968	9.90	Sept. 1968	8.13	0.77
Electric debentures	June 1970	9.21	Aug. 1971	7.46	1.85
DDK debentures	June 1970	9.37	Aug. 1971	7.30	2.07

Note: Electric debentures=interest-bearing debentures of electric power companies;
DDK debentures: interest-bearing debentures of Nippon Telegraph & Telephone public corporation.

Corporate Bond Issues by Industry

	Fiscal 1970 actual ¥ billion	Fiscal 1971 planned ¥ billion	Rate of increase 1971/1970 %
Textiles	21.1	51.5	144.1
Chemicals	21.0	67.2	220.0
Iron & steel	69.5	158.3	127.8
Electric machinery	38.9	91.8	136.0
Transportation machinery	41.8	70.7	69.1
Land transportation	38.0	54.4	43.2
Electric power	278.2	385.0	38.4
Gas	14.1	25.6	81.6
Special bonds	32.0	39.0	21.9
Other	53.6	148.7	177.4
Total	608.2	1,092.2	79.6

Based on survey of the bond underwriting syndicate covering 310 companies.

Purchases of Bonds of Steel Companies by Individuals

	Total issues		Purchases by individuals			
	Fiscal 1969 ¥ billion	First half of fiscal 1970 ¥ billion	Fiscal 1969		First half of fiscal 1970	
			Amount ¥ bill.	% of total	Amount ¥ bill.	% of total
Nippon Steel Corporation	19.5	14.0	3.51	18.0	6.84	48.9
Nippon Kokan	6.4	4.3	1.44	22.5	1.16	27.0
Sumitomo Metal Industries	5.45	4.3	0.55	10.1	1.27	29.5
Kawasaki Steel Corporation	5.45	4.3	0.79	14.5	1.05	24.4
Kobe Iron Works	4.8	2.1	0.89	18.5	0.51	24.3

Outstanding Amounts of Bonds
March 1971
(In millions of yen)

National bonds	3,597,462
Short-term government bills	1,941,433
Food bills	1,293,169
Foreign exchange fund bills	648,265
Registered local public bonds	1,660,414
Underwritten by government	26,490
Corporate bonds	15,725,880
Debentures of public corporations	6,237,145
Discount bonds	637,004
Bank debentures	6,337,677
Discount debentures	1,881,685
Industrial Bank	2,006,781
Long-Term Credit Bank	1,708,728
Japan Hypothec Bank	1,064,361
Bank of Tokyo	133,027
Central Coop. B. of Ag. & For.	566,666
Shoko Chukin Bank	858,113
Industrial bonds	3,151,095

Source: Bank of Japan, Economic Statistics Monthly.

Outstanding Amounts of Foreign Bonds
March 1971

Government bonds		
	£1,000	10,797
	$1,000	23,741
	DM 1,000	280,000
	Swiss frcs. 1,000	110,000
Local public bodies		
	$1,000	37,040
	DM 1,000	800,000
Public corporations		
	$1,000	51,051
Bank debentures		
	$1,000	66,507
	DM 1,000	200,000
	Swiss frcs. 1,000	50,000
Industrial bonds		
	$1,000	401,988
	DM 1,000	263,450

Source: Bank of Japan, Economic Statistics Monthly.

Outstanding Issues of Industrial Bonds, March 1971

	(In millions of yen)
Domestic issues, total	3,751,095
Manufacturing	1,344,126
Mining	46,978
Transportation	385,510
Communications	22,773
Electric power & gas	1,270,867
Commerce	22,113
Foreign currency issues total ($1,000)	473,969*
Manufacturing ($1,000)	349,694*
Transportation ($1,000)	14,125
Communications ($1,000)	13,000
Commerce ($1,000)	28,843
Electric power & gas (DM 1,000)	250,000

Note: * Including issues in DM.
Source: The Industrial Bank of Japan.

3 THE CAPITAL MARKET

6 INVESTMENT TRUSTS

From March 1964 to September 1969, the outstanding balance of investment trusts declined almost without interruption. The balance reached a high of ¥1,432.3 billion at the end of July 1964, and it was only in June 1971 that the balance surpassed this mark and rose to ¥1,459,289 million. The basic reason for the slump was the sales policy of the securities companies, which, for stocks as well as investment trusts, had attracted largely short-term funds. Fluctuations in the economy, therefore, caused a sudden increase in cancellations, and the lethargic condition of the stock market made it impossible to rekindle investor interest. At the end of 1960, the outstanding balance of investment trusts (¥604.2 billion) was higher than that of loan trusts, now the most important fund source of the trust banks (¥512.7 billion); at the end of 1970, loan trusts amounted to ¥4,372.4 billion, while investment trusts totaled ¥1,315.3 billion, not even one-third. In 1961, investment trusts accounted for 6.9 percent of personal financial assets, whereas, in 1970, their share had dropped to 1.8 percent; the share of loan trusts, on the contrary, rose from 2.9 percent in 1961 to 5.7 percent in 1970. An important factor in keeping the investment trusts going was the favorable development of the bond investment trusts. In July 1964, bonds constituted 13.4 percent of the outstanding balance of investment trusts; in August 1971, their share was 44.0 percent. The fixed interest rate of the bond investment trusts was credited with the popularity of these trusts. In 1968, stock prices moved upward and contributed to the recovery of the investment trust business. The securities companies tried to improve the image of investment trusts by launching new types of trusts, such as installment trusts, uncancellable trusts, and international trusts, which, in July 1971, accounted for 41.6 percent of the outstanding balances of open-end trusts. For installment investment trusts, the securities companies tied up with banks and the postal transfer system so that investors could have their payments transferred automatically. The companies have also changed their approach and now stress the savings aspect not only of investment trusts but also of securities in general; all companies have organized a securities savings section.

In 1964, the Ministry of Finance urged a reorganization of investment trusts so as to check the deteriorating situation. By reducing the share of stocks in the trusts to 60–75 percent, the ministry wanted to create "balanced funds," and, from January 1965 on, unit trusts, too, were switched to balanced funds. A number of funds, however, diverted increasingly large amounts into the call money market, where returns were better and risks less. In 1965, bond investment trusts suffered a temporary decline but, for the year as a whole, new contracts were higher than cancellations. On account of the lower bond yields, however, distributions on bond investment trusts were reduced from 7.77 percent to 7.45 percent.

The debacle of Yamaichi Securities greatly affected the investment trust business; in May 1965, cancellations amounted to ¥32 billion; in June, to ¥47.8 billion; and, in July, to ¥42 billion; it was only in September that cancellations dropped below ¥30 billion.

The slump in stock prices reduced the market value of closed-end trusts below the nominal value (¥5,000) of the certificates. In July, the seven leading securities companies handling closed-end investment trusts decided to postpone repayment of the funds maturing in that month by one year, so as to protect investors from losses. In September, however, the stock market went up, and Daiwa, Oi, and Osaka securities companies redeemed matured trusts without waiting a year. In October 1966, the Securities Investment Trust Association proposed to defer the redemption of the unit trusts which matured in 1965 for another year. Because the contracts provided only for a one-year postponement, the association asked the Ministry of Finance for permission to charge the terms of the contracts. Actually, however, the situation in October 1967 was not much better, and the Ministry of Finance decided that repayment should be made regardless of conditions as there was no assurance that the situation would improve. Hence, nine closed-end investment trusts set up by six different companies were redeemed below face value, the first time since 1951 that investors in unit trusts had suffered a loss. Yamaichi's ninety-fifth issue (set up in October 1965) paid out ¥4,024.44 on a ¥5,000 certificate.

The securities companies made a few changes in their management: they reduced the number of stock issues selected for their funds from 400 or 500 to about 100, reduced the share of stocks to about 75 percent, and increased their reserves for price fluctuations. Starting January 1966, the smallest denomination of trust certificates was raised from ¥5,000 to ¥10,000 and a fee of ¥500 was levied in addition to the price of the certificate. In November 1966, the Investment Trust Association called for an improvement of the investment trust system: (1) the investment trust companies should be not only nominally but also actually independent of the securities companies; in particular, the stocks to be purchased should be bought through the securities company that had sold the certificates; (2) the Investment Trust Association should be transformed into a self-regulatory organ of the industry; (3) the ceiling on stocks in the investment portfolio should be reduced from 75 percent to 70 percent.

In the latter half of 1965 and the first months of 1966, the situation remained unsatisfactory for investment trusts despite the recovery of the stock market. Cancellations exceeded new investments by about ¥20 billion each month, and, for the entire year 1966, the outstanding balance of investment trusts declined by ¥153 billion. In 1967, cancellations were higher than new investments in all months except January; in March, the excess amounted to over ¥30 billion. For the entire year, the outstanding balance shrank by ¥87.1 billion in 1967 and ¥57.7 billion in 1968; it rose again in 1969. At the end of 1967, stocks made up 47.1 percent of the assets of unit trusts and slightly over half of all trust assets. The increase in stock prices in 1969 brought the market value of closed-end trusts to the par level and made the redemption of overdue trusts possible; by September, all matured unit trusts had been redeemed. For bond trusts, new contracts had already been higher than cancellations in 1967, but, for stock investment trusts, it was only at the end of 1969 that, for the first time in six years, the outstanding balance increased. New stock investment trusts set up in 1971 amounted to ¥361,118 million, cancellations came to ¥161,325 million, and repayment of matured trusts to ¥30,651 million; the outstanding balance at the end of the year amounted to ¥900,841 million. The value of new bond investment trusts set up in 1971 was ¥291,650 million and cancellations amounted to ¥157,600 million; the outstanding balance at the end of the year came to ¥717,673 million.

In the spring of 1968, a plan to establish American type mutual funds was discussed. The securities companies thought that the flood of cancellations could be avoided if investors owned, instead of investment certificates, stock in a company managing mutual funds. New legislation would be necessary to make this type of investment company possible, and the downfall of IOS may have finished these plans.

Since October 1969, cancellations have declined and, in 1970, they fell to about half the 1969 level; the change to buying and selling open-end funds at the basic price on the day of the transaction and the condition for the new types of funds excluding cancellations in the first two years contributed to the improvement.

On April 4, 1970, the Ministry of Finance made it possible to acquire foreign securities for investment fund portfolios. A ceiling of $100 million was fixed for all funds; the four large securities companies being allocated $70 million. The Securities Investment Trust Association fixed a limit of 30 percent on the share of foreign stocks in the assets of each stock trust; on April 1, 1971, the limit was raised to 50 percent. The four large securities companies started buying stocks on the New York market, and later added stocks traded on the exchanges in London, Toronto, and Frankfurt to their funds. In April 1971, two medium-sized funds, Taiyo and Asahi (managed by Shin-Nippon and Nippon Kangyo Kakumaru, respectively), were given permission to acquire foreign securities up to $5 million for their investment trusts; three other medium-sized funds, Shin-Wako, Eguchi, and Nihon, were allowed to buy foreign securities in July. But the volume of foreign securities actually incorporated into investment trusts remained very small; at the end of March 1971, it was about $20 million, not even 1 percent of the outstanding balance. In April and May, the large securities companies started international investment trusts, for which they made larger purchases of foreign securities, including, for the first time, Australian and French stocks in their purchases. Up to July 20, 1971, the securities companies had bought a total of $56,336,000 of foreign stocks; they sold $11,430,000 and retained about $45 million.

The large companies usually set up a new unit fund each month; Taiyo, Shin-Wako, Fuji, and Nippon funds are established less regularly. Asahi investment trusts are relatively few.

Open-end funds number forty-six; nine companies operate these funds. The trust managers have followed a policy of keeping down investment in stocks and diverting larger funds into the call money market. At the end of June 1971, the average share of stocks in stock trusts was 59.9 percent; it was 47.9 percent for closed-end and 73.9 percent for open-end trusts. The stock trusts had ¥254.2 billion in call money, equivalent to 31.5 percent of the outstanding balance; thereafter, however, the amount decreased considerably due to the slack demand for funds. Bond trusts are managed by six companies; their outstanding balance in August 1971 was 4.2 times higher than at the end of 1961.

On account of the downtrend in the yield of bonds, the securities companies intended to reduce the dividend rate on bond trusts, which had been restored to 7.7 percent, to 7.5 percent. If the trust fee (paid to the trust companies for managing the trust funds, at present twenty ten-thousandths) is included, the companies need a yield rate of 7.9 percent on bonds in order to break even, but, since about May 1971, the securities companies have been unable to buy bonds with such a yield rate. On the other hand, the trust companies want to have their fee raised to thirty-five ten-thousandths because their costs have risen. This would impose a further burden on fund management, all the more because the companies want to change prepayment of the commission (¥50 per ¥10,000) to payment at termination.

Together with insurance companies and pension trusts, investment trusts are Japan's most important institutional investors. With the tendency to diversify and to decrease investment in stocks, their portfolios, which represented about 10 percent of the total value of listed stocks in 1961–63, accounted for only 2 percent of the value in 1970. As mentioned above, the investment trusts tend to select the same issues. Usually, the top ten issues in each fund include at least three issues that are the same and only two or three that are not among the top ten of other funds. The investment trusts have closely reflected the trends and moods of the stock market. In November 1969, the four large investment trusts held 53.6 percent of all shares of electrical machinery manufacturers; they increased their holdings of Sony from 3,780,000 shares at the end of April 1968 to over 7 million shares at the end of April 1969, and their holdings of TDK Electronics from 5,130,000 shares at the end of November 1968 to over 9 million shares at the same time in 1969. In December 1970, the investment trusts started to decrease their holdings of growth stocks (in particular, electronics, precision instruments, chemicals, and pharmaceuticals) and to increase their investments in housing, construction, printing, banking, and insurance. At times, the funds have been very successful; between the stock market low of March 16, 1968 and the high of November 20, 1969, the market value of the four large open-end funds increased 2.09 times, whereas the Dow-Jones average rose by 65.2 percent; but, at the end of 1970, the market value of the funds was down 33.4 percent, and, at the end of August 1971, the net asset value of all open-end investment trusts was below par.

In February 1971, the industry commemorated the twentieth anniversary of the beginning of investment trusts, and the Ministry of Finance availed itself of this occasion to invite the industry representatives to a consultation, which produced the following guidelines: (1) diversify fund investment; stop short-term buying and selling; invest long-term for earnings and not for gains from market fluctuation; (2) divide all funds into three categories: (a) capital funds (investments in open-end trusts that cannot be cancelled), (b) income funds (investment in stocks of large companies), (c) capital income funds (unit trusts, installment and balanced trusts); in capital income funds, investment in one issue should be limited to 5 percent of the fund balance (generally, the ceiling is 10 percent); (3) report ratio of value of stock traded to market prices (simple average of market price at the end of each month or period) of stocks in the portfolio; report average fees; (4) report to the Ministry of Finance quarterly trading in each issue, including number of shares traded and price; (5) limit dividend payments on open-end funds (except installment funds and funds that cannot be cancelled) if the price before distribution is below the value of the trust fund as shown:

Ratio of standard price before distribution to average value of trust fund	Maximum dividend rate	
	Capital funds	Balanced & income funds
80 – 90%	5%	6%
70 – 80%	4%	5%
under 70%	3%	4%

Note: % p. a. of average value of trust funds; before tax.

(6) block offers of stocks to trust companies should be limited to four per month.

The Ministry of Finance wanted to reward a better performance than the Dow-Jones average and punish funds falling below the average; but, so far, there is no agreement on the standard by which performance of investment trusts should be measured. In June 1971, the four large securities companies proposed the following norms: (1) increase or decrease in standard price (i.e., net asset ratio); (2) comparison between the changes in the standard price and the stock market index; (3) for unit trusts: earnings of matured trusts (including cancellations).

The chief reward or punishment would be the higher or lower dividends that the funds would be allowed to distribute, but the implementation of the system would require a strict classification of the various types of investment trusts.

The Ministry of Finance advised the securities companies not to sell investment trusts to business corporations. Usually, about 90 percent of the investment trusts are sold to individuals and 2–3 percent to nonprofit corporations (mostly schools and religious bodies), but, in July 1971, local banks, credit associations, prefectural federations of credit cooperatives, and mutual aid societies purchased about ¥1 billion of investment trusts. Due to the monetary relaxation, these institutions possessed considerable idle funds, but few stocks and bonds with good yield rates were available on the market; demand for call money was sluggish and call money rates were low. The ministry was afraid that the financial institutions would cancel their holdings in investment trusts if money became scarce and that these cancellations would have an undesirable influence on the investment trust business.

Nomura plans a new type of open-end trust in which investment in stocks will be limited to 50 percent (the other 50 percent is to be invested in bonds or used for call loans) and the smallest trading unit will be ¥1,000. In addition to attracting small savers, the fund is intended to qualify for tax exemption given to savings up to ¥1.5 million. Instead of charging a commission of ¥30 per unit when the certificate is bought and ¥20 when it is sold, Nomura wants to charge a commission of ¥50 or less when the certificate is sold. Daiwa, Nikko, and Yamaichi are searching for a form of investment trust that will be eligible for tax exemption and preferential treatment under the Law for Workmen's Property Formation. The transformation of the present balanced funds into cumulative funds (incorporation of earnings into capital) for the absorption of small savings is under consideration.

Investment Trusts

(In millions of yen)

Year	Unit trusts				Open-end trusts			Open-end bond trusts			Total			
	New trusts	Cancel- lations	Redemp- tions	Outstand- ing balance	New trusts	Cancel- lations	Outstand- ing balance	New trusts	Cancel- lations	Outstand- ing balance	New trusts	Cancel- lations	Redemp- tions	Outstand- ing balance
1959	145,330	58,876	3,219	265,048	37,150	—	65,033	—	—	—	182,480	58,876	3,219	330,081
1960	246,930	85,832	—	426,146	115,136	2,113	178,056	—	—	—	362,066	87,945	—	604,202
1961	391,190	130,082	9,910	677,443	197,015	25,669	349,402	244,490	88,470	156,020	832,695	244,221	9,810	1,182,865
1962	222,625	135,156	14,161	750,751	124,491	94,018	279,875	83,819	107,160	132,679	430,935	336,334	14,161	1,263,306
1963	287,569	137,155	17,884	883,280	44,304	137,071	287,108	109,857	71,021	171,515	441,730	345,247	17,884	1,341,903
1964	174,592	168,238	45,415	844,219	155,566	125,335	317,339	122,332	84,811	209,036	452,490	378,384	45,415	1,370,594
1965	183,773	235,669	42,556	749,765	13,056	113,832	216,563	120,665	110,132	219,569	317,494	459,634	42,556	1,185,897
1966	168,000	231,241	75,976	610,548	36,071	62,372	190,262	87,381	74,942	232,008	291,454	368,556	75,976	1,032,818
1967	133,060	224,243	45,929	473,435	82,297	75,500	197,059	120,693	77,513	275,188	336,051	377,257	45,929	945,682
1968	150,763	185,450	104,426	334,322	81,064	*97,056	181,067	210,854	113,442	372,600	442,683	395,919	104,456	887,989
1969	174,594	143,165	34,462	331,288	214,319	*166,599	228,787	252,416	135,824	489,193	641,330	445,225	34,825	1,049,268
1970	172,382	91,662	23,660	388,347	170,969	*56,405	343,351	258,978	164,547	583,624	602,329	312,249	24,026	1,315,322

Note: * including redemptions.
Source: The Investment Trust Association.

Fund Management of Investment Trusts

(In millions of yen)

End of year	Unit trusts					Open-end trusts				
	Call loans	Stocks	Bonds	Other assets	Total assets	Call loans	Stocks	Bonds	Other assets	Total assets
1959	60,899	230,485	12,771	3,223	307,389	21,146	45,253	1,129	311	67,841
1960	65,676	389,758	40,721	8,125	504,282	44,432	129,399	10,735	2,107	186,674
1961	80,909	569,998	113,573	14,206	778,687	38,885	229,626	57,170	7,155	332,837
1962	60,729	647,905	83,135	17,201	808,972	49,682	272,147	36,625	3,277	361,832
1963	75,833	789,950	49,603	26,080	941,467	18,296	209,203	10,204	3,684	241,389
1964	96,422	700,088	41,084	21,784	859,380	29,643	222,793	20,841	2,798	276,076
1965	116,665	526,121	55,567	21,679	720,033	21,955	145,713	10,580	2,607	180,856
1966	119,472	369,093	90,824	11,844	591,234	14,852	137,824	9,455	1,835	163,969
1967	127,472	229,885	109,078	5,147	471,584	27,204	124,585	25,130	1,478	178,397
1968	73,259	190,783	84.255	4,192	352,490	21,326	141,776	18,581	1,990	183,673
1969	114,801	177,299	65,561	7,790	365,453	29,959	219,487	13,066	4,821	267,335
1970	160,080	184,565	64,881	2,697	412,223	41,407	225,683	17,356	2,456	286,902

	Open-end bond trusts				Total				
	Call loans	Bonds	Other assets	Total assets	Call loans	Stocks	Bonds	Other assets	Total assets
1959	—	—	—	—	82,046	275,738	13,901	3,544	375,231
1960	—	—	—	—	110,109	519,158	51,456	10,232	690,957
1961	15,005	145,010	3,417	163,433	134,801	799,624	315,754	24,778	1,274,958
1962	12,090	122,898	3,412	138,401	122,503	920,053	242,659	23,891	1,309,107
1963	34,372	139,932	3,851	178,155	128,502	999,154	199,740	33,616	1,361,012
1964	41,098	171,652	4,534	217,285	167,164	922,881	233,578	29,117	1,352,741
1965	15,720	207,205	5,167	228,093	154,341	671,834	273,353	29,455	1,128,983
1966	15,209	220,153	5,188	240,552	149,535	506,918	320,434	18,869	995,756
1967	16,113	263,300	5,457	284,871	170,790	354,470	397,509	12,084	934,853
1968	26,803	351,799	7,426	386,030	121,389	332,560	454,636	13,609	922,194
1969	37,058	460,558	9,235	506,852	181,819	396,787	539,186	21,847	1,139,641
1970	35,025	557,927	12,393	605,345	236,507	410,249	640,165	17,550	1,304,471

Notes: 1. Stocks and bonds are given at book values.
2. Other assets include money in trust, accrued dividends, accrued interest, and other receivables.

Source: The Investment Trust Association.

Investment Trust by Funds
August 31, 1971

Fund	New trusts	Cancel-lations	Redemp-tions	Outstand-ing bal-ance	Net asset value	Ratio of net asset value to outstand-ing balance	Ratio of stocks to total portfolio
	¥ mill.	¥ mill.	¥ mill.	¥ mill.	¥ mill.	%	%
Unit trusts							
Nomura	6,170	2,369	1,299	161,023	170,856	106.1	47.0
Nikko	3,500	2,771	540	87,351	86,902	99.4	42.7
Yamaichi	3,113	1,833	118	64,941	64,274	98.9	43.5
Daiwa	3,212	1,822	222	83,698	83,388	99.6	44.4
Taiyo	509	215	32	6,802	7,338	107.8	42.0
Shin-Wako	442	405	0	7,830	8,094	103.3	32.0
Asahi	0	130	30	6,408	6,517	101.7	38.0
Nippon	1,747	511	0	10,361	10,462	100.9	30.9
Total	18,694	10,057	2,243	428,418	437,835	102.2	44.3
Open-end trusts							
Nomura	1,506	1,252	—	139,644	119,539	85.6	80.3
Nikko	2,732	972	—	81,824	67,358	82.3	70.5
Yamaichi	1,294	2,233	—	57,811	49,468	85.5	70.1
Daiwa	892	974	—	73,401	63,292	86.2	73.9
Taiyo	420	200	—	18,615	17,813	95.6	67.6
Shin-Wako	225	500	—	11,840	10,070	85.0	62.1
Eguchi	220	540	—	7,960	5,951	74.7	60.7
Asahi	760	280	—	12,480	10,776	86.3	68.7
Nippon	0	170	—	7,345	6,374	86.7	65.4
Total	8,030	7,122	—	410,923	350,646	85.3	73.7
Total of stock trusts	26,724	17,180	—	839,341	788,481	93.9	57.4
Open-end bond trusts							
Nomura	8,770	5,293	—	295,093	305,368	103.4	—
Nikko	4,557	3,037	—	133,363	137,949	103.4	—
Yamaichi	4,970	2,420	—	97,928	101,291	103.4	—
Daiwa	3,924	1,630	—	112,028	115,977	103.5	—
Taiyo	391	0	—	5,138	5,335	103.8	—
Asahi	959	659	—	21,493	22,249	103.5	—
Total	23,571	13,039	—	665,043	688,173	103.4	—
Grand total	50,296	30,219	2,243	1,504,384	1,476,654	—	—

Source: Nihon Keizai Shimbun.

Composition of Open-end Investment Trusts

1. Top Twenty Issues in Open-end Investment Trusts of Four Large Securities Companies
(Market value in millions of yen)

End of December 1970		End of June 1971	
Issue	¥ million	Issue	¥ million
Matsushita Electric Works	2,772	Matsushita Electric Works	3,942
Fujitsu	2,709	Fujitsu	3,237
Fuji Photo Film	1,668	Sony	2,774
Toto	1,651	Toto	2,486
Mitsui Real Estate	1,640	Daiwa House	2,377
Oki Electric	1,625	Mitsui Real Estate	2,314
Daiwa House	1,539	Eidai Sangyo	2,274
Ricoh	1,509	Matsushita Electric Ind.	2,269
Sony	1,508	Nippon Gakki	2,211
Kajima Construction	1,418	Fuji Photo Film	2,199
Nippon Gakki	1,409	Toyota Motor	1,695
Nippon Kogaku	1,400	Kajima Construction	1,592
Shiseido	1,277	Oki Electric	1,547
Sharp	1,261	Tokio Marine & Fire Ins.	1,523
Matsushita Electric Ind.	1,230	Maeda Construction	1,513
Eidai Sangyo	1,189	Mitsukoshi	1,456
Canon	1,114	Daifuku Machinery	1,399
Tokio Marine & Fire Ins.	872	Nippon Denso	1,389
Mitsukoshi	866	Nippon Kogaku	1,228
Ebara Mfg.	864	Shiseido	1,184

Note: Aggregate values of the Open-end Trust No. 1 of each of the four companies, Nomura, Nikko, Daiwa, and Yamaichi.

Composition of Open-end Investment Trusts (cont.)

2. Increase and Decrease in Holdings of Leading Issues.

Increases	Number of shares 1,000	Decreases	Number of shares 1,000
Nomura			
Tokio Marine & Fire Ins.	1,300	Mitsubishi Estate	1,400
Maeda Construction	1,200	Ricoh	1,100
Mitsui & Co.	1,000	Nippon Electric	1,020
Mitsukoshi	860	Sharp	770
Matsushita Electric Works	810	Ebara Mfg.	730
Meiji Seika	500	Japan Dev. & Construc.	600
Toyota Motor	480	Sumitomo Bank	560
Oki Electric	480	Hitachi Seiki	520
Daiwa House	400	Komatsu Mfg.	430
Nikko			
Toyota Motor	1,120	Nippon Oil	1,050
Dai Nippon Printing	600	Fujitsu	700
Nippon Gakki	600	Fujikoshi Steel	670
Yamaha Motorcycle	510	Shinetsu Chemical	650
Eidai Sangyo	510	Sharp	650
Mitsui Mining & Smelting	500	Takeda Chemical	600
Maeda Construction	470	Ricoh	570
Mitsubishi Estate	300	Denki Kagaku Kogyo	300
Ishii Iron Works	300	Nippon Oil	300
Daiwa			
Mitsui-OSK Line	900	TDK Electronics	600
Kirin Brewery	620	Sumitomo Metal Ind.	500
NYK	500	Kajima Construction	320
Mitsubishi Estate	300	Denki Kagaku Kogyo	300
Ishii Iron Works	300	Nippon Oil	300
Yamaichi			
Sumitomo Electric Inc.	840	Nippon Sanso	450
Mitsui Mining & Smelting	700	Calpis Food	330
Ajinomoto	600	Komatsu Mfg.	300
Mitsubishi Metal Mining	500	Kashiyama	300
Dowa Mining	500	Nakagawa Electric	290
C. Itoh & Co.	500	Taisei Construction	280
Mitsui & Co.	450	Banyu Pharmaceutical	270
Mitsukoshi	450		

Note: Increases or decreases between the end of December 1970 and June 1971 in the Open-end Trust No. 1 of the four large companies.

Net Asset Value of Open-end Investment Trusts
December 27, 1971

	Fund	Net asset value (¥)
Nomura	Fund No. 1	756
	Fund No. 2	951
	New Large-Scale Fund	1,121
	New Fund	1,478
	Installment Fund	882
	International Joint Fund	10,205
Nikko	Fund No. 1	695
	Fund No. 2	764
	Fund No. 3	1,386
	New Large-Scale Fund	1,144
	Balanced Fund	1,293
	Installment Fund	936
	International Fund	10,216
Yamaichi	Fund No. 1	762
	Fund No. 2	879
	Fund No. 4	1,028
	New Large-Scale Fund	1,054
	Fund No. 6	1,070
	Installment Fund	903
	Common International Fund	10,268
Daiwa	Fund No. 1	721
	Fund No. 2	729
	Fund No. 3	1,027
	Large-Scale Fund	967
	Balanced Fund	1,242
	Installment Fund	952
	Uncancellable Fund	959
	International Fund	10,267
Taiyo	Fund No. 1	945
	Fund No. 2	1,057
	Balanced Fund	1,124
	Large-Scale Fund	1,035
	Installment Fund	895
Shin-Wako	Fund No. 1	787
	Fund No. 2	1,012
	Balanced Fund	1,157
	Installment Fund	911
Asahi	Alps Fund	833
	Blue Fund	852
	Balanced Fund	997
	Large-Scale Fund	1,055
Fuji	Fund No. 1	740
	Balanced Fund	992
Nippon	Nippon Fund	890
	Balanced Fund	964

Note: Face value of certificates of international funds ¥10,000; all others ¥1,000.
Source: Nihon Keizai Shimbun.

4 THE CALL MONEY MARKET

From the end of the inflation and the suspension of the activities of the Reconversion Finance Bank until the adoption of the new fund supply system in 1962, central bank credit constituted the main form of currency supply. Because the advances of the Bank of Japan were not given directly to the ultimate borrowers but to the city banks, the supply of "growth currency" (the expression used in the discussions on these problems) created the overloan situation of the city banks. In fact, the central problem of financing the strong expansion of the economy was the supply of long-term funds required for capital investment, but nominally short-term funds were widely used for long-term investment, and the money market had to make up for the insufficiencies of the capital market. Although the enormous expansion of the money supply was not without inflationary side effects, the rate of inflation was much less serious than in the immediate postwar period. An important reason for the different behavior of the economy was the entirely different supply-demand situation. The emphasis on the rehabilitation of key industries had left an immense consumption demand unsatisfied (the decision to start the reconstruction of the economy with the rebuilding of basic industries seemed theoretically sound from a long-range point of view but had disastrous practical consequences), whereas the economic expansion in the sixties was accompanied by a rapidly growing supply of goods.

The new fund supply system made open market operations the main form of currency supply. Actually, these operations were not based on a real market. The supply of bonds eligible for these operations was limited and the price underlying the operations was based on a bilateral agreement between the Bank of Japan and the banks. This part of the money market, therefore, was regulated by official policy and not shaped by market forces. Central bank credit always supplemented the market operations, and, in 1970, about 70 percent of the currency supply was in the form of open market operations and 30 percent in advances.

Another source of short-term funds that has gained in importance in recent years is the foreign exchange fund. An export surplus results in an equivalent surplus of yen funds flowing into the economy. On the other hand, the foreign exchange fund as well as the food control special account raises funds by issuing bonds (maturity two months). Due to the government's tax policy, the expansionary phase of the business cycle brings a large excess of government receipts from overpayments to the public, and it was only on account of the large payments out of the foreign exchange fund in the previous three years that the Treasury accounts with the public registered an overall excess of payments.

Basically, therefore, central bank credit remained the main source of growth currency, while the call money market chiefly served to correct the so-called fund dislocation.

The call money market became important in the years following the Iwato boom. The average balance of borrowed funds rose from ¥165,681 million in 1957 to ¥1,263,063 million in 1965 and ¥1,645,301 million in 1970; the volume was around ¥2 trillion in the first half of 1971. The call market operators are six short-term brokers: Ueda Tanshi, Tokyo Tanshi, Yamane Tanshi, Nippon Waribiki, Yagi Tanshi, and Nagoya Tanshi. The first four firms are based on Tokyo, the fifth on Osaka, and the sixth on Nagoya. They are subject to the Law for the Control of Acceptance of Investments, Deposits and Interest Rates (1954), which actually regulates money lending. The business of the short-term brokers comprises the following transactions: (1) lending and borrowing of call money; (2) buying and selling of bills; brokerage; (3) buying and selling of national bonds; brokerage; (4) handling of foreign drafts. As a rule, the call market operators work as brokers and all transactions are handled by phone. In September 1971, the four largest firms increased their capital from ¥100 million to ¥300 million; half of the new capital was to be taken over by the city banks. The Bank of Japan wanted the capital increase for the following reasons: (1) the newly created bill market implied a considerable enlargement of business; (2) the Bank of Japan expected the call brokers to buy the short-term notes issued for absorbing the large funds flowing into the economy through the payments from the foreign exchange fund; (3) transactions in foreign exchange had reached sizeable proportions; (4) the Bank of Japan planned to strengthen the call brokers' function as dealers (i.e., carrying out transactions on their own account).

The type of loans on the call money market are: half-day loans (repayment on the same day), overnight loans (repaid the next day unless renewed), unconditional loans (called at will with one day's notice by the lender or repaid by the borrower), and over-the-month loans (repayment on a fixed day in the following month). The rates are worked out by the call brokers and *Sanmeikai*, a committee on which all city banks are represented, and approved by the Bank of Japan, and are largely unrelated to actual fund demand; they are Japan's second official discount rate. From the change to percentage rates until July 1971, the unconditional rate had been kept 0.25 percent and the over-the-month rate 0.75 percent higher than the overnight rate. The rates for borrowers are a uniform 0.25 percent higher than those for lenders (call brokers' margin) and rates go up with the length of time.

Average Balances of Call Money in 1970

(In billions of yen)

	Lending	Borrowing
City banks	2	1,405
Local banks	258	14
Trust banks	390	23
Mutual banks, credit associations, National Federation of Credit Assocs.	361 ⎫	
Financial institutions for agriculture and forestry	343 ⎬	251
Foreign banks	7 ⎪	
Others	332 ⎭	
Total	1,692	1,693

Note: "Others" includes insurance companies and investment trusts.
Source: Bank of Japan.

Securities are used as collateral; national bonds, government-guaranteed debentures, first-rate bonds of local governments or public corporations, corporate bonds (particularly bank debentures) and commercial bills are used for this purpose.

City banks are the most important borrowers in the call money market, while local banks, trust banks, and the financial institutions for small business and agriculture are the main lenders.

Due to their almost chronic fund deficiency, the city banks became permanent borrowers of over-the-month funds, which usually constituted about 90 percent of all call money. The call market, therefore, lost its function of adjusting short-term fund imbalances, and, as mentioned above, corrected the structural fund dislocations in the financial system. In January 1971, the organization of a bill discount market was proposed. According to the original plan, the Bank of Japan was to add commercial bills, drawn by first-rate enterprises and discounted by commercial banks, to the paper eligible for open market operations, while, at the same time, drafts with a maturity of over sixty but under ninety days were to be shifted from the call money market to the new bill market. On April 7, 1971, the governor of the Bank of Japan announced that, on account of the monetary situation, the new system would not be put into effect "for the time being" (which made it doubtful whether the authorities had planned the new system for a permanent structural adjustment or only as a temporary measure for providing additional credit). But the financial institutions decided to create a bill market independent from the market operations of the Bank of Japan and on May 20, 1971, the bill market came into existence. The parties are exactly the same as in the call money market; the bills handled are: (1) commercial paper (drafts drawn by manufacturers or traders); (2) first-rate one-name notes; (3) drafts drawn by financial institutions to their own order. The bills must have a maturity of from sixty to ninety days. Contracts are concluded on the preceding day or in the morning of the day of the transaction. Interest on call loans is paid when the loan matures, but the bills are discounted so that the actual interest rates are higher than the call rates.

	Bills	Over-the-month
Seller's (borrower) nominal rate	7.250%	7.250%
actual rate	7.375%	
Margin of bill broker	0.125%	0.250%
Buyer's (lender) nominal rate	7.125%	7.000%
actual rate	7.250%	

As is the case for call money, the smallest transaction is ¥10 million; in fact, most transactions are of the order of ¥100 million.

The reluctance of the Bank of Japan to be drawn into the bill market was at least partly due to several unsolved problems: (1) there are no accepted standards for the credit rating of enterprises and the eligibility of commercial bills; (2) the rates at which bills are discounted by the banks are not uniform. In order to solve these difficulties, the proposal was made that the bill market should handle only bills drawn by the city banks for which the commercial bills would serve as collateral. Another problem was whether the Bank of Japan would accept bills on the same footing as the paper presently eligible for open market operations (national bonds, etc.), or only for financing above a certain ceiling and at less favorable rates (i.e., a new form of penalty rates). The most decisive reason why the Bank of Japan did not want to become involved in the bill market may have been the opposition of the long-term credit banks. They contended that, if commercial bills were to be used for open market operations, bank debentures should also be included.

In fact, the bill market was started under inauspicious circumstances. Fund demand was stagnant and interest rates were going down. Transactions on May 20, 1971, amounted to ¥35.5 billion, but the total for the month was only ¥67.4 billion. The smallest amount was ¥300 million; the interest rate (seller's rate), 7.125 percent. The city banks (including the Bank of Tokyo) were sellers, local banks; trust banks, mutual banks, the National Federation of Credit Associations, and the Central Cooperative Bank of Agriculture were buyers. Actually, the bill market shows the same structure as the call money market and the lack of free interest rates remains an obstacle to a more flexible adaptation to the prevailing monetary situation. To a certain extent, the bill market may have contributed to the shift from over-the-month to unconditional loans, although the monetary relaxation was the basic cause. Whereas, until March 1971, over-the-month loans accounted for 90 percent of all call loans, the share of unconditional loans rose to 60 percent in June and 80 percent in August.

The monetary relaxation caused a large inflow of funds into the call market, but, because lenders and borrowers did not agree on terms, large amounts remained in the hands of the brokers. The lenders wanted to lend over the month, the borrowers wanted to borrow unconditionally, and the brokers were reluctant to accept funds because they did not want to get stuck with the interest differential. Beginning in April 1971, the difference between the average balance of funds lent and funds borrowed became uncomfortably large and pointed to the disequilibrium caused by the excessive liquidity in the money market.

Call Money: Average Balance by Lender and Borrower, June 1971

(In millions of yen)

	Lender	Borrower
Total	2,213,531	1,584,179
City banks	1,833	1,366,538
Local banks	537,336	475
Trust banks	449,576	18,000
Long-term credit banks	27,924	19,923
Foreign banks	11,531	
Mutual banks	115,578	
Credit associations & Federation of Credit Associations	474,422	
Financial institutions for agriculture & forestry	302,350	
Securities companies	41,176	6,429
Life & nonlife insurance companies	150,473	
Others	101,332	172,814

Source: Bank of Japan

Occasionally, the Bank of Japan supplies the short-term bill brokers with funds under the system of "special financing in the form of general loans"; for example, in 1957, in 1964 and again in December 1965, when the central bank lent ¥16 billion to the call brokers in order to prepare the flotation of national bonds. In 1966, the Bank of Japan suspended its usual market operations but began to buy short-term treasury bills from the bill brokers. At that time, the short-term money market was in confusion, because, on account of the supplementary budget passed at the end of December 1965, the bank found it impossible to adjust the money supply by market operations involving long-term bonds. It was the first time that the Bank of Japan had undertaken market operations for short-term bills.

Generally speaking, the Bank of Japan has pursued the policy of keeping the call money rate stable and there have been relatively long periods in which the rate remained unchanged: from April 1954 to May 1955 (fourteen months), the unconditional rate was 2.2 *sen*; from November 1961 to September 1962 (eleven months), the unconditional rate was 2.4 *sen*; and from October 1965 until the end of 1966 (fifteen months), the overnight rate was 1.5 *sen*, the unconditional rate 1.6 *sen*, and the over-the-month rate 1.8 *sen* (all lender's rates). If the call market rate goes up, the interest rates on bonds (particularly national bonds and government-guaranteed debentures) become relatively unfavorable and make the flotation of bonds difficult. In January 1967, for instance, the over-the-month rate was raised by 0.05 *sen* to 1.85 *sen*, and by another 0.05 *sen* in February, which made the over-the-month rate (1.9 *sen* = 6.935 percent) higher than the yield of national bonds to subscribers (6.795 percent). In April, the call rate was reduced to the level before the January raise, but it rose in June, July, and September (together with the increase in the official discount rate), and again in December, when the over-the-month rate rose to 2.2 *sen* (8.03 percent). Due to the strong fund demand, the call rate rose to 2.5 *sen* (9.125 percent) in 1968 and was upped to 9.25 percent with the change to the percentage system in 1969. It was only in the last three months of 1970, that a definite downtrend set in, and the over-the-month rate declined from 9.25 percent in September 1970 to 7.0 percent in May 1971.

On account of the slow demand for over-the-month money, the rate was lowered by 0.25 percent on July 8, 1971 (lender's rate 6.75 percent), while the other rates were left unchanged. This altered the previous interest structure, in which the difference between the over-the-month rate and the unconditional rate was twice as large as that between the unconditional and the overnight rate. The structure remained the same when all rates were lowered by 0.25 percent on July 28, 1971. The new rates (lender's rates) were: over-the-month, 6.5 percent; unconditional, 6.25 percent; and overnight, 6.0 percent. The discount rate for the bill discount market (bill brokers' selling rate) was lowered from 6.75 percent to 6.5 percent. The reduction brought the call rates down to the lowest level since 1956, which represented a decline of 2.75 points compared with September 1970. This situation created great difficulties for the banks, who pay 6.0 percent on eighteen-month deposits.

In former years, the Bank of Japan supplied the short-term financing agencies (which, in addition to the call money brokers, include the securities finance companies) with funds by market operations at the borrower's call money rate. In August 1971, the Bank of Japan sold notes in the call market in order to soak up the excessive liquid funds. The notes have a maturity of three months and an interest rate equal to the unconditional call rate. The first issue, on August 20, amounted to ¥170 billion. The stagnation in the demand for funds induced the short-term brokers to reduce the call money rate by another 0.25 percent in August and by 0.5 percent effective October 15, 1971. Together with the reduction of the official discount rate on December 29, the call rate was lowered. The new lender's rates were: overnight, 5.5 percent; unconditional, 5.25 percent; and over-the-month, 5. 25 percent. On December 31, overnight and unconditional rates were reduced by another 0.25 percent.

Call Market Money
Average Monthly Balances, May 1970–July 1971

(In millions of yen)

	Average balance during month	
	Funds lent	Funds borrowed
1970, May	1,783,497	1,428,659
June	1,710,149	1,659,435
July	1,628,371	1,732,822
August	1,505,110	1,615,303
September	1,547,107	1,568,469
October	1,763,194	1,689,824
November	1,949,034	1,681,345
December	1,778,296	1,845,669
1971, January	2,080,810	2,037,136
February	2,028,924	2,116,600
March	1,867,558	1,881,448
April	2,240,373	1,754,904
May	2,258,401	1,427,685
June	2,213,531	1,584,179
July	2,074,141	1,706,788

Source: Bank of Japan, Economic Statistics Monthly.

Call Money Market, June 1971

(In millions of yen)

		Balance at end of month		
		Total	Tokyo	Osaka–Nagoya
Total		2,032,127	1,634,574	397,553
Overnight		10,234	10,000	234
Unconditional		580,881	452,324	128,557
Over-the-month		1,441,012	1,172,250	268,762
Average balance during month		2,313,531	1,764,990	448,541
Highest:				
Total	May 1971	2,231,382		
Unconditional	Apr. 1971	721,764		
Over-the-month	Nov. 1971	2,043,386		
Average month	May 1971	2,258,401		

Tokyo Call Rates, December 1970–July 1971

(In percent per annum)

	Overnight			Unconditional			Over-the-month		
	Lowest	Average	Highest	Lowest	Average	Highest	Lowest	Average	Highest
1970, December	7.250	7.750	7.750	7.500	8.000	8.000	8.250	8.750	8.750
1971, January	7.000	7.250	7.250	7.250	7.500	7.500	8.000	8.250	8.250
February	7.000	7.000	7.000	7.250	7.250	7.250	8.000	8.000	8.000
March	7.000	7.000	7.000	7.250	7.250	7.250	8.000	8.000	8.000
April	6.500	6.500	6.500	6.750	6.750	6.750	7.500	7.500	7.500
May	6.250	6.250	6.500	6.500	6.500	6.750	7.000	7.000	7.500
June	6.250	6.250	6.250	6.500	6.500	6.500	7.000	7.000	7.000
July	6.000	6.250	6.250	6.250	6.500	6.500	6.500	6.750	7.000

Source: Bank of Japan.

A FINANCIAL HISTORY OF THE NEW JAPAN

5 CONSUMER CREDIT

1 CREDIT

Consumer credit, in the widest sense, includes all financial arrangements that make the purchase of consumer goods and services possible without immediate cash payment in full. It may be divided into two broad fields: first, consumer credit in the strict sense, i.e., total or partial replacement of cash payment directly connected with the purchase of specific consumer goods or services; and, secondly, consumer financing, i.e., bank loans for the purchase of consumer goods or services. The most common forms of consumer credit in the strict sense found in Japan are: (1) consumer credit given by ordinary retail stores (sales "on the cuff," credit accounts; usually restricted to selected customers); (2) sales by installment department stores; (3) credit given by credit companies; (4) credit given by the credit associations of specialty stores (3 and 4 are referred to as ticket sales); (5) installment credit given by sales companies organized directly or indirectly by manufacturers.

Around 1960, the city banks concluded tie-ups with leading department stores that were basically credit card arrangements limited to a particular store. The customer must open an account with one of the banks connected with the department store. Usually, a fixed rate repayment system is used (e.g., Mitsukoshi, Isetan, Keio), but the Daimaru Excel Card System (for which Daimaru signed up twelve banks) provides for a fixed sum of ¥10,-000 being paid monthly in addition to the payment of 10 percent of the balance due or ¥50,000, whichever is lower. The balance payable is treated like a bank loan, and interest at a monthly rate of 0.8 percent is charged on it. The ceiling on one purchase is ¥300,000. The total number of installment sales department stores is about seven hundred; the most important in Tokyo are Marui (thirty-three stores; sales, fiscal 1970, ¥49.5 billion), Midoriya (forty-four; ¥40.0 billion), and Maruko (twenty-one; ¥11.8 billion). Japan's leading credit company is Nippon Shinpan (Japan Credit Sales), whose main business was the collection of payments due to retailers for merchandise sold under the coupon (ticket) system. Nippon Shinpan now also functions as a credit card agency; the firm undertakes credit investigation, issuance of credit cards, and collection, and takes over the risk of credit sales. In 1969, Nippon Shinpan became a member of the Interbank Card Association. In the beginning of October 1971, Nippon Shinpan concluded an agreement with the First National City Bank for the establishment of a joint venture for consumer credit, particularly for home and car purchases. Specially stores often form associations, which organize credit, using coupons, passbooks, or checkbooks. The associations belong to regional federations (the Tokyo Regional Federation comprises sixteen associations of specialty stores), and the regional federations, in turn, belong to the Japan Federation of Specialty Store Associations. In 1968, the regional federations in Tokyo, Utsunomiya, and Kawasaki adopted common coupons,

Sales of Nippon Shinpan Co.

(In millions of yen)

	April– Sept. 1970	Oct. 1970– March 1971
Total sales	17,093	20,849
Credit sales	5,171	6,180
Sales financing	4,913	6,704
Home loans	3,565	3,571
Real estate sales	507	1,051
Credit guarantees	2,737	3,182
Other	197	159

Increase in Consumer Credit

End of year	1965 ¥ billion	1966 ¥ billion	1967 ¥ billion	1968 ¥ billion	1969 ¥ billion	1970 ¥ billion	1970/1965 times
Total outstanding loan balances (A)	19,217.9	22,046.0	25,323.0	29,032.8	33,784.4	39,479.3	2.1
Total outstanding consumer loan balances (B)	59.7	105.9	190.6	346.0	625.9	943.1	15.8
Loans for consumer goods & services	30.4	49.2	75.0	129.6	247.1	320.2	10.5
Loans for consumer goods	28.9	47.2	71.6	122.5	233.4	302.2	10.5
Loans for passenger cars	19.6	32.2	43.7	61.2	96.0	114.4	5.8
Loans for electric appliances	2.1	4.7	14.1	42.5	110.7	156.3	74.4
Loans for services	0.9	1.2	1.5	3.0	6.4	9.2	10.2
Home loans	29.2	56.6	115.5	216.3	378.7	622.8	21.3
B/A (%)	0.3	0.5	0.8	1.2	1.9	2.4	

Source: Bank of Japan, Economic Statistics Annual.

and the national federation followed their example. In the following year, however, the national federation changed from coupons to credit cards.

Large manufacturers have also adopted the credit card system for their credit sales. In 1969, Toshiba (Tokyo Shibaura Electric Co.) together with its sales company, Toshiba Shoji, set up the Toshiba Credit System, which allows credit purchases at over fourteen thousand stores carrying Toshiba's electric appliances. One of Toshiba's competitors, Hitachi, Ltd., organized a new system for which a sales company called Hitachi Credit was set up in April 1970. The purchaser wishing to buy on the installment plan makes a down payment, which is subtracted from the purchase price; the balance is treated as a loan for which the "add-on" system is used. Interest at a yearly rate of 6 percent is added to the remaining balance, which is paid in equal installments. The system enables Hitachi to fix the same price for cash and credit sales.

Although the banks give auto loans, most of the installment sales of motor cars are handled by the sales and finance companies set up by the car manufacturers. The purchaser gives a promissory note which is used by the sales companies as collateral for obtaining bank credit. The sales company retains title to the car until the car is fully paid for (the same is true for other consumer durables paid on the installment plan), and the car is registered in the name of the sales company.

The Japan Diners Club was organized in 1960 and became the pioneer of the credit card movement. Not only ordinary cash loans but also loans for foreign travel, golf, and parties have been made available since April 1970; amounts range from ¥100,000 to ¥1.2 million. Foreign travel loans are given for travel with seventeen air lines, or travel arranged through the Japan Travel Bureau. Interest rates vary with the number of installments in which repayment is made. If repayment is made in six installments, the interest rate is 4 percent; it is 7 percent for twelve installments and 14 percent for twenty-four installments. The "add-on" system is used. For golf loans, the interest rate is 6 percent if the loan is repaid in installments, 8 percent for twelve, and 16 percent for twenty-four installments. Loans for parties can be repaid in three (8 percent), six (10 percent), or twelve installments (12 percent).

Credit cards issued jointly by bank groups are the Union Credit card (issued by eighty-six financial institutions, accepted by 50,000 stores; 750,000 cardholders) and the card issued by the Japan Credit Bureau. Credit cards issued by individual banks are the Diamond Card (Mitsubishi), Sumitomo Credit, Million Card Service (Tokai), and HCB (Hokkaido Taku-shoku). In fiscal 1969, sales of the seven credit card companies amounted to ¥65.8 billion. Five of the seven card systems have tie-ups with foreign credit card companies. The Tokyu group plans to issue a joint credit card in cooperation with Nippon Shinpan. The holder will be entitled to installment purchases at all the establishments connected with the group (main enterprises: Tokyu Department Store, Tokyu Hotel chain, Toko Store chain). Sales efforts will be chiefly directed to the 40,000 members of the Tokyu Family Club (customers of Tokyu Department Store). A more limited joint card is planned by the three New Otani hotels and the eleven hotels belonging to the New Osaka hotel chain.

One of the basic difficulties common to all forms of consumer credit in Japan is the lack of reliable credit investigation and credit rating. On the other hand, protection of borrowers is also insufficient (no truth-in-lending legislation). The charges of dumping levied against imports of Japanese electric appliances into the United States led to an inconclusive investigation of the dual price system (purely nominal list prices and much lower actual prices), and the practices connected with installment sales; another problem is the protection of purchasers of real estate making installment payments in case of insolvency of the real estate company or developer before the transfer of title.

With the diffusion of credit cards, their fraudulent use (defaulting cardholders, use of stolen or lost credit cards) is putting an increasing burden on the credit card companies. Until 1968, there were about ten cases per month per company of unauthorized use, and the companies found the circulation of lists of defaulting cardholders (which were sent twice a month to all affiliated stores) relatively efficient. Since 1969, however, there has been a sharp increase in the fraudulent use of cards, and many card companies have stopped sending such lists. Stolen cards are mostly used on the days immediately following the theft, and notification comes too late. The card companies pay a premium of ¥10,000 for the discovery of a fraudulently used card. Insurance against liabilities from the use of lost or stolen cards is available; the premium is low, ¥100 a year, which covers liabilities of ¥350,000–400,000 for a period of ten to thirty days after the loss. In order to prevent abuse, the Japan Credit Bureau affixes the photo of the cardholder to the credit card if the cardholder so desires.

Until 1970, funds for the settlement of international credit card payments had to be deposited beforehand; since April 1970, these payments can be settled afterwards. In 1969, payments arising from the use of credit cards by Japanese abroad amounted to $65,000; foreigners used credit cards in Japan to the extent of $3.5 million.

Generally speaking, Japanese consumers continue to pay cash for the bulk of their purchases. Checks are seldom used by private individuals; they are more used by enterprises; the same is true for postal transfers and bank remittances. In 1970, 294 million checks were used in Japan, only 1.7 percent of the number used in the United States. But the automatic transfer system, by which periodic payments are directly recycled into the banks, is widely used. The city banks started it in 1959 for telephone and electricity charges; in 1962, NHK, the official broadcasting system, began to use it for the fees payable by the owners of television sets (it is now used by about 20 percent of all households). Large enterprises have started to pay the salaries of their employees by automatic transfer to the employee's bank account. Future plans of the banks foresee an integrated real-time system, in which terminals in department stores and other important retail outlets will be directly connected with an all-bank computer system and the account card of the bank customer will replace credit cards.

While the bank's consumer credit business has been growing rapidly, an old credit institution is going out of business. Pawnshops are closing down in great numbers because of poor business. Not only private but also cooperative and municipal pawnshops, which were very popular in the immediate postwar period, are unable to earn enough to pay their expenses.

5 CONSUMER CREDIT

2 FINANCING

Consumer financing takes two forms, loans given directly to consumers and loans given to retailers in order to finance installment sales or other forms of consumer credit given by retailers. Usually, only the first form is regarded as consumer credit, but, in the absence of finance houses, the second form is of great importance in Japan because it supplies a large part of the credit that the sales companies of the manufacturers, particularly the automobile manufacturers, give to the public.

Japanese banks began to pay greater attention to the field of consumer credit in 1960, when the first auto loans were given. In 1961, housing loans, education loans, and saving for travel were started. Auto loans had been generally accepted by 1963 and piano loans and loans for the purchase of electric appliances were introduced that year. Savings clubs for a variety of purposes were founded in 1964, and beds were added to the consumer durables for which the banks gave consumption loans. Loans for travel, particularly foreign travel, were started in 1966, but the unfavorable balance of payments in the following year forced the banks to deemphasize these loans. Initially, the banks were much more interested in collecting deposits in connection with the various new forms of consumer services than in lending money to individual customers, and it is only since 1965 that consumer credit has become more important. From 1965 to 1970, the balance of outstanding consumer credit increased 15.8 times, but, despite this spectacular growth, the outstanding balance of consumer credit constitutes only 2.4 percent of the outstanding balance of all bank loans. Housing loans account for 70 percent of the total balance of direct consumer credit, but loans for financing automobile sales make up about 74 percent of the credit to retailers.

There are three types of housing loans: installment saving loans, tied loans, and general housing loans. In the first type, the prospective borrower saves a specified amount each month during a period from one to five years (a larger amount may be deposited from the semiannual bonus); then, he is given a loan from twice to four times the amount of the accumulated funds and continues to pay in the same monthly amount in order to repay the loan. This system qualifies for exemption from income tax on the interest paid on the deposit. Instead of the installment saving plan, the borrower may deposit a lump sum (minimum ¥1 million) for at least six months. In the tied-loan system, the bank ties up with a contractor or construction firm. The borrower is given a loan with which he buys a house from the particular contractor or pays for the home built for him by the contractor; the contractor guarantees the loans. General housing loans are ordinary bank loans for the purpose of buying or building a house.

Although housing loans may range from ¥100,000 to ¥10 million, the borrower must usually supply about 30–40 percent of the required capital from his own funds. According to a survey by the Ministry of Construction, over 50 percent of all persons buying or building new homes borrow from relatives. Employees of large firms frequently borrow from their company against their prospective retirement allowance. The Japan Housing Finance Corporation, a government organ (loan program for fiscal 1971, ¥125.7 billion) requires as a prerequisite for a loan that the borrower has already purchased or rented the land for building the home. In large cities, the corporation lends ¥62,700 per *tsubo* (6 sq. ft.) up to a maximum of ¥950,000 for wooden houses and ¥69,300 per *tsubo* up to a maximum of ¥1,050,000 for ferroconcrete houses. The corporation also makes loans up to ¥1.5 million for the purchase of a flat in an apartment house. Actually, the construction costs of wooden houses are between ¥150,000 and ¥200,000 per *tsubo*.

Frequently, the banks also require a guarantee. The guarantor must have assets and an income at least equal to that of the borrower. The borrower must have an income which allows him to use 10–20 percent of the income for the repayment of the loan. Usually, the loan is limited to two or three times the yearly income of the borrower.

For the tied loans, the borrowers often become members of an association. Qualifications are as follows: they must be between twenty-five and sixty years of age and able to complete repayment of the loan before they reach the age of seventy; their yearly income must be at least ¥1 million; if they are employees, the company for which they work must have a capital of at least ¥5 million and they must have completed five years of service (individual proprietors must have been at least five years in business).

Maturity may be between ten and twenty-five years. For loans up to ten years, the monthly interest rate is 0.74 percent (yearly rate 8.88 percent); for loans over ten years, the rate is 0.77 percent (yearly rate 9.24 percent). On loans maturing in twenty-five years, the interest rate is over 11 percent. In April 1970, the insurance companies raised their interest rate on home loans from 9 percent to 9.5 percent. Methods of repayment are equal repayment of capital and interest, repayment of capital in equal installments, and repayment in increasing installments. Usually, larger repayments are made out of the bonus.

Banks usually take out a mortgage on the land or house bought with the bank loan, but, in many cases (particularly for short-term loans), the mortgage is not registered (and therefore legally no mortgage); the borrower merely deposits the title deed to the land or house with the bank. If the mortgage is registered, banks insist on a first mortgage; this sometimes creates difficulties for the borrower who has also borrowed from other sources (e.g., his employer).

Of special interest are the joint enterprises set up by groups of financial institutions for the purpose of home loans. On June 17, 1971, the Japan Home Finance Co. (*Nippon Jūtaku Kinyū*) was established by the Japan Credit Bureau group. Its capital is ¥400 billion; subscribers include five city banks (Sanwa, Mitsui, Kyowa, Kobe, and Hokkaido Takushoku), two local banks (Chiba and Yokohama), two trust banks (Mitsui and Toyo), the three long-term credit banks (Industrial, Long-Term Credit, and Hypothec), five life insurance companies (Chiyoda, Daido, Dai-Ichi, Mitsui, and Nippon), and eight nonlife insurance companies (Asahi, Dai-Tokyo, Dowa, Koa, Nichido, Nippon, Nisshin, and Taisho). The main differences in the business practice of the new company from the business methods of the banks are: (1) no deposit (or installment saving) will be required; the loan will be given to qualified borrowers without waiting; (2) repayment within twenty-five years (banks usually ten to fifteen years); (3) amounts will be higher than those given by banks (usually limited to ¥10–20 million); (4) the interest rate will be about 11 percent. The institution expects to have ¥100 billion in outstanding loans after three years. In addition to home loans, the company will also act as agent for credit and loss insurance and enter the secondary mortgage market should such a market develop.

On September 1, 1971, the Union Home Finance Co. (*Union Jūtaku Kinyū*) was founded. Its capital, ¥600 million, was subscribed by thirty-three financial institutions, comprising six city banks (Fuji, Mitsubishi, Dai-Ichi, Kangyo, Saitama, and Taiyo), three trust banks (Yasuda, Mitsubishi, and Nippon), the three long-term credit banks (Industrial, Long-Term Credit, and Hypothec), eleven life insurance companies (Asahi, Dai-Hyaku, Dai-Ichi, Fukoku, Kyoei, Meiji, Nippon, Nissan, Taiyo, Toho, and Yasuda), and ten nonlife insurance companies (Dowa, Koa, Kyoei, Nichido, Nippon, Nissan, Taisei, Taiyo, Tokio, and Yasuda). In addition to loans and guarantees, the company expects to be active in the emission and sale of mortgage bonds if and when this becomes possible.

The third joint enterprise in this field is the Joint Trust Home Center (*Shintaku Gōdō Jutaku Center*), set up in October 1971 by the seven trust companies (Mitsui, Mitsubishi, Yasuda, Toyo, Chuo, Nihon, and Sumitomo) with an initial capital of ¥500 million. The company will give loans and loan guarantees, purchase home loan contracts, take over the management of home loans from other banks, act as an insurance agency, and engage in the real estate business. Also contemplated is the issuance of mortgage bonds. The trust banks expect a revision of the Loan Trust Law that will enable them to use these funds for home loans. Interest rates will be between 10.5 percent and 11.5 percent; a yearly business volume of ¥10 billion is foreseen for the first years. The Tokai Bank group may also organize a joint company for home loans, but, so far, Sumitomo Bank has not announced any plans in this field.

The main reason for the establishment of these joint enterprises is the rationalization of management. Most home loans are relatively small long-term loans whose collateral requires expert knowledge. Moreover, there is great interest in issuing mortgage bonds and creating a secondary mortgage market. At present, legal provisions exist for mortgage certificates (Mortgage Certificate Law of 1931), but not for negotiable mortgage bonds (except secured industrial debentures). On July 5, 1971, the parties interested in the creation of a mortgage market (financial institutions, construction companies, real estate companies, manufacturers of prefabricated houses, and politicians) founded the Japan Mortgage Bond Association (*Nippon Teitō Shōken Kyōkai*).

Under an agreement signed April 1, 1970, by Nippon Shinpan and a number of credit associations, Nippon Shinpan undertakes credit guarantees, investigation, and the administration of home loans ranging from ¥500,000 to ¥10 million (some associations ¥5 million) with a maturity from one to fifteen years and an interest rate of 9.5 percent. The Seibu group worked out a special arrangement with the Japan Housing Finance Corporation for the sale of apartments in its Shin-Tokorozawa residential estate. The development comprises 331 units, of which 291 (three rooms, dining-kitchen) are priced between ¥4.3 million and ¥5.4 million and 40 units (three rooms, living-dining-kitchen) between ¥5.45 million and ¥6.55 million. No downpayment is needed; the purchaser can obtain a loan of ¥1.5 million (maturity thirty-five years, interest rate 5.5 percent, repayment in monthly installments of ¥8,050) from the Japan Housing Finance Corporation and an additional loan of up to

70 percent from the Seibu group. The monthly interest rate is 0.76–0.85 percent; repayment in monthly installments (for a ¥4.3 million loan, ¥9,068 in ordinary months, ¥97,573 when the bonus is paid).

The government has taken a number of measures not only for financing the construction of homes but also for encouraging home-ownership. The second five-year housing construction plan foresees the erection of 9.5 million units from 1971 to 1975, of which 5.2 million will be individually owned. This program will require a yearly investment of ¥3,200 billion in residential construction and create a strong demand for funds in this field. For fiscal 1971, four new programs were initiated for encouraging home building, viz., the savings system for "agricultural towns," a home installment savings system within the postal savings system, and loans given by the Japan Development Bank to private developers. The savings systems for the so-called formation of workers' capital, modeled after the German *Bausparkasse*, basically consists of installment savings (up to ¥1 million tax-free) and building loans given by financial institutions; for fiscal 1971, the government provided interest subsidies amounting to ¥600 million. The working of the system is illustrated below. The Employment Promotion Corporation is an agency set up and financed by the government for peripheral projects in labor relations; it was a substitute for a "Workers' Home Building Association" for which the Ministry of Labor failed to secure the necessary funds.

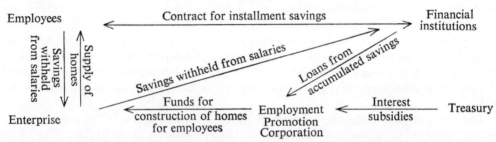

"Agricultural towns" is used to designate a project aiming at inducing farmers to build houses for rent on land withdrawn from rice cultivation under the government's plan for reducing the acreage planted with rice. Land in the suburbs of the large cities, or in other areas in which housing is insufficient, is to be financed by the agricultural cooperatives; a subsidy of ¥52 million was allocated in the fiscal 1971 budget to reduce interest rates by 3 percent on the loans necessary for building 2,000 units.

The home installment postal savings system means an installment savings plan for home building that provides for building loans from the Japan Housing Finance Corporation on preferential terms.

The Ministry of Construction wants to introduce tax rebates for home loans. The plan foresees the subtraction of 10 percent of the yearly income of the taxpayer from the yearly amount of repayments of home loans. The remainder can be subtracted from taxable income. This rebate would not apply to incomes over ¥5 million, buildings with a floor space exceeding 120 sq.m. or land larger than 300 sq.m. To give an example, a taxpayer earning ¥2.5 million a year who has to repay ¥600,000 a year on a home loan could subtract ¥350,000 (600,000–250,000) from his taxable income. This would reduce his income tax (in the case of a family of four) from ¥162,300 to ¥105,900; the tax rebate of ¥56,000 would be equivalent to a 1 percent decrease in total indebtedness (capital and interest).

Consumer Loans

		Total				Consumer goods & services			
		New loans		Outstanding balances		New loans		Outstanding balances	
		Number of loans	Value	Number of loans	Value	Number of loans	Value	Number of loans	Value
Institution	Term	1,000	¥ mill.	1,000	¥ mill.	1,000	¥ mill.	1,000	¥ mill.
	1970								
All banks	Jan.–Mar.	500.5	162,565	2,426.0	705,874	455.7	86,036	2,128.9	272,904
	Apr.–June	497.2	176,923	2,713.1	793,143	454.5	90,065	2,386.9	298,245
	July–Sept.	529.0	180,726	2,897.4	868,164	485.2	92,892	2,544.3	313,101
	Oct.–Dec.	461.7	181,596	3,042.5	943,130	414.4	83,519	2,655.4	320,271
	1971								
	Jan.–Mar.	489.9	190,164	3,213.4	1,016,280	426.4	81,064	2,778.8	315,469
City banks	**1970**								
	Jan.–Mar.	245.4	71,470	1,221.9	290,051	234.0	43,570	1,135.6	141,576
	Apr.–June	242.7	76,221	1,353.3	324,395	229.9	44,180	1,258.8	151,726
	July–Sept.	264.1	78,719	1,394.2	353,856	251.4	46,794	1,289.0	157,987
	Oct.–Dec.	223.7	78,583	1,453.0	385,338	209.0	41,103	1,336.6	160,791
	1971								
	Jan.–Mar.	223.0	74,101	1,514.5	405,522	209.5	39,198	1,387.7	156,109
Local banks	**1970**								
	Jan.–Mar.	227.1	64,793	1,087.1	283,525	211.4	40,404	1,135.6	141,576
	Apr.–June	232.4	75,891	1,227.0	318,405	213.8	43,672	1,076.8	139,957
	July–Sept.	242.6	76,292	1,360.0	346,693	222.9	43,874	1,197.0	148,049
	Oct.–Dec.	220.6	76,772	1,434.3	373,064	199.3	40,850	1,259.6	152,615
	1971								
	Jan.–Mar.	228.2	72,477	1,518.7	390,904	211.1	40,698	1,333.1	153,234
Trust banks, long-term credit banks, trust accounts	**1970**								
	Jan.–Mar.	27.9	26,302	116.8	132,297	10.2	2,061	44.9	6,049
	Apr.–June	22.0	24,810	132.7	150,342	10.6	2,212	51.2	6,561
	July–Sept.	22.3	25,714	143.1	167,613	10.8	2,224	58.2	7,064
	Oct.–Dec.	17.3	26,240	155.1	184,727	6.0	1,565	59.3	6,865
	1971								
	Jan.–Mar.	38.6	43,585	180.1	219,854	5.6	1,166	56.9	6,125
Mutual banks	**1970**								
	Jan.–Mar.	48.2	19,009	229.2	89,816	40.9	7,870	167.8	24,113
	Apr.–June	53.1	22,968	261.4	99,438	44.2	8,886	195.4	27,646
	July–Sept.	64.5	28,385	306.3	112,195	54.3	11,289	229.8	31,762
	Oct.–Dec.	54.8	28,511	238.7	124,041	43.7	9,140	249.0	32,230
	1971								
	Jan.–Mar.	54.6	25,620	344.3	132,001	45.2	9,187	265.8	33,249
Credit associations	Oct. 1969– Mar. 1970	111.0	71,538	272.5	168,449	72.7	15,607	136.3	22,949
	Apr.–Sept.	217.1	107,174	534.5	270,401	172.9	31,781	354.5	48.526
	Oct. 1970– Mar. 1971	221.6	109,978	662.8	315,363	176.8	32,375	463.4	56,810

Consumer Loans (cont.)

Consumer goods & services (cont.)								Housing			
Consumer goods						Services		New loans		Outstanding balances	
Subtotal		Passenger cars		Electric household appliances							
New loans	Outstanding balances	New loans	Outstanding balances	New loans	Outstanding balances	New loans	Outstanding balances	No. of loans	Value	No. of loans	Value
¥ mill.	¥ mill.	¥ mill.	¥ mill.	¥ mill.	¥ mill.	¥ mill.	¥ mill.	1,000	¥ mill.	1,000	¥ mill.
81,349	257,422	28,700	100,289	44,644	129,156	2,475	7,528	44.7	76,529	297.0	432,969
86,088	282,078	34,363	109,412	43,537	143,975	1,918	7,829	42.7	86,857	326.2	494,898
88,601	296,461	33,477	113,212	46,777	153,238	2,248	8,180	43.8	87,832	353.1	555,063
77,930	302,230	30,066	114,442	38,550	156,328	3,202	9,272	47.2	98,076	386.9	622,858
76,234	296,640	26,856	109,967	41,112	154,938	2,796	10,034	63.5	109,100	435.6	700,811
40,487	131,172	13,260	48,001	22,809	68,664	1,558	4,167	11.4	27,899	86.2	148,474
41,574	140,692	15,188	50,953	22,001	75,545	1,097	4,495	12.7	32,041	94.5	172,669
43,667	145,917	14,857	51,527	24,234	79,439	1,631	5,418	12.7	31,924	105.1	195,869
37,154	147,492	13,159	51,541	19,150	80,082	2,371	6,482	14.6	37,479	116.4	224,547
36,103	142,462	11,846	48,811	19,995	77,695	1,783	6,976	13.4	34,903	126.8	249,412
38,930	120,604	14,662	49,989	20,906	57,875	821	3,011	15.6	24,388	138.8	158,247
42,406	135,224	18,386	55,944	20,544	65,542	734	2,972	18.5	32,218	150.1	178,448
42,875	143,946	17,834	59,062	21,562	70,659	483	2,345	19.5	32,418	163.0	198,644
39,352	148,348	16,411	60,438	18,774	73,232	737	2,376	21.2	35,921	174.6	220,449
39,101	148,560	14,617	59,063	20,670	74,549	897	2,621	17.0	31,778	185.6	237,669
1,932	5,644	777	2,298	928	2,616	95	349	17.6	24,240	71.9	126,247
2,107	6,160	788	2,513	991	2,887	86	361	11.3	22,597	81.4	143,781
2,059	6,597	785	2,622	979	3,139	133	416	11.5	23,489	84.9	160,548
1,423	6,389	495	2,462	625	3,013	93	412	11.3	24,675	95.7	177,861
1,029	5,617	392	2,093	445	2,692	115	437	32.9	42,418	123.2	213,729
7,137	21,052	2,512	8,647	3,946	9,931	265	1,022	7.2	11,138	61.3	65,702
7,920	24,226	2,941	9,451	4,225	12,077	274	1,026	8.8	14,082	66.0	71,791
9,551	27,263	3,512	10,133	5,034	14,099	272	1,063	10.1	17,096	76.4	80,432
8,023	28,612	2,946	10,337	4,065	15,057	342	1,155	11.0	19,370	74.6	91,810
7,793	29,190	2,712	10,269	4,496	15,738	288	1,141	9.4	16,433	78.4	98,752
21,668	29,691	8,770	13,630	11,917	14,344	1,170	2,109	41.9	66,626	156.9	181,928
29,226	43,334	10,463	16,802	17,583	24,483	982	2,143	44.1	75,393	180.0	221,875
29,181	50,887	10,018	17,854	17,807	30,654	1,408	2,527	44.8	77,602	199.3	258,553

Notes: 1. Services: education, travel, medical expenses, etc.
2. Housing: purchases of land or houses, construction or remodeling of homes.
Source: Bank of Japan, Economic Statistics Monthly.

Source (for table on next page): Bank of Japan, Economics Statistics Monthly.

Outstanding Balance of Loans for Working Capital of Retailers Selling on Credit

(In millions of yen)

Institution	End of	Total outstanding balances	Installment credit				Retailers issuing coupons			Construction companies	Lending secured by automobile paper
			Subtotal	Automobile sales companies	Installment dept. stores	Other	Subtotal	Credit sales companies	Assocs. of specialty stores		
All banks	March 1970	1,093,980	961,182	834,281	28,750	98,151	46,567	21,548	25,019	86,229	640,348
	June	1,137,991	995,586	863,267	31,688	100,630	50,158	22,971	27,186	92,246	666,579
	Sept.	1,161,629	1,012,437	870,716	29,252	112,468	49,527	23,110	26,417	99,664	673,031
	Dec.	1,204,373	1,038,953	895,234	29,660	114,059	55,755	24,633	31,121	109,664	682,968
	March 1971	1,218,959	1,042,450	896,444	30,391	115,615	54,457	25,548	28,908	122,052	677,924
City banks	March 1970	487,219	454,060	374,361	15,249	64,449	19,550	10,992	8,558	13,608	286,614
	June	507,053	472,189	390,723	17,998	63,468	20,939	11,260	9,679	13,924	296,506
	Sept.	517,089	481,555	393,746	15,707	72,102	20,772	11,444	9,328	14,761	298,979
	Dec.	533,196	491,403	405,226	14,331	71,844	23,805	12,049	11,756	17,987	302,125
	March 1971	536,668	491,342	402,827	16,435	72,080	22,947	12,736	10,211	22,377	296,223
Local banks	March 1970	380,692	351,884	312,751	10,700	28,433	22,855	6,801	16,054	5,951	248,064
	June	391,398	359,775	317,371	10,412	31,991	24,772	7,702	17,070	6,849	257,045
	Sept.	403,427	372,046	326,720	10,150	35,176	24,120	7,538	16,582	7,260	264,788
	Dec.	422,534	386,441	338,723	10,968	36,749	27,520	8,691	18,829	8,572	272,377
	March 1971	426,937	390,221	341,451	10,624	38,146	26,937	8,755	18,182	9,778	275,146
Trust banks, long-term credit banks & trust accounts	March 1970	226,068	155,237	147,168	2,800	5,268	4,161	3,754	407	66,669	105,669
	June	239,540	163,620	155,172	3,277	5,170	4,446	4,009	437	71,472	113,028
	Sept.	241,111	158,834	150,249	3,394	5,191	4,634	4,127	507	77,642	109,263
	Dec.	248,642	161,109	151,283	4,359	5,465	4,429	3,893	536	83,104	108,464
	March 1971	255,355	160,886	152,166	3,332	5,388	4,572	4,057	515	89,896	106,554
Mutual banks	March 1970	231,109	195,263	178,362	4,103	12,797	5,332	3,027	2,305	30,513	146,130
	June	242,363	201,993	182,763	4,209	15,020	5,293	3,189	2,103	35,077	151,201
	Sept.	242,441	204,126	183,954	4,414	15,758	5,424	3,103	2,321	32,890	151,073
	Dec.	248,166	209,797	188,485	3,738	17,573	5,563	3,282	2,281	32,804	158,039
	March 1971	248,528	209,107	188,985	3,894	16,227	6,122	3,588	2,533	33,297	158,690
Credit associations	March 1970	97,096	66,760	59,532	4,121	3,107	6,405	3,974	1,942	18,393	—
	Sept.	101,216	74,998	68,245	3,269	3,484	6,939	4,527	2,411	28,279	—
	March 1971	118,776	84,466	77,698	2,819	3,949	7,653	4,770	2,882	26,656	—

Notes: 1. Automobile sales companies: large sales and finance companies affiliated with automobile manufacturers.
2. Installment department stores: member stores of the Federation of Installment System Department Stores Associations.
3. Construction companies: dealers specializing in sales of private homes and residential land on the installment plan.
4. Lending secured by automobile paper: lending secured by bills payable in installments for purchasing automobiles, including discounts of bills. Lending secured by automobile paper is not included in the total.

6 LEASING

Japan's first general leasing firm was organized in 1963, but it was only in 1969 that leasing began to play a major role. As far as the functional aspects of the leasing business are concerned, finance leasing is the prevalent type in Japan, while maintenance leasing is used to a certain extent for automobiles, electronic computers, and office machines. Operating leases are rarely used. Banks have been the chief promoters of the leasing business (Nos. 2–8 in the list of leasing companies), but trading companies (Nos. 9–12) and manufacturers have also taken the initiative. Altogether, there are about sixteen general lease companies, but leasing of special equipment is also important. The leasing of domestically produced computers is in the hands of the Japan Electronic Computer Co., while the importers handle sales or leases of foreign computers. A wholly-owned subsidiary of IBM leases, IBM products, and Control Data Corporation established a joint venture with C. Itoh & Co., called CDC Japan Corp., for importing and leasing CDC's computers and data processing systems. Sperry Rand works through Nippon Univac and Nippon Remington Rand (joint enterprises with Mitsui & Co.), Burroughs through Takachiho Koheki, and Bull-General Electric through Mitsubishi Corporation. The regional construction machinery associations have formed special lease departments, and the manufacturers of machine tools planned a lease company for numerically controlled machine tools. The value of lease contracts concluded in 1970 amounted to ¥210.6 billion; the eight leading firms accounted for 60 percent of the total.

The reasons for the use of leasing are the same as elsewhere: to avoid large capital expenditures and the fixation of capital. Of a certain importance is the fact that Japanese companies rely to a large extent on borrowed funds for capital investment; leasing relieves them of the necessity of finding their own credit, while the difference in interest costs is not very large. The rapid technological progress, which created a costly difference between the legally and economically useful lives of depreciable property, also furthered the shift to leasing.

Rentals are based on the purchase price of the equipment, interest on capital required for purchase, taxes, insurance premiums, depreciation or residual value, and the number of months for which the lease is concluded. Usually, the rental is reduced when the lease is renewed. The participation of financial institutions in the leasing companies facilitates the procurement of the required funds, while Japan Electronic Computer Co. (JECC) illustrates the difficulties which leasing without sufficient financial backing encounters. JECC was set up in 1961 by the government and six Japanese computer manufacturers (Nippon Electric, Fujitsu, Hitachi, Toshiba, Oki Electric, Mitsubishi Electric). The company buys the computers from the manufacturers and either sells or leases them. The company tried to meet the rapidly growing fund demand through increases in its capital (from ¥1,050 million in 1961 to ¥59.7 billion in 1971) and larger loans from the Japan Development Bank, but fell behind in its payments to the manufacturers. In March 1970, JECC ceased to handle small computers in order to save its resources for large computers. Hitachi wanted to take over the leasing of its own computers, but was not allowed to do so, and Nippon Electric, which belongs to the Sumitomo group, would like to use General Lease. At the end of fiscal 1970, JECC's arrears in payments to the manufacturers amounted to about ¥50 billion, but the monetary relaxation, in the summer of 1971, enabled the company to reduce the arrears to ¥200 million. In order to help JECC, the Ministry of Finance reduced the useful life of computers in several stages from six years to five years.

Foreign enterprises have shown great interest in the Japanese leasing business. Two subsidiaries of the Bank of America participate in Sumitomo's General Lease, and two subsidiaries of First National City Bank acquired 10 percent each of the capital of Fuyo General Lease Co. Originally, Chase Manhattan Bank was to acquire 25 percent of the capital of Mitsubishi's Diamond Lease, but the Fair Trade Commission informed Mitsubishi that such an arrangement would not be approved because, according to Article 11 of the Antimonopoly Law, banks can hold no more than 10 percent of the shares of another enterprise; this, the commission said, also applies to foreign banks. Hence, three subsidiaries of Chase Manhattan acquired 10 percent each of the capital of Diamond Lease. A subsidiary of Manufacturers Hanover Trust Co. was to participate in Nippon Kangyo's Tokyo Lease Co. Together with thirteen manufacturing companies, the Industrial Bank of Japan and the First National Bank of Boston founded Pacific Lease, which was to operate not only in Japan but also in the entire Pacific area.

Leasing of industrial equipment, construction and office machinery (including teletype and telefax machinery), motor vehicles (including refrigerated trailers), aircraft, vessels, and automatic vending machines has made up the bulk of the leasing business. Particularly noteworthy developments in recent years have been the increase in leases of store equipment, particularly to supermarkets (connected with the efforts of the large trading companies to gain a controlling influence over supermarkets), and the extension of leasing (as distinct from short-term renting) to the consumer durables sector. Tokyo Lease handles color TV sets, stereo sets, air conditioners (¥8,000 per month in summer, ¥2,000 in winter), electric typewriters, sewing machines, pianos, and furniture. Sony leases its video tape recorders. Through its sales company, Hitachi Credit, Hitachi leases TV sets, refrigerators and stereo sets not only to households but also to hotels, restaurants, and beauty parlors. The lease term is three years, with a one year extension possible. Rentals are fixed specifically for each kind of appliance, e.g., ¥2,000 a month, for a 17-inch black-and-white TV receiver; ¥3,000, for a model R-5150S refrigerator. Ordinary households pay the first installment in cash, but the following payments are made by automatic transfer from a bank account.

A field which remains undeveloped is factoring. Nippon Shinpan operates a factoring system using coupons. Based on its credit investigation, the factor (Nippon Shinpan) issues coupons to the retailers, who use them for ordering merchandise from wholesalers. The wholesalers send the coupons with their bills to the factor who pays the bills and collects from the retailers.

In September 1970, the six largest trading companies (Mitsubishi, Mitsui, Marubeni-Iida, C. Itoh, Nissho-Iwai, Sumitomo) began to investigate the possibility of introducing factoring into Japan. Mitsui & Co. has been negotiating with James Talcott and Bankers Trust over the foundation of a joint venture for factoring. The Sanwa group plans to form a factoring company with First National Bank of Boston. Until recently, the banks and trading companies were of the opinion that Japan's peculiar financial structure made factoring difficult; the large firms did not need it for their dealings with other large firms, and the problematic credit worthiness of small enterprises seemed to make factoring uneconomical. But the large expansion of the economy has made the burden of credits and collections too heavy for the trading companies, and they would welcome special organs to take over these functions.

Principal Leasing Companies

Date of foundation	Company	Major shareholders		
		Financial institutions	Trading companies	Manufacturers, etc.
Aug. 1963	Japan Lease	Fuji B., Sumitomo B., Mitsubishi B., Sanwa B., Tokai B., Long-Term Credit B., Industrial B., Mitsubishi Trust, Sumitomo Trust, Mitsui Trust, Yasuda Trust, Chuo Trust.	Mitsubishi Corp., Mitsui & Co., Marubeni Corp. Tomen Okura Shoji	Komatsu Mfg. Mitsubishi H.I., (altogether 29 companies)
Aug. 1964	Tokyo Lease	Kangyo B., Long-Term Credit B., Nissan Fire Ins.		Kangin Real Estate, Nanei Shoji
May 1969	Central Lease	Tokai B., Chuo Trust, Chiyoda Life Ins., Chiyoda Fire Ins., etc.	Tomen	Meitetsu, etc.
July 1969	Century Leasing System	Dai-Ichi B., Nihon Life Ins., Asahi Life Ins.	C. Itoh & Co.	
June 1968	Jusho Lease Kosan		Sumitomo Shoji	
Apr. 1969	Showa Lease	Kyowa B., Chiyoda Life Ins., Dai-Ichi Life Ins., Yasuda Life Ins., Nisshin Fire Ins., Dai-Tokyo Fire Ins.	Ataka & Co.	Shinwa Shoji, Shinyokai
March 1967	Mitsui Lease	Mitsui B., Mitsui Trust, Mitsui Life Ins., Bank of Tokyo	Mitsui & Co.	
June 1968	Hitachi Lease	Fuji B., Yasuda Trust, Yasuda Fire Ins.		Nissei Sangyo, Hitachi

Principal Leasing Companies (cont.)

Date of foundation	Company	Major shareholders			
		Financial institutions	Trading companies	Manufacturers, etc.	Foreign partners
Apr. 1964	Orient Lease	Sanwa B., Toyo Trust, Kangyo B., Kobe B., Industrial B., Daiwa B., Nippon Life Ins.	Nissho-Iwai, Nichimen Jitsugyo		U.S. Leasing
Oct. 1968	General Lease	Sumitomo B.	Sumitomo Shoji	Nippon Electric, Sumitomo Machinery	Bamerical International Finance Corp., Finabai Société Financière, Ameribas Holding
Jan. 1971	Pacific Lease	Industrial B., Nippon Life Ins.		Hitachi, Toshiba, Mitsubishi H.I., Nissan Motor, Yawata Iron & Steel, Fuji Iron & Steel (Yawata and Fuji are now Nippon Steel Corp.)	First National Bank of Boston
Apr. 1971	Diamond Lease	Mitsubishi B., Mitsubishi Trust	Mitsubishi Corp.		Chase Manhattan, Overseas Banking Corp., Berkeley Service Corp., Dovenmuehle Inc.
May 1969	Fuyo General Lease	Fuji B., Yasuda Trust, Yasuda Life Ins., Yasuda Fire Ins.	Marubeni Corp.	Fuyo Development	First National Overseas Investment Co., Citicorp Leasing International

7 THE FINANCIAL ROLE OF TRADING COMPANIES

The large general trading companies are a typically Japanese institution without parallel elsewhere. Historically, their position dates back to the Meiji era, and their predecessors are the merchants of the Tokugawa period, who were at the same time traders and bankers. The fourteen largest trading companies form the Trading Companies Association (established in 1966), and the managers of the business departments hold regular meetings (called *suiyōkai*, which means both Wednesday Club and Wednesday Meeting). Generally speaking, the trading firms concentrate on forming the connecting link between producer and customer, but, in the years since the Iwato boom (1959–61), their activities have experienced a tremendous expansion. The large trading companies have left behind the stage of mere wholesale trade and have become organizers of industry, credit institutions, intelligence agencies, and coordinators of international marketing. They have played an important role in the development of overseas raw material sources. Not only are many long-term contracts for the supply of raw materials concluded by or through the trading companies, but these firms also participate in numerous joint ventures and other investment projects for the exploitation of raw material reserves. Petroleum, natural gas, coal, iron ore, nonferrous metals, salt, timber, and agricultural products are some of the fields in which the trading companies have organized Japanese participation in the exploration and exploitation of new resources. In some cases, the trading companies have worked together with the firms of their own group interested in certain raw materials; in other instances, they have led a group of enterprises in a given industrial sector. Although keen competition exists between the various companies (particularly bitter is the rivalry between Mitsubishi and Mitsui for the top spot), there is a great deal of cooperation. Almost all large trading companies cooperate with one another and with the large steel manufacturers in the importation of iron ore (to a lesser degree in coking coal imports) and the development of overseas iron ore deposits. The enormous funds required for development projects, the necessity of finding large markets, the advantages of using large carriers, and the growing involvement of Japanese enterprises as partners or competitors with international capital are some of the factors accounting for the tendency toward cooperation among the trading companies.

Thanks to their numerous foreign branch offices or subsidiaries, the trading companies are generally well informed on the economic situation and market conditions in other countries, and are in a position to advise Japanese enterprises on the possibilities of supplying plant and equipment to foreign customers. They often organize groups of manufacturers, who submit joint bids to foreign tender invitations. In this way, the Japanese manufacturers avoid competing with one another, and are often able to submit low bids because every one of the manufacturers involved takes over the part of the bid for which he can offer the most favorable conditions.

Of special interest are the attempts of the trading companies at diversification (particularly their efforts at establishing direct connections with the retail trade), their participation in the leasing business, and their activities in the field of residential construction. The trading companies became involved in residential construction partly as a result of their cooperation with real estate companies in the building of new stores, and partly on account of the participation of the *zaibatsu* and other groups in housing developments, the construction of high-rise apartments, and prefabricated housing. The groups are able to raise the capital required for large-scale development projects, to secure large tracts of land, and to organize the simultaneous construction of numerous units. The firms belonging to the same group handle the construction work, the supply of building materials, fixtures, and other equipment, and the real estate companies take over the sale, leasing, or maintenance of the buildings.

Other fields in which the trading companies are interested but in which activities have not gone beyond preliminary research are the development of submarine resources, space exploration, and communications satellites.

The main reason for the expansion of the activities of the trading companies is the greater profitableness of these new operations; many of them are less liable to cyclical fluctuations than the more traditional forms of trade, and in a number of cases quick depreciation is possible. Due to the severe competition in traditional forms of trade, the margins are very thin and sometimes even insufficient to cover all costs. Moreover, most of the investments for the exploitation of raw material sources abroad are not far enough advanced to bring a profit; on the contrary, many projects require additional capital. Since the trading companies rely to a large extent on borrowed capital, they must find a number of operations which bring quick results.

For most firms connected with the trading companies, the financing of their transactions is almost as important as the distribution or supply channels provided by the trading firms. Through their credits, the trading companies divide their own bank credit among their customers or suppliers and, at the same time, take over credit rating and risk. For many enterprises, financing by the trading firms is more advantageous because the banks are not only more exacting with regard to collateral but also demand compensating balances. Even giant enterprises use the credit facilities of the trading companies; in this way they can reduce their own costs in buying and selling and finance payments to their subcontractors or subsidiaries. For the banks, the business practices of the trading companies are far from ideal. Most credits of the banks to the trading companies are labeled loans for operating capital, but a considerable part of these loans serves for financing deferred payments (e.g., for machinery). The system enables industrial enterprises to indulge in an unhealthy expansion of credit. They can obtain loans directly from the banks for the purpose of investing in equipment and, at the same time, use the credit of the trading companies for purchasing raw materials or selling their finished products. For this reason, the trading companies have suffered much more from the growing number of bankruptcies than the banks.

In most cases, the banks have sufficient collateral in the form of deposits, securities, or mortgages, while the trading companies often rely on warehouse receipts, bills of lading, and similar security, and the liquidation of this type of collateral often involves losses. It is relatively simple for the banks to stop their credits when the situation of their clients becomes risky, but the trading companies often find it impossible to cut off their connections. Apart from long-term contracts, the nature of their transactions entails a closer involvement in the business of their clients. The trading companies have tried to adapt their financing to their clients and the different kinds of merchandise, but the risks inherent in the system remain very great. The losses of the large trading companies are sometimes caused by the collapse of small or medium-sized traders who, in turn, have become insolvent on account of the difficulties of small industrial enterprises. In times of recession, the financial needs of most enterprises grow rapidly, while official policy usually restricts credit. The industry must finance huge inventories accumulated through the overproduction preceding the recession; moreover, the curtailment of production creates additional financial needs. The collapse of one enterprise may cause a chain reaction and lead to the bankruptcy of twenty or thirty other firms (this occurred, for instance, in the insolvency of Sanyo Special Steel, Sun Wave, Harima Steel, and Showa Metal Industries). At any given time, the trading firms have outstanding advances amounting to two or three times their monthly sales; often they have given guarantees for the loans of their clients. All these circumstances combine to make the impact of bankruptcies on the trading firms extremely severe.

For their financial needs, the trading firms rely on bank loans, and their borrowings are always a multiple of their net worth. At the end of the term from October 1970 to March 1971, Mitsubishi Corporation's current liabilities stood at ¥1,413,573,719,310 and its fixed liabilities at ¥214,810,379,458. These liabilities included ¥667,702,251,188 in bills payable, ¥324,276,260,955 in accounts payable, ¥309,569,102,177 in short-term loans, and ¥209,544,692,827 in long-term loans. Net worth (capital accounts) amounted to ¥56,124,279,086. Liabilities, therefore were about twenty-nine times and bank loans almost nine times the net worth of the firm. Receivables amounted to ¥640,288,526,966, and drafts received in payment to ¥575,978,971,947 (drafts discounted, ¥228,437,282,341). Guarantees given by the company amounted to ¥97,731,712,954, short-term claims against subsidiaries to ¥39,183,311,840, and long-term claims to ¥10,117,345,603. The investment account of the firm was ¥107,106,238,510, including ¥19,144,748,209 in shares of and contributions to subsidiaries. Mitsubishi's sales during the six-month term amounted to ¥2,125,761,395,712, and its net profit to ¥4,208,941,316.

The fourteen large trading companies handle about 50 percent of all Japanese exports and 60 percent of the imports; in the total transactions of the companies, exports and imports account for about 20 percent each, domestic transactions for 55 percent, and triangular trade for 5 percent. The trading companies were concerned about the yen revaluation long before President Nixon's announcement of his new economic policy. For two terms, Mitsui set aside reserves for possible exchange losses, but it dissolved this account for the March 1971 settlement, because the government said that the yen would not be revalued and there was no need for a taxable reserve. The companies tried to protect themselves by accepting advance payments for exports and deferring payments for imports (leads and lags). This resulted in a large inflow of cash, and the trading companies invested considerable sums in treasury bills. Shortly before Japan's switch to a floating rate, the trading firms converted large amounts of dollars into yen, but the floating yen rate brought negotiations for new export orders to a standstill. In July 1971, the volume of export orders amounted to ¥403.2 billion, but in the month following the Nixon shock new contracts fell below 10 percent of the July volume. The traders, who grew up in the postwar period, are not accustomed to variable exchange rates and apparently thought it safer to do nothing than to do something wrong. Since three to six months elapse between the conclusion of the contract and the shipment of export goods, the decline in contracts had no immediate effect on actual exports. The trading companies were among the first to press the government for an early return to fixed exchange rates and compensation for exchange losses. The aggregate exchange losses of the ten largest trading companies in the term from April to September 1971 amounted to ¥12.3 billion; exchange losses for the six-month term ending March 1972 were estimated at ¥15 billion. The traders have asked the manufacturers to bear the exchange losses. In the case of steel, there seems to be a justification for this request; for exports, the contracts between the trading companies and the steel manufacturers are on a yen basis, but those between the trading companies and the foreign buyers are denominated in dollars. For imports, however, the contracts between the trading companies and the steel makers are in dollars, so that the manufacturers will get the benefit from a lower dollar rate.

The suspension of future contracts made it impossible to hedge against currency fluctuations. While the yen floated, the trading companies concluded contracts based on a rate of ¥310 or ¥320 to the dollar. They asserted that the yen was not sufficiently accepted abroad to conclude contracts on a yen basis (although some shipbuilding companies have done this), and they seemed afraid of the old gimmicks such as a gold clause.

IV

THE ERA OF

INTERNATIONALIZATION

1 POSITION IN THE INTERNATIONAL COMMUNITY

1 JAPAN AND WORLD POLITICS

Until President Nixon's new economic policy, "internationalization" was one of the most widely discussed subjects in Japanese economic circles in general and in banking circles in particular. The meaning of this term was rather vague; it referred to the greater involvement of Japan in world affairs, the advance of Japanese enterprises abroad, outward foreign investment, participation in foreign businesses, and operations in foreign capital markets, especially in the Eurodollar market.

A quarter of a century has elapsed since the termination of the Second World War, but Japan finds herself in a position of growing uncertainty and isolation. Formally, she is committed to a defense partnership with the United States, first spelled out in the U.S.-Japan Security Treaty which went into effect in April 1952, was renewed in 1960, and extended "automatically" in 1970. The official policy of the Japanese government invariably affirms the country's basic alignment with the West. The Left has never ceased to denounce this commitment, but in the conservative camp, too, doubts have been expressed with increasing frequency whether this policy is in the nation's best interest. To a certain extent, these misgivings are the result of resurging nationalism and the search for greater national identity. But even among Japanese friends of the United States, the problems involved in Japan's present situation have prompted a reexamination of the policies pursued until today. Two nagging doubts seem foremost in the minds of responsible people: first, has not the alliance with the United States biased Japan's relations with other nations; second, will the policy of the United States, and particularly her defense policy, protect Japan against war or aggression?

In evaluating Japan's position, it should not be overlooked (but also not overemphasized) that her alignment with the United States means a complete reversal not only of her war policy but of her entire modern history. To defend the independence of the nation against the dangers arising from the advance of the Western powers in the Far East was the basic policy of the early Meiji era, and the alliance with Great Britain was meant to stop Russia's advance, not to promote British influence. The victory over Russia was hailed as the beginning of the liberation of Asia from Western domination, while the West reciprocated by conjuring up the specter of the "yellow peril." After World War I, Japan appeared more and more as a dangerous rival, initially in the field of commerce, but increasingly in terms of military power. Neither the League of Nations nor the Washington and London conferences provided solutions, and neither the pursuit of national interests nor the conceptions of international order appear to have been the only possible or even the most advantageous policies. Japan's war against China was imperialistic in aim and motive, and the greatest weakness in the calculations of the Japanese army was the misunderstanding of Chinese nationalism. The war with the United States was a clash of two imperialisms; and while the disparity of economic resources was decisive for its final outcome, Japan's underestimation of the willingness of the Americans to fight a long and costly war was a major factor in the fatal decision to resort to force. No problem remains from this collision of interests because Japan was forced to abandon her imperialism, but it would have been astonishing indeed to have foreseen that Japan's defeat would result in such an identity of interests as the U.S.-Japan Security Treaty and the foreign policy in line with it seem to imply. Without the Cold War and the Korean conflict, Japan would hardly have achieved such a quick rehabilitation from her pariah status to a member of good standing in the international community.

Territorial expansion for the sake of providing living space is a dead issue, even for the new nationalism, but the problems of securing raw materials and access to markets involve Japan in a basic collision of interests with both the industrialized and the developing countries. Political freedom of action to protect her own economic order, while trying to promote a rational accommodation to the different and seemingly conflicting economic interests of the various nations is essential to Japan. In this respect, Japan finds her freedom of action severely limited by her political alignment with the West. Her economic interests, seemingly unique, have isolated her; she is treated, on the one hand, by the industrialized Western countries chiefly as a competitor and not as an integral part of the world economy, and, on the other, is regarded by the developing nations as a thoroughly selfish and greedy trader.

Japan belongs to no economic bloc; she is a member of all important international organizations, hosts innumerable international conferences, spends enormous sums on prestige projects such as the Tokyo Olympics or the Osaka World Fair, engages public relations firms to analyze the Japanese image abroad, and trades with the entire world, but is alone, isolated, and distrusted. Out of the seventy-eight member nations of GATT, twenty-two apply Article 35 (direct restrictions on imports) against Japan. As of March 1971, they included the following (figures based on the four-digit Brussels Tariff Nomenclature): France retained import restrictions on 70 items; West Germany, on 38; Britain, on 25; Italy, on 18; the Benelux countries, on 12; and the United States and Canada, on 5. As of June 1971, the number of positions (on the basis of the four-digit BTN) subject to discriminatory restrictions imposed on Japanese imports by European countries (including the restrictions under the Long-Term Cotton Textiles Agreement) was: Spain, 336; Portugal, 250; Austria, 74; Sweden, 52; Italy, 46; France and Britain, each 44; Norway, 33; the Benelux countries, 27; West Germany, 21; Greece, 13; and Denmark, 8.

As related above, Japan reduced the number of imported products subject to quotas from eighty in January 1971 to forty at the end of September. Generally speaking, however, Japan's liberalization, publicized by the government and the business community as a sign of the country's awareness of its international obligations, failed to impress its business partners. The reasons are not difficult to find. Japan removed restrictions on imports and capital transactions only grudgingly and under immense pressure. Instead of aiming at equality or reciprocity in the treatment of other nations, the liberalization programs were neatly worked out by the bureaucracy to suit Japan's domestic situation, the "industry first" and "the consumer be damned" policy of MITI's paternalistic protectionism and the Liberal-Democratic party's need for the farm vote. The liberalization retained irritating restrictions (e.g., the fifty-fifty rule for foreign investment) and did nothing to eliminate the impression of bad faith given to other countries by the lack of economic rationality in many of the control measures, the ridiculous interpretations of international agreements, and the amount of red tape that remains after the so-called liberalization (even now, it takes about twenty minutes of paperwork to send one dollar abroad). It is largely these irrational irritants which have exacerbated the present disagreement with the country's only ally and most important trading partner, although President Nixon's shotgun diplomacy must be blamed for the perturbation of the international monetary system and the threat to the stability of world trade.

1 POSITION IN THE INTERNATIONAL COMMUNITY

2 JAPAN'S RELATIONS WITH CHINA

President Nixon's rapprochement with the People's Republic of China not only took the Japanese by surprise but made a difficult problem infinitely more difficult. For a long time, the Japanese government officially ignored the problem of Japan's relations with China, perhaps in the secret hope that a change in the world situation would bring a solution. The Left naively asserted that Japan's repudiation of her allegiance to the Western camp would automatically establish complete harmony and prosperity in Japan and China. Successive conservative governments have made the avoidance of an outright choice between Red China and Taiwan their chief endeavor. Japanese politicians have defended the renunciation of any policy with regard to China by asserting that any understanding between Japan and China would presuppose an understanding between Chiang Kai-shek and Mao Tse-tung—which would be the most convenient way for the problem to disappear. Until the admission of the People's Republic of China to the United Nations, the government's official stand on the China issue had two aspects: Japan would conform to the decision of the United Nations regarding the recognition of the Peking government as the legitimate government of China and its seating in the United Nations; and Japan would, simultaneously, pursue a policy of "friendly" relations with the two "peoples," while promoting trade under the formula of the separation of politics and economics. A considerable number of politicians inside the Liberal-Democratic party have become critical of the government's handling of the China issue. The United States, they think, anticipated the defeat in the United Nations and changed her policy beforehand; Japan's change in her policy toward China now appears to be a result of America's reorientation, and confirms China's appraisal of Japan as a "lackey of American imperialism."

Japanese businessmen are falling over each other in their rush to gain admission to the Celestial Empire. To the Kwangchow (Canton) Fair, which opened on October 15, 1971, a total of 1,457 Japanese firms sent 2,300 representatives (compared with 791 firms and 1,408 representatives attending the spring fair). On September 20, 1971, the Bank of China informed Fuji Bank and Mitsubishi Bank that it had terminated its correspondence agreements with the two banks because their representatives had attended the general meeting of the Japan-Republic of Korea Cooperation Committee held in July. On October 8, Fuji Bank informed the Bank of China that it would henceforth abide by Premier Chou En-lai's "four trade principles" and requested resumption of correspondence relations. The Bank of China notified Fuji Bank on November 10 that it would reopen exchange transactions with Fuji Bank starting December 1. Fuji Bank, which has a branch office in Seoul, may open a representative office in Peking in the near future. Mitsubishi Bank followed Fuji's example in accepting the four trade principles and asking for reestablishment of correspondence relations. Sanwa Bank sent representatives to the Kwangchow Fair on a "fact-finding" mission; together with Sumitomo, Mitsubishi, and Tokai banks, Sanwa will take part in a mission to be sent to Peking by the Japan Productivity Center.

The four trade principles were formulated in April 1970 by Premier Chou En-lai as conditions for doing business with mainland China. They are prohibitions: (1) thou shalt not make large capital investments in Taiwan and Korea; (2) thou shalt not maintain close ties with American interests (e.g., joint ventures); (3) thou shalt not assist any attempt by the Chiang Kai-shek regime to invade the Chinese mainland or any South Korean plot against North Korea; (4) thou shalt not supply munitions to Indochina.

An increasing number of firms have made the profession of faith, and, as earlier in the selection of "friendly firms" admitted to the trade with China, the Chinese have permitted themselves a considerable degree of discretion in applying the four principles. Toyota Motor Co. is doing a nice amount of business with China although it has a tie-up with a Korean auto manufacturer and holds a share of nearly 80 percent in the Korean auto market; Toyota is also heavily involved in Taiwan. Hitachi, Ltd., one of Japan's leading manufacturers of electrical machinery, was found eligible despite its almost ¥1.5 billion worth of investments in Taiwan, but Teijin, Japan's second largest producer of synthetic fibers, was turned down on account of its investment in Taiwan (¥1.7 billion). Nippon Steel Corporation is doing business with Peking although it is helping with the construction of a huge steel mill at Pohang in Korea, and Fuji Bank has a joint consulting enterprise with First National City Bank.

But businessmen are almost as divided as the politicians on the question of China. A number of enterprises in the Mitsubishi group, notably Mitsubishi Heavy Industries, which has tie-ups with Caterpillar and Chrysler and is heavily engaged in defense production, hesitated to accept the four principles, but, recently, Yoichiro Makita, the late president of Mitsubishi Heavy Industries, declared that the firm would make no new investments in Taiwan without the consent of Peking and that the Mitsubishi group would send some of its executives to China in 1972. The four largest trading companies (Mitsubishi, Mitsui, Marubeni-Corp., and C. Itoh) have stayed away from the Japan-Taiwan Cooperation Committee, but they have not accepted the four principles and remain excluded from the China trade. Other large trading companies, however, have explicitly agreed to observe Peking's conditions and intend to use dummies for their trade with Taiwan, reversing the former practice of trading with China through subsidiaries.

A delegation of the Dietmen's League for Normalization of Japan-China Relations, which visited Peking in the beginning of October 1971, signed a communiqué stating four political principles: (1) China is represented by the Peking government; (2) Taiwan is an integral part of China; (3) the Japan-Republic of China Peace Treaty is null and void; (4) all rights of China in the United Nations, including the permanent seat in the Security Council, must be restored to the Peking government. The last has been rendered irrelevant by the action of the world body; the third principle, however, may open the pandora's box of reparations (which the Nationalist government forewent in its peace treaty with Japan). Then, there are the Senkaku Islands (eight small islands northeast of Taiwan) and the continental shelf (with its potential oil deposits) over which Japan, China, South Korea, and Taiwan are already advancing conflicting claims. This means that a normalization of relations with China involves so many awkward problems that Japan will move very cautiously. At the present stage, Japan does not want to break off relations with Taiwan and the government will wait and see what kind of arrangement the United States, while maintaining her ties with Taiwan, will make to establish some kind of relationship with China. In the meantime, the government hopes, "private" contacts with China will grow to such an extent that both governments will find it convenient to overlook certain untidy chinks in their relations. It is not as if there were no channels of communication between the two governments at present. Under the so-called Memorandum Trade Agreement, trade offices were established in Tokyo and Peking in 1964, and one of the Japanese representatives in Peking has been an official of the Ministry of Foreign Affairs serving "in a private capacity."

As far as trade is concerned, businessmen always emphasize the long-term potential of the Chinese market. But it is difficult to define exactly what this long-term potential means. In the foreseeable future, China will not become an open market for the kinds of consumer goods Japan is now exporting to the West, i.e., automobiles, electric appliances, and textiles. The sort of market penetration Japan tried in the twenties, and which led to the clashes in the thirties, is entirely out of the question. China is undoubtedly interested in capital goods and technology, but the volume of this trade will be strictly controlled and nowhere in proportion to the country's population. China will be willing to sell large quantities of farm products, such as soybeans or pork, but, when it comes to industrial raw materials, ideological roadblocks come into play. Premier Chou En-lai told a mission of businessmen visiting China, in November 1971, of his apprehensions that Japanese militarism might be revived in order to secure the raw materials needed for Japan's economic expansion. Such a repetition of pre–World War II policies is unthinkable at present, but the Chinese leadership's deep distrust will not easily be dispelled.

On the other hand, the thought that, some day, they will have to make some hard decisions on military preparedness sends shivers down the spines of the leaders of Japan. "Atomic arms or no atomic arms?"—that is this modern Hamlet's question. The invariably strong nuclear allergy would incline the vast majority of the people to answer with a passionate no, and no politician would dare to defend an unqualified yes. To the Japanese it seems that the United States, the Soviet Union, and the People's Republic of China each have a definite status, and that each of these contestants should recognize the others' position and be satisfied with his own lot. Naturally, such a static hierarchical order is a puerile dream in a world that has reverted to power politics, and the preoccupation of China's leaders with world hegemony bodes ill for the stability of the international order.

Although the Supreme Court has upheld the government's interpretation of the constitution and decided that the establishment of the self-defense forces did not violate the antiwar clause, the issue remains uncertain. The popular abhorrence of anything atomic has prevented a serious development of military missile capacity. The government planned a substantial increase in defense outlays under the fourth defense program (1972–76), but the recession has already forced a downward revision from the original total of ¥5,400 billion to ¥4,900–5,000 billion. The Defense Agency has not yet been raised to the status of a ministry, and most military units, because of recruitment difficulties, are below their authorized strength. The switch of trained personnel (e.g., pilots) to civilian jobs is a constant drain on available manpower, and there is no effective organization of reserves. For the moment, therefore, Japan possesses neither the will nor the capacity to become a military power. From a technical point of view, Japan's acquisition of a nuclear weapon capability would constitute no problem and could be effected in a relatively short period. But any government that openly adopted a program of nuclear armament would run the risk of a massive popular uprising. Furthermore, any substantial increase in Japan's military power would become a political liability, because it would arouse suspicion not only in China but in most of the countries in Southeast Asia.

It is against this background that the coolness of Japan to suggestions for a greater Japanese contribution to the Far Eastern defense system must be understood. Japan had no voice in the formulation of the strategy underlying the American defense system, including the defense of Japan, and the basic concepts of the American strategy are incompatible with Japan's position. But Japan has not yet worked out a strategy of her own. In the foreseeable future, the country cannot rely on its own military power either for defense or for influencing the course of world politics. As a basic option, therefore, the country must support an international order that bans the use of force and affirms the possibility of achieving international understanding. This abstract formula (the essence of the United Nations' Charter), although accepted by all nations, is subject to different, and at times diametrically opposed, interpretations. The attempts to impose particular value systems by force prove that mankind is far from agreeing on a universally recognized order of values ("peace" or "aggression" means something different for each of Japan, the United States, the Soviet Union, and the People's Republic of China). Japan's present policies, therefore, are based on something that should, but actually does not, exist, and hence are based on wishful thinking; small wonder that other nations have little trust in Japan.

A number of secondary issues further complicate Japan's international position: no peace treaty has been signed with the Soviet Union—Japan's demand that Russia return the islands of Habomai and Shikotan and the Soviet refusal even to consider territorial questions have so far proven insurmountable obstacles to a normalization of relations; Peking will demand a new settlement of Sino-Japanese relations; and neither North Vietnam nor North Korea will be bound by the agreements reached with the governments of the southern parts of these countries. These unsolved issues are, in effect, so many political liabilities which weaken Japan's position.

The inference from these considerations seems that Japan's economic might is the only real basis of her political influence. Unlike such unaligned nations as India, Indonesia, and Egypt, Japan is committed to "the Free World" and cannot make a bargaining weapon of her political loyalties. The nation's conservative leaders would be the last to threaten the United States with neutralism or all-out adherence to the Communist bloc. They can plead for greater understanding and for more or less token concessions to obviate domestic criticism of their foreign policy, but they would not even dream of going it alone, to say nothing of a complete sellout to the Communists. Hence, although the West would hardly like to see Japan's economic potential fall under Red domination, and although China would gain significantly from controlling Japan's productive apparatus, these eventualities are barely possible and, under present circumstances, not at all probable. The truth, therefore, is that Japan's economic power carries no positive political weight. Japan finds it hard to gain economic concessions from countries such as the United States, Australia, and Canada, for whom Japan is a very important customer, and she cannot in the least exert any political influence or pressure on them. The same considerations are applicable to Japan's relations with the Communist countries and all other nations for whom she is a marginal buyer or supplier.

The conclusion, however, is not that Japan is unable to take any initiative in international relations but that she is forced to espouse such causes, movements, and proposals which deserve universal acceptance. Many Japanese commentators emphasize the country's role as a bridge between West and East and North and South. Although the art of compromise is highly developed in Japan, Japanese diplomats have hardly excelled as "honest brokers" or trusted mediators. Among Japanese, more importance is attached to the matter of saving face than to an appraisal of the substantive merits; solutions acceptable to West and East can only be found if a common basis, i.e., common values, can be detected and presented in a form which brings out their rationality and objective validity. Unfortunately, in this respect, Japan's tradition warrants no optimism. Nevertheless, the beginning of a real contribution to international understanding could be made if politicians and diplomats would rid themselves of the facile notion that Japan can be a bridge because she borrowed from everywhere—that by being nice to everybody or by sending goodwill missions to every corner of the globe international problems can be solved. Of the many top business leaders and prominent conservative and socialist politicians who have visited Peking, not one has contributed anything helpful towards finding a point of departure for a settlement of the pending issues. They merely report the claims that the New China News Agency has repeated often enough not to be forgotten. The same is true of the banalities expressed in the joint communiqués issued after the U.S.-Japan consultations. In her modern history, Japan has never produced a charismatic leader such as Ghandi or a demagogue such as Sukarno whose personality could influence the march of world history. But she has enough able men who, through thinking and hard work, could give her a more than nominal role in world affairs. Unfortunately, the present system, with its rotation of party bigwigs in the formal national leadership and with its bureaucrats serving as the chief purveyors of national policies, offers little chance of producing more than inane verbiage.

1 Position in the International Community

3 JAPAN AND THE DEVELOPING COUNTRIES

The Japanese businessman sees his country's position in the international community as an environmental factor of his business. His main concern, of course, is the maintenance of such conditions as will assure expanding export markets and investment opportunities and a steady supply of raw materials, fuels, and food. Peace and political stability are considered most important, and very few Japanese businessmen are interested in a war boom although the munitions industry and the manufacture of military aircraft have grown considerably. The expansion of export markets receives much attention, and although Japan cannot hope to compete with the United States in the development of multinational enterprises, the feasibility of such undertakings has been and is being studied by a number of concerns. Until now, the exploitation of raw material sources or economic cooperation with developing countries has been given the chief emphasis in foreign investment. Multinational enterprises require a far-reaching redirection of the flow of investments, and probably would give greater weight to political factors. In present business thinking, foreign investment and economic cooperation have little political connotation because both have been more or less a matter of opportunity rather than planning or politics. A number of countries have welcomed Japanese investment, notably Brazil, Thailand, Kuwait, Indonesia, Canada, the United States, and Australia. The exploitation of raw material sources was the objective of Japanese investments in Kuwait, Indonesia, Alaska, Canada, the Philippines, Malaysia, Peru, and Australia. In some cases, Japan has sought outlets for its manufacturing industry, e.g., through the building of assembly plants for motor cars in Thailand, the Philippines, Mexico, and Peru, and in these as well as other branches (textiles, fishing nets) Japanese firms compete with one another in developing foreign markets. MITI therefore, has admonished industry to avoid "excessive competition" in foreign investment. The scarcity of capital and the restrictions on capital movements have retarded the international advance of Japanese industry. The government's foreign policies, generally, have been innocent of any attempts to facilitate the establishment of foreign subsidiaries. In this respect, the postwar development differed greatly from the prewar pattern of economic penetration backed up by diplomatic and, if necessary, military pressure.

Japan's raw material imports seem politically neutral. With an 84.84 percent share in the 1970 imports of crude petroleum (and 90.99 percent of the raw petroleum oil imports), the Middle East is Japan's chief supplier of petroleum, but imports from Indonesia have increased greatly in recent years (1970, 13.91 percent). For cotton, Japan relies on the United States and some Latin American countries such as Mexico, El Salvador, and Brazil; in addition, cotton is bought from Pakistan and India as well as from Egypt and Ethiopia, while wool is imported from Australia and to a certain extent from New Zealand and South Africa. Australia has become Japan's most important supplier of iron ore, followed by India, Chile, Peru, and Brazil. Nonferrous metals come from Zambia, the United States, Malaysia, the Soviet Union, Chile, Canada, Australia, and South Africa. The United States is Japan's chief supplier of coking coal; other sources are Australia, Canada, and the Soviet Union. A number of other products have similarly diversified origins; timber is imported from the United States, the Philippines, the Soviet Union, Malaysia, Indonesia, and Canada; sugar from Cuba, Australia, the Ryukyu Islands, and South Africa; and soybeans from the United States and the People's Republic of China. The countries listed above are only the main sources of industrial raw materials, fuels, and foods, but they seem to prove the non-political nature of Japan's import pattern. In its recent "White Book on Raw Material Sources," MITI forecast growing competition among the industrial nations for the control of raw material sources, and said the lack of political influence may jeopardize Japan's supplies. The absence of political bias suggests that the Japanese businessman himself does not follow a definite political line and is not under pressure to show political preferences. Imbalances in Japan's trade with certain developing countries have given rise to complaints by these trading partners as well as to various schemes to stimulate Japanese imports from or investments in these countries. But these problems were economic in nature and involved trade policies rather than political relations.

Generally speaking, Japan exhibits the same nonpolitical tendencies in her export trade. Japan trades with the Arab nations as well as with Israel, with South Africa as well as the anticolonial African states. The United States is Japan's main export market, but in the last decade her trade with the Soviet Union and Eastern Europe has expanded rapidly. Trade relations with the People's Republic of China have suffered from the on-again, off-again policy of the Chinese, which was largely politically inspired. Japan's imports from the Soviet Union have been much higher than her exports, but both sides were eager to increase the exchange of goods, and the same applies to the East European countries. Compared with the high sophistication of trade with the United States and some Western nations, in which purely commercial aspects such as price, quality, and delivery dates constitute the basis of Japan's competitiveness, trade relations with the Communist countries look somewhat primitive and clumsy and slow to adapt to changing conditions. On the whole, trade relations with the Soviet Union and other Communist countries are more openly influenced by direct political considerations as well as by the politically inspired economic systems of such countries. How trade with those nations will affect the political future of Communism, either domestically or internationally, seems of little concern to the Japanese businessman.

To a certain degree, the Japanese are aware of the problems of the less-developed countries but are rather unwilling to assume a larger responsibility in solving them. Theoretically, the necessity of cooperation not only with Asian but with all developing nations is recognized, but little is done to implement this cooperation. In Japan, as in other advanced countries, the fact that the difficult and seemingly unsolvable social problems of the developing countries are common problems of the international community remains a purely academic proposition. Here, as in other spheres, the progress from national to international or supra-national thinking is slow, and the progress in action is slower still. Japan, like other advanced nations, is inclined to save her conscience and her money by referring to her cooperation with international organs and agencies, such as, in addition to the United Nations, the

World Bank, the International Development Association, the Colombo Plan, and the Development Assistance Committee (DAC) of the Organization for Economic Cooperation and Development. According to MITI's "White Book on Economic Cooperation," Japan provided a total of $1,824 million in foreign aid in 1970, up 44.4 percent over the preceding year. The amount, equivalent to 0.93 percent of Japan's GNP, was the second highest after the United States, but, in the composition of the aid, Japan compared unfavorably with the average of the countries represented on DAC. Only $458 million, 25.1 percent of the total, was official development aid, corresponding to 0.23 percent of GNP, far below the goal of 0.7 percent adopted by the United Nations. The share of outright grants, 6.7 percent, was particularly low. Export credits (longer than one year) given by the government, financing of direct investment, contributions to international agencies, and other official payments totaled $694 million (38 percent), while private export credits (longer than one year), direct investments, and other private capital flows reached $672 million (36.9 percent).

In addition to the small amount of direct grants, the stringent terms of Japan's assistance have often been criticized. The average interest rate on Japanese loans was 3.59 percent, compared with an average of 2.7 percent for the DAC. Japan's bureaucrats want to ensure the effectiveness of the aid given by the government (which is understandable in view of the tendency in some developing countries to dream up unrealistic projects) and treat foreign countries more or less the same as they treat their Japanese subjects. Japan often refers to

Net Flow of Funds from Japan to Developing Countries and Contributions to International Development Agencies, 1966-1970

(In millions of yen)

	1966	1967	1968	1969	1970
Official development assistance	285.3	385.3	356.2	435.6	458.0
Other official funds	198.9	215.5	322.1	375.8	693.6
Private funds	140.9	196.8	371.0	451.7	632.3
Total	625.1	797.5	1,049.3	1,263.1	1,824.0
Ratio of total foreign aid to GNP (%)	0.62	0.67	0.74	0.76	0.93

Comparison of Japan's Economic Aid with DAC Average (1970)

	Japan %	DAC average %
Official development assistance	25.1	46.2
Grants	6.7	22.4
Development loans	13.7	16.7
Intergovernmental aid	4.7	7.6
Other official funds	38.0	7.9
Private funds	36.9	45.9
Export credit	21.2	14.8
Direct investment, etc.	15.7	31.1

her reparations programs as proof of her sincere efforts to help less-privileged nations. In Japan and elsewhere, much greater seriousness is needed in dealing with social disorders in developing countries. The problems are far more pressing and difficult than the sonorous and sterile pronouncements would admit. OECD officials may state with a straight face that it may take at least 200 years for developing countries in Asia, Africa, and some parts of Latin America to attain the living standards of the United States and other leading Western industrial nations (actually, the gap between poor and rich nations is widening), but responsible political leaders should realize at once that such a situation cannot be permitted to continue and that the present methods of handling these problems are entirely inadequate. For many developing countries, President Nixon's new economic policy has meant, as Takeshi Watanabe, president of the Asian Development Bank, put it, "less aid and less trade." The growing indebtedness of developing countries and the difficulties in their balance of payments position point to the insufficiency of the present approach to their development problems. Measures such as preferential tariffs, although laudable in themselves, are out of proportion to the needs. Naturally, a great many of the developing nations would have to change their attitudes by "getting off their high horses" and allowing their ills and shortcomings to be treated as common problems.

What the industrial countries have been calling "aid for the underdeveloped nations" has been, in practice and motivation, aid for their own heavy industries. Together with other advanced countries, Japan has given long-term credits to less-developed countries not out of charity but out of self-interest. Rather than lose orders, the exporting countries prefer to let credits run longer because the poorer countries cannot afford to buy large capital equipment on any other basis.

From fiscal 1951 to fiscal 1969 (ended March 31, 1970), Japanese overseas investment totaled $2,683 million; of this sum, $1,567 million, equivalent to 58 percent, flowed into developing countries. The developing regions attracting the largest funds were Southeast Asia with $604 million and Latin America with $513 million. Manufacturing industries accounted for nearly half of the total and investments were also large in mining.

Direct outward investment has shown a considerable increase in recent years, from $122 million in 1968 to $200 million in 1969 and $408 million in 1970. The development of raw material sources for import into Japan and the construction of factories as well as the organization of distribution channels for securing overseas markets were the main objectives of private overseas investment. On account of the rising labor costs in Japan, overseas investment in labor-intensive industries is on the increase.

The accusations of "economic aggression" have made the Japanese more aware of the problems involved in overseas projects. Industry now recognizes, theoretically at least, that the exploitation of raw material sources must contribute to the economic development of the host country, create new employment opportunities, improve business management, and promote technology. A significant change in attitude is reflected in the recent agreements for the development of oil deposits with Nigeria and Iran. Until now, MITI and the industry have stressed the "independent" development of foreign oil sources by Japanese firms; the recent agreements provided for the "joint" development in a way which conforms to the demands of OPEC (Organization of Petroleum Exporting Countries). Nigeria obtained a 51 percent interest in a joint development; in the fifty-fifty joint venture with the National Iranian Oil Co., Iran will share in the "downstream" business, i.e., refining and sales.

1 POSITION IN THE INTERNATIONAL COMMUNITY

4 JAPAN'S POSITION IN WORLD TRADE

In the last decade, Japan's exports increased 4.8 times, from $4,054.5 million in 1960 to $19,317.7 million in 1970. This corresponds to an average yearly rate of increase of 17.0 percent. Imports rose from $4,491.1 million in 1960 to $18,881.2 million in 1970, a 4.2 fold increase, corresponding to an average yearly rate of increase of 15.5 percent. During the same period, world exports increased 2.6 times, at an average yearly rate of 10.1 percent, and world imports somewhat less than 2.4 percent, at an average yearly rate of 9.1 percent. Japan's share in world exports, therefore, rose from 3.6 percent in 1960 to 6.6 percent in 1970, and her share in world imports from 3.8 percent in 1960 to 6.8 percent in 1970.

Changes in the structure of exports and competitive prices may have been the principal factors which made the rapid growth of Japanese exports possible. In 1970, heavy industrial and chemical products accounted for 72.4 percent of Japan's exports and contributed 87.4 percent to the increase over the preceding year. The large expansion of productive capacity and the progress in technology enabled Japan to aim at mass markets and, at the same time, to respond to the qualitative changes in world demand. Supported by a broad home market, Japan could supply a wide range of modern consumer goods, while in many fields of industrial equipment, Japan's technology has reached the international level, enabling her manufacturers to compete not only in developing countries but to sell in the most advanced countries. Because the large increases in wage rates could be offset by even greater increases in labor productivity, export prices remained competitive.

There has been some change in the structure of Japanese exports by destination, but the concentration on the United States and Southeast Asia has remained its most characteristic feature (see overleaf).

In the structure of Japanese imports by commodities, industrial raw materials and fuels account for over half of Japan's imports, but manufactured products also play an important role (see overleaf).

The United States supplies almost 30 percent of Japanese imports because she is a major supplier of raw materials as well as of machinery, but the position of the United States in Japan's foreign trade is unique. Many countries from which Japan procures raw materials or fuels show a large favorable balance in their trade with Japan. This applies to advanced countries such as Canada, Australia, and New Zealand, to Latin American countries such as Chile, Peru, Brazil, Argentine, Cuba, Ecuador, Bolivia, and a few others, and to a number of countries in the Middle East, Iran, Saudi Arabia, Kuwait, etc. (in 1970, the trade balance in favor of the Middle East amounted to $1,703.5 million). Many countries in the Middle East with sparse populations hardly represent a market for Japan's consumer products and it would be preposterous to expect a bilateral balance in the trade with these countries (actually, some of the countries in the Middle East contend that oil exports should be disregarded in calculating the trade balance). In view of the structure of Japan's trade, a bilateral balance with each trading partner is perfectly out of the question. In 1970, Japan's trade showed a favorable balance with 22 advanced countries, 102 developing countries, and 5 Communist countries; the trade balance was unfavorable with 8 advanced countries, 51 developing countries, and 7 Communist countries. Naturally, trade is only one factor determining the international money flow; services, transfer payments, and capital movements may result in a completely different balance.

Increase in World Trade

(Percentage increase over preceding year)

Year	World trade (except Japan) A	Japanese exports B	Elasticity coefficient B/A	Yearly average
1960	8.1	14.0	1.7	
1961	4.5	5.0	1.1	
1962	5.3	15.9	3.0	1.94
1963	10.9	12.5	1.1	
1964	9.7	27.5	2.8	
1965	10.5	21.4	2.0	
1966	7.5	14.1	1.9	
1967	4.5	8.2	1.8	
1968	11.3	24.2	2.1	1.80
1969	13.9	23.3	1.7	
1970	16.1	20.8	1.3	

Composition of Japanese Exports by Destination

(In percent)

	1955	1960	1965	1970
North America	26.8	33.2	34.7	33.7
U.S.A.	22.8	27.1	29.3	30.7
Europe (incl. Eastern Europe)	10.3	13.2	15.4	17.4
West Europe	9.8	11.6	12.9	15.0
EEC	4.1	4.3	5.7	6.7
EFTA	4.5	5.6	5.4	5.5
Asia (incl. Communist countries)	41.9	36.0	32.5	31.2
Southeast Asia	28.1	24.6	19.2	27.8
Latin America	7.4	4.4	2.9	6.1
Africa	10.2	8.7	9.7	7.4
Oceania	3.4	4.5	4.8	4.2
Communist countries	(2.0)	(1.8)	(5.6)	(5.4)

Structure of Japanese Exports by Merchandise Categories, 1970

	$ million	%
Total	19,317.7	100.0
Food	647.7	3.4
Raw materials	198.9	1.0
Heavy industrial & chemical products	13,981.1	72.4
Machinery	8,941.3	46.3
Automobiles (except parts)	1,337.4	6.9
Ships	1,409.6	7.3
Electrical machinery	2,864.7	14.8
Metal products	3,805.3	19.7
Steel materials	2,843.7	14.7
Chemicals	1,234.5	6.4
Light industrial products	4,335.4	22.4
Textiles	2,407.5	12.5
Nonmetallic mineral products	372.4	1.9
Others	1,555.5	8.1

Source: Ministry of Finance, Customs Statistics.

Structure of Japanese Imports by Merchandise Categories, 1970

	$ million	%
Total	18,881.2	100.0
Foods	2,574.1	13.6
Raw materials	6,676.7	35.4
Raw materials for textiles	962.7	5.1
Raw materials for metals	2,696.3	14.3
Other	3,017.7	16.0
Mineral fuels	3,905.5	20.7
Coal	1,010.1	5.3
Crude oil	2,235.6	11.8
Petroleum products	549.8	2.9
Manufactured goods	5,633.5	29.8
Heavy industrial & chemical products	4,590.0	24.3
Machinery	2,297.7	12.2
Chemicals	1,000.5	5.3
Other	1,291.9	6.8
Light industrial products	1,043.4	5.5
Textiles	314.5	1.7

Source: Ministry of Finance, Customs Statistics.

Structure of Japanese Imports by Origin, 1970

	$ million	%
Total	18,881.2	100.0
North America	6,488.5	34.4
U.S.A.	5,559.6	29.4
Western Europe	1,934.1	10.2
EEC	1,116.9	5.9
EFTA	750.2	4.0
Southeast Asia	3,013.2	16.0
West Asia	2,273.4	12.0
Latin America	1,373.2	7.3
Africa	1,098.7	5.8
Oceania	1,812.2	9.6
Communist countries	887.5	4.7
Advanced countries	10,429.5	55.2
Developing countries	7,563.7	40.1

Source: Ministry of Finance, Customs Statistics.

Contribution of Leading Industrial Nations to Expansion of Exports of Developing Countries

(In percent)

Exports to	Period	Developing countries total	Latin America	Africa	Southeast Asia	Middle East
Japan	1955–60	11.9	1.7	4.8	24.7	14.8
	1960–65	15.0	9.5	3.7	25.0	26.3
	1965–69	19.2	17.8	9.7	14.0	38.3
U.S.A.	1955–60	11.4	15.3	−3.4	15.6	6.6
	1960–65	8.8	−2.8	6.0	28.0	2.7
	1965–69	19.6	20.8	5.8	37.4	−0.6
Britain	1955–60	13.3	30.5	−0.6	8.4	18.4
	1960–65	2.6	−2.4	11.9	8.3	7.1
	1965–69	5.6	4.5	6.7	0.6	12.3
EEC	1955–60	28.8	57.6	48.3	−5.2	23.8
	1960–65	29.2	25.4	49.8	11.3	26.8
	1965–69	26.6	24.8	47.6	7.6	30.5

Note: Percentage share of increase in exports of developing countries to respective industrial country in total increase of exports of developing countries during period indicated.

Source: MITI, White Book on Trade, 1971.

Structure of Japan's Trade with Developing Countries, 1969

(In percent)

	Exports						Imports					
	Total	Developing countries	Africa	Latin America	Southeast Asia	Middle East	Total	Developing countries	Africa	Latin America	Southeast Asia	Middle East
Percentage composition of total	100.0	42.6	5.7	5.8	27.7	3.4	100.0	41.4	4.7	7.7	15.9	13.1
Percentage composition of trade with developing countries		100.0	12.6	13.0	60.7	8.0		100.0	10.9	18.6	36.8	30.8
Trade structure	100.0	100.0	100.0	100.0	100.0	100.0	100.0	100.0	100.0	100.0	100.0	100.0
Raw materials	4.6	5.6	0.9	0.9	7.1	1.8	69.4	86.2	47.2	85.9	86.4	98.9
Foods	3.6	4.3	0.9	0.7	5.3	1.6	14.3	13.0	9.5	28.3	14.0	0.6
Industrial raw materials	0.7	0.7	—	0.1	0.9	0.2	34.8	37.2	35.1	54.6	58.5	0.8
Fuels	0.3	0.6	—	0.1	0.9	—	20.3	36.0	2.6	3.0	13.9	97.5
Labor-intensive industrial products	24.4	22.2	16.1	16.8	22.5	35.2	4.7	2.6	0.1	1.0	5.6	0.8
Consumer goods	10.9	5.0	6.1	6.5	3.2	7.3	2.1	0.7	—	—	1.8	—
Producer goods	13.5	17.2	10.0	10.3	19.3	27.9	2.6	1.9	0.1	1.0	3.8	0.8
Capital-intensive industrial products	70.4	71.7	82.8	82.0	69.7	63.1	25.5	10.7	51.8	12.2	7.3	0.1
Consumer goods	19.9	11.9	7.1	14.4	11.3	14.5	2.4	0.1	—	0.1	0.2	—
Producer goods	24.9	24.9	10.5	31.2	27.0	25.0	13.3	10.0	50.3	11.1	6.4	0.1
Capital goods	25.6	34.9	65.2	36.4	31.4	22.6	9.8	0.6	1.5	1.0	0.7	—

Source: MITI, White Book on Trade, 1971.

Japan's Trade Balance with Developing Countries and Development Aid

Region	Year	Japanese exports $ million	Japanese imports $ million	Trade balance $ million	Development aid $ million	Ratio of development aid to trade balance %
Developing countries	1960	2,055.8	1,782.1	273.7	220.0	80.4
	1965	3,671.7	3,455.6	216.1	431.3	199.6
	1969	6,888.2	6,263.3	624.9	1,091.6	174.8
Africa	1960	294.8 (219.5)	106.4	188.4 (113.1)	−0.4	—
	1965	679.7 (315.7)	227.3	452.4 (88.4)	7.5	1.7 (8.5)
	1969	875.2 (407.9)	684.0	191.2 (−276.1)	56.2	29.4
Latin America	1960	304.4 (280.0)	311.3	−6.9 (−31.3)	51.4	—
	1965	487.8 (459.5)	707.3	−219.5 (−247.8)	89.4	—
	1969	943.9 (875.2)	1,162.4	−218.5 (−287.2)	77.3	—
Southeast Asia	1960	1,306.6	914.9	391.7	140.2	35.8
	1965	2,194.9	1,406.2	788.7	320.8	40.7
	1969	4,448.0	2,381.0	2,067.0	848.2	41.0
Middle East	1960	141.8	421.2 (15.0)	−279.4 (126.8)	28.6	— (22.6)
	1965	286.3	1,074.2 (37.5)	−787.9 (248.8)	13.2	— (5.3)
	1969	559.2	1,930.6 (62.9)	−1,371.4 (496.3)	109.1	— (22.0)

Notes: 1. Figures in parentheses: Africa—without ship exports to Liberia; Latin America—without ship exports to Panama; Middle East—without oil imports.

2. Trade on customs clearance basis; bilateral aid.

Source: MITI, White Book on Trade, 1971.

2 ROLE IN INTERNATIONAL FINANCE

1 PARTICIPATION IN INTERNATIONAL ORGANIZATIONS

In the euphoric optimism of the expansion prior to the "Nixon shock," Japanese bankers talked confidently about Tokyo as an emerging capital market. In 1969, Mitsubishi Bank predicted that a Tokyo dollar market would develop whether the government liked it or not and called on the government to promote this development by relaxing the world's "tightest exchange controls and restrictions on capital transactions." The confidence of the Japanese banking community was reinforced by the successful flotation of bonds of the World Bank and the Asian Development Bank and the first long-term impact (untied) loan to a foreign enterprise (Transocean Gulf) denominated in yen. The basic reason for this optimism was the change in Japan's position from a debtor to a creditor nation, which took place in 1968. In that year, the large ($2,529 million) favorable balance on trade account offset the deficits on services (−$1,306 million), transfer payments (−$175 million), and long-term capital trans-actions (−$239 million) and brought the overall balance to $1,102 million, the first time that the balance had exceeded the $1 billion mark (it had registered a deficit of −$571 million in the preceding year). The swing raised the value of long-term as well as short-term assets above that of liabilities and gave, for the first time in the postwar period, a favorable assets balance. As far as long-term capital transactions were concerned, the large increase in trade credit was mainly instrumental in creating a favorable balance. Foreign loans, foreign investment in Japanese securities, and bonds floated abroad represent the largest categories of long-term liabilities, whereas direct Japanese outward investment is higher than direct foreign investment in Japan.

For many years after the end of World War II, Japan was preoccupied with her domestic problems and her participation in international organizations was rather passive. Nonetheless, Japan has gained a strong position in some international bodies and has played a leading role in the establishment of the Asian Development Bank.

1 INTERNATIONAL MONETARY FUND

Japan joined the International Monetary Fund (IMF) and the Bank for Reconstruction and Development (World Bank) on August 13, 1952. Japan's IMF quota was originally fixed at $250 million. Following Japan's membership in the IMF, the par value of the yen was fixed, on May 11, 1953, at 2.46853 mg. of gold fine (¥360 = $1). Compared with the parity of ¥1 = 750 mg. of gold fine fixed in 1897 by the Currency Law (which constituted a devaluation of 50 percent compared with the value of the yen laid down in the New Currency Regulations of 1871, ¥1 = 1.500 mg. of gold), the value of the yen had decreased to about

1/307, but on the basis of the wholesale price index, the yen's purchasing power had declined to 1/770.

Due to Japan's precarious balance of payments position, the country was temporarily exempted from observing Article 8 of the IMF agreement prohibiting direct restrictions on payments based on current transactions.

On April 1, 1964, Japan assumed the obligations of Article 8, but retained restrictions on tourist travel.

At its annual meeting in September 1969, the IMF adopted the system of Special Drawing Rights (SDRs), which had been about five years in the making. The SDRs, often referred to as "paper gold," were meant to have a threefold function: to serve as an international standard (1 SDR = $1 = 0.888671 mg. of gold fine), to increase international liquidity (reserve assets), and to serve as a means of settlement. It was actually a halfway measure because the leading nations, particularly the Group of Ten that is often said to run the IMF, was not ready for an international currency and an international central bank.

Each of the 104 nations which participated in the first allocation of SDRs in January 1970 received 16.8 percent of their quota with the fund at the end of 1969. Japan's allocation amounted to $121.8 million, the seventh largest amount (the total allocation was $3,414 million). The general meeting also instructed the board of governors to study the advisability of increasing the fund's capital.

In December 1969, the IMF called for an increase by an average of 35 percent, but Japan's share was increased by 65.5 percent, bringing it from $725 million to $1.2 billion, which made Japan the fifth largest contributor (after the United States, Britain, West Germany, and France; Japan had asked for a share at least equal to that of France, $1.5 billion).

This entitled Japan to nominate an executive director (the five largest contributors each appoint one of the fund's twenty executive directors, the others are elected); the government chose Hideo Suzuki, a former bureau chief of the Ministry of Finance who was serving as director of the IMF and the World Bank. Since one-fourth of Japan's additional quota of $475 million had to be paid in gold and Japan's gold holdings at that time amounted to only $360 million, Japan purchased $100 million of gold from the United States, which IMF then redeposited with the United States. Payment was completed by October 31, 1970.

In September 1970, the IMF announced that it would sell $257,490,000 of gold and $67,510,000 in SDRs to acquire the currencies of twelve member nations. Japan was one of the countries whose currencies were purchased and thus was able to add $56,840,000 to its gold reserve (bringing it to $530 million). In the second allocation of SDRs in January 1971 (total $3 billion), Japan received $128.4 million. As of August 31, 1971, Japan's fund position in the IMF was as follows:

Subscription	$ million
Gold	300
Currency	900
Quota	1,200
SDRs	millions of SDRs
Allocations	
January 1, 1970	121.8

January 1, 1971	128.4
Net acquisitions	26.3
Holdings	276.5

	$ million
Net drawings or net fund sales of currency	− 189.8
Currency	710.2
Reserve position in fund	489.2
Gross fund position	1,689.9
Currency available for fund borrowing	250.0

In a new distribution of SDRs on January 2, 1972, Japan received an allocation of SDRs 127.2 million, equivalent to 10.5 percent of her quota in the fund.

In order to prevent a too rapid accumulation of foreign exchange, the Bank of Japan gave two yen loans of ¥36 billion ($100 million) each to the IMF, on February 12 and March 24, 1970; the yen were immediately changed into dollars. In June and July 1970, Japan took over $250 million in loans which Italy had lent to the IMF. This brought the fund's total borrowings from Japan to $440 million, $190 million under the general agreements to borrow (GAB) and $250 million under bilateral arrangements. The fund repaid $125 million of the bilateral loans in April 1971; in August 1971, the fund also repaid Japan $76 million which had been borrowed under the GAB. In another replenishment of the fund's currency holdings of fourteen members in August 1971, the fund sold $29,200,000 gold to Japan.

2 INTERNATIONAL BANK FOR RECONSTRUCTION AND DEVELOPMENT

In the latter part of the fifties and in the beginning of the sixties, loans from the Bank for Reconstruction and Development (World Bank) were an important source of funds for financing public works, notably railroad and road construction. A loan from the World Bank for the purchase of thermal generating equipment obtained in 1953 was the first long-term foreign loan after the war; the usual way of arranging these loans from the World Bank was for the Japan Development Bank to borrow from the World Bank and then to pass on the loans to the ultimate borrower. The usual conditions were an interest rate of 5.5 percent and a term of twenty-five years. Up to 1961, Japan had been given a total of $500 million in loans from the World Bank and the bank intimated to the Japanese authorities that it no longer considered Japan eligible for loans and would use its resources for financing projects in developing countries. But as late as 1966, the World Bank granted a $100 million loan for the construction of the Tomei Expressway (for which it had already given a loan of $75 million in 1963); total advances to Japan amounted to $857,041,004; as of October 30, 1971, the balance of outstanding loans to Japan was $459,619,794.

In 1970, the roles changed and Japan began to extend credit to the World Bank. On February 22, 1970, the Bank of Japan gave the World Bank a loan of ¥36 billion ($100 million) at 7.14 percent, repayable after a period of grace of three years in five equal installments in two years. A second loan in the same amount and under the same conditions was given on March 25, 1970. The Bank of Japan had already repaid $163 million of outstanding loans of the World Bank in advance.

Other loans of $100 million each were given by the Bank of Japan in January and March 1971; the last two loans carried an interest rate of 7.43 percent and were repayable in three equal installments in one year after a grace period of four years.

In June, an agreement was reached for the flotation of bonds in Japan between the World Bank and a Japanese syndicate of underwriters headed by Nomura Securities and a bank group led by the Industrial Bank of Japan. The issue had been planned for the World Bank's fiscal year 1972 (July 1971–June 1972), but was moved up to June 1971. The amount of the issue was ¥11 billion, the issue price ¥99.50 and the coupon rate 7.75 percent; this gave subscribers a yield of 7.839 percent. The bonds are redeemable at par in equal installments of ¥1.1 billion from 1977 through 1980 with a final installment of ¥6.6 billion payable on July 10, 1981. The conditions were somewhat more favorable than those for the bonds of the Asian Development Bank floated in December 1970, the first bonds issued in Japan by a foreign institution. Unlike the bonds of the Asian Development Bank, of which 80 percent was taken over by financial institutions, the bonds of the World Bank were offered to the public. The bonds will shortly be listed on the Tokyo Stock Exchange.

The World Bank had intended to float $50 million in bonds; in order to make up the difference, the Bank of Japan agreed to a loan of ¥7 billion at 7.43 percent, repayable in three installments between June 1975 and June 1976.

In November 1970, the World Bank established an office in Tokyo; the office is headed by Aritoshi Soejima, a former counselor to the secretariat of the minister of finance.

In January 1971, Japan completed payment of $250.4 million which brought Japan's total contribution to the bank to $1,230 million and made Japan the fifth largest contributor.

3. BANK FOR INTERNATIONAL SETTLEMENTS

Japan had been a member of the Bank for International Settlements (BIS) since its foundation in 1930 but had relinquished her rights in the Peace Treaty of San Francisco. She returned as an observer in 1961 but wanted to become a regular member. In 1969, the BIS decided to increase its capital and offer 200,000 new shares to Japan and Canada (which had also been an observer). The Bank of Japan, therefore, was readmitted to the BIS in January 1970, when it paid in 7.5 million Swiss francs, one-fourth of the face value of the shares. The stockholders of the BIS, which has developed from an agency handling Germany's reparations after World War I into an institution for international monetary cooperation, are the central banks of twenty-nine nations, not the governments. Strangely enough, the shares originally held by Japan were not owned by the Bank of Japan but by a syndicate of thirteen commercial and special banks; they were sold in October 1951.

4. ORGANIZATION FOR ECONOMIC COOPERATION AND DEVELOPMENT

The Organization for Economic Cooperation and Development (OECD) is not a financial institution but plays an important role in the liberalization of capital and trade. It is a successor institution to the Organization for European Economic Cooperation which administered the Marshall Plan. The Development Assistance Committee (DAC) mentioned above has promoted economic cooperation with the developing countries.

Japan joined the OECD on April 1, 1964, and although she agreed to the basic obligation of liberalizing capital movements, she was allowed to enter reservations on eighteen items of the liberalization code (which was rearranged in July 1964). Since the complete liberalization of capital movements would presuppose a more or less complete economic integration, the OECD's code distinguishes two categories: category A, items for which reservations are allowed when joining the OECD, but for which no new reservations can be made later without special reason, and category B, items for which reservations can be added or canceled. Japan entered nine complete or partial reservations with regard to the twenty-seven items on List A, and nine with regard to the ten items on List B. Details are given below.

List A	List B
Direct inward capital investment by foreigners	Flotation of foreign bonds by Japanese
Direct outward foreign investment by Japanese	Flotation of bonds by foreigners in Japan
	*Purchase and sale of unlisted securities by foreigners
*Purchase and sale by foreigners of securities listed on Japanese exchanges	*Purchase and sale of unlisted securities by Japanese
*Purchase and sale by Japanese of securities listed on foreign exchanges	Acquisition of real estate by foreigners in Japan
*Acceptance of foreign trade (export-import) credit	Acquisition of real estate by Japanese abroad
*Granting of foreign trade (export-import) credit	Granting of credit for triangular trade (trade between third countries)
*Loans among family members	Acceptance of financial credit
*Gifts	Granting of financial credit
*Right of emigrants to take their assets with them when leaving the country	

*: partial reservation.

As explained above, certain controls have been lifted but a great many restrictions remain. Japanese officials who can no longer appeal to the country's precarious balance-of-payments position as a reason for retaining outdated restrictions now cite the necessity of preventing unwanted inflows of short-term capital and the possibility of tax evasion as reasons for keeping capital movements under strict control.

5 ASIAN DEVELOPMENT BANK

The establishment of an Asian Development Bank was first proposed by a three-man committee organized on the basis of a resolution adopted by the United Nation's Economic Commission for Asia and the Far East (ECAFE) in 1960 and reaffirmed by a seven-member committee in 1963. Based on the report of a committee of experts, ECAFE decided to establish the Asian Development Bank (ADB) in its twenty-first session in 1965. The inaugural meeting of the board of governors was held in Tokyo in November 1966; Manila was chosen as the site of the head office of the bank, which started its business on December 19, 1966.

ADB's original members were the eighteen countries represented in ECAFE and twelve nonregional members; admission of new members requires the consent of two-thirds of three-fourths of the total voting power of the member nations. The authorized capital of the bank had been fixed at $1.1 billion which had been divided into $550 million in paid-in shares and $550 million in callable shares. Payment of 50 percent of the subscriptions to the original paid-in capital had to be made in gold or convertible currency and 50 percent in the currency of the member. Regional members were to subscribe to at least 60 percent of the authorized capital, nonregional members to 40 percent. Actual subscriptions originally amounted to $965 million of which regional members contributed $615 million and nonregional members $350 million. With $200 million each, Japan and the United States were the largest subscribers among the regional and nonregional members, respectively. Member countries now number thirty-six.

The organization of the bank largely followed the pattern of the Inter-American Development Bank. The decision-making organ of the ADB is the board of governors on which each member is represented by a governor and an alternate, but the voting power is based on a system which gives each member an equal number (778) of basic votes and an additional number of proportional votes (one vote for $10,000) equal to the number of shares held by that member. A board of directors is responsible for the direction of the general operations of the bank; it is composed of ten members of whom seven are elected by the governors representing regional members and three by the governors representing nonregional members. The president of the bank, who must be a national of a regional member, is elected by the board of governors for a term of four years. The first president was Takeshi Watanabe, former adviser to the Japanese Ministry of Finance; he was reelected to a second term in April 1971.

The funds of the bank are divided into ordinary capital resources, i.e. authorized capital and funds raised by borrowing which are to be used for financing on a commercial basis, special funds up to 10 percent of the paid-in capital which can be used for soft loans, and special funds placed under the administration of the bank by member countries. The bank now operates two funds belonging to the last category: the multipurpose special fund and the technical assistance fund.

In 1970, the ADB raised a loan of 130 million Austrian schilling through a consortium led by Creditanstalt Bankverein. In April 1971, an agreement was reached with Kuhn, Loeb & Co. and the First Boston Corporation to float $25 million worth of bonds and an equal amount of notes in the United States. Three Swiss banks, the Union Bank of Switzerland, the Swiss Bank Corporation, and Crédit Suisse, underwrote a bond issue of S. francs 40 million. The issue price was S. francs 99, the interest rate 7 percent, and maturity fifteen years. The bonds were offered to the public in denominations of S. francs 1,000 and 5,000.

As mentioned above, the ADB was the first foreign institution to float bonds in Japan. The first bond issue amounting to ¥6 billion was agreed on in November 1970. The issue price was ¥99 and the coupon rate 7.4 percent, giving the subscriber a yield of 7.619 percent. The bonds will mature in seven years, but redemption will start in 1973. The four leading securities firms, Nomura, Daiwa, Nikko, and Yamaichi acted as underwriters, the Bank of Tokyo, Fuji Bank, and the Industrial Bank took over the sale of the bonds and the Industrial Bank was to handle payment of interest and principal. A second bond issue, agreed upon in October 1971, amounted to ¥10 billion; conditions were less favorable, issue price ¥99.75 and interest rate 7.4 percent, thus reducing the yield rate to 7.454 percent. On December 1,

1971, ADB offered a bond issue of 400 million Belgian francs with an interest rate of 7.5 percent and a maturity of twelve years. The issue was underwritten by five Belgian banks. ADB planned to issue a total of $20 million in short-term (1 year) dollar bonds to be taken over by the governments of the region so as to increase the dollar holdings of the countries in the area.

In February 1970, Representative Otto Passman fiercely damned ADB's management, summing up his castigation with the exclamation: "I think this is the most mismanaged outfit I have ever had anything to do with!" The main findings which aroused Passman's ire were these. Although the bank had assets of $452 million, less than $140 million in loans had been approved. In more than three years of operations, the bank had disbursed only $9.3 million against loan commitments but had spent $11.6 million for administrative expenses. The bank had 438 people on the payroll, not counting the top executives. The U.S. Export-Import Bank, with six times its assets, had only 364 employees. At the end of 1969, ADB had a total of $129,363 outstanding in personal loans at 5 percent to seventy-seven members of its staff under a "compassionate loan" program designed to assist employees to get settled in Manila; an additional $178,000 had been repaid during 1969. Income reported for 1969 amounted to $12.9 million, but less than 2 percent came from interest, the rest coming from investment income. Administrative expenses were $5.6 million, about 45 percent of the income. In contrast, the U.S. Export-Import Bank spends only 5 percent on overheads. The bank reported $44,000 for entertainment expenses, up from $24,000 in the preceding year. What particularly angered Congressman Passman, the Democratic Representative from Louisiana,was that ADB had $100 million invested in American securities and yet borrowed additional money.

The House Banking and Currency Committee, without refuting Mr. Passman's allegations, declared that there was no basis for criticism of the bank's activities and recommended congressional approval of a U.S. contribution of $100 million for the bank's special funds to be used for concessional lending. Not mentioned were ADB's numerous and costly surveys and missions which are of dubious value. While a bank should check the data submitted by its customers, the formulation of technical programs by a financial institution is a highly questionable procedure.

In 1970, a Philippine newspaper reported that Filipino officials had discussed with other Asian diplomats the idea of setting up a regional development bank from which Japan would be excluded, and Rep. Gary Brown (R-Mich.), on his way to ADB's fourth annual meeting in Singapore in April 1971, was quoted as having said: "Member countries of the ADB have asked the United States to take greater interest in counterbalancing Japanese influence in the bank's affairs."

In the five years from its foundation until the end of 1971, ADB lent a total of $638,460.000. The bank's advances comprised fifty-seven conventional and twenty-eight concessional loans for eighty-one different projects in sixteen member countries. Moreover, technical assistance valued at $8,080,950 was provided for projects in sixteen member countries.

Bond and note issues added about $160 million to ADB's loanable funds. Bonds amounting to $122 million were floated in Austria, Belgium, Japan, Switzerland, and the United States. The board of governors approved an increase in the bank's capital which is to be raised to $2,750 million.

6 THE PRIVATE INVESTMENT COMPANY FOR ASIA, S.A. (PICA)

The Private Investment Company for Asia, S.A. (PICA) was founded in February 1969 with a capital of $16.8 million. American and Japanese interests took over one-third each of the capital; the other third was subscribed to by enterprises from Australia, Canada, Britain, France, West Germany, Italy, Sweden, and Norway. Subscriptions range from $100,000 to $400,000. The company's legal domicile is Panama, but most of the actual business is done in Tokyo. PICA was sponsored by the Federation of Asian Chambers of Commerce and Industry and inspired by ADELA, the investment bank for Latin America.

Although Japan is the only Asian country represented by stockholders, the company has formed a consultative committee to get the views of Asian countries. PICA's main business is the promotion of economic development in Asian countries by investing in promising private undertakings. So far, PICA's main investments have been in Malaysia and Indonesia. In 1970, PICA joined with Malaysian and Indian interests in investing in India Malaysia Textile Berhad; in July 1971, the company acquired M$3 million worth of shares in the Kuala Lumpur Hilton Hotel. In May 1971, the company decided to invest $4,624,000 in cable, steel tube, and glass container manufacturing in Indonesia, $1,914,000 in chemicals and shipping in the Philippines, and $1,500,000 in an integrated textile mill in Taiwan. In July 1971, PICA joined with Continental International Finance Corporation, Nikko Securities, and Banque de l'Indochine in the China Investment and Trust Co., Ltd. of Taipei.

An international syndicate including the Bank of America, First National City Bank, four Japanese banks (Tokyo, Mitsui, Sumitomo, and Sanwa) and other banks with branches in Singapore will give PICA an "Asian dollar" loan of $10 million for four years. The interest rate is still undecided but may be 0.75 percent higher than the 6-month rate on Eurodollars. The Bank of America will act as the manager of the syndicate.

Net Increase or Decrease in Long-Term Capital

(In millions of dollars)

Year	Total	Direct investment	Trade credits	Loans	Securities	Foreign bonds	Other
Assets							
1962	309	78	195	12	0		24
1963	298	122	104	61	—		11
1964	451	56	337	49	—		9
1965	446	77	243	115	0		11
1966	706	107	401	149	1		48
1967	875	123	481	221	4		46
1968	1,096	220	586	237	3		50
1969	1,508	206	674	336	1		291
1970	2,031	355	787	628	62		199
Liabilities							
1962	481	45	36	269	59	72	—
1963	765	88	58	383	114	153	−31
1964	558	83	82	255	16	154	−32
1965	31	47	−9	18	−61	72	−36
1966	−102	30	−30	−18	−25	−25	−34
1967	63	45	−32	29	70	−13	−36
1968	857	76	−15	478	229	119	−30
1969	1,353	72	3	385	730	200	−37
1970	440	94	7	80	252	44	−37

Foreign Balance

(In millions of dollars)

	End of 1962	End of 1965	End of 1968	End of 1970	May 1971	June 1971	September 1971	December 1971 (estimate)
Assets								
Long-term assets	4,534	7,667	11,995	19,881	23,695	24,516	30,336	31,715
Direct investment	1,476	2,714	5,168	8,745	9,658	9,868	10,425	11,200
Deferred payments for exports	393	639	1,087	1,647	1,801	1,835	1,920	2,050
Loans	633	1,315	2,775	4,270	4,657	4,715	4,960	5,300
Investment in securities	64	287	893	1,859	2,160	2,235	2,346	2,450
Contributions to international agencies	0	0	0	69	82	120	155	200
Other assets	386	327 / 146	413	371 / 529	958	963	614 / 430	700 / 500
Short-term assets	3,058	4,953	6,827	11,136	14,037	14,648	19,911	20,515
Foreign exchange banks	1,155	3,015	3,828	6,599	7,037	6,965	6,443	5,200
Other private assets	62	41	108	84	84	84	84	80
Foreign exchange reserves	1,841	1,899	2,891	4,399	6,916	7,599	13,384	15,235
Assets of government & Bank of Japan	—	—	—	56	0	0	0	0
Liabilities								
Long-term liabilities	5,198	8,559	10,984	14,089	15,721	16,055	18,020	18,340
Direct investment	2,428	4,144	4,717	6,326	7,261	7,400	7,612	7,540
Deferred payments for imports	274	522	651	837	895	901	1,019	1,050
Foreign bonds	37	162	81	103	101	101	99	100
Loans	327	708	789	1,033	1,068	1,064	1,066	1,070
Investment in securities	1,144	1,703	2,403	2,654	2,690	2,696	2,670	2,670
Reparations	156	231	504	1,485	2,312	2,443	2,563	2,670
GARIOA, EROA	490	389	289	214	195	195	195	200
Short-term liabilities	2,770	4,415	6,267	7,763	8,460	8,655	10,408	10,800
Foreign exchange banks	1,854	3,452	4,617	5,539	5,881	5,803	6,791	6,800
Other private liabilities	336	614	1,296	2,224	2,507	2,631	3,181	3,500
Liabilities of government & Bank of Japan	580	349	354	0	72	221	436	500
Net assets	−664	−892	1,011	5,792	7,974	8,461	12,316	13,375

2 ROLE IN INTERNATIONAL FINANCE

2 OVERSEAS OPERATION OF JAPANESE FINANCIAL INSTITUTIONS

In prewar times, Japan's official foreign exchange bank, the Yokohama Specie Bank, as well as some of the major commercial banks possessed overseas branches. After the war, the government favored the Bank of Tokyo in the allocation of foreign branches (the Bank of Tokyo has almost as many overseas branches as all other banks together); it was only in the sixties that the rapid expansion of Japan's foreign trade induced the Ministry of Finance to allow more foreign branches. The close cooperation between banks, trading companies, and manufacturers naturally extends to foreign business, and the customers of a particular bank prefer to deal with a representative of that bank wherever they do business. Until recently, European banks generally relied on correspondent banks for the largest part of their foreign business (this does not apply to the former British and French colonies); American banks are following the foreign business of American firms, but the pattern of cooperation differs greatly from the Japanese way of doing business for which the domestic group affiliations and the relations with the trading companies are very important.

Financing of foreign trade was the main objective of the establishment of foreign branches, but with the development of the Eurodollar market, the induction of foreign capital gained in importance. In recent years, the banks have evinced increasing interest in the investment business while the securities companies have established foreign subsidiaries or foreign branches for underwriting and investment in foreign securities.

The main forms the banks use for establishing themselves abroad are branch offices, representative offices, subsidiaries, participation in foreign banks, in international finance companies, and in consortium banking which began around 1964. Branches can engage in the usual banking operations while representative offices are not allowed to accept deposits or give loans and must restrict their activities to liaison, information, and negotiations. Due to the banking legislation of the State of New York, Japanese banks do not set up branches but "agencies" (the Bank of Tokyo and the Industrial Bank have a joint subsidiary in New York, called The Bank of Tokyo Trust Co). On account of the restrictions on the deposit business of foreign branches, Japanese banks applied for permission to set up subsidiaries in California (Mitsubishi Bank, Sanwa Bank) and Chicago (Dai-Ichi Kangyo Bank). Australia banned the foundation of branches or subsidiaries of foreign banks within its borders in 1941; Japanese banks, therefore, have bought into Australian financial institutions. In December 1971, six Japanese trust banks (Mitsubishi, Mitsui, Sumitomo, Yasuda, Toyo, and Chuo) established a joint representative office in New York, comprising a representative of each of the six firms.

The greatest conglomeration of foreign branches and representative offices is found in

London where, in addition to an office of the Bank of Japan, fourteen banks and five securities companies are represented, the second largest foreign group after the Americans. London also hosts the offices of thirty-five Japanese trading companies, ten manufacturers of electrical machinery, ten shipping companies, fourteen shipbuilding and engineering companies, and nine insurance companies. As of the end of 1970, the number of representatives of Japanese banks, trading companies, and manufacturers (not included are news media, students, etc., but family members residing abroad are included) permanently stationed abroad amounted to 38,747; the largest contingent was living in the United States (11,965), followed by Thailand (2,848), West Germany (2,410), Britain (1,828), Hong Kong (1,485), and Australia (1,468). Japanese business representatives (including family members) were most numerous in New York (6,470); next came Bangkok, London, Los Angeles, and Hong Kong. A few examples of the size of foreign representation are given below.

	Number of offices	Number of representatives
Mitsui & Co.	102	779
Mitsubishi Corporation	78	633
C. Itoh & Co.	95	510
Bank of Tokyo	66	332
Fuji Bank	8	60
Japan Air Lines	53	465
Nippon Yusen Kaisha (NYK)	26	70
Japan Travel Bureau	7	33
Ishikawajima-Harima Heavy Industries	21	70
Sony Corporation	15	150

Notes: 1. Offices include branches, representative offices, and subsidiaries; Japanese employees permanently assigned to foreign offices only.
2. As of December 31, 1970.

In violation of a basic principle of modern law, territoriality, the Ministry of Finance imposed severe restrictions on the operations of foreign branches of Japanese banks. Initially, the restrictions were motivated by considerations of Japan's balance of payments position, later by considerations of monetary policy. The main restrictions were ceilings on loans and loan guarantees given overseas by overseas branches. The loans were chiefly to trading companies and foreign subsidiaries of Japanese enterprises; the loan guarantees, for loans granted by foreign banks to foreign subsidiaries of Japanese firms. The reason for the restrictions is clear; the credit of the foreign branches is backed up by the home office, but this does not change the fact that the Japanese government has no right to control business operations conducted entirely on foreign territory. Naturally, the Japanese deny that they do any such thing; the "administrative guidance" is given to the Japanese banks who then "voluntarily" instruct their overseas branches to observe the ceilings fixed by the Bank of Japan—not as fixed by the Bank of Japan but as fixed by the home office. It is "perfectly legal" procedures like these which have earned the Japanese a reputation for duplicity. The actual ceilings, based on "administrative guidance" by the Bank of Japan, were kept secret; specific approval was required for all loans for longer than six months. The ceiling on lending and guarantees was raised by about 10 percent in January 1970, bringing the total loan limit of the foreign branches of the foreign exchange banks to $792 million, and the ceiling on guarantees to $244 million. On February 25, 1970, "automatic" approval was substituted for "specific" approval of loans with a maturity exceeding six months, and, on August 1, all restrictions on the amounts which could be lent or guaranteed by the overseas branches of the foreign exchange banks were abolished. At about the same time, controls on the borrowing of Eurodollars and other short-term funds by Japanese banks were relaxed; the limitations on funds brought into Japan were replaced by limitations on the differential between inflows and outflows. The reason for these controls was that the deposits with the foreign branches of Japanese banks were transferred to the home offices and deposited in free-yen accounts which, together with Eurodollar and other short-term funds borrowed through the foreign branches and converted into yen, were used for domestic lending.

The most notable development was the entry of Japanese banks into international financing. The Bank of Tokyo became the first by setting up, in 1968, Banque Européenne de Tokyo S.A. Of the initial capital of Fr. francs 25 million, the Bank of Tokyo owned 80 percent, and Bank of Tokyo Holding 20 percent. In August 1970, the capital of Banque Européenne de Tokyo was increased to Fr. francs 75 million and the three long-term credit banks and three city banks (Kyowa, Kobe, and Saitama) were given shares in the bank. The Bank of Tokyo and the Industrial Bank now own Fr. francs 22.2 million (30 percent) each, Bank of Tokyo Holding Fr. francs 11 million (15 percent), and the other five banks Fr. francs 19.5 million (25 percent). At the same time, the capital of the Bank of Tokyo Holding was increased to $3 million of which the Bank of Tokyo owns 80 percent and the Industrial Bank 20 percent.

On December 11, 1970, four city banks (Sanwa, Kangyo, Mitsui, and Dai-Ichi), together with Nomura Securities Co., established the Associated Japanese Bank (International) Ltd. The capital of the bank is £3.5 million to which each of the five participants contributed in the form of subordinate loans of £700,000 each. The London-based bank will raise long- and medium-term funds on the European capital market for investment in overseas ventures of Japanese enterprises. The bank obtained a license as an authorized bank in April 1971.

A third investment bank was established, also in London, on December 17, 1970. This was the Japan International Bank; to its capital of £3.6 million, four city banks (Fuji, Mitsubishi, Sumitomo, and Tokai) each contributed £720,000, and three securities companies (Daiwa, Nikko, and Yamaichi) each £240,000. The foundation of the bank was held up by a dispute on the interpretation of Article 65 of the Securities Transaction Law which limits the underwriting of securities to securities companies. The securities companies contended that this article should also apply to the activities of the London bank (which is typical of the muddled legal thinking caused by the authorities' habit of regulating the activities of foreign subsidiaries of Japanese enterprises). The Ministry of Finance decided that Article 65 would not apply to foreign foundations, but in order to placate the securities companies the city banks agreed that, "for the time being," the bank would not act as underwriter but limit its activities to other forms of raising capital for investment in foreign businesses of Japanese firms.

Fuji Bank agreed with Banco America do Sul of São Paulo (in which Fuji owns a 12.6 percent interest) to set up an investment bank in Brazil. The South American Trust Bank (a subsidiary of Banco America do Sul in which Fuji also owns 11.11 percent of the capital) will become the nucleus of the new bank which will also absorb four minor Brazilian investment companies. Fuji Bank will contribute 40 percent of the capital of 25 million cruzeiros, Banco America do Sul, its affiliates, and other investors the remaining 60 percent.

In January 1971, the Bank of Tokyo announced its participation in the establishment of an international finance bank for promoting trade with Communist countries. The foundation, Centropa Finanzierung-Vermittlungs Handels-Treuhand G.m.b.H., has a capital of 7 million Austrian schilling, contributed in equal shares by the Bank of Tokyo and six European banks: Bank für Arbeit and Wirtschaft A.G. (of Austria), Banco di Sicilia (of Italy), Banque Occidentale pour l'Industrie et le Commerce (of France), Bank Kleinwort, Benson (of Britain), Banco Popular Español (of Spain), and Bank Handlowy Warszawie S.A. (of Poland).

The Industrial Bank of Japan signed a contract in March 1971 for participation in the Rothschild Intercontinental Bank, an international investment bank organized by the Rothschild group and three American Banks. The Industrial Bank acquired an interest of £1,035,000, equal to 12.5 percent of the undertaking. In July 1971, the Long-Term Credit Bank was authorized to buy 5 percent of the stock of Manufacturers Hanover Ltd. of Britain, a subsidiary of the American bank of the same name, for providing clients with medium- and long-term Eurodollar loans.

In the last three years, Japanese banks have acquired shares in eight financial institutions set up in Australia, causing the opposition Labor Party to speak out against the "financial invasion" of Australia by Japanese banks. The Bank of Tokyo is interested in two institutions, Partnership Pacific Limited and Beneficial Finance Corporation. In November 1970, Mitsubishi Bank joined four other banks, the Australia and New Zealand Banking Group, Bank of Montreal, Crocker-Citizens National Bank of San Francisco, and Irving Trust Co. of New York, which had established Australian International Finance Corporation in June of that year for financing development projects in Australia and the Pacific basin. The capital of the firm was increased by one-fourth to give each partner a 20 percent share.

Sanwa Bank acquired a 14.66 percent share in Commercial Continental Bank which had been set up by Australian, American, British, and French interests in July 1970 (Commercial Banking of Sidney, Mutual and Citizens Insurance, Continental Illinois National Bank and Trust Co. of Chicago, Crown Agents, and Crédit Commercial).

An international group of seven banks cooperated in the foundation of Euro-Pacific Finance Corporation, organized in 1970 with an authorized capital of A$20 million and a paid-up capital of A$2.5 million. The bank does not accept deposits but is engaged in supplying capital for development and industrial projects in Australia and will eventually serve the entire Pacific area. The shares of the partners in the capital of the bank are: the Commercial Bank of Australia, 25 percent; Midland Bank, Fuji Bank, and United California Bank International, 15 percent each; Deutsche Bank, Amsterdam-Rotterdam Bank, and Société Générale de Banque, 10 percent each.

Tokai Bank joined Australian, American, and French interests in establishing Patrick Intermarine (Australia) Ltd., which will finance the development of mineral resources in Australia and also engage in the underwriting and sale of securities as well as consulting. Patrick Partners of Sidney and the Marine Midland Bank of New York each contributed 20 percent of the capital, Tokai Bank and L'Union Européenne Industrielle et Financière 10 percent, and other Australian securities companies the remaining 40 percent.

The Industrial Bank of Japan took over the share of Lazard Brothers of Britain which withdrew from Australian United Corporation, an enterprise set up in 1953 by Morgan Guaranty Trust, Morgan Grenfell, Lazard Brothers, Australian United Investment, Jan Potter, and the Bank of New South Wales.

In August 1971, Dai-Ichi Bank and Nomura Securities Co. applied for approval to acquire a 2.5 percent interest each in the Merchant Bank and the Development Finance Corporation as well as to participate in the foundation of a new investment bank to whose capital (A$1 million) Development Finance Corporation will contribute 60 percent and Dai-Ichi Kangyo Bank and Nomura Securities each 20 percent. Dai-Ichi's move was prompted by the establishment of an Australian subsidiary of the Furukawa group (Furukawa Australian Development Co.), which relies for financial support on Dai-Ichi Kangyo Bank. This was the second foreign venture in which Nomura, which used to have close ties with Sanwa and Mitsui banks, joined with Dai-Ichi.

In December 1970, the formation of trust banks became possible in Taiwan, and Japanese institutions were invited to participate in the foundation of the first trust bank set up by Taiwanese securities companies with a capital of NT$200 million. Nippon Kangyo Bank subscribed to 10 percent of the capital and Nikko Securities Co. to 3 percent.

Not only the banks but also the securities companies have been very eager to establish foreign offices and participate in foreign ventures. The most significant development may have been the admission of four Japanese securities firms to the Boston Stock Exchange. On November 25, 1969, the exchange admitted Yoshio Terasawa, executive vice-president of Nomura Securities International Inc., the first Japanese to sign the Boston Exchange Constitution (in Chinese characters) as he took possession of the seat and paid $14,000. Nomura Securities International Inc. started in 1953 as the New York branch office of the mother firm and became a wholly owned subsidiary in 1969. It operates branch offices in Los Angeles and Honolulu. Nomura had chosen Boston because the New York Stock Exchange does not accept membership applications from foreign securities firms. Boston already had three foreign members (German, French, and Swiss). On January 12, 1970, the American subsidiaries of the remaining three of the "Big Four" Japanese securities firms, (Yamaichi Securities Co. of New York, Inc., Daiwa Securities Co. America, Inc., and Nikko Securities Co. International Inc.) likewise purchased (also at $14,000) seats on the Boston Exchange. On November 30, 1970, these three firms were also admitted to the Pacific Coast Stock Exchange. All four, Nomura, Yamaichi, Nikko, and Daiwa, have established joint ventures in Hong Kong.

Initially, the main foreign operations of the Japanese securities companies were connected with the flotation of debentures or the sale of shares of Japanese enterprises (e.g., a convertible debenture issue of C. Itoh & Co. and issues of European Depository Receipts of Olympus Optical Co. and Sanyo Electric Co.), but in the beginning of 1971 the Ministry of Finance stopped all foreign issues in order to slow down the accumulation of foreign exchange. The securities firms, therefore, tried to participate in issues of foreign enterprises. From October 1970 to September 1971, the four large securities firms handled 322 underwriting contracts; their business volume from these contracts was $49.6 million, more than double the amount in the preceding year. In the two months of October and November, underwriting contracts numbered 111, with $23.3 million of business.

In May 1971, the Tokio Marine and Fire Insurance Co. formed a British subsidiary, Tokio Marine and Life Insurance Co. (U.K.) Ltd., with a capital of £250,000. The firm underwrites marine and aviation insurance through the agency of Willis, Faber, and Dumas.

Japanese banks extended their overseas activities also to related fields. Sanwa Bank acquired a 5.3 percent interest in Euro-Finance, an economic and investment research organization, and the Industrial Bank of Japan participated in the foundation of Diebold Group International, Inc., sponsored by the Diebold Group, Inc., an American management consultant firm. The international subsidiary was incorporated in Liberia and was to operate in Asia, Africa, Oceania, the Middle East, and Latin America.

Foreign Branches of Japanese Banks
December 31, 1970

	Branches	Agencies	Rep. offices
Dai-Ichi Bank	2	1	3
Daiwa Bank	2	1	1
Fuji Bank	2	1	4
Hokkaido Takushoku Bank	—	—	1
Bank of Kobe	2	1	1
Kyowa Bank	—	—	1
Mitsubishi Bank	4	2	2
Mitsui Bank	5	1	1
Nippon Kangyo Bank	3	1	2
Saitama Bank	—	—	1
Sanwa Bank	4	1	2
Sumitomo Bank	3	1	3
Tokai Bank	2	1	2
Bank of Tokyo	28	—	31

Note: The Bank of Tokyo has 11 affiliated and associated banks in the United States, Europe, and Australia; new branches or subsidiaries are planned in the Netherlands, Italy, and New Zealand.

New branch offices approved by the Ministry of Finance in January 1971 were: Dai-Ichi Bank—Chicago, Fuji Bank—Zurich, Mitsubishi Bank—Los Angeles, Sanwa Bank—San Francisco.

The trust banks have set up a joint representative office in New York.

Participation of Japanese Banks
in Australian Financial Institutions

Financial institution	Location	Capital	Japanese banks	Share	Date of participation
Partnership Pacific Ltd.	Sidney	A$6 million	Bank of Tokyo	33.33%	Feb. 1969
Beneficial Finance Corporation	Adelaide	A$5,555,000	Bank of Tokyo	20.4%	Aug. 1970
Australian International Finance Corporation	Melbourne	A$6,220,000	Mitsubishi B.	20%	Nov. 1970
Commercial Continental Ltd.	Sidney	A$5 million	Sanwa Bank	14.66%	Dec. 1970
Euro-Pacific Finance Corporation	Melbourne	A$2,500,000	Fuji Bank	15%	Jan. 1971
Patrick Intermarine (Australia) Ltd.	Sidney	A$2 million	Tokai Bank	10%	Feb. 1971
Australia United Corporation	Melbourne	A$4,024,000	Industrial B.	4%	Mar. 1971

Participation of Japanese Banks in Foreign Financial Institutions

Foreign institutions	Location	Capital	Japanese bank	Share	Date of participation
Bank of Tokyo of Calif.	Los Angeles	$9.9 million	Bank of Tokyo	52.11%	Feb. 1953
Bank of Tokyo Trust Co.	New York	$16,279,000	Bank of Tokyo	70.11%	Oct. 1955
			Industrial Bank	29.81%	
Iran-Japan Int'nal Bank	Teheran	$2,572,000	Bank of Tokyo	30%	Oct. 1959
Chicago-Tokyo Bank	Chicago	$2,320,000	Bank of Tokyo	4.91%	Apr. 1964
Banco São Paulo-Tokyo S.A.	São Paulo	$146,000	Bank of Tokyo	100%	May 1965
Banque Européenne de Tokyo S.A.	Paris	Fr. francs 25 million	Bank of Tokyo	80%	Aug. 1968
			B. of T. Holding	20%	
		Fr. francs 75 million	Bank of Tokyo	30%	Aug. 1970
			Industrial Bank	30%	
			B. of T. Holding	15%	
			Long-Term Credit B.	5%	
			Japan Hypothec Bank	5%	
			Kyowa Bank	5%	
			Kobe Bank	5%	
			Saitama Bank	5%	
Bank of Tokyo Holding	Luxemburg	$3 million	Bank of Tokyo	80%	Nov. 1968
			Industrial Bank	20%	
B. of Tokyo (Schweiz) A.G.	Zurich	$4,574,000	Bank of Tokyo	99.9%	July 1971
Centropa Finanzierung-Vermittlung Handels-Treuhand G.m.b.H.	Wien	Austrian schilling 7 million	Bank of Tokyo	1/7	Jan. 1971
B. of Tokyo (Holland) N.V.	Amsterdam	G12 million	Bank of Tokyo		Mar. 1972
Banco America do Sul	São Paulo	$4,840,000	Fuji Bank	12.6%	Oct. 1940
S. American Trust Bank	São Paulo	$1,239,000	Fuji Bank	11.11%	Dec. 1961
Ind'l Development B.	São Paulo	$7,349,000	Fuji Bank	4.25%	Feb. 1967
Sumitomo Bank of Calif.	San Francisco	$8,050,000	Sumitomo Bank	57.27%	Nov. 1952
Central Pacific Bank	Honolulu	$2,250,000	Sumitomo Bank	15%	Feb. 1953
Banco Sumitomo Brasiliero	São Paulo	$1,220,000	Sumitomo Bank	100%	Oct. 1958
Tosan Bank	São Paulo	$1,951,000	Mitsubishi Bank	40%	1933
Chekiang First Bank	Hong Kong	$1,701,000	Dai-Ichi Bank	33.33%	Aug. 1950
Banco Finansa	São Paulo	$5 million	Industrial Bank	4.76%	July 1958
Associated Japanese Bank (International) Ltd.	London	£3.5 mill.	Sanwa Bank	20%	Dec. 1970
			Kangyo Bank	20%	
			Mitsui Bank	20%	
			Dai-Ichi Bank	20%	
			Nomura Securities	20%	
Japan International Bank Ltd.	London	£3.6 mill.	Fuji Bank	20%	Dec. 1970
			Mitsubishi Bank	20%	
			Sumitomo Bank	20%	
			Tokai Bank	20%	
			Daiwa Securities	6.67%	
			Nikko Securities	6.67%	
			Yamaichi Securities	6.67%	
First Pacific B. of Ch.	Chicago	$2 million	Dai-Ichi Kangyo B.	98.8%	Jan. 1972
Mitsubishi Bank of Calif.	Los Angeles	$3 million	Mitsubishi Bank		June 1972

2 ROLE IN INTERNATIONAL FINANCE

3 FOREIGN BANKS IN JAPAN

The first foreign banks which opened offices in Japan after the war chiefly served the needs of the occupation forces, but in December 1949 they were given a business license based on the Bank Law which enabled them to engage in ordinary banking business. They were also recognized as authorized foreign exchange banks under the Foreign Exchange and Foreign Trade Control Law of 1949 and, in the absence of overseas branches of Japanese banks, were practically the only channels for Japan's transactions with the outside world. They played an important role in the induction of foreign capital and the transmission of information. For many years, the foreign banks had almost a monopoly on import usances, but their share declined from 91 percent in 1965 to 69 percent in 1970. The foreign banks in Japan were particularly helpful in times of large deficits in the balance of payments because they were able to arrange substantial impact (untied) loans.

The banking license given to foreign banks does not cover savings, trust business, and secured corporate debentures. They do not belong to the Federation of Bankers Associations and are not bound by the "voluntary" interest rates of the federation, but they must observe the interest ceilings on loans fixed under the Temporary Money Rates Adjustment Law and the guidelines of the Bank of Japan on deposits. They can give no loans under a year, and their loan volume (including loans in foreign currency) is also regulated. As in the case of the Japanese banks, a ceiling is fixed on the increase in free-yen deposits and on foreign exchange holdings. They are practically shut out from the money market because they need case by case permission for lending in the call money market—Japan is probably the only major industrial country enforcing such a restriction.

In addition to banking, foreign banks have branched out into peripheral business such as credit cards, leasing, and consulting, The Union Bank of Switzerland established an investment consulting firm and, as mentioned above, First National City Bank set up a joint consulting firm with Fuji Bank.

In addition to foreign banks, three American securities firms have opened offices in Japan: Merrill Lynch, Pierce, Fenner, and Smith, Arthur Lipper Corporation, and Burnham & Co. Japan enacted a special law regulating the business of foreign underwriters and securities dealers (the Japanese expression used in the title of the law, *Gaikoku Shōken Gyōsha ni Kansuru Hōritsu*, includes individuals and companies engaged in underwriting or trading in securities). No foreigner can engage in any transaction without obtaining a license from the minister of finance. But foreign underwriters who have not obtained a license for underwriting can, with the permission of the minister of finance, participate in the master contract covering the issuance of securities and engage in other domestic business to the extent specified by cabinet order. The Enforcement Order for the Law on Foreign Securities Firms (Cabinet Order No. 267 of August 13, 1971) defines the transactions in which foreign underwriters can engage with the permission of the minister of finance as follows: "those engaged in the securities business can participate in the master underwriting contract if they do not hold prior consultations with the issuer or owner of the securities and do not engage in the domestic sale of said securities" (Article 12). Provided, therefore, that the securities are offered for sale abroad, a foreign underwriter can sign his name to the underwriting contract if he obtains permission from the minister of finance. In order to make sure that the permission is not asked, Article 19 of the Ministerial Ordinance concerning Foreign Securities Firms (Ordinance No. 61 of the Ministry of Finance, 1971) lays down that the provisions regarding standards of investigation, reasons for refusal, and cancellation that the law fixes for a license are applied to the permit that is required for each individual transaction. On account of the reasons for refusal, the documents which must be attached to the application are quite bulky but, with the consent of the minister of finance, part of this documentation may be dispensed with.

Also represented in Japan are the British Insurance Group and American International Underwriters.

Operations of Foreign Banks in Japan, 1970

(In billions of yen)

Allocation of Funds

	American banks	European banks	Asian banks	Total
Foreign currency accounts				
Cash, deposits	0.2	0.9	1.0	2.1
Advances	222.7	0.5	1.4	224.6
Discounts	20.5	0.0	0.0	20.5
Loans	201.4	0.5	0.6	202.5
Overdrafts	0.8	0.0	0.8	1.6
Foreign remittances	13.9	8.1	11.6	33.6
Loans to branches	0.6	0.9	0.2	1.7
Other assets	2.9	0.1	0.2	3.2
Subtotal	240.3	10.5	14.4	265.2
Converted into yen	99.1	31.2	14.8	145.1
Total	339.4	41.7	29.2	410.3
Yen accounts				
Cash, deposits	35.7	7.2	1.2	44.1
Call loans	1.8	1.3	6.7	9.8
Advances	244.7	88.3	34.5	368.0
Discounts	10.3	6.5	8.3	25.1
Loans	225.2	36.1	24.2	285.5
Overdrafts	9.2	46.2	2.0	57.4
Foreign remittances	0.1	0.2	0.9	1.2
Other assets	2.7	2.0	1.0	5.7
Total	285.0	99.5	44.3	428.8

Supply of Funds

	American banks	European banks	Asian banks	Total
Foreign currency accounts				
Deposits	164.4	1.6	1.7	167.7
Borrowings	0.0	4.5	10.2	14.7
Foreign remittances	0.4	0.1	1.6	2.1
Borrowing from other branches	15.3	0.5	8.8	24.6
Overdrafts between head & branch offices	148.0	34.9	6.7	189.6
Other liabilities	11.3	0.1	0.2	11.6
Total	339.4	41.7	29.2	410.3
Yen accounts				
Deposits	120.3	15.7	18.4	154.4
Borrowings	0.1	0.3	0.1	0.5
Call money	2.0	0.0	0.0	2.0
Foreign remittances	0.0	0.0	0.0	0.0
Overdrafts between head & branch offices	0.0	0.1	1.3	1.4
Other liabilities	22.8	5.9	2.0	30.7
Subtotal	145.2	22.0	21.8	189.0
Free-yen accounts	40.7	46.3	7.7	94.7
Deposits	10.0	3.9	1.9	15.8
Borrowings from head office	30.5	42.4	5.8	78.7
Borrowings from other branches	0.2	0.0	0.0	0.2
Converted from other currencies	99.1	31.2	14.8	145.1
Total	285.0	99.5	44.3	428.8

Source: Ministry of Finance, Banking Bureau, Yearly Report on Finances.

Number of Foreign Bank Offices in Japan
June 30, 1971

	Branches		Representative offices	
	Number of banks	Number of branch offices	Number of banks	Number of representative offices
U.S.A.	6	14	17	17
Canada	—	—	5	5
Latin America	—	—	3	3
Britain	3	9	5	5
West Germany	1	1	3	3
France	1	1	4	4
Other European countries	1	3	5	5
South Korea	2	3	3	3
Other Asian countries	5	8	3	3
Oceania	—	—	5	5
Total	19	39	53	53

Source: Ministry of Finance, Banking Bureau, Yearly Report on Finances.

Number of Foreign Banks Operating in Japan

	Branches		Representative offices	
	Number of banks	Number of branch offices	Number of banks	Number of representative offices
July 1962	14	34	8	8
July 1965	15	35	17	17
July 1968	15	34	19	19
June 1969	17	36	28	28
December 1969	18	37	41	41
December 1970	18	38	49	50
June 1971	19	39	53	53
August 1971	20	40	55	56
December 1971	22	42	56	57

**Branch Offices of Foreign Banks
in Japan**

Bank	Location of branch offices
A. Under Occupation	
Bank of America	Tokyo, Osaka, Yokohama; later Kobe
Chase National Bank	
(later Chase Manhattan)	Tokyo, Osaka
National City Bank	
(later First National City Bank)	Tokyo, Osaka, Yokohama; later Kobe
Hongkong & Shanghai Banking Corporation	Tokyo, Yokohama, Kobe; later Osaka
Chartered Bank	Tokyo, Yokohama, Osaka, Kobe
McIntyre Bank (later closed)	Tokyo, Osaka
Banque de l'Indochine	Tokyo
Dutch-India Bank (later closed)	Tokyo, Kobe
Bank of China (Int'l. Comm. Bank of China)	Tokyo
Algemene Bank Nederland N.V.	Tokyo, Osaka
B. Later Foundations	
American Express International	
Banking Corporation	Tokyo
Bangkok Bank	Tokyo, Osaka
Bank Negara Indonesia 1946	Tokyo
Bank of India	Tokyo, Osaka
Continental Illinois National Bank	
& Trust Co. of Chicago	Tokyo, Osaka
Deutsche Überseeische Bank	Tokyo
Hanil Bank	Tokyo
Korea Exchange Bank	Tokyo, Osaka
Manufacturers Hanover Trust Co.	Tokyo
Mercantile Bank, Ltd.	Nagoya (Osaka Branch closed 1968)
Morgan Guaranty Trust Co. of New York	Tokyo
Overseas Union Bank	Tokyo
Wells Fargo Bank	Tokyo

Note: Security Pacific National Bank of Los Angeles has received approval for converting its representative office into a branch which will open in the spring of 1972.

2 ROLE IN INTERNATIONAL FINANCE

4 INDUCTION OF FOREIGN CAPITAL

▲1 FOREIGN LOANS

The chief forms of the induction of foreign capital are foreign loans, sale of Japanese securities, and the flotation of external bonds. Foreign loans are either tied loans, i.e., loans granted for a specific purpose or untied loans, usually called impact loans. Prominent among the tied loans were the loans given by the World Bank for so-called development projects such as the construction of roads and railroads, but also for blast furnaces, strip mills, tube mills, and plate mills (total for the steel industry from 1955 to 1960, $157 million). Also important were the loans given by the U.S. Export-Import Bank for financing imports of American products. The bulk of these loans covered imports of machinery, including industrial equipment (e.g., for the steel industry, petrochemicals, machine tools), aircraft, and computers, but also agricultural products (each year, e.g., the U.S. Export-Import Bank makes available a credit of about $75 million for the import of cotton; originally, this credit was given in the form of a revolving credit). Some of the loans of the U.S. Export-Import Bank were given to the Industrial Bank for financing the purchase of American equipment by small manufacturers. Very often loans for financing imports of American equipment are arranged by the American manufacturers (the same applies to some European manufacturers) and are not only given by banks but also by insurance companies and underwriters.

The induction of impact loans was influenced by many factors, particularly the dollar rate, foreign and domestic interest rates, the situation in the domestic money market, and the restrictions imposed by the authorities. Furthermore, the American equalization tax (1963), which practically put an end to the flotation of bonds and the issue of ADRs in the American market, and the emergence of the Eurodollar market produced significant changes in the pattern of capital induction.

Although the dollar rate was relatively stable, the possible margin of fluctuation was sufficiently large to make foreign borrowing attractive. In 1968, for example, the dollar fell to the lowest level since January 5, 1965; in that year, medium- and long-term impact loans reached about $620 million, almost double the $330 million registered in 1963, which had been the largest yearly total of such loans so far. Generally speaking, foreign interest rates used to be considerably lower than Japanese interest rates, particularly if the effective interest burden arising from the requirement of compensating balances was taken into account. It was only in 1969 that the interest rates on Euro-currencies rose sharply above Japanese rates. All foreign loans have to be validated by the Ministry of Finance and the ministry did not approve loans if it considered interest rates too unfavorable to the Japanese borrower. Since July 1961, the Ministry of Finance has had a standard interest rate (which is not published) for measuring the appropriateness of interest rates on foreign loans. On straight loans, the gross bank margin is around 1.25 percent (sometimes as low as 1.1 percent); the commission of the leading Japanese banks for the loan guarantee is 1 *rin* (0.365 percent). In fiscal 1970, five major shipbuilders borrowed a total of $31,235,000, four for shipyard expansion and modernization and one for working capital. The single loans ranged from $500,000 to $5.5 million, interest rates from 7.5 percent to 8.25 percent, and maturity from three to five years. Japanese effective interest rates were over 10 percent.

Impact loans began to play a significant role in 1960 when the rapid economic expansion created a strong demand for funds and the government's move toward liberalization opened the way for the induction of loans. About the same time, the Eurodollar market assumed greater importance and facilitated the borrowing of foreign capital. The limitations on interest rates imposed on American banks by Regulation Q was one of the factors responsible for the formation of the Eurodollar market, but in Japan the call money rate was around 10 percent, so that interest rates of 7–8 percent were considered low. Actually, the Japanese banks (i.e., their London branches) sometimes paid a higher rate (referred to as the "Japanese rate") than the going rate; the usual differential was 0.125–0.25 percent but occasionally it jumped to 1 percent. A large advantage of the Eurodollar loans was that they required no collateral, no credit line, and no compensating balances. Usually, the loans were for three months, but there has been a gradual shift to longer terms and in recent years, medium- and long-term financing has brought a basic change to the Eurodollar market.

The volume of Eurodollars which moved into Japan never assumed very large proportions and was actually small compared with the country's total money stock. In April 1971, the outstanding balance of foreign funds borrowed by the banks on the Euro-currency market amounted to about $1.6 billion; another $600 million must be added for Euro-currencies in free-yen accounts. The outstanding balance of Euro-currency loans to enterprises was about $1.4 billion, and there was a certain amount, which is difficult to estimate, invested in Japanese securities.

Most Eurodollar loans were taken up by the London branches of the Japanese foreign exchange banks, sent immediately to the head office in Japan, changed into yen, and used for domestic loans, because this was the most profitable way for the banks to use these loans. It was also the reason for most restrictions placed by the Japanese authorities on the induction of impact loans (as a banker put it, "the history of the Eurodollar in Japan is the history of restrictions") because the influx of foreign funds seemed to threaten monetary policy (which, as explained above, was the main anticyclical tool used by the authorities). In 1962, the Ministry of Finance ordained that the banks had to keep part of the free-yen deposits and unsecured loans as liquid reserves in foreign currency. This regulation, called the "foreign currency deposit reserve system," froze up to 35 percent of the funds borrowed from abroad and made the costs prohibitive. In 1966, the interest restrictions were abolished and the deposit reserve ratio was lowered. The official money managers, who, like their Western colleagues, had previously regarded Eurodollars merely as hot money, began to take a more realistic look at Eurodollars as a supplementary fund source for temporary deficiencies in money supply and balance of payments deficits. In 1967, the Bank of Japan fixed a ceiling of $1.1 billion on the induction of impact loans by the banks and advised them to borrow from American banks instead of borrowing in the Eurodollar market (the American controls on impact loans were relaxed in April 1967). In January 1968, however, the restrictions on foreign lending by American banks were made more stringent and the American banks borrowed Eurodollars through their foreign branches for the loans they made to Japanese enterprises. The devaluation of the British pound in November 1967 raised new concern over the pool of hot money attacking currencies and staging a gold rush. In February 1968, new limitations were imposed which limited the inflow of short-term funds as well as the amounts which could be converted into yen and used for domestic financing. As a rule, no increase was allowed in free-yen accounts and in the amounts which could be converted into yen and used for domestic financing. In connection with the credit restraints imposed in September 1969, the restrictions were tightened. No new loans with a maturity of less than three years were allowed and for short-term loans already contracted the maturity was to be extended if possible; despite the high foreign interest rates, the interest rates on loans for three to five years were to be kept below the standard rate (8.2 percent for dollar loans). The flotation of foreign bonds was to be restricted to "good" issues; as a general rule, the inflow of foreign capital was to be held to the same level as the outflow through outward investment and economic cooperation. The last rule reflected the concern of the authorities over the rapid increase in Japan's foreign exchange reserves, and, from this point of view, the restrictions on Eurodollar loans and free-yen accounts were changed from an overall volume basis (limitation of total volume of funds inducted) to a net increase basis (the difference between inflows and outflows had to remain the same). As part of the yen shift in foreign financing, the Bank of Japan advised the Japanese banks to borrow in the call market and repay Eurodollar loans with foreign exchange which the Bank of Japan made available. This served the twofold purpose of tightening domestic credit and decelerating the increase in official reserves. In this way, $250 million in short-term funds were repaid from April to June 1969.

In 1971, the authorities tried again to keep the increase in impact loans to a minimum. For the April–June quarter, the ceiling on the increase in bank-guaranteed impact loans was fixed at about $40 million, and for the July–September quarter the increase was to remain 15 percent less than in the preceding quarter. The Bank of Japan wanted to abolish bank-guaranteed impact loans altogether. In May 1971, the Ministry of Finance advised the foreign exchange banks to curb their lending abroad and stop guaranteeing loans by their foreign branch offices. All other companies were similarly advised to refrain from guaranteeing loans by their branch offices abroad. Demand for impact loans was particularly strong on the part of trading companies; their requests were six to seven times higher than the ceiling desired by the Bank of Japan. Although the monetary situation in Japan was relaxed, interest on foreign loans was still lower if the compensating balances were considered. The banks themselves were also eager to increase their foreign liabilities as a hedge against a possible yen revaluation (they did not want to be caught with an excess in dollar holdings).

 2 FOREIGN INVESTMENTS IN JAPANESE SECURITIES

Foreign investment in Japanese securities takes the following forms: purchase of Japanese stocks, bonds, and investment trust certificates in Japan, purchase of Japanese stocks abroad, and purchase of bonds floated by Japanese public agencies or private corporations abroad. In the official statistics, the total investment in stocks includes the acquisition of stocks "for participation in management," which means direct investment in Japanese enterprises and is basically different from investment in securities. As explained above, the latest relaxation of the restrictions on direct foreign investment effected on August 4, 1971, left seven industries "subject to specific screening" and provided for automatic approval of foreign investment up to 100 percent of the capital in 228 industrial branches and up to 50 percent in all others. At the same time, the limit on the acquisition of stock by a single investor was raised from 7 percent to "below 10 percent" of the shares issued by one company; the ceiling on total foreign investment remained "below 25 percent" for nonrestricted and "below 15 percent" for restricted industries.

Foreign investment in Japanese stocks reached a high in 1963 but dropped to less than half in the following year. It was only in 1968 that purchases rose again. The statistics on validation of the acquisition of securities do not reflect actual stockholding. A report of the Tokyo Stock Exchange stated that at the end of September 1970 Japanese corporations listed on the exchange in which foreign investors owned more than 1 percent of all issued stocks numbered 153 (118 listed on the First and 35 on the Second Section). The highest proportion of foreign stock ownership (other than joint ventures) was in Sony Corporation (31.15 percent). For the end of March 1971, Wako Securities Co. reported that the number of shares of the 899 companies on the First Section of the Tokyo Stock Exchange owned by foreigners was 3,414,000, equal to 3.29 percent of all stocks; foreign stockholders numbered 30,670. The number of shares owned by foreigners exceeded 10 million in such well-known companies as Hitachi, Nippon Electric, Nippon Oil, Mitsubishi Estate, Mitsubishi Petrochemical, and Taisei Construction.

In November 1971, foreign investment in Japanese stocks was estimated at $2.5–3 billion, about 4 percent of the market value of all listed Japanese stocks.

In fiscal 1969, the induction of foreign capital rose to an all-time high. Loans declined by about 17 percent, but stock purchases increased 3.7 times over the preceding fiscal year, resulting in a 90 percent increase in the total induction of foreign capital. In fiscal 1970, the total declined by 25 percent; the main reason for the drop was the decrease in the stock purchases for portfolio investment, which were 40 percent lower than in fiscal 1969. The acquisition of stock for participation in management rose from 300 cases and $54 million in fiscal 1969 to 350 cases and $91.1 million in fiscal 1970. The foundation of wholly owned subsidiaries and joint ventures or foreign participation in existing Japanese enterprises increased from 174 cases in fiscal 1969 to 290 cases in fiscal 1970. The flotation of external bonds decreased sharply, from eleven issues valued at $235 million in the preceding fiscal year to seven issues (private corporations five, government-guaranteed debentures two), valued at $122 million.

In anticipation of the yen revaluation, foreign purchases of Japanese securities increased in the beginning of 1971, punctuated by occasional waves of selling. An additional factor in the buying of Japanese bonds was the large decline in the interest on Eurodollars which, for three-month loans, fell from 11.375 percent in September 1969 to 5.5 percent in February 1971. Until 1970, foreign investors showed little interest in Japanese bonds, but in July 1970, buying orders for bonds began to rise, while the gloomy business outlook prompted foreign investors to sell stocks (in 1970, foreign purchases of stocks amounted to $1,019.9 million, sales to $863.8 million). Acquisition of bonds redeemable within one year is exempt from the American equalization tax, but under Japanese regulations proceeds from bond sales can only be repatriated after a six-month waiting period and purchases are limited to bonds listed on the stock exchanges or traded over the counter. In May 1971, the Ministry of Finance prohibited foreign investment in unlisted Japanese bonds. In the beginning of September 1971, the Ministry of Finance ordered the six largest securities firms to keep foreign investment in Japanese securities handled by them to $100 million a month.

There is a great difference between the figures reported by the Ministry of Finance for "validation of foreign investment," actual purchases of securities, and the net increase or decrease in foreign investment. According to the Foreign Investment Law, "validation" (*kyoka*) is required for the acquisition of corporate bonds and interest-bearing bank debentures with a remaining maturity of longer than one year, whereas "approval" (*ninka*) is sufficient for bonds maturing within less than one year, discount bank debentures, national bonds, government-guaranteed debentures, and debentures of Nippon Telegraph & Telephone public corporation. Different from the figures given by the Ministry of Finance for validated bond purchases, the ministry reported the following amounts for actual purchases of Japanese public bonds and corporate debentures: March 1971, $102.4 million; April, $104.0 million; May, $128.6 million; June, $28.3 million. Foreign investment in Japanese stocks amounted to $132.9 million in March, $106.8 million in April, $77.7 million in May, and $201.35 million in June. In the latter month, sales of stocks by foreign investors amounted to $101.8 million, so that the net investment amounted to $99.45 million. For the six months from January to June 1971, the net increase in foreign investment in Japanese stocks was $428 million. The increase resulted mainly from purchases by middle-sized mutual funds, pension funds, and insurance companies. The most important portfolio investors are funds specializing in Japanese issues, such as Pacific Fund, Robeco, Japan Selection Fund, Japan Fund, and Tokyo Capital Fund. The first time that Japanese stocks were incorporated in a foreign investment trust was in 1959, when a German investment trust bought about DM124 million worth of Japanese securities. A foreign investment trust specializing in Japanese stocks was established in Hong Kong in June 1961 under the name of International Investment Trust Corporation.

In November 1961, Yamaichi Securities Co. and Vickers da Costa of London jointly set up the Anglo-Japanese Investment Trust, a closed-end investment trust made up of about 20 million shares. In April 1962, the Japan Fund Inc. was organized in the United States with 1,250,000 shares. The Tokyo Fund was set up by Nikko Securities, the Bank of Tokyo, and the Nelson Fund. In May 1971, Nikko Securities Co. tied up with Investors Securities Management Co. of Canada to establish a fund called Investors Japanese Growth Fund. In August 1971, the Save and Prosper Ltd. group stopped sales of their Save and Prosper Japan Growth Fund units on account of the difficulty in assessing the value of the fund.

Due to the rise in Japanese stock prices, net foreign investment dropped sharply in July; purchases amounted to $147.6 million, sales to $141.8 million, leaving a net increase of $5.8 million. Net acquisition by foreign investors of Japanese bonds declined from $28.3 million in June to $8.1 million in July. So far, the largest excess of sales over purchases of stocks was registered in May 1970, when the IOS debacle resulted in net sales of $80 million of Japanese stocks by foreign investors; the next largest was in October 1971, when sales ($125 million) exceeded purchases ($50 million) by $75 million. The largest single sell order came from International Investment Trust, an IOS subsidiary, which, in July 1970, sold 30.3 million shares of Kubota through Nikko Securities Co.

In order to facilitate foreign investment in Japanese stocks, the system of American Depositary Receipts (ADR), originally used for European stocks, was adopted for Japanese issues. Under this system, the shares are deposited with Japanese depositary banks (trust banks); against these shares, American trust banks issue ADRs which are then offered to the public by underwriters. The first Japanese firm for whose shares ADRs were issued was Sony Corporation (June 1961). Smith, Barney & Co. and the American subsidiary of Nomura Securities bought 2 million shares (face value ¥100 million) newly issued for this purpose. Against these shares, Morgan Guaranty Trust Co. issued ADRs which were sold by the underwriters. For Toshiba (February 1962), old shares were bought on the market. ADRs now traded in New York include Matsushita Electric, Honda, Tokio Marine & Fire Insurance, Fuji Photo Film, Hitachi, Ltd., Nippon Electric, Mitsubishi Heavy Industries, Nissan Motor, Toyota Motor, Mitsui & Co., Kansai Electric, and Japan Air Lines. Sony has been listed on the New York Stock Exchange since September 1970 and Matsushita since December 1971.

In March 1963, the London Stock Exchange formally approved Honda Motor's application for listing on the exchange, the first Japanese stock to be officially traded in Europe. In 1964, Taisho Marine and Fire Insurance issued London depositary receipts. In February 1969, Pioneer offered the first European depositary receipts; other firms whose stocks are traded in this form are Olympus Optical, Sanyo Electric, and Mitsumi Electric. Sekisui House Co. is listed on the Amsterdam Stock Exchange. There are also Hong Kong Depositary Receipts.

The first foreign bond issue after the war was placed in the United States in February 1959, when the government raised $30 million for electric power projects. The government guaranteed a $20 million bond issue of the Nippon Telegraph and Telephone public corporation in April 1961 and two issues of the Japan Development Bank, the first, $20 million, in October 1961, and the second, $17.5 million, in May 1962. Japanese bonds were floated for the first time in Europe in February 1962, when the Prefecture and City of Osaka placed a DM100 million issue in Germany.

Private bond offerings were first sanctioned in 1961; as a rule, issues of corporate bonds were much smaller than issues of public bonds. The imposition of the American equalization tax made issues in the United States practically impossible, and after November 1964 issues of bonds of private corporations were shifted to Europe. In 1965, the government obtained an exemption from the equalization tax of ¥100 million a year in issues of public bonds. In December 1963, Takeda Chemical became the first Japanese company to offer convertible debentures in Europe, and numerous other firms followed Takeda's example. With the development of the Eurodollar market, a greater variety of forms of lending appeared. In addition to convertible bonds, bonds with stock purchase warrants were used; long-term bonds with a maturity of over eight years were supplemented by medium-term bonds with a maturity of three to seven years and certificates of deposit of over three years. Besides public offerings, private placements of bonds and notes were used. The interest rates reflected conditions in overseas capital markets. The first bonds floated in the United States after the imposition of the new equalization tax were debentures of the Nippon Telegraph and Telephone Corporation offered in April 1965; the issue was raised from $20 million to $22.5 million on account of the favorable reception, although the yield to subscribers had been reduced from the 6.08 percent of former issues (1963) to 6.03 percent (issue price $97.25, interest rate 5.75 percent, maturity fifteen years). A bond issue of the metropolis of Tokyo in

July 1965 sold at $95.25, had a coupon rate of 6 percent and yielded 6.5 percent if held to maturity (fifteen years); an issue of the Japan Development Bank in November of the same year had an issue price of $97.75, an interest rate of 6.5 percent and matured in fifteen years. Yields to subscribers of issues of private corporations were as low as 7.56 percent and as high as 8.25 percent. The Japanese government does not levy a tax on interest payments on bonds denominated in foreign currencies and issued abroad if the interest is paid in foreign currency to foreign individuals or corporations and the maturity of the bond is longer than three years.

In 1966, no external bonds were issued on account of the unfavorable situation in foreign money markets and the Ministry of Finance kept issues down in 1967. For 1971, the ministry authorized issues in Germany of two municipalities, Yokohama and Kobe, and, despite a ban on issues by private corporations, of Kansai Electric Power Co. (DM100 million, interest rate 7.75 percent, maturity fifteen years).

The main outflows of capital from Japan are direct foreign investment, loans and other credits, particularly deferred payment for exports and the acquisition of foreign securities. At the end of March 1970, the total value of approved outward investment amounted to $2,683 million (number of approved cases of foreign investment 3,167). The highest amount, $1,282 million, was for loans, followed by acquisition of securities $1,035 million, direct investment $339 million, and opening of branch offices $27 million. These figures do not include government aid. By objectives, the highest amount, $1,003 million, was for trading; development projects accounted for $959 million and manufacturing for $722 million. By region, the largest share of the investment capital, $720 million, went to North America, $604 million to Southeast Asia, $513 million to Latin America, $306 million to the Middle East, $303 million to Europe, $158 million to Oceania, and $79 million to Africa. The regional distribution of investments for development reflected Japan's endeavor to secure raw material sources; the Middle East ranked first with $302 million, Southeast Asia second with $266 million, North America followed with $129 million, Latin America with $96 million, and Africa with $57 million. In investments for trade, North America accounted for by far the largest share, $431 million; other large investments went to Europe ($287 million), Latin America ($168 million), and Southeast Asia ($105 million). The government has established two organs for financing foreign development projects, the Overseas Mineral Resources Development Co. and the Petroleum Development Corporation. The establishment of an Industrial Development Cooperation Corporation for promoting direct investment in developing countries is under consideration. As mentioned above, the ceiling on direct foreign investment by Japanese enterprises was abolished July 1, 1971.

Portfolio investment in foreign securities is of very recent origin. It was completely prohibited until February 1970, when investment trusts were allowed to acquire up to a total of $100 million in foreign securities for incorporation into their trust assets. In October 1970, the insurance companies were given the same permission. Investment in foreign securities was liberalized on July 1, 1971, but direct purchases of foreign securities by individual investors were not allowed. The customer places his order with a domestic securities company which relays the order to its foreign branch. The branch has its broker buy the securities on the stock exchange and turns them over to a depositary bank. The bank informs the securities company of the acquisition and the securities company hands the customer a "depositary receipt" for the securities. For payment, the customer must open a foreign securities transaction account with the securities company for which he pays a yearly fee of ¥15,000. He pays the price of the securities, including commissions and other fees, in yen which the securities company transmits in foreign exchange to the depositary bank which, in turn, pays the broker. The commission payable by the customer to the Japanese securities firm is ¥9,000 plus 0.5 percent of the value of the transaction for transactions below ¥10 million, 0.5 percent of the value for transactions between ¥10 million and ¥25 million, 0.45 percent for transactions between ¥25 million and ¥50 million, 0.4 percent for transactions between ¥50 million and ¥100 million, and 0.35 percent for the part of the transaction exceeding ¥100 million. The depositary bank collects the dividends and sends them to the Japanese securities firm.

Since November 1, 1971, the securities companies have been allowed to hold foreign securities on their own account and the Securities Dealers Association has made preparations for over-the-counter transactions in about 200 foreign issues. Initially, purchases were restricted to securities issued in the United States, Britain, Canada, West Germany, France, the Netherlands, Switzerland, and Australia.

The securities companies had started to add foreign securities to their investment funds in April 1970; in April 1971, the Securities Investment Trust Association raised the ceiling on foreign securities in Japanese stock investment trusts from 30 percent to 50 percent. In the same month, the four large securities companies started so-called international investment trusts. Since the foreign securities are deposited abroad, the arrangement involved a combination of foreign depositary banks and Japanese trust banks holding the trust assets. Moreover, the securities companies appointed foreign securities companies as advisers. Nomura Securities Co. established an associated Japanese international fund which is sold in Japan through fifty-six firms. The banks cooperating with the fund are Daiwa Bank and its New York agency; Toyo Trust & Banking Co. and Bankers Trust; and Mitsui Trust & Banking Co. and Bank of Tokyo Trust Co. The fund's advisers are Merrill Lynch, Pierce, Fenner, and Smith, Bankers Trust, and N. M. Rothschild & Sons Ltd. The fund includes 200 Japanese issues and 134 foreign issues. The Daiwa International Fund is sold in Japan by about a hundred firms; the banks connected with it are Sumitomo Trust & Banking and Bank of Tokyo Trust Co. and the three trust banks, Mitsubishi, Sumitomo, and Yasuda, on the one side and First National City Bank on the other. Advisers are Dreyfus and Morgan Grenfell. The fund comprises a total of 350 issues, made up of 215 Japanese, 100 American, 18 Canadian, 10 German, and 7 Dutch issues. The Nikko International Fund is handled domestically by 115 firms; Mitsubishi Trust & Banking serves as trustee and Morgan Guaranty Trust as depositary bank, as well as adviser. Another adviser is S. K. Warburg. Yamaichi established a Joint International Trust Fund, sold by 107 domestic firms. Cooperating with the fund are Mitsubishi Trust & Banking and Bank of Tokyo Trust Co., Lehman Brothers, and Kleinwort, Benson are advisers to the fund which includes about two hundred Japanese and one hundred foreign issues.

Loans to foreign governments by the Japanese government have been fairly numerous, and a number of loans were made for balance of payments reasons. In November 1968, the government bought $100,006,000 of bonds of the U.S. Export-Import Bank and the Bank of Japan purchased $80 million of certificates of the bank in 1970. The Japan Export-Import Bank has given a series of loans to the Inter-American Development Bank. The first loan of ¥3.6 billion ($10 million) was given in June 1966; the second, for the same amount, in October 1968. These loans had to be used for the purchase of Japanese products. For some of the loans, the Export-Import Bank cooperated with commercial banks, e.g., in October

1968, with the Bank of Tokyo for a loan of $5,882,353 to Argentina's State Industrial Bank and in July 1969 with thirteen foreign exchange banks for a ¥3.6 billion credit to Taiwan Electric Co. In September 1971, the Export-Import Bank extended a loan of ¥7.2 billion to IADB (its fourth), and, at the same time, the Bank of Japan signed a loan agreement for $10 million with the Bank of Tokyo. Furthermore, a syndicate of forty Japanese commercial banks agreed to a loan of ¥7.2 billion. IADB intends to float debentures in Japan. In May 1971, seven foreign exchange banks granted loans amounting to $49.5 million to the Korea Exchange Bank; a loan of $50 million had been given in May 1970 by a consortium of fifteen commercial banks to the Central Bank of the Philippines. The most significant development, however, was an agreement concluded on December 2, 1971, between Transocean Gulf Oil Co., a Delaware subsidiary of Gulf Oil Co., and a syndicate for a ¥5 billion loan. The syndicate included the Bank of Tokyo, the Industrial Bank, the Japan Hypothec Bank, the Long-Term Credit Bank, the Bank of Yokohama, and the Tokyo Branch of Morgan Guarantee Trust Co. Maturity is seven years (including a grace period of four years), the interest rate 8.2 percent.

The emission of bonds in Japan by the World Bank and the Asian Development Bank has been mentioned above; South Korea wanted to issue bonds for financing the construction of a subway in Seoul, and Taiwan, the Philippines, and Australia were reported to be interested in floating bonds in Japan. Almost all bonds issued in Japan by private industrial companies (i.e., other than bank debentures) are secured by mortgages; unsecured bonds made their first appearance with the flotation of the bonds of the Asian Development Bank and the World Bank. These issues fell under the exemptions from the provisions of the Securities Transaction Law laid down in Article 3 of this law. But private companies must file an application with the Ministry of Finance and prepare a prospectus. For private offerings, a simple notification is sufficient.

Validation of Foreign Investment I

(In thousands of dollars)

Fiscal year	Total	Acquisition of stock or other proprietory interest Total	Participation in management	Beneficiary certificates	Deben- tures	Loans	External bonds
1952	44,751	10,123	7,166	146	25	34,457	—
1953	54,926	5,002	2,687	562	—	49,362	—
1954	19,307	3,970	2,467	58	—	15,279	—
1955	52,214	5,101	2,309	52	7	47,054	—
1956	103,302	9,520	5,360	115	15	93,652	—
1957	135,597	11,490	7,282	128	—	123,979	—
1958	272,967	11,350	3,698	116	28	231,473	30,000
1959	154,890	27,031	14,561	214	30	127,615	—
1960	211,658	74,151	31,593	555	20	127,132	9,800
1961	577,529	116,142	40,170	1,280	77	387,605	72,425
1962	678,823	164,668	22,619	650	86	358,419	155,000
1963	884,302	185,262	42,656	798	247	503,945	194,050
1964	912,784	84,845	30,645	1,828	851	650,760	174,500
1965	528,506	83,331	44,643	398	2,726	379,551	62,500
1966	457,097	126,735	39,812	390	261	329,711	—
1967	847,787	159,836	29,778	284	123	637,544	50,000
1968	1,836,645	670,008	52,701	253	32	947,372	218,980
1969	3,488,240	2,462,897	53,777	233	524	789,602	234,984
April–Dec. 1970	1,785,227	1,008,677	66,857	227	25,017	681,621	79,685

Source: Ministry of Finance.

Validation of Foreign Investment II

(In millions of dollars)

Fiscal year	Total	Acquisition of stock or other proprietory interest Total	Participation in management	Beneficiary certificates	Deben- tures	Loans	External bonds
1970	2,623.8	1,555.6	91.1	0.6	99.7	845.9	122.0
1971, April	567.5	311.1	3.1	0.4	30.2	198.6	27.3
May	328.8	202.7	3.3	0.8	42.1	83.3	—
June	351.1	300.1	83.1	0.4	8.2	42.5	—
July	252.6	203.2	2.5	0.1	3.0	46.3	—
Aug.	361.6	271.0	15.3	0.1	2.6	60.6	27.3
Total 1950–Aug. 1971	15,767.3	7,071.7	646.5	10.4	190.7	7,115.5	1,378.9

Source: Ministry of Finance.

External Bonds of Private Corporations

(In thousands of dollars)

	Total		Manufacturing		Transportation		Communications		Commerce		Electric power & gas	
	New issues	Outstand-ing balance	New issues	Outstand-ing balance	New issues	Outstand-ing balance	New issues	Outstand-ing balance	New issues	Outstand-ing balance	New issues	Outstand-ing balance
1960	4,000	4,000	4,000	4,000	—	—	—	—	—	—	—	—
1961	10,225	14,225	10,225	14,225	—	—	—	—	—	—	—	—
1962	59,500	73,725	49,500	63,725	—	—	10,000	10,000	—	—	—	—
1963	88,400	158,299	48,400	108,299	15,000	15,000	15,000	25,000	10,000	10,000	—	—
1964	69,500	225,107	57,000	162,607	—	15,000	—	25,000	12,500	22,500	—	—
1965	10,000	228,175	10,000	168,477	—	15,000	—	23,000	—	21,699	—	—
1966	—	217,854	—	162,778	—	14,525	—	21,000	—	19,552	—	—
1967	15,000	219,542	15,000	169,264	—	14,425	—	19,000	—	16,853	—	—
1968	75,000	270,204	75,000	224,541	—	14,125	—	17,000	—	14,538	—	—
1969	219,983	445,690	124,000	306,305	—	14,125	—	15,000	30,000	41,954	250,000	250,000
1970	70,000	469,972	55,000	341,683	—	14,125	—	13,000	15,000	32,858	—	250,000

Note: Includes issues in German marks.
Source: The Industrial Bank of Japan.

3 FOREIGN BUSINESS OF JAPANESE BANKS

1 FOREIGN EXCHANGE CONTROLS

The main fields comprising the foreign business of Japanese banks are: (1) financing of foreign trade; (2) induction of foreign capital; (3) financing of Japanese undertakings abroad; (4) business with foreign enterprises operating in Japan; (5) participation in international financing; (6) information. In the years immediately following the war, foreign exchange was under the control of the occupation and the entire foreign exchange business was in the hands of the branches of foreign banks operating in Japan under the control of the occupation authorities. On April 25, 1949, a fixed exchange rate ($1 = ¥360) was adopted in connection with the measures, known as the Dodge line, for halting the inflation. The Dodge line intended to make up for the lack of domestic purchasing power by an expansion of exports; this was also to improve the balance of payments which had so far been manipulated by a variety of exchange rates. A foreign trade special account replaced the trade fund in April 1949, but its receipts and payments for imports or exports of goods and services were in yen only and had no direct connection with foreign currency. On December 1, 1949, the Foreign Exchange and Foreign Trade Control Law (*Gaikoku Kawase oyobi Gaikoku Bōeki Kanri-hō*) was promulgated which, together with the Law Concerning Foreign Capital (*Gaishi ni Kansuru Hōritsu,* usually called Foreign Investment Law) enacted on May 10, 1950, still forms the basis of Japan's foreign exchange system. The law provided for the so-called concentration of foreign exchange, which made it illegal for anyone to hold foreign exchange except with the permission of the government and ordered all foreign exchange to be turned over to the foreign exchange special account (renamed foreign exchange fund special account in April 1951) set up under the law. Exports were transferred from the government corporations (*kōdan*) which had conducted them so far to private operation on December 1, 1949, and imports followed on January 1, 1950. At the same time, responsibility for foreign exchange control was transferred from SCAP (supreme commander for the Allied powers) to the Japanese government together with the equivalent of $67 million in U.S. dollars and pounds sterling on SCAP's commercial account. Accounts in the name of the Foreign Exchange Control Board were opened with foreign banks; this board was to exercise control over foreign exchange transactions for SCAP. It was abolished in July 1952 and its business was taken over by the Ministry of Finance. The foreign exchange holdings deposited with foreign banks on FECB accounts were transferred to accounts opened in the name of the minister of finance (MOF a/c).

When private foreign trade had been reopened (on a very limited scale) in August 1947, nine city banks were designated as foreign exchange banks and authorized to handle documentary export bills. Under the Foreign Exchange and Foreign Trade Control Law of 1949 eleven city banks and the ten foreign banks possessing branches in Japan were recognized as "authorized foreign exchange banks." Administratively, these banks were called "Class A" foreign exchange banks; they were empowered to establish correspondence relations with foreign banks (they numbered forty-two when the distinction was abolished in August 1970) and (forty-eight) "Class B" foreign exchange banks (trust banks and local banks) which were not allowed to conclude correspondence contracts with foreign banks. In 1950 the Japan Export Bank was established (mainly for financing exports of plant and equipment); its function was enlarged to include import financing in 1952 when its name was changed to the Japan Export-Import Bank. The bureaucrats revived the tradition of "special banks" in 1954, when the Foreign Exchange Bank Law was enacted; the Bank of Tokyo, the successor firm to the Yokohama Specie Bank, was transformed into the sole foreign exchange bank organized under this law.

The foreign exchange banks were allowed to hold a limited amount of foreign exchange in June 1952; this was initially limited to dollars. Some restrictions were removed in 1956 and, in July 1960, free-yen accounts for nonresidents were introduced. With Japan's declaration that she would observe Article 8 of the International Monetary Fund Agreement in April 1964 and Japan's admission to the Organization for Economic Cooperation and Development, the country was committed to a more liberal policy. As a result of these changes, the Class A foreign banks were authorized to open foreign exchange accounts with banks in Japan and abroad and to open foreign exchange accounts for correspondent banks and nonresidents. All current and capital transactions go through the foreign exchange banks, which can sell or buy foreign exchange to settle balances arising from transactions with their customers in the domestic or foreign exchange markets. Connected with the foreign exchange business are certain functions which the foreign exchange banks (and the Bank of Japan) exercise as agents of the government, such as certification of export declarations and of import licenses and transactions related to foreign trade, e.g., foreign exchange contracts, overseas remittances, rediscount, refinance, and interbank transactions in foreign currency.

In the course of the liberalization of foreign exchange transactions, trading companies were allowed to hold foreign exchange starting in January 1966. In February 1970, this regulation was extended to manufacturers possessing foreign branches and directly engaged in foreign trade. The trading companies and manufacturers can buy foreign exchange from the foreign exchange banks (originally, a ceiling of $100 million was fixed); they can open foreign exchange deposit accounts with domestic foreign exchange banks in which they can deposit receipts from merchandise trade and services and keep these funds for a period of three months within which the foreign exchange was received (i.e., a maximum of six months) and use these funds for paying for imports. At present, the Bank of Japan undertakes no foreign exchange transactions in its own name except with the foreign exchange fund; it acts, however, for the minister of finance in the administration of the Foreign Exchange and Foreign Trade Control Law, and is entrusted with intervention in the foreign exchange market and the administration of the restrictions on banking activities (ceiling on holdings of foreign exchange, conversion of foreign exchange into yen, and induction of short-term funds).

3 FOREIGN BUSINESS OF JAPANESE BANKS

2 FOREIGN EXCHANGE MARKET

Japan's foreign exchange market is very limited because it still operates within the restrictions of the system of concentration set up by the Foreign Exchange and Foreign Trade Control Law. Foreign exchange can only be kept by the government (foreign exchange fund special account), the Bank of Japan, and the authorized foreign exchange banks. Residents (corporations and individuals) are not allowed to retain foreign exchange; as a rule, foreign currency must be sold to the government through the foreign exchange banks, money-changers, or post offices (the last two institutions play no role) within one month of the acquisition of the foreign currency. Within this month, individuals returning from abroad can now use the money brought back or received from abroad for foreign travel or remittances. In addition to the exceptions for trading companies and manufacturers mentioned above, airlines and shipping companies can retain income from international fares and freight. The concentration system comprised not only foreign exchange (the official designation is foreign means of payment) but also precious metals, claims in foreign currency, and foreign securities. Under the Regulations for the Concentration of Foreign Exchange (originally fixed by the Foreign Exchange Control Board in 1950 but often revised since 1952 by the Ministry of Finance), banks could hold for their foreign exchange operations only "designated currencies"; they were, as of May 1, 1971, the U.S. dollar, the Canadian dollar, the Australian dollar, the English pound, the German mark, the Dutch guilder, the Austrian schilling, the French franc, the Swiss franc, the Belgian franc, the Swedish krona, the Norwegian krone, the Danish krone, the Portuguese escudo, and the Italian lira.

The foreign exchange fund buys and sells foreign exchange against yen. The fund acquires the yen required for its buying operations (inventory financing) from appropriations on the general accounts of the budget (not done in recent years), borrowing from the Trust Fund Bureau, emission of short-term bonds (foreign exchange fund bills), and sales of foreign exchange not required for current operations to the Bank of Japan. The foreign exchange fund also intervenes in the foreign exchange market, but the actual operations (as all other operations) are carried out by the Bank of Japan. The funds of the foreign exchange fund are partly invested in foreign securities (e.g., treasury bills) or deposited with American or British banks in MOF accounts (sometimes called foreign exchange concentration accounts). Since June 1970, funds of the foreign exchange fund have been used for import financing by the foreign exchange banks, first in the form of loans in foreign currency and, since March 1971, in the form of deposits of foreign currency with foreign exchange banks.

There is no restriction on the kind of currencies in which payments can be received from or made abroad, but the concentration system under which the foreign exchange fund buys unlimited amounts of currency at a fixed rate applies only to dollars. Foreign exchange banks cannot sell other currencies directly to the foreign exchange fund; they must convert them in overseas markets in which these currencies can be converted into dollars. The concentration system does not apply to futures.

In addition to the foreign exchange fund and the foreign exchange banks, the foreign exchange market includes the foreign exchange brokers. The brokerage business started in 1952 as an appendage to the short-term fund (bill brokerage) business; this is the reason why of the seven foreign exchange brokers, four are bill brokers (Nippon Waribiki Tanshi, Tokyo Tanshi, Ueda Tanshi, and Yamane Tanshi); only three specialize in foreign exchange (Hatori Shokai, Minami Shokai, and Osaka Gaitame). These firms act strictly as brokers for interbank transactions and do not engage in transactions on their own account; they cannot hold foreign currency and there are no cash and delivery transactions. The foreign exchange fund (i.e., the Bank of Japan), however, uses the brokers for intervention in the foreign exchange market (e.g., buying excess foreign exchange for which the brokers can find no buyers). The foreign exchange market has no physical place; all transactions are handled by telephone. Tokyo and Osaka are the only foreign exchange markets in Japan, with over 90 percent of all transactions taking place in Tokyo. The exchange brokers handle 90 percent of the interbank transactions; the buyer pays a commission of 3 *sen* per dollar. After the adoption of free-yen accounts for nonresidents in 1960, and the possibility of settling foreign trade transactions in yen, small markets in free yen began in New York and London.

The operations of the banks in the foreign exchange market are mainly for two purposes: adjustment of funds and avoidance of risks. Operations are different for dollars and for other currencies because dollars can always be sold to the foreign exchange fund at the MOF concentration rate. Since the foreign exchange fund does not buy other currencies and the domestic market is narrow, other currencies are usually sent abroad.

The interbank transactions on the foreign exchange market take three forms: spot transactions, forward transactions (futures), and swap transactions. Spot transactions include delivery on the same day (about 30 percent of all transactions) and delivery on the following day (about 70 percent of all transactions). Forward transactions are for a fixed day or for delivery in a set time. Most contracts remain within six months; delivery in a certain month is specified in about 80 percent of all forward contracts. It may be set for the first or latter half of the month, or in the first, middle, or latter ten days. Swap transactions include spot buying and forward selling or spot selling and forward buying. A bank uses the first when it is oversold and the latter combination when it is overbought. On account of the chronic fund shortage and the high domestic interest rates, the Japanese foreign exchange banks tended to be oversold, but as a result of the large export surplus the banks became overbought. The restrictions on the holding of foreign currency were relaxed in September 1960; on the basis of the overall position of the bank, i.e., the total of spot and futures for all foreign currencies, the Ministry of Finance fixed limitations on the amounts of assets and liabilities. At present, the Ministry of Finance fixes ceilings on the amounts of oversold or overbought currencies on the basis of the overall net position of each bank for all currencies; the swap transactions, therefore, are a means of remaining within the ceilings. As explained above, the foreign exchange banks borrowed foreign funds at low interest rates and converted them into yen; since the authorities considered this a threat to their monetary policy, the foreign exchange reserve deposit system was introduced in June 1962.

Under Article 4, Paragraph 3, of the International Monetary Fund Agreement, a margin of 1 percent either way was allowed for spot transactions with no restrictions on forward rates. In Japan, no fluctuations were allowed in the forward rate until 1954 and in the spot rate until 1956. The margin for transactions of the foreign exchange banks with the foreign exchange fund was first 0.50 percent either way; it was raised to 0.75 percent in April 1963 and remained that way until August 28, 1971. Because the foreign exchange fund was always ready to buy or sell within these limits, this rate was also the basic rate for all transactions of the banks with their customers. The main rate categories in Japan were the basic rate, the arbitrated rate, the MOF concentration rate, the interbank rate, and the rates for the transactions of the banks with their customers.

The basic rate is the rate registered with the International Monetary Fund; it was fixed in December 1949 by ministerial notification based on Article 7, Paragraphs 1 and 2 of the Foreign Exchange and Foreign Trade Control Law at ¥360 = $1. The arbitrated rate is the rate of all currencies other than the U.S. dollar based on the ministerial notification. The actual rate is posted on the authority of the minister of finance in the head office of the Bank of Japan for ten currencies (all registered with the IMF): the British pound, German mark, French franc, Italian lira, Belgian franc, Dutch guilder, Swedish krona, Norwegian krone, Danish krone, and Austrian schilling. For all member countries of the IMF, the arbitrated rate is based on the dollar parity of their currencies; for nonmember countries it is fixed on the market quotations of their currencies against the dollar.

The rate for transactions between the foreign exchange banks and the foreign exchange fund (actually the Bank of Japan as agent of the minister of finance) is called the MOF concentration rate which is based on Article 2 of the Regulations for the Concentration of Foreign Exchange. The band of ±0.75 percent in effect since April 1963 corresponds to ±¥2.70, so that the ceiling on the MOF concentration rate was ¥362.70 and its floor ¥357.30. The MOF concentration rate was also the intervention rate; the Bank of Japan does not intervene in futures. Transactions between foreign exchange banks had been subject to various restrictions which, however, were gradually removed so that the rates for spot as well as forward transactions became free. Actually, for spot transactions, the MOF concentration rate used to be more favorable than the interbank rate. For currencies other than the dollar, no upper or lower limits were fixed; generally for currencies with a registered parity, a band of ±0.7–0.75 percent was recognized. Actual transactions, however, were based on arbitrated rates and market fluctuations occurred within a band of 1.5 percent both ways. The rates in the forward exchange market depend on supply and demand and interest rates. Supply and demand were the most important factors in the forward market for dollars and pounds; for other currencies, their forward rates in other markets against the dollar and the forward rate of the dollar in the domestic market were taken into account.

The only interbank rate is the telegraphic transfer (TT) rate; in the transactions of the banks with their customers, different rates are in effect for TT, sight drafts, time drafts, import settlement bills, and D/P (documents against payment) drafts. The TT rate is the only pure exchange rate; all other rates involve interest rates. The banks have been free to fix the TT rate since April 1963; according to an agreement among the banks, the rate was based on the interbank rate of the preceding day and a commission of 50 *sen* was charged one way (buying or selling). Until the flotation of the yen, therefore, the TT rates for customers were as follows:

Selling rate: upper limit ¥363.20
lower limit ¥357.80
Buying rate: upper limit ¥362.20
lower limit ¥356.80

The main instruments bought by the banks from their customers are sight drafts and time drafts for exports; the main instruments sold are bills for the settlement of imports. For drafts, the commission had been fixed by agreement among the banks at 62 *sen* per dollar and at ¥1.87 per pound sterling. The rates were fixed on the TT rate and interest for the days in transit. For sight drafts, the upper ceiling was ¥361.58, the lower ceiling ¥356.18; for import settlement bills, the upper ceiling was ¥363.82, the lower ceiling ¥358.42. The most common payment terms of time drafts are 30, 60, 90, 120, and 150 days after sight. If a bank buys usances (i.e., drafts payable after a certain time) from its customers, the interest for the period, the margin of the bank, and the margin between the spot rate and the forward rate have to be considered in addition to the exchange rate. The foreign exchange banks can borrow foreign exchange funds from the Bank of Japan at 5 percent (the Bank of Japan discounted export usance bills in yen at 5 percent); the interest charge, therefore, was based on this rate. The banks were free to fix the margin between spot and forward rates. For import usance bills, the banks borrow from foreign banks and the interest rate on import usance bills is based on the American bankers' acceptance (B/A) rate. This rate, therefore, changes very frequently. It was fixed at 6.625 percent for three and four month usances with letters of credit and at 6.875 percent for usances without letters of credit on January 11, 1972; at their height in July 1969, the rates were 11.25 percent for three- and four-month usance bills with letters of credit and 11.5 percent for usances without letters of credit. These changes, as all changes in interest rates on foreign funds (e.g., the loans given by the foreign branches of Japanese banks), are decided by the *Nisui-kai*, the meeting of the chief managers of the foreign divisions of the fifteen city banks.

For D/P drafts, if accompanied by L/C, the exchange rate, based on an agreement among the foreign exchange banks, is 30 *sen* lower than the rate for purchases of sight drafts accompanied by L/C. The upper limit was ¥361.28, the lower limit ¥355.88.

Volume of Transactions in Foreign Exchange Market

	1960	1963	1965	1967	1968	1969	1970
American dollars							
(In millions of dollars)							
Spot	330	1,310	2,163	2,149	3,109	4,258	4,845
Forward	318	1,083	1,844	1,806	2,636	2,926	4,241
Swap	48	511	829	618	727	1,229	2,611
Total	696	2,904	4,836	4,573	6,472	8,413	11,697
English pounds							
(In millions of pounds)							
Spot	59	75	88	95	68	50	31
Forward	21	9	14	14	5	1	2
Swap	3	1	4	12	1	1	—
Total	83	85	106	121	74	52	33

Source: Bank of Japan

Bands of Dollar Rates

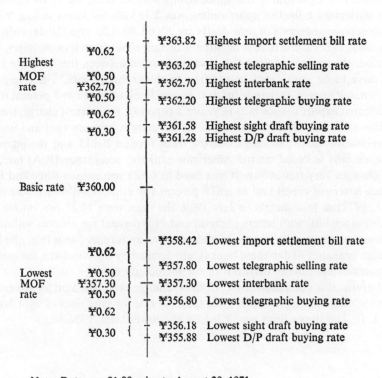

Highest MOF rate	¥0.62	¥363.82 Highest import settlement bill rate
	¥0.50	¥363.20 Highest telegraphic selling rate
	¥362.70	¥362.70 Highest interbank rate
	¥0.50	¥362.20 Highest telegraphic buying rate
	¥0.62	
	¥0.30	¥361.58 Highest sight draft buying rate
		¥361.28 Highest D/P draft buying rate
Basic rate	¥360.00	
Lowest MOF rate	¥0.62	¥358.42 Lowest import settlement bill rate
	¥0.50	¥357.80 Lowest telegraphic selling rate
	¥357.30	¥357.30 Lowest interbank rate
	¥0.50	¥356.80 Lowest telegraphic buying rate
	¥0.62	
	¥0.30	¥356.18 Lowest sight draft buying rate
		¥355.88 Lowest D/P draft buying rate

Note: Rates per $1.00 prior to August 28, 1971.

3 FOREIGN BUSINESS OF JAPANESE BANKS

4 FOREIGN TRADE FINANCING

In order to cope with the difficulties of the postwar era, Japan imposed severe restrictions on foreign trade and exchange. From the end of the war to the enforcement of the Foreign Exchange and Foreign Trade Control Law (December 1, 1949), trade financing was purely domestic financing and, for the largest part, export financing. But it involved no foreign exchange, which was under the control of the occupation. All transactions went through the Board of Trade which represented the Japanese government. Export advance financing, the most important form of export financing, was essentially stopgap financing until the exporter could deliver his goods to the Board of Trade or until he could take his foreign draft to a foreign bank doing business in Japan and receive payment in yen from trade funds. Preferential treatment was provided through the Bank of Japan Foreign Trade Bill System (put into effect on August 30, 1946). The Bank of Japan gave preferential treatment, first, because funds available from city banks were insufficient and had to be supplemented by central bank credit and, secondly, because under the government trade system, manufacture and assembly of export goods were based on orders placed by the Board of Trade and were considered less risky than domestic transactions. The same kind of preferential treatment to these bills (Class 1 Foreign Trade Bills) was extended to export commodity purchase funds (Class 2 Foreign Trade Bills) and funds to cover export charges (Class 3 Foreign Trade Bills).

On July 1, 1947, four foreign trade public corporations came into being and took charge of placing orders instead of the Board of Trade. The export bill system was abolished and replaced by "foreign trade stamp bills" (renamed "foreign trade bills" on the eighth of the same month). The bills became eligible as collateral by being stamped by the Bank of Japan instead of being approved by the Board of Trade.

Private foreign trade was sanctioned again on August 15, 1947, although under severe restrictions. Immediately, fund demand for prospective export production and assembly (prior to the conclusion of export contracts) became very brisk, while small enterprises needed capital for equipment investment. For these ends, a system under which the Board of Trade certified the fund demand of the export industry was set up (October 1947) which comprised credits negotiated through the good offices of the Bank of Japan and credit given or guaranteed by the Reconversion Finance Bank. In the beginning, all foreign trade bills were only eligible as collateral (interest charges were somewhat above the official discount rate and advances were limited to a certain part, about 80 percent, of the face value of the collateral), but, on April 1, 1948, exporters were given permission to discount them if they were accompanied by a letter of credit. Manufacturers and jobbers were given the same discount facilities on May 20, and, on July 4, funds advanced against such bills were exempted from the application of the penalty rates (charged by the Bank of Japan against loans exceeding a certain ceiling).

All imports were government imports. Importers needed credit for purchases from the Board of Trade. If the commodities constituted the raw material for exports, the foreign trade bill system was used. Processing of cotton or wool for the government could be paid out of foreign trade funds. For imports of raw materials for domestic consumption, a system of bills stamped by the Bank of Japan set up in August 1946 was used. For import charges, the Class 3 foreign trade bills mentioned above were used.

Export financing in foreign currency was revived on December 5, 1949, when the foreign exchange banks were licensed to buy documentary export bills. At first, all export bills were sight drafts, but time drafts became possible in 1953. On February 2 of that year, a system under which the Bank of Japan gave credit on the security of foreign bills of exchange was set up. The credits were granted to foreign exchange banks which gave sight drafts as collateral. The system was intended to promote exports by making low-interest usance facilities available to foreign importers; at the same time, it supplied exchange banks with exchange funds and enabled them to buy time drafts. Together with the deposit of government-held foreign currency with exchange banks (put into practice for U.S. dollars on December 8, 1947; for English pounds on March 2, 1948); it helped the Japanese banks to obtain foreign exchange and strengthened their position in the face of foreign competition.

The system of foreign trade drafts, which made domestic financing possible before documentary export bills could be drawn, remained in use and was also resorted to for goods supplied to the U.S. Forces and special procurement orders. The foreign trade drafts for exports were renamed "export advance bills" on February 2, 1953. When, on July 1, 1960, the yen was added to the list of currencies in which trade accounts can be settled (the "designated currencies"; the arrangement is known as "yen exchange"), the Bank of Japan also extended the preferential treatment accorded to export advance bills to export contracts on a yen basis. They received the same treatment as bills payable in foreign currency as far as rediscounts or advances secured by these bills were concerned. In particular, the system applied to export drafts payable in yen, which were eligible for rediscounting. At the same time, the name of the export advance bill system was again changed to "export foreign trade bill system."

When imports were reopened to private business in January 1950, their financing became the sole responsibility of the importer. Since at that time the banks were not permitted to hold foreign exchange, they had to buy foreign exchange from the foreign exchange special account with high-interest yen funds. This made it impossible for the Japanese banks to compete with the foreign banks doing business in Japan, which operated with lower interest charges. When applying for a letter of credit, 50 percent of the amount had to be deposited with the foreign bank as "margin money." This situation prompted the opening of accounts of the Foreign Exchange Control Board with Japanese foreign exchange banks in which the surplus funds of the board were deposited and made available at the same low interest rates as those of the foreign banks. As mentioned above, these accounts (known as FECB a/c) were transferred to the minister of finance upon the dissolution of the board on August 1, 1952 (they were then designated MOF a/c). Letters of credit were opened with the FECB a/c as collateral, and the margin money was transferred from the same accounts. Foreign drafts were sight drafts and were settled by transfers from the FECB a/c. The Japanese importer concluded a forward exchange contract together with the opening of the letter of credit; the foreign exchange bank hedged by a forward purchase from the FECB. When the goods arrived, settlement was effected in yen at the forward rate. The forward rate was officially fixed and included a 5 percent per annum interest charge for the customer and a 4 percent per annum interest charge for the foreign exchange bank. This system came into effect on January 16, 1950. The concentration system was revised on July 10, 1950, and the foreign exchange banks were allowed to retain a certain amount of foreign exchange, but their chronic fund shortage prevented the banks from taking full advantage of this concession.

In order to finance the settlement of import bills after the arrival of the goods, the Bank of Japan's foreign trade draft system was extended to cover these transactions on January 20, 1950, under the designation of import foreign trade drafts. They received preferential treatment and were eligible for rediscount with terms up to sixty days after the arrival of the goods (for imports from the "open account" area, i.e., the area outside the dollar and pound areas and the area for which settlement was in Belgian currency, ninety days after the arrival of the shipping documents).

A further measure was the extension of credit by the three American banks operating in Japan (First National City Bank of New York, Chase Manhattan, and Bank of America) in the form of dollar usances. The banks entered into credit arrangements with individual Japanese foreign exchange banks by which each bank was given a credit line. Based on these credits, letters of credit could be opened. The foreign exporters drew time drafts on the Japanese exchange banks; the terms of the usances varied between 30 and 120 days; the interest rate was 4 percent per annum for the banks and 5 percent per annum for the customers. Besides the usance system, settlement by sight drafts and refinancing by the exchange banks (which drew refinancing drafts on the foreign banks) were also practiced.

These systems (letters of credit secured by FECB a/c, the import foreign trade draft system, and the dollar usance system) were abolished when, on September 25, 1950, the Bank of Japan foreign exchange credit system (also styled Bank of Japan usance system) was introduced. It comprised two categories, the first covering the period from the opening of the letter of credit to the arrival of the shipping documents for which the margin money was required; the second, the usance stage, extended to 90 days (in case of imports from distant points, 120 days) after that date. The Bank of Japan's advance covered both periods; the interest rate was 4 percent per annum for the bank and 5 percent per annum for the customer. For imports from the open account area, only the second category was in use. Actually, the financing for the usance period under the second category was in yen, but it received preferential treatment by fictionally considering it as a foreign exchange transaction. The same was true for the special foreign credit system which was in effect from February 18, 1952, to March 10, 1954. Since loans in the first category (until the arrival of the shipping documents) were automatically transferred to the second, the result was the release of large funds outside the Bank of Japan's credit controls. For this reason, the second loan category was abolished on November 1, 1951, and the system of import foreign trade drafts revived (with terms of three to four months). Their name was changed to "import settlement bills" on February 2, 1953, and the bills were downgraded to being eligible as collateral (i.e., no longer for rediscount) on January 16, 1954, while their term was shortened to two to three months.

With the adoption of the "yen exchange" system on July 1, 1960, the system was extended to comprise not only sight drafts payable in yen but also time drafts. The appellation was changed back to import foreign trade drafts.

The dollar usance system, abolished with the implementation of the Bank of Japan usance system, was revived for the importation of crude oil in October 1950. A pound usance system started on January 23, 1951; under this system, credit was extended not to the individual exchange banks but to the FECB. The pound usance system was applicable to imports of twelve commodities, including raw cotton, raw wool, and crude oil, from the sterling area. The term was 120 days and it took the form of acceptances in London. Since imports from the sterling area were large, the credit line was soon exhausted and operations were suspended on April 26, 1951. The dollar system, too, came to a halt on December 5 of the same year. From then on, import financing was on a strictly domestic basis, though the pound usance system was revived on May 21, 1953, and the dollar usance system on November 11, 1954. Import financing in foreign currencies again replaced yen financing.

The revival of the pound usance system was prompted by the difficulties arising from the decrease in the government's sterling holdings, and the individual banks entered into credit arrangements with foreign banks. No limitation was put on the commodities for which the usances could be bought. The term was ninety days, originally from the day of acceptance of the draft in London or the day of settlement but, from April 1, 1959 on, from the day of arrival of the shipping documents. For the importers, however, the system was more expensive than special foreign loans or import settlement bills, and the balance of usances never exceeded the ¥400 million level. A relaxation of British foreign exchange controls brought an extension of the term to 120 days (August 6, 1953) and the interest rate on these usances was lowered when the Bank of England reduced the bank rate from 4 percent to $3\frac{1}{2}$ percent (September 17). In order to restrict imports, the government barred the use of import settlement bills for nonessential commodities (October 15, 1953); all these factors contributed to a greater use of pound usances. The restrictions on imports became more stringent in 1954; the system of special foreign loans was abolished and import settlement bills were, as mentioned above, downgraded to being eligible as collateral only and the terms of the bills were shortened by one month. When the Bank of England lowered the bank rate to 3 percent (May 13, 1954), the interest burden for the importer fell below that of import settlement bills.

In November 1954, the system of dollar usances was revived on a limited scale (first for certain raw materials for steel manufacture and materials to be processed for exports; after April 1, 1955, for fourteen other categories, including raw cotton and raw wool). The term was ninety days after the arrival of shipping documents. Because the pound usance system had been adopted in order to avoid a drain on the government's reserve of English pounds, credit sources had been limited to "foreign banks situated abroad"; when the dollar usance system was reintroduced, the exchange crisis was over and Japanese banks were also allowed to extend this type of credit. When the dollar usance system was implemented, nonessential commodities (foodstuffs other than staple foods, clothing, household goods, etc.) were excluded from the application of the pound usance system (just as for import settlement bills). When holdings of pound sterling increased, Japanese banks were authorized to give credit in the form of pound usances (April 1, 1955). But the deterioration in the balance of payments situation in 1957 brought another round of restrictions on import financing. The term of pound usances was shortened to ninety days and their use limited to thirty-three categories of commodities (May 14). On September 20 of the same year, the Bank of England prohibited banks located in Britain from extending refinancing facilities to nonresidents. Since over half of the Japanese usances were for refinancing, this prohibition resulted in a large contraction of pound usances (total balance at the end of June 1957 £116.5 million, of which refinancing was £66.9 million; total balance at the end of December £39.6 million). Heavy oil, which had so far enjoyed preferential financing (the longest term, five months for shipper's usances or stand-by credit) was transferred to the usance list on October 1, 1958.

Toward the end of 1958, Japan's entire system of trade financing was overhauled in view of the restoration of convertibility of European currencies. The difference between hard and soft currencies was abolished and dollar and pound usances were combined into a single system (April 1, 1959). The usances were made applicable to a total of sixty commodities, and the requirement of opening a letter of credit was dropped; this made it possible to issue usances on a collection basis. On February 22, 1960, the usance system was extended to all commodities with the exception of some nonessential goods (the same as the import settlement bill system) and all restrictions on the commodities for which it could be used were removed on August 1. On November 16, the usance term was extended to 120 days.

After the war, the U.S. government had made special arrangements for exporting cotton to Japan. The initial American cotton shipments were based on a Commodity Credit Corporation (CCC) agreement involving several government agencies: the Department of the Army, Department of Agriculture, Department of Commerce, CCC, and the U.S. Commercial Company. The shipments started in June 1946. In order to put the shipments on a private basis, it was later agreed that the agreement should expire automatically upon the settlement of the balances due to CCC and USCC; in its place, shipments of cotton to Japan were to be financed by a cotton loan of $60 million for which SCAP concluded an agreement with a consortium of five American banks on May 15, 1948. The loan was secured by the "occupied Japan export-import revolving fund" set up in 1947 and collateralized by Japan's gold and silver holdings, amounting to about $137 million, under sequestration by the occupation authorities. With the exception of the U.S. Export-Import Bank, the consortium was composed of private banks. It was the first postwar loan given Japan by private lenders; and although it was secured by the revolving fund, its conditions were very strict: only 40 percent of the finished products could be sold on the domestic market and the proceeds of all exports had to be paid into the SCAP cotton textile account.

The loan agreement expired at the end of 1950, and with the U.S. fiscal year 1952 (July 1, 1951), all further aid to Japan was cut off in anticipation of the signing of the peace treaty. In view of the larger cotton crops expected for 1951 and 1952, the U.S. Export-Import Bank reestablished a U.S. cotton revolving fund of $100 million and the Bank of Japan concluded the first cotton loan agreement ($40 million) with the U.S. Export-Import Bank on December 21, 1951. In addition to the cotton loans, the Export-Import Bank gave other loans totaling $115 million for the purchase of agricultural products in 1957. American surplus agricultural products were imported under the Agreement Concerning the Purchase of Agricultural Products signed by the American and Japanese governments on March 8, 1954. It was one of four agreements based on the Mutual Security Act passed by Congress in 1951. The purchase price of the commodities (¥18 billion = $50 million) was paid into an account opened in the name of the U.S. government; 20 percent of this sum was given outright to the Japanese government and transferred to the economic aid fund special account set up in fiscal 1954 for payments to the defense industry. The remaining 80 percent was used to pay for goods and services procured in Japan under the U.S. military aid program.

On July 10, 1954, the U.S. Congress passed the Agricultural Trade Development Act, which was intended to lessen the fiscal burden and stabilize agricultural prices by selling or giving away as part of the foreign economic aid program about $6 billion worth of agricultural commodities held by CCC. Based on this law, the Japanese government concluded two agreements for surplus agricultural commodities: the first (May 31, 1955) covered purchases amounting to $85 million and gifts of $15 million, the second (February 10, 1956) provided for $65.8 million of purchases. Yen funds equivalent to the purchase prices stipulated in the agreements were paid into a special account; 80 percent of the first and 73 percent of the second purchase total were converted into dollars by the Bank of Japan and lent to the Japanese government as a forty-year loan through the U.S. Export-Import Bank. For the import of wheat and barley, the import settlement system was used; for raw cotton, the swap system of the Bank of Japan was used for the first agreement and the dollar usance system for later shipments.

As mentioned above, government imports received preferential treatment through the Bank of Japan's stamp bill system, and the same preferential treatment was accorded private transactions for certain commodities (crude oil, raw materials for steel, hides, hemp, and raw cotton for absorbent cotton). Gradually, however, this preferential treatment was restricted and it was abolished completely on June 30, 1955.

Preferential treatment through the stamp bill system was given to the financing of import charges (freight, insurance, stevedoring) from January 1950 to March 1954. An import foreign trade draft system set up on January 24, 1950, was made applicable to imports on an FOB basis for freight and insurance on November 1, 1951. These bills were styled import freight bills.

The Bank of Japan revised its refinancing system effective August 10, 1955. Export advance bills accompanied by an irrevocable letter of credit were discounted at a preferential rate, initially 1.6 sen (5.84 percent), 4 rin (1.46 percent) lower than the official discount rate (applicable to commercial bills); the differential became 6 rin (2.19 percent) when the official discount rate was raised on May 8, 1957, but the rate remained the same on export advance bills. The latter rate was lowered by 1 rin (0.365 percent) on June 20 of that year, bringing the difference to 7 rin (2.555 percent). The official discount rate was reduced by 2 rin on June 18, 1958, while the rate was left the same on export advance bills which made the difference 5 rin (1.825 percent), and this difference remained the same until July 22, 1961. Export advance bills without an irrevocable letter of credit were not discounted but accepted as collateral for loans on which the interest rate was 1 rin (0.365 percent) higher than the discount rate for export advance bills. Import settlement bills and freight bills were likewise only eligible as collateral for loans on which the interest rate was the same as the official discount rate. As explained above, these facilities were not available to traders but only to banks entitled to direct transactions with the Bank of Japan for refinancing.

The Bank of Japan instituted another revision of its discount and loan system which went into effect with the reduction of the official discount rate on August 24, 1960. As far as foreign trade was concerned, the new system comprised export trade bills accompanied by an irrevocable letter of credit eligible for discount, and export trade bills and import trade bills eligible as collateral. The discount rate on export trade bills first was 5 *rin* (1.825 percent) lower than the official discount rate; on July 22, 1961, the official discount rate was raised to 1.9 *sen* (6.94 percent), while the discount rate on export trade bills was reduced to 1.2 *sen* (4.38 percent) and remained at that level until March 20, 1969, when it was lowered by another 1 *rin* (0.365 percent) to 1.1 *sen* (4.02 percent). It remained at that level through all changes in the official discount rate until September 1, 1969 (the beginning of the credit restraints). The interest rate on loans secured by export trade bills (not accompanied by an irrevocable letter of credit) remained 1 *rin* (0.365 percent) higher than the discount rate on export trade bills and moved in unison with that rate. The expression "import trade bills" was adopted as a collective appellation of import settlement bills, import freight bills, and import usance bills in yen; the rate on loans secured by these bills was the same as the discount rate. On January 8, 1966, the Bank of Japan suspended the import trade bill system.

On September 1, 1969, the Bank of Japan switched to interest rates fixed in percent; the official discount rate was raised from 1.6 *sen* (5.84 percent) to 6.25 percent, the discount rate on export trade bills went up from 1.1 *sen* (4.02 percent) to 4.25 percent, and the interest rate on loans secured by export trade bills was fixed at 4.5 percent. Due to the favorable expansion of exports, the government considered the preferential treatment of export refinancing less urgent; the pressure for a revaluation of the yen resulting from Japan's growing exchange reserves was an additional reason. On May 19, 1970, the Bank of Japan introduced new categories into its export refinancing; they were export usance bills in yen and bills for pre-export financing eligible for discount and loans secured by bills for preexport financing. While the official discount rate remained the same, the discount rate on export usance bills in yen (part of the yen shift discussed below) was fixed at 5 percent, the discount rate on bills for preexport financing was 5.25 percent, and the rate on loans secured by bills for preexport finance was 5.5 percent. On July 31, 1971, the rate on loans secured by bills for preexport financing was reduced to 5.25 percent; otherwise, the rates remained the same until August 10, 1971, although the official discount rate was reduced in several steps from 6.25 percent to 5.5 percent. On August 10, 1971, the Bank of Japan raised the discount rate on export usance bills in yen to 5.25 percent, making all rates for export financing uniform.

When trading firms extended their overseas operations, the first method approved for providing on-the-spot working capital was borrowing from local banks on the strength of stand-by credits arranged by Japanese banks. Loans on the basis of stand-by credits were used not only for working capital in connection with imports to and exports from Japan but also for financing wool purchases in Australia, hedging cotton purchases, performance bonds, bid bonds, etc.

Stand-by credits were also used as a preferential measure for petroleum imports. Japanese oil refineries and sales companies connected with foreign interests were given shipper's usances with the longest possible term of five months after customs clearance through the foreign firms with which they were affiliated. In order to provide credit for Japanese firms with no foreign connections, Japanese banks set up stand-by credits under which domestic letters of credit were opened to cover shipper's usances issued by foreign banks. The importers settled these bills five months after customs clearance by telegraphic transfers. This preferential treatment, however, was discontinued after October 1, 1958, when the terms of shipper's usances and stand-by credits were shortened.

On December 8, 1952, the government deposited part of its foreign exchange reserves with the twelve Class A foreign exchange banks which were given permission to lend, through their overseas branches or correspondent banks, a certain part of the dollar funds to Japanese trading firms as working capital for their foreign operations. The same permission was given on April 1, 1955, for the English pound.

When Japan's balance of payments position worsened in 1957, the government greatly reduced its deposits with the foreign exchange banks (only the Bank of Tokyo was not affected). In July 1957, the overall ceiling on foreign advances by the twelve exchange banks was lowered by 30 percent for U.S. dollars (from $110 million to $85 million) and 50 percent for English pounds (from £4 million to £2 million). The validity of stand-by credits was shortened from six to three months. This tightening put a severe strain on the financial situation of the overseas branches of trading firms. By May 1958, however, the original framework had been restored for on-the-spot advances.

Originally, stand-by credits and on-the-spot loans were two different systems; the former had to be approved individually for each firm, while, for the latter, a global ceiling had been fixed for each foreign exchange bank. Since, however, both systems essentially served the same purpose, they were unified on October 1, 1958. Each foreign exchange bank was allowed to give on-the-spot loans or extend stand-by credits within the limits of its overall ceiling, which was abolished on August 31, 1960.

Starting in January 1956, the twenty largest trading companies were allowed to hold a total of $6.5 million in foreign currency (this ceiling was gradually raised). On April 1 of the same year, the current account system between the head offices and the foreign branches of these firms was introduced. After August 1, 1960, other trading companies possessing foreign branches could apply for permission to retain foreign currency. The interfirm current account system was extended to all trading firms possessing foreign branches on February 8, 1960. On April of that year, all commercial firms were allowed to have deposits in foreign currency in the same way as trading firms. If the foreign branches of trading companies did not rely on loans, guarantees, or stand-by credits of Japanese banks but borrowed or received guarantees from nonresident foreign banks based on a letter of guaranty from their head office, they had to obtain permission if the total of such credit exceeded $300,000 per branch (permission for a credit total under $300,000 had been unnecessary since October 1959). The ceiling was removed on August 1, 1960.

Of great importance for the financing of exports were the loans given by the Japan Export-Import Bank discussed above. These loans were of particular importance for ship exports, and the interest rate on these loans originally was 4 percent. The rate was raised to 4.75 percent for new loans after April 1, 1969, and, in 1970, the share of financing by the Export-Import Bank was reduced. The usual arrangement for financing the building of ships for export was to demand a down payment of 20 percent of the price from the customer; the city banks financed 8 percent of the price and the Export-Import Bank 70 percent of the remaining 72 percent (i.e., 50.4 percent of the total price). This share was reduced to 60 percent (i.e., 43.2 percent of the total) effective April 1, 1970, which increased the interest burden of the shipbuilder from about 6 percent to about 6.5 percent. The OECD as well as the EEC has often called for a reduction of government support for shipbuilding; the latest proposal of the EEC wants to limit government aid to shipbuilding to 3 percent of the selling price of a vessel.

One of the ways in which the government has promoted exports is the system of export insurance. This insurance is available in two forms, individual insurance and collective insurance. Collective insurance contracts are concluded each fiscal year between the government (the insurance division of MITI) and the export association for the products for whose export this insurance can be taken out (e.g., textiles, machinery and equipment, rolling stock, ships, automobiles, and bicycles). The insurance covers emergency risks and credit risks; special insurance is available against impossibility of collection and nonpayment of drafts. The foreign exchange banks can charge the entire costs of the export bill insurance to the drawer of the bill. The insurance covers 80 percent of the insured amount; the premiums vary for different kinds of bills (documentary bills, sight draft, D/A, and D/P bills) and different countries. A number of prefectures and municipalities have adopted supplementary insurance systems.

For trade with the People's Republic of China, export and import contracts are made out in Japanese yen or Chinese yuan but accounts are actually settled in British pounds. All documents, therefore, including letters of credit and trade bills, quote Japanese or Chinese currency and the Bank of China accepts purchase contracts for yuan futures though neither side actually uses these currencies for settlement. The Japanese banks agreed to this method under three conditions: (1) the Japanese traders take the exchange risk in case of a parity change; (2) import letters of credit in yuan issued in Japan must state expressly that the yuan is to be converted into sterling at specific rates; (3) provision must be made for dishonored bills.

3 FOREIGN BUSINESS OF JAPANESE BANKS

5 THE YEN SHIFT

Despite the adoption of free-yen accounts and the yen exchange system in July 1960, the actual use of yen for foreign trade financing was small and accounted for only 1 percent of all export and import payments. The Ministry of Finance and the Bank of Japan were basically opposed to the use of yen for trade financing for three reasons: first, because the use of yen in international transactions might encourage the influx of hot money; second, because the increase in the balance on free-yen accounts posed a threat to monetary policy (which was usually a policy of tight money); third, because the use of yen in international transactions would make control of the exchange rate more difficult. But in times of monetary relaxation and low Japanese interest rates, the use of yen funds for foreign trade transactions increased. Such a "yen shift" occurred in 1966 when the call rate (over the month) dropped to 1.80 *sen* (6.57 percent). A new element was injected into the situation by the worsening of the balance of payments of the United States and the growing foreign exchange reserve of Japan. At the Honolulu Conference in February 1968, Japan promised to cooperate with the United States by reducing loans from American banks, but at that time money was scarce and the Bank of Japan had just made its "position guidance" more severe by imposing loan ceilings not only for the end but also for the middle of the month. In 1966, the yen shift reduced the increase in the foreign exchange holdings, and the official reserves decreased in 1967. But in 1969, MITI pressed for a yen shift for the following reasons: first, despite Japan's growing economic strength, only an insignificant fraction of its foreign trade is settled in yen whereas the leading European countries use their own currencies to a large extent; second, in view of the impending adjustment of international parities, the use of yen can lessen the foreign exchange risks of Japanese traders; third, Japan's strong competitive position makes it possible for Japan to use yen. MITI wanted to increase the share of the yen in the settlement of trade accounts to 5–6 percent and demanded better conditions for yen drafts from the Bank of Japan. At the same time, MITI accused the Japanese foreign exchange banks of favoring drafts in foreign exchange over yen drafts on account of the commission connected with the foreign exchange drafts. The Ministry of Finance supported the yen shift for the banks and advised the banks to repay their high-interest Eurodollar loans, and, in September, the Bank of Japan agreed to a yen shift for trading and manufacturing companies. This was in spite of the increase in the official discount rate and the credit restraints.

In June 1969, the Bank of Japan allowed the replacement of dollar import credits by yen through special arrangements by the importers with their banks. Due to the rise in foreign interest rates, the steel manufacturers had formally applied for yen loans, and the petroleum industry also wanted yen credits. In July 1969, Nissan Motor Co. decided to settle accounts with its British subsidiary, Nissan-Datsun, Ltd., in yen instead of pounds.

On June 1, 1970, the Bank of Japan set up a special system of import financing in order to reduce the interest burden of Japanese importers. Under this system, the Bank of Japan made yen loans available to the Class A foreign exchange banks up to 15 percent of the total amount of the yen usances issued by the foreign exchange banks to the importers. If the banks provided national bonds or government-guaranteed debentures as collateral, the interest rate on these loans was 6.35 percent (the official discount rate); it was 6.75 percent in case other collateral was provided. The term of the loans was four months. The bank also accepted import drafts (issued by the importers against import usances) as collateral (interest rate 6.75 percent). These loans were outside the credit lines of the banks and did not come under the Bank of Japan's position guidance. These measures were expected to replace about $80–120 million of the $800 million which were needed in four months for new import financing and reduce the interest burden of the importers from over 10 percent to about 8 percent. Independently of these measures, the Bank of Japan authorized the foreign exchange banks to discount import usance bills on New York directly instead of through American banks; but the Bank of Japan admonished the banks to avoid "friction" with American banks.

In addition to the discount of export bills and loans secured by export bills, the Bank of Japan provided loans in foreign currency from the foreign exchange fund for the time between loading and collection (interest rate fixed at 5 percent on May 15, 1970) and discounted export usance bills in yen at the same rate of 5 percent (term six months after shipment or five months after acceptance). The bank ceased to purchase bills denominated in foreign exchange and issued by foreign banks on November 30, 1970.

Until the fall of 1970, foreign interest rates were high so that borrowing from American banks decreased; but when the American B/A rate came down to 4.375 percent, borrowing in Japan became less advantageous. Because a "dollar shift" would bring an increase in short-term funds, the Ministry of Finance and the Bank of Japan decided to reduce the actual costs of borrowing without changing the nominal interest rates. In February 1971, the swap costs (0.25 percent) for import loans were no longer computed separately, and, on March 11, 1971, the share of import financing was raised from 15 percent to 30 percent of the total amount of yen usances at the same interest rate as the B/A rate. At that time, the B/A rate was 3.875 percent; together with commissions, the borrowing costs amounted to 5.375 percent; the interest rate for the yen loans was fixed at 4.75 percent.

In the meantime, the currency crisis had pushed the forward rates up and in order to stabilize the market, the Bank of Japan, which had set a ceiling on purchases of export bills in November 1970, decided to increase its purchases of export bills and increase the deposits of foreign exchange with the foreign exchange banks in order to correct their overbought position (which, in May 1971, was about $3 billion). Moreover, the Ministry of Finance and the Bank of Japan tried to lessen the pressure on forward rates by depositing large funds with the foreign exchange banks. After the flotation of the yen, a special fund of $50 million was assigned for buying export bills of small enterprises. These funds were to cover up to 90 percent of the contract price; the interest rate was 3.625 percent; with a commission of 0.25 percent, the borrowing costs were 3.875 percent. The term was for three months (from contract to shipment). Eligible were (1) small enterprises in designated export districts or designated export industries (export share at least 10 percent of shipments); (2) small enterprises in other districts if the export ratio of the industry was at least 30 percent; (3) small enterprises belonging to industries in which products of small enterprises accounted for 50 percent of shipments and exports for 10 percent; (4) other small enterprises deserving consideration.

Originally, the deposits of foreign currency with the foreign exchange banks was for short-term financing, but the promotion of imports became part of the eight-point program adopted by the government to avoid a yen revaluation. This program envisaged imports of large equipment, such as atomic reactors or aircraft, and the funds made available under the foreign exchange loan system were to replace funds formerly borrowed from the World Bank or the U.S. Export-Import Bank. Hence, in addition to the foreign exchange banks, these funds were to be deposited with the Japan Development Bank and the Japan Export-Import Bank. The Ministry of Finance wanted to link this system with the financing of the development of raw material sources.

4 BALANCE OF PAYMENTS

The increase in Japan's foreign exchange reserve during the year 1971 attracted much attention. A large part of this increase resulted from the international currency situation but it also reflected a qualitative change in Japan's balance of payments position which began in 1968. After the war, Japan literally started from scratch as far as foreign exchange and overseas assets were concerned. For about fifteen years, the country's balance of payments position was always precarious and items of little importance by Western standards (e.g., special procurement orders) were vital for offsetting the drain on the country's foreign exchange reserves resulting from the requirements of economic growth. For the entire period up to 1966, the balance of payments was the most serious and often the only limiting factor on the expansion of the economy. The modernization of industry made the importation of equipment necessary because, at that stage, Japanese manufacturers were unable to produce much of the advanced machinery required for the country's steel mills, shipyards, oil refineries, petrochemical *kombinats*, and the manufacture of electrical machinery and automobiles. Originally, most of the import restrictions were imposed for balance of payments reasons although their protectionist function has grown stronger in the last ten years.

It was only in 1964 that the trade balance definitely turned favorable and in 1968 that it became large enough to offset the deficits on almost all other accounts. This was the year in which Japan, for the first time since the war, became a creditor nation. This fact was an indication of the maturity of Japan's economy and it also suggested that the country's foreign exchange problems had changed. The yen had become a strong currency, and the threat to the authorities' monetary policy created by the in- and outflows of short-term funds as well as the mounting pressure for a revaluation of the yen superseded the anxieties over balance of payments deficits. In contrast to the credit restraints imposed in 1954, 1957, 1961, and 1964, the monetary restrictions decreed in September 1969 were not occasioned by an adverse international payments balance but by the excessive tempo of the expansion. At that time, OECD's third working party (which busies itself with international financial problems) warned Japan (as it did West Germany) that the credit restraints would lead to an excessive accumulation of foreign balances. There can be no doubt that Japan's foreign exchange reserves have grown much too fast, but whether it was for the reasons given by the OECD is a different question.

The discussions on the revaluation of the yen expressly or tacitly assumed that Japan's favorable balance on trade account was due to the undervalued yen. Never have prominent people uttered more arrant nonsense than in this debate. Price is the basic factor in international competition, but the competitiveness of Japanese prices did not depend on the parity of the yen. It is certainly true that the price structure of Japanese products is as opaque as black ink, but the estimate given by Yasusaburo Hara, president of Nippon Kayaku Co., Ltd., that Japanese-made ships, automobiles, and electric machinery and appliances "have an average 20 percent edge on their foreign counterparts in terms of price" may not be far off the mark. The basic reason for Japan's international competitiveness was the flexibility of her industry which was not due to any government planning or the foresight of her businessmen (on both counts, Japan's performance has been poor) but to a coincidence of conditions which is usually described as luck. Luck has been with the Japanese ever since the Korean War. Because she had not (as the United States) an immense stock of plant and equipment rapidly becoming obsolescent, Japan was able to reorient her resources according to the requirements of a rapid technological advance while keeping the disruptive effects of the changes on the older sectors of the economy to a minimum. The ruthless disregard of environmental health (for which the country is starting to pay now), the official contempt for the consumer's interest, the deplorable social security system, the containment of wage increases within the limits of productivity gains, and the absence of a costly military establishment—all these factors contributed to the competitiveness of Japanese industry. An aspect worth mentioning is the enormous concentration in foreign trade. According to MITI, the top 28 Japanese trading firms handled 68.3 percent of Japan's total exports and 77 percent of all imports in 1970. The 28 firms, all of which reported annual sales exceeding ¥100 billion, constituted only 0.6 percent of the 8,801 firms engaged in foreign trade (56.8 percent of them in export, 26.8 percent in export and import, and 16.4 percent in import). This concentration has made Japan's foreign trade system the most effective in the world and has contributed much more to the country's competitiveness than the imaginary advantages of an undervalued yen. Japanese export prices have gone up, but not to such an extent as to jeopardize their competitiveness. Furthermore, Japanese products have become more competitive in quality and performance, and Japanese manufacturers generally have a good record in meeting delivery schedules.

In sharp contrast to the surplus on trade account stands the ever-increasing deficit on services. In 1960, the Ministry of Transportation "sold" the Ministry of Finance an enormous state-supported shipbuilding program with the promise that the implementation of the program would increase the ratio of goods carried in bottoms flying the Japanese flag to above 70 percent and produce a favorable balance on invisibles. Nothing of the sort happened. The deficit on services has grown from $35 million in 1960 (deficit on freight and insurance, $90.4 million) to $1,798 million in 1970 (deficit on freight and insurance, $1,227 million). The problem is made difficult by the enormous difference in the volume of exports and imports. Due to the large imports of industrial raw materials and fuels, the quantitative ratio of imports to exports is ten to one. In 1970, the total volume of exports amounted to 42,008,000 m.t. (the totals include air cargo); Japanese-flag vessels carried 18,274,000 m.t. (43.5 percent), foreign flag vessels, 23,663,000 m.t. (56.3 percent). The total volume of imports was 435,924,000 m.t.; Japanese-flag vessels carried 200,411,000 m.t. (46.0 percent), foreign-flag vessels 235,464,000 m.t. (53.5 percent). Furthermore, the types of ships used for exports and imports differ; exports are carried more and more in container ships (naturally, they are also used for some imports), whereas giant tankers (very large crude carriers) and bulk carriers predominate in the import trade. Although the Ministry of Transportation is drawing up ever more grandiose plans for the merchant marine, the quantitative imbalance and qualitative difference between exports and imports makes the economics of a 70 percent self-sufficiency in shipping very doubtful.

In addition to freight and insurance, Japan's payments exceed receipts for such items as travel, patent royalties, management and agents' fees, and interest and dividends from investment. Thanks to the income from military transactions (offshore procurement orders), the government's account is in the black.

In some critical years (1961, 1963, and 1964), the favorable balance on long-term capital account helped to offset part of the deficit on current account, but since 1965 the balance has been unfavorable. The outflow of capital was, at least partially, the result of official policy promoting outward foreign investment, particularly for the development of raw material sources. More important, however, was the large increase in deferred payments for exports and loans. Since 1966, the increase in these accounts has been remarkably steady compared with the erratic performance of capital inflows into Japan. Significant for the development in recent years was the increase in foreign investment in securities and in the flotation of external bonds.

In 1962, the surplus on long-term capital account helped to turn the basic balance favorable; 1965 and 1966 and again from 1968 to 1970, the basic balance showed a surplus despite the deficit on capital account. The surplus was very large, $1,964 million, in 1969 but shrank to $417 million in 1970 due to the enormous outflow of long-term capital ($1,579 million).

The control of short-term capital movements has been called the key to the management of international payments, but in this field the Japanese authorities have not been altogether lucky. Most of the measures taken were protective reactions to real or imaginary threats and it is impossible to find a consistent pattern except for the fact that most of the measures were restrictions and prohibitions. They seldom solve anything but, as someone said, "it is more satisfactory for the authorities to repel rather than try to offset inflows of hot money." Broadly speaking, the government tried to prevent an excessive accumulation of foreign exchange (and thereby lessen the foreign pressure for the revaluation of the yen) in five ways: (1) measures for decreasing foreign exchange holdings; (2) restrictions on the inflow of foreign capital; (3) restrictions on the inflow of short-term funds; (4) liberalization of the outflow of capital; (5) liberalization of imports. Most of these measures have been discussed elsewhere; suffice it to point out that the risk involved in the accumulation of dollars had been clearly recognized long before it became acute. Thus in November 1970 the Bank of Japan stopped buying export trade bills from the foreign exchange banks. Until then, the bank had bought exports bills denominated in dollars at the B/A rate; this had been part of the preferential export financing of the bank. These purchases grew rapidly in 1970 on account of the drop in the B/A rate and the Bank of Japan abolished this type of financing on the grounds that no other central bank assumed the foreign exchange risk for the commercial banks. In the same year, the phenomenon of "leads and lags" received wide publicity. Importers in the weak currency countries tend to "lead," i.e., accelerate their payments to foreign supplies, while foreign importers will "lag" their payments for goods from weak currency countries. Exporters in strong currency countries try to accelerate collections; exporters in weak currency countries tend to delay them. The "leads and lags" in foreign trade settlements were said to have accounted for $400 million of the $1.9 billion rise in Japan's currency reserves in May 1971, and the direct restrictions on short-term fund transactions at least partially served the purpose of preventing the banks and the trading companies from using export financing for speculative purposes. On the other hand, the authorities themselves provided the means for some speculation. The foreign exchange funds deposited with the foreign exchange banks, ostensibly for promoting imports, actually for reducing the foreign exchange holdings, could be used for financing exports. The banks paid the official discount rate plus 0.25 percent on these deposits, which at the end of June 1971 came to 6 percent, the same as the B/A rate on four-month loans. The foreign banks considered these deposits as a kind of export promotion; on August 10, therefore, preferential treatment of export financing was abolished and the discount rate on bills for preexport financing and the interest rate on loans in foreign currency raised. But, when the dollar was floated, the Japanese authorities continued to buy dollars at the old official rate. Between August 16 and August 28, spot transactions in dollars on the Tokyo foreign exchange market totaled $5,627 million, and the increase in the official reserves in August 1971, $4,587 million (equivalent to Japan's total foreign exchange holdings at the end of January 1971), indicates the extent to which the banks and the trading companies were able to shift the exchange risk on to the monetary authorities. The foreign exchange funds deposited with the banks for reducing the official reserves were quite useful in this operation.

According to a report of the Ministry of Finance to the Diet, fourteen of the foreign exchange banks sold 3,490 million of dollars to the foreign exchange fund during the twelve days from August 16 to August 27 when the government attempted to maintain the fixed exchange rate of the dollar. The Bank of Tokyo sold the largest amount, $602 million, followed by Mitsubishi Bank with $492 million and Fuji Bank with $394 million. The ten largest trading companies collected a total of $884 million in prepayments for exports; the largest amounts were reported by Mitsui & Co. with $331 million, Marubeni-Iida with $142 million, and Nissho-Iwai with $85 million. The ministry estimated "speculative" selling at $2,500 million, the amount the banks had borrowed from foreign banks and the trading companies had collected in advance payments for exports from their foreign customers. The opposition parties branded the sales as "unlawful" and "speculative"; since the government was fully aware of the opportunity it gave to the banks and trading companies to protect themselves against exchange losses; these accusations are groundless, but the government certainly acted highly irresponsibly.

Below are the figures reported by the Ministry of Finance.

1. Excess of Spot Sales of Foreign Exchange Banks,
August 16-27

	$ million		$ million
Bank of Tokyo	692	Kobe Bank	75
Mitsubishi Bank	492	Kyowa Bank	61
Fuji Bank	394	Industrial Bank of Japan	29
Sumitomo Bank	364	Hokkaido Takushoku Bank	15
Mitsui Bank	352	Saitama Bank	15
Dai-Ichi Kangyo Bank	341		
Sanwa Bank	315	Subtotal	3,490
Tokai Bank	233	Other	405
Daiwa Bank	112	Total	3,895

2. Inflow of Prepayments for Exports August 17–31
(single payments exceeding $50,000)

	$ million		$ million
A. Prepayments as reported by banks		B. Prepayments as reported by trading companies	
Bank of Tokyo	267	Mitsui & Co.	331
Mitsui Bank	221	Marubeni-Iida	142
Fuji Bank	194	Nissho-Iwai	85
Sumitomo Bank	151	Sumitomo Shoji	64
Sanwa Bank	128	C. Itoh & Co.	61
Dai-Ichi Kangyo Bank	77	Mitsubishi Corporation	59
Tokai Bank	62	Nichimen Jitsugyo	53
Mitsubishi Bank	57	Tomen	42
Daiwa Bank	24	Ataka & Co.	30
Kobe Bank	22	Kanematsu Gosho	17
Kyowa Bank	11		
Industrial Bank of Japan	10	Subtotal	884
Hokkaido Takushoku Bank	8	Other	518
Saitama Bank	5	Total	1,402
Subtotal	1,237		
Other	165		
Total	1,402		

1. Measures for Decreasing Foreign Exchange Reserves

1969, April		Yen shift (about $1 billion).
	August, December	Subscription to capital of Asian Development Bank ($50 million).
	October–December	Increase in participation in World Bank ($170 million).
1970, January		Purchase of beneficiary certificates of U.S. Export-Import Bank ($80 million).
	February	Yen loan to World Bank ($100 million).
	March	Yen loan to World Bank ($100 million).
	June	Italian loan to IMF taken over ($125 million).
	July	Italian loan to IMF taken over ($125 million).
	June	Import financing by loans from the foreign exchange fund (about $700 million).
	September	"Yen shift operations" of Bank of Japan (purchase of securities from foreign exchange banks to enable them to repay short-term loans from foreign banks prior to maturity; about $40 million a month).
	October	Purchase of beneficiary certificates of U.S. Export-Import Bank ($40 million).
	December	Flotation of yen bonds of Asian Development Bank ($17 million).
1971, January		Yen loan to World Bank ($100 million).

June-September	Deposit of funds of the foreign exchange fund with foreign exchange banks for import financing ($500 million).
June	Flotation of yen bonds of World Bank ($32 million).
	Yen loan to World Bank ($18 million).
	Eight-Point Program.
October	Flotation of yen bonds of Asian Development Bank ($28 million).
December	Yen loan to Transocean Gulf Oil ($14 million).

2. Restrictions on Inflow of Foreign Capital

1969, September	Restrictions on impact loans.
October ⎫ 1970, January ⎭	Suspension of flotation of external bonds of government agencies.
1971, February	Suspension of flotation of external municipal and corporate bonds (exceptions: German mark bonds of the cities of Kobe and Yokohama and Kansai Electric Power Co.).
March	Suspension of purchase of government bills by nonresidents; "administrative guidance" on their acquisition of securities; prevention of "dollar shift" in trade financing.
May	Prohibition of acquisition of unlisted bonds by foreign investors.
September	Securities firms to keep foreign investment in Japanese securities within $100 million a month.

3. Restrictions on Inflow of Short-Term Funds

The four major measures concerning short-term transactions are:

(1) Foreign Exchange Reserve Deposit System (*Gaika Junbikin Seido*).
(2) Restrictions on Acceptance of Short-Term Foreign Exchange (*Tanki Gaika Tori-ire Kisei*).
(3) Restrictions on Conversion into Yen (*Yen Tenkan Kisei*).
(4) Restrictions on Holdings (*Mochidaka Kisei*).

The Foreign Exchange Reserve Deposit System has been in force since 1962; it requires the foreign exchange banks to keep a certain percentage (at present 15 percent) of short-term foreign funds of high liquidity as reserve; subject to the reserve requirements are short-term liabilities such as Eurodollar and call money deposits, clean loans from foreign banks, and nonresident free-yen accounts. Liquid foreign exchange assets counted as reserves include cash, deposits, call loans, securities issued by foreign governments or international organizations, and bills accepted by first-rate banks.

Together with the flotation of the yen, payments into free-yen accounts were stopped; on September 1, 1971, the foreign exchange banks were advised to keep conversions of dollars borrowed from abroad into yen at the level of August 31; not to accept prepayments for exports ("leads") by trading companies; and to exercise "self-restraint" in spot sales of dollars. On September 6, 1971, these rules were formalized; balances of foreign funds converted into yen had to remain the same every day (instead of in the middle and at the end of the month) and balances of short-term foreign funds and of free-yen accounts had to be kept at the level of September 6 (i.e., restrictions on funds borrowed from abroad as well as on remittances). As related above, these rules proved unworkable and had to be relaxed. On September 1, 1971, the six securities firms handling foreign investments in Japanese securities were advised by the Ministry of Finance not to increase their balances of "securities yen." The securities companies receive the purchase price together with the orders; the securities companies convert the foreign currency into yen which are deposited in a special account ("securities yen") until the securities are paid for (for ordinary way transactions, settlement is on the fourth day).

4. Liberalization of Capital Outflows

1969, October	"Automatic" approval of direct outward investment up to $300,000.
1970, February	Ceiling on foreign exchange holdings of trading firms and manufacturers raised.
March	Travel allowance for tourists raised to $1,000.
April	Investment in foreign securities by securities companies ($100 million).
September	"Automatic" approval of direct outward investment up to $1 million.
December	Expenses for establishing overseas branches allowed up to $1 million.
1971, February	Allowance for business travel raised to $3,000.
June	Allowance for tourists raised to $3,000.
	Abolition of limitations on foreign exchange holdings of trading companies and manufacturers; ceiling on funds retained by air lines and shipping companies raised.
July	Ceiling on direct outward investment abolished. Investment in foreign securities and acquisition of real estate abroad by individuals permitted.

5. Import Liberalization

1970, November	Restrictions on imports reduced to ninety items.
1971, March	Restrictions on imports reduced to sixty items.
	Revision of tariff schedule.
August	Adoption of preferential tariffs for developing countries.
September	Restrictions on imports reduced to forty items.

Balance of Payments

(In millions of dollars)

Year or month	Balance on current transactions	Visible trade Balance	Exports	Import	Services	Transfer payments	Balance on capital transactions[1] Long-term	Short-term[2]	Errors & omissions	Overall balance	Changes in gold & foreign currency	Changes in other assets
1965	932	1,901	8,332	6,431	−884	−85	−415	−61	−51	405	108	297
1966	1,254	2,275	9,641	7,366	−886	−135	−808	−64	−45	337	−33	370
1967	−190	1,160	10,231	9,071	−1,172	−178	−812	506	−75	−571	−69	502
1968	1,048	2,529	12,751	10,222	−1,306	−175	−239	209	84	1,102	886	216
1969	2,119	3,699	15,679	11,980	−1,399	−181	−155	178	141	2,283	605	1,678
1970	1,970	3,963	18,969	15,006	−1,785	−208	−1,591	724	271	1,374	903	593
1971	5,898	7,900	23,650	15,750	−1,748	−254	−1,161	2,993	−53	7,677	10,836	−3,031
1971 Jan.	−185	−2	1,228	1,226	−179	−8	−192	13	55	−309	133	−314
Feb.	182	367	1,613	1,246	−171	−14	99	17	91	389	336	53
Mar.	453	702	2,091	1,389	−191	−58	−101	101	76	529	590	−61
Apr.	377	547	1,863	1,316	−137	−33	67	−88	65	421	319	102
May	417	579	1,887	1,308	−159	−3	165	604	−3	1,183	1,139	44
June	498	652	2,015	1,363	−137	−17	−55	144	97	684	683	1
July	613	788	2,116	1,328	−164	−11	−181	10	53	495	328	167
Aug.	820	866	2,053	1,187	−31	−15	−74	582	1,976	3,304	4,587	−1,283
Sept.	680	860	2,070	1,210	−167	−13	−109	−42	−268	261	870	−690
Oct.	571	727	2,084	1,357	−138	−18	−220	−11	−207	133	714	−581
Nov.	474	636	2,031	1,395	−150	−12	−295	120	−28	271	738	−467
Dec.	985	1,172	2,577	1,405	−132	−56	−325	102	−445	316	399	−83

Notes: 1. Minus sign indicates outflow of capital (increase in Japanese assets held abroad or decrease in foreign currency claims).
2. Transactions for the settlement of balances are not included.
3. Minus sign indicates decrease in assets or increase in liabilities.

Source: The Bank of Japan, Economic Statistics Monthly.

Japan's Foreign Exchange Reserves

End of year or month	$ million	End of year or month	$ million
1952	930	1968	2,891
1953	913	1969	3,496
1954	637	1970	4,399
1955	738	1971, January	4,532
1956	941	February	4,868
1957	524	March	5,458
1958	861	April	5,777
1959	1,322	May	6,916
1960	1,824	June	7,599
1961	1,486	July	7,927
1962	1,841	August	12,514
1963	1,878	September	13,384
1964	1,999	October	14,098
1965	2,107	November	14,836
1966	2,074	December	15,235
1967	2,005		

Note: As of the end of March, 1952–1955; excluding IMF gold tranche position prior to 1964.

Changes in Short-Term External Assets and Liabilities
of Foreign Exchange Banks

(In millions of dollars)

	Assets		Liabilities		Net
1971	Change in total assets	Change in export usances	Change in total liabilities	Change in import usances	position
January	−455	−348	−213	−212	−242
February	27	75	5	−26	22
March	109	161	83	−58	26
April	112	−4	−64	−104	176
May	645	109	531	173	114
June	−72	132	−78	149	6
July	−186	−31	−361	−326	175
August	251	85	1,335	746	−1,084

Note: Figures from April to August are provisional.
Source: Bank of Japan.

Short-Term External Assets and Liabilities of
Foreign Exchange Banks

(In millions of dollars)

	End of July 1971	End of August 1971
Assets, total	6,779	7,030
Denominated in foreign currency	6,759	7,008
Export usances	4,999	5,084
Denominated in yen	20	22
Liabilities, total	5,442	6,777
Denominated in foreign currency	4,587	5,838
Import usances	1,849	2,595
Denominated in yen	855	939
Net assets, total	1,337	253
Denominated in foreign currency	2,172	1,170
Denominated in yen	−835	−917

Source: Bank of Japan.

Export and Import Price Indices

(1965 average=100)

Year or month	Price indices on contract basis (1)		Price indices on customs clearance basis (2)	
	Export	Import	Export	Import
1962	96.9	98.2	103.7	94.5
1963	99.2	101.0	102.5	95.6
1964	100.6	102.6	101.3	97.9
1965	100.0	100.0	100.0	100.0
1966	100.1	102.1	100.1	100.7
1967	100.5	101.0	103.2	100.4
1968	101.0	101.5	103.3	99.0
1969	103.7	103.8	107.9	98.8
1970	108.7	107.3	113.9	103.2
1970, June	109.2	107.6	115.3	101.8
July	109.3	107.5	115.7	103.4
Aug.	109.0	106.6	117.4	104.7
Sept.	108.7	107.0	116.9	104.7
Oct.	108.6	106.5	115.1	103.4
Nov.	108.5	107.3	115.4	104.6
Dec.	108.6	107.0	114.8	104.1
1971, Jan.	108.7	107.5	115.2	105.2
Feb.	108.9	107.9	116.6	104.1
Mar.	109.1	108.6	116.0	105.3
Apr.	109.5	109.2	117.0	105.3
May	109.7	108.5	118.8	106.5
June	109.9	109.0	119.4	107.1
July	110.1	109.5	122.1	106.9
Aug.	110.1	109.4	123.3	104.7
Sept.	109.8	106.3	—	—
Oct.	109.2	104.4	—	—

Source: (1) The Bank of Japan; Economic Statistics Monthly.

(2) Ministry of International Trade and Industry; Monthly Foreign Trade Statistics.

5 YEN REVALUATION

The revaluation of the yen began to be discussed in 1968, and the discussions were taken more seriously after the revaluation of the German mark in October 1969. There was unanimous agreement among the Japanese that a revaluation of the yen was out of the question, although there was no agreement on the reasons why the yen should not be revalued. The argument most frequently advanced contended that it was premature to regard Japan's balance of payments as stabilized—as recently as 1967, the basic balance had shown a deficit of $1,002 million and the overall balance had been $571 million in the red, so that there had even been rumors of a yen devaluation (the British pound had been devalued in November 1967 and the gold rush in March 1968 had sparked speculation on a possible devaluation of the dollar). All commentators stressed the difference between Japan and West Germany with respect to the structure of foreign trade, the balance of payments, and foreign exchange reserves.

Japan's seemingly flourishing exports involved a number of uncertainties. Despite the enormous progress in the sixties, the share of heavy industrial products in the total value of exports was below the level of the advanced industrial countries in the West. In order to promote exports of capital goods, Japan had to give higher credits and longer terms for deferred payments to the developing countries. The shift to capital goods in the export structure, therefore, was bound to have an adverse influence on the balance of payments. A further negative factor was the large dependence of Japan's exports on the American market and a revaluation of the yen would make Japan less competitive at a time when competition on the part of the developing countries in such fields as textiles, footwear, and electronics was becoming stronger. The growth of exports has hardly changed Japan's position as a marginal supplier, notably in the American market. The talk of "internationalization" notwithstanding, Japan's economy still retains many traits of a closed economy and is far from being integrated in the world economy. The practical effect is that a slowdown in demand in any part of the world has a direct impact on Japanese exports. Even twenty years of expansion do not make a mature economy (there remains a hiatus between Japan's quantitative and qualitative development) and the coincidence of rapid expansion and a favorable balance of payments is no criterion for the value of a country's currency.

Until the beginning of 1971, Japan's foreign exchange reserves had been relatively low; although there was no reason for anxiety and Japan would have been able to overcome temporary liquidity problems, the foreign exchange holdings did not correspond to the size of the country's foreign trade. At the end of March 1971, the reserves were equivalent to 4.2 times the average monthly value of imports in the first quarter of the year. Moreover, with $539 million, the share of gold in Japan's official reserves was extremely low, while short-term liabilities, although more than offset by short-term assets, exceeded the foreign exchange reserves.

Many commentators emphasized that Japan's favorable balance of payments developed under circumstances which could not be expected to last. The yen was not freely convertible and the restrictions on short- and long-term capital transactions and the limitations on imports still afforded a certain protection (although it proved ineffective after August 15). Japan had just started to liberalize direct outward investment and faced the enormous task of financing large-scale capital investments for the development of raw material sources. The eventual dismantling of the protective apparatus and Japan's greater international engagement, particularly in the developing countries, were bound to affect her balance of payments position. The Japanese government and the business leaders, therefore, were of the opinion that the question of revaluing the yen could only be considered after the yen had been "stripped naked" and had been able to retain its strong position outside the greenhouse of official protection.

In order to avoid a revaluation of the yen and to ease the mounting tension with the United States, the authorities resorted to the measures outlined above. In the face of increasing pressure, on June 4, 1971, the government announced its "eight-point program," which envisaged the following measures: (1) reduction of import restrictions to forty items by the end of September; enlargement of existing import quotas to 5 percent of domestic consumption (to be applied to about thirty items); (2) preferential tariffs on imports from developing countries (put into effect August 1); (3) tariff reductions primarily on imported consumer goods; reduction of excise tax on large passenger cars; (4) liberalization of outward investment (implemented July 1); liberalization of direct inward investment (implemented August 4); lending system for Japanese firms engaged in development of foreign raw material sources to be organized; support of bank loans to foreign institutions; (5) removal of non-tariff import barriers; imports of items subject to automatic import quotas (AIQ, thirty-seven items) to be freed "on principle" by the end of the year; rescission of restrictions on items subject to prior approval (six items) to be taken into consideration; (6) promotion of economic cooperation; development aid of the government to be raised to the standard of the DAC; effective utilization of the Overseas Economic Cooperation Fund; easier terms for government loans; more untied loans; (7) promotion of "orderly" exports and imports; abolition of the tax privileges for exports to be taken into consideration; (8) effective operation of fiscal and monetary measures.

The government floated the yen on Saturday, August 28, 1971, and on that day the yen rose by 5.478 percent computed by the IMF formula (ratio of difference between fixed parity and quoted price to quoted price). Initially, the exchange banks refused all transactions in foreign currencies except the cashing of travelers' checks or dollar notes, and the restrictions imposed by the Ministry of Finance confused the foreign exchange market until the middle of September. It was only on October 28 that the Bank of Tokyo resumed forward transactions. The Bank of Japan intervened frequently to keep the dollar rate from plunging too fast which brought angry protests from abroad against the "dirty float." In the first week following the flotation of the yen, the dollar fell to ¥338.30, a decline of 6.41 percent; the volume of transactions was nearly $900 million. The decline was less sharp during September but accelerated at the end of the month; on September 28, the rate dropped to ¥335.88, a decline of 7.18 percent; it sank further to ¥332.90 on October 2, bringing the rate of revaluation to 8.14 percent. The faster rise in the value of the yen was caused by the decision of the Bank of Japan to end the managed float and let market forces determine the value of the yen. On October 11, the dollar was quoted at ¥330.05, 9.07 percent above parity; during the rest of the month, the dollar registered occasional gains but weakened toward the end of the month; and, in both October and November, the percentage gain of the yen exceeded that of the mark. On November 29, the yen's value against the dollar was 10.07 percent above parity and, with little intervention by the Bank of Japan, the dollar declined sharply in the following two weeks. On December 11, the dollar was quoted at ¥323.10, equivalent to a revaluation of the yen by 11.42 percent, only fractionally lower than the rise of 11.8 percent in the value of the German mark.

The question that has still to be answered is the "why" of the decline of the value of the dollar as against the yen. Actually, there has been no satisfactory explanation for the revaluation of currencies, neither for the revaluation of the German mark in 1969 nor for the wave of revaluations which began in May 1971. In his *Money and Foreign Exchange After 1914* (1922), Gustav Cassel wrote: "The discussions on the variations in exchange rates and their true explanation . . . has been chiefly characterized by a remarkable lack of clearness on the question as to what really determines the exchange rate between two independent currencies." The same may be said about the recent discussions on the revaluation of the mark or the yen, at least in the sense that there was no convincing explanation as to why or by what standard these currencies were overvalued. The inference from a large surplus in the balance of payments or on trade account to a "basic disequilibrium" in the parity of the currency is an obvious petitio principii until it is shown that the surplus was the effect of the exchange rates—which has not been demonstrated and probably will not be demonstrated. Generally speaking, the actual devaluations and revaluations since the end of World War II have shown a decreasing importance of purely monetary factors and a growing influence of economic considerations, notably considerations of foreign trade, the balance of payments position, and political objectives. Most postwar currency adjustments have reflected the inflationary depreciation of the value of the domestic currency, and in many cases the devaluations in Southeast Asian and Latin American countries still fall into this category. But for some of the leading European countries, the improvement of the balance of payments became a far more prominent aspect than the adjustment of the nominal parity to the actual value (whatever this may be). Through this shift in emphasis, what had merely been an effect of a currency devaluation has now become its objective. In Goschen's theory on the currency value, the supply-and-demand situation results in a change in the price of one currency in terms of another currency, but this change can only take place in a free currency system which allows a more of less automatic adjustment of parities, a condition which was not present in the Bretton Woods system.

If the currency value can be manipulated in order to erase a deficit in the balance of payments, it can also be changed in order to reduce a surplus. Deflationary conditions may increase the value of a currency, but Professor Schiller's expectation that a revaluation of the currency would contain inflationary pressures (which was his objective in revaluing the mark) has hardly been borne out by subsequent developments. Outside Germany, the accumulation of a large official reserve was considered the result of a basic disequilibrium in the exchange rate and the revaluation of the mark was urged as a means of rectifying this disequilibrium. As stated above, just as the devaluation of a currency can improve the balance of payments by lowering export prices in terms of the currency of importing countries, a revaluation, which diminishes the price competitiveness of the country in export markets, can achieve a reduction of a balance of payments surplus. But it is not clear, it is indeed a completely gratuitous assumption, that a large surplus on trade account is caused by the undervaluation of the exporting country's currency. Without doubt, price is a basic factor although by no means the only factor, in the competitiveness of merchandise in international markets, but until now nobody has furnished any proof that the exchange rate had anything to do with the price competitiveness of German or Japanese products. On the contrary, the German experience seems to indicate that the change in parity had only a temporary effect on the competitive position of German export goods and the increase in Japanese exports in subsequent months (validated exports in October, 17.7 percent higher than the level a year earlier, and 31 percent higher in November) embarrassed a Japanese government that had decried the lethal effect of the American import surcharge and the flotation of the yen. On the other hand, the assertion that America has priced itself out of the export market may not be without foundation. The overvaluation of the dollar may not be without influence, but there are numerous other reasons why the prices of American industrial products are high apart from tariffs in importing countries.

The reversal of the cause-effect relationship in the currency adjustment gambit means that currency rates are used for regulating foreign trade, and foreign pressure for a revaluation of the yen was aimed *solely* at smashing Japan's competitive position, an objective for which the United States could count on the cooperation of the Europeans. In terms of domestic purchasing power, the value of the yen has been declining ever since its parity was fixed at $1 = ¥360 in 1949. According to Pick's Currency Yearbook 1970, the yen's domestic purchasing power declined by 42 percent in the sixties while monetary circulation increased 368 percent. The black market value of the yen, however, rose from a low of $1 = ¥875 in March 1946 to a high of ¥363 in April 1970, which reflected the acceptance of the yen as a usable currency rather than its domestic purchasing power.

The exchange rates of many Western currencies go back to their values under the gold-standard system and still reflect in a faint way the value of their gold coins prior to the First World War. There was no particularly compelling reason for fixing the par value of the yen at $1 = ¥360; it was one possible choice among others. Actually, on the basis of the Bank of Japan's wholesale index, a rate of ¥330–350 had been considered appropriate and the lower rate was chosen because the official wholesale price index did not take into account black market prices which indicated a higher degree of inflation. Up to the adoption of a single exchange rate (which went into effect at 0001 hours, April 25, 1949), the yen-dollar exchange rate had been fixed separately for each particular branch of industry, which had the same effect as paying subsidies in order to make exports possible. The multiple exchange system which had been in force prior to October 1948 permitted exporters to disregard high domestic production costs in quoting export prices. To the extent that devaluations or revaluations represent manipulations of international prices, they are artificial corrections of costs which have nothing to do with the value of the currency in the sense of its domestic purchasing power. The correction of export surpluses by revaluation or the stimulation of exports by devaluation (which upset economic cost-price relations for nonmonetary reasons) points to the emergence of a dichotomic currency value, its domestic value (on which Cassel based his purchasing power theory) and its value in international settlements (which is influenced by the balance of payments and the movements of short-term capital). James W. Angell has already pointed out that movements in private commercial and banking operations, and particularly movements in governmental finance, produce fluctuations in prices and exchange rates. The institutional rigidity of the Bretton Woods system largely neutralized the impact of market forces, and the downfall of the system was not caused by the strictly controlled settlements in international trade but by the freely moving Eurodollars, which assumed such enormous proportions that they far exceeded not only the gold reserves of the United States but also her liquid assets. Although the total foreign assets of the United States greatly surpass her liabilities (U.S. direct investment abroad rose to $78.1 billion in 1970), her monetary assets were obviously insufficient to satisfy the over $40 billion in claims held abroad. However, it was not this "credibility gap" which brought down the system but the contradiction between the fictious value of the dollar ($1 = 0.888671 g. gold) and the market price of gold which, if not proof, was at least a sufficient indication that the dollar was overvalued by about 20 percent. Since the entire Bretton Woods system had become dependent on a fictitious value, it had to collapse. The basic mistake had been to build the system on a national currency whose domestic value could not be made immune to erosion by inflation and whose international value was jeopardized by political and military overcommitments. Unfortunately, the present readjustment of parities on the basis of a "central rate" promises a repetition of the same incongruity.

The approach of the Japanese to the problem of revaluing the yen has undergone a few changes. As mentioned above, government and business were opposed to a yen revaluation even after President Nixon's announcement of his new economic policy. There had been some voices calling for an adjustment of exchange rates. On July 10, 1971, the exchange policy study group of the "Modern Economists" (who had also attacked the Yawata-Fuji merger) published a manifesto which was hardly free from ideological bias and facile assumptions about the working of the exchange market. The group attacked the accumulation of large foreign reserves as harmful to the economy on the grounds that the interest income from the accumulated funds was practically zero because the value of the dollar was sinking and that a favorable basic balance meant that the value created by national resources (labor, capital, land) was given to deficit countries (above all the United States), i.e., the surplus in the balance of payments diminishes consumption and investment in the surplus country and increases consumption and investment in the deficit countries; the inflow of foreign funds imports inflation; and the international currency instability hinders international cooperation, provokes protectionism, and causes unnecessary friction.

The group considered a large change in parity undesirable because it would have a severe impact on exports and partially also on imports; it would be difficult to fix an appropriate parity; if the increase were too small (West Germany was cited as an example), a second revaluation would become necessary, but on the other hand, a one-step revaluation would lead to speculation and hedging. The group advocated a series of small revaluations, about 1 percent every three months or 2.4–4 percent in one year. These revaluations would be continued until the exchange rate had been raised to a suitable level, i.e., until the reserves had decreased to a tolerable size. During this "period of contrived instability," the Bank of Japan would intervene to protect the equilibrium. As an alternative, the group proposed small adjustments of 0.2–0.3 percent each month. The gradual adjustment, the group claimed, would not provoke large movements of short-term funds because it would not be accompanied by speculation or hedging; on account of the gradualness of the change, industry could easily adapt itself to the realignment. It would not be necessary to fix the level in advance, and the process could be protracted over three or four years.

The business leaders, who had previously opposed any change in the parity, naturally demanded a return to fixed exchange rates after the flotation of the yen. The naiveté of their demands was unbelievable, but even more outrageous were the demands that the government should reimburse industry for the exchange losses. There can be no doubt that the decline in the value of the dollar caused losses to enterprises with large outstanding claims denominated in dollars and the government was certainly to blame in that it created a false sense of security by its repeated assurances that the yen would not be revalued, but the demands of industry were simply preposterous. Business reacted as if the world had never known anything else but fixed exchange rates. As usual, the plight of small enterprises was emphasized, but the large enterprises will reap the benefits from any concessions.

After the first weeks of uncertainty, trading companies and the manufacturers of electrical machinery, automobiles, and textiles were concluding new export contracts, some denominated in yen but most based on privately fixed exchange rates, usually 10–12.5 percent higher than the old parity. Many businessmen wanted to be given the possibility of hedging against exchange losses by (1) the reopening of the futures market, (2) the introduction of a system of loans in foreign currencies, and (3) the relaxation of the controls on prepayment of exports ("leads") and conversion of dollars into yen. Some trading companies and automobile manufacturers proposed the adoption of a double exchange rate similar to the French system with fixed exchange rates for commercial bills. Common to most proposals was the demand that the state should cover the exchange risk. The shipbuilders wanted compensation for exchange losses, deferment of repayment of loans from the Export-Import Bank, and tax relief. The desire of the businessmen for a fixed exchange rate was understandable, but a fixed exchange rate based on wrong premises is dangerous. In their eagerness to reach an accommodation with the United States, the Japanese have made a blunder even more disastrous than the infelicitous lifting of the gold embargo (restoration of the gold standard) in 1930.

The agreement reached by the finance ministers of the Group of Ten in Washington on December 19, 1971, fixed the parity of the yen against the dollar at $1 = ¥308, a revaluation of 16.8831 percent by the IMF formula. In terms of gold, the value of the yen was increased by 7.66 percent. The meeting adopted a margin of 2.25 percent each way for possible fluctuations from the basic rate so that the exchange rate of the yen against the dollar can move between ¥314.93 and ¥301.07. The rate of revaluation was much higher than the government and the business leaders had expected; on December 18, the dollar quotation on the Tokyo exchange had been ¥320.60, 12.29 percent above the old dollar parity. It was Japan's second "unconditional surrender" and, next to the declaration of war in December 1940, the most irresponsible decision ever made by a Japanese government. The failure to carry out a radical liberalization of trade and exchange was the main cause of the debacle.

What made a solution to the problem of a yen revaluation so difficult was that it was not a currency problem but a matter of the political, military, economic, and financial position of the United States in the world. Although Japan has been suffering from inflation ever since the growth policies adopted in the beginning of the sixties, the government has never tried to stop the inflation by a deflationary monetary policy, which was reserved for restoring external equilibrium. In this sense, Japan had no domestic currency problem, and the problem was thrown at her by the United States. President Nixon's "game plan" was based on the theory that the limitation of total demand can reduce the pace of inflation. This theory may work in the case of a demand-pull inflation when an excessive supply of means of payment creates excessive demand, but it does not work in the case of a cost-push inflation that does not imply an excessive money supply and which gets worse when the high costs of money add to the price pressure. While the new economic policy brought a reversal in the strategy for containing the rise in costs, the American administration was reluctant to resort to the remedy of a devaluation for restoring the balance of international payments. Except for the fact that the dollar was actually overvalued, the decision was right in the sense that the deficit in the balance of payments was only partially attributable to the decline in American competitiveness (although the decline was real enough); the largest deficit was caused by political and military spending. But the administration also decided that America's trading partners, friends, and allies were to contribute to the improvement of the American balance of payments by revaluing their currencies against the dollar. By suspending the convertibility of the dollar into gold, the dollar became a paper currency, by no means worthless but worth less than it was supposed to be. At the same time, however, the United States refused to admit that the dollar was no longer equivalent to 0.888671 g. of gold.

It has been argued that it makes no difference whether the stronger currency is upvalued or the weaker currency devalued because the result is the same. A devaluation of the dollar in terms of gold would merely benefit the gold producing nations (South Africa, the Soviet Union) and the gold hoarders (France, Switzerland) and penalize countries that cooperated with the United States and refrained from converting dollars into gold (Japan, West Germany). But these countries have been penalized and were forced to agree to a realignment which fixed parities on the basis of a currency with a fictitious value. One of the freaks of the Bretton Woods system was the duty of the central banks in countries with strong currencies to intervene on behalf of weak currencies for whose weakness they were not responsible and which they could not cure. No central bank will want to collect another pile of paper dollars, but fixed exchange rates imply the intervention of central banks to maintain the rates. There had been much talk of a realignment on the basis of SDRs because this would have been a less painful way of reducing the value of the dollar. Unfortunately, the SDRs are no international currency and the IMF is no international bank free to control international credit.

The demand of the secretary of the treasury, John Connally, that the alignment of parities should produce a shift of $11–13 billion in the American balance of payments showed the contradictions to which the reversal of the cause and effect relationship in international payments can lead. In fact, American foreign investment (which increased by $7.1 billion in 1970) was equal to half of the dollar drain that Mr. Connally was hoping to halt. Theoretically it should be possible to slow down that investment.

The fallacy of judging the exchange relations between two countries merely on the basis of the visible trade figures has been pointed out recently by the United States-Japan Trade Council. According to Nelson Stitt, director of the council, Japan, in addition to purchasing $4,600 million worth of goods directly from the United States in 1970 (the Japanese customs statistics give $5,559,579,000 as the value of Japanese imports from the U.S.A. in that year), bought goods worth about $3,000 million from American-owned firms in third countries. Since the U.S. equity in these firms averages 65 percent, the indirect dollar inflow into the United States amounted to $1,900 million. Moreover, Japan's payments on services (deficit in 1970, $1,785 million), transfer payments (deficit in 1970, $208 million), and capital transactions (in 1970, balance on long-term capital transactions, a deficit of $1,591 million; on short-term capital transactions, a surplus of $724 million) involve large surpluses in favor of the United States resulting from the repayment of loans, repatriation of profits, royalty payments, shipping charges, and other payments. Moreover, Japanese trading companies buy a considerable quantity of American products for resale in third countries—Stitt estimated the value of such sales in 1970 at $400 million.

In his column in the *Japan Times*, Joseph Z. Reday pointed out that the trade council presented a one-sided picture "by failing to mention indirect contributions by Japan to the deficit side of the U.S. trade and payments picture" (*Japan Times*, December 5, 1971). The sale of third country products to the U.S. by Japanese trading companies is one of these negative factors, and another is Japan's trade with countries in Southeast Asia, such as Vietnam and Thailand, whose heavy trade deficits with Japan are financed by American aid and military spending in those countries. Hence, that trade should be added to the U.S. deficit with Japan as should all other trade in which Japan sells more to a country than it buys and the U.S. buys more than it sells.

Balanced bilateral trade is an impossible postulate, and one of the reasons for the international movements of capital is the need to offset import deficits which cannot be compensated by exports. That a number of countries in Southeast Asia obtain the necessary funds by America's political and military spending is not Japan's fault and the United States is in a position to change it by changing her policies. (As mentioned before, there is no reason why Japan should contribute to policies on which she has not been consulted and over which she has no control.)

In the sale of American products to third countries by Japanese trading companies, the price at which these products are bought in the United States is entered on the credit side of the American balance of payments, while the price of products of third countries sold by Japanese trading companies in the United States does not figure in Japan's balance of payments; only the profit of the trading companies can increase Japan's foreign assets. Furthermore, the triangular transactions of Japanese trading companies are rather limited (they accounted for 5.1 percent of the entire sales of the ten largest trading companies in the term from October 1970 to March 1971) and can hardly be compared with some of the imports into Japan from third countries in which American companies have a stake. In 1970, the share of the six largest American oil companies supplying Japan with crude oil (Caltex, Esso, Mobil, Gulf, Union, and Getty) amounted to 52.2 percent. The value of imports of petroleum and petroleum products in 1970 amounted to $2,785.5 million; direct imports from the U.S. were valued at $111.4 million (of which petroleum products, above all liquified petroleum gas and liquified methane gas, amounted to $109.5 million), which leaves $2,674.1 million in imports from third countries of which American firms supplied more than half. The profits from these sales increase American foreign assets. American firms also have a substantial interest in third country enterprises (e.g., in Australia) selling iron ore, coal, bauxite, and nonferrous metals to Japan. Of the ships entering Japanese harbors, relatively few fly the American flag because many of the ships owned by American capital are registered in Liberia, Panama, or other flag-of-convenience countries, but a large part of the $2,814 million which Japan paid in 1970 for transportation (deficit on this account $1,174 million) went to American-owned companies. American firms were the main recipients of investment income (Japanese payments in 1970, $917 million, deficit $211 million). On the other hand, offshore procurement by the U.S. Forces resulted in a net inflow of $661 million into Japan. Nelson Stitt also mentioned tourism as a factor to be considered. Undoubtedly, the number of Japanese tourists visiting the United States has increased rapidly; according to the U.S. Department of Commerce, 207,455 Japanese visited the States in 1970 and in the first six months of 1971, Japanese visitors, 145,569, outnumbered those from Great Britain (125,606), thus becoming the most numerous group of foreign visitors to the United States (not counting Canadians and Mexicans). But, in 1970, American visitors to Japan numbered 359,107, so that the balance was in Japan's favor although, overall, the balance on travel showed a deficit of $83 million in 1970.

In addition to an increase in the parity of the yen, the United States wanted abolition of Japanese restrictions on imports and the purchase of weapons by Japan to offset American military expenditures in Japan. As far as Japan's import restrictions are concerned, her record is hardly enviable. Import restrictions on agricultural products have penalized the Japanese consumer and the government should long ago have adopted a more sensible policy for helping agriculture (governments elsewhere have done even worse than the Japanese government). But in some cases, American demands appear unreasonable to both the Japanese government and industry Perhaps they are! In any case many Japanese industrialists are nervous over the extent of American penetration into what they consider their own preserve. Moreover, the United States, while stressing reciprocity, is maintaining quota limitations on imports of oil, meat, dairy products, cotton textiles, and steel, which comprise one-fourth of all U.S. imports. The United States has as yet to fulfill an important provision of the agreement she negotiated with the Common Market in the Kennedy round, the abolition of the "American selling price" system which assumes fictitious high prices for certain chemicals for the assessment of duties. As far as Japan is concerned, the forceful manner in which President Nixon caused the Japanese government to conclude an agreement for "voluntary" quotas on exports of textiles other than cotton is still fresh in the memory of the Japanese people. Japanese textile exports to the United States are still substantial (value in 1970, $596,587,000) but account for only 2 percent of the American market (total imports make up about 8 percent) and American imports of synthetic fibers from Japan are less than 1.5 percent of total consumption. The American textile industry never proved any damage caused by imports from Japan, and, as told by Jack Anderson, the Tariff Commission, asked by the then vice-president, Hubert Humphrey, about the needs of the textile industry found the industry had "enjoyed a period of unparalleled growth since the early 1960s" and that "there has been a marked expansion in sales, employment, and new investment in plant and equipment." According to the same source, the textile industry contributed some $300,000 to Mr. Nixon's presidential campaign. Japan's politicians and businessmen are polite enough not to pass on to President Nixon rumors that his quota demands were in payment of a political debt, but the Japanese textile industry knew that the concessions by the Japanese government were without rhyme or reason and presented a bill asking for ¥463,210 million in government assistance over a period of three years. The industry may recoup some of the damage, if it suffered any, from Mr. Nixon's actions, but the damage done by the irresponsible rhetoric that Japan's greedy commercialism has deprived thousands of American textile workers of their jobs will not be repaired.

The demand that Japan buy more military hardware from the United States is contrary to Japan's best interests. Japan still has to work out a defense policy suitable for her position in the new power constellation in Asia. The fourth defense program has been drawn up on premises that seem no longer valid, although the government appears to be determined to carry it out, despite the fact that its position has been subjected to a vigorous assault both from the opposition parties and from dissenting elements within the Liberal-Democratic party. This combined attack has forced some concessions from the government.

In the course of the debate on the realignment of parities, Japan and the European countries have often been accused of black ingratitude. The rehabilitation of Japan and Europe was in the best interests of the United States, and it is in the best interests of Japan that America regain her social and economic health.

One of the objections to the Washington agreement is its failure to come to grips with the roots of the currency problems. Nothing is said about the convertibility of the dollar into gold, so that a paper currency has been made the cornerstone of the international currency system. No assurance has been (or could be) given that the inflationary erosion of the value of the dollar will not continue and that the policies which were responsible for the imbalance in the American international payments position will be changed. The most crucial issue, the flow of short-term funds, has been passed over in silence, and the disposal of the large dollar balances (including the 60 billion in Eurodollars) has been left to the vicissitudes of the international money market. Time was far too short to work out a replacement for the Bretton Woods system, which had obviously failed to work.

Dollar Holdings of Central Banks
December 1971

	$ billion
Japan	13.4
West Germany	11.7
United Kingdom	4.3
Canada	3.8
Switzerland	3.7
France	3.2
Italy	3.2

Source: Morgan Guaranty Trust Co.

The Washington conference marks the beginning of a new era of in which exchange rates appear to have become a political football. Protectionism never was dead, but this has been the first time that power politics have been used for imposing exchange rates that do not necessarily reflect monetary values. The United States wanted the new parities as a short-cut to remedy economic ills that should have been cured by means unpalatable to the administration in view of its national and political goals.

Japan's direct losses caused by the yen revaluation are substantial but by no means fatal. At the end of November 1971, the country's official reserves amounted to $14,836 million, which included gold, SDRs, the gold tranche, and small amounts in currencies other than dollars (pounds, German marks, French francs, etc.). But the bulk of the reserves, about $13 billion, was in dollars of which about $2.3 billion had been bought at an average discount of 10 percent. The Bank of Japan, therefore, may suffer a loss of about $64 billion from the lower value of its dollar holdings and additional losses from the change in the price of gold (1 ounce of gold = $38, an increase of 8.57 percent). Actually, on December 21, the first day of trading after the Washington conference, the dollar opened at ¥314.20 for overnight and ¥314.50 for immediate delivery. The latter quotations temporarily approached the limit of ¥314.93, but the Bank of Japan did not intervene.

The major Japanese trading companies estimated their net losses resulting from the change in exchange rates at ¥15 billion, but the heaviest losers were the shipbuilders. The yen value of their outstanding credits representing deferred payments for ship exports etc. was reduced by ¥257 billion. According to the Commercial Code, such losses have to be written off within two years, but this would force the major shipbuilding companies to cut their dividend rates. They want to be given ten years to write off these losses. The yen value of the outstanding liabilities of the oil companies will be reduced by about ¥130 billion, but the price increases already obtained by OPEC added about twice this amount to the cost of crude oil (of which the oil companies will have to bear about half). OPEC is demanding further price increases as compensation for the devaluation of the dollar.

Sumitomo Bank calculated the effect of the currency readjustment on export and import prices. The table inserted below is based on the weight of exports to or imports from the most important trading partners in 1970 (customs statistics of the respective countries) and shows the average rate of increase or decrease in the value of the country's currency in foreign trade transactions.

	Nominal change in parity %	Change in currency value for exports %	Change in currency value for imports %
Japan	16.88	13.51	12.99
West Germany	13.58	6.19	6.27
Canada (floating rate)	7.50	4.52	5.37
Belgium	11.57	2.19	2.79
Netherlands	11.57	1.96	2.90
Britain	8.57	1.94	2.17
France	8.57	0.10	−3.03
Sweden	7.49	−0.62	−0.81
Italy	7.48	−0.63	0.06
Switzerland	6.36	−1.27	−2.73
United States	8.57*	−7.48	−7.74

* increase in price of gold

The actual rate of increase in the value of the yen for exports is twice as high as the rate of increase of the Deutsche mark. The difference of 7.32 points will make it almost impossible for Japanese machinery (e.g., machine tools) to compete with German products in the American market. With a spread of 20.99 points, Japanese products will lose their price competitiveness as against American products which, of course, was the objective of the exercise in "international cooperation." As far as Japan was concerned, the Europeans were largely in agreement with the Americans (as were the United States and France as far as Germany was concerned). The result of the Washington conference reflected Japan's isolation—as did the result of the Washington Conference in 1921–22 (which limited Japan's influence in China and fixed the ratio of the capital ships of the United States, Britain, Japan, France, and Italy at 5:5:3:1.75:1.75).

There is, however, no agreement on the effects of the currency realignment on Japan's foreign trade and on her economy in general. Forecasts of the increase in the dollar value of exports in fiscal 1972 range from a low of 5.0 percent (forecast of the Economic Planning Agency) to a high of 12.7 percent (Hokkaido Takushoku Bank). The stagnation of the economy will keep the increase in imports down in the first half of the fiscal year although they will rise somewhat faster in the latter half. The balance of payments is expected to show a surplus of $7–8 billion on trade account and of $4–5 billion on current account in fiscal 1972.

The impact of the yen revaluation will be different not only for various industries but also for each enterprise. Masaru Ibuka, president of Sony Corporation, confidently predicted that the yen revaluation would have no influence on the export business of his company because its products would be bought regardless of price. Generally speaking, tape recorders, stereo sets, motorcycles, and large tankers will remain sufficiently competitive, but for all other products the competitive position of Japanese manufacturers will suffer. Most severely affected will be steel, synthetic fibers, petrochemicals, machine tools, heavy electrical machinery, aluminum, fertilizers, dyes, and toys.

Japan is a great country for taking strange ideas seriously. During the debate on the yen revaluation, the argument was advanced that Japanese workers work too hard and that the export surplus would be reduced if the Japanese would take it easier. The five-day week, which had been tentatively adopted on a limited scale by a few enterprises, received a great boost. Actually, for the Japanese worker, an increase in income is far more urgent than a reduction in working hours. Given the Japanese way of working, a direct comparison of working hours in Western countries and in Japan may sometimes be misleading.

Another slogan which was given much publicity advocated the transfer of resources from exports to the promotion of national welfare. How this can be accomplished was not explained, but the government eagerly took up this proposal and revived its old recipe of higher burdens for higher welfare. The government wants higher spending for its anticyclical measures; very little money will be left for improving social conditions and the small embellishments will contribute nothing to a solution of basic social problems.

Although the yen revaluation has created an entirely new situation and changed the premises of all existing policies, the government has given no indication of a basic rethinking. The budget plans announced so far promise more massive spending for old programs; the appropriateness of the old policies seems to be taken for granted. The government as well as most economic commentators regard the inflationary threat as remote, probably because the inflation apparent in consumer prices is not considered an inflation. (The government recently started a new series of consumer price indices with 1970 as base year so as to lessen the impression of inflationary price increases.)

In the field of foreign exchange, the old restrictive legislation making prohibition the rule and liberalization the exception will apparently not be scrapped although this policy has been one of the main causes of the recent upheaval.

As has happened before, the lack of clearness leads to the adoption of contradictory policies. The Financial System Research Council recently recommended the "improvement" of the reserve deposit system; the ceiling of the reserve rate is to be raised from 10 percent to 20 percent; for free-yen accounts of nonresidents, the ceiling will be lifted to 10 percent. The ceiling of 10 percent has had nothing to do with the effectiveness of the system (the highest rate ever imposed was 3 percent), but it made little sense to demand high reserve deposits as long as the Bank of Japan provided credit to make the overloans of the city banks possible. At present, the government wants to reduce interest rates; the increase in fund costs caused by higher reserve deposit requirements will hardly serve this purpose.

The stagnation in the economy continued after August 15, 1971. According to a revised estimate of the Economic Planning Agency published in December, the real rate of increase in GNP in fiscal 1971 would be 4.3 percent. A forecast by the Economic Research Center was more optimistic and put the rate at 7.2 percent. Production and shipments went up in September but declined in October (indices 1965 = 100: mining and manufacturing production: September, 233.2; October, 227.6; shipments: September, 226.0; October, 214.9; inventories: September, 238.8; October, 242.4). Machinery orders and housing starts declined in October and wholesale prices weakened (index: September, 110.6; October, 110.0; November, 109.8). Bankruptcies also became more numerous in October (bankruptcies involving liabilities exceeding ¥10 million: September, 742, ¥47,295 million; October, 841, ¥64,300 million; November, 778, ¥51,190 million; December, 767, ¥62,148 million; the total number of bankruptcies from January to December 1971 was 9,206, the highest number in postwar years).

The settlement of accounts for the term from March to September 1971 showed a general decline in profits. Sales of the 380 companies listed on the First Section of the Tokyo Stock Exchange increased by 3.9 percent over the preceding six months, but operating profits decreased by 14.5 percent and net profits by 16.0 percent. The manufacturing firms (281) among these companies reported particularly depressing results; sales were up, but only by a mere 1.7 percent, while operating profits were down by 21.0 percent and net profits by 21.9 percent. Nonmanufacturing firms increased their sales by 5.4 percent, but their operating profits declined by 3.3 percent and their net profits by 5.1 percent. The companies listed on the Second Section suffered an even worse decline in profits; sales rose by 1.4 percent, but operating profits dropped by 28.1 percent and net profits by 24.5 percent. Particularly bad were the performances of steel and metal products, chemicals, machinery, electrical machinery, pulp and paper, petroleum, and textiles. Numerous industries applied for permission to form depression cartels; particularly noteworthy was the depression cartel for crude steel (the first time that a cartel had been recognized for an intermediate product).

The securities companies, however, were able to report favorable business results; the operating profits of the eight largest securities companies for the year from October 1970 to September 1971 rose by 28 percent. Commissions increased by 6.3 percent: commissions from stock transactions rose by only 4.1 percent, but those from bonds rose by 18.8 percent.

In September, the Dow-Jones average regained the ¥2,400 mark and rose to ¥2,432.50 on October 2, but it quickly sank below ¥2,300 and was down to ¥2,224.52 on November 6. But a new rally brought the average back to over ¥2,400 and the high for November was ¥2,450.74 reached on the twenty-ninth.

In the latter half of December, speculative buying, large purchases by foreign investors, and the monetary relaxation pushed the Dow-Jones average up to ¥2,527.76 on December 21, to ¥2,621.77 on December 23, and to ¥2,713.74 on December 28, the last trading day of the year. This was only slightly below the all-time high of ¥2,740.98 reached on August 14, 1971, before the Nixon shock. Effective December 27, the Tokyo, Osaka, and Nagoya stock exchanges raised the margin requirement from 30 percent to 40 percent; margin requirements were increased to 50 percent for ten issues and to 70 percent (of which 40 percent in cash) for Sanko Steamship Co. whose price had risen by 692.0 percent over the year. Special restrictions on margin trading were in effect for twelve issues.

On January 1, 1972, the smallest trading unit on the Second Section became 1,000 shares, the same as on the First Section.

The economic stagnation which began in the latter half of 1970 was accompanied by a slower increase in banknote circulation, the rate of increase dropping from about 19 percent in the first half of fiscal 1970 to 16 percent in the second half. The excess of payments of the foreign exchange fund over receipts for the period from April to October 1971 reached ¥3,378.9 billion, and these payments were the main cause of the monetary relaxation. The unfavorable business results affected tax revenues from the corporation tax, and the income from customs duties suffered on account of the stagnation of imports. In the same April–October period, central bank credit decreased by ¥2,011.7 billion, which reduced the excess liquidity in the money market. As one of the means of absorbing liquid funds, the Bank of Japan added sales of its own notes to its customary buying operations, but the bulk of the excess funds was used for repaying loans from the central bank, so that the balance of outstanding advances of the Bank of Japan dropped from ¥2,429.1 billion at the end of March 1971 to ¥740.0 billion at the end of October. The remaining credits represent lending for foreign trade or special financing programs, so that general advances by the Bank of Japan have actually become zero, thus ending the overloan situation which started in 1956 and lasted for fifteen years.

The monetary relaxation caused the call money rate (over-the-month lender's rate) to fall from a peak of 9.25 percent in September 1970 to 5.25 percent from December 25, 1971, a decline of four points. The rate was the lowest since 1956. This situation impaired the earnings of the mutual banks, the credit associations, and the financial institutions for agriculture, the chief lenders in the call market; these institutions diverted part of their funds to loans or investment in securities. Since the over-the-month call rate was lower than the interest rate on interbank time deposits (6 percent per annum), funds began to flow into time deposits after the cut in the call rate on October 15. Between April and October, the fund balance of the call market declined by ¥435.0 billion (if adjusted for the balance of the discount market, by ¥225.4 billion). The sharp increase in time deposits prompted the authorities to revise the guidelines for interest rates on interbank deposits; instead of the previous uniform 6 percent rate, two steps were introduced effective November 19; a maximum rate of 5 percent for deposits between three and six months and a maximum rate of 6 percent for deposits over six months.

Deposits with the eighty-six commercial banks reached ¥30,201.1 billion on November 30, 1971; "actual" deposits were ¥27,622.4 billion. Interest rates, which had been slow in declining in the beginning of the year, dropped more sharply after August and their decline equaled about 40 percent of the decline in the official discount rate.

Noteworthy were the reductions in the interest rates on housing loans by the city banks and the trust banks which went into effect on December 1, 1971. The new rates were as follows:

Tied loans:	up to 5 years	9.3 percent per annum
	5–10 years	9.6 percent per annum
	10–15 years	9.9 percent per annum
Untied loans:	up to 5 years	9.0 percent per annum
	5–10 years	9.3 percent per annum
	10–15 years	9.6 percent per annum
Trust banks:	9.84 for loans up to 20 years.	

Interest rates on loans to small enterprises were reduced by 0.3 percent–1.1 percent; on loans guaranteed by the credit associations, the interest rate was reduced by 0.62–1.2 percent (typical rates for loans to small enterprises: loans up to ¥10 million, maturity eighteen months, 7.2 percent–7.8 percent). A reduction of 0.5 percent in the official discount rate, accompanied by a reduction in the interest rates on demand deposits, had been scheduled for December 25 but was postponed because the Ministry of Posts and Telecommunications objected to a reduction of the interest rates on postal savings. The official discount rate was lowered by 0.5 percent to 4.75 percent effective December 29, the lowest level in the entire postwar period. The government intends to push its low-interest policy by reducing not only interest rates on demand deposits (probably in February 1972) but also on long-term bank lending.

The decline in interest rates and hedge buying by foreign investors brought an increase in bond prices. As a result, the yield differential between market prices and the prices of newly issued bonds disappeared and even after the revision of the issue conditions in September 1971, a reverse gap (market prices higher than issue prices) continued. In December, however, bond prices declined. In accordance with the government's low-interest policy, the issue prices of industrial bonds were lowered effective January 1972. The new issue conditions were as follows:

	Issue price ¥	Interest rate %	Yield rate to subscriber %
Grade A bonds	99.50	7.4	7.508
” A' ”	99.25	7.4	7.563
” B ”	99.0	7.4	7.619
” C ”	99.25	7.6	7.765
10-year national bonds	98.90	7.0	7.189

In order to stimulate the economy, the government plans a large increase in fiscal expenditures in 1972. The general accounts of the budget for fiscal 1972 will provide for expenditures of ¥11,470.4 billion, an expansion of 21.8 percent over the original budget for fiscal 1971; the fiscal loan and investment program is to be brought to ¥5,635 billion, 31.6 percent higher than in fiscal 1971. Issues of national bonds will amount to ¥1,950 billion, 60 percent higher than in fiscal 1971 (¥1,220 billion) and equivalent to 17 percent of the budgetary expenditure.

In this era of change and confusion, Japan is confronted with some serious and fundamental questions. These include the problem of economic balance between production and consumption, the problem of social balance between high and low income classes, the problem of balance between the private and the public sectors, and the problem of balance between domestic and international requirements.

A solution to these problems supposes a clear and accepted value system and a definite set of priorities, but the vagueness of such values and priorities as exist is one of the causes of the present uncertainties. For a hundred years, the government has favored the producer over the consumer and has pursued the aggrandizement of the state without regard to the quality of life and the requirements of human culture. Money has become the sole measure of value and, while the establishment makes sure that it gets plenty of it, the social security system fails to provide even a minimum standard of living to those unable to provide for themselves. The government keeps repeating that the funds for infrastructural facilities are insufficient but goes on spending money on unnecessary subsidies and hundreds of public corporations and commissions. As for public works, the benefits accruing to industry frequently seem to be a more important consideration than their usefulness to the public welfare.

Industry knows that the limitations on raw material sources and markets will severely restrict the quantitative expansion of the economy and make it imperative to shift from selling merchandise to selling services and technology, but there is no indication that the business leaders are aware of either the importance or the immensity of this task.

Japan has still to develop an international policy that will protect the country's trade and finance while allaying the fears of economic imperialism among the developing nations. Even if there were a U.S. commitment to China to prevent Japan from again building a significant military establishment and particularly a nuclear capability, this would do little to establish a working relationship between Japan and China. Since her relations with the Soviet Union are also plagued by unsolved problems, Japan can hardly afford to lose the partnership with the United States. There will hardly be complete identity of interests between the two nations, and at times they will have to reconcile real or imaginary national interests with the requirements of cooperation.

INDEX

Advertising expenditures, 228
Agricultural credit institutions, 115, 126, 300, 340, 388, 390, 391, 396, 415, 534
Agricultural cooperatives, 115, 426
Agricultural policy, 234, 529
Agricultural towns, 426
Aircraft industry, 225
American International Underwriters, 476
Asian Development Bank, 392, 463–65, 489
Auto loans, 420–21, 423
Automatic transfer of recurrent payments, 125, 422, 431
Automation of banking operations, 147–49, 152, 159, 422
Automation of operations of securities companies, 176
Automation of operation of stock exchange, 192
Automobile industry, 215, 217, 221, 224, 236, 240, 258, 259, 260, 263, 264, 265, 272, 273, 288, 372, 395
Automobile insurance, 202, 204, 205, 316

baikai, 186, 187
Balance of payments, 27, 28, 64, 65, 66, 67, 78, 79, 214, 215, 229, 230, 231, 232, 234, 235, 236, 256, 269, 270, 273, 279, 280, 305, 306, 307, 309, 311, 362, 481, 511–20, 521–22, 523, 532
Balance on services, 232, 235, 512–13
Balanced funds, 402, 405–406
Banks
 Bank of Japan, 12, 25, 36, 37, 49, 55, 58, 59, 61, 65, 66, 68, 73, 78, 83, 99–103, 120, 125, 127, 131, 133, 134, 163, 171, 182, 198, 199, 200, 229, 237, 248, 250, 251, 253, 254, 259, 268, 273, 282, 283, 299, 300, 303, 304, 305, 308, 309, 310, 311, 314, 315, 340, 363, 365, 388, 389, 390, 391, 413, 414, 415–16, 462, 473, 481, 482, 488, 489, 493, 494–97, 499–502, 504–505, 508, 509, 522, 523, 534
 advances, 28, 30, 32, 37, 55, 65, 73, 75, 78, 79, 127, 129, 171–72, 198, 199, 236, 278, 299, 303, 305–306, 307, 317, 320–21,

355–56, 390, 391, 413, 416, 501, 533, 534
 functions, 99–103
 "neutrality" of central bank, 100–102
 penalty rates, 66, 78, 102, 230, 306, 307, 311, 415, 500
 Policy Board, 58, 99, 131, 171
 sale of notes, 417, 534
 City Banks, 48, 49, 58, 59, 61, 66, 73, 91, 102, 103, 104, 105–106, 107, 108, 111, 125, 127, 128, 129, 130, 135, 148, 149, 154, 156, 157, 159, 163, 164, 171, 198, 199, 200, 230, 237, 239, 267, 278, 300, 304, 305, 307, 308, 311, 312, 313, 339, 340, 355, 364, 373–74, 388–89, 390, 391, 392, 393, 397, 414, 415, 416, 419, 422, 430, 492–93, 496, 499, 533, 535
 Bank of Tokyo, 48, 91, 105, 108, 159, 181, 416, 432, 464, 466, 468, 470, 471, 473, 474, 484, 489, 506, 514, 515, 522
 Dai-Ichi Bank, 105, 109, 156, 157–58, 159, 160, 218, 425, 470, 471, 474
 Dai-Ichi Kangyo Bank, 105, 111, 157–58, 161, 163, 468, 472, 474, 514, 515
 Daiwa Bank, 105, 109, 158, 159, 161, 488, 514, 515
 Fuji Bank, 105, 127, 147, 148, 152, 158, 159, 160, 161, 163, 171, 172, 174, 218, 219, 238, 425, 432, 433, 444, 464, 470–71, 473, 474, 475, 514, 515
 Hokkaido Takushoku Bank, 12, 59, 67, 73, 75, 104, 157, 159, 420, 423, 512, 513, 532
 Kobe Bank, 105, 109, 157, 160, 238, 424, 433, 470, 474, 514, 515
 Kyowa Bank 105, 158, 159, 160, 161, 424, 432, 470, 474, 514, 515
 Mitsubishi Bank, 105, 125, 127, 130, 148, 156, 158, 159, 160, 161, 171, 172, 238, 421, 425, 431, 432, 433, 444, 445, 459, 468, 470, 473, 474, 514, 515
 Mitsui Bank, 105, 125, 147, 156, 158, 159, 160, 238, 424, 432, 466, 470, 474, 514, 515
 Nippon Kangyo Bank, 12, 49, 58, 59, 73, 75, 104, 105, 157–58, 159, 160, 161, 173–

537

74, 389–90, 425, 431, 433, 434, 470, 474
Nomura Bank. *See* Daiwa Bank.
Saitama Bank, 91, 105, 157, 158, 160, 161,
    425, 470, 474, 514, 515
Sanwa Bank, 49, 105, 109, 127, 158, 159,
    160, 218, 424, 432, 433, 445, 466, 468,
    470, 471, 472, 473, 514, 515
Sumitomo Bank, 105, 127, 130, 147, 148,
    156, 158, 159, 161, 421, 425, 433, 434,
    445, 466, 470, 474, 514, 515, 531
Taiyo Bank, 91, 105, 157, 158, 159, 160,
    161, 425, 514, 515
Teikoku Bank, 49, 105
Tokai Bank, 105, 109, 127, 158, 159, 160,
    421, 425, 432, 445, 470, 471, 473, 474,
    514, 515
Yasuda Bank. *See* Fuji Bank.
Commercial banks, 104, 122, 155, 299, 462,
    488, 489, 534
Foreign exchange banks, 65, 100, 120, 163,
    248, 249, 251, 252, 253, 254, 283, 475,
    489, 492, 494–96, 499–501, 506, 507,
    508–510, 514–15, 516
Local banks, 48, 58, 91, 103, 104, 106–107,
    111, 127, 135, 148, 149, 154, 156, 158,
    159, 163, 198, 199, 242, 308, 312, 341,
    373, 388, 396, 406, 415, 416, 493
    Bank of Yokohama, 158, 159, 242, 424,
      489
    Chiba Bank, 158, 159, 424
    Chiba Kogyo Bank, 158
    Suruga Bank, 158
    Yoyo Bank, 242
Long-term credit banks, 67, 75, 69–70, 91,
    103, 104, 107–108, 152, 157, 162, 341,
    388, 393, 396, 416
    Industrial Bank of Japan, 12, 48, 49, 58,
      59, 73, 75, 108, 109, 128, 161, 171, 172,
      181, 199, 238, 425, 431, 432, 433, 462,
      464, 468, 470, 471, 473, 474, 480, 489,
      514, 515
    Japan Hypothec Bank, 67, 75, 104, 108,
      181, 425, 470, 474, 489
    Long-Term Credit Bank, 67, 75, 104, 108,
      181, 199, 310, 425, 432, 470, 474, 489
Mutual loan and savings banks, 103, 105,
    112–13, 125, 126, 132, 154, 155, 157,
    158, 159, 162, 163, 304, 308, 340, 373,
    388, 416, 534
    Chubu Mutual Bank, 158
    Heiwa Mutual Bank, 158–59
    Kofuku Mutual Bank, 159
Ordinary banks, 91, 104, 131–32, 148, 155,
    157, 162, 342
Savings banks, 105, 106
Special banks, 12, 59, 73, 104, 108, 462
Trust banks, 58, 91, 103, 104, 108–111, 126,
    132, 152, 157, 162, 165, 168, 199, 202,
    278, 308, 310, 312, 363, 388, 391, 396,
    402, 404, 415, 416, 425, 493, 535

Chuo Trust & Banking Co., 109, 432, 468
Mitsubishi Trust & Banking Co., 109, 111,
    171, 425, 432, 433, 468, 488
Mitsui Trust & Banking Co., 108–109,
    160, 289, 424, 433, 468, 488
Nippon Trust & Banking Co., 109, 425
Sumitomo Trust & Banking Co., 109, 111,
    432, 468, 488
Toyo Trust & Banking Co., 109, 111, 160,
    424, 468, 488
Yasuda Trust & Banking Co., 109, 111,
    171, 424, 431, 433, 468, 488
Foreign banks operating in Japan, 253
    Algemene Bank Nederland N. V., 479
    American Express International Banking
      Corporation, 479
    Bangkok Bank, 479
    Bank of America, 466, 479, 501
    Bank of China (International Commer-
      cial Bank of China), 479
    Bank Negara Indonesia 1946, 479
    Bank of India, 479
    Banque de l'Indochine, 479
    Chartered Bank, 479
    Continental Illinois National Bank &
      Trust Co. of Chicago, 479
    Deutsche Überseeische Bank, 479
    Dutch-India Bank, 479
    Chase Manhattan Bank, 431, 479, 501
    First National City Bank, 161, 419, 431,
      466, 475, 479, 488, 501
    Hanil Bank, 479
    Hongkong & Shanghai Banking Corpo-
      ration, 479
    Korea Exchange Bank, 479, 489
    Manufacturers Hanover Trust Co., 431,
      479
    McIntyre Bank, 479
    Mercantile Bank, Ltd., 479
    Morgan Guaranty Trust Co. of New
      York, 479, 489
    Security Pacific National Bank of Los
      Angeles, 479
    Overseas Union Bank, 479
    Union Bank of Switzerland, 112, 475
    Wells Fargo Bank, 479
Banks, administrative control, 102–103, 156,
    163
    branch offices, 104, 154, 156–58, 163
    business lines, 123, 155–56, 160–61
    cooperation, 158–60
    foreign branches, 468
    foreign branches, transactions of, 251, 468,
      469–70, 482
    foreign subsidiaries, 468, 470–71
    investment in securities, 130, 146–47, 534
    irregularities, 152
    operating methods, 147–49, 152
    operating costs, 149, 163

participation in foreign financial institutions, 469–72

profits, 149, 152, 163

Bank debentures, 164, 181, 278, 385, 388, 391, 393. *See also* financial debentures.

Bank deposits, 30, 36, 37, 73, 75, 78, 130, 278, 307, 309, 325, 327, 328, 339–40, 534–35

Bank deposits, types, 123–27, 131, 133, 162

Bank-guaranteed checks, 159

Banking, liberalization of, 260

Banking system, development of, 12–13, 91, 105, 130, 155, 161–64

Bank loans, 30, 36, 37, 63, 73, 75, 78, 130, 164, 278, 307, 308, 309, 325–26, 339–41

Bank loans, types, 125, 127, 161–63, 423

Bank management, 106

Bank mergers, 106, 154–58

Bank for International Settlements (BIS), 267, 462

Bankers Trust Co., 432

Bankruptcies, 65, 78, 79, 237–39, 240, 275, 279, 308, 309, 310, 435, 436

Bill brokers. *See* call money brokers.

Bill market, 314, 414, 415–16

Blocked accounts, 30, 31, 33, 39, 40

Bond exchange center, 392

Bond investment trusts, 168, 169, 387, 388, 402, 403, 404

Bond Issuance Adjustment Council, 49, 51, 58, 83

Bond market, 40, 49, 55, 58–59, 73, 75–77, 82–83, 179, 180, 181–82, 200, 300, 305, 385–401

Bond prices, 40, 175, 300, 387, 390, 391, 392, 393, 395–97, 485, 535

Bonds, local government, 41, 49, 51, 52, 75, 83, 168, 179, 181, 182, 292, 387, 388 389, 393

Bonds, national (government bonds), 30, 32, 34, 37, 41, 49–51, 54, 73, 147, 179, 181, 262, 265, 293, 298–302, 311, 388–89, 390, 392–93, 395, 535, 536

British Insurance Group, 476

Brokers, 165, 173, 175, 177, 186, 194, 195, 196. *See also* securities companies.

Budget, 32, 34, 37, 53–55, 67, 78, 230–31, 241, 243, 262, 264, 270, 271, 276, 287–93, 299, 300–301, 302, 392–93, 494, 532, 535–36

Business cycle, 213–214

Business tie-ups (teikei), 221. *See also* banks, cooperation.

Call money brokers (short-term fund dealers, bill brokers), 299, 414, 416–17, 495

Call money market, 108, 198, 204, 278, 308, 309, 311, 317, 320–21, 396, 402, 404, 413–18, 475, 482, 534

Call money rates, 79, 134, 135, 265, 278–79, 300, 308, 310, 312, 313, 314, 315, 373, 396, 414, 417, 481, 534

Capital Increase Adjustment Council, 82

Capital accumulation, 56, 66, 213, 296, 325–28

Capital Funds, 405–406

Capital increases. *See* emission of new shares.

Capital structure of enterprises, 340, 378, 383

Capital transactions, 215, 250, 442, 480–82, 513

Capital transactions, restrictions on, 463, 480–82

Cartels, 221, 240, 247

Central Bank for Agriculture and Forestry, 49, 115, 181. *See also* Central Cooperative Bank of Agriculture and Forestry.

Central Bank for Commercial and Industrial Cooperatives (Shoko Chukin Bank), 59, 75, 91, 108, 114–15, 148, 153, 181, 316

Central Cooperative Bank of Agriculture and Forestry, 58, 59, 75, 91, 104, 108, 115, 159, 388, 416. *See also* Central Bank for Agriculture and Forestry.

Certificates of deposit, 162

Checks, 123, 422

Chemical industry, 35, 36, 216, 222–23, 231, 263, 273, 371

China, Japan's relations with, 444–48, 507, 536 trade with, 232

Clearing system, 152–53

Closed-end trusts. *See* unit trusts.

Closed Institutions Custodian Commission, 40, 44

Closed Institutions Liquidation Commission, 22, 25, 44

Coal mining, 34, 35, 36, 79, 215, 216, 225–26, 231, 249, 293

Collateral, 131

Collective transactions (group trading), 38, 45–46, 57, 61

Commercial bills, 127, 147

Commissions on securities transactions, 175, 178, 180–81

Company savings plans, 328

Compensating balances, 131, 135–36, 152, 311, 435, 480, 482

Computers, 224, 430–31

Computers installation by financial institutions, 147–48, 152, 159, 160, 176

Concentration in business, 217–21, 266–67, 512

Concentration of foreign exchange, 492, 494–95, 501

Consulting, 160, 161, 475

Consumer credit, 228, 418–19

Consumer demand, 215, 217, 227–28, 239–40, 272

Consumer durables, 239–40, 272, 275, 325

Consumption expenditures, 227, 263, 269, 272, 311, 325

Controls on Foreign exchange transactions, 215
Convertible corporate debentures, 59, 75, 179, 180, 182, 191, 193, 206, 379, 383–84, 393, 485
Corporative business results, 231, 236, 240, 263, 265, 272, 275, 314, 351, 356, 361, 362, 367–69, 370–71, 372–73, 533
Corporate debentures, 168, 179, 182, 393, 395. *See also* industrial debentures, financial debentures, bank debentures.
Corporate fund demand, 310, 313, 320, 339–40
Correspondent banks, 444–45, 493
Credit associations, 103, 105, 112–14, 132, 154–55, 157, 162, 163, 308, 340, 373, 388, 396, 406, 534
Credit cards, 159–60, 419–22, 475
Credit Cooperatives, 112, 114, 115, 132, 155, 157, 163, 304, 396, 406
Credit Guarantee Association, 242
Credit, regulation of, 36–37, 55, 66, 103, 149, 306, 307, 312
Credit restraints, 27, 55, 66, 68, 73, 78, 79, 214, 229, 231, 237, 240, 265, 273, 300, 306, 307, 308, 309, 313, 314, 395, 511
Credit transactions (margin trading), 68–69, 175, 180, 187–88, 195–96, 348, 352, 356, 362, 364, 366, 368, 371, 374, 534
Cumulative voting, 191
Currency reform of 1946, 31–34, 39, 120
Currency supply. See money supply.
Currency Stabilization Board, 36, 44

Dealers, 165, 173, 175, 177, 186, 187, 195, 196. *See also* securities companies.
Deconcentration, 25–26, 218
Deflation, 27, 28, 30, 55, 56, 66, 68, 78, 79, 214, 231, 235, 236, 265, 267–68, 305, 349, 354, 387, 523
Delisting, 377
Department stores, 419
Deposit insurance, 114, 156, 163, 200
Depositary receipts, 256, 353, 378, 485
Deposits Bureau, 55, 56, 73, 91, 116, 120, 201. *See also* Trust Fund Bureau.
Developing countries, investment in, 449, 452, 523
Developing countries, Japan's trade with, 449–50, 452, 453–58
Development Assistance Committee (DAC), 451, 462, 522
Dichotomic structure, 219–20
Direct inward investment, 255, 257–62, 280, 483
Disclosure requirements, 189–90, 191
Discount rate, official, 51, 66, 79, 80, 100, 102, 131, 133, 134, 135, 155, 229, 230, 235, 265, 268, 273, 276, 278–79, 300, 303, 304, 305, 306, 307, 308, 309, 310, 312, 313, 314, 315, 504–505, 535

Dividend rates, 342, 356, 362, 365, 380, 382–83, 384
Dodge line, 27, 53–55, 61, 73, 492
Dow-Jones average, 61, 68, 79, 80, 82, 171, 190, 192–93, 231, 239, 240, 276, 279, 282, 347–48, 349, 350, 351–56, 362–69, 371, 375, 405, 534

Economic Council, 216, 285, 286
Economic developments, 27–29, 43, 64–67, 78–79, 80, 213–17, 229–32, 234–36, 239–40, 262–80, 303, 304, 310, 311, 313, 315–16, 349, 533–36
Economic planning, 216, 242–43, 264, 267–68, 285–87
Economic Planning Agency, 131, 255, 266–68, 285–86, 288, 365, 532, 533
Economic policy 230, 283, 285–86, 287–88
Economic Stabilization Board, 34
Eight-point program, 177, 252, 280, 510, 522
Electric power industry, 25, 35, 54, 79, 263, 265, 277, 393, 397
Electrical machinery and electronics, 28, 215, 217, 224, 227, 231, 239–40, 272, 273, 316, 374, 395, 430
Emission market, bonds, 37, 41, 49, 51, 58, 59, 61, 73–74, 75, 77, 82–83, 147, 300, 341, 385, 387, 388–89, 391, 392–93, 395, 396–97, 417
Emission market, stocks, 40, 48, 63, 71, 82, 347–48, 378–84
Emission of new shares, 189, 193, 197–98, 341, 342, 377, 384
Emission of new shares at market prices, 164, 190, 206, 342, 351, 380–81
Employee stock ownership, 363
Employment structure, 234, 326
Enterprise Groups, 128, 146, 218–19, 340, 434, 435
Environmental problems, 216, 240–42, 279
Equipment investment, 28, 29, 56, 61, 67, 72, 79, 82, 130, 162, 213, 214, 215, 216, 222, 226, 230, 231, 236, 237, 240, 262–63, 264, 269, 273, 277, 278, 286, 287, 305, 311, 313–4, 325–26, 372, 435, 499
Equipment trusts, 111
Eurodollars, 129, 480–82
Exchange rates, 54, 253, 492, 496–98, 501, 509, 523–25
Exports, 64, 78, 79, 222, 223, 224, 225, 229, 231–32, 264, 265, 269–70, 273, 277, 368, 436, 437, 450, 453–58, 492, 499, 512–13, 521, 532
Export controls, 249. *See also* textiles, restrictions on exports to the U.S.
Export insurance, 507

Factoring, 431–32
Fair Trade Commission, 63, 82, 131, 146, 158, 192, 266–67, 431

Farm income, 234, 275
Farming population, 234
Federation of Bankers Associations of Japan,
    66, 106, 132, 133, 135, 148, 149, 152,
    159, 268, 303, 308, 312, 313, 314, 385,
    389, 392, 475
Federation of Economic Organizations (*Kei-
    danren*), 190, 191, 254, 259–60, 391,
    396
Federation of Securities Dealers Associations
    of Japan, 86–87, 165, 186
Finance corporations, 91
Financial debentures, 51, 73–74, 83, 92, 108,
    147, 305, 341, 385, 387
Financial System Research Council, 35, 44–45,
    100, 101, 147–48, 154–56, 162–63, 164,
    200, 533
Fire insurance, 201, 202, 204
First National Bank of Boston, 431, 432
Fiscal loan and investment program, 262, 264,
    271, 276, 291, 535–36
Fiscal policy, 230, 242–43, 287, 293, 298–99,
    300
Fixed capital formation, 325
Floating exchange rates, 253, 282, 283, 316,
    436–37, 509, 514, 522–23
Flotation of yen bonds by foreign institu-
    tions, 392, 459, 464, 489
Food control special account, 55, 79, 181,
    288, 292, 293, 413
Foreign aid, 451–52
Foreign balance, 459
Foreign banks in Japan, 475–79, 492–93, 500
Foreign bonds, 256, 270, 341, 482–86
Foreign exchange brokers, 495
Foreign Exchange Control Board, 492, 494,
    500, 502
Foreign exchange controls, 251–54, 282, 283,
    316, 463, 470, 480–82, 492–93, 516–17
Foreign exchange fund special account,
    64, 65, 79, 100, 120, 181, 254, 316, 317,
    321, 324, 413, 492, 493, 494, 495, 496,
    500, 514
Foreign exchange fund bills, 67, 120, 181,
    494
Foreign exchange loans, 65, 494, 509
Foreign exchange market, 282, 493–95, 514–
    15
Foreign exchange reserves, 27, 28, 66, 67, 235,
    270, 279, 282, 366, 492, 508, 511, 514,
    515–19, 521–22, 530–31
Foreign exchange reserves, measures for de-
    creasing, 515–17
Foreign exchange transactions, 492–95
Foreign interest rates, influence on Japan, 312,
    314–15
Foreign Investment Council, 70, 255, 257,
    259–60, 262
Foreign investment in Japanese securities, 70–
    71, 194, 253, 254–55, 257, 258, 261,

276, 363, 366, 367, 368, 371, 387, 393,
    482–86
Foreign loans (to Japanese borrowers), 255–
    56, 270, 480–82, 483, 503
Foreign securities dealers and underwriters,
    entry into Japan, 177, 475–76
Foreign securities, investment in, 176–78, 251,
    252, 253, 404
Foreign technology, induction of, 256, 257,
    259, 260
Foreign trade, 64–65, 453–58, 512–13. *See also*
    exports and imports.
Foreign trade financing, 499–510
Free yen, 248, 253, 254, 475, 481, 495
Fuji National City Consulting, 161
Fukuda, Takeo, 162
Fund dislocation, 317, 413, 415
Fund supply. *See* money supply.
General Agreement on Tariffs and Trade
    (GATT), 235, 249, 442
Government control over economy, 248–49
Governmental financial institutions, 116–22
    Export-Import Bank of Japan, 67, 91, 100,
        117, 122, 292, 488–89, 493, 506, 510
    Hokkaido and Tohoku Development Fi-
        nance Corporation, 310, 316
    Housing Loan Corporation, 120, 292
    Japan Development Bank, 67, 117–18, 120–
        21, 222, 242, 292, 310, 316, 426, 485,
        486, 510
    People's Finance Corporation, 120, 121,
        292, 316, 340
    Reconversion Finance Bank, 34, 35, 54,
        55, 58, 120, 499
    Small Business Credit Insurance Cor-
        poration, 316
    Small Business Finance Corporation, 121,
        308, 316, 340
Government financing of private enter-
    prises, 341–42
Government-guaranteed debentures, 82–83,
    147, 168, 169, 181–82, 265, 311, 385,
    387, 388, 393
Gross national product (GNP), 27, 28, 29, 67,
    262, 263, 264, 265, 269, 274, 286, 291,
    304, 311, 533
Group trading (collective transactions), 38,
    45–46, 57, 62
Growth companies, 171, 183
Growth industries, 215, 216, 217, 222–26, 405

Holding Company Liquidation Commission
    (HCLC), 23–25, 44
Housing, 227, 242, 243, 272–73, 286, 287,
    325, 326, 327–28, 426, 434–35
Housing loans, 111, 203, 273, 423–26, 535
Ikeda, Hayato, 29, 67, 69, 216, 230, 286, 304,
    348, 353
Impact loans, 480–82
Import restrictions, 244–47

Imports, 64–65, 78, 79, 214, 215–16, 226, 229, 235, 264, 269, 273, 277, 278, 436, 449–50, 453–58, 492, 500, 512–13, 532
Income, family, 326–27
Income, funds, 405–406
Indemnity payments, 32, 33, 34
Indirect financing, 134, 161, 339–42
Industrial debentures, 51, 73, 83, 182, 226, 385, 387, 388, 391–92, 393, 395, 397, 489
Industrial investment special account, 117–18
Industrial parks, 217
Industrial structure, 216–17, 219–20
Inflation, 19, 22, 27, 31, 34, 36, 53–56, 64, 101, 164, 273, 330, 523, 524, 525, 526–27, 532
Information business, 160–61, 219
Infrastructure, investment in, 242–43, 286, 287, 293
Insider trading, 189
Installment investment trusts, 174
Insurance companies, 132, 146, 176, 201–207, 304, 308, 310, 312, 362, 380, 487. *See also* life insurance companies, nonlife insurance companies.
Insurance companies, foreign, operating in Japan, 253
Insurance systems, governmental, 201, 287, 288
Insurance, types of, 201, 202, 203, 204, 421
Inter-American Development Bank, 488–89
Interest rates, 49, 51, 66, 67, 79, 83, 103, 116, 121, 125, 126, 131–36, 155, 162, 163, 230, 231, 248, 267, 269, 278, 279, 303, 304, 305, 308, 309, 310, 311, 312, 314, 315, 316, 395, 396, 417, 421, 424, 425, 480–81, 509, 534–35. *See also* call money rates discount rate.
International Bank for Reconstruction and Development (World Bank), 70, 121, 226, 256, 461–62, 480
Internationalization, 441, 459
International investment trusts, 176–77, 402, 404, 484
International Monetary Fund (IMF), 249, 264, 270, 281, 459–61, 493, 496
Inventories, 230–31, 236, 305, 314
Inventory investment, 214, 216, 235
Investment trusts, 68, 69–70, 80–82, 124, 165–69, 174, 175, 179, 199, 305, 348, 355, 356, 387, 402–12, 487
Inward foreign investment, 254–62
Ishibashi, Tanzan, 31
Iwasaki, family, 23
Iwato boom, 124, 206, 213, 215, 232, 239, 366, 376
Japan National Railways, 226, 243
Japan Securities Finance Co., 61, 69, 176, 195–98, 200, 348, 349, 350, 352, 354, 355–56, 371, 390, 391

Japan Credit Bureau, 158, 159, 160, 421, 424
Japan Diners Club, 159, 421
Japan Housing Finance Corporation, 424, 425, 426
Japan Home Finance Co., 424
Japan Joint Securities Co., 199–200, 239, 355–56, 362, 364
Japan Joint Securities Foundation, 200, 390
Japan Mortgage Bond Association, 425
Japan Securities Holding Association, 199–200, 240, 356, 362, 364
Japan-U.S. relations, 245, 282–84, 441–43, 526–30, 536
Jimmu boom, 27–29, 213, 215
Joint deposit cards, 158–59
Joint Trust Home Center, 425

Keidanren. See Federation of Economic Organizations.
Keiretsuka, 219, 220
Kennedy round, 245, 247, 264, 280
Kennedy shock, 199, 239
Kishi cabinet, 349, 351
Kombinats, 128–29, 215, 220, 223
Korean War, 27, 64, 66, 213, 214, 215, 222

Land reform, 26, 217
Labor, 213, 216–17, 220, 233–34, 240
Labor credit associations, 115
Laws and ordinances
    Agricultural Cooperative Association Law, 115
    Antimonopoly Law. *See* Law Relating to the Prohibition of Private Monopoly and Maintenance of Fair Trade.
    Assets Revaluation Law, 71, 73
    Automobile Liability Insurance Law, 205
    Bank Law, 104, 105, 123, 124, 475
    Bank of Japan Law, 58, 99, 100–102, 171
    Bank of Japan Notes Deposit Ordinance, 31
    Bank of Japan Regulations, 99
    Basic Public Hazards Countermeasures Law, 241
    Capital Tax Law, 44
    Commercial Code (*Shoho*, "Commercial Law"), 48, 57, 59, 71, 73, 164, 190, 191, 193, 531
    Commodity Price Control Ordinance, 31
    Cooperative Association Law, 115
    Corporation Tax Law, 82, 110, 149, 164, 176
    Credit Association Law, 112
    Currency Law, 459
    Deconcentration Law. *See* Law for the Elimination of Excessive Concentration of Economic Power.
    Emergency Commodity Supply Control Law, 34
    Emergency Food Measures Ordinance, 31
    Emergency Fund Adjustment Law, 22, 49

Liberalization of foreign investment in automotive industry, 258–259, 260
Liberalization of foreign trade, 235–36, 244–47, 442, 517, 522, 529
Liberalization of inward foreign investment, 254–62, 280, 442–43
Life Insurance Association, 203
Life insurance companies, 126, 199, 200, 201–207, 364, 373, 388, 424, 425
    Asahi Mutual Life Insurance Co., 425, 432
    Chiyoda Mutual Life Insurance Co., 424, 432
    Daido Mutual Life Insurance Co., 424
    Dai-Ichi Mutual Life Insurance Co., 424, 425, 432
    Dai-Hyaku Mutual Life Insurance Co., 425
    Fukoku Mutual Life Insurance Co., 425
    Kyoei Mutual Life Insurance Co., 425
    Mitsui Mutual Life Insurance Co., 424
    Nissan Mutual Life Insurance Co., 425
    Nippon Life Insurance Co., 424, 425, 433
    Taiyo Mutual Life Insurance Co., 425
    Toho Mutual Life Insurance Co., 425
    Yasuda Mutual Life Insurance Co., 425, 432, 433
Loan trusts, 111, 396, 402

Margin trading. *See* credit transactions.
Marine insurance, 201, 202, 204–205
Medium-term credit, 134, 162
Meiji era, 12–13, 434, 441
Meiji Life Insurance Co., 289, 425
Meiji Restoration, 12
Mergers, 174, 218, 221, 266. *See also* bank mergers.
Ministry of Agriculture, 245, 246
Minister of finance, 13, 31, 36, 37, 56, 99, 100, 111, 114, 115, 130, 132, 165, 167, 171, 174, 187, 190, 191, 196, 198, 201, 202, 251, 253, 476, 492, 496, 500
Ministry of Finance, 25, 38, 40, 45, 49, 52, 58, 69, 91, 99, 100–103, 104, 108, 111, 117, 120, 124, 125, 126, 129, 131, 134, 135, 149, 152, 156–57, 158, 160, 162, 163, 164, 165, 167, 170, 173, 174, 176, 183, 186, 187, 189, 190, 191, 192, 194, 200, 203, 230, 248, 250, 251–52, 253, 256, 257, 260, 262, 268, 282, 287, 288, 291, 299, 300, 304, 305, 307, 310, 311, 315, 341, 348, 350, 351, 352, 364, 376, 384, 388, 391, 392, 396, 397, 403, 404, 405, 406, 467, 470, 480–81, 482, 484, 486, 489, 495, 508, 509, 510, 514, 517
Minister of international trade and industry, 115
Ministry of International Trade and Industry, (MITI), 54, 117, 121, 220, 221, 223, 256, 257, 260, 305, 442, 449, 508
Mitsubishi group, 23–24, 129, 193, 218, 445
Mitsui group, 23–24, 129, 160–61, 218

Mizuta Mikio, 393
Monetary policy, 230, 278, 304–317, 481. *See also* credit restraints.
Money market, 28, 51, 79, 276, 278, 304, 313, 413–17, 534
Money supply, 103, 306, 315, 317, 320, 339–42, 413
Money trusts, 109–110, 111, 396
Morinaga, Teiichiro, 186, 380
Mortgage bonds, 160, 425
Mortgages, 423, 425
Mujin, 105, 112
Mutual Funds, 404

National Association of Local Banks, 159, 308
National Association of Mutual Banks, 159
National Central Association of Credit Cooperatives, 114, 157
National Federation of Credit Associations, 105, 114, 155, 388, 416
National Federation of Securities Dealers Associations, 45
National Federation of Securities Associations, 45
National Clearing House Federation, 152
National debt, 301, 302
National Mutual Insurance Federation of Agricultural Cooperatives, 204
New Financial Adjustment System (new fund supply system), 306, 307, 309, 314, 315, 320, 413
Nippon Shinpan Co., 160, 419, 421, 425, 431
Nisui-kai, 497
Nixon shock, 281–84, 374, 393, 396, 436
Nonlife insurance companies, 201–07, 373, 424, 425
    Asahi Fire & Marine Insurance Co., 424
    Chiyoda Fire & Marine Insurance Co., 432
    Dai-Tokyo Fire & Marine Insurance Co., 424, 432
    Dowa Fire & Marine Insurance Co., 424, 425
    Koa Fire & Marine Insurance Co., 424, 425
    Nissan Fire & Marine Insurance Co., 425
    Nichido Fire & Marine Insurance Co., 424, 425
    Nippon Fire & Marine Insurance Co., 424, 425
    Nisshin Fire & Marine Insurance Co., 424, 432
    Taisho Marine & Fire Insurance Co., 424
    Taiyo Fire & Marine Insurance Co., 425
    Tokio Marine & Fire Insurance Co., 425, 472–73
    Yasuda Fire & Marine Insurance Co., 425, 432, 433
Note issue, 31, 32, 36, 49, 53, 55, 56, 65, 101, 103, 126, 303, 306, 309, 321, 534
Nuclear power, 226

Occupation of Japan after World War II, 19–
27, 66, 499, 503
Occupation policies, 20–27, 30, 42–45, 71, 214
Odd-lot trading, 183
Off-market transactions, 187, 194
Okinawa, financial institutions, 158
Open-end trusts, 165, 168, 169, 402, 403, 404,
405, 406
Open market operations, 56, 58, 59, 66, 73,
100, 102, 147, 182, 226, 306, 307, 308,
309, 310–11, 314, 413, 415, 416–17
Organization for Economic Cooperation and
Development (OECD), 235–36, 249–
50, 462–63, 493, 506, 511
Outward foreign investment, 251–53, 434, 449,
452, 487–91, 517
Overdrafts, 125, 127, 159
Overloans, 36, 65, 66, 73, 75, 79, 102, 127,
129, 230, 306, 317, 321, 341, 413, 533,
534
Over-the-counter trading, 40, 45, 61–62, 68,
179, 182, 183, 190, 387–88, 390, 393

Pacific war, 13–14, 17–19
Pawnshops, 422
Payment conditions, 237, 278, 341
Peace Treaty of San Francisco, 17, 43, 66, 462
Pension plans, 110, 202, 206, 376
Per share earnings, 369–70, 380
Personal loans, 159
Petrochemical industry, 28, 219, 223, 236, 263,
265
Plan for Doubling National Income, 216, 230,
286, 353
Pollution Prevention Corporation, 241
Position guidance, 103, 312, 314, 391, 509
Postal annuities, 41, 118, 201
Postal Life Insurance, 41, 118, 201
Postal savings, 73, 91, 116, 118–19, 124, 125,
132, 326, 425
Postal Transfer System, 118
Potsdam Declaration, 14, 19
Prefectural Mutual Insurance Federations of
Agricultural Cooperatives, 204
Preferential tariffs, 245, 247, 264, 280, 522
Pressure groups, 245–46, 288, 291
Prices, 31, 34, 43, 53, 54, 64–65, 78, 79, 214,
227, 228, 229, 232–34, 235, 245, 262,
265, 268, 269, 272, 273, 277, 286, 287,
311, 313, 325, 512
Price-earnings ratio, 365–66
Price maintenance, 220
Price manipulations, 376. *See also* support
buying.
Pricing system, 241, 421
Private Investment Company for Asia, the,
(PICA), 466
Private placement of bonds, 389–90, 393
Production, 29, 43, 65, 67, 78, 79, 164, 213,

214, 216, 229, 230, 231, 235, 236, 239–
40, 265, 273, 276–77, 305
Productivity, 219, 233, 234, 274
Profitability, 372–73, 435

Radcliffe Report, 101–102
Rearmament, Japan's, 446–47
Recessions, 27, 79–80, 214, 225, 239–40, 276–
79, 349
Reparations, 42–43
Reserve deposit system, 100, 103, 229, 230,
268–69, 303, 305, 306, 307, 309, 533
Reserve requirements, 113, 114
Reserve requirements, foreign currency de-
posits, 251, 481, 495, 516, 533
Revaluation of assets, 71–72, 82
Revaluation of yen 252, 254, 270, 276, 279–80,
282–83, 436–37, 482, 511–12, 521–32
Rice production and distribution, 233, 268, 288

Saitorinin, 57, 87, 186, 192
Sanmeikai, 312, 413
Saving, 34, 36, 44, 45, 68, 112, 118, 123, 124,
167, 202, 274, 300, 325–28, 402, 406, 423
Second Section, 61, 179, 183, 216, 349, 355,
356, 365, 366
Securities Commission, 52, 57, 72
Securities companies, 61, 63, 69–70, 86–87,
108, 112, 162, 165, 170–72, 173–78, 186,
187, 188, 189, 195, 199, 200, 239, 253,
299, 300, 305, 350, 351, 355, 356, 364,
367, 374, 379, 380, 384, 388–89, 390,
391, 393, 395–96, 402–406, 487, 488,
517, 533
Daiwa Securities Co., 38, 40, 58, 59, 69–70,
165, 167, 170, 174, 176, 177, 178, 190,
198, 199, 253, 305, 363, 388–89, 403,
404, 405, 406, 464, 470, 472, 474, 488
Nikko Securities Co., 38, 40, 58, 69–70, 165,
167, 170, 174, 176, 177, 178, 190, 198,
199, 253, 305, 363, 388–89, 404, 405,
406, 464, 466, 470, 472, 474, 484–85,
488
Nomura Securities Co., 38, 40, 58, 69–70,
165, 167, 170, 174, 176, 177, 178, 190,
198, 199, 253, 305, 365, 373, 388–89,
404, 405, 406, 462, 470, 472, 474, 485,
488
Yamaichi Securities Co., 37, 38, 39, 40, 57,
58, 68–69, 69–70, 165, 167, 170–72, 173,
175, 176, 177, 178, 190, 198, 199, 253,
305, 356, 363, 364, 367, 388–89, 403,
404, 405, 406, 464, 470, 472, 474, 484,
488
Daisho Securities Co., 167, 170, 173
Eguchi Securities Co., 167, 174, 404
Eguchi-Nitto Securities Co., 174
Kakumaru Securities Co., 167, 173–74
Nippon Kangyo Kakumaru Securities Co.,
173–74, 178, 253, 389

Nitto Securities Co., 174, 178
Oi Securities Co., 70, 167, 170, 171–72, 403. *See also* Wako Securities Co.
Okasan Securities Co., 167
Osakaya Securities Co., 70, 167, 170, 178
Osaka Shoji, 70, 403
Shin-Nippon Securities Co., 173, 174, 178, 253, 389, 404
Tamazuka Securities Co., 167, 173
Toichi Securities Co., 174
Toyama Securities Co., 376
Wako Securities Co., 172, 174, 175, 178, 365, 367, 404
Yamakano Securities Co., 167, 173
Yamatane Securities Co., 174, 175
Yamazaki Securities Co., 167, 170
Securities companies (foreign) in Japan, 475–76
 Arthur Lipper Corporation, 475
 Burnham & Co., 475
 Merrill Lynch, Pierce, Fenner, and Smith, 475, 488
Securities companies, foreign operations, 176–178
Securities Coordinating Liquidation Committee (SCLC), 26, 44, 46, 47, 63, 71
Securities finance companies, 180, 187, 188, 195–98, 305, 365, 417
Securities Investment Trust Association, 87, 167, 174, 403, 404
Securities transaction tax, 180
Securities yen, 253, 517
Seibu group, 425
Shipbuilding industry, 224–25, 232, 263, 277, 316, 372, 437, 481, 506–507, 531
Shipping industry, 54, 221, 232, 249, 277, 293
Shoko Chukin Bank. *See* Central Bank for Commercial and Industrial Cooperatives.
Short-term fund dealers. *See* call money brokers.
Shoup Tax Mission, 71, 124, 294, 296
Small Enterprise Promotion Corporation, 316
Social Welfare Promotion Association, 203
Soviet Union, Japan's relations with, 232, 447, 450, 536
Specified stocks 182, 191
Special accounts, 292
Special drawing rights (SDR), 264, 270, 460–61
Special procurement, 64, 67, 78, 500, 529
Standard interest rate, 132, 134, 135, 303, 313, 314
Standard of living, 227–28, 536
Steel industry, 28, 34, 35, 36, 65, 79, 215, 216, 221, 222, 231, 237, 263, 265, 266, 273, 278, 316, 372, 395, 434, 437, 508
Stock exchange, kinds of transactions, 179–80
Stock exchanges, 37–38, 56–57, 86, 87, 179–94
 Fukuoka Stock Exchange, 38, 57, 179, 196
 Hiroshima Stock Exchange, 57, 179

Kobe Stock Exchange, 38, 57, 179
Kyoto Stock Exchange, 38, 57, 179
Nagoya Stock Exchange, 38, 39, 45, 57, 61, 87, 179, 183, 195, 198, 216, 349, 387
Niigata Stock Exchange, 38, 57, 179, 196
Osaka Stock Exchange, 38, 39, 45, 61, 69, 87, 179, 183, 195, 198, 216, 349, 387
Sapporo Stock Exchange, 57, 179, 196
Tokyo Stock Exchange, 37, 38, 39, 45, 57, 61, 68, 69, 80, 87, 165, 179, 183, 186–87, 188, 189, 191, 193, 194, 195, 196, 198, 216, 279, 349, 363, 365, 374–76, 377, 387
Stock exchange, organization, 87, 170, 182, 183, 186, 187, 197
Stock market, 61, 68, 79–80, 82, 169, 199, 202, 239, 264, 275–76, 279, 347–57, 362–70, 374–77, 405
Stock prices, 38, 40, 45–46, 61, 62, 68, 69, 79–80, 82, 183, 187, 239, 348, 350–57, 362–71, 375–77
Stock transfer agency, 111
Stock ownership, 146–47, 193–94, 376
Stock transfer, 193
Structural loans, 222
Subcontractors, 216–17, 219, 237, 238, 240, 278, 436
Suez crisis, 28, 80, 82
Sumitomo group, 23–25, 193, 218, 431
Support buying, 189–190, 191, 363, 391
Supreme commander for the Allied powers (SCAP), 20, 37–38, 41, 42, 44, 46, 51, 52, 53, 54, 56, 61, 62, 65, 69, 70, 87, 117, 492

Take-over bids, 190–91, 192, 193, 215, 257
Tanaka, Kakuei, 156, 270, 284, 288, 393
Tariffs, 247
Taxation, 54, 66, 71–72, 82, 109, 111, 124–25, 126, 155, 189, 193, 229, 242, 243, 270–71, 287, 291, 292, 293, 294–97, 307, 328, 406, 413, 423, 426, 486, 534.
Tax System Research Council, 296, 304
Technological innovation, 213, 214, 215, 216, 225
Textile industry, 65, 215, 216, 217, 223–24, 231, 236, 280, 371
Textiles, restrictions on exports to the U.S., 280, 282, 283–84, 529–30
Tokuyakuten, 220
Tokyo Bankers' Association, 106, 131, 152
Tokyo Clearing House, 106, 152, 153
Tokyo Securities Association, 87
Tokyo Securities Dealers Association, 40, 45, 62, 165, 170, 397
Tokyo Stock Exchange, constitution, 186, 187
Tokyo Stock Exchange, members, 186
Tokyo Stock Exchange, trading posts, 182
Tokyo Stock Exchange Association, 38
Tokyo stock price index, 192
Tokyu group, 421